LORD ABERDEEN

Lord Aberdeen

A political biography

MURIEL E. CHAMBERLAIN

LONGMAN
London and New York

Longman Group Limited,
Longman House, Burnt Mill, Harlow, Essex CM20 2JE, England
and Associated Companies throughout the World.

Published in the United States of America
by Longman Inc., New York

© Longman Group Limited 1983

First published 1983

British Library Cataloguing in Publication Data

Chamberlain, Muriel E.
Lord Aberdeen.
1. Aberdeen, George Gordon, Earl of
2. Prime Ministers – Great Britain – Biography
I. Title
941.081'092'4   DA536.A2

ISBN 0-582-50462-7

Library of Congress Cataloging in Publication Data

Chamberlain, Muriel Evelyn.
Lord Aberdeen.

Bibliography: p. 535
Includes index.
1. Aberdeen, George Hamilton Gordon, Earl of,
1784–1860. 2. Statesmen – Great Britain – Biography.
3. Diplomats – Great Britain – Biography. 4. Great
Britain – Foreign relations – 19th century. I. Title.
DA536.A2C45   941.081'092'84 [B]   82-273
ISBN 0-582-50462-7   AACR2

Set in 11/12 pt Linotron 202 Garamond
Printed in Singapore
by
Kyodo Shing Loong Printing Industries Pte Ltd.

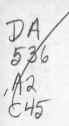

Contents

List of plates	vii
List of maps	viii
List of abbreviations	ix
Note on referencing system	x
Acknowledgements	xi
Family tree of Gordons of Haddo	xiv
Introduction	1
1. The Gordons of Haddo	13
2. Athenian Aberdeen	30
3. Devonshire House or Bentley Priory?	46
4. The scholar	61
5. The improving landlord	79
6. Entry into politics	91
7. Acceptance of the Vienna Embassy	105
8. Teplitz and Leipzig	122
9. The Frankfort proposals	139
10. Frankfort to Paris	155
11. Return to private life	172
12. Wellington's government	193
13. The Eastern Crisis, 1828–30	205
14. Reaction and Revolution, 1828–30	229
15. A Conservative at home	251
16. A Conservative abroad	268
17. A Scottish interlude	289
18. Foreign Secretary again	297
19. The Ashburton–Webster negotiations	310
20. The Oregon Crisis	331
21. Britain's 'natural rival'	343
22. The 'good understanding' with France	357
23. The collapse of the *entente*	379
24. Revolution and reaction, 1848–50	390

25. The survival of the Peelites 414
26. The formation of the Aberdeen coalition 441
27. Liberal–Conservatism in action: the legacy of Pitt and Peel 455
28. The Eastern Crisis, 1853–54 472
29. The War 497
30. Last years 517
    Conclusion 531

Bibliography 535
Maps 543
Index 553

List of plates

1. Lord Aberdeen by Sir Thomas Lawrence.
2. Lord Aberdeen's Father, Lord Haddo, by Pompeo Batoni.
3. Haddo House. William Adam's elevation of the entrance front.
   Haddo House as it is today.
4. Catherine Hamilton, Countess of Aberdeen, by Lawrence.
   Harriet Douglas, Countess of Aberdeen, by Lawrence.
5. Lord Aberdeen's daughters by George Hayter.
6. Buchan Ness by James Giles.
7. Lord Aberdeen by John Partridge.
8. What everybody thinks. – *Punch*.
   Aberdeen smoking the pipe of peace. – *Punch*.
9. The destruction of the Turkish squadron at Sinope.
10. The ministerial split. – *Punch*.
    What it has come to. – *Punch*.
11. Lord Aberdeen in the uniform of Lord Lieutenant of Aberdeenshire.
12. The Aberdeen Cabinet deciding on the Expedition to the Crimea.
13. The road from Balaclava to Sebastopol during wet weather.
14. Not a nice business. – *Punch*.
    'You are requested not to speak to the man at the wheel.' – *Punch*.
15. How to get rid of an old woman. – *Punch*.
    Austria still plays on the old Scotch fiddle. – *Punch*.
16. Lord Aberdeen. Marble bust by Matthew Noble.

List of maps

1. The Aegean in the early 19th century 544
2. The closing phases of the Napoleonic Wars 546
3. The Ottoman Empire at the time of the Crimean War 548
4. The Maine boundary dispute, 1783–1842 549
5. The Oregon boundary dispute, 1819–46 550

List of abbreviations

AAE	Archives du Ministère des Affaires Etrangères, Paris
Add. MSS	Additional Manuscripts in Manuscript Department of the British Library
BFSP	British and Foreign State Papers
CO	Colonial Office
FO	Foreign Office
HH	Haddo House
MSS. Clar. Dep.	Clarendon Papers
NLS	National Library of Scotland
PRO	Public Record Office
RA	Royal Archives, Windsor
SRO	Scottish Record Office

Note on referencing system

Some of the letters quoted have previously been published. Where the publication is complete and accurate as in E. Jones-Parry's *The Correspondence of Lord Aberdeen and Princess Lieven 1832–1854*, reference is given to the published volumes. Where the publication was selective, or edited, as is the case with most Victorian biographies, reference is given, wherever possible, to the manuscript source. Lord Stanmore had copies made of some letters in connection with his own biography of his father. Where these are referred to, they are indicated as 'copies'. The only important examples of this are the letters from Aberdeen to Augustus Foster at Haddo House (although some of the originals survive in the National Library of Scotland) and some of Metternich's letters to Aberdeen, the originals of which were returned to Metternich's family. These copies are in Add. MSS 43128.

Acknowledgements

My first thanks must be to the present Marquess of Aberdeen and Temair for his help and encouragement, and more particularly for reading the manuscript and saving me from a number of errors. I should also like to thank June, Marchioness of Aberdeen and Temair, for her kind hospitality when I was working on the papers at Haddo House, and Mrs Longley for her assistance in using the Haddo archives. I am grateful to Lord Harrowby and Mr David Gurney for their friendly help when I consulted family papers in their respective possession.

I owe a great deal to many archivists, among them the Royal Archivists, especially the Registrar, Miss Jane Langton, who gave me much help. Despite my strictures on some of their predecessors, I should like to thank the present staff of the Manuscripts Department of the British Library for their unfailing assistance, especially in helping me to find letters in the still uncatalogued Wellington Papers; and that thanks must be extended to the staff of what is now the Official Publications Library and the Greek and Roman Department of the British Museum. The Scottish Record Office was also most helpful and, without their preliminary sorting, the papers at Haddo would have been virtually unusable. I must pay tribute to the superb cross-referencing system of the National Library of Scotland, without which many scattered papers would be untraceable. I also received every assistance from the staff of the Public Record Office, the Royal Commission on Historical Manuscripts, Lambeth Palace Library, the Royal Society, the Society of Antiquaries, the Bodleian Library, Aberdeen University Library, Nottingham University Library, Norwich Record Office, Leeds City Libraries Archives Department, and the *Archives Nationales* and the *Archives du Ministère des Affaires Étrangères* in Paris. I should like to thank the National Library of Ireland, Dublin, the Northern Ireland Public Record Office, Belfast, the *Haus-, Hof-u. Statsarchiv*, Vienna, and the West Yorkshire Record Office, Wakefield, for supplying me with important information; and Lord Blake of the Queen's College, Oxford, for facilitating my consultation of the Derby Papers.

I am most grateful to Professor W. B. Stanford of Dublin for reading and commenting on part of the manuscript and to various colleagues and former colleagues at University College, Swansea, who supplied information or gave me other help, especially Emeritus Professor Cecil Price, Dr David Howell, Dr Marianne Elliott, Dr Hugh Dunthorne and Professor Richard Shannon, who also read the manuscript.

Finally, I should like to thank Mrs P. M. Thomas, Mrs Rhian James and Mrs June Morgan of University College, Swansea, who typed the manuscript admirably and at great speed, and the staff of Longman who saw it through the press.

We are indebted to the following for permission to reproduce copyright material:

The Marquess of Aberdeen for extracts from papers and letters of Lord Aberdeen; The Earl Bathurst and The British Library for extracts from the Bathurst papers; The British Library for extracts from the Wilson papers; The Earl of Clarendon and The Bodleian Library for extracts from the Clarendon papers; The Earl of Derby and Liverpool City Libraries for extracts from the Derby papers; Sir William Gladstone and The British Library for extracts from the Gladstone papers; Sir Charles Graham and The Bodleian Library for extracts from the Graham papers; David Q. Gurney and The Norfolk Record Office for extracts from the Gurney Journal and papers; The Earl of Harewood for extracts from the Canning papers; The Sixth Earl of Harrowby and the Harrowby Manuscript Trust for extracts from the Harrowby manuscripts; Lord Heytesbury and The British Library for extracts from the Heytesbury papers; The Archbishop of Canterbury and the Trustees of Lambeth Palace Library for extracts from the Howley, Wordsworth and Longley papers; The Earl of Leven and The Scottish Record Office for extracts from the Levin and Melville papers; Lord Liverpool and The British Library for extracts from the Liverpool papers; Ministry of Culture Management of France's Archives for extracts from the Guizot papers; The Trustees of the National Library of Scotland for extracts from the Aberdeen papers; Nottingham University Council for extracts from the Newcastle papers in the Nottingham University Library Manuscripts Department; The Earl Peel and The British Library for extracts from the Peel papers; Public Record Office of Northern Ireland for extracts from the Castlereagh papers; the gracious permission of Her Majesty The Queen for extracts from the Royal Archives; Scottish Record Office for extracts from the Haddo papers; Society of Antiquaries of London for extracts from their manuscripts; Society of Dilettanti for extracts from their manuscripts; Duke of Wellington, The British Library and Her Majesty's Treasury (The Royal Commission on Historical Manuscripts) for extracts from the Wellington papers.

Acknowledgement is also due to the following for permission to reproduce illustrations:

The National Trust for Scotland for Lord Aberdeen by Lawrence, Lord Haddo by Batoni, Haddo House (Adam's elevation), Haddo House as it is today,

Catherine Hamilton by Lawrence, Harriet Douglas by Lawrence, Lord Aberdeen's daughters by Hayter, Buchan Ness by Giles, and Lord Aberdeen in uniform; the National Portrait Gallery, London, for Lord Aberdeen by Partridge, and The Aberdeen Cabinet by Gilbert; Punch Publications Ltd for Aberdeen smoking the pipe of peace. Other *Punch* cartoons are reproduced by courtesy of Essex County Libraries, Victorian Studies Centre at Saffron Walden. The destruction of the Turkish squadron and The road from Balaclava are reproduced by courtesy of the Trustees of the British Museum; and the marble bust of Aberdeen by courtesy of the Dean and Chapter of Westminister.

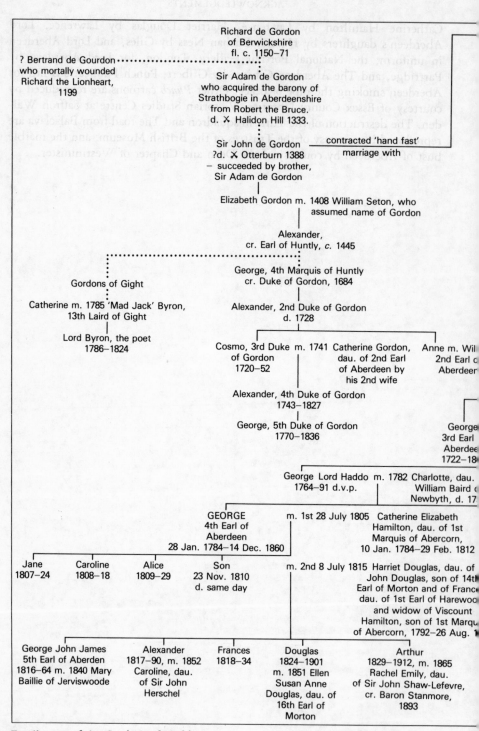

Family tree of the Gordons of Haddo

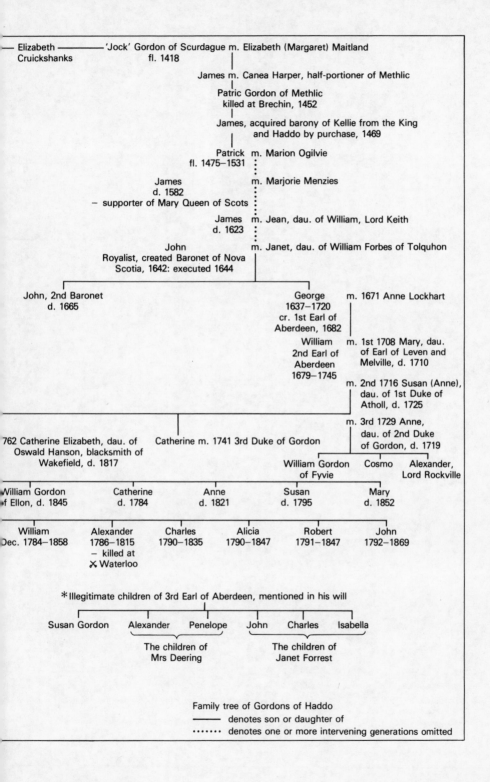

Elizabeth ———————— 'Jock' Gordon of Scurdague m. Elizabeth (Margaret) Maitland
Cruickshanks   fl. 1418

James m. Canea Harper, half-portioner of Methlic

Patric Gordon of Methlic
killed at Brechin, 1452

James, acquired barony of Kellie from the King
and Haddo by purchase, 1469

Patrick m. Marion Ogilvie
fl. 1475–1531 ⋮

James   m. Marjorie Menzies
d. 1582   ⋮
— supporter of Mary Queen of Scots ⋮

James m. Jean, dau. of William, Lord Keith
d. 1623 ⋮

John   m. Janet, dau. of William Forbes of Tolquhon
Royalist, created Baronet of Nova
Scotia, 1642: executed 1644

John, 2nd Baronet   George   m. 1671 Anne Lockhart
d. 1665   1637–1720
                                          cr. 1st Earl of
                                          Aberdeen, 1682

                                          William   m. 1st 1708 Mary, dau.
                                          2nd Earl of   of Earl of Leven and
                                          Aberdeen   Melville, d. 1710
                                          1679–1745
                                                    m. 2nd 1716 Susan (Anne),
                                                      dau. of 1st Duke of
                                                      Atholl, d. 1725

                                                    m. 3rd 1729 Anne,
762 Catherine Elizabeth, dau. of   Catherine m. 1741 3rd Duke of Gordon   dau. of 2nd Duke
Oswald Hanson, blacksmith of   of Gordon, d. 1719
Wakefield, d. 1817   William Gordon   Cosmo   Alexander,
                                          of Fyvie   Lord Rockville

William Gordon   Catherine   Anne   Susan   Mary
f Ellon, d. 1845   d. 1784   d. 1821   d. 1795   d. 1852

William   Alexander   Charles   Alicia   Robert   John
Dec. 1784–1858   1786–1815   1790–1835   1790–1847   1791–1847   1792–1869
                 – killed at
                 ✗ Waterloo

*Illegitimate children of 3rd Earl of Aberdeen, mentioned in his will

Susan Gordon   Alexander   Penelope   John   Charles   Isabella

The children of   The children of
Mrs Deering   Janet Forrest

Family tree of Gordons of Haddo
——— denotes son or daughter of
······· denotes one or more intervening generations omitted

Introduction

The fourth Earl of Aberdeen was determined that his papers should be published. When he died, just before Christmas 1860, he left them all neatly bundled and docketed and he gave clear instructions to his youngest son, Arthur, about their publication. The project had often been discussed between father and son and indeed some volumes, relating to the period up to 1845, were printed during the father's lifetime.[1]

Aberdeen was well aware that he had finally left public life, after a long and honourable career in high office, judged a failure and even a traitor. He believed that he had been the victim of a peculiarly vicious smear campaign, organised by his political opponents, which had convinced the public that he was, at best, an incompetent who had allowed the country to muddle into the Crimean War and then conducted the war so inefficiently that thousands had died unnecessary and squalid deaths in the Crimean winter or in the hospital at Scutari or, at worst, a traitor who was prepared to sacrifice England's interests to the foreigner.

But Aberdeen had been a classical scholar before he became a politician and – except in the last rather dreadful months of his life when he seems to have suffered some kind of nervous breakdown – he awaited the verdict of posterity calmly. It was natural, he said, that the public should seek a sacrifice for a war which had gone badly and he and his Secretary of State for War, the Duke of Newcastle, were the obvious victims. He was convinced that, once the dust of contemporary controversy had settled, the truth would emerge. His correspondence – and he had kept almost every letter he received and copies of a high proportion of his outgoing letters from an early age – would show more clearly than anything else could, the part that he had really played in British public life from August 1813, when he went as British Ambassador to Vienna, during the closing stages of the Napoleonic Wars, to January 1855, when he resigned as Prime Minister. The acquittal never came. More than a hundred and twenty years after his death, his reputation stands scarcely higher than it did in 1860.

His papers were never published. The man who prevented their publication was William Gladstone. Aberdeen, fearing that his son's comparative inex-

1

perience might lead him into indiscretion, laid down in his Will that his two old and close friends, Sir James Graham and William Gladstone, should have a power of veto.[2] Graham was enthusiastic for the publication but he died in 1861. Gladstone, although expressing the utmost goodwill, twice subsequently prevented any publication. By 1870, Arthur Gordon had prepared the volume relating to his father's embassy to Austria. Gladstone raised a number of objections, mostly relating to the editing. Gordon complained that his father had only meant Gladstone to restrain political indiscretions and that literary decisions were in his hands.[3] Unfortunately, Gordon was in a weak position to argue. His own career depended entirely on Gladstone's political patronage. Early in 1871 he sailed to become Governor of Mauritius and the project went into abeyance.

Gordon, Lord Stanmore as he became, spent most of his active life as a colonial governor.[4] As Governor General of Ceylon in the 1880s he continued to try to discharge what he regarded as the 'sacred trust' left to him in his father's will. More volumes of the papers were prepared and privately printed, some in Colombo. When he returned to England, he again tried to publish. He had also been asked to write a short *Life* of his father for a series edited by Stuart Reid, and a full–length biography of a political colleague of his father, Sidney Herbert, by Herbert's widow. Gladstone once again intervened. Aberdeen and Herbert were dead but Gladstone was still a practising politician. Some probable revelations were likely to be very embarrassing. He took particular exception to two points in Gordon's draft life of his father. Gordon had referred to Gladstone's opposition to parliamentary reform in the 1850s and told again the story of the Neapolitan letters of 1851. Gladstone disliked the reference to the latter – an episode about which he always felt uncomfortable[5] – but the former was the politically damaging revelation. When challenged, Gordon proved from Gladstone's own letters that Gladstone had opposed parliamentary reform, not only in 1852 but even in 1857. Gladstone had gone far beyond his jurisdiction in objecting not only to the publication of Aberdeen's correspondence, but even of Gordon's biographies of Aberdeen and Herbert. In the end he had to limit his intervention to a request that none of his own letters should be published without his specific permission. Gordon grimly pressed ahead with the publication of his father's *Life*, which came out in 1893, but the Herbert biography was delayed until 1906.[6] Aberdeen's complete Correspondence was never published.[7] No doubt Gordon could have challenged the extent of Gladstone's legal powers under his father's Will but in practical terms he was never in a position to do so. His own career still depended on Gladstone. The rather acrimonious correspondence about publication in 1891 ended with Gordon's request for Gladstone to support him if he stood for Parliament for Cambridge.[8]

Gordon's biography of his father is an important source in its own right. In the 1850s he had acted as his father's private secretary. He had charge of his father's papers, been present at important meetings and acted as a confidential intermediary. His status for this period is thus not only that of a biographer but that of an eye-witness. Detailed examination of the papers shows how often his rather cryptic asides are based on very sound information. But valuable although it undoubtedly is as a memoir of his father, it has its limitations and they are not always the obvious ones. Gordon himself admitted that no man could be entirely impartial in writing about his father.[9] The *Life* was to some extent avowedly an *apologia*, the case for the defence, but it was a judicious *apologia*, rarely going beyond what could be proved. Its limitations are more subtle.

Arthur Gordon was Aberdeen's youngest son, born when his father was already forty-five. His recollections are plainly of an elderly man. This comes out very clearly when, in 1871, Gladstone suggested that a bust of Aberdeen should be placed in Westminster Abbey. Gordon took exception to the idea that the bust should be a copy of that executed by Nollekens in 1813 which was 'simply detestable' and showed his father as 'a young man'.[10] Gordon's view of his father was of the archetypal Victorian *paterfamilias*. This pervades his biography and no doubt accorded with the popular recollections of the septuagenarian Prime Minister. It leaves out whole dimensions in Aberdeen's life, the adventurous young man who had explored Turkey, the popular figure in the frivolous, and not particularly moral, society of Bentley Priory. More importantly, it ignores the fact that Aberdeen was already fifty-three when Victoria came to the throne. He was not a Victorian. Like Castlereagh he was a man of the eighteenth century. His attitudes to politics, both domestic and foreign, were much more those of the eighteenth century than of the nineteenth.

In other ways too Gordon imposed his own picture upon his father's memory. By the time he came to write the memoir, he was committed to the Liberal party. He seems to have felt impelled to identify his father's position with his own, to state categorically that his father was always a Liberal at heart and that only unfortunate accidents of early association stranded him in the Tory camp.[11] There is just enough truth in this to make it plausible. Aberdeen had Liberal friends, whom he greatly valued, all his life. He was remarkably open-minded on many questions of practical reform. But there was also a very strong streak of Toryism in his character which cannot be ignored without distortion.

Gordon died in 1912. Aberdeen still had no full–length biography. His family seem to have felt that his name would never be cleared until the whole story was told to the world. They sought a biographer. No one seemed keen to undertake the job.[12] In the end, the choice fell on Lady Frances Balfour, the daughter of Aberdeen's young political colleague, the eighth Duke of Argyll. It was an unhappy choice. Lady Frances performed the task perfunctorily. The result was two volumes of random selections from Aberdeen's correspondence, loosely held together by extracts from Gordon's memoir. The standard of editing was deplorable. Letters were misdated and misattributed, or more often, not dated or attributed at all. But worse than that was the random nature of the selection. Striking passages, torn out of all context, and published, added up to a picture of a very strange man indeed. Aberdeen's reputation was, if anything, worse after the publication of the Balfour biography than before.[13]

There was by now a considerable danger that Aberdeen's papers, which he

3

had left so carefully arranged, would themselves be broken up and begin to disappear. An unhappy accident had befallen them quite early when a number of papers, which related to Aberdeen's youth (including letters from Lord Melville and the Younger Pitt) were left on a billiard table and a housemaid, supposing them to be rubbish, had begun to use them systematically to light fires.[14] Aberdeen's will, although entrusting the task of publication to his son, Arthur Gordon, had provided that the papers were ultimately to be returned to the eldest son, Lord Haddo, and his heirs, but some became mixed up with Gordon's own papers and some seem to have been accidentally retained, at least for a time, by Lady Frances Balfour.[15]

In 1932, the fourth Earl's grandson, the first Marquess of Aberdeen, presented the papers to the Manuscript Department of the British Museum. Even then some curious treatment followed. A number of the papers were returned as 'too private'.[16] There was perhaps an arguable case for returning those that related to his disagreements with his second wife in the 1820s, although more than a hundred years after the event it might seem to speak of undue delicacy. But it is hard to justify other decisions on any grounds. All his letters to his sister–in–law, Lady Maria Hamilton, in 1813 which related to his courtship of Anne Cavendish were returned. This interrupts his sequence of letters to Maria about the closing stages of the Napoleonic Wars and makes his wish to return home on 'private grounds' puzzling. If it was meant to conceal anything it was inept because most of the story of his unsuccessful courtship of Anne Cavendish is also told in his letters to his brother, Robert, which were retained. It is even harder to understand why some of Aberdeen's brothers' letters were returned on the grounds that there was no point in reviving scandals about the Duke of Wellington.[17]

As a result of the extraordinary scrupulosity of the Manuscript Department of the 1930s, Aberdeen's letters were divided between what is now the British Library and his family home in Aberdeenshire, Haddo House.

After Lady Frances Balfour's biography in 1923 another fifty years were to pass before Mrs Lucille Iremonger published her biography in 1978. Mrs Iremonger was the first scholar to use the extensive papers still at Haddo. Her purpose was avowedly to present the case for the defence and to give a picture of the private man who had attracted the warm admiration, and indeed love, of the small circle who had really known him. In this she succeeded admirably.

It may be said that, as a private man, Aberdeen needs little further defence. He remained remarkably unembittered during a long life which was marked from beginning to end by personal tragedy. Orphaned at an early age, left to make his own way in the world, he knew brief happiness with his adored first wife before she succumbed to tuberculosis. Aberdeen nursed the three talented and delightful daughters of his first marriage, and the only daughter of his second, with a quite extraordinary tenderness and devotion until, one by one, they succumbed to the same disease. His second marriage was stormy and his four sons all contrived to torment their father in one way or another. He died with the bitter knowledge that his eldest son was a dying man, unlikely to survive his father for very long. Yet he faced it all with what he hoped was

Christian resignation (although his Christianity always bordered on agnosticism) but which, to an outsider, looks more like Stoicism. He was an admirable husband and father, dealing with great patience with his hysterical second wife and his often wayward sons and step-sons. He extended his paternal relationship to a number of other young men, including Viscount Canning, the eldest surviving son of George Canning (although it could be argued that George Canning himself had never treated Aberdeen well), and even William Gladstone himself.

He felt the same sense of paternal obligation to his Scottish estates. Arthur Gordon rather disliked Scotland[18] and consistently played down the Scottish dimension which was in fact very important to his father. Much as he disliked speaking in the House of Lords, nothing brought Aberdeen to his feet quicker than what he saw as an attack upon the Scottish legal system, marriage laws or banking system. When he took over his estates they were badly neglected. By the end of the nineteenth century they were among the show estates of Scotland[19] and most of the transformation had taken place in the time of the fourth Earl. His record here was far and away better than that of many nineteenth–century statesmen, whose public reputation has always stood much higher.

There are other aspects of Aberdeen's career which have never been given their due, largely because they were of little interest to his original biographer. As a young man, Aberdeen was a classical scholar of great promise and no little achievement. His investigations into the archaeology of the Eastern Mediterranean were remarkably scientific for that period, and his contributions to the *Edinburgh Review tours de force* for so young a man. He played a very important role in the Society of Dilettanti, which was the most important patron of classical archaeology in the period. He was originally a very active President of the Society of Antiquaries, however negligent he may have become when he was Foreign Secretary. He was also active as a member of the Council of the Royal Society, a Trustee of the British Museum and a Trustee of the National Gallery. His judgement was always independent and his recognition of the merits of the Elgin Marbles was to be of crucial importance.

And yet one cannot ignore the fact that his contemporaries themselves drew some distinction between the private man, whose record was almost wholly admirable, and the public man who seemed to have some fatal flaw or weakness, which led him to disaster. Was this judgement unjust, the result simply of the fact that Aberdeen's case was never properly put to the public? Two things may be said at the outset. First, it passes belief that a man who was the kind of naive fool that Aberdeen is sometimes portrayed as being, could have been regarded as an exceptionally promising protegé by the Younger Pitt and as a trusted friend by men as diverse as the Duke of Wellington, Sir Robert Peel and William Gladstone.

Secondly, there is no doubt that he was quite extraordinarily unlucky in the presentation of his case. Not only was he deprived of the publication of his own papers and the tribute of a substantial biography, which was accorded to practically all the other major statesmen of the period, but also a great deal of what was published soon after his death gave the point of view of his enemies. Lord Ellenborough's *Political Diary*, which covered Aberdeen's first period at the Foreign Office from 1828 to 1830, was published in 1881. It dripped with venom from the pen of the man who felt that Aberdeen was keeping him, Ellenborough, out of the Foreign Office. Seven years later came Lane-Poole's *Life* of Stratford Canning which, as a fighting defence of Canning, almost inevitably cast Aberdeen as the villain. Aberdeen himself was perfectly correct in thinking that he had been the victim in 1852–55 of a well–orchestrated campaign by political enemies, who may or may not have disliked him as a man, but who certainly saw him as the 'keystone' or the 'bond'[20] of a political coalition which, so long as it endured, frustrated all their own ambitions. Coming as it did at the end of his public life, Aberdeen had no time to rehabilitate himself. Once cast as the villain or scapegoat, he seems to have continued to play that role, certainly in the popular mind and sometimes in scholarly works as well. Unfavourable contemporary references tend to be repeated from book to book, favourable ones are rarely mentioned. To take but one example, more than one historian has remarked that in her *Journals* Mrs Arbuthnot twice called Aberdeen 'a fool', even a 'pompous fool'. No one seems to have noticed that there are numerous references to him throughout the *Journals*, practically all of them favourable, or that the 'pompous fool' remark came after he had got the better of her in an argument.[21]

Aberdeen did not come from the charmed circle of English political families who had dominated British politics for generations. Despite their marriage connections with the Dukes of Gordon, the Gordons of Haddo had not previously aspired to play a prominent part in English politics. From modest beginnings in the fifteenth century, they had built up a very strong local base in Aberdeenshire until, by the end of the eighteenth century, they were the largest landowners in the county. Only the accidental death of the future fourth Earl's father and subsequent family quarrels brought him to England, made him the ward of the Younger Pitt and convinced him that high politics were the most honourable career a man could follow.

Aberdeen himself had no skill in the management of public relations. From the time he turned tail and failed to deliver his maiden speech, he was an extraordinarily bad speaker in the House of Lords, nervous, inaudible and easily rattled by a skilful opponent. He had little press backing. When Delane chose to bring the great weight of *The Times* to bear on his side, as he did frequently in the 1840s, it was an enormous asset, but one which Aberdeen could never count upon. It deserted him altogether in the 1850s.

Aberdeen was not an immediately impressive figure who could command an audience. A man of medium height, with dark curly hair and a rather unusual face with remarkably high cheek bones, as a young man (if Thomas Lawrence's portrait is to be trusted) he greatly resembled his kinsman, Lord Byron. Whether or not Lord Aberdeen was handsome tended to be a matter of amused speculation by young ladies, even royal ones. Queen Victoria wrote in her Journal in February 1839: 'We had great fun about Lord Aberdeen, who Lord M[elbourne] would have was very handsome, and asked several of the Ladies if they didn't think Lord Aberdeen was very handsome, and nobody did; "Oh! he has a beautiful magnificent expression; a sweet expression," said Lord M.'[22]

As he grew older, Aberdeen seems to have become heavy and rather awkward. A visiting American referred to him as 'clumsily made'. Aberdeen, who was not a vain man, was rather amused by the description and told his old friend, Hudson Gurney, that he had never noticed his clumsy make but perhaps it became more apparent after the age of fifty. The American had also commented on his careless dress and Aberdeen admitted to Gurney that he had been wearing a very threadbare coat that day.[23]

Aberdeen always had a strong sense of humour and an acute sense of the comic, which he shared with his first wife and their daughters. He laughed uproariously on one occasion when, accompanying the Queen on the royal yacht, Lord Liverpool accidentally locked himself in his cabin and it seemed likely that they would have to pull him out through the porthole 'like a cork out of a bottle'.[24] On another occasion he scandalised the young Duke of Argyll by being unable to contain his mirth in the Queen's presence at the sight of Sir Robert Inglis, a vehement Protestant, taking the required oaths against Popery.[25] Aberdeen's letters are full of a quiet sardonic humour. When under pressure he could become unpleasantly sarcastic. He was often accused in Parliament of 'sneering'. Those with the wit to do so, like Benjamin Disraeli, tended to retaliate with interest.

Criticism followed Aberdeen almost from his earliest days. He was the target of a considerable press campaign, when British Ambassador to Austria in 1813–14, for being ready to concede too much to France in a negotiated peace. Aberdeen did make mistakes as Ambassador but much of the fire was totally misdirected. The British public, with their eyes firmly fixed on Wellington's victories in Spain, thought that Bonaparte was defeated long before he was and that Britain could dictate the settlement of Europe. This was nonsense and Aberdeen knew it. To the Continental Powers Spain was a sideshow. The decisions would come in Germany where Britain had no army. Before Aberdeen arrived at allied headquarters in September 1813, Britain had been almost ignored in the Allies' counsels and had not even been told the terms of the treaties between the other Powers. The great danger was that the other Powers would conclude a 'Continental' peace, which would totally ignore British interests. Aberdeen saved a good deal when his bargaining position was very weak. To blame him for not insisting on depriving France of Antwerp at a time when Napoleon still controlled the whole of the Low Countries, or for letting a reference to 'maritime rights' (an issue on which the whole Continent was united against the British position) slip in, reveals the unrealism of the British public rather than the weakness of Aberdeen.

His experiences as a young man, his embassy to Austria, together with his travels in the Ottoman Empire and his journey through France in 1802–03, did a great deal to mould Aberdeen's views of foreign affairs for the rest of his life. His views were independent of party and conflicted with many of the favourite prejudices of his countrymen. He had many continental friends and was exceptionally well informed about the real situation in various European countries. While, as he angrily said himself on several occasions, his own patriotism was never in doubt, he never succumbed to nineteenth–century jingoism. A doctrine of 'My country, right or wrong' had no attraction for him. His view remained essentially a European one and he believed that, generally speaking, what was good for Europe was good for Britain.

Aberdeen was the only British Prime Minister of the nineteenth century, apart from the Duke of Wellington himself, who had ever seen a battlefield. He conceived a great horror of war as he surveyed the field of Leipzig and followed the retreating French army across Europe. He understood the full tragedy of the Crimea much better than the public did. But he never became a pacifist. He always held that a country had not only the right, but the duty, to defend its vital interests. As Foreign Secretary he would have taken his country into war on more than one occasion, if necessary. His sense of guilt about the Crimean War sprang not from any belief that it was wrong for Britain to go to war to defend Constantinople, but from the fear that war had been resorted to before diplomacy was exhausted; this offended against both his private morality as a man and his training as a diplomat.

Aberdeen also emerged from his early experiences with a deep horror of revolution and the bloodshed which was likely to follow. He did not regard the Vienna Settlement of 1815 as perfect or immutable but he never became more staunchly Tory than when he believed that it was in imminent danger of violent destruction, as in 1830 and 1848. In the eyes of his countrymen he became the friend and supporter of despots. He stood in his place in the House of Lords and defended the actions of Radetzky in Italy and of the Tsar in Hungary. He always believed that France, and above all a revolutionary or a Bonapartist France, represented the greatest real threat to the peace and stability of Europe. In one sense his commitment to the French *entente* of 1843–46 was an aberration, attributable to his conviction that Louis Philippe and Guizot were the best guarantees of a stable and pacific France for whom great sacrifices must be made. He went very far in 1849–50 in his efforts to bring about a *fusion* of the Legitimist and Orleanist branches of the French royal house and to keep out Louis Napoleon. None of this finds any place in Gordon's biography.

There was a considerable element of eighteenth–century *realpolitik* in Aberdeen's policy. He was quite familiar with and entirely unperturbed by the 'dirty tricks' departments of the times, such as the 'Secret Department' of the Post Office in Abchurch Lane, which intercepted and opened foreign mail – until it was so unfortunately revealed to the public by the friends of Mazzini. He was not shocked by the deception of the Sultan in the Convention of Alexandria in 1828, nor by the use of the 'secret maps' to put pressure on interested parties during the Ashburton–Webster negotiations.

It was a favourite charge brought by radical critics against the 'secret diplomacy' before the First World War, that ambassadors were given instructions in private letters which never appeared in the official despatches. Whether or not this was true of the period immediately before 1914, it was certainly true of the first half of the nineteenth century. Palmerston and Clarendon did it as well as Aberdeen.[26] As Foreign Secretary, Aberdeen seems to have been constantly at cross purposes with his own ambassadors. This was by no means always his fault. The ambassadors themselves were sometimes of doubtful quality and the slowness of communications meant that they sometimes received instructions urging action, just as they were being countermanded from London. But Aberdeen did constantly modify his official instructions in his private letters. This was usually because he had been unable to persuade his Cabinet colleagues to adopt officially the line he really wanted to pursue. The most striking example of this was in his correspondence with Stratford Canning in 1828–29. Aberdeen generally had little sympathy with nationalism but there was one exception to this. He did sympathise with Greek nationalism. The Prime Minister, the Duke of Wellington, on the other hand wanted to subordinate all other considerations to the upholding of Turkish power. In the end it was Canning who suffered.[27]

This tendency to use private channels of communication meant that really sensitive material was often kept out of the official archives – not least because the Foreign Office was very prone to 'leak'. The full story of Aberdeen's quarrel with Canning in 1829 was suppressed. Much that Aberdeen wrote to Castlereagh in 1813 never went to the Foreign Office. The extraordinary activities of the British Ambassador to Paris, Stuart de Rothesay, on behalf of the French Legitimists in 1830, were entirely concealed.[28] Only very occasionally were documents already in the archives changed, although this did happen in the aftermath of the Tahiti crisis so that the official records should tally with what Peel called 'the producible controversy'.[29] Two very important (or what came to be regarded as very important) documents, the Nesselrode Memorandum of 1844 and Guizot's memorandum of 27 February 1846 on the Spanish marriage question, were not deposited in the Foreign Office at the time.[30] Each subsequently surfaced in the most embarrassing circumstances: the Nesselrode Memorandum when *The Times* published it, having learnt of it from the *St Petersburg Gazette*, and Guizot's memorandum when the French used it as an excuse for arranging the simultaneous marriages of the Queen of Spain and her sister, later in 1846. Generally, however, secrecy spared rather than caused embarrassment and the Aberdeen Papers are often a richer source of what really happened than are the official records. Gordon, if he knew of these episodes, was careful to suppress them – for obvious reasons. Their revelation in the different moral climate of late nineteenth–century England would have added to the condemnation of his father rather than rehabilitated him. But this would be to misunderstand the situation. There was nothing unique in what Aberdeen did. He was simply following the normal practice of his time.

Aberdeen's defence of 'despotism' is a rather different question. Here he put himself completely at odds with the growing national and liberal temper of the times. Palmerston, a much more adroit politician, knew how to capture it for his own purposes. Aberdeen's viewpoint is an interesting one, if only because it makes the modern reader stop and reconsider many of the assumptions of nineteenth–century liberal historiography. Aberdeen was probably right in thinking that the Portuguese wanted Miguel as their King in the 1830s or that Piedmont was an ambitious and self-seeking state, but it took a bold man to say so. In the end, Aberdeen exasperated even his own close friends such as Sir James Graham, until Graham complained to Peel that, although he was a 'liberal' at home, Aberdeen was a 'zealot' (for despotism) abroad.[31]

The contemporary press had already dubbed Palmerston 'a Tory at home but a liberal abroad',[32] and the opposite paradox does indeed seem to have been true of Aberdeen. The pupil of Pitt and the friend of Peel, Aberdeen never opposed what he regarded as well considered reform. At the time of the first Reform Act, he tried to bring about a compromise. During the next few years he suffered a rather sharp reaction, perhaps understandably brought about by the fact that the expenses of post–Reform Act elections ruined his finances and one of his brothers was seriously injured by a radical mob, but even in the 1830s his private letters show that he was giving serious thought to many social questions. He believed in the power of education as zealously as any Benthamite and he eventually came to the conclusion that the Great Reform Act had left the representative system in an even worse state than before and that only further reform would remedy the situation.

It is less surprising than it might at first seem, that he emerged in December 1852 as the leader of a coalition government which, if it had not been overtaken by the Crimean War, had all the makings of a great reform administration. Contemporaries saw with some astonishment that Aberdeen had no intention of being a mere figurehead and that he had more 'pluck' than many of his usually bolder colleagues. The public knew little of his thinking on domestic questions but there was one episode in his earlier career, to which very little attention has ever been paid, which might have given a clue to his role as Prime Minister. Very briefly, in Peel's short administration of 1834–35, Aberdeen had been Colonial Secretary. He had not much enjoyed the job as he found the administration of the patronage involved tedious. Yet in those few months he had shown all the makings of a very good Colonial Secretary. He was in office during the critical months when the Act emancipating the slaves throughout the British empire took effect. He had to face serious problems in both South Africa and Canada. If his policy had been carried through, great future difficulties would have been avoided in both countries.

Aberdeen was almost sixty-nine when the coalition was formed in 1852. Even in foreign affairs, if he and his great rival and almost exact contemporary, Lord Palmerston, had retired at the conventional age of sixty-five, their post-humous reputations would have been very different. Palmerston's handling of the crises of 1848–49 had aroused widespread distrust. Aberdeen, although not without his critics, was still generally remembered as a cautious and states-manlike figure who had always kept the peace. Kingsley Martin, writing after the Second World War, once compared Aberdeen to Neville Chamberlain.[33] It was a natural comparison to make and, in some ways, profoundly true. Aberdeen, like Chamberlain, was not, as many contemporaries supposed, merely a weak man resorting to appeasement as the easiest policy. On the contrary, he was an obstinate man who believed that he could perceive a path to safety if he could persuade his colleagues to follow it. But there was one vital difference. Chamberlain was tragically wrong in 1938–39, Aberdeen was probably right in 1853–54.

NOTES

1. HH 1/28, Alexander Gordon to Lord Haddo, 25 Dec. 1860; *Selections from the Correspondence of the Earl of Aberdeen*. Privately printed. Of the 13 volumes in the British Library, 4 were printed before 1860.

2. SRO RD5/1116, pp. 256–9. Holograph Codicil to the Will of the 4th Earl of Aberdeen, dated 16 Nov. 1857.

3. Add. MSS 44320, Arthur Gordon to Gladstone, 30 Dec. 1870, 4, 20 Jan., 3 Apr. 1871, Gladstone to Gordon, 2, 6, 29 Jan. 1871; Add. MSS 49326, Arthur Gordon to O. C. Waterfield, 2 Apr. 1871.

4. There is a good biography of Arthur: J. K. Chapman, *Arthur Hamilton Gordon, First Lord Stanmore*, Toronto, 1964.

5. See below pp. 404–6.

6. Stanmore, *Sidney Herbert*. Stanmore's preface praising Gladstone is heavily ironic (vol. 1, pp. vii–viii); cf. Add. MSS 44322, Gladstone to Gordon, 22 Apr. 1891, Gordon to Gladstone, 22 Apr. 1891.

7. The *Edinburgh Review* obtained some of the privately printed volumes and Henry Reeves reviewed them in 1883, clviii (1883), pp. 547–77.

8. Add. MSS 44322, Gordon to Gladstone, 22 Apr., 15, 29 June, 27 Aug. 1891, Gladstone to Gordon, 18 July 1891; Add. MSS 49209, Gladstone to Gordon, 17, 21 Feb. 1893, Gordon to Gladstone, 19 Feb. 1893.

9. Stanmore, pp. 322–3.

10. Add. MSS 44322, Gordon to Gladstone, 2 June 1871.

11. Stanmore, pp. 312–3.

12. HH 1/32, 1st Marquess of Aberdeen to George F. Hill, 2 Dec. 1932.

13. For example, C. K. Webster's strictures in his *Castlereagh 1812–1815* draw on the Balfour biography. Although not uncritical, he had taken a much more judicious view of Aberdeen in the *Cambridge History of British Foreign Policy*, written a little earlier, see especially vol. 1, p. 412.

14. HH 1/32, Marquess of Aberdeen to Hill, 2 Dec. 1932.

15. SRO RD5/1116, pp. 258–9; HH 1/32, Marquess of Aberdeen to Hill, 2 Dec. 1932, Hill to Aberdeen, 6 Dec. 1932.

16. HH 1/32. Hill to Aberdeen, 19 Nov. 1932, Aberdeen to Hill, 2 Dec. 1932. Various bundles of letters at Haddo House are still tagged as being so returned e.g. HH 1/28, 'Letters from Lord A. to Lady Maria Hamilton, his sister-in-law 1813. Selection made. These to be returned as very private.'

17. HH 1/32, Hill to Aberdeen, 19 Nov. 1932, Aberdeen to Hill, 2 Dec. 1932.

18. See his Journals in Add. MSS 49253–6 and 49269. He was prone to complain that his countrymen could not even run a railroad.

19. PP, XVI (1896) Royal Commission on Agriculture, pp. 489–99, 516–7; cf. Ch. 5 below.

20. 'Keystone' was Gladstone's word, 'bond' Aberdeen's own; Add. MSS 44319, Gladstone to Arthur Gordon, 28 July 1854; Gurney Papers, RQC 334/124, Aberdeen to Gurney, 22 Feb. 1855.

21. *The Journal of Mrs Arbuthnot 1820–32*. The 'pompous fool' reference is on 20 Mar. 1821 (vol. 1, p. 84). On another occasion for example she wrote, 'Ld Aberdeen is a very sensible, amiable man who will . . . keep peace & harmony in our foreign relations' (4 June 1828, vol. 2, p. 191).

22. RA, Queen Victoria's Journal, 8 Feb. 1839.

23. N. P. Willis, *Pencillings by the Way*, quoted *Quarterly Review*, liv (1835), p. 463; Gurney Papers, RQC 334/84, 85, Aberdeen to Gurney, 19 Oct., 27 Nov. 1835.

11

24. V. Surtees, *Charlotte Canning*, p. 92.
25. Argyll, *Autobiography and Memoirs*, vol. 1, p. 416.
26. For example some of Clarendon's private letters to Stratford, such as those of 26 May and 1 June 1853 (Stratford Canning Papers, PRO, FO 352/36) are less than consistent with the suspicions he was expressing to his colleagues. He excused this to colleagues on the grounds that Stratford was such a difficult man that he must be placated.
27. See below Ch. 13.
28. See below pp. 238–40.
29. See below p. 367.
30. The status of the Nesselrode Memorandum has attracted much subsequent interest. Puryear's belief in its binding nature (*England, Russia and the Straits Question*) is generally rejected. Cf. Temperley, *England and the Near East*, pp. 253–7 and Bolsover, 'Nicholas I and the partition of Turkey', *Slavonic and East European Review*, 27 (1948–49) 115–45. On Guizot's Memorandum see Jones-Parry, *The Spanish Marriages*.
31. Add. MSS 40452, Graham to Peel, 7 Apr. 1850.
32. *Morning Herald*, 17 Dec. 1853.
33. B. Kingsley Martin, *The Triumph of Lord Palmerston*, pp. 25–6.

CHAPTER ONE

The Gordons of Haddo

The Gordons of Haddo liked to trace their descent from the Bertrand de Gourdon whose arrow fatally wounded Richard the Lionheart at the siege of Chalus
in 1199. The fourth Earl believed the story and told the editor of Douglas'
Peerage of Scotland in 1808, 'The current tradition and belief is that the immediate descent is from that Bertrand de Gourdon, who shot Richard the first in
Normandy & that my crest with the motto (two arms ready to let fly an arrow
from a bow & *fortuna sequatur*) allude to that event, and the words with which
it was accompanied.' But the fourth Earl, normally a most careful scholar, was
an incurable romantic about the history of his own family.[1] There were certainly
Gordons living in Scotland before the death of Richard I and the Richard Gordon, who is a more probable ancestor of the Gordons of Haddo, was already
settled in Berwickshire about 1170 but the tradition that the family had a
foreign origin would be compatible with the possibility that they sprang from
one of the Norman families whom the House of Canmore brought into Scotland
in the eleventh and twelfth centuries. Adam Gordon, a descendant of Richard
Gordon of Berwickshire, obtained the lands of Strathbogie in Aberdeenshire
from Robert the Bruce and it was one of his descendants, Alexander Gordon,
who became Earl of Huntly about 1445. His descendant George Gordon,
Fourth Marquis of Huntly, became the first Duke of Gordon in 1684.[2]

Nineteenth century reference books usually politely described the Haddo
Gordons as a cadet branch of the family of the Dukes of Gordon. More strictly,
they represented an older but illegitimate line of the family, although the
illegitimacy was itself the matter of some dispute. The Sir John Gordon of
Strathbogie, who flourished between 1376 and the 1390s, contracted a 'handfast' marriage with Elizabeth Cruickshanks, the daughter of the Laird of
Aswanley. Handfast marriages were common throughout the Highlands but
they were not recognised by the law or the Church. When Sir John died, his
estates passed to his brother, Sir Adam, and eventually from the failure of male
heirs to Sir Adam's daughter, Elizabeth. In 1408, Elizabeth married Alexander
Seton, who assumed the surname of Gordon, and it was their son who became
the first Earl of Huntly. Sir John had, however, left two sons not recognised
by the law, 'Jock' and 'Tam'. Jock, or John, was a man of some property. A

13

charter of 1418, which described him as the natural son of the late Sir John of Gordon, Knight, granted him the lands of Ardlach with the mill of Bady-chale 'in the barony of Aberdour and the sheriffdom of Aberdeen', which were to descend to his lawful heirs male or, failing them, to his natural sons, Alexander, Adam and Thomas. In fact, John married and had three legitimate sons, John, William and James. The Haddo Gordons were descended from James. The Fourth Earl firmly pointed out to the editor of Douglas's *Peerage* that the Dukes of Gordon descended from the female line and were really Setons and 'it might be mentioned that my descent is continued in the male line'.[3]

James acquired an interest in the lands of Haddo on the river Ythan in the parish of Methlic, some twenty-five miles north west of Aberdeen, through his marriage to Canea Harper, 'half-portioner', that is co-heiress, of Methlic, and his son, Patrick, was described as 'Gordon of Methlic' when he was killed at Brechin on Ascension Day 1452, fighting under the Earl of Huntly against the Earl of Crawford. Robert II had granted Methlic to the Foulerton (or Foullar-ton) family in 1382, and various grants from the Foulertons to the Gordons culminated on 22 June 1469, when William Foulerton of Abberruthven made over to James de Gordon, probably the grandson of the first James, all his lands of Haddo and half of Meikle Methlic. James's son, Patrick, extended his prop-erty when on 24 October 1479, David Annand of Ochterellon transferred pos-session of all the lands of the Park of Kelly with the lands of Overhill and 'pertinents' lying in the parish of Methlic.[4] These lands of Haddo and Kelly, acquired in the fifteenth century, still remained the heart of the estate in the nineteenth. Although they extended their possessions greatly in the intervening centuries, the family never showed much interest in acquiring lands outside Aberdeenshire.

The sixteenth century was a time of consolidation rather than of spectacular advance in the fortunes of the Gordons of Haddo. The Gordons made discreetly advantageous marriages with neighbouring families and gained some useful acquisitions, such as the town of Tarves in 1550 and the lands of Savock (Saphak) in 1560–61.[5] As a later descendant, Lord Stanmore, observed: '. . . these Lairds of Haddo were a tough and exceedingly long-lived race. Excepting those who came to a violent end on the battle-field or the scaffold, there were few of them who did not attain or exceed the allotted age of man.'[6] Patrick Gordon, who had had seisin of Methlic as son and heir in April 1475, did not die until 1531 when he was succeeded by his grandson, James. James continued in possession until 1582, when he too was succeeded by his grand-son, another James. James lived until 1623 and was once again succeeded by a grandson, John.

It was this John Gordon who brought the family into public prominence. He committed himself wholeheartedly to the Stuart cause during the Civil War and was the first Royalist judicially executed in Scotland. In 1639 Charles I had appointed him second in command to the Marquis of Huntly over the army raised to fight the Covenanters and three years later he created him a Baronet of Nova Scotia by a patent dated at York, 13 August 1642. In March 1643 Sir John led a spectacular raid on the city of Aberdeen but vengeance quickly followed. The Marquess of Argyll attacked him in his house of Kelly. The house was sacked and Sir John himself carried off to Edinburgh, where he was confined for a time in a small cell in the Tolbooth prison, which came to be known as 'Haddo's hole'. He was beheaded on 10 July and his estates confiscated. On the scaffold he commended his soul to God and his six children to the king, for whose cause he was dying.[7]

Charles II did not hasten to repay the debt although the family estates were restored to Sir John's eldest son, another Sir John, by the Scottish Parliament in 1661. The second Sir John died in 1665, leaving only a daughter, and the title and estates passed to his next brother, George. George had been bred to the law. He had studied at King's College, Aberdeen, and abroad and was reputed to be a brilliant man. He distinguished himself both in the Scottish parliament, where he opposed the idea of a legislative union between England and Scotland, and in the courts. He eventually found a patron in the Duke of York, later James II, who came to administer Scotland on his brother's behalf in 1680. Sir George became President of the Court of Session in October 1681 with a salary of £500 a year and the following May he was appointed High Chancellor of Scotland with a princely salary of £1500 a year. On 30 November 1682, he was raised to the peerage of Scotland as the first Earl of Aberdeen. But the new Earl did not long remain in favour with the Duke of York. Two versions exist of his fall from grace. According to Crawfurd, although the Earl had no personal sympathy with the Covenanters, he refused to see the law abused to persecute them and, in particular, opposed a measure to make husbands and fathers responsible for the opinions of their wives and daughters. According to Bishop Burnet's less charitable explanation, the earl belatedly sought to find favour with the Covenanters after his rapacity had led to an intrigue against him at court. He resigned the Chancellorship in May 1684, but, whatever the true cause of his quarrel with the court, he did not approve of the Glorious Revolution of 1688. He refused to take the oaths of allegiance to William and Mary and, as a result, was imprisoned for a time in Edinburgh Castle. On his release he retired completely into private life on his Aberdeenshire estates. He took the oaths to Anne and again played some part in public affairs.[8]

Apart from his official salary, the first earl had married a wealthy heiress, Anne Lockhart of Torbrex, and in the early 1680s he added substantially to his estates, buying Over Ardlethan, Auchneve, Auchmalladie, Rawkstone (Raxton), Nether Ardlethan, Oykhorne and Tillicairn, as well as property in the city of Aberdeen. His last important acquisition was the barony of Tolquhon in 1717. He died in 1720 in his eighty-third year.[9]

His only surviving son, William, had been born in 1679. William held even more markedly Jacobite opinions than his father. In the first general election after the Union, that of 1708, William was returned as the Tory member for the county of Aberdeen but, in December of that year, the Commons resolved that as the eldest sons of peers had not been eligible to sit in the Scottish parliament and, as the Act of Union provided that each country should retain its own electoral customs, they could not now sit in the Union parliament. In

January 1709, William's election was held to be invalid, together with that of the eldest son of the Marquis of Annandale.[10] The decision was legally a dubious one and the real objections to the young Lord Haddo were his Jacobite views. After his father's death he was twice elected as one of the sixteen representative peers of Scotland, in 1721 and 1722, and during his brief time in the Lords amused himself by consistently opposing all government measures on principle.

Debarred from a public career by his opinions, the second Earl devoted himself to his family and his estates. He married three times: first, in 1708, Mary, the daughter of the Earl of Leven and Melville; second, in 1716, Susan, the daughter of the Duke of Atholl; and third, in 1729, Anne, the daughter of the Duke of Gordon. By his three wives he had seven sons and three daughters. Tradition describes him as a prudent, religious and cultured man. He was able to make considerable additions to his estates, for example, Crichie in 1722, Fedderat in 1723–4, Ballogie in 1726, the Boddam estate between 1726 and the 1740s, Tarland in 1729 and Ruthvens in 1742.[11] He had a fierce pride in his family and his land, which caused him to tie up his property in the complicated entail which was fashionable in eighteenth–century Scotland, but which gave later generations of heirs many problems. The estates were to remain intact through almost every conceivable line of descent and his descendants were to have no power to alter his dispositions. His heirs were to continue to use the name of Gordon and all the resonant family titles, Earl of Aberdeen, Viscount Formartine, Lord Haddo, Methlic, Tarves and Kellie, even if they were advanced to a higher title. If they failed to do so, they would forfeit the property. His successors were to have certain limited rights to provide for their widows and younger children from the income of the property but such charges were not to exceed 50,000 merks Scots money at any one time. If this amount of money was already committed, the next heir could make no provision for his dependents. He had no right to sell, mortgage, exchange or in any way alienate the property.[12] It was this sort of provision which caused a report of 1814 to say that a Scots heir at entail was no more than a 'life renter' of his property.[13] The fourth Earl was to suffer a good deal from his great grandfather's rigid views on the future of his estates.

It was the second Earl who built the present Haddo House, to replace the house damaged during the Civil War. In 1731 he employed the Scottish architect, William Adam, the father of the two famous Adam brothers, Robert and James, to design it for him. This was not long after Leoni's edition of the works of Andrea Palladio and Colen Campbell's *Vitruvius Britannicus* had made the Palladian style fashionable in England, and Adam built the second Earl one of the first Palladian houses in Scotland. It was a house of dignified simplicity with the family arms and the names of William and his third wife, Anne, the daughter of the Duke of Gordon, placed on the front. Its merits have come to be appreciated in the twentieth century[14] but, unhappily, William's immediate successors were more impressed by the inconvenience of transplanting a style, which depended on sweeping out-door stair-cases and entrance doors which opened directly into main living rooms, from Italy to the bleaker climate of north-east Scotland. The fourth Earl spent much time and money on making his ancestral home more comfortable.

William died in Edinburgh in March 1745. He had gone there intending to join the Young Pretender but he was a cautious man and, as Lord Stanmore succinctly puts it, 'he was still only talking about it when, fortunately for the interests of the family, he died somewhat suddenly'. Stanmore also relates that his eldest son, George, had 'according to the prudent custom then prevalent in great Scottish families, been bred a Whig'.[15] He certainly found no difficulty in coming to terms with the Hanoverians but he never achieved a high place in British politics. He was a Scottish representative peer from 1747 to 1761, but he felt that his services were not appreciated by the government. He several times asked the Duke of Newcastle for the 'green ribbon' (the Order of the Thistle) to which he felt entitled as a prominent Scottish nobleman. In March 1761 he protested that, if he were to be left out of Parliament after fourteen years loyal service, during which time he had never been given office, he ought to have some mark of royal favour.[16] He again sat as a representative peer from 1774 to 1790 but he voted against Pitt's Regency Bill in 1788, and was not returned again after 1790. In 1794 he was passed over for the Lord Lieutenancy of Aberdeenshire, which would normally have come to him as the county's largest landowner.

His descendants believed that his lack of success in public life was due to his reprehensible character. Many years later Lord Melville explained to the fourth Earl that his grandfather had had to be passed over for the Lord Lieutenancy because of his scandalous life.[17] The fourth Earl was brought up by his widowed mother and her circle of friends to think very badly of his grandfather. He passed this version on to his son, Arthur, Lord Stanmore, on whose biography of his father all subsequent work has been based. Even the *Complete Peerage* refers to the fourth Earl's 'harsh and negligent grandfather', and in a brief family history written by his descendant, Cosmo Gordon of Ellon, in 1958, he features as 'the wicked Earl'.[18] The rather scanty surviving evidence, mainly letters now in the Scottish Record Office, does not entirely bear out the received version.[19] There is no question that the third Earl was a rake, notorious even by the easy standards of the eighteenth century but, far from being harsh and negligent towards his family, he seems to have been generous, affectionate and imbued with a strong, if unorthodox, sense of justice.

He married Catharine Elizabeth Hanson of Wakefield. If a local Wakefield tradition is to be believed (and the information about the Hanson family appears to be correct) this was literally a shotgun marriage:

George, 3rd Earl of Aberdeen, came on a visit in 1762 to John and Esther Hatfeild of Hatfeild Hall, Stanley, and having reached Wakefield late in the evening, he stayed at the Strafford Arms for the night, and partook of some mutton chops for supper. They were cooked so much to his taste that he asked to see the person who had cooked them, and went into the kitchen for that purpose. He was so greatly struck with the fine appearance of the cook, Catharine Hanson, then 29 years old, the daughter of Oswald Hanson, blacksmith, of Sandal, that he at once began to make love to her. After his visit to Hatfeild Hall was ended he went once more to the Strafford Arms, and again saw Catharine, who followed him to his bedroom at night with a loaded pistol, and threatened to shoot him if he did not marry her. He consented and married her according to promise . . .[20]

By her he had two sons, George and William, and four daughters, Catherine, Anne, Susan and Mary.

He also kept a number of mistresses and fathered a number of illegitimate children. His principal crime in the eyes of society seems to have been the openness with which he acknowledged them. Two of the mistresses are well documented, Mrs Dering or Diring (or in one version Miss Dairam, said to be of German extraction) by whom he had two children, Alexander and Penelope, and Mrs Janet Forrest, by whom he had three children, John, Charles and Isabella. He had bought the Ellon estate, confiscated after the '45 Rebellion, in 1752, and he installed Mrs Dering and Mrs Forrest in Ellon Castle on the road from Aberdeen to Peterhead, a few miles from Haddo. He also had an older illegitimate daughter, Susan Gordon, who lived in England and in whom the Earl apparently had great confidence since he made her one of the Trustees of his Will. She may be the daughter of another mistress who, according to family tradition, lived at Wiscombe Park in Devon but who is otherwise completely mysterious.[21]

Although the third Earl's concern for the welfare of his illegitimate children was to be a thorn in the side of his lawful kin, for many years he seems to have remained on good terms with his wife and legitimate sons. When he was away from Haddo his younger son, William, wrote to thank him for presents, to assure him that 'Mama, my Sisters and I are all very well & happy with the thoughts of seeing you here soon' and to ask him for instructions on running the estate. The cattle and horses, he told him, were well looked after, the hay put in the stables and barn, and his orders about the oats carried out but as they had already killed the two hogs, as the Earl had ordered, and were running short of pork and beef, what should they kill next? His daughter, Susan, wrote to him while on a visit to London, full of the delights of the big city and hoping that her father would soon be able to join her. The Earl's letters do not bear out the other family tradition that he was so vain that he always referred to himself by the royal 'We'. Apart from some legal documents they are written in the normal first person singular.[22]

Except for one unfortunate episode, the third Earl was also on excellent terms with his elder son, Lord Haddo. In 1773 he sent him on the Grand Tour, in the care of a Captain Livingstone, with careful instructions about the boy's morals, honour and health although he allowed that Livingstone was a better judge of his studies. He enjoined him to incur all proper expenses for one of his son's rank but without extravagance. The Earl had some reason to worry about the expense and it may have been from Livingstone that Haddo learnt of the extravagance that angered his father and embarrassed his son. When they reached London, Livingstone wrote apologetically,

We dined this day at the Star and Garter in New Bond Street. We had only a fowl boiled, some beef . . . and a bottle of wine. The Bill came to 18 shillings which certainly was very dear. I trouble your Lordship with this detail to show you how the money goes fast away.

Haddo wrote full of excitement to tell his father that they had spent the night at Hatfield rather than proceed after dark because 'Lord Seaforth was robbed between Barnet and London' at about that time of night. The letter is an affectionate and informal one which suggests a warm relationship with his father. Unfortunately later letters, describing the Tour, do not seem to survive but Haddo acquired a liking for all things Italian and some competence in the language. His portrait by Pompeo Batoni, mentioned by Livingstone, now hangs in Haddo House.[23]

By 1782, Haddo, still only eighteen, had run up large debts and had to apply to his father for assistance. His father agreed but made conditions. Haddo must give up his house at Chesterhall, sell all except three or four of his horses, accept a reduced income of £650 a year and enter into a proper legal agreement with his father 'on stamped paper', in the presence of witnesses. Haddo was furious and humiliated, particularly at the last condition. Moreover, he had just made up his mind that he wanted to get married. He wrote to a brother officer that he would have to resign from his regiment and go abroad. He complained he had been 'most cruelly used . . . All I ask'd or wish'd for from Ld A. after my debts were pay'd was his consent to marry and to settle what he thought proper upon us.'[24]

The quarrel does not seem to have lasted long. Within a matter of weeks, Haddo had married Charlotte (or Charles), the daughter of William Baird of Newbyth and the sister of General Sir David Baird, and in 1787, the third Earl purchased the neighbouring estate of Gight for his son for the sum of £17,850. The estate had belonged for generations to another branch of the Gordon family. The last 'Laird' of Gight was Catherine Gordon, who married Captain John Byron, the eldest son of Admiral the Hon. John Byron, in 1785. Captain Byron was a man of notorious extravagance and quickly ran through his wife's fortune, forcing the sale of the Gight estate. There was supposed to be an ancient prophecy by Thomas the Rhymer,

> When the heron leaves the tree
> The laird o' Gight shall landless be

and family legend insisted that, shortly before the sale, a number of herons which had nested for years at Gight, flew over to Haddo, where Lord Haddo was supposed to have said 'Let the birds come, and do them no harm, for the land will soon follow.' The next year Catherine Byron gave birth to her famous son, George Gordon Byron, the poet. The paths of Lord Byron and of the fourth Earl of Aberdeen were to cross on a number of occasions until the former's death in 1824, and perhaps some of Byron's attacks upon Aberdeen were fuelled by a sense, however unjustified, that Aberdeen's family had stolen his mother's lands.[25]

Lord Haddo made his home at Gight, or Formartine as it was more usually called in this period. He was a cultured man who retained his love of Italian literature but he also immersed himself in all the sporting activities of a Scottish laird. His eldest son commented wistfully in later years, 'My father certainly contrived to make himself the most popular character in this county, chiefly I believe by conforming to the pursuits of the country, and by the art of concealing when necessary, the *learning and rationality*, he possessed, of which indeed few people had more. This appears to me enviable.' Haddo was a convivial man, a leading Freemason and, in that capacity, he even laid the foundation stone of the South Bridge at Edinburgh in July 1785.[26]

Haddo's eldest son, George, the future fourth Earl, was born in Edinburgh on 28 January 1784, his father's twentieth birthday. His birth was quickly followed by that of five more sons, William, Alexander, Charles, Robert and John, and one daughter, Alicia. The last child, John, was born posthumously, some months after his father's sudden death on 2 October 1791 at the age of twenty-seven. Inevitably, legends gathered round the tragedy, including the belief that it was the fulfilment of yet another prophecy by Thomas the Rhymer but the most circumstantial contemporary account, which was accepted as accurate by his eldest son, who was probably at Gight at the time, is in the *Gentleman's Magazine* of October 1791:

At Formartine-house in Scotland, Lord Haddo. The unfortunate accident which occasioned his death is very singular. After handing Lady H. and her sister into her postchaise, to go to attend Aberdeen races, which commenced next day, his Lordship had just mounted his horse, and in leaning forward, the animal struck him a violent blow with his head on his chest, which stunned him so much he fell. His groom ran immediately to his assistance, and in a few minutes he was so far recovered as to be able to mount his horse with apparent ease; but before he had proceeded a few yards, the servant perceived him to be seized with a sudden giddiness, and he fell to the ground motionless. The bursting of a blood-vessel is supposed to have been the immediate cause of his death.[27]

Haddo's death was followed by a serious quarrel between the third Earl and his daughter-in-law. Lady Haddo took her seven children and went south to London. She turned for help to an old friend of her husband, Henry Dundas, later Lord Melville, who was then Home Secretary in William Pitt's first administration. Dundas and his wife, Jane, showed great kindness to the Gordon children but they seem to have played a significant part in totally estranging the new Lord Haddo from his grandfather. Lady Haddo's health failed and she died at Clifton, at that time a spa rivalling Bath, on 8 October 1795. Dundas and his wife then became virtually substitute parents to the young Gordons. The Baird family seem to have taken little responsibility although Sir David Baird, who was in India at the time of his brother—in—law's death, later took charge of Alexander, and perhaps of Charles, who both made their career in the army.

George had begun his education at preparatory schools on the outskirts of London, first at Barnet and subsequently at Parsons Green. He went to Harrow in June 1795. According to the *Harrow School Register*, his brothers, William, Alexander and Charles, entered with him but, in view of Charles' age it seems unlikely that he actually accompanied his brothers to school. William left to join the navy in July 1797.[28]

George believed that his grandfather was very reluctant to pay for him to go to Harrow and probably refused to pay for him to go to Cambridge.[29] He seems to have felt some bitterness for this all his life but a draft of the third Earl's will, apparently drawn up in November 1791 soon after his son's death, puts the matter in a rather different light. In this document the Earl named a number of highly suitable men to be the curators or guardians of his grand-children in the event of his own death. 'I name,' he said 'for tutors and curators of my grandchildren, sons and daughters of George, Ld Haddo, my son, he not having named any, His Grace the Duke of Gordon, Marques of Huntly, my son William Gordon, General Gordon, Col Cosmo Gordon, Lord Rock-ville, my brothers, and Lady Haddo, while unmarried.' Any three of these were to form a quorum. When Henry Dundas heard of the provision, some ten years later, he responded with unbounded indignation. To nominate guardians for her children was, he insisted, a breach of promise to Lady Haddo. 'The whole is so gross an outrage on your mother's memory', he wrote to the fourth Earl, 'it is impossible to think of it without indignation.' Dundas' anger seems exaggerated. The nominees were the obvious and proper men to look after the interests of an infant heir to great estates and the third Earl had himself acted as guardian to the Duke of Gordon during the latter's minority. Among various financial arrangements, including provision for Lady Haddo and George's younger brothers, the third Earl also laid down, 'I . . . recommend that my grandson Ld. Haddo be partly educated in Scotland that he do not despise his own country'. This suggests a rather different interpretation of the third Earl's reluctance to see his grandson educated at Harrow and Cambridge. It may also explain the reported opinion of an old family retainer in 1804 that the young Earl would have been a fine man 'gin they hadna ta'en him to England, and spoiled his education'.[30]

Whatever the truth of the matter the young George naturally believed the version told to him by those who surrounded him. At the age of fourteen he availed himself of his right under Scots law to choose his own guardians and applied to Dundas and Dundas' friend, William Pitt. Pitt liked the young Scots boy and willingly accepted. Thereafter he lived alternately with them. In a sense his whole later political career sprang from those critical years.[31]

An ambiguous sentence in Stanmore's Life has led later writers to suppose that Haddo lost all contact with Scotland between the ages of eight and twenty-one. This was not so. Dundas was frequently at Dumira in Perthshire and Haddo accompanied him there. He told Hudson Gurney in 1802, 'I always fix my headquarters [at Dumira] when in Scotland.' Dundas even gave him a small house for his own use, his 'Vall Ombrosa', for which he cherished the deepest affection. Other letters show that, as he grew up, he went to Scotland for the shooting; on at least one occasion with Frederick Robinson, later Earl of Ripon. Haddo always felt great affection for Dundas but over the years their relationship subtly changed. At first the younger man depended very much on his guardian for practical and business advice but later he came to assume almost a protective role towards him as when he organised the Scottish peers to try to retrieve Dundas' ruined finances after the debacle of the impeachment.[32]

There was no such ambiguity in his relations with Pitt. His loyalty and admiration for Pitt endured until the end of Aberdeen's own life. The time he spent in Pitt's house in Wimbledon remained vivid in his mind. It was here that he came into contact with high politics and made up his mind that his own destiny must lie there. But for this almost accidental association there was no reason why he should have done so. His own family had not been prominent in national politics. His own temperament was conspicuously not that of a politician. Sometimes he had doubts and considered striking out on a different course but he always returned to the view that the public service was really the highest calling. These early associations had another effect too. Aberdeen expected to enter politics at the top and to talk to any man on equal terms. He was a patrician in what was still an age of patricians. Despite the major blow to his career which resulted from Pitt's early death in 1806, he was very largely able to do what he expected.

At Harrow he met three other future Prime Ministers, Frederick Robinson, Henry John Temple, later Viscount Palmerston, and Robert Peel. Peel, however, was four years younger and it seems improbable that they had more than the most superficial acquaintance at this time. But Temple, like Robinson, was his almost exact contemporary. No doubt, like Temple, he studied Caesar, Terence, Ovid, Virgil and Horace, as well as Homer and the Greek Testament.[33] Like Temple too he contrived to learn some Italian, perhaps inspired by his dead father's interest. He may have acquired his passion for the theatre from the then headmaster, Joseph Drury, although William Pitt was a devotee too. His grounding in English seems to have left much to be desired. As a young man his spelling and grammar were idiosyncratic, although his later style was impeccable. His son, Arthur, may be right in believing that he was a 'quiet and studious boy'[34] but it sounds suspiciously reminiscent of the lectures which Aberdeen was prone in later life to address to his adolescent sons. Harrow School was a tough place in the late eighteenth century. Drinking and swearing were the fashionable pastimes and boys were expected to prove their manliness by fisticuffs. As Palmerston's biographer, Jasper Ridley, rightly points out, anecdotes of the relations of the two boys, including the well known one of the pillow fight in which Temple worsted Haddo, are somewhat suspect when they date from after the Crimean War. In any case, the pillow fight anecdote is balanced by another in which Haddo locked Temple in an inner room without a candle until he was heard pleading, 'Lighten our darkness, we beseech thee, O Lord.'[35]

There seems no particular reason to believe that Haddo, a robust and adventurous young man, good at most outdoor pursuits, as his travels a few years later demonstrated, fared badly at Harrow. He retained an affection for the school and became a very active governor. He later took the credit for the appointment, in the face of much opposition, of Dr Vaughan as Headmaster.

Vaughan was only twenty–eight at the time of his appointment in 1844, but, in Aberdeen's view, he brought Harrow from a state of decay to one of prosperity in a few years. In 1859, however, Aberdeen failed to secure the appointment of Barry, the Headmaster of Leeds Grammar School. The fact that Barry was not a public school man – which Aberdeen considered unimportant – was fatal to his chances.[36]

In June 1800, Haddo left Harrow for St John's College, Cambridge. He only resided in Cambridge regularly in the session 1800–1 and, less regularly, 1801–02. As a peer he was automatically entitled to a degree without an examination – the regrets he later expressed about this circumstance again sound a little like routine paternal exhortations. He did not repine at the time. His two years at Cambridge were a golden interlude to which he always looked back with pleasure.[37] He was a scholar by nature and he plunged happily not only into classical, but also into Renaissance, studies. He began to collect books and laid the foundations of an impressive library. For the first time he found himself in a circle of like-minded young men with whom he could exchange ideas, prominent among them Hudson Gurney and George Whittington. Gurney was one of the great Quaker banking family, although himself a member of the established Church. He professed rather radical politics although, as Aberdeen cynically pointed out, he did not seem to find them incompatible with making 'hogsheads' of money.[38] The two men remained friends for life and exchanged letters on every conceivable subject, including Aberdeen's financial difficulties, until Gurney's death in 1858. Whittington, who was preparing for the Anglican ministry, was probably Aberdeen's closest friend and, with Gurney, accompanied him on his tour of France and Italy in 1802–03.[39] He was a shrewd counsellor and his premature death in 1807 robbed Aberdeen of a staunch friend, whose loss he always felt. A Harrow friend, Lord Royston, the son of the Earl of Hardwicke, joined Aberdeen at Cambridge in 1801. He too died prematurely in a shipwreck off Memel in 1808.[40] Another Harrow friend, Lord Binning, the son of the Earl of Haddington, although he did not go to Cambridge, remained a member of the group.

They all had literary ambitions and freely exchanged verses, essays and translations of then fashionable authors. Aberdeen, after much urging, sent some of his own 'Juvenalia' with suitable apologies and disclaimers to Gurney. But by now he had quite a good opinion of himself as a literary critic. He poked fun at some recent unfortunate translations of the scriptures and derived a good deal of amusement from one which ran,

> 'Tis like the precious ointment that
> Was poured on Aaron's head,
> Which from his beard, unto the skirts
> Of his rich garment spread.

'Such', he remarked, 'is the translation of one of the finest psalms of David.' He told Gurney that he was proposing to erect a cenotaph to John Barbour, Archdeacon of Aberdeen: 'a Scotchman who wrote better and more intelligible

English than his contemporary Chaucer, and it is a curious fact that most of the Scotch writers of that period excelled the English in purity of language'.[41] He does not seem to have carried out the project.

Aberdeen was also thinking of competing for two university prizes, although he asked Gurney not to mention the fact because 'no one wishes it to be known that they write'. For one he was composing an English ode on the Column a Pompeii. The snag was that for submission it would have to be translated into Latin. The other required an essay on the internal evidence of the New Testament. Aberdeen did not, at this time, have much taste for theological debate and he complained to Gurney that he was 'immersed in the streams (often mud ponds) of divinity'.[42]

Not all their writings were on this intellectual plane. They also composed satirical, not to say Rabelaisian, verses about Cambridge life. One entitled 'College confusion', which seems to be in Aberdeen's own hand, poked fun at new regulations on dining and on chapel. It ran in part,

> Gentle College, Gentle College
> Gentle now thou art no more;
> Bachelors with bloody noses,
> Drunken Deans distain thy floor . . .
> He'll restore the loved rice puddings
> Which Sir Isaac long denied.
> Trace Sir Isaac's opposition
> To the FUNDAMENTAL cause,
> He knew costiveness and rice were
> Linked by nature's certain Laws.

A milder verse teased Whittington. It began,

> I have known many skill'd in canonical law,
> Who said Graces curtail'd very small,
> But Sir you are the first that ever I saw
> Who really said nothing at all.

It went on to hope that Whittington would increase in Grace 'while with conduct judicious and sage, You your path to a Bishopric Trace'.[43]

George's career at Cambridge was interrupted in August 1801 by the death of his grandfather, in his eightieth year, at Ellon Castle. The new Lord Aberdeen travelled north to Haddo for the reading of his grandfather's Will. When he learnt its contents he was torn between furious anger, a certain sense of humour and perhaps a grudging recognition that his grandfather had his own sense of fair play. He wrote the next day, 'I yesterday attended the opening of the papers at Ellon Castle, and surely never was such a will opened in Scotland.'[44]

The third Earl had a very twentieth–century attitude to the rights of illegitimate children, or perhaps he was only reverting to the views of the fifteenth century, Sir John Gordon, that the rights of natural children were only slightly inferior to those of the legitimate line. It was a point of view that his legitimate heirs could hardly be expected to appreciate. The fourth Earl was to inherit, as he was legally bound to do, all the lands entailed by the deed of 13 July 1765 by the second Earl, and the third Earl had added very considerable properties to the original entail, including the lands and Barony of Gight. He entailed the Ellon estate on his younger son, William, and his heirs. But he divided other recently acquired estates among his natural sons – Auchmedden to Alexander, the son of Mrs Dering; Cairnbulg to John, and Boddam with its fishing rights to Charles, the sons of Mrs Forrest. If William died without heirs, Ellon too was to pass to the third Earl's natural children. William had considered this unfair and had argued with his father that it ought to revert to his nephew, William, the fourth Earl's next brother, but the old man was unmoved. His legitimate heirs had good reason to complain that, while he had stipulated that all financial settlements on his widow and on the younger children of the family should be charges on the entailed estate, he had found ways of milking the estate to provide considerable sums for his illegitimate children. In November 1791, he had executed Bonds of Provision for his natural children of £3,000 for Susan, £5,000 for Alexander, £5,000 for Charles, £5,000 for John, £2,000 for Penolope and £2,000 for Isabella. On his death he provided a further £2,000 for Susan and £5,000 for Charles. On his death too, Mrs Dering and Mrs Forrest were to receive modest annuities and some of his estates, not subject to the entail, were to be sold, along with the London House in Tilney Street, to pay his debts and to provide for the education of his natural children, some of whom were still very young.[45]

It was a long and extremely complicated Will but his grandson quickly grasped the essentials. He wrote to his lawyer the following day,

I send you enclosed an account of all the settlements we discovered; by which you will see that he has added several estates to the original entail, but has left me burdened to the amount of about 26,000 exclusive of my Father's debts which amount to seven thousand. I am to pay Lady Aberdeen's jointure, which amounts to about a thousand yearly–2,000 to each of my Brothers–10,000 to Mr G. [the third Earl's son, William] to be given to Lady Anne and L. Mary and the rest in various Legacies. To Mr Gordon he has left Ellon etc. and the hard part is that he has entailed it upon his natural children, failing Mr G. in male issue; after passing thro' his three natural sons, *it then is to come to my brother* William and that series of heirs, failing male issue in the above mentioned children. Upon his eldest he has settled upwards of 26,000, upon his second, 10,000 with an estate of 1,200 a year, and the same upon his third. For the daughters he has provided handsomely in proportion . . . Everything is in the most confused state, no accounts, no receipts or anything of the kind to be found, and his accounts have not been settled since the year 90 . . . if you think the Law can alter anything tell me if you wish to be possessed of copies of any of the settlements and they shall be sent.[46]

Aberdeen was already thinking ahead to possible alterations of the settlement. 'There was no contract of marriage', he commented, 'between the late Lord and his wife, and certainly I should think she might claim a larger provision from his personal estate, and if she is inclined to wave [sic] her claims

in favour of my brothers I should think something might be done for them.
Lady A. however was a party to the deed, and accepted the annuity in full of
her claims.' Aberdeen did not mention that the family plate, consisting of seven
dozen plates and twenty-eight dishes, had also been conveyed to Lady Aberdeen
and after her death were to go to William, not to the heir at entail.

Aberdeen did not view his own prospects too despondently. 'My estate', he
wrote, 'when new lett [sic] will not fall short of sixteen or seventeen 000£ so
that the burthens may be payed during my minority.' Moreover, the 'Great
part of the estates is very improvable and will soon amount to 20,000.' But it
was a disappointing home-coming. 'Concieve [sic] my sensations at seeing this
place after an absence of twelve years!' he wrote.[47] He did not remain there,
but quickly went to consult Dundas at Dumira. There was the less reason to
remain because he could not control his estate until he came of age in 1805.
His grandfather had appointed as trustees, his son William, his son-in-law,
Edward Place (the husband of his daughter, Anne), his daughter 'Susan Gordon', John Burnett (Advocate in Edinburgh) and Alexander Shand and Alexander Crombie (Advocates in Aberdeen). His legitimate daughter, Susan, had
died in 1795 and since this will was not drawn up until 1798, Susan Gordon
must be his illegitimate daughter. Perhaps she was appointed to watch the
interests of the natural children. Her father was particularly anxious that she
should attend meetings of the trustees and provided for special payments when
she had to travel from England.

Dundas was extremely indignant when he heard the terms of the Will,
although he had already told the young heir that it would probably not be to
his liking and he should feel under no obligation to go to the funeral, unless
his grandfather had left specific directions that he should do so. He advised
him to take immediate legal advice and recommended the services of a Mr
Manchope and of Mr Blair, the Scottish Solicitor-General. A month or two
later he wrote to Manchope,

I have desired Mr Crombie to be in Edinburgh in the course of November as the Chief
Baron, yourself and I must have a very minute consideration of the whole of Lord
Aberdeen's Affairs, in order to advise him in what manner to proceed. He will one day
have a fine fortune: but his Grandfather has contrived to keep him underground as long
as possible. I hope my young friend will become an enthusiast in his own Affairs, for
from the short view I had of it, he has a noble Field to work upon.[48]

The third Earl's Will proved, however, to be good in law and Aberdeen had
to resign himself to leaving his affairs in the hands of the trustees for the next
few years. In fact, the trustees were conscientious and efficient. The papers now
in Aberdeen University Library relate principally to the administration of the
affairs of the natural children and their education which, ironically, the trustees
decided should be in England. But William exerted himself to get the estate
in order for his nephew and Alexander Crombie stayed on as Aberdeen's trusted
man of business for many years.[49]

NOTES

1. NLS, MS 2251, f. 3, Aberdeen to the Editor of the *Peerage of Scotland*, 30 May [1808]. This story was incorporated in the 1813 edition with Normandy corrected to the Limosin. For other evidence of Aberdeen's interest in family traditions, especially connections with the House of Stuart, see below pp. 32, 75.

2. This account is based mainly on R. Douglas, *The Scots Peerage* (1907 edition) vol. 1, pp. 82–99, vol. IV, pp. 506–62; but see also 1813 edition (ed. J. P. Wood), vol. 1, pp. 16–23.

3. NLS, MS 2251 *ibid.* This point was incorporated in the 1813 edition.

4. SRO, Haddo House Papers, GD 33/36/1–6, 33/30/1, 5. The Gordons held the lands of Kelly from the Earls of Crawford until 17 July 1575, GD 33/30/22.

5. SRO, GD 33/52/2, 33/43.

6. Stanmore, p. 2.

7. Crawfurd, p. 230; Douglas (1813 edition),p. 19.

8. Crawfurd, pp. 230–3; Burnet, vol. 1, pp. 581–3; *Complete Peerage*, vol. 1, pp. 14–18; SRO, GD 33/no number.

9. SRO, GD 33/6/11, 17, 33/8/3, 33/9/17, 33/37, 33/39, 33/41, 33/54, 33/57/16. If a rather scurrilous ballad, 'Cauld Kail in Aberdeen' (R. Chambers, *Songs of Scotland*, pp. 144–6) is to be believed his last years were notorious for a love affair with a young girl.

10. *Parliamentary History*, vol. 1, pp. 757–8.

11. SRO, GD 33/14/7, 33/24, 33/52, 33/59/5.

12. SRO, GD 33/28/24, see also SRO CC 1/6/26. Sir John Gordon, the royalist, had also entailed the estate but less stringently, SRO, GD 33/61.

13. J. Sinclair, *General Report*, vol. 1, pp. 101–5.

14. It is now in the care of the National Trust of Scotland.

15. Stanmore, p. 4.

16. Add. MSS 32877, Aberdeen to Newcastle, 20 Jan. 1758; Add. MSS 32881, The same, 24 June 1758; Add. MSS 32884, The same, 10 Oct. 1758 Add. MSS 32919, the same, 5 Mar. 1761: copies in HH 1/21.

17. Add. MSS 43227, Melville to Aberdeen, 1 Nov. 1807.

18. *Complete Peerage*, vol. 1, p. 17; C. Gordon, *A Souvenir of Haddo House*, p. 12.

19. The letters are in SRO, GD 33/63/IX.

20. J. W. Walker, *Wakefield, its history and people*, vol. 2, pp. 530–1. I am indebted for this reference to the West Yorkshire County Record Office, who also supplied corroborative information about the Hanson family.

21. The best source of information is the Earl's own Will, SRO, CC1/6/64, but see also Aberdeen University Library, MS 1061, Sederunt book of Lord Aberdeen's Trusts in favour of his natural children; notes by Sir James Reid in HH 1/27 and C. Gordon, *Haddo House*, pp. 12–3.

22. SRO, GD 33/63/IX, William to his father, 24 Feb., 6 Mar. 1773, Susan to her father, 2 Mar. 1773; C. Gordon, p. 13.

23. SRO, 33/63/IX, Aberdeen to Capt. Livingstone, Feb. 1773, Livingstone to Aberdeen, 28 Feb. 1773, Haddo to his father, 28 Feb. 1773. Haddo was extraordinarily young for the Grand Tour, only eleven, but the dates on the letters seem to be correct. The Batoni portrait is dated 1775.

24. HH 1/22, Haddo to Laggan, 14 May 1782. Haddo resigned his captaincy in the N. Fencibles in 1782, J. M. Bulloch, vol. II, p. 111.

25. J. M. Bulloch, vol. 1, pp. 291–4; For the later relations between the fourth Earl and the Lord Byron see below, pp. 69–70.
26. Norfolk Record Office, Hudson Gurney Papers, RQC 334/26, Aberdeen to Gurney, 3 Nov. 1809; *Aberdeen Journal*, 1 Aug. 1785. HH 1/38 contains a copy of Haddo's 'Gight Book' of 1791, in which visitors were expected to write contributions (some are in Italian or Latin) with instructions that they were not to be immoral, irreligious or political.
27. *Gentleman's Magazine*, 61, pp. 971–2.
28. *Harrow School Register, 1571–1800*, pp. 77, 81.
29. Stanmore, pp. 4–7.
30. HH 1/27, the draft Will is undated but a memorandum summarising its provisions is dated 6 Nov. 1791; Add. MSS 43227, Dundas to Aberdeen, 27 Aug. 1801; Gurney Papers, RQC 334/26, Aberdeen to Gurney, 3 Nov. 1809 – Aberdeen expressed sympathy with the old huntsman's views.
31. Stanmore, p. 6.
32. Stanmore, p. 11; Balfour, vol. 1, pp. 23–4; Gurney Papers, RQC 334/2, Aberdeen to Gurney. 10 [Sept. 1802]; Aberdeen to Augustus Foster, 22 Sept. 1804, printed Vere Foster, *The Two Duchesses*, pp. 188–9; Add. MSS 43229, Whittington to Aberdeen, 22 Aug. 1802. For his reaction to the impeachment see below pp. 91–2.
33. Palmerston's letter describing life at Harrow survives and is printed in Bulwer, vol. 1, pp. 7–8; none of Aberdeen's letters of this period survives – perhaps because of the careless housemaid.
34. Stanmore, p. 6.
35. Ridley, p. 10; *Edinburgh Review*, clviii (1883), p. 549.
36. Bodleian Library, MSS Clar. dep. c525, Aberdeen to Clarendon, 29 Sept., 7, 8 Nov. 1859. He also played a part in the choice of Christopher Wordsworth to succeed Dr Longley in 1836. Lambeth Palace Library, Longley Papers, Aberdeen to Longley 1 Apr. 1836; Wordsworth Papers 2141, Aberdeen to Wordsworth, 31 Mar. 1836.
37. Stanmore, p. 7; Add. MSS 43229, Whittington to Aberdeen, 25 Sept. 1805, Aberdeen to Whittington, 27 Sept. 1805.
38. Gurney Papers, RQC 334/28, 30, Aberdeen to Gurney, 16 Jan. 1810, 7 Jan. 1811.
39. Whittington did not take priest's orders until 1805, HH 1/19 Aberdeen to Foster, 24 Sept. 1805. He was not, as has sometimes been stated, Aberdeen's 'tutor' see below, p. 61.
40. Few letters from Royston survive but he too had literary pretensions and some of his writings were published posthumously.
41. RQC 334/7, 8, Aberdeen to Gurney, 'Monday 14th' [July 1802]; Dumira, 24 Sept. 1802.
42. RQC 334/4, 6, Aberdeen to Gurney, 9 Mar., 18 Apr. 1802.
43. Add. MSS 43347, 'College Confusion' and 'The Revd Mr Whittington. On his grace after meals'.
44. NLS MS 3418, f. 13, From Aberdeen, Haddo House, 28 Aug. 1801. The letter is to an unnamed lawyer, probably Manchope.
45. SRO, CC1/6/64, will of the third Earl of Aberdeen, died 13 Aug. 1801 (dated Haddo, 30 Oct. 1798), and accompanying papers.
46. NLS, MS 3418, *ibid*.
47. *Ibid*.

48. Add. MSS 43227, Dundas to Aberdeen, 'Sunday' [Aug. 1801], 27 Aug. 1801; NLS, MS 3834, Dundas to (?) Manchope, 27 Aug., 2 Sept., 18 Oct. 1801, 14 Mar. 1802.
49. Aberdeen University Library, MS 1061, Sederunt Book of Lord Aberdeen's Trust in favour of his natural children.

CHAPTER TWO

Athenian Aberdeen

Since he could not enter immediately into his inheritance, Aberdeen returned for another rather desultory year at Cambridge. He was already thinking of travelling and in December 1801, when Britain and France had entered into peace negotiations, he applied to William Pitt for suitable introductions. Pitt was happy to oblige but Aberdeen postponed his travels until the autumn of 1802.[1]

The Peace of Amiens was signed between England and France on 25 March 1802 and, for the first time since the French war began, in 1793, the continent was once again open to young Englishmen who wished to make the Grand Tour. Aberdeen initially planned to go to Florence with Hudson Gurney but Gurney suddenly announced that he was unable to leave on the agreed date. Whittington had already expressed great interest in the Florence venture and Aberdeen now offered him the spare seat in his chaise. Aberdeen told Gurney that he had 'chalked out the finest tour possible' and, at the last moment, Gurney changed his mind and came too. Whittington went as a personal friend and not, as has sometimes been supposed, as Aberdeen's tutor but he had a good deal of influence on the choice of itinerary.[2] Whittington was passionately interested in Gothic architecture. Aberdeen himself preferred the classical style but together the three young men visited many of the great Gothic cathedrals of France on which Whittington was later to base his book, *The Ecclesiastical Antiquities of France*, which Aberdeen edited after his death.

Aberdeen approached his travels in a serious spirit. He kept a diary, part of which he later began to work up into a more coherent journal, and also a note book in which he recorded his impressions of politics, religion, agriculture, trade and manufacturers, manners and dress, literature and the fine arts, theatres, and public buildings. For a young man, still only eighteen, he showed remarkable maturity of observation, especially of politics. His interest in agriculture probably reflected his realisation that he would soon be responsible for his own Scottish estates. Like many travellers of the time he also had a keen eye for the bargains in paintings and sculpture, which might be picked up cheap in a war-torn Europe.[3]

Aberdeen and his party left London on Friday, 19 November 1802, and arrived at Dover the same evening, but they were then detained by contrary winds. They took the opportunity to explore Dover and Aberdeen made some notes on the architecture of the castle. Architectural enthusiasm, however, soon had to give way to more immediate concerns. He noted in his diary, 'After having witnessed the wreck of a French Vessel, a sight perfectly novel to me, and not very encouraging, we sailed.' The weather continued bad. The passage took nine hours, the vessel was crowded, everyone was sick and they had great difficulty in getting in to Calais harbour. Aberdeen added wryly that he might have found it 'amusing', if he had not been extremely ill himself.

Calais and its people reminded him very much of Scotland, although one wonders what picture of his native land he carried with him, since he also noted, 'The rapacity of the Municipal officers is inconceivable. I was obliged to pay 220 Livres before even my carriage was suffered to pass.' According to Gurney the trouble arose from the twelve pairs of leather breeches Aberdeen had brought with him. The French customs officials could not believe that they were all for his own use. From Calais they went to Boulogne and Montreuil. At Boulogne he had some conversation with people who remembered Nelson's attack upon the harbour the previous summer and concluded, with youthful iconoclasm, that Nelson 'added nothing to his fame by that Business'. It had been badly planned and the British sailors inadequately armed. At Montreuil he made his first attempt to buy a picture from the convent but was foiled 'as it is national property, I am a little at a loss to whom to apply.'

From Montreuil they went to Abbeville where his experiences were entirely unhappy. 'I lost my poor dog Tag in this town', he recorded. 'I despair of ever discovering him, as the town is so large and populous.' Only the cathedral was in good repair and the town was full of beggars. They surrounded him in the cathedral and 'from the number of sturdy fellows, howling women, and noisy children, I began to grow rather alarmed, and departed.' On his way back to his hotel some women hissed him 'probably from my being in regimentals.' Wearing British army uniform in France in the autumn of 1802 was probably not the most tactful thing to do but Aberdeen could never resist a 'red coat', especially when abroad. Presumably in 1802 he was wearing the uniform of the 3rd Aberdeenshire Militia which his grandfather had raised and which Aberdeen subsequently commanded.

Amiens and Rheims were more pleasant. The party admired the cathedrals and Aberdeen, who seems to have considered himself an Englishman or a Scot as the fancy took him, recalled with pride that it was the English who built Rheims cathedral. Chantilly brought them back to the realities of the revolution and no doubt it was during this early visit to France that he first conceived the horror of revolutionary upheavals which remained with him all his life. He described it as 'one of the most distressing scenes in France'. The magnificent chateau had been destroyed and the stables were inhabited by what he at first simply called a regiment of cavalry but which he later amended to 'a band of Regicidal Freebooters'. St Denis, the burial place of the French kings, was also marked by the revolution, although Aberdeen found it impressive despite its being despoiled of all its ornaments. They descended to the royal vaults where the custodian told them how in the time of Robespierre the vaults had been opened and the bodies taken out of the lead coffins. He assured them that the body of Henri IV had been perfectly preserved and that it had been possible to see the wound made by the assassin's dagger. Even at such an affecting moment, the young Aberdeen's acquisitive instincts were still working. He was impressed by the marbles and put down a note, 'Mem. to see if I can get a table made of the different marbles.' Versailles too was devastated although the town seemed reasonably prosperous but when Aberdeen talked to some of the tradespeople he found them nostalgic for the Court.

Aberdeen's party arrived in Paris on 27 November. He made copious notes on the public buildings. The Tuileries was in surprisingly good repair and he was impressed by the pictures in the Louvre, especially Raphael's Transfiguration. But what interested him most of all was the Scotch College. All the Jacobite traditions of his family suddenly came to the surface and he was fascinated to learn that the College was the depository of the papers of the 'unfortunate house of Stuart' and that some of their adherents were buried there.

During his short stay in Paris, Aberdeen contrived to visit all the major theatres which were open, the *Théâtre de la République*, which he visited twice, once to see *Cupid and Psyche*, where he found the singing execrable but the *corps de ballet* good; the *Opéra Comique*, where in contrast the singing was good and the design beautiful; the *Opéra Buffe*, the only Italian opera in Paris; the *Théâtre Louvois*, where he saw 'Tom Jones à Londres', which was tolerably well acted; and the *Théâtre Francais*, where he saw La Harpe's 'Mélanie'. Mlle. Bourgois played Mélanie and Aberdeen commented that he had never seen even Mrs Siddons die better.

Politics, however, was the great preoccupation. Even when first planning his expedition the previous winter, before the peace had been finally signed, Aberdeen had approached Pitt on the possibility of an introduction to Bonaparte himself. At Amiens he had seen Lord Cornwallis and been invited to dine with Joseph Bonaparte but declined the invitation, hoping to see him in Paris 'when after a little Practice I should be able to speak French more fluently'. As the ward and protegé of William Pitt, Aberdeen was of sufficient importance for Napoleon Bonaparte, then still enjoying the modest title of First Consul, to invite him to dine at Malmaison. Aberdeen told his youngest son many years later that he was captivated by Napoleon. 'I have often heard him say', Stanmore recalled, 'that Napoleon's smile was the most winning he ever saw, and that his eye was wholly unlike that of any other man.'[4] Napoleon's charisma did not blind Aberdeen to the realities of the situation. He analysed it very coolly in his Journal. Bonaparte was undoubtedly popular but mainly because people were grateful to him for turning out the Directory. He thought he detected a return to both royalist and religious sentiment and was surprised to find how much freedom of discussion there was. 'You may hear', he noted at Versailles, 'a party of Jacobins railing at the present Government, and complaining of their being deluded with only a show of Liberty etc. etc., a Party of Contents, and of Royalists all in the same Coffee house, talking most vociferously.' He appreciated that the prevailing military rule in which the generals were looked up to in the place of the old nobility was a prelude to Bonaparte's restitution of a hierarchy of titles in which he would himself occupy the highest place. He was already First Consul of France and Italy and would probably assume that title in the Helvetic and Batavian Republics too. Bonaparte had suffered an unexpected check in establishing his Civil Code and Aberdeen analysed with interest the way in which he was eliminating all the deputies who had opposed him from the legislative body.

Aberdeen's keen observation of politics extended to economic questions too. He noted that French finances were in such a state of confusion that the government did not know whether or not they were in deficit. French commercial development was uneven. In some ways they were a century behind the British, in others they excelled them. He foresaw serious competition from the reviving French wool industry, especially the fine cloths of Abbeville. He was critical of some aspects of French agriculture but he was delighted by the apple orchards of Picardy and fascinated by the wheeled ploughs which he considered much better than the usual British kind.

The cultural state of France puzzled him. He found the youth of Paris frivolous and interested only in dress. Despite the Revolution the lower classes were generally 'remarkably civil and obliging' but 'they seem to have lost some of their national gaiety, which renders them still more like the Scotch'. This observation gave him an excuse for a rather doubtful historical speculation that the first contact between the French and the Scots was in the time of Mary Queen of Scots when 'the gloomy and savage disposition of the Scotch was greatly softened down and improved by the mixture of the gaiety with which Mary was surrounded.' He acknowledged that the fine arts had not only survived but even flourished during the Revolution and attributed this to the fact that painters and sculptors enjoyed government as well as private patronage. While in Paris he visited Jacques Louis David and found him an extraordinary 'old man' who had just finished a series of designs for the Life of Cupid. Aberdeen had no hesitation in pronouncing the works of David, Girard and Proudhon 'unrivalled'.

Aberdeen, Gurney, and Whittington left Paris on 7 December and travelled south by way of Lyons and the Rhone valley to Avignon. They were shocked once again by the revolutionary excesses which had been perpetrated at Lyons and Avignon. Aberdeen described those at Avignon as 'almost inconceivable' and noted that practically all the churches were destroyed or mutilated. They arrived at Aix-en-Provence on 20 December. It had one fine street but 'the rest of the town is occupied by narrow and dirty Lanes, where the filthy custom which formerly characterised Edinburgh prevails universally' – presumably that of throwing slops from the window. Perhaps that was why they then visited the warm baths. Fréjus interested them as the place where Bonaparte first landed in France and they proceeded to Nice by way of Cannes and Antibes. They left Nice for Genoa on 31 December. They had meant to go by sea but the winds were contrary so 'we went by the corniche, a horrible road'. Aberdeen conceded, however, that the scenery was beautiful and Menton 'very fine'. His horse fell between Savona and Genoa and Aberdeen injured his knee severely.

When they arrived at Genoa on 4 January 1803, Aberdeen, like many other Mediterranean travellers, 'was taken ill . . . with a pain in my bowels' and had to be attended by doctors. But his misfortunes did not prevent him from spending some time visiting the fine collection of pictures in the Duke's Palace. He noted in particular three fine paintings by Giordano, several by Van Dyke and a portrait of Anne Boleyn, said to be by Holbein. He was half fascinated, half disgusted by a picture of Juno sticking the eyes of Argos on to a peacock's tail.

By this time the sea had apparently moderated and they left Genoa in a local boat, a felucca. Their next important stopping place was at Pisa, where, despite Whittington, his remaining anti-Gothic prejudices surfaced. 'The Cathedral', he commented, 'is a wonderful building considering the age in which it was built' but he was better pleased by the Campo Santo, 'an immense cloister of beautiful Gothic work'. For the first time he began to think seriously of writing something for publication. The 'curious frescoes' in the cloister ought, he thought, to be recorded before they decayed.

From Pisa they followed the Arno to Florence. Aberdeen was delighted by the countryside which he described as very rich and thickly planted with olives, mulberries, vines and corn, and entranced by Florence, 'the most beautiful town I have ever seen.' His son records that he spent 'some interesting evenings' at the house of the Pretender's widow, the Countess of Albany and there met the Italian poet, Alfieri, with whom the Countess had lived since her separation from Bonnie Prince Charlie in 1784. Alfieri was surprised to find that Aberdeen spoke Italian so well and had a good knowledge of Italian poetry and, contrary to his usual custom, went out his way to be agreeable to the young man.[5]

Aberdeen left Florence on 29 January for Rome. His classical studies now began to come to life. He remembered that Virgil had said that even the Romans considered Cortona, the former capital of Etruria, ancient, and spent some time trying to date a sarcophagus in the cathedral. But his diary becomes rather brief at this point, although he was apparently still writing dutiful accounts of his travels to Lady Melville and to his uncle, William, and also, not very successfully, trying to make sketches of things which interested him.[6]

Aberdeen's appetite for classical antiquities was by now thoroughly whetted and, instead of returning to Britain, he decided to extend his tour to Greece and the Levant. Although a handful of British and French travellers had begun to penetrate those regions by 1800, it was still an adventurous and potentially dangerous undertaking. His son says that Pitt and Dundas reluctantly gave their consent, but Aberdeen can have had little time to consult them, for in March he was already in Naples ready to set out. An excellent chance had presented itself because a fellow Scotsman, William Drummond of Logie Almond, was on his way out to Constantinople to succeed yet another Scot, Lord Elgin, as British ambassador to Turkey.

The diary which Aberdeen kept, and which is now in the Greek and Roman department of the British Museum, was meant to be a great deal more than a simple record of places visited.[7] He was already well read in the many controversies which had been generated during the previous half century about the location of the sites mentioned in classical literature, notably the position of Troy,[8] and he meant to see for himself and form his own judgements. He visited many virtually unknown sites and excavated some with more care and thoroughness than was usual at this early date. The information which he was later able to supply on demand to other scholars shows that he must have had a considerable body of detailed notes but unfortunately these have for the most part disappeared. The careful copies of a large number of inscriptions, some now destroyed, to which his son refers[9] have also apparently not survived. Of the actual artefacts he brought back, some subsequently went to the British Museum but others, including several of the most interesting, have disappeared without trace.[10] Aberdeen's primary concern at this time was with the remains of classical civilisation but he was also keenly interested in the contemporary politics of the region, which was still under the control of the Ottoman empire. Much of Aberdeen's subsequent career in British politics was to be dominated by the Eastern Question, fundamentally the problem of the decay of the Ottoman empire and the European rivalries about what was to replace it. His position in 1803, as the friend and companion of the British ambassador, gave him the entrée into the highest Turkish political circles. The view he formed of the Turkish empire was deeply unflattering and essentially he never wavered from it even when he was Prime Minister, fifty years later. It could be argued that Aberdeen did not make sufficient allowance for changes brought about by time but it could not be denied that he had a first–hand knowledge of the area and its peoples, which was unusual among British politicians.

Aberdeen's new diary begins in a business-like manner. 'Naples. March 1803. On the fifteenth of March, about ten in the evening, I embarked on board the Medusa, Capt. Gore. In company with Mr Drummond, ambassador to the Porte, Ld Brooke – Messrs Fenwick, Gordon & Findlay.' Charles Gordon was to be his companion during the first part of his eastern tour. It is clear from Aberdeen's own references and from Drummond's letter enquiring anxiously about Gordon's whereabouts, after the two men had parted company, that he could not have been, as has often been assumed, Aberdeen's brother Charles. He might have been Charles Gordon of Abergeldie, a man who carried out a number of confidential missions for the British government in this period, but the identification is not certain.[11]

Aberdeen's tendency to sea-sickness had not left him and he ruefully recorded the next day, 'I was extremely ill the whole of this day, but afterwards got better.' On 17 March, they saw the volcano of Stromboli which 'never ceases emitting both Flames and smoke in great quantities'. On 18 March they passed through the Straits of Messina and Aberdeen began to exercise his detective faculties to identify the famous places of antiquity. He wrote,

The town of Scylla is just above the old rock and presents a picturesque appearance, it is on the Italian side, and just at the entrance of the Straits. What they pretend is Charybdis, is not opposite, but some miles further, close under the Lighthouse of Messina; we sailed through it in a boat, and perceived a little eddy. The whole of the channel is occasionally filled with whirlpools, which are never stationary. When the wind blows strong they are dangerous for smaller vessels, but in fine weather not perceptible. Capt. Gore informs me he has seen in bad weather a very tremendous one precisely opposite Scylla.

The following day, after 'a noble prospect of Etna which appears prodigious', although not in eruption, they landed at Syracuse. He explored the antiquities very thoroughly and was fascinated to see the women washing clothes at the fountain of Arethusa. 'It is curious', he commented, 'to recollect that in the same spot, two thousand years ago, the very same operation was going forward.' By now he was thoroughly caught up in the past and wrote with enthusiasm, 'I observed the spot where Marcellus must have entered the town [during the Punic Wars], it is so circumstantially described, that I could not be wrong.' They also visited the 'cave' of Dionysius and in a spirit of enquiry, perhaps mixed with youthful high spirits, discharged a pistol in the cavern to test the echo. It made a satisfying 'great noise'.

By 20 March they had arrived at Malta, where they remained until the 28th. Aberdeen visited the ancient fortifications of St Elmo and St Angelo. He also studied the agriculture and noted the method of terracing used to prevent the soil being carried away. While at Malta, he received his first lessons in diplomacy. On 26 March he dined with General Oakes, 'where I got into a terrible scrape by speaking my mind too freely concerning Caraccioli [the Neapolitan diplomat] & the King of Naples'. The following day Drummond read him the despatch he had just written concerning Malta. Drummond recommended that the British should continue to occupy the island, even though this was contrary to the Peace of Amiens and might precipitate a new war with France – as, in fact, it did. But Drummond argued that French plans to invade Greece were already well advanced and, if Britain evacuated Malta, it would only expedite the French descent on the Morea, which would in any case lead to war. Aberdeen apparently realised the significance of the despatch because it is the only time he records Drummond's diplomatic proceedings in his Diary.

The *Medusa* reached Melos on 1 April. They were detained there for several days by adverse winds. On 2 April there was a hurricane and they doubted whether their anchor would hold. Aberdeen and his companions spent some time ashore, shooting the abundant birds, snipes, quails, plovers, partridges and hawks. They also saw storks and hoopoes but, to Aberdeen's disappointment, could not 'get at' them.

On 17 April they anchored at Piraeus and the following day, for the first time, Aberdeen walked to the Parthenon. They remained in Athens until 28 April. Aberdeen determined to visit everything within reach and his Diary becomes illegible in his desire to note everything down. On 22 April, they travelled the fourteen miles to Eleusis, stopping on the way at the Greek convent at Daphnis, which had been plundered by a band of Albanians shortly before they arrived. They then 'proceeded along the via sacra to Eleusis, which is finely situated on the sea-side, having the Island of Salamis directly opposite'. Aberdeen saw immense fragments of columns scattered over Eleusis but could make out few architectural details. He discovered some inscriptions of which he made copies. Eleusis, sacred to the goddess Demeter, always fascinated Aberdeen.

On 24 April, he went to the Parthenon again and had time to record his impressions at more leisure than on the first visit. 'From whatever side we arrive', he wrote, 'the Parthenon rises above the Acropolis and forms the most striking object from every point of view . . . The Propylaea was built by Pericles from the designs of Mnesikles, it cost near 11,000,000 [illegible] – more than the annual revenue of the republic.' His descriptions of buildings are always precise and factual, rather than lyrical. He could wax far more poetical about country scenes, particularly wooded ones. He was, however, seriously concerned by the destruction he saw. At the Parthenon on 24 April, he noted, 'Saw destruction committed, which is indeed continual.' He had already noted some days earlier, 'Ionic temple on the banks of the Ilissos . . . published by Stuart is completely gone.' He also visited the Pnyx, the traditional meeting place of the people of Athens in classical times, which was to engage his attention on his return later in the year but where on this occasion he contented himself with trying out the acoustics: he 'spoke and tried the effect of the voice which is admirable'. Two days later he visited the Academy of Plato and marvelled at the immense olive trees. He concluded regretfully that they could not flatter themselves that they had seen the very trees under which Plato taught but he hoped that they might be their descendants. He spent some time scouring Athens to 'procure antiquities but could scarcely pick up anything'. From a passing reference to his 'Greek Master', he may also have embarked on his study of modern Greek.

They sailed from Athens early on the morning of 28 April and later that day had another example of the lawlessness of the region. They saw pirates making for a brig which fired guns for their assistance. Aberdeen laconically recorded, 'We fired one eight and twenty pounder, at the sound of which they made off.'

On 1 May they arrived off the Dardanelles but, like many travellers in the days of sailing ships, had to wait some days for suitable winds to sail through the Straits. They could not go ashore 'on account of the Plague which raged'. This did not deter Aberdeen from doing business with some traders, who presumably came to the ship, and he bought some coins, adding to the small collection he had begun in Athens. By 8 May, they had got as far as Gallipoli where Aberdeen noted 'the doors of the Greek houses are not four feet high, in order to prevent the Turks riding in'. On 11 May he [mistakenly] thought that he saw Mount Olympus 'very distinctly', although at a distance of nearly 70 miles. He was still carefully comparing his observations with travellers' tales and commented acidly, 'The notion of the top being white marble, it is needless to say is perfectly absurd'.

They finally arrived in the harbour of Constantinople on 13 May. Aberdeen immediately fell in love with the city and the surrounding countryside, which no doubt explains why he was so anxious to return there in later years as ambassador. He was astonished by his first sight of the city and more especially by the beauty of the Palace of the Seraglio and its gardens, while 'the country . . . has charmed me more than anything I have ever seen'. He spent the next few weeks visiting the famous mosques of the city and riding out into the countryside with its profusion of woods, shrubs and flowers. As in Malta he took particular note of the crops. He also visited the slave market, where he seems to have felt curiosity rather than indignation. There were both black and white slaves on offer and of the Georgian women, 'the Turks say that some of their skins are so clear that the water in drinking may be seen pouring down their throats like pearls'.

On 21 May, when Drummond had his formal audience with the Sultan, Aberdeen was permitted to accompany him. He had to rise before four in the morning, and be 'in motion' by five. When they arrived at the Seraglio Palace, the Vizier ordered dinner although, as Aberdeen commented in amazement, it was not yet eight o'clock. Drummond and the Vizier ate at one table, Drummond's friends at another. All, however, had to use their fingers. Half an hour later they were taken to see the Sultan. The Sultan, magnificently clad, sat on a throne shaped like a bed and covered with pearls and precious stones. Drummond made a speech and the Sultan replied. Aberdeen understood that this was unusual and a sign of particular favour towards the English.

A day or two later, Aberdeen jotted down his impressions of the state of the Ottoman Empire, which are of interest in view of his later concern with its destiny. He praised the then Sultan, Selim III. He was right in regarding him as a reformer but unduly optimistic in thinking that he had broken the power of the Janissaries who in fact secured his overthrow in 1807. Aberdeen's final conclusion was, however, pessimistic. The power of the crescent was on the wane and, despite the strong fleet Selim had built up, Constantinople would probably fall 'a second time'.

Having explored Constantinople and its environs, Aberdeen was anxious to be off on his travels again. He secured permission from the Turkish authorities to do 'what he liked' at Troy, Rhodes and Cyprus, and letters of introduction to enable him to see Jerusalem. In particular the Captain Pacha lent him an officer to 'superintend and facilitate' whatever he wished to do at Troy.

New interest in the site of Troy had been aroused by the publication in 1767 of Robert Wood's *An Essay on the Original Genius and Writings of Homer: with a comparative View of the Ancient and Present State of the Troad.* Wood had visited the Troad in 1750 and compared Homer's text with the local topography. He published a map of the region but did not attempt to identify the site of Troy on it. Wood's findings interested the Comte de Choiseul-Gouffier, who was appointed French ambassador to the Porte in 1784, and he went out with a team of artists and scholars, intending to probe the problem further. His embassy was interrupted by the French Revolution and his thunder was stolen by one of the scholars who had accompanied him, Jean Baptiste Le Chevalier. Le Chevalier left Constantinople in 1788 and being himself forced to flee from the Revolution, presented his findings to the Royal Society of Edinburgh in 1791. His paper was first published in translation by Andrew Dalzel, the Professor of Greek in Edinburgh, under the title, *Description of the Plain of Troy, with a Map of the Region.* Le Chevalier managed to confuse the issue considerably. The location of Troy depended largely on the correct identification of the

two rivers, mentioned by Homer, the Scamander and the Simois. The Scamander was normally identified with the modern river Menderes. Le Chevalier,
however, believed the Menderes to be the Simois and identified the Scamander
with a small brook near the village of Bournabashi (the modern Pinarbasi) and
originated the theory that Bournabashi itself occupied the site of ancient Troy.
There were many difficulties about the theory, not least that Homer represented
the Scamander as a greater river than the Simois and that Bournabashi was too
far inland to fit Homer's descriptions of continual coming and going between
Troy and the Greek camp on the shore. One reply to Le Chevalier came from
Jacob Bryant, the secretary to the Duke of Marlborough, who had edited the
definitive edition of Wood's *Essay* in 1775. Bryant, however, took the extreme
position of doubting whether Troy had ever existed, believing the whole war
to have been an exercise in poetic imagination, perhaps based on a real war in
Egypt. Another scholar, John Morritt, who visited the Troad in 1794, replied
in 1798 in *A Vindication of Homer* . . . in which he insisted on the 'exact concurrence' between the topography of Homer and the present state of the country. The controversy thundered on through the pages of the *British Critic* and
elsewhere. The location of the site of ancient Troy was thus a lively issue when
Aberdeen embarked on the *Hannah*, with Mr Gordon and the artist, Preux,
on 2 July.

On 6 July, after various misadventures, which included running aground
and being fired upon by mistake, they anchored off the coast of Asia Minor.
Aberdeen immediately went ashore and during the next few days examined a
number of tombs which were confidently stated to be those of the heroes of the
Trojan war, including Antilochus, Achilles, Patroclus and Ajax. Aberdeen
maintained a healthy scepticism, pointing out that the cement on Ajax's tomb
was 'quite modern'. Like other enquirers, Aberdeen found it difficult to identify
the two Homeric rivers, the Scamander and the Simois. Homer had provided
a valuable clue when he said that the Scamander rose from two sources, one
hot one cold. Aberdeen had taken the precaution of bringing a thermometer
with him. He recorded on 7 July: 'We crossed the plain of the sources of the
Scamander, of which I felt 20, all precisely the same temperature, 57: then six
at 75, bathed in what is called the Hot Source.' They slept at Ayas, after
supping on yoghourt and figs.

Aberdeen had an introduction to Osman Bey, the Turkish governor of the
region, and most of his subsequent explorations were carried out with his
assistance. They spent the night of 8 July at Bournabashi, and set out early
the next day for Osman Bey's residence at Bayramic. Aberdeen's journal for the
day alternates between sarcastic references to Chevalier's errors, admiration for
the countryside and surprise at the 'extraordinary' music and dancing with
which the Turks entertained them. When they reached Bayramic, Osman Bey
would not see them that evening 'but ordered us an excellent dinner, and an
admirable Tenedos wine. I got quite drunk . . .'

But he was ready for an early start the next day. He wrote in his diary, '10th
early we paid Osman Bey a visit, drank coffee, smoaked a pipe, were entertained with two young bears from Mt Ida – and returned to our own appart-

ment to breakfast, after which Osman Bey accompanied us with about 100 attendants towards the sources of the Scamander.' The journey took a day and a half. The tents went astray and they had to sleep in the open air 'but none the less such was the mildness of the climate, we undressed entirely. I slept very comfortably.' The road was very beautiful with fine woods of oak and plane trees but the first 'source' he was shown proved disappointing.

It was a miserable Spring, in a rock on the side of the river, the thermometer stood at 75 on one side, precisely the heat of the air, and at the other sixty five. This discovery I made, as it was necessary to crawl under a low sort of natural arch, to where the water gushes out. The water is considered highly medicinal. We encountered forty people from the town of Scylla in Anatolia, 13 days journey off, and several from Constantinople who had come to bathe in & drink the water.

He noticed quantities of rags hanging above the warm spring and realised that they must be votive offerings. For the first time he recognised the significance of some of the bas reliefs he had seen in Greece. After a pause for refreshments they climbed higher to the 'real sources', which proved more satisfying. 'The immense scale which everything is on', Aberdeen commented, 'is astonishing.'

The following day they ascended to Gargaron, one of the summits of Mount Ida. Aberdeen wrote, 'I found the summit covered with violets, thistles, creeping Heath, wild Parsley, and various ariomatick plants. We descended to the principal source of the Simois which is one of the most magnificent sights I have ever beheld.' It rose in a grotto of white marble. Regrettably, Aberdeen carved his name on it. Osman Bey did likewise and Aberdeen was moved to wonder whether the custom was an ancient one. The visit to the 'Sources' was the high spot of Aberdeen's visit to the Troad, although he subsequently enjoyed some excellent hospitality from the Bey and some interesting conversation with Osman and his 'dervish' about the Islamic religion.

On 15 July they sailed for Alexander Troas. 'I never in my life beheld such a mass of ruins', Aberdeen wrote that day. 'The Turks whenever they want to build a palace even from Constantinople had to dig here for marble, in the doing of which Inscriptions and antiquities are dayly discovered. Learned some excavations to be made and got an inscription and some coins.' It took him two days and an expenditure of £20 to get the inscription aboard the *Hannah*. The collecting instinct was now strongly established in Aberdeen and at Mytilene he tried hard to secure a Gospel and a manuscript of the tenth century but the local priests refused to let him have it 'as it is said to perform miracles'.

On the evening of 20 July, they anchored in the harbour of Smyrna, after being alarmed by many whirlwinds as they sailed down the Gulf. His expedition from Smyrna to Sardis, sixty miles away, taking Preaux with him, was not without its difficulties. After eating 'some hard bread steeped in rum and water', Aberdeen became very ill and had to rely on the ministrations of a local doctor whom he found 'very ignorant'. Camping out at Sardis, they were attacked by mosquitoes and rose with 'prodigious swellings'. Aberdeen did not let this divert him from his purpose. While Preaux drew, he traced the plan of an Ionic temple and inspected a three chamber tomb which had been recently opened. His attempt to excavate another tomb was thwarted by the fact that the workmen had no suitable tools. From Sardis he went to Magnesia but, arriving back at Smyrna on 30 July, he recorded, 'Though I am happy to have made this journey, yet I think it is scarcely worth the fatigue'.

A few days later at Scio (Chios) the nineteen year old Aberdeen met a new hazard. He found 'The women are extremely free in their manners. We were invited at several places to pass the night.' He does not say whether any of the party accepted the invitation but he found the women 'very handsome', very tall and wearing a singular dress which he attempted, not very successfully, to sketch.

On 13 August they arrived at the nearest port to Ephesus and, although the plague had recently been raging, they hired horses and set off for Ephesus itself. They arrived just as it got dark for one of their most hair-raising adventures. 'The extent of the ruins and appearance of desolation,' wrote Aberdeen 'struck us forcibly. The village is composed of about a dozen cabins so filthy that we could not enter one of them.' They could find nothing to eat but, with difficulty, persuaded one of the villagers to boil some mullet, which they had bought earlier in the day. 'We laid down in our clothes, but I did not close my eyes during the night. I never saw such a quantity of mosquitoes, nor found them so painful. Wolves and jackals were howling around us in prodigious numbers all night, we were guarded by some dogs who kept them off.'

The next day they made an exhaustive tour of the extensive but ill-preserved ruins. Preaux drew the most interesting. Aberdeen found Spon's plans nearly correct and satisfied himself that he had identified the temple of Diana, one of the seven wonders of the world, and the theatre in which St Paul caused the riot of the Ephesian silversmiths. He recorded a number of inscriptions. They visited the supposed Grotto of the Seven Sleepers but did not enter it lest, as Aberdeen drily commented, they be taken by 'a slumbering fit'.

A new shock awaited them they returned to Scala Nova where they had left their ship. Presumably because of weather conditions, the captain had moved the *Hannah* to the other side of the bay. They hired a local boat to reach it but a heavy sea came up and nearly swamped them. Aberdeen himself had to seize the helm and get them back to land. They were condemned to another night with little food, plenty of mosquitoes and 'the roaring of camels'.

They had a more civilised day on Samos the following day 'and breakfasted on eggs and Samos wine very comfortably'. The next day they visited Patmos, and Aberdeen tried to secure some manuscripts from the monastery of St John but, although he offered 'a great sum', the monks refused to sell. On 20 August Gordon and Preaux departed for Jerusalem but Aberdeen decided to return to Greece. The passage to Athens was a stormy one. Aberdeen noted, 'Everything was broke.' One member of the crew 'promised a large wax candle to the virgin if he escaped'. The danger was real but on the 29 August they sighted Cape Sounion and its famous temple and the following day they were back in Athens.

On his return to Athens, Aberdeen struck up a friendship with Giovanni Battista Lusieri, Lord Elgin's agent, who was still superintending the removal of the sculptures from the Parthenon on behalf of his patron, although Elgin himself was by this time a prisoner of war in France, having been trapped there when the Peace of Amiens ended. Lusieri tells the story of 'two very rich English gentlemen' who, about this time were prepared to offer 50,000 piastres (£4000) for the frieze from the Parthenon. Lusieri does not name them but some authorities have speculated that Aberdeen was one of them. If he was, the other was probably Augustus Foster, the son of Lady Elizabeth Foster, who joined him in Athens about this time. Lusieri persuaded them that this was impossible without firmans from the Porte and that, in any case, Elgin had prior claims.[12] Aberdeen did apparently secure one relic of the Parthenon, a foot of Hercules from one of the metopes. It is mentioned among the goods he shipped home[13] but has unfortunately disappeared. If Lusieri did see Aberdeen as a rival it would explain why, when they were walking together on 31 August, he suggested to Aberdeen that he might turn his attention to the Pnyx. Aberdeen regarded the idea with favour and spent the early days of September excavating, or at least clearing, the Pnyx.

At this point Aberdeen's diary becomes scrappy. He carried out a number of excavations in the vicinity of Athens and must have made detailed notes. Four years later, when another Cambridge friend, Edward Clarke, who was distinguished both as a scientist and a classicist, asked his permission to use an engraving of a head of Medusa which Aberdeen had found, to illustrate a book, he was able to furnish him with a very detailed account of its provenance. It came, he said, from a tumulus, south east of Athens, nearly on the site of the ancient village of Axone. It had been a square chamber, eight feet in diameter and five feet high, with walls composed of large blocks of white calcareous stone, no other specimen of which he had seen in the country. In each corner of the chamber was a head. Round one of them connected by small wires, was a species of chaplet or band entirely composed of the Medusa heads which Clarke wished to use. They were of fine earthenware and it was possible to see traces of gilding, although many were mutilated. The tomb had also contained vases, chests of burnt bones, mirrors, strigils, and paterae. Aberdeen was convinced that the tomb must have been connected with the Eleusian mysteries, partly from the subjects depicted on the vases, and partly from the presence of marble eggs and of a leaden medal with the head of Ceres. Aberdeen's letter to Clarke shows that he had gone into the subject of the Eleusian mysteries with considerable care.[14] Unfortunately, the notebooks in which he must have made his original recordings do not seem to be among those which have survived either in the British Museum or at Haddo.

Aberdeen left Athens on the evening of 26 September, intending to return to Constantinople, but the wind was contrary and he persuaded the captain to put him ashore at Egina, where he went to see the ruins of the temple of Jupiter. 'Amongst them a thought struck me, it was no less than to change all my plans, and instead of going to Constantinople, to make the tour of the Morea and return by way of Venice.' The following day the captain landed him at Epidaurus. It was a mad undertaking. When William Drummond, not a cautious man, heard of it he told him frankly, 'I should not have ventured on such a journey.'[15] The Morea was generally held to be a wild and savage region.

That first night, Aberdeen arrived at a village on the road to Corinth, called Angelo Castro, where only one man had seen a 'Frank' before. Aberdeen was refused admittance at several houses but at last a man, who had been to Athens and even knew Lusieri, took pity on him and let him in.

A Scene ensued perfectly like what we read of in the voyages to the South Sea Islands etc. Men, women & children came and examined me & my clothes with the greatest curiosity. When they saw my conveniences for sleeping and dressing, a man asked if people ever died in my country, at least, he said, with so many comforts they must live two hundred years!! The people were honest, and I was altogether much pleased.

He visited Corinth, Argos and Tiryns, where he was immensely impressed by the cyclopean walls. On 6 October he reached Mycenae. He was puzzled and impressed by what is now called the Treasury of Atreus but which was then known as the tomb of Agamemnon and described it in great detail. He saw the Lion Gate and thought it 'one of the very finest specimens of art in Greece', although at that time earth had almost reached the top of the door. A week later he was at Sparta and gives an unusual insight into his own reactions:

I confess I was glad to find that Sparta excelled its rival as much in picturesque beauty, as in virtue and valour. I always view that proud preeminence to which Athens [aspired] in works of Genius and Art with an admiration mixed with a certain degree of Envy, and it gives me pleasure to learn that the unlettered Spartan strolled unconcerned amidst the taste, the wealth and dissipations of the conquered city of Minerva.

In his enthusiasm his usual scepticism seems to have been in abeyance and he persuaded himself that he had found the tomb of Leonidas, the hero of Thermopylae. In his excursion from the town he did find two bas reliefs, representing articles of womens' toilet, which were to be at the centre of a lively academic controversy a few years later.[16]

Aberdeen had one stroke of luck at Sparta. The Turkish governor, or Voivode, on finding that Aberdeen had friends in high places in Constantinople, loaded him with hospitality, offered him the choice of his collection and provided him with a janissary as escort. Aberdeen had no illusions about the dangers of the country. He noted: 'The most famous robber at present is one Zacheriah', and he was amused by one particular anecdote: 'Some time ago a maniote in ambush, shot a traveller. When he came to examine him, and found he had no money, he exclaimed, " 'tis a pity I've lost a ball".'. Aberdeen was undeterred, and recorded on 18 October, 'We made an expedition into the country of the Maniotes, passed some stupendous ravines of the Mount Tagites, and although everyone told us the danger was great we met with no harm'.

He visited Mistra, Megapolis and Messene, where he 'procured a head, well preserved.' This is the well known 'Aberdeen head', now in the British Museum.[17] From Messene, he set off northwards for Patras. He was now travelling faster, sometimes riding for nine hours a day. They were still living rough, hunting (one day they killed a kid which they had for supper) and sleeping on the ground. Occasionally he was entertained by a local dignitary.

43

The country was beautiful but the season was now advanced and the only important archaeological site where Aberdeen paused for any length of time was Olympia, which he was disappointed to find already 'pretty well explored'. His arrival at Patras marked his return to civilisation, and he dined with the Russian and Austrian consuls.

His movements after leaving Patras are obscure. Some notes, dated January 1804, concerning the guerrilla warfare which the Greeks were already waging against the Turks in Crete, seem to imply that he doubled back to the island. But he certainly then made his way to Corfu and Venice and returned to England by way of Vienna and Berlin. He wrote to Gurney from Vienna, in April 1804, that he had found Venice 'the most pleasant town in the world'. He had come by way of Padua, Verona and then through the Tyrol and Carinthia. Nothing could exceed the 'picturesque beauty' of Carinthia. Vienna too was beautiful but 'as it naturally requires some little time to blush off the shyness in a new society, I shall probably not taste its pleasures to their full extent'.[18]

By the time Aberdeen reappeared in Vienna, his friends (particularly Drummond, who no doubt felt responsible for him) had become alarmed by his prolonged disappearance. Drummond, now back in England, reproached Aberdeen for staying abroad so long 'at so interesting a moment' in British politics.[19] Aberdeen himself, still only twenty, also felt that it was time to return, to begin his public career and take personal charge of his Scottish estates.

NOTES

1. Add. MSS 43229, Whittington to Aberdeen, 7 Oct. 1801, Pitt to Aberdeen, 20, 23 Dec. 1801. The *Aberdeen Journal*, always keenly interested in his activities, confidently announced on 6 Jan. 1802 that the Earl of Aberdeen had gone to Paris.
2. Gurney Papers, RQC 334/2, 8, 10, Aberdeen to Gurney, 'Saturday, 10th' [Sept. 1802], 24 Sept. 1802, 'Monday' [Sept. 1802]; Add. MSSS 43229, Whittington to Aberdeen, 10 Aug. 1802. Gurney kept a Journal, still in the possesion at his family, which is an interesting parallel to Aberdeen's account.
3. The following account is based on the Diary, which forms Add. MSS 43336, and the Journal and notebook, which form Add. MSS 43335. There are extensive quotations from the Journal in Balfour, vol. 1, pp. 15–22 but she appears not to have seen the Diary since she makes the patently incorrect statement that Aberdeen gives no dates.
4. The story that Aberdeen dined at Malmaison rests entirely on Stanmore's testimony (p. 9). Aberdeen's Journal speaks only of his meeting Bonaparte at a public review at which they had some conversation. The Diary may be defective at this point. It is in a disordered state and was bound up out of order before coming into the possession of the MSS Department of the British Museum. Gurney, who comments on Aberdeen's absorption in the Louvre, does not mention Napoleon.
5. This story too rests on Stanmore's account. Unfortunately, there is a gap in Gurney's Journal from 13 January, when they left Genoa, to 29 January, when they left Florence.

6. The sketches and draft letters are in Add. MSS. 43336. There are some better sketches by Aberdeen of architecture and costumes in Gurney's Journal.

7. The following account is based on that diary. It was not used by Stanmore or Balfour. Vol. 1 covers Mar.–Sept. 1803 and vol. 2, Sept.–Nov. 1803. There are some notes relating to January 1804 in vol. 1. There is also a volume of miscellaneous notes.

8. Apart from the works on Troy, mentioned below, pp. 38–9, the principal works with which Aberdeen seems to have been familiar and with which he constantly compared his own observations were P. Brydone's *A Tour through Sicily and Malta* (1773), Richard Chandler's *Travels in Asia Minor* (1775), Jacob Spon's *Voyage* (1678) and G. Wheler's *Journey* (1682). He also had a good knowledge of classical sources, notably Pausanias's *Itinerary*.

9. Stanmore, pp. 10–11.

10. The sculptures he brought back, which were subsequently acquired by the British Museum, are nos 632, 633, 644, 646, 710, 802, 808, 811, 812, 1600, 1697 and 2341 in the *British Museum Catalogue of Sculpture*. They are mostly sepulchral monuments and votive reliefs. Cf. B. F. Cook, *Guide to Greek and Roman Art in the British Museum*. The rest were probably disposed of by the fifth Earl and his wife.

11. I owe this suggestion to the present Lord Aberdeen. Cf. Add. MSS 43229, Drummond to Aberdeen, 24 Apr. 1804; J. M. Cook, *The Troad*, p. 28; J. M. Bulloch, *House of Gordon*, vol. 1, pp. 30–2. A letter from Aberdeen to his son (H.H. 1/22, Aberdeen to Haddo, 23 Jan. 1838) seems to state clearly that Gordon of Cluny was his companion but he was John, not Charles, Gordon, cf. J. M. Bulloch, *The Gordons of Cluny*, p. 33.

12. W. St Clair, *Lord Elgin and the Marbles*, p. 141; H. H. 1/19, Aberdeen to Foster, 20 Nov. 1804, 6 Apr. 1805 (copies); NLS. MS. 1808, Aberdeen to Foster, 4 Mar. 1805. Foster had also been with him for a time in France and Italy, Gurney, Journal, 21 Dec. 1802, 4–13 Jan. 1803.

13. Add. MSS 43256, f. 6, Lists of objects of antiquity, collected by Lord Aberdeen; embarked at Malta 24 Sept. 1808 on the vessel, *Standard*: '2° un très beau pied d'un Hercules d'une des metopes du Parthenon à Athènes.'

14. Add. MSS 43229, Aberdeen to Clarke, 22 July 1807.

15. Add. MSS 43229, Drummond to Aberdeen, 24 Apr. 1804.

16. *British Museum Catalogue of Sculpture*, nos 811 and 812, see below pp. 62–3.

17. *British Museum Catalogue of Sculpture*, no. 1600.

18. Gurney Papers, RQC 334/11, Aberdeen to Gurney, 12 Apr. 1804.

19. Add. MSS 43229, Drummond to Aberdeen, 24 Oct, 1803, 24 Apr. 1804.

CHAPTER THREE

Devonshire House or Bentley Priory?

Aberdeen returned to Haddo in the summer of 1804. It was a dispiriting home-coming, in some ways worse than that for the reading of his grandfather's will three years earlier. He had by now travelled widely and seen some of the most beautiful cities in the world. He found Scotland bleak, barbarous and unin-viting by contrast. He chronicled his dismay to his close friend, Augustus Foster. He arrived in Edinburgh on 13 August in what must have been a peculiarly unpleasant summer. Edinburgh, he assured Foster, was 'of all places the most horrible; there is a most plentiful crop of grass in the streets which the painter of the Panorama has omitted much to the injury of the Rurality of the scene.' From his red nose and sore lips he would have supposed it to be Christmas but 'five or six gloomy months must pass' before that festival arrived. He was about to leave for Aberdeenshire and 'If I am not lost and benighted on my own deserts, I will write shortly.' He tried to persuade Foster who was waiting for a diplomatic appointment to join him and promised him some shooting, although without enthusiasm. 'What a country,' he remarked, 'where murder is the only amusement.'[1]

A week later he was more cheerful and told Foster, 'I do not find this country so horrible as I imagined . . . and there is a sensible pleasure at standing to look around one and being able to see nothing but one's own.'[2] But the task was a daunting one. His house was neglected, with stacks of fuel and lumber piled up against the walls. Marshy swamps and peat-moss came to within a few yards of the house itself. Despite the efforts of the trustees, the estates were still neglected and unproductive. For a short time he considered attempting to break the entail and selling up, but the legal difficulties would have been formidable and a sense of pride in his ancestral lands and of duty to his tenants and dependents also restrained him. He remained at Haddo until the following February, planning improvements on his estates and drawing up model leases for his tenants which incorporated all the best modern ideas of estate manage-ment.[3]

He escaped occasionally to the Duchess of Gordon's cottage in the High-lands, to Blair Atholl 'to massacre a few red deer' and to his own retreat at Dumira. He attended a county meeting at Perth, rather to the amusement of

46

Drummond who assured him that he would have come himself if he had known Aberdeen planned to be there but 'I had no great anxiety to hear the squabbling of our Perthshire *Lairds*.' Drummond and other friends, among them Whittington and Sir William Gell, urged him to come away, but Aberdeen insisted that he must stay, at least until the celebration of his coming of age in January 1805. Whittington understood the importance of the occasion. 'I am quite reconciled', he wrote, 'to your stay in the North, *on account of the gala*, if you had cut the natives at such a crisis you would certainly have undone half a year's exertions.'[4] Aberdeen's majority was celebrated with due ceremony and suitable feasting and drinking for all. Aberdeen told Gurney, 'I feted about seven or eight hundred of my people, as well as the principal Gentlemen of the County' and confessed that he had been so 'completely immersed' in port and claret that he could scarcely write or even think. According to the *Aberdeen Journal*, the bells were rung at all the neighbouring churches, the volunteers paraded on the lawn and fired three volleys, in the evening there was a display of fireworks and bonfires were lit on all the hills; eight hundred people enjoyed a 'plentiful' dinner in a building especially erected for the purpose and the tenants danced to the bagpipes until seven o'clock the following morning. Aberdeen also marked the occasion by suitable charitable donations and gave money to clothe twenty-eight poor children in Methlic. His tenants had every reason to feel that their young landlord understood his obligations in a proper spirit.[5]

Aberdeen, however, had no intention of remaining permanently in residence at Haddo. The possibility of his going as British ambassador to Russia had been raised. Like many a young Scot of the period he also considered going to recoup his fortunes in India. But the most enticing programme was a return to Greece or Turkey. In September 1804 Aberdeen was quite undecided. In a cryptic letter to Foster he told him that he might 'walk the olive groves of Academe,' or freeze 'midst hyperborean snows or inhale the smoke of London.' Academe might mean Greece or Cambridge since he did not finally decide against returning to the university until the summer of 1805 and the hyperborean snows might equally well mean Haddo or St Petersburg.[6]

Gell was the most pressing for an immediate return to Greece. 'Why not', he wrote in October in his usual ebullient style,

relinquish your solitary honours of the arctic circle . . . Think no more of waiting till spring is over, do you not well know that They [the *hoi polloi*] the blatant beast will never think of suffering you to quit England at the London time of the year? . . . Why not hybernize in the Morea and become acquainted with every foot of it? If the people don't kill me outright, I shall have I flatter myself a most copious topographical knowledge of the country before the winter is over . . . No time could be so favourable as the present. Russians and all conspire to favour us & France & Turkey are not very friendly so we are not so likely to be shot by the Imperial order of Bony.

He and two friends were ready to sail by the first fair wind after 30 October. Aberdeen still had time to join them and they could always hire a ship of their own 'without much expense'.[7] It was a tempting invitation to a young man of Aberdeen's temperament but he resisted it.

In February 1805, he was still hesitating. He told Gurney, 'Greece is before my eyes, but my right hand points to India, and my left to Petersburgh.'[8] In the opinion of some of his friends, Aberdeen should have been considering another possibility too, marriage. The Duchess of Gordon had already made an attempt to secure him for her daughter. In his friends' eyes, Aberdeen was a susceptible young man. Drummond was much more suspicious than Whittington of his motives for remaining in Aberdeenshire for the winter. He wrote, 'As your *real* and *urgent* business obliges you to remain in your recesses I have nothing to say; but to indulge such suspicions as are often formed, when a young man happens to be so much occupied, will not, I trust, be forbidden me. Do you remember the fuss I was in at that charming place Barynkdene, when you were so enamoured of a beautiful Arabian Miss, whose name I can neither pronounce, nor spell?' Gurney was equally suspicious and Aberdeen had to assure him, 'I am not married, nor have I any immediate intention of amusing myself by the completion of that ceremony . . . My Heart is equally divided, one part is at Corfu, the other at Venice.'[9]

When Aberdeen finally came to London in March 1805, to lodge at 5 Cleveland Row, he was still in a state of indecision as he told Foster, who by this time had departed to the British mission at Washington. 'It is but two days', he wrote on 4 March, 'since I emerged from obscurity, and resumed my place amongst the constellations which adorn Babylon . . . As for my Plans, they are far from being decided, whether I go to Happy Climes, or remain here; whether I roam in liberty amongst the Beauties of the Day, or content myself with the possession of one object.' He warmed to his theme a little later in the letter, 'It is a great consolation that your women are pretty. As for their expecting you to be enamoured at the first glance it is no objection, provided they comply equally soon . . . . If you meet with the seeds of Plants which are very rare in this country send me a few, for a beautiful Dame who has nothing but vulgar Roses and Lilies in her cheeks.'[10]

Aberdeen had resisted the attempts to embroil him with the Duchess of Gordon's daughter but he now became deeply enamoured of Lady Harriet Cavendish, the younger daughter of the fifth Duke of Devonshire. Augustus Foster was enthusiastically in favour of it.[11] Unhappily, Harriet was a lively young lady who could not resist teasing the handsome but stiff and shy young Scotsman. Aberdeen wrote gloomily to Foster, 'The Thermometer of my affections is not very far from the freezing point, and what is worse, I fear the mercury is still sinking.'[12] He persisted for some time and in April, Lady Elizabeth Foster wrote to her son, 'Your friend Lord *Aberdeen* braves the Duchess of Gordon and flirts with Harriet more than ever! I admire his spirit, but I am sorry the papers have got hold of it and amiable and delightful as he is, he would not be a good match for her.'[13] In the end he became discouraged, greatly to the chagrin of Harriet who, as her brother Hartington realised, was not nearly so indifferent as she had pretended to be.[14] The ill success of Aberdeen's courtship of Harriet Cavendish was to have a permanent effect on his political career because it drove him into the arms of another powerful family, the Abercorns.

London life, political, social and literary, centred on a number of great houses, Devonshire House, the home of the Dukes of Devonshire in Piccadilly, Holland House, the home of Lord Holland in Kensington, and Bentley Priory, the home of the Abercorns at Stanmore in Middlesex. Although Devonshire House and Holland House were accounted Whig and Bentley Priory, Tory, there were no sharp divisions between their habituéś. Many frequented all three, as Aberdeen himself did. Political parties were, in any case, inextricably intermixed at this time, as a result of most politicians of all shades of opinion rallying to Pitt after the outbreak of the French war. As Lord John Russell reminded Aberdeen many years later, Pitt called himself a Whig to the end of his days.[15]

Bentley Priory has left less mark on history than Holland House, partly because it flourished for a much shorter period, but for a generation it played an important part in the intellectual life of the capital, presided over by a remarkable man, John James Hamilton, first Marquess of Abercorn. Abercorn was a man who could perhaps only have flourished in the eighteenth century, a proud and imperious aristocrat, who despised the drudgery of office but who exercised more political influence than many cabinet minsters. William Pitt, a lifelong friend, admired his talents. His moral reputation was bad, but it was a tolerant society. At Bentley Priory he gathered round him many of the most talented men of the age, among them Sir Walter Scott, Richard Sheridan, Thomas Lawrence (who painted a charming portrait of Abercorn's mistress, Mrs Maguire, and their son, exhibited at the Royal Academy in 1806), John Kemble, the actor, and Richard Payne Knight, the antiquarian. Scott later described Bentley Priory as 'the resort of the most distinguished part of the fashionable world' and invitations were keenly sought. Pitt introduced Aberdeen and he soon became a welcome guest. Scott related how Abercorn, Payne Knight and Aberdeen 'made evenings of modern fashion resemble a Greek symposium for learning and literature'.[16]

Abercorn had three beautiful daughters, Catherine, Maria and Frances. The story which Lady Frances Balfour recounts of Uvedale Price seeing a number of children come out of a house in Grosvenor Square and being so struck by their beauty that he asked the porter whose children they were refers not, as she states, to Aberdeen's daughters but to Catherine and her sisters.[17] The girls were also talented and accomplished, well read, and skilful musicians.[18] Stanmore calls Catherine a 'bright and rare being'[19] and her personality radiates even from her few surviving letters, the earliest of which were written to her father at the age of fourteen.[20] She was bubbling over with life and a keen sense of humour, undaunted in the face of any difficulty, but also quickly compassionate and sympathetic to anyone in need. Unlike Harriet Cavendish she did not snub the shy young man who quickly transferred his affections to her.

It was a whirlwind courtship. Cooler heads, such as Melville and Lord Abercorn, began to worry about marriage settlements, rendered the more necessary by the strict terms of the entail which made it difficult to provide for widows or younger children but, after taking legal advice, Melville told Aberdeen, 'I am certain it will be best to marry upon articles without waiting the execution of formal Deeds.' Abercorn had promised to make 'a handsome provision in the name of jointure' and further security could be provided for Catherine and her children 'by insurance of your lives, and an appropriation for that purpose of a part of your income'. A 'regular marriage settlement' could come later, if necessary. But Aberdeen was compelled to undertake the long journey to Aberdeenshire to collect all the relevant papers from Alexander Crombie. Even when all parties were agreed that the match was highly suitable, two great families could not be united in the early nineteenth century without careful practical provision.[21]

Aberdeen became almost ill with the intensity of his emotions. He poured out his feelings to Whittington who replied with a light-hearted but basically serious letter:

Really you should act prudently & cautiously during this preliminary interval instead of raving and racketting about, sitting up till day light, & drinking an enormous quantity of wine, claret too of all things! . . . but, seriously, I hope & trust that in this storm & tempest of your passions, you will not forget that you are a *man*, & moreover a man of by no means a strong constitution.

He sent, as Aberdeen had requested, a prescription 'to remove acid from the stomach'.[22]

The anguish was not to last long. Aberdeen and Catherine were married on 28 July 1805, at Stanmore. Aberdeen had hoped that Whittington would perform the ceremony but, by this time, Whittington himself was ill. Aberdeen did not yet have a London house and he rented Melville's Wimbledon villa as his and Catherine's first home. They were soon urging their closest friends, Whittington, Gurney and Drummond, to visit them and share their happiness.[23]

They were so obviously in love that even hard-bitten Regency London was touched. Even Harriet Cavendish at first took the marriage well. She wrote to her sister, Georgiana, at the time, 'It seems to be a very happy match and he looks almost blooming upon it' and a few months later,

You will be . . . surprised to hear that I now grant him all the perfections I once denied him, beauty not excepted. He is more improved than I could have believed possible. The Abercorns have quite cured him of shyness and 'embarras', which is as advantageous to his manners as to his person, and he no longer dresses his hair so [illustrated by a drawing of hair 'en brosse']. He must be very happy, for his countenance, voice and smile are all as animated as they were once doleful and one can almost believe in the spirits Lord Brooke expatiated upon.[24]

Unfortunately Harriet assumed in the free moral climate of the time that they could soon resume their flirtation, despite Aberdeen's marriage. She was quickly snubbed by both Aberdeen and Catherine and, for a time, her letters became waspish about them. Unhappily her letters were published in 1940, and the unfavourable picture incorporated into the Aberdeen legend. Although in October she avowed that she had lost interest in Aberdeen since he had become a good husband and 'sits in one chair with his chère moitié', in December she grumbled that Catherine 'is grown more cross and grave than any person ever was', although she heard that 'they are as conjugal as ever'. She complained bitterly of the possessiveness of the Abercorns and told her sister:

The Bravo [her nickname for Aberdeen] and I had a short conversation, but his *sposa* is so constantly on the watch, that I, out of consideration, walked off, upon which he went to Lady Jersey, which redoubled her watchfulness, especially as the latter was making her fine eyes and really looked quite beautiful; but the tenaciousness of Lord Aberdeen's attentions is quite as great on the Abercorn part as before the marriage, and you would imagine that they were still trying to gain him. He is constantly surrounded with some part of the family.

She inadvertently betrayed, however, that her opinions were not generally held. In the same letter, after a rather spiteful description of Catherine's dress and appearance, she continued:

Caroline and I agreed in a whisper that she looked ugly *pas du tout*. Lady Jersey, Lady H. Villiers, Lady Castlereagh and a long train came up to us in the course of the evening – 'Look at that lovely creature, did you ever see anything so beautiful? Oh, she is the most beautiful creature I ever beheld', and we, *pour cause*, were obliged to be in raptures. Such is the triumph of Grecian symmetry, gems, antiques, stamped by Lord Haddo's taste.

Aberdeen never took Harriet's jealousy too seriously and wrote to Foster in November 1805, 'I mean to go to Chiswick [another Devonshire house] very soon: though not married to Lady Harriet Cavendish there is no one I like better.'[25] Harriet later married Lord Granville and good relations continued.

Lady Elizabeth Foster had given her son her version some months earlier: 'Lord Aberdeen is, I am afraid, in a grand flirtation with Lady Catherine Hamilton . . . as it is a connection as to Politicks that his friends would like I dare say it will do, but he is too good for them [the Abercorns]: I don't say for her, for she is pretty and, I believe, amiable . . . I think him delightful.' Lady Elizabeth's sentiments seem to have been known to Catherine since she added a mischievous postscript to a letter from her husband to Augustus: 'I say, Mr Foster will say, that Aberdeen has not slipped on the noose already – yours C. Aberdeen, otherwise the amiable Lady C.H.'[26]

High spirits were the most marked characteristic of the young people who gathered at Bentley Priory in the summer and autumn of 1805. They were young, affluent, full of life and health, and uncommonly talented. Many were Whigs, since Lord Abercorn made it clear that he considered party allegiance unimportant as long as his guests were clever and sociable. Writing comic or sentimental verse was fashionable and passing references to 'the Editor' suggest that they had some kind of house journal. One 'song' was plainly at Aberdeen's expense. It began:

> Sweet on the Doric Fane to gaze
> By Athens high Acropolis,
> And sweet to trace the winding Bays
> By famed Constantinople

and continued in a later verse,

> I know who thinks it sweeter much
> To roll the ogling eye away

And loll with Spouse upon the couch
In happy Bentley Priory.

Other gems included an ode to Maria on pouring tea; a lament to be sung to
the Welsh air Nos Galen for 'The withered Violet' and dedicated to 'Julia',
who had gathered it; a comic dialogue between Lord Abercorn's glove and Lord
Aberdeen's boot; and a reproach to Mrs Siddon for preferring sculpture to painting. Aberdeen himself probably wrote the poem on the proposed inscription
for the entrance gate of Lady Catherine Hamilton's flower garden. The second
verse gives its flavour:

> Far from the senseless joys of crowded scenes
> Here Catherine wooes the scientifick page
> With studious thought the fact historic gleans
> Or treads with Shakespeare's muse the buskined Stage.[27]

The theatre, both professional and amateur, was the ruling passion. While
Aberdeen was in Scotland in the winter of 1804–05, Whittington kept him
informed of all the theatre news, including the prodigious success of the 'young
Roscius', 'the boy, Betty', that is William Henry Betty, whom Whittington
considered superior to Kemble. Aberdeen was less impressed. He told Foster
in November 1805, 'The Theatre is in great glory. Kemble and Mrs Siddons
every night'. After 'being made sick with an automate of a Boy all last year',
he heard that a girl of seven or eight was coming out that week at Covent
Garden.[28] Aberdeen remained a devotee of the professional theatre and the journals that he intermittently kept show that, at least as a young man, he tried
never to miss an important opera or dramatic production.

In the winter of 1805–06 there was an even more compelling attraction, a
small theatre at Bentley Priory, built under the direction of John Kemble himself, in which they were to perform their own plays. Aberdeen had already
established a reputation as an amateur actor. He told his son how, while he
was still an undergraduate at Cambridge, he and two friends presented themselves under assumed names to the manager of a theatre in Canterbury and
persuaded him to engage them to play the principal parts in Shakespeare's *King
John*. The manager was so pleased with their performance that he offered to
retain them as permanent members of his company.[29]

All the young men were anxious both to write and to act. Drummond wrote
the *Medea*, in which he hoped that Aberdeen would play Theseus; and Whittington wrote *Rumpled Wigs*, a satire on famous actors. Whittington also found
a new play, *Ethwald*, by a then fashionable playwright, Miss Joanna Baillie,
being performed in Norwich and persuaded the theatre manager to let him
have a copy. *Ethwald* was heavily derivative from *Macbeth* but it had a scene
which greatly appealed to the young men, in which the weird sisters appeared
in a mist-filled cavern. They were, however, compelled to admit that they
would have difficulty in staging the scene in which a character was decapitated
on stage and his head held up to the audience. They delighted in spectacular

effects and one cryptic letter from Whittington to Aberdeen is intriguing. 'Don Kemble', he wrote 'is certainly an object of legitimate curiosity, & I have no doubt that the blowing up of Michael Angelo for Sir Joshua [Reynolds] before Lawrence will be received with as much astonishment as a sceptical observation on Moses would be by Dr Majendie [a very conservative Cambridge don].' Eventually the wilder suggestions were rejected and on 4 November, Aberdeen could report progress to Whittington: 'We are settled here. The theatre is finished and the Rehearsals are begun.' The two main plays were to be *Oroonoko*, in which Aberdeen was to be Oroonoko, and *The Rivals*, in which Aberdeen was to be Falkland. William Lamb, the future Lord Melbourne, was to be Captain Absolute and Thomas Lawrence, Sir Lucius O'Trigger. Lamb's brother, George, wrote a farce, *Whistle for it, or the Cave of the Banditti*, in which Aberdeen took a part and he played Rosenburgh to William Lamb's 'Basil' in the play of that name. Aberdeen's young brother, Robert, was present and was found small parts. Early in December, Aberdeen could write to Whittington, 'We have rehearsed both Oroonoko and The Rivals before Kemble – fancy how tremendous.'[30]

Melville had become alarmed by Aberdeen's total absorption in his new hobby and wrote to him, suggesting that it was not quite proper for one of his rank and prospects to indulge in these entertainments and that he ought to be turning his attention to embarking upon a public career. Aberdeen was perturbed and wrote to Pitt for advice. Pitt, perhaps aware that his protegé's Achilles heel would always be his nervousness in public speaking, took a very different view. He replied:

Your Character for attention to real Business cannot I am sure suffer in my Eyes, nor I think in those of others, from taking a Part in the Amusements of the Priory. They will I hope only be a prelude for graver Exhibitions, and whenever an Opportunity may arrive, you will be ready to obey the summons you may remember in Tacitus, 'Nunc ego Te ab Auditoriis et Theatris, in Pulverem atque Aciem et ad vera Proelia voco'.[31]

Melville was correct in thinking that the forthcoming entertainment had attracted wide publicity. Whittington, who had been invited to the rehearsals, wrote on 8 December, 'I cannot tell you how much I am desirous of seeing you "knock at your heart" & slap your breeches before you do it in publick . . . you have already obtained the title of *Roscius* among the newspaper critics.'[32] Fashionable London almost fought for places for the entertainment. Only the most favoured obtained accommodation at the Priory. The unlucky had to make cold and difficult journeys back to London in the small hours.

The pièce de resistance was undoubtedly *The Rivals* and Sheridan attended in person. He wrote to his wife afterwards, 'Well they play'd the Rivals really extremely well indeed . . . I don't know when I have sat out a Play before.'[33] Even Harriet Cavendish was amused and commented, 'The Rivals was acted even to satisfy Mr Sheridan who was forced to laugh at all his own jokes and applaud all his own sentiments.' But she could not resist some digs at Aberdeen. A few days earlier she had attended one of the other plays when she wrote, 'The "Bravo" looked hideous as a ruffian. In the farce, which was "Cross Purposes", he was rouged, which made his face worse than ever in my opinion, but mama was in raptures.' Of his performance as Falkland she thought his actions were 'ugly and awkward' but 'his voice is clear and distinct and he certainly acted with a great deal of feeling and a perfectly just conception of his part.'[34] The press, which published very full accounts, was kinder. The *Morning Post* commented, 'The Earl of Aberdeen's Falkland was much admired. This noble Lord certainly possesses very strong natural recommendations, and has all the graceful elegance and ease necessary to exhibit them to full advantage.'[35]

During the spring and early summer of 1806, Aberdeen and Catherine remained at Wimbledon. Catherine was now pregnant and, although Aberdeen wished to visit Haddo, Lord Abercorn was adamant that his daughter should not be removed to what he always regarded as ultima Thule. Aberdeen too had doubts about the wisdom of such a journey but Catherine was now anxious to see her Scottish home and outwitted her husband and father by persuading her doctor, Dr Croft, to give it as his opinion that such an expedition would be an excellent idea. Aberdeen reluctantly agreed that they should leave on 25 August and travel north in gentle stages of not more than forty miles a day and break their journey at Melville's home at Dumira.[36]

He was able to tell his father–in–law on 27 September that they had arrived safely at Haddo, both perfectly well. They stayed a fortnight at Dumira amid 'unparalleled beauties' and he had re-visited his own favourite retreat of Vallombrosa. It had re-awakened mixed feelings about Haddo. 'We are now', he said, 'removed to a very different scene, yet certainly to me not without its attractions.' After some questions about Abercorn's visit to Ireland, where he had been attending to the business of his own estates in Tyrone, Aberdeen added, 'I hope to perform something of the same kind . . . I hope you will sometime come here and give me a great deal of advice about Planting, Water, etc. but I do not much want you at present, nor until some little alterations are made, which perhaps if you knew all, you might thank me for.'[37]

'Cat', as she was known to both her father and her husband, was enchanted by all she saw and added a breathless postscript to Aberdeen's letter:

Dear Papa,

You need not believe one word of what Ld. Aberdeen says about this place, for I can assure you that there is nothing to complain of. I was never so surprised in my life as when I first saw it, for I had been told so much about it by every body, that I expected a thing not fit for a human being to live in, placed in the middle of a barren, bleak, moor, without a Tree, or anything near it but a bog, instead of that I saw a great many very good trees about the House which is not regularly beautiful on the outside, but very comfortable in the inside, from the windows you see nothing but trees, and this fine weather it is as cheerful as possible. It is really very strange that everybody should have thought it so despairing; they said it was useless to do anything but build, for that we could never make it tolerable, but with a good chair and Sopha or two, and new curtains to the Drawing Room I do not wish for anything better.[38]

Catherine, who loved animals, and at Wimbledon had been cherishing a 'land tortoise' brought home by William Gell, was delighted by new pets. 'What do you think,' she wrote to her father, 'I have two little tame Fawns.' But she could not conceal her mirth at the plantations Aberdeen had just begun, 'as for the plantations here they are just like those in Castle Rackrent, I have not perceived them yet, but I am told they will be magnificent ten years hence.' At this point her husband added a note 'Gentlemen who plant at the rate of one million trees per ann. cannot afford to put in very large and umbrageous machines.' Cat concluded with a mocking threat that if the Abercorns would not come to Haddo next year, then they would not come to Baron's Court.[39]

Aberdeen was mildly amused by his wife's enthusiasm but a friend, Stuart Wortley, wisely told him that he should not consider Catherine's 'liking it better than she had been taught to expect' as of little importance. 'I know no circumstances that can contribute more to the prosperity of your temporal concerns than that she should not object to a residence there a certain portion of every year. "The eye of the Master maketh the Horse fat" you know – & so it does by an Estate & I much mistake your lordship's situation and inclination, if you will not have full use for all that it can yield, even in the large proportion of the usual increase of Scotch Estates.'[40]

Abercorn was of a very different opinion. He told Aberdeen that, although he did not disapprove of 'occasional visits at Haddo, your time of Life, Habits, Tastes, & everything, make the balance overpoweringly against your considering it as a residence or scene for enjoyment, or *main* object'. He assured him 'My main object is to have you fixed here again in as few weeks as may be.'[41]

Nevertheless Aberdeen and Catherine remained until November. They had one alarm. While Aberdeen had gone to attend the Aberdeen race meetings, Catherine was taken ill and he hastened back with 'an approved accoucheur' but it turned out only to be a 'cursory visit from King Agrippa.' Catherine added reassuringly, 'Nota bene. King Agrippa means Gripes, which is nothing very alarming though his Lordship makes such a fuss about it, in short I am perfectly well.' Aberdeen's paternal anxiety was not altogether allayed. He told Abercorn that there were 'no embryo feats of activity' yet but 'I am persuaded the being is quick although the motions are not yet perceptible.'[42]

Aberdeen's anxiety was, however, unfounded. The following February he was able to write to Whittington, 'Early this morning Cat, with the assistance of the learned Dr Croft, produced a young Lady, (as all say) of most comely appearance and ample dimensions. They are both as well as possible. I should like very much to have her made a Christian by you, for many reasons, and I hope you will do it.' Whittington was a little dilatory and Aberdeen wrote again, 'I am glad you will come to town and perform the office I mentioned as the young Lady is above a fortnight old, I believe the business should be over in a week at farthest.'[43]

Aberdeen was delighted by his baby daughter, who was christened Jane for Lady Melville. Jane's birth was followed by that of two more daughters, Caroline in 1808 and Alice in 1809. From the point of view of the succession, a son would have been more convenient and, because of the strict entail, daughters could only be the source of financial anxiety. This worried other people, including Lord Abercorn, but only once did Aberdeen himself admit – to a close friend, William Howley, later Archbishop of Canterbury but then an Oxford don – that he was disappointed that Alice was not a boy. Even then he immediately rebuked himself, remembering that the baby was perfect and the mother healthy.[44] He spoke very tartly to his brother Alexander who regretted that Alice was not the desired 'son and heir'. Aberdeen adored his three small daughters and spent far more time with them that did the average nineteenth century father. He regularly recounted their activities and their sayings to Alexander, then serving in Spain, who responded by sending trinkets for them.[45] Their mother's tragic death in 1812 only served to bind him more closely to her daughters.

This tragedy was still hidden in the future when Aberdeen rejoiced over his first-born and faced the practical problems of providing a town house for his family. An attempt to buy Lord Winchester's house in Portman Square for 12,000 guineas failed and, in 1808, he finally purchased Argyll House, the former home of the Dukes of Argyll, off Oxford Street, which was to remain his London residence for the rest of his life. Lady Melville wrote to congratulate him on acquiring 'an uncommonly desirable' house but added gloomily that she feared it was but a shell '& sad experience makes me tremble for friends who must put themselves into the hands of Tradesmen'.[46]

Aberdeen embarked upon a most ambitious conversion with the aid of his friend, William Wilkins, the architect who helped to popularise the Greek style in England – despite Lord Abercorn's complaints that the innovations which Wilkins had suggested at Bentley Priory had proved unsafe. The most elaborate room was to be the salon and Wilkins regretfully conceded that, if Lady Aberdeen wished to use the room the next year, the columns must be done in wood and painted, although they would be much better done in alabaster. Boileau designed the frieze for the salon, and apparently one for Catherine's boudoir, and went frequently to Lord Elgin's 'to study the character of the figures'. These were presumably the Elgin Marbles which had recently gone on public, or semi-public, display for the first time. Much effort was also expended on installing stoves of the continental type which Aberdeen had admired on his travels, to heat the bedrooms. While this work was being carried out, Argyll House was uninhabitable and, although in October 1809 Wilkins expressed the hope that they would be able to move in the following February, it was not until April 1811 that Aberdeen could tell Alexander, 'The House is quite finished.'[47]

The renovation of Argyll House was not the only major expense which Aberdeen was then incurring. He was still an ardent collector and anxious to furnish and beautify his property in the best traditions of the times. His principal ally in this quest was Richard Payne Knight. Knight was the son of a wealthy Shropshire family who had travelled regularly in Italy since 1767. His writings had attracted the attentions of Goethe, who had translated some of them. The description of him in the *Quarterly Review* of 1816, as 'the arbiter of fashionable virtu' was meant sarcastically but a little earlier it would have been the literal truth. He was regarded by well-informed men as the final authority on the classical collections which so many young aristocrats were intent on acquiring. This was the more surprising because Knight was not a cautious man. In 1786, encouraged by fellow members of the Dilettanti Society, he had published a pioneering work on phallic worship among the ancients. Copies of this, which he sent to many leading men, including the Prince Regent, caused a sensation.[48] Politically he was a supporter of Charles James Fox and reproached Aberdeen for his commitment to Pitt. Nevertheless the two men became close friends and went into partnership to acquire various collections of coins and medals which interested them, some discovered by Aberdeen's old friend Drummond, who went as the British envoy to Sicily in 1807.[49]

On one occasion the more experienced Knight rescued the young Aberdeen from an embarrassing situation. Ever since 1802 Aberdeen had been hankering to build up an impressive collection of pictures. The French Revolution and the subsequent wars had brought many masterpieces on to the market which in normal times would never have been sold. In February 1807, Aberdeen fell in with a picture dealer with an illegible signature (apparently Radzlock), operating from Portland Place. Aberdeen selected three pictures and offered 4000 guineas for them. Radzlock pressed him hard to take others and suggested a kind of hire purchase agreement. If Aberdeen would take pictures worth 10,000 guineas, he would be prepared to accept 2,000 guineas cash and allow him to pay the rest 'on mortgage' in five equal instalments in the course of the year. He airily quoted the immense sums which patrons like the Duke of Bridgewater had paid to acquire the Rubens and Correggios which were coming on to the market. Aberdeen had a great admiration for Rubens and would dearly have liked to have acquired a Correggio but he was beginning to smell a rat. He sent Knight round to see Radzlock. The latter described the visit as 'mortifying' and reproached Aberdeen for betraying him, since he had only agreed to do business if it could be kept secret. Aberdeen sent a polite letter but the transaction lapsed. Knight told him, 'I had in my youth some dealings with gentleman jockeys. I thought their professional morals rather lax, but they are quite rigid compared with those of gentleman picture dealers.' He directed Aberdeen's attention to more reputable, if less enticing, dealers.[50]

Aberdeen took full advantage of the foreign travels of his brothers to try to acquire bargains. Alexander and Charles were with the army in Spain. Robert, who declined to go into the Church as had originally been intended, turned to the diplomatic profession and was sent out to Teheran with Sir Gore Ouseley. Alexander was instructed to look out for Greek marbles and, on one occasion, was told 'If the Castor and Pollux can be had for money, do not let them escape.' Aberdeen even had wild hopes of acquiring part of the King of Spain's famous picture collection, surmising that they might be sold to pay for army supplies, and considering going out to Madrid himself to try to negotiate.[51] He was to be disappointed in this ambition. Many of the pictures he coveted ended up in the collection of the Duke of Wellington, after being captured in Joseph Bonaparte's baggage train at the battle of Vitoria, and are now in Apsley House.

He was also unsuccessful in some less ambitious projects. The family plate had been willed to the Dowager Countess and Aberdeen was anxious to replace it. Alexander and Charles were instructed to make good the deficiencies in Spain but there were difficulties arising from the strict wartime controls on the import of bullion. The first consignment met with disaster. Alexander, who had been instructed by his brother to make sure of the plate even during the retreat of 1810 and to keep it in his own baggage, unless he could entrust it to a friend in a man-of-war, gave it into the charge of Charles, who was coming home on sick leave. It included a large oval dish or salver with embossed edges, a 'handsome waiter', and antique jug, a sugar basin and a punch bowl. Charles unhappily proved to be an incompetent smuggler. In February 1811, an indignant Aberdeen told Alexander, 'You have heard of the calamity about the Plate, and I fear there is no chance of getting it released. It was very ill-managed, for God's sake be more careful. I told you frequently that the greatest caution must be used, and yet Charles says he never knew it was contraband.' Aberdeen, however, had not given up. In January, Alexander had brought a further 120 dollars worth of old plate, mainly flat dishes and salvers, and Aberdeen assured him, 'I should like anything fit for a sideboard that is highly wrought and embossed with figures, animals, flowers etc.' Alexander went on buying plate but it is not clear how much reached London safely. Certainly, the second consignment too ran into difficulties. Aberdeen warned his brother, 'The Plate which Arbuthnot brought in is not yet landed: there is very great danger: that which Charles brought is entirely confiscated.'[52] Alexander was also commissioned by his brother to buy wine in Spain and Portugal, and in November 1809, sent him a pipe of port wine.[53]

Robert encountered other difficulties in Teheran. He pointed out that as the making of wine was forbidden by Moslem law, it required the influence of an ambassador to get any that was drinkable, and he had not been able to procure any. He had, however, got some handsome manuscripts cheaply and some silver coins. Even from that distance Aberdeen seems to have expected a tribute of classical pieces and Robert wrote to him in December 1811, 'I trust you will have received the most valuable Persepolitan remains that ever left this Country.'[54]

Apart from trying the patience of his brothers, Aberdeen also made a systematic collection of interesting classical pieces that appeared in the sale rooms, some of which attracted public attention. Whittington congratulated him on acquiring an important group, possibly by Piombo, for £550.[55] By this time Aberdeen was already establishing a reputation for himself as a connoisseur and scholar.

NOTES

1. HH 1/19, Aberdeen to Foster, 14 Aug. 1804 (copy).
2. HH 1/19, Aberdeen to Foster, 20 Aug. 1804 (copy).

3. For his management of his estates see Ch. 5 below.
4. HH 1/19, Aberdeen to Foster, 22 Sept. 1804 (copy); Add. MSS 43229, Drummond to Aberdeen, 5 Oct., 13 Nov. 1804; Whittington to Aberdeen, 16 Dec. 1804, 27 Jan. 1805.
5. Gurney Papers, RQC 334/12, Aberdeen to Gurney, 2 Feb. 1805; *Aberdeen Journal*, 6, 13 Feb. 1805.
6. HH 1/19, Aberdeen to Foster, 22 Sept. 1804 (copy). Whittington sent Aberdeen's effects, including his substantial library, from Cambridge in August 1805. They consisted of '7 large cases of books, 2 small cases (viz., the book for Athens, & the prints), a small trunk (containing your papers) and 3 packages in mats'. Some things which he could not pack, such as 'Bonaparte's head', he promised to bring himself, Add. MSS 43229, Whittington to Aberdeen, 21 Aug. 1805.
7. Add. MSS 43229, Gell to Aberdeen, 22 Oct. 1804
8. Gurney Papers, RQC 334/12, Aberdeen to Gurney, 2 Feb. 1805.
9. Add. MSS 43229, Drummond to Aberdeen, 13 Nov. 1804; RQC 334/12, Aberdeen to Gurney, 2 Feb. 1805,
10. NLS, MS 1808, Aberdeen to Foster, 4 Mar. 1805. The 'beautiful Dame' was probably Lady Harriet Cavendish.
11. It was Augustus Foster, the son of Lady Elizabeth Foster, who was first the mistress and then the wife of the Fifth Duke, who introduced Aberdeen to Devonshire House, Vere Foster, pp. 232–3. The Duchess of Gordon's daughter, Georgina, married the sixth Duke of Bedford and thus became the step-mother of Lord John Russell.
12. NLS, MS 1808, Aberdeen to Foster, 4 Mar. 1805.
13. Lady Elizabeth Foster to Augustus Foster, 5 Apr. 1805, Vere Foster, p. 211.
14. Lady Elizabeth Foster to Augustus Foster, 5 June 1805, Vere Foster, pp. 224–5; Leveson-Gower, *Hary-O*, pp. 116–7.
15. Add. MSS 43066, Russell to Aberdeen, 21 Aug. 1852.
16. *Quarterly Review*, 34 (1826) pp. 213–4.
17. Add. MSS 43228, Uvedale Price to Aberdeen, 6 Feb. 1818 (on Abercorn's death); cf. Balfour, vol. 1, p. 194.
18. The contemporary press was full of the doings at Bentley Priory and *The Morning Post* (18 Apr. 1805) commented on Catherine playing the 'very fine organ' there.
19. Stanmore, p. 19.
20. These are in HH 1/29. The letters to her father are docketed 'Cat'.
21. Add. MSS 43227, Melville to Aberdeen, 29 June, 9 July (2 letters) 1805.
22. Add. MSS 43229, Whittington to Aberdeen, 12 July 1805.
23. Add. MSS 43229, Whittington to Aberdeen, 30 July, 3 Aug. 1805, Drummond to Aberdeen, 13 Aug., 'Friday' Aug. 1805; Gurney Papers, RQC 334/13, Aberdeen to Gurney, 4 Aug. 1805.
24. Leveson-Gower, pp. 117, 123
25. *Ibid.*, pp. 130, 141, 147; HH 1/19, Aberdeen to Foster, 20 Nov. 1805 (copy).
26. Vere-Foster, pp. 224–5; HH 1/19, Aberdeen to Foster, 24 Sept. 1805. Lady Elizabeth Foster also reassured her son that Catherine 'likes Petrarch; that is something to redeem her with you', Vere-Foster p. 262.
27. Add. MSS 43347, ff. 46–7, 38, 41, 43, 58, 40.
28. Add. MSS 43229, Whittington to Aberdeen, 16 Dec. 1804, 27 Jan. 1805; HH 1/19, Aberdeen to Foster, 20 Nov. 1805 (copy).
29. Stanmore, p. 14.
30. Add. MSS 43229, Drummond to Aberdeen, 22 Nov., 5 Dec. 1805; Whittington

to Aberdeen, 11 Sept., 25 Sept., 9 Oct., 27 Oct., 8 Nov. 1805; Aberdeen to Whittington, 27 Sept., 4 Nov., 1 Dec. 1805.

31. Add. MSS 43227, Melville to Aberdeen, 17 Oct. 1805; Add. MSS 43229, Pitt to Aberdeen, 27 Oct. 1805.
32. Add. MSS 43229, Whittington to Aberdeen, 8 Dec. 1805.
33. C. Price, *Letters of R. B. Sheridan,* vol. 2, p. 250.
34. Leveson-Gower, pp. 136–7, 140.
35. *Morning Post,* 23 Dec. 1805; cf. *Courier,* 25 Dec. 1805.
36. HH 1/29, Aberdeen to Abercorn, 14 Aug. 1806.
37. HH 1/29, Aberdeen to Abercorn, 27 Sept. 1806.
38. Postscript to above.
39. *Ibid.*
40. Add. MSS 43229, Stuart Wortley to Aberdeen, 'Saturday Oct. 1806'.
41. HH 1/29, Abercorn to Aberdeen, 9 Sept. n.d.
42. HH 1/29, Aberdeen to Abercorn, 13 Oct. 1813
43. Add. MSS 43229, Aberdeen to Whittington, 11, 27 Feb. 1807.
44. Howley Papers, 2186A, Aberdeen to Howley, 15 July 1809.
45. Add. MSS 43223, Alexander to Aberdeen, 30 Oct. 1808, 3 July, 19 Oct. 1809, 22 Aug. 1810, Aberdeen to Alexander, 25 July 1810, 9, 30 Apr. 1811, 4 June 1811.
46. HH 1/29, Aberdeen to Abercorn, 14 Sept. 1807; Add. MSS 43227, Lady Melville to Aberdeen, 24 Feb. 1808.
47. Add. MSS 43229, Bonome to Aberdeen, 4 June 1808, followed by plans; Add. MSS 43230, Wilkins to Aberdeen, 10 Oct., n.d. Oct. 1809; Add, MSS 43223, Aberdeen to Alexander, 9 Apr. 1811, HH 1/29, Aberdeen to Abercorn, 13 Oct. 1806, 19 Feb. [1813].
48. *DNB,* xxxi, pp. 259–61; *Quarterly Review,* 14 (1816) p. 533.
49. The voluminous correspondence on this is in Add. MSS 43229 and 43230, beginning with Knight to Aberdeen, 28 May 1808.
50. Add. MSS 43229, ?Radzlock to Aberdeen, 16, 18, 20, n.d., 23, 26 Feb. 1807; Knight to Aberdeen 27 Feb. 1807.
51. Add. MSS 43223, Alexander to Aberdeen, 15 Aug. 1810, Aberdeen to Alexander, 25 July 1810, 8 Oct., 24 Dec. 1812
52. Add. MSS 43223, Aberdeen to Alexander, 25 July, 28 Aug., 21 Sept., 27 Oct., 1 Dec. 1810; 13 Feb., 13 Mar., 21 Apr., 4 June 1811; for the full story see Iremonger, pp. 37–8.
53. Add. MSS 43223, Aberdeen to Alexander, 28 Aug., 17 Nov. 1810.
54. SRO GD 33/63/IX, Robert to Aberdeen, Teheran, 2 Dec. 1811.
55. Add. MSS 43229, Whittington to Aberdeen, 12 Apr. 1805.

CHAPTER FOUR

The scholar

In 1805 almost all Aberdeen's friends seemed to be writing for publication. Whittington wrote jokingly that when he came to London, 'I shall expect to find you half obscured by books & papers at your official table in your back drawing Room, and about a dozen meagre looking authors each with a prospectus in his pocket, besieging the staircase in every direction.'[1] Whittington himself had determined to write a history of Gothic architecture, with particular reference to the French cathedrals which he and Aberdeen had visited together and the two young men discussed the project at length.

Whittington had already had his Hulse Prize essay published. This was a reasonable and moderate work in which he argued that the historical evidence for the events of the New Testament was as good as that on which the history of most of the classical period rested.[2] Aberdeen no longer regarded divinity as entirely 'mud ponds' and occasionally discussed such subjects with Whittington and Gurney. Basically, they agreed that the New Testament was a matter of history but the Old Testament a mixture of poetry, legend and primitive myth. It was a judgement with which they delighted to shock an older generation of Cambridge dons.

Aberdeen was jolted into a more serious consideration of such subjects in 1808. He had been deeply shocked by the death of Whittington, apparently from peritonitis, in Cambridge in the summer of 1807, followed the next year by that of Royston. He turned to William Howley, an old friend of the Abercorn family, who, until his own death in 1848, remained one of Aberdeen's closest friends and in a sense his spiritual adviser, to whom he turned in his successive bereavements. He wrote to him in November 1808 suggesting that he should come to Oxford to talk to him on 'a matter of deep interest which has been the subject of much unsatisfactory reflection with me'. He hoped Howley could 'lessen the state of religious uncertainty in which I find myself'. He seems to have envisaged a regular course of instruction and asked Howley to set aside an hour to see him on several mornings.[3]

Aberdeen considered himself, *ex officio* as it were, a member of the Presbyterian Church and he certainly played a very active role in the affairs of the Church of Scotland. He once told William Gladstone that he had no intention of leaving that Church although he rather thought that sooner or later he would be thrown out. At the same time he told Gladstone that he preferred the 'sister church' and privately he considered himself an Anglican. In London he always attended St. James's, Piccadilly, and he never took communion outside the Church of England.[4] Like most men of his time he believed in infrequent communion and always took it (rather contrary to usual practice) on Good Friday.[5] He had all his children baptised as Anglicans. To the end of his days he lamented that his attitude to religion remained one of intellectual assent rather than of lively belief but despite the pressures put upon him by two of his sons, one of whom became an extreme Evangelical and the other an aesthetic Anglo-Catholic, he never wavered from his rational, indeed eighteenth–century, approach.

His own comparative orthodoxy did not make him unsympathetic to the unorthodox. On the contrary, he always seems to have had a weakness for the way-out thinker, whether in the sphere of religion or politics. Another friend, William Drummond, certainly belonged among the unorthodox. In 1805 he published his *Academical Questions*. 'I have attempted', he told Aberdeen in October 1804, 'to veil its real meaning; but I am afraid that our bigots will take alarm . . . I have avoided all remarks upon our peculiar religion. The constitution of the country has given us a creed . . . We must expect the hoi polloi to be under the guidance of some superstition or another; and I do not think ours the most mischievous I know.'[6] Drummond's forebodings proved correct. His book was severely handled in the periodicals and he was threatened with prosecution. His speculations grew wilder and in 1811 he printed, for private circulation, *Oedipus Judaicus*, in which he attempted to prove that the whole Old Testament was an extended astrological allegory. Aberdeen was not shocked but he was amused and Drummond reproached him for laughing at his ideas with a mutual friend, reminding him that he had only shown him the manuscript in strict confidence.[7]

Most of Aberdeen's friends were classicists, rather than theologians. One such was Robert Walpole, the grandson of Horatio Walpole, who brought out his *Memoirs relating to . . . Turkey in 1817* and his *Travels in various Countries of the East* in 1820. Aberdeen contributed to both. In the *Memoirs*, he and Walpole wrote a joint chapter on 'The Mines of Laurium' in which they discussed the types of silver coinage used in Attica and speculated on the relationship of gold and silver coinage. Aberdeen's other contribution to the *Memoirs* was a trenchant piece, 'Remarks on Two sculptured Marbles brought from Amyclae, by the Earl of Aberdeen'. This apparently innocuous title was the prelude to a tremendous attack on the sensational work of the Abbé Fourmont, who claimed to have discovered a temple dedicated to the goddess Oga or Onga, near Amyclae, where human sacrifice was carried out. Aberdeen's publication of the marbles on which Fourmont's 'evidence' had been based, showed that they were really ornamented with articles of female toilet and attire, such as mirrors, combs and slippers, and certain plants usually associated with Bacchus. Aberdeen concluded that they came originally from the temple of Bacchus at nearby Brysea, which Pausanias said was served by priestesses, and probably represented votive offerings made by a priestess on entering upon her duties. Aberdeen's friend, Payne Knight, had also tangled with Fourmont and his French supporters to expose his 'literary frauds', and Aberdeen returned to the attack in Walpole's *Travels* in 1820 in a 'Letter from the Earl of Aberdeen to the Editor, relating to some statements made by M. R. Rochette, in his late Work on the Authenticity of the Inscriptions of Fourmont'. He would, he said, leave Payne Knight to reply on the general question of Fourmont's credibility as a source but he could testify from his own visit to Amyclae in 1803, when very few travellers had been there, that Fourmont's descriptions in no way conformed to reality.[8]

Aberdeen first ventured into print in July 1805, when he and Drummond contributed their joint review of their friend, Gell's, book, *The Topography of Troy*, to the *Edinburgh Review*.[9] Aberdeen had from the first been fascinated by the mystery surrounding the lost site of Troy. His speculations interested Drummond who, although expressing a curious delicacy about recommending publication 'to one of your rank', gave it as his opinion that it would be quite proper to publish the results of a scholarly enquiry.[10]

Gell published his sumptuous *Topography of Troy*, based on his travels in the Troad in the winter of 1801–2, in 1804. Although he spent only a few days there he was a talented draughtsman and he had the advantage of the use of a *camera lucida*. He succeeded in producing over forty very remarkable topographical plates which are the book's real claim to fame. The accompanying text was both enthusiastic and naive, with travelling details mixed up with archaeological speculations. Gell was entirely convinced that he had found the warm and cold sources of the Scamander (although a more sceptical friend accompanying him thought the two springs of equal temperature) near the village of Bournabashi. Bournabashi must therefore be Troy. 'It being perfectly established,' wrote Gell 'that this is the warm spring, it will be easily admitted, that the Scaean gate cannot be far distant from it.' He was equally sure that he had found the tombs of Ajax and Hector, the site of the Greek encampment and other locations mentioned by Homer. He thought he might even have found more. They saw some marble capitals of columns which 'almost persuaded us, that we had found some of the original marbles of Troy'.[11] It is hardly surprising that Aberdeen, who had explored the area and made a careful study of the authorities, raised his eyebrows at all this.

The review has frequently been misunderstood. Its sardonic tone has made an unfortunate impression on some modern scholars and contributed to the belief that Aberdeen was a sarcastic and unpleasant man,[12] but this is to take it out of its context. Up to a point it was a serious work, intended to put the record straight, but at another level it was almost an undergraduate joke at the expense of a friend. Aberdeen's contribution to the review has also sometimes been underestimated, and it has been assumed that he merely added suggestions to Drummond's draft. In fact, Francis Jeffrey, editor of the recently founded *Edinburgh Review*, had discussed the possibility of a review with both Aberdeen and Drummond but in April 1805, when Aberdeen realised that he could not finish his piece in time, he wrote to Jeffrey suggesting that he incorporate his material with that of Drummond. His only stipulation was that it should be made clear that it was written by someone with first hand knowledge of the area – this seems to have been the immediate origin of Byron's quip at the 'travelled Thane'. Aberdeen subsequently sent Foster a copy in which he marked the parts which he had contributed but this does not seem to have survived. Aberdeen's notes, however, suggest that a substantial part of the final version originated with him. [13]

The review begins with a brief but competent survey of the current state of the controversy, apparently contributed by Aberdeen. The reviewers insisted (correctly) that contemporary commentators had confused the Simois and the Scamander. Only the Menderes (believed by contemporary travellers to be the Simois) fitted the Homeric description of the Scamander as a mighty river which had nearly drowned Achilles, and it was the Menderes which rose at the correct place among the Idaean range of hills. Aberdeen wrote a glowing account of the true source; 'The water rises in a vast cavern of white marble, and gushes out by two apertures in the rock, forming, in its fall, a magnificent cascade; and the surrounding precipices being covered with pine, oak, and plane trees, render the whole scene eminently beautiful and imposing.' They totally rejected Bournabashi as Troy and became very sarcastic at Gell's claim to have found actual relics or to have identified 'a large conic heap of stones' with grass on top as Hector's tomb. They could not resist teasing Gell for some of the slightly comic personal touches he had added, such as the Turks' alleged astonishment at his toothbrush and his unfortunate eruption into the harem when exploring the house of the Aga of Bournabashi, which had nearly led the whole party to disaster. Their comments that the blues and greens of the famous coloured plates were too vivid for Asia Minor, although a little ungracious, were entirely just.

The fact that they did not advance any alternative theory as to the site of Troy has led some scholars to conclude that Aberdeen should be numbered among those who did not believe in its historical existence but this is not so. Aberdeen dismissed as 'fanciful' Bryant's theory that Troy existed only in mythology and accepted the essential 'geographical exactness of Homer'. He told Jeffrey that 'from a series of ocular proofs' he had arrived at a solution no one else had so far advanced but, unfortunately, he was not confident enough of it to publish it and it cannot now be reconstructed. [14]

Payne Knight, who was in the secret, was much amused by the review and wrote to Drummond,

You and Lord A. have been very sharp upon poor Gell: but if he has any Sharpness in him, which he does not appear to have, he may retaliate with Interest; & to hunt down an Earl & Privy Councillor in the Character of Reviewers would be a fine sport for a true blood hound of a Critic. [15]

Gell did find out but it in no way impaired their friendship. He visited Aberdeen at Wimbledon in July 1806, on his return from Greece, and Aberdeen told Whittington that he was 'crammed with Grecian news, for Gell is come, with views, sketches, Panoramas etc. He really has done a great deal.'

A few months later, Gell wrote mockingly to Aberdeen as 'My dear Ld. Aberdeen, grand Duke of Athens, Cousin of Theseus & intimate friend of Pericles.' Gell's first direct reference to the review is in a letter written from Gibraltar in 1809, in which he tells Aberdeen, 'The gay Drummond who assists you to gain your bread by reviewing, has retired to Malta.' Some years later, Aberdeen helped Gell to obtain the finance for a new expedition to Greece and subsequently assisted him in his publication of an account of the Sacred Way to Eleusis. [16]

If Aberdeen's first excursion into print, although controversial, passed off good-humouredly, this was not to be true of his second. Jeffrey obviously considered that he had a valuable discovery in the learned young Earl, who had first hand knowledge of the Near East, and urged him to contribute further reviews. Aberdeen was then planning a history of Greek architecture and he agreed to review a book by M. L. Dutens, *Recherches sur le Tems, le plus récule de l'Usage des Voûtes chez les Anciens*. Dutens was a distinguished scholar and a Fellow of the Royal Society but the book was a rash attempt to prove that the arch had been in use among both the Greeks and the Egyptians from the second millenium B.C. Aberdeen had seen many of the examples which Dutens cited solely on the evidence of drawings, and knew that they could not support his thesis. Dutens, for example, had used the so-called tomb of Agamemnon at Mycenae as an example of the arch, describing it as 'bâti en voûte conique, dôme, ou coupole'. Aberdeen in reply described the structure in detail as he had observed it in 1803. He pointed out that the capstone was missing and yet the building still stood, which would have been impossible if it had been the keystone of a true arch. Aberdeen made short work of Dutens' examples from Egypt and Asia Minor, pointing out that the only authentic arches there were Roman work. 'We know', he wrote 'that Ephesus, Miletus, Magnesia, Mylasus, and in particular Troas Alexandria, were flourishing and extensive colonies, and in each of these the traveller will, with difficulty, be able to discover any remains which are not strongly marked by the distinguishing characteristics of the age and manner of the Romans.' Aberdeen dealt with equal severity with Dutens' supposed examples from Athens and Rome. [17]

Aberdeen did not confine himself to archaeological evidence. He challenged Dutens on philological and literary grounds too. The words *apsis* and *tholos* could not always be taken to imply an arch. Dutens had grossly mistranslated a passage in Plutarch's *Life of Pericles* to suggest that there was a 'dome' above the sanctuary of the Parthenon. He had made Plato speak, improbably, of 'une voûte oblongue', or 'oblong arch'. The passage he had quoted from Aristotle came from *De Mundo*, which the best authorities did not believe to be Aristotle's work. His Hebrew was no more reliable than his Greek or Latin. He had not appreciated that ⵏⵏⵏ *gobim* related to the fact that Solomon's temple was roofed with cedar planks, 'which excludes any idea of masonry, or of an arch'. Aberdeen's refutation was a very effective hatchet job. It was also a learned *tour de force* from a young man of barely twenty–two.

Dutens did not take it quietly. He wrote angrily to Jeffrey and he printed a reply to Aberdeen in subsequent editions of his book, complaining of this 'unfair attack upon my work'. His language had originally been stronger. He had burst out against 'la malignité qui règne dans les attaques dirigées contre l'Auteur'. He and Aberdeen corresponded for some time, at first through Jeffrey, then, since Aberdeen disdained to preserve his anonymity, directly. Aberdeen, in whom the future diplomat can surely be seen emerging, courteously told him of the first projected public protest, 'With what you have written I feel myself satisfied with the exception of a single word. A person may be *unfair* through chance, ignorance or negligence, but to be *disingenuous* implies a radical quality of mind much to be deprecated.' Dutens settled for 'unfair'. Aberdeen was also agreeable to continuing the argument in private although 'such is my dislike of all controversy, and being sensible of the ridicule which might attend one of this unimportant description, that I mean only to print and not to publish, whatever I shall propose'. Aberdeen did draft some further replies, even more devastating to Dutens' position, but neither printed nor published them.[18]

Aberdeen consulted Whittington and Payne Knight while preparing his article. Payne Knight took up a trenchant position and insisted that there was no proof that the arch was employed before the time of Augustus.[19] Aberdeen rejected Payne Knight's late date, as decisively as he had rejected Dutens' early one. 'The age of Augustus,' he wrote in his review, 'although some have supported it, is certainly too late for the period of its invention.' He himself believed that, although there may have been barrel vaults and a primitive kind of pointed arch, made by overlapping stones, at an earlier date, the use of true arch in the classical world dated from the time of Alexander the Great − an opinion not far removed from that of some modern scholars.[20] His independence from his mentor, Payne Knight, on this question is interesting in view of his much more significant rejection of Payne Knight's judgement on the Elgin Marbles some years later.

Aberdeen was now becoming known as a scholar and connoisseur. In 1806 he became involved in a small but irritating disagreement with the University of Cambridge. He was asked to write to the distinguished Italian sculptor, Canova, to ask him whether he would undertake a statue of Pitt for the University, only to discover, after he had done so, that the University now favoured a rival artist, Nollekens. Gell said that he would rather drink hemlock than see Nollekens get the commission. Presumably Aberdeen did not feel so strongly as that, since he employed Nollekens to make his own bust a few years later, but he felt that he had been put in a false position. Failing Canova, both men would have preferred John Flaxman but the commission went to Nollekens.[21]

In May 1805, Aberdeen was elected to the Society of Dilettante[22] which had been founded about 1732 by Sir Francis Dashwood, of Hell Fire Club fame, and his personal friends. It originally consisted of wealthy young men who had undertaken the Grand Tour, and its earliest meetings may well have been in Italy. Later, it was to add distinguished artists and scholars to its membership but it remained primarily a society of patrons. Its early reputation was for conviviality and hard-drinking but its members came to be taken more and more seriously as connoisseurs, especially of classical antiquities.

The Society financed James Stuart's and Nicholas Revett's expedition to Athens and the publication, in 1762, of the first volume of *The Antiquities of Athens*, which first made Greek architecture fashionable in Britain. British interest in the collection of classical antiquities had begun in the seventeenth century and rivalry, spiced by national antagonism, had quickly developed between British and French collectors. The Society had been prominent in this. They financed the expedition of Richard Chandler (a Fellow of Magdalen College, Oxford) to Asia Minor and Greece in 1764. Chandler brought home various marbles, including a fragment of the frieze of the Parthenon, which were subsequently presented to the British Museum. Sir William Hamilton, the British envoy in Naples and the complaisant husband of Nelson's Emma, who acquired the fine collection of Greek vases, terra cottas, bronzes and gold ornaments, which formed the nucleus of the British Museum's Department of Greek and Roman Antiquities, was a member of the Society. So too was Charles Townley, who brought home a magnificent collection of bronzes, vases, gems, coins and marbles. The marbles, which he sold to the British Museum in 1805 for £20,000, formed the foundation of their collection of ancient sculptures.

Aberdeen and some of his friends, notably Augustus Foster, had toyed with the idea of founding an Athenian Society for the select few who had travelled to Greece but it never really got off the ground and, after his election to the Dilettanti, he gradually lost interest.[24] He was a very active member of the Dilettanti until the early 1820s, although after he became Foreign Secretary, in 1828, he never again found time to play much part. He was probably introduced to the Society by Lord Abercorn. Other members included the fifth Duke of Devonshire, Thomas Lawrence, William Drummond, William Gell, Joseph Banks, the President of the Royal Society, and, a little later, Sir Robert Peel, himself a connoisseur of considerable distinction.

In 1808 Payne Knight proposed Aberdeen's election to the Publication Committee. The Committee was then finalising the publication of the *Select Specimens of Antient Sculpture preserved in the several Collections of Great Britain*. A high proportion of the specimens, twenty-three out of sixty-three, came from Payne Knight's own collection. It was to be a sumptuous production 'in the most magnificent style' and the Society paid £2000 for the engraved copper plates alone. The first volume was ready in 1810.[25]

In 1811 Aberdeen became chairman of the Ionian Committee, which was formed to finance Gell's third expedition to the Eastern Mediterranean, and which was responsible for drawing up his instructions. These were closely modelled on those given by the Society to Chandler in 1764; in particular he was to make plans of buildings, accurate drawings of bas-reliefs and ornaments and copy inscriptions. The results of Gell's expedition were published by the Society in the *Antiquities of Eleusis* and the *Antiquities of Attica*.[26]

His membership of the Society of Dilettanti led Aberdeen into the great controversy concerning the Elgin Marbles. The first part of the collection arrived in England in 1804. The artists and sculptors appreciated their quality almost from the beginning but the same was not true of the connoisseurs and patrons.[27] When they first went on view to a select public, in 1807, Payne Knight scribbled Aberdeen a note of staggering casualness, suggesting that Aberdeen might like to see 'Lord Elgin's things',[28] which in his opinion were interesting but not outstanding. Knight and Elgin had already clashed on the matter. It was probably Knight who vetoed Elgin's application to the Dilettanti in 1803 for financial assistance in bringing home his collection, and his remark to Elgin when Elgin returned home, 'You have lost your labour, my Lord Elgin. Your marbles are over–rated: they are not Greek: they are Roman of the time of Hadrian', was the talk of London.

It might have remained a private quarrel but Elgin still wanted financial assistance. Like Hamilton and Townley before him he wished to sell his collection to the British Museum, not least because he was having the utmost difficulty in housing it. His original asking price was £62,000. As early as May 1809, Aberdeen was being spoken of as a possible member of a committee to determine a fair price, but in fact he had little to do with the abortive negotiations of 1810–11. By 1815 the whole question had become one of urgency to Elgin. The marbles were then in Burlington House, but Lord George Cavendish, who had just bought it, wanted them removed. Elgin approached the Speaker of the House of Commons and the Trustees of the British Museum. The Trustees met in April, and set up a committee to negotiate with Elgin and the government. It consisted of Charles Long, the Paymaster-General, Aberdeen and Knight. It could not have been worse from Elgin's point of view. Long had been associated with the unsuccessful negotiations of 1811. Knight was his severest critic and Aberdeen apparently Knight's faithful disciple, although so far Aberdeen had maintained a cautious silence on the Marbles. Aberdeen went to see William Richard Hamilton, Elgin's former private secretary who was now permanent Under-Secretary at the Foreign Office. Aberdeen had already demonstrated his personal regard for Hamilton by securing his election to the Dilettanti in the face of some opposition. He now told Hamilton that he thought the nation would purchase the Marbles but he warned Hamilton, on Long's advice, that £35,000 was the maximum which could be got through the Commons. Payne Knight thought £20,000 would be excessive.[29]

Hamilton tried rather clumsily to influence Aberdeen. He told him that Ennio Quirino Visconti, the Director of the Louvre, had written enthusiastically but he received a crushing reply. 'There could be no doubt', said Aberdeen, 'that Visconti was the best practical Antiquary in the world, and that his independent unbiased opinion would be of great weight anywhere, but that it was equally well known that he would write anything he was asked for £10.' Perhaps Aberdeen's suspicion of attempted bribery was not altogether unfounded. Hamilton now advised Elgin to sell Knight and Aberdeen a collection of ancient coins they had long coveted. Fortunately, Elgin had a better appreciation of how Aberdeen was likely to react to such a proposal and turned the suggestion down flat.[30] Aberdeen was, however, beginning to come to his own conclusions. Payne Knight's influence was strong on the one side but on the other side were men whose opinion Aberdeen also respected, Canova, Flaxman, Nollekens, Thomas Lawrence and Benjamin West, the President of the Royal Academy.

A state of deadlock ensued and in February 1816, Elgin petitioned the House of Commons to appoint a Select Committee to examine the question. As a member of the House of Lords, Aberdeen was not eligible to sit on the Committee but he did appear before it as a witness. His evidence caused a minor sensation because he rejected Knight's views. He thought the sculptures were undoubtedly of the antiquity attributed to them and might well have been done under the direction of Phidias, the almost legendary Athenian sculptor, although they were probably executed by different artists and therefore varied in quality. He was unwilling to concede that they were of better workmanship than the Phygalia marbles, for which the British Museum had paid £15,000, but he thought them of greater interest because they had come from the Parthenon and he would place them in 'the highest class of art'. He suggested the quasi-official sum of £35,000.[31] This was the sum which Elgin, protesting strongly, was eventually compelled to accept.

During the parliamentary enquiry the scope of the discussions widened considerably. The Committee was instructed to enquire, not only into the merits of the Marbles, the importance of their becoming public property and the proper purchase price, but also into the authority under which Elgin had acquired them. By now charges of vandalism, and even theft, were being levelled against Elgin.

The public attack was led by no less a figure than Lord Byron and Byron had no hesitation in classing Aberdeen with Elgin. He combined the view that the Parthenon marbles were late, and certainly not of the age of Pericles and Phidias, with a scornful condemnation of the despoilers. *English Bards and Scotch Reviewers* (1809), contained not only the well-known (and in its context venomous) reference to 'the travelled Thane, Athenian Aberdeen' but also the lines,

> Let Aberdeen and Elgin still pursue
> The shade of fame through regions of virtu;
> Waste useless thousands on their Phidean freaks,
> Misshapen monuments and main'd antiques;
> And make their grand saloons a general mart
> For all the mutilated blocks of art.

Byron attacked Elgin still more ferociously in *Childe Harold's Pilgrimage* in 1812. The hero contemplates the ruin of the Parthenon and muses,

> The last, the worst, dull despoiler, who was he?
> Blush, Caledonia! such thy son could be . . .
> But most the modern Picts' ignoble boast,
> To rive what Goth, and Turk, and Time hath spared.

Perhaps Byron had seen the graffito in the Erechtheum, 'Quod non fecerunt

Gothi, hoc fecerunt Scoti'.[32] He had at first intended to include an even more offensive reference to Aberdeen. Stanza fourteen of Canto II originally began:

> Come then ye classic Thieves of each degree,
> Dark Hamilton and sullen Aberdeen,
> Come pilfer all that pilgrims love to see,
> All that consecrates the fading scene . . .

Byron toned down the allusions to Aberdeen while *Childe Harold* was passing through the press, leaving only the comparatively innocuous allusion to 'another noble Lord [who] has done better because he has done less'. This was apparently because Clarke told him that Aberdeen was about to propose Byron for membership of the Athenian Club. J. W. Ward, later Lord Dudley, acted as intermediary in resolving Aberdeen's objections to Byron's derogatory references to his former agent, Gropius, in the same poem. Ward told Aberdeen that Byron had been very civil and promised a correction. Byron had been misled in Greece where 'The Prussian Freebooter, tho' you have deplored the alliance and discontinued the subsidy, still goes on making depredations in your name' and Byron had 'transferred to his supposed employer a considerable part of the indignation which it appears was exclusively due to his unauthorised misdeeds'.[33]

Elgin's depredations were deplored by many contemporaries, notably E. D. Clarke and Edward Dodwell, who had had every chance to make personal observations. Some made a realistic distinction between the morality of removing sculptures which were already on the ground and in imminent danger of destruction, and of damaging buildings to remove others which were comparatively safe. Elgin's principal offence was that he had inflicted substantial damage on the Parthenon in removing the metopes. Aberdeen made what defence he could of Elgin before the Select Committee. The sculptures were neglected and in bad repair. He believed them to be in imminent danger, although he was quite blunt that the danger came not from the Turks but from 'travellers' who wished to collect them. He had one dramatic piece of evidence on this. While he was there himself workmen had knocked off and smashed the so-called head of Hadrian from the western pediment, while trying to sell it to a visitor.[34] This head was a particularly important piece of evidence. Sir George Wheler, who had seen the Parthenon before the great destruction when a Turkish powder magazine blew up there in 1687, believed it to have been inserted at a late date as a compliment to the Emperor Hadrian. Payne Knight later claimed that it was a misunderstanding on this point which had led him into his extreme view of the lateness of the sculptures.

But Aberdeen felt that it would be impossible to curb the predatory habits of collectors, or the impoverished natives' willingness to make money by selling their relics. He went to the heart of the problem when he said that, if Elgin had not secured the metopes, the French would have done so, and he, Aberdeen, was therefore glad to see them in London. The despoiling of the Parthenon was due to Anglo-French rivalry and the weakness and venality of the Ottoman government.

70

Aberdeen's disagreement with Knight about the artistic merits of the Elgin Marbles led him to think profoundly about what constituted beauty. The taste of several generations of educated Britons had been formed on the basis of the Graeco–Roman sculptures which they had seen on the Grand Tour in Italy and, in some cases, acquired for themselves. The ideals were the Apollo Belvedere, the Laocoon in Rome and the Medici Venus in Florence. By comparison the Parthenon sculptures seemed crude. To be able to see the bone structure of a figure was accounted a fault. B. R. Haydon, on first seeing them, was amazed to be able to clearly make out the ulna and radius in a female wrist. A completely new perspective was needed and men like Knight shrank from reconsidering the whole canon of taste and casting doubt on all the standards in which they had been carefully nurturing British patrons. Younger men, however, had to begin to think afresh.

In 1812, Aberdeen wrote an introduction to William Wilkins' new edition of Vitruvius' *De Architectura*. Wilkins was one of the leaders of the fashion for Greek architecture and Aberdeen had given him his warm support and helped him to secure commissions. In 1822, Aberdeen published a revised edition of this introduction as a separate work under the title, *An Inquiry into the Principles of Beauty in Grecian Architecture: with an Historical View of the Rise and Progress of the Art in Greece*. The first part was concerned with aesthetics. Why, he asked, did men admire Greek architecture? Was it due to its intellectual associations or was it spontaneous? He concluded that it sprang from the second, although it was enhanced by the first. If it arose only from intellectual associations it would appeal only to educated men but this was not the case. What then constituted beauty which men spontaneously recognised? Here he took issue with other writers, including Burke's *Philosophical Inquiry into the Origin of our Ideas of the Sublime and the Beautiful*. Aberdeen contended that, in architecture, magnitude was one necessary constituent of beauty. He instanced the 'grandeur of the Egyptian pyramids . . . although the pyramidal form is not in itself peculiarly impressive, as is proved by the insignificant appearance of that of Caius Cestius at Rome, and of all others of small dimensions'. A building need not be simple. 'A great profusion of ornament is far from being incompatible with [sublimity]. A Gothic cathedral, with its lofty and slender proportions, and endless variety of parts, – a Grecian edifice with all its decorated regularity and order, will produce similar sensations of wonder and admiration.' No buildings could differ more than the Great Pyramid, York Minster and St. Peter's Rome, but 'as each possesses the efficient cause of grandeur each excites these feelings which partake of sublimity'. His belief that 'grandeur' was a necessary part of architectural beauty led him to reject Burke's definition of beauty as inadequate. For Burke, beauty must be small, smooth and delicate. All these were feminine characteristics. Ideals of female beauty arise, Aberdeen contended, from 'the sexual affections and sympathies implanted in our nature' but they were clearly irrelevant to architecture. Many of these criteria would not apply to the Parthenon itself. It was large, angular and dazzling white, certainly not delicate in form or colour. This was very relevant to the controversy about the Parthenon sculptures. Their realism was exciting to some, disturbing to others.

They entirely lacked the smoothness and delicacy of, say, the Apollo Belvedere. Contemporaries were beginning to refer to them as 'masculine' and the first part of Aberdeen's *Inquiry* is really a plea for the reassertion of the masculine element in beauty, against the prevailing dominance of the female aspect, which could all too easily become insipidity.[35]

The rest of the book shows wide knowledge, maturity of judgement and catholicity of taste. Having rejected Burke, Aberdeen aligned himself with Aristotle, contending that beauty lay in magnitude and order. Real beauty required consistency. His passage on this recalls a poem from Bentley Priory days, inspired by Wyatt being elected President of the Royal Academy:

> All forms, all fancies, and all fashions please,
> Egyptian, Gothic, Grecian and Chinese,
> When ev'ry Artist, ev'ry stile [sic] will risk,
> Here a Pagoda, there an Obelisk.[36]

Aberdeen condemned the contemporary taste for mixing styles. He also pleaded for something like functionalism. The test must be 'fitness and utility'. Ornament would be unsatisfying and even tawdry if it was seen to originate in 'an ostentatious desire for splendour'.[37]

The *Inquiry* showed appreciation of Gothic styles as well as classical. In 1809 his thinking had not progressed so far. In that year he had written a preface to Whittington's *Ecclesiastical Antiquities of France*, which had been left uncompleted at Whittington's premature death. He even expressed regret that so excellent a writer should have confined his talents 'to a discussion of so limited and partial an interest as the progress of Gothic architecture'. Whittington's book contained a number of speculations which would not be accepted today but it was an important pioneering study based on a wide knowledge of literary as well as archaeological sources.

In his Preface, Aberdeen explained the origins of the book. Whittington had set out to refute those writers, supported by the Society of Antiquaries, who believed that Gothic architecture originated in Britain and should be called 'English architecture' – an important misconception which later misled the Oxford Movement. Whittington had no doubt that the style developed in France and illustrated his argument with a detailed study of a number of French churches and, in particular, a detailed comparison of the cathedrals of Amiens and Salisbury. Whittington did not live to complete the last section of his book in which he had intended to advance his own theories on the origin of the style and Aberdeen tried to reconstruct it. Aberdeen rightly rejected any connection with the Goths, remarking that it was only called Gothic 'out of a silly contempt'. But he fell into the trap of another contemporary theory. All scholars had been puzzled by the suddenness with which the Gothic style developed and it was tempting to link it with another contemporary event, the Crusades. Aberdeen himself believed that it was imported into the West by the Crusaders and that they should seek for its origins among eastern architecture.

Although modern scholarship would not here support his speculations, his rejection of the received opinions of the Society of Antiquaries again shows the same independence of judgement as his rejection of Payne Knight's views on the Elgin Marbles. Aberdeen was by this time a member of the Society and soon to become its President. He had been elected on the proposal of William Hamilton in June 1805.[38] The President was then the Earl of Leicester, later Marquess Townsend, who had held the position since 1784. He died, still in office, in 1811. The Council proposed Sir Henry Englefield as his successor but Englefield was a controversial figure, who had played a leading role in the dispute about Wyatt's 'restoration' of Durham cathedral some years earlier, and his opponents, led by Samuel Lysons, determined to block his election. At a meeting on 14 November 1811 strong support began to emerge for Aberdeen, despite the Duke of Norfolk's protest that he would never be satisfied with 'a Scotchman' as President. Lysons campaigned hard for Aberdeen and, although it was a strongly contested election, when the vote was held on St. George's day 1812, Aberdeen topped the poll with 251 votes out of 453. He remained President until 1846.[39]

He began with the best of intentions. In December 1811 he told Hudson Gurney, who was to become a Vice-President of the Society in 1819, that if he were elected, 'something should be attempted for the improvement of the Society'.[40] On the face of it he was an ideal choice, combining the qualifications of a prominent nobleman with those of a distinguished antiquarian. But his interest in the Society was somewhat intermittent, although he was not so negligent as his critics, then or later, have assumed. His letters to Gurney show that he was still active in the affairs of the Society and watchful for its interests, even when public affairs or private griefs prevented his regular attendance. Criticisms began a few years after his election, when he went on his mission to Vienna. His opponents compared him unfavourably with Sir Joseph Banks, the President of the Royal Society, and Francis Douce complained that what they really needed was a President who had 'an almost exclusive interest in the Society's welfare and direction'.[41] It was unrealistic to expect that from Aberdeen and some of the difficulties arose from the fact that the Society could not make up its mind whether it did want that or whether it wanted an honorary figurehead.

In fact, Aberdeen was a very active member for long periods. Between 1818 and 1824 he assiduously attended the regular Thursday meetings and sometimes supplied material for discussion from his own collections, for example a gold ring with a runic inscription found near Carlisle, or the Household Book of James V for the year 1538–39, which he had in his own library.[42] During his term of office, important publications were undertaken. *Archaeologia* and the *Vetusta Monumenta* continued to appear regularly and it was these handsome books which attracted many artists and architects to the Society. In 1826 the Society undertook an interesting, although financially unsuccessful, publication of surviving Anglo-Saxon texts. While Aberdeen did not directly inspire these ventures, he took a continuing interest in them. He was particularly anxious to see a satisfactory edition of the Anglo-Saxon Chronicle produced and hoped that Hudson Gurney would undertake it. He even discussed the details of the translation with him and one exchange sheds some light both on nineteenth century prudery and on Aberdeen's relaxed attitude towards it. Gurney was worried as to how he could translate the Anglo-Saxon word for 'castrate'. Aberdeen suggested 'mutilate' since women would take it at its face value, while men would realise its real meaning. Aberdeen could not resist adding one of the smoking room stories he had brought home from his eastern travels. The Sultan ordered a Pasha to collect men for a battle. Unfortunately a secretary misplaced a vowel point in the verb and the Pasha castrated the men and delivered them to the appointed place in no state, as Aberdeen put it, for any sort of action.[43]

The finances of the Society were always a problem and Aberdeen was seriously worried by challenges from potential rivals, such as the newly founded Royal Society of Literature. He feared that the high subscription rate of four guineas a year, in addition to the entry fee, kept out many worthy men although he feared that, if they lowered it, they would not be able to supply the lavish publications, which were one of the principal attractions of the Society. He canvassed, although without success, the possibility of an associate membership with lower rates and fewer privileges than Fellows.[44]

In the 1830s Aberdeen's interests began to shift from antiquarianism to science. In 1835 he told Gurney,

The truth is, however, that for some years, my interest in all matters of antiquity has considerably diminished. Ancient rubbish, whether Greek, Roman or English has lost its charm; and I have rather inverted the usual order of things, and have been a zealous Antiquary only in my youth. Natural history, and especially the branch of Botany, has, by way of amusement, been more attractive; and this has been increasing for the last twelve or fifteen years.

The word 'rubbish' requires some explanation. It was an ironic word, long in use between Aberdeen and Gurney, dating from the time when Aberdeen had been taunted by his critics for bringing home 'ancient rubbish'. In 1818 he had asked Gurney about the progress of his new building to house his books and 'rubbish'.[45]

Aberdeen still tried to do his duty by the Society. In 1834, after the death of his second wife, he promised to dine the Auditors on his return to Town. It would, he said, be 'a compulsory recommencement of the dismal business of life in London'. The following year he promised Gurney to be more regular in his attendance on Thursdays, 'which formerly on my part was certainly most exemplary'.[46] In 1837–38 he smoothed over a serious quarrel between William Hamilton and Nicholas Carlisle, the Secretary, which threatened to split the Society. He told Gurney in November 1837, 'Matters look very warlike' but, in April 1838, he was able to congratulate himself that he had settled the dispute by doing nothing hastily and allowing full time for the desired effect to be produced. He told Gurney: 'This is the true course in all negotiations. You know that I am the pupil of Metternich; and I recollect him telling me long ago that the secret of success in everything was *une saine lenteur*.'[47] This was Aberdeen's last major service to the Society. His attendance thereafter diminished to vanishing point, although he still discussed the Society's affairs regularly with Gurney. His continued absence when he was Peel's Foreign Secretary in the 1840s attracted so much criticism, the force of which he recognised, that he did not stand for re-election as President in 1846. Right at the end of his life he resumed his antiquarian pursuits to a limited extent and drew the Society's attention to the Black Stone of Essar-Haddon, now in the British Museum.[48]

Aberdeen's connection with the British Museum was even more lasting than his connection with the Society of Antiquaries, although it began with a fiasco. Early in 1812, when a vacancy occurred on the Board of Trustees, the then Archbishop of Canterbury and the Prime Minister, Lord Liverpool, pledged themselves to support Aberdeen. His election was regarded as so certain that Liverpool did not bother to attend the meeting. Unexpectedly, the Chancellor and the Speaker of the House of Commons produced a rival candidate who was chosen. Liverpool wrote abject apologies to Aberdeen but Aberdeen, who was in an extremely vulnerable frame of mind after the death of his first wife, was distressed out of all proportion to the cause.[49] Nevertheless he agreed to serve when the next vacancy occurred in December 1812, and became a very active Trustee. He declined Lord John Russell's invitation in 1847 to head the Royal Commission which was about to be appointed to enquire into the British Museum, because he felt that it would be improper for him to sit in judgement on his colleagues.[50] But the Journals which his son, Arthur, kept in the eighteen-fifties, show that his father still spent a good deal of time at the Museum on various business.[51]

Sometimes Aberdeen was able to combine his antiquarian concerns with his continued interest in the House of Stuart. During the Napoleonic Wars he was successful in preventing Linlithgow Palace, the birthplace of Mary Queen of Scots, from being turned into a prisoner of war camp. Some years later he enlisted the help of Sir Walter Scott to stop the destruction of Gosford's Close in Edinburgh, the surviving relic of the palace of Mary of Guise, the wife of James V. He tried to enlist Scott's help in a more important venture, the publication of the Stuart Papers, that is, the papers of the Old Pretender and his two sons, which had been acquired by the Prince Regent. A Commission under J. W. Croker, appointed in 1819, had made only limited progress in examining them and, in 1829, while Foreign Secretary, Aberdeen virtually sacked the Commission and entrusted the papers to Scott, assisted by J. G. Lockhart and a Dr Gooch. Lockhart set to work arranging them but they were only published by the Historical Manuscripts Commission this century.[52]

In April 1808 Aberdeen became a Fellow of the Royal Society and three times served on its Council, in 1812–13, 1817–18 and 1821–22.[53] Membership did not then carry the same implications of interest or distinction in science, in the modern sense, as it would do today but Aberdeen did have a lively interest in the development of science and its philosophical implications. He discussed the new discoveries in geology at some length with Gurney. Since one of his closest friends in his declining years was Samuel Wilberforce, Bishop of Oxford, it would be interesting to know what was his reaction to Darwin's *Origin of Species*, but that only appeared in 1859, by which time Aberdeen was writing few letters. His open-mindedness on earlier controversies[54] suggests that his would have been a very different reaction from the Bishop's.

Aberdeen was always a man of his time, whose interest shifted to some extent in accordance with the fashion of the moment. His interest in science, particularly in botany, had in part a very practical origin in his concern for the good management of his own estates.

NOTES

1. Add. MSS 43229, Whittington to Aberdeen, 16 Mar. 1805
2. *A Dissertation on the external evidences of the truth of the Christian religion*, 1805.
3. Howley Papers, 2186A, Aberdeen to Howley, 27 Nov. 1808. A number of notebooks in H. H. 1/39 contain jottings on the evidence for Christianity.
4. Add. MSS 44088, Aberdeen to Gladstone, 10 Dec. 1840. In 1853 he had great pleasure in nominating the Rector of St James's, Mr Jackson, (a broad Churchman) to be Bishop of Lincoln, Add. MSS 43046, Aberdeen to Victoria, 28 Feb. 1853.
5. Add. MSS 49256, Stanmore's Diary, 2 Apr. 1858.
6. Add. MSS 43229, Drummond to Aberdeen, 5 Oct. 1804.
7. Add. MSS 43229, Drummond to Aberdeen, 24 Apr. 1804.
8. *Memoirs*, pp. 425–46, 446–51; *Travels*, pp. 489–503. The marbles are nos 811 and 812 in the BM Catalogue of Sculpture.
9. *Edinburgh Review*, 6 (1805), pp. 257–83
10. Add. MSS 43229, Drummond to Aberdeen, 24 Oct. 1803.
11. *Topography*, esp. pp. 8–9, 39, 41, 75, 93.
12. Cook, p. 28. ·
13. Add. MSS 43229, Drummond to Aberdeen, n.d. [early Jan. 1805], Whittington to Aberdeen, 28 Apr. 1805; Add. MSS 43344, Aberdeen to Jeffrey, 8 Apr. 1805, preceded by detailed notes; H. H. 1/19, Aberdeen to Foster, 24 Sept. 1805 (copy).
14. Cook. p. 28; Add. MSS 43344, Aberdeen to Jeffrey, n.d.
15. Add. MSS Drummond to Aberdeen, 13 Aug. 1805, encl. Knight to Drummond, 10 Aug. 1805; cf. Drummond to Aberdeen, 'Friday' [mid Aug. 1805].
16. Add. MSS Aberdeen to Whittington, 26 July 1806, Gell to Aberdeen, 1 Dec. 1806; Add. MSS 43230, Gell to Aberdeen, 12 Jan. 1809; and see below pp. 67–8.
17. *Edinburgh Review*, 7 (1806), pp. 441–56
18. The copy of Dutens' book in the British Library is dated 1805 but includes a copy of his letter to the Editor of the *Edinburgh Review* of 1 Apr. 1806. It has an MS note, 'A second or rather 3rd edition with many additions at page 4th and an alteration of the Postscript'; Add. MSS 43229, Jeffrey to Aberdeen, 19 Jan. 1806, Aberdeen to Dutens, 26 Aug. 1806 and attached papers; SRO, GD 33/63/IX, Aberdeen to Dutens, 11 Mar. 1806; H. H. 1/39, Notebook on the history of the arch.
19. Add. MSS 43229, Knight to Aberdeen, 10 Sept, 1805; Whittington to Aberdeen, 27 Oct. 1805, Aberdeen to Whittington, 4 Nov. 1805.

THE SCHOLAR

20. *Edinburgh Review*, 7 (1806),pp. 455–6; cf. T. D. Boyd, 'The arch and the vault in Greek architecture', *American Journal of Archaeology*, 82 (1978), pp. 83–100
21. Add. MSS 43229, Canova to Aberdeen, 15 Oct., 18 Oct. (2 letters) 1806; Gell to Aberdeen, 1 Dec. 1806, Aberdeen to Whittington, 11 Feb. 1807; Add. MSS 43338, Aberdeen's journal, 3 May – 1 June 1813.
22. Society of Dilettanti, Minute Books, vol. 5, 12 May 1805.
23. For the history of the Society see L. Cust and S. Colvin, 1898.
24. H. H. 1/19, Aberdeen to Foster, 20 Nov., 6 Apr. 1805 (copy); NLS MS 1808, Aberdeen to Foster, 4 Mar. 1805.
25. Society of Dilettanti, Minute Book, vol. 5, 6 Mar., 3 Apr. 1808, 4 Mar. 1810.
26. Society of Dilettanti, Minute Book, vol. 5, 2 June 1811, 3 Jan., 6 June 1813, 5 Feb. 1814, vol. 6, 2 Mar. 1817, 24 June 1821, 26 May, 6 June 1824; DMSS 2 (1800–30), ff. 70, 99, 146, 150, 161, 303; DMSS 3 (1831–4) f. 52, Gell's instructions.
27. For the history of the controversy see A. H.Smith, 'Lord Elgin and his collection', *Journal of Hellenic Studies*, 36 (1916) pp. 163–370 and W. St. Clair, *Lord Elgin and the Marbles*.
28. Add. MSS 43229, Knight to Aberdeen, 'Saturday' [July 1807].
29. Smith, pp. 321–2; St. Clair, p. 223.
30. Smith, pp. 318, 322; St. Clair, p. 224.
31. PP. III (1816) 95–9 (8 Mar. 1816).
32. Quoted St. Clair, p. 193.
33. St. Clair, pp. 189–91; Add. MSS 43230, Ward to Aberdeen, 15 May 1812, Egerton MSS 2869, Byron to Clarke, 19 Jan. 1812.
34. PP, III (1816) 96.
35. *Inquiry*, pp. 7, 8, 19.
36. Add. MSS 43347, f. 48, 'Taste, a poem'.
37. *Inquiry*, pp. 26, 31–3.
38. Society of Antiquaries, Minute Book, vol. 30, 20 June 1805.
39. J. Evans, *History of Society of Antiquaries*, pp. 219–20, 225–51.
40. Gurney Papers, RQC 334/34, Aberdeen to Gurney, 9 Dec. 1811.
41. Evans, p. 241.
42. Evans, pp. 240–2; *Archaeologia*, 21 (1827), pp. 25–30, 22 (1829) pp. 1–12.
43. Gurney Papers, RQC 334/39, Aberdeen to Gurney, 21 Sept. 1818, /40, 19 Oct. 1818.
44. Gurney Papers, RQC 334/50, Aberdeen to Gurney, 14 Nov. 1823, /51, 23 Nov. 1823.
45. Gurney Papers, RQC 334/86, Aberdeen to Gurney, 21 Dec. 1835, /40, 19 Oct. 1818.
46. Gurney Papers, RQC 334/73, Aberdeen to Gurney, 8 Mar. 1834, /86 21 Dec. 1835.
47. Gurney Papers, RQC 334/92, Aberdeen to Gurney, 10 Sept, 1837, /94, 23 Nov. 1837, 395, 26 Apr. 1838.
48. Society of Antiquaries, Occasional Papers II, Presidents of the Society.
49. Add. MSS 43230, Liverpool to Aberdeen, 31 July 1812.
50. Add. MSS 43066, Russell to Aberdeen, 8 Apr., 22 Apr. 1847.
51. Add. MSS 49269, Stanmore's Diary, e.g. 10, 15 May 1856.
52. NLS MS 868, Aberdeen to Scott, 24 Nov. 1824, MS. 869, Aberdeen to Scott, 1 July 1829; H. M. C. Report 56, 'Calendar of the Stuart Papers', 7 vols, 1902–23.

53. Royal Society, Journal Book, 28 Apr. 1808. I am indebted to the Librarian of the Royal Society for this information.
54. He accepted Buckland's views on the extreme antiquity of fossils and thought it remarkable that the discovery should have been reserved for their own time. Gurney Papers, RQC 334/88, Aberdeen to Gurney, 2 Nov. 1836.

CHAPTER FIVE

The improving landlord

Aberdeen was not a rich man, certainly not so when his income was balanced against his many obligations, and several times during his life he was on the verge of serious financial embarrassment. He told his eldest son's wife in 1846, when Peel's government fell, that the loss of his official salary was a substantial blow.[1] When out of office his income derived entirely from his Aberdeenshire estates and, although an income of £2,000 a year was enough to make a man accounted a great landowner in Scotland, in England Lord Durham gave it as his opinion that a man could jog on with £40,000. Aberdeen's income rarely exceeded £20,000 and often did not reach that figure. But it was by English standards that he had to judge his resources. He wanted to cut a figure in London, to move easily in circles like Devonshire House and Bentley Priory, and to pursue a political career. As a young man he had expensive tastes. He wanted to travel – and in his circle men thought nothing of hiring a ship for their own use –[2] to collect expensive *objets d'art*, to build and lay out pleasure grounds comparable to those of English peers. As Stuart Wortley told him bluntly in 1806, his estates would have to pay well if they were to support their master's inclination.[3]

Aberdeen's main obligations were to his family and to the tenants of his estate. He took both sets of obligations seriously. Even before he had children to raise and settle in life, he had five younger brothers and a sister with claims upon him. All his brothers had careers. William went into the navy and rose to be Commander-in-Chief at the Nore, with some help from his elder brother when Prime Minister. Alexander, who was always very close to Aberdeen, became the hero of the family. He joined the army and acted as A.D.C. to his uncle, General Sir David Baird, at the capture of the Cape of Good Hope in 1806. He was on the Copenhagen expedition and served throughout the Peninsula War, becoming the Duke of Wellington's A.D.C. He was to be killed at Waterloo in June 1815. Charles's career closely followed that of his elder brother. He too served in the Peninsula and acted as Wellington's A.D.C. The campaign almost ruined his health and, for a time, it seemed that he would have to leave the army but he recovered and rejoined his regiment, the Black Watch, but died prematurely in 1835 returning to duty in Corfu. Robert struck out on a different course and became a diplomat, serving all over the world, until his death in 1847. John, the youngest son, also went into the navy but he seems to have had a constitutional inability to obey orders and was the subject of many despairing letters between his elder brothers. His career nearly ended with a bang when he was court-martialled in 1847 for sailing his ship home from Valparaiso without orders. Aberdeen managed to save him from the worst consequences and he remained in the service to become an admiral. Even Aberdeen's sister, Alicia, in a sense had a career, since she became a Lady of the Bedchamber to Princess Sophia Matilda.[4]

The third Earl's will had settled small sums upon the younger children but all their lives they looked for some support from their eldest brother and running battles, sometimes rather comical, developed between him and them about their supposed extravagence. While Aberdeen was still a minor, the brunt fell on Melville. In April 1803 he told his lawyer that the brothers should be 'peremptorily informed' that their bills would not be met beyond their 'positive Allowance'. For William, Alexander and Charles this should be £150, made up of £50 from Aberdeen in addition to their own £100. Fortunately, Robert and John were still at school and so were not yet incurring major expenses. But Alexander, who had been in Brunswick and Brussels, studying German and the military arts, had been running up bills. Charles had just arrived home on H.M.S. *Romney* and was, no doubt, considerably indebted to his captain, Sir Home Popham. Melville had to pay out an extra £20 for William because he feared he would not be able to go to sea without it. He arranged for an extra £300 to be credited to Alicia which, with her own £100, ought to be adequate even when her education was at 'its most expensive'.[5]

When Aberdeen took charge of his own affairs, it was his usual habit to transfer a portion of his income, usually £5,000 a year, to Coutts Bank in London and his brothers had permission to draw upon it when necessary but, in October 1811, Aberdeen told Alexander, 'At this moment I have not a single farthing at Coutt's and am in considerable difficulty besides.'[6] It is not quite clear whether Aberdeen was genuinely in difficulties – as he might well have been after the large sums he had been spending on Argyll House – or whether this was meant to curb Alexander, who had been complaining for some time that he was not paid regularly, that he was much in debt at home, and that he needed a loan of 100 guineas to make good the wear and tear to his equipment, pay his servants, and meet his expenses on horses. His elder brother told him severely, 'Give me leave to say a word here about your expense.' The other day he had been with Charles, who was home on leave, to order a new scabbard for Alexander. The man in the shop had said that the type Alexander wanted would cost as much as solid silver. 'Surely', commented Aberdeen, 'this would be ridiculous in any one however rich, but to a person in your situation is absurd in the last degree.' Charles changed the order. Aberdeen, however, very quickly repented, remembering that his brother might be killed any day, wrote to apologise and started to look for suitable horses for him.[7] Similar scenes were played out with other brothers over the years. Whether or not his brothers were as extravagant as Aberdeen supposed, James Brebner's meticulous accounts show that his commitments to them were quite substantial. In the early 1830s he was making a half–yearly allowance of £450 to William, £125 to Charles and John, and £250 to his sister Alicia.[8]

But his brothers' extravagance was a minor problem compared with the very large debts which Aberdeen had inherited from his father and grandfather. He consulted his old friend Hudson Gurney about them in 1810. He had devised a grand scheme for re-organising his estates and paying off his debts. His debts, he told Gurney, amounted to about £30,000 and although they did not particularly press (he could meet the regular interest and, if one person required payment, he could get it from another) he had decided to pay them off, if possible. He wrote:

I am determined as soon as possible to clear off every debt I have . . . Instead therefore of renewing leases at advanced rents, I mean to take a fine for renewal. To give an instance – suppose the increased value of a farm to be £500, what would this sum be worth for 19 years and what for 30? In fact it is the same as if I were to give you an annuity of 500 a year for 19 years for a stipulated sum. In this view of the matter, I should imagine that by surrendering the annual value of a farm amounting to £500, I ought to get in principal six or seven thousand. Is it not so?

Gurney persuaded him that the plan would not be 'prudent' and Aberdeen dropped it but a few weeks later he had thought of a new way. He suggested that he put aside £400 or £500 each year to pay off his debts. This sum would come from the 'certain increase' of his rents. He could afford to put aside a higher sum but he wanted to enjoy some of the present benefit from his improved rents because 'riches would be much less enjoyable ten years hence, than they are at present'. He asked Gurney how long it would take him, at compound interest, to pay off the whole sum. His own calculations suggested that he would be clear of debt by 1819. He added that he disliked discussing such matters and would not consult anyone else.[9]

Gurney's reply does not survive but Aberdeen seems to have adopted the scheme. He was, however, too optimistic. He made his calculations during the agricultural boom of the Napoleonic wars, and, although his estates did not suffer so badly as some English estates after 1815, the boom could not last. In the 1830s he was still paying some charges on debts contracted by his grandfather.[10]

The really intractable problem, however, was the estates themselves. They were extensive, in excess of 50,000 acres, and fairly compact, but much of the land was poor and little of it was in good heart. Aberdeen had no illusions, referring to himself in 1822 as the owner of poor land and contrasting it gloomily with the Abercorn estate near Edinburgh, which he was then administering, which commanded so much higher rents.[11] The chief problems were bog and stones. They were common to much of Scotland. Later in the century, Aberdeen's friend, the eighth Duke of Argyll, complained that he had spent £30,000 on drainage, but, because it was all below ground, no one appreciated the effort involved.[12] Because of the rather unusual way in which responsibility for drainage was distributed between landlord and tenants on the Haddo estates, it is difficult to estimate what Aberdeen spent[13] but the estimate for simply draining the bog nearest the house in 1808 was £1200.[14] Clearing the ground of stones was an even more formidable undertaking. Aberdeen wrote despairingly to Abercorn, in July 1808, that near Aberdeen it cost £100 an acre to clear level ground of stones, not rocks, and 'a large portion of my hills would require I should think five times that sum'.[15]

Aberdeen had nearly one thousand tenants. Very few of them had holdings of over 100 acres and a high proportion had between 5 and 20 acres. There was considerable continuity of tenure; leases were usually for 19 years and some-times for as long as 38 years. His tenantry were much more like a peasantry than were agricultural tenants in contemporary England. Most of them must have been desperately poor but, thanks to the kirk, they were surprisingly well educated. Most could sign their names – which would certainly not have been true in England – and Aberdeen commented with pleasure to his wife that many could also write a good letter.[16] Aberdeen was very conscious of the difference between his Scottish tenants and the ignorant condition of the Irish tenants on the Abercorn estates in County Tyrone.

When Aberdeen inherited his estate, however, their condition was generally deplorable. Aberdeen's own belief that his grandfather had shamefully neglected his estates derives support from a number of contemporary sources. Andrew Wight recorded censoriously of Ellon in 1784:

I cannot admire the husbandry, though the soil is excellent, capable by good cultivation of making great returns, particularly of turnip, cabbage, red clover, etc. It is within reach of lime . . . Yet all these advantages are neglected, the tenants poor, and the crops still poorer. The Earl of Aberdeen possesses great tracts of land in this part of Aberdeenshire, which, lying in a state of nature, must be low rented. It is a great misfortune to be too rich; for it makes many men negligent as to the improvement of their estates.[17]

Wight may have been optimistic both about the quality of the soil and the third Earl's financial position.

The surviving estate papers of the third Earl are in great confusion, although they seem to indicate occasional bursts of energy when attempts were made to clear up the mess. They also reveal the Earl in frequent disputes with his ten-ants, such as the fishers of Cairnbulg, 'an unreasonable Sett'. On one occasion he sued two tenants, Alexander Cowie and James Gaul, in the sheriff's court at Aberdeen for £50 damages for carelessly burning off stubble and endangering a valuable peat moss. The bad harvests of the 1780s led to a proliferation of distraints against tenants' goods and stock. But towards the end of his life the Earl had employed the two Aberdeen lawyers mentioned in his Will, Alexander Shand and Alexander Crombie, who seem to have tried to do something to reduce the estate to order.[18]

The third Earl's negligence had meant that no major improvements had been undertaken on the estate, comparable to those undertaken by many Scottish landowners in the eighteenth century, notably by Aberdeen's near neighbours, the Grants of Monymusk. On the Haddo estate, the houses, which so appalled the fourth Earl, were no doubt exactly like those described earlier in the century at Monymusk, consisting of walls six feet high of rough stones packed with earth and topped with a foot or two of peat. The roofs were 'tiled' with thinly pared peat, overlaid with heather. The 'lumb', or chimney, was simply a wooden box, let into the roof and open at both ends to allow the smoke to escape as best it could. These cottages were usually grouped in 'farm touns' of eight or ten dwellings, the number being related to the size of a plough team because a tenant's strips of land would be scattered and the work still done communally. Report after report in the eighteenth century complained of the exhaustion of the soil because Scottish farmers did not understand that they must either rotate their crops scientifically or allow the land to lie fallow for substantial periods.[19] The scene was almost medieval and Aberdeen had no doubt that improvements must be speedily put in hand.

During his minority, his Trustees did take steps to find out the true position and introduce more efficient methods. Melville kept up a constant pressure but William Gordon and Alexander Crombie pulled their weight as well. At Melville's suggestion a Mr Low was employed to make a complete survey of the estate and many of his plans survive.[20] An accountant, Matthew Martin, was engaged to investigate all the factors' accounts. As a result the Trustees were able to make a good estimate of the income of the estate at the harvest of 1801. The lands entailed by the second Earl in 1745 yielded £4,684 16s. 0½d. in money rents and £3,133 3s. 4¾ in kind; the new lands entailed by the third Earl, £1,632 15s. 6d. in money and £673 0s. 3¾ in kind. In addition the lands assigned to the Dowager Countess yielded a little under £900. In other words Aberdeen, or at least the Trustees on his behalf, received just over £10,000 of which only a little over £6,000 was in cash. It was slightly better than the £9,000 which Aberdeen had been led to expect but it was not a great deal in ready money. Aberdeen believed that the annual income of the estate, when 'new lett', would be £16–17,000 and that it could be raised without too much difficulty to £20,000.[21]

He was fortunate in that a high proportion of his leases were due for renewal within a few years of his succeeding to the estate. Apart from being rather longer, Scottish leases, or 'tacks', of this period still contained many features which were obsolete in England. On the Haddo estates in the 1780s rents had still been paid partly in money, partly in kind, and partly in labour services. Labour services, except for the occasional obligation to provide 'carriage', that is, transport for certain goods, do not appear in the fourth Earl's leases but rents in kind remained very important. Tenants were commonly expected to supply quantities of meal, both 'farm meal' and 'white meal', and sometimes other items such as 'bear' (barley), malt, lambs, capons, hens, peat and eels.[22]

Aberdeen set about the problem with his usual methodical thoroughness. He consulted experts and built up a library on agricultural matters. On his return to Haddo in the summer of 1804, one of his first acts was to draw up a set of model regulations, 'Articles and Regulations settled by George Earl of Aberdeen: To be observed by the Tenants on the Lands belonging to his Lordship whose Tacks shall be made to bear relation to the same'. Some of the clauses appear in leases drawn up by Shand and Crombie in 1799 for the newly acquired lands in the parish of Cruden, but some of the most interesting, including the provisions for neutral arbitration in certain cases, are innovations and almost certainly derive from Aberdeen himself.[23]

Article I dealt with the succession to leases. Aberdeen gave his tenants considerable freedom. Except in the case of certain special tenancies, such as those of heirs portioner where the eldest daughter had the right to inherit, a tenant might nominate any of his children, son or daughter, to succeed him or, if he had no suitable child, any other person so long as he or she fulfilled all the obligations of the original Tacksman. Succeeding articles defined these obligations in great detail. Article II laid down, 'Tenants must reside with their families upon their farms and always have sufficient stock thereupon'. Article III made careful provision for the rotation of crops. Turnips, cabbages and potatoes were to be interspersed with grass and cereal crops, such as oats, 'bear' and wheat. A certain proportion of land must lie fallow each year and lime or dung be applied to the ground. The degree of detail may be gauged from the stipulation that fallow land, which did not receive dung, was to be limed at the rate of at least twenty bolls (bushels) of shell lime or sixty bolls of slaked lime (at 128 Scotch pints to the boll) each acre. Tenants who contravened the regulations as to the rotation of crops were to pay an extra £3 rent for each acre managed contrary to the regulations, and comparable penalties were to be exacted for failure to lime or manure. Tenants must allow their own cattle to consume all the straw and fodder grown on their land and must lay on the land all the dung made by the cattle. There was a penalty of 5s. for each threave of straw or fodder and each cart load of dung sold or given away.

Detailed regulations were laid down for the management of a holding during the last year of a lease and for the method of handover from the old to the new tenant. If a tenant made improvements such as the enclosing of any part of his farm with 'dykes', that is, substantial stone walls, provided it was done with the consent of the proprietor and conformed to certain (again detailed) standards, he was to be compensated on leaving the property, the sum to be determined 'by neutral men of judgement and skill to be mutually chosen by the Landlord and Tenant'. Tenants were to be obliged to keep houses, farm buildings, gates, drains etc. in good condition. If they put up additional buildings they were again to receive compensation at 'a fair valuation' either from the proprietor, or the incoming tenant, when they left. On the other hand, if buildings were neglected, the proprietor, or his factor, had the right to repair them and charge the tenant.

Other clauses reserved the landowner's right to make minor boundary changes; to own all game and fish on the estate and to 'hunt, shoot, fish and sport thereon at all times and seasons'; and to own all minerals, including coal and lime. The proprietor had the right to do what was necessary to work such minerals but, if it adversely affected a tenant, he had the right to damages and an abatement of rent as determined by 'two neutral persons'. Similar provisions applied if the proprietor wanted to take part of a tenant's property for the construction of a new road or a plantation of trees. Finally, the tenants' obligation to have their corn ground at particular mills was to be phased out; labour services were usually to be confined to the transport of materials for the building and repairing of the kirks, kirkwards, manses and school houses; and the tenants were to have the right to cut peat, but only in the places determined by the proprietor or his factor.

These were indeed model regulations, incorporating many of the best features of the 'improving leases' granted on progressive Scottish estates in the eighteenth century, and so far as they related to the compensation due to tenants for improvements, and the provisions for its impartial assessment, anticipating provisions which did not become legally binding in Britain as a whole until the Agricultural Holdings Acts of the 1870s and 1880s. That they were not merely pious aspirations is demonstrated by the fact that they were still being written into tacks agreed with tenants thirty years later. To take but one typical example, on 8 March 1830, Lewis Mowat agreed to take that part of Denmore which had lately been possessed by William Taylor for nineteen years, beginning from Whitsunday 1830, for a yearly rental of nine guineas. 'Both parties agree to adopt Lord Aberdeen's regulations as their rule of management', which were to be as binding as if they were inserted in the contract.[24] Only one point had generally been modified. The swinging fines suggested for breaches of the regulations had had to be modified to the more practical provision that double rent was due on any acres not farmed according to the agreement. It is amusing to note that both landlord and tenant had a cavalier attitude to the stamp duty since most tacks contained a provision that the agreement would be put upon stamped paper at mutual expense 'when requisite'.

By the end of the nineteenth century when a later factor, George Muirfield, gave evidence about the Haddo estates to a Royal Commission, these very detailed leases, laying down exactly how a tenant was to farm, had come to be regarded as fetters on the initiative of an enterprising farmer but, at the beginning of the century, they were very important means of education.

When a holding did become vacant Aberdeen and his factors went to great trouble to find a suitable tenant and one rule which Aberdeen laid down, which was still being followed in 1894, was that the man must have sufficient capital to work his land efficiently.[25] But he also set great store by continuity. When his eldest son came of age in 1837, he looked round his assembled tenantry and remarked that he was sorry that there were not more present who had been at his own coming of age in 1805, but it was a consolation that no one was missing because he had been turned off the estate. After his death the *Banffshire Journal* called him 'a most indulgent landlord', who never distrained for rent nor turned anyone off for non-payment. Some of his tenants, it said, had, with their landlord's help and co-operation, become wealthy men themselves.[26]

Aberdeen also adopted a paternal attitude to his tenants' housing. The decrepit cottages were gradually replaced by granite houses, each built according to most precise specifications in relation to the size of a tenant's holding. Later in the century, the estate assumed responsibility for putting up buildings but originally the work was done by the tenants in return for considerable rent abatements. But even in the early part of the century the detailed quality control of the sort of plaster or the thickness of the door jambs which were to be used was such as might be expected from the 1804 regulations.[27]

Aberdeen's responsibilities did not stop with the upkeep of his estates themselves. As the sole 'heritor' of a number of parishes, he was responsible for the maintenance of the parish churches, the manses and the school houses, and for the stipends of the ministers and school masters. In many instances he supplemented the stipends above the agreed level.[28] He also had the appointments in his gift but this could sometimes be an embarrassment rather than a privilege. Old family scandals raised their heads when he told Crombie in 1832, in connection with appointments to the churches at Tarves and Ellon, that, considering Mrs Dering's connection with the family, he could hardly avoid naming Mr Murray but it was 'not the sort of arrangement I much like'.[29] In addition, charity was always expected from the big house and each winter the accounts included items for clothing and blankets for the aged and infirm.

The 'heritor' originally had extensive judicial functions and, as late as the 1850s, Aberdeen's youngest son remembered his father 'sitting at the gate' in the traditional manner to hear complaints and resolve disputes. At noon on Saturdays he would appear at the head of the horseshoe stairs on the west side of the house to receive all who wished to speak with him. By the 1850s the custom had become a social and ceremonial one, as much as a practical one, and when Aberdeen returned to Haddo after an absence many tenants came simply to see him but the continued custom had its use as an expression of the solidarity of the estate.[30]

So far as possible Aberdeen applied scientific methods to his estates. He consulted the experts – and sometimes the eccentrics – and pestered friends and relatives abroad for information and specimens. One of the problems of Scottish agriculture at this time was that not enough hay was produced for winter fodder, and livestock sometimes finished the winter too weak to stand. Some progress was being made in the introduction of the so-called 'artificial grasses', that is, grasses grown from seed, which produced better hay. Aberdeen's regulations of 1804 laid down specific rules for the growing and harvesting of clover seed and perennial rye grass.[31] He also became interested in the possibilities of fiorin grass, which was being tried out in Ireland, and corresponded at length with its leading advocate, William Richardson. Richardson urged him to scientific experiments, trying the grass on both 'wet' and 'dry' land, and involving irrigation schemes which Aberdeen rightly called 'formidable'. He carried out at least some of the suggested experiments but had no more long term success with fiorin than did the Irish farmers.[32]

He constantly looked for new stock. Alexander, when in Spain, was instructed to look out not only for plate and classical relics but also for merino sheep. He duly bought two rams and three ewes in Lisbon for twenty dollars and two rams and eight ewes in Badajoz. The unfortunate Charles was detailed to bring them home. Even Robert in Teheran was asked to get some goats. Later, Aberdeen established the herds of shorthorns and Aberdeen Angus, which were flourishing by 1894.[33]

He experimented, without much success, with exotic fruits such as figs, which he also begged from acquaintances abroad,[34] but he was entirely successful in the cultivation of more homely fruit and vegetables. Large vegetable gardens and glasshouses were eventually established, but as early as October 1806 he was able to tell Abercorn triumphantly that he had just finished an 'enormous' dinner of french beans, green peas and gooseberries.[35] This was no minor achievement. The introduction of a wider range of fruit and vegetables into the Scottish diet at this period was an important factor in the beginning of a rise in the standard of living, and knowledge of their cultivation spread from the great houses such as Haddo.

But above all, Aberdeen became known for his tree planting. He estimated himself that he planted 14 million trees. He did so partly because he loved trees. On his foreign travels he always made careful notes of the trees he saw. The treeless nature of his own property was one of the things which most depressed him in his early years there and much of the planting was undertaken for purely ornamental purposes. But there were practical reasons too. Lack of woodland had been recognised as a major problem in Scotland for a hundred years. It meant that the fields lacked shelter and there was a chronic shortage of timber for building and other purposes. Timber was so precious that, at the beginning of a tenancy, an inventory was taken of all the wood on the property and the tenant was expected to account for it at the end. Timber was also a good financial investment. In 1754, for example, the Monymusk estate had two million trees, which, it was calculated, would be worth £50,000 in thirty years.[36] In September 1808, Aberdeen sent Abercorn a list of the trees he had planted since the previous January. In all they numbered 698,610, of which the greatest number, 440,000, were Scotch firs but they also included a wide variety of deciduous trees, beech, oak, ash, and elm.[37] Some years later, he begged bushels of acorns from Payne Knight in Herefordshire and Lord Ashburnham in Sussex.[38]

Aberdeen was likely to need capital. Although he came to accept and eventually to love his Scottish home, he always seems to have felt a sense of inferiority when he compared it with the houses of his English friends, such as the delightful Sandon Park of Lord Harrowby, or Bentley Priory itself, and indeed some of his friends made rather disparaging remarks. Lord Clarendon once told Queen Victoria that it was a very plain house.[39] Aberdeen set out to make quite extensive alterations in the house, some of them designed to improve its comfort rather than its appearance, but more especially to soften its appearance by creating beautiful grounds. Particularly in the grounds he drew a good deal of his inspiration from Lord Abercorn's properties, both at Bentley Priory and at Baronscourt in Ireland. He was also influenced by his friend Uvedale Price whose views of the 'picturesque' were highly regarded.[40]

The main alterations to the house were undertaken in the 1820s and 1830s. The two most ambitious projects were an external flight of twenty granite steps, leading up to the first floor drawing room on the east side of the house to balance the original external stairway on the west side, and an entirely new kitchen wing and courtyard. The first was completed in 1822, the second begun in 1827 or 1828 and probably completed with the erection of the clock in 1833.[41] Two architects were employed, Archibald Simpson and John Smith. A few years later John Smith was employed to design the new kitchen offices and other buildings at Balmoral, which Aberdeen's brother, Robert, was at this time leasing from the Fife Trustees. Prince Albert acquired the lease from Aberdeen, who had inherited it at Robert's death, in 1848.[42] The alterations at Haddo gave considerable satisfaction. In 1825 Aberdeen's daughter, Alice, wrote that the house now looked very pretty, covered in ivy and Aberdeenshire roses, and the new steps were 'handsome'. It was less bleak now the trees had grown up.[43]

The great pride of the grounds was the lake. 'Artificial waters' were an important element in the picturesque and, in this instance, also provided a practical means of dealing with an intractable bog. The lake was finally finished in 1836, covering twenty acres and 'converting an ugly marsh into a very handsome and delightful object'.[44] In 1837 Gladstone offered Aberdeen a pair of swans to put on it but Aberdeen politely declined because, since Gladstone's visit the previous year, he had acquired four swans, 'very peaceful birds, living together in great amity' and he feared that Gladstone's 'warlike pair' might eject them.[45]

Gladstone was only one of many politicians who visited Haddo over the years. As Aberdeen progressed from scholar and landowner to important politician, Haddo, despite its comparative remoteness, became for a time one of the important political country houses.

NOTES

1. HH 1/29, Aberdeen to Lady Haddo, 23 Sept. 1846.
2. Add. MSS 43229, Gell to Aberdeen, 22 Oct. 1804.
3. Add. MSS 43229, Wortley to Aberdeen, 'Saturday' [Oct. 1806].
4. Bulloch, *Gordons under Arms*, pp. 33, 67–8, 215–16; 335; Lodge, *Peerage, Baronetage and Knightage* (1908 ed.),p. 131, *DNB*, XXII, p. 166
5. NLS, MS. 3834, from Melville, 3 Dec. 1802, 25 Apr., 20 May, 31 Dec. 1803, 31 Jan. 1804; Col. A. Hope to Melville, 2 Oct. 1803.
6. Add. MSS 43223, Aberdeen to Alexander, 10 Oct. 1811.
7. Add. MSS 43224, Alexander to Aberdeen, 14 Aug. 1811; Aberdeen to Alexander, 10, 21 Oct. 1811.
8. HH 4/7, 'State of Disbursements made by James Brebner, Advocate in Aberdeen, on account of the Earl of Aberdeen . . . 1832–33'.
9. Gurney Papers, RQC 334/28, Aberdeen to Gurney, 16 Jan. 1810, /29, 4 Feb. 1810.
10. HH 4/7, 'State of Disbursements . . . 1832–33'. The statement that he paid off his father's debts, although not legally compelled to do so, seems to relate only to one particular debt of £500 that he paid off in 1821, HH 1/30, Aberdeen to Harriet, 12 Oct. 1821, cf. Iremonger, p. 122.
11 Gurney Papers, RQC 334/49, Aberdeen to Gurney, 31 Nov. 1822. Abercorn's land was rented at 6 guineas an acre.

12. Argyll, vol. 1, p. 292.
13. There is very full information on the Haddo estates in PP, XVI Pt 2 (1894) 489–99 and PP, XVI (1896) 516–7, being evidence presented to the Royal Commission on Scottish agriculture. The Haddo records there quoted go back to 1842. They confirm the impression of the more fragmentary records of the earlier period in HH 1/45, 2/49–61, 3/28–35, 4/5–8, 6/1–3.
14. HH 7/1.
15. HH 1/29, Aberdeen to Abercorn, 30 July 1808.
16. HH 1/30, Aberdeen to Harriet, 20 Sept. 1822.
17. A. Wight, *Present State of Husbandry in Scotland*, vol. 3, Pt 2, pp. 607–8.
18. The papers relating to these cases are in HH 2/49 in no particular order.
19. H. Hamilton (ed.), *An Aberdeenshire Estate*, pp. ix, xiii–xvi, xxix, xli, liv–lvii; J. Sinclair, *General Report* . . . vol. 1, pp. 30, 127, 424.
20. NLS, MS 3834, from Dundas, 18 Oct. 1801; Add. MSS 43227, Melville to Aberdeen, 9 July 1805. The original plans are in the Muniment Room at Haddo but there are photocopies in West Register House in Edinburgh.
21. HH 2/49, M. Martin to A. Shand, 29 Oct. 1801; HH 5/6, Abstract Rental of the Earl of Aberdeen's Estate, Crop 1801; NLS MS 3418, Aberdeen to (?) Manchope, 28 Aug. 1801.
22. There are examples of the old tacks, dating from 1780, 1784 and 1794 in HH 2/49, of the new in HH 5/6 and 6/1.
23. SRO GD 33/65/106, 'Articles and Regulations . . . 1804'; HH 2/49, Commission to Shand and Crombie, Ellon Castle, 16 Mar. 1799 . . .
24. HH 6/1, 1830, Lewis Mowat.
25. HH 4/6, Aberdeen to Crombie, 24 Jan. 1831; PP, XVI, Pt 2 (1894), 491.
26. HH 1/22, Aberdeen to Haddo, 5 Oct. 1837 encl. *Aberdeen Journal; Gentleman's Magazine*, 3rd ser., 10 (1861) p. 207.
27. PP, XVI, Pt 2 (1894), 490; for detailed specifications of a house dating from 1841 see HH 6/1.
28. HH 4/6, Aberdeen to Crombie, 21 Oct. 1829; HH 4/7, State of Disbursements made by James Brebner . . . Nov. 1832–June 1833.
29. HH 4/6, Aberdeen to Crombie, 27 Apr. 1832.
30. Stanmore, pp. 189–90.
31. SRO, GD 33/65/106, 'Articles and Regulations . . . 1804'.
32. Add. MSS 43229, Richardson to Aberdeen, 13 Sept. 1808; Add. MSS 43230, n.d. Sept., 10 Oct., 20 Oct., 9 Dec., n.d. Dec., 14 Dec, 1809.
33. Add. MSS 43223, Aberdeen to Alexander, 25 July 1810, Alexander to Aberdeen, 27 Oct. 1810; SRO GD 33/63/IX, Robert to Aberdeen, 2 Dec. 1811; pp XVI, Pt 2 (1894), 402.
34. HH 1/30, Aberdeen to Harriet, 2, 3 Sept. 1822; HH 4/6, Aberdeen to Crombie, 21 May 1828.
35. HH11/29, Aberdeen to Abercorn, 13 Oct. 1806. For the later successful but expensive establishment of the garden (it cost £1200 to level the ground) see HH 1/30, Aberdeen to Harriet, 27 Sept. 1821.
36. H. Hamilton, pp. xlvi–xlix; J. Sinclair, vol. 1, p. 118.
37. HH 1/29, Aberdeen to Abercorn, 10 Sept. 1808.
38. Add. MSS 43230, Knight to Aberdeen, 2 Nov. 1817, 28 July, n.d. Sept. 1818; Ashburnham to Aberdeen, 25 Nov., 7 Dec., 23 Dec. 1818.
39. RA B16/79, Clarendon to Victoria, 14 Sept. 1857; Cf. Aberdeen's lament to Gurney, 'The desolation of the exterior is only equalled by the badness of the

House', Gurney Papers, RQC 334/23, Aberdeen to Gurney, 8 Oct. 1809.
40. Price's correspondence with both Abercorn and Aberdeen is in Add. MSS 43228.
41. The building plans are at Haddo but are listed in SRO NRA 55, plans 2–6; HH 1/30, Aberdeen to Harriet, 29 Aug. 1822; HH 4/6, Aberdeen to Crombie, 24 Jan. 1831.
42. RA Vic. Add. MSS Q1/99, memorandum, 14 June 1868. Smith's plans for Balmoral are SRO, NRA 55, Plans 146–8. It was John Smith's son, William, who carried out the major alterations at Balmoral for Prince Albert.
43. HH 1/14, Alice to Mrs Gale, 16 Aug. 1825.
44. Gurney Papers, RQC 334/88, Aberdeen to Gurney, 2 Nov. 1836.
45. Add. MSS 44088, Aberdeen to Gurney, 4 Sept. 1837.

CHAPTER SIX

Entry into politics

Pitt and Dundas inspired Aberdeen with an interest in politics and a conviction that the public service was the only proper stage for a man of talent and position. As a Scottish peer, Aberdeen was not automatically entitled to a seat in the House of Lords and a Scottish peer, unlike an Irish one, was not eligible to stand for election to the Commons. But it seemed that an easy solution would be found since Pitt had promised that Aberdeen should be given a United Kingdom peerage as soon as it could decently be done after he attained his majority.

Long before he came of age, Aberdeen was listening to debates in both the Lords and the Commons and discussing politics with friends with avid interest, and the confidence of inside knowledge. Aberdeen and Whittington might laugh at their friend Robinson, later Earl of Ripon, for returning from Ireland in 1805, talking 'politics mysteriously like a man in office',[1] but Aberdeen would often have been open to the same charge. When Hudson Gurney thought of contesting a Norwich election, Aberdeen became a keen partisan. Gurney withdrew but the result did not please Aberdeen who wrote that a place must be bad indeed, which set aside two men 'eminent for Ability, Uprightness and Conscientiousness of Principles . . . to make way for a public Traitor and a private Thief'.[2] He wrote to Gurney the same year, 1802, that the people in Cambridge thought that there would be war again but Pitt had said nothing to him about it.[3] He told Foster in 1804, 'I have always been of opinion that Russia will do nothing [in the war against Napoleon]' and the following year that, although the continental alliances and naval victories had come to Pitt's assistance, there would be sharp debates in Parliament.[4] Aberdeen had no intention of being a mere spectator of politics. He had returned from his eastern travels as his majority approached, not only to take charge of his estate, but also to take what he felt to be his rightful place on the public stage; as Drummond put it, 'Mr Pitt . . . is more popular than ever. Why do you stay abroad at so interesting a moment?'[5]

All these bright prospects of early advancement seemed likely to be dashed by the disgrace of Melville and the death of Pitt. In April 1805, the radical, Samuel Whitbread, moved his resolutions in the Commons, which amounted

91

to accusations of financial misconduct against Melville when Treasurer of the Navy. The resolutions passed on the Speaker's casting vote. The decision was a severe blow to Pitt who was compelled to allow Melville to resign from office. Melville was impeached the following year, and, although he was eventually acquitted, his career was in ruins and it was clear that he could do little further to help Aberdeen. Aberdeen was greatly distressed by his trials and even Aberdeen's more cynical friends at Devonshire House accepted that this was because of his deep affection for Melville, rather than from any calculation of the effect upon his own political prospects. As Lady Elizabeth Foster told her son, Augustus, 'Lord Melville was so kind to him, and he has so much heart' but she also suspected that the Abercorns had used the affair to drive the wedge between Aberdeen and Devonshire House.[6]

Melville was financially ruined by the scandal. Aberdeen was persuaded to play a leading role in discreetly organising a fund to raise the mortgage from Melville's East India Company pension so that he might at least have a competence to live upon. In view of Aberdeen's sensitivity about financial affairs and his dislike of begging favours, only his devotion to Melville could have persuaded him to undertake the enterprise. His correspondence on the matter reveals incidentally how wide his acquaintance with Scottish society already was, despite his exile during his formative years. Only occasionally was he compelled to plead that he did not know the potential subscribers. It was not an easy task. Some, like Lord Kellie, immediately volunteered generous amounts. Others were difficult to pin down. The Duke of Gordon wrote from Bath that he would contribute but had not yet made up his mind how much. Several months later Stuart Wortley was suggesting to Aberdeen that he wrote 'dryly' to Gordon and tell him where he could lodge his subscription, if he were still of the same mind.[7]

With unconscious irony, Augustus Foster had replied to his mother in June 1805, 'I am sorry for this affair of Lord Melville's. He would have held out a very good ladder for Aberdeen in politics. Now he has only got Mr Pitt, but he, you will say, is everything.'[8] But in January 1806 Willian Pitt was dead. He was only forty-six but long years in office had taken their toll. His health had given his friends anxiety for some months, but his death, when it came, was still a great shock. For Aberdeen it was a shattering personal blow, which must have recreated the trauma of his own father's death. He wrote at once to Whittington, who was abroad, in quite uncharacteristically emotional terms, in which personal distress and anxiety for the national loss merged.

With mingled sentiments of greif [sic] and horror, I now write to you, Mr Pitt is no more. The Country has lost its only support in this dreadful time of disasters; and I have lost the only Friend to whom I looked up with unbounded Love and Admiration. The sun is indeed set, and what can follow but the blackest night! . . . Everybody in the streets looks as if they had lost a father and Protector; and they are right; they have . . . To think that I am writing at a Table, where I have seen him a thousand times, is indeed agony. What will become of the country, torn by differing factions. While he lived, whether in or out of place, there was at least one object, to which all eyes were directed, and which might have united all hearts in time of danger. But now, it is all void, a blank; on whom can be put our trust? Where can the mind repose with confidence?

He begged Whittington to return to England; 'For God's sake come to England. If I do not close my eyes, which I have not these last two nights, I shall soon be as miserable in body as in mind. The Blow is so dreadfully fatal, because wholly irreparable, and admits of no alleviation.'[9]

Aberdeen was, however, compelled to control his own grief in order to comfort Lord and Lady Melville, who were distraught by the loss, coming when Melville's impeachment was still unresolved. He and his wife moved for a few days from Melville's villa in Wimbledon, which they were still renting at this time, to Berkeley Square, because the Wimbledon associations were unbearable. He told Whittington, 'I am more composed since I left it, for there every object tended to provoke greif [sic]. Being so near the spot where he lived, my imagination deprived me of sleep while I staid.'[10]

But Aberdeen was still a resilient young man and very soon he was beginning to think how politics must develop and how he must rebuild his own future now that his trusted leader was irrevocably lost. Two days after Pitt's death he resolved to keep a journal, which he began by noting the circumstances of Pitt's death and his own feelings of desolation.[11] He only kept the journal for a little over two months but it affords interesting evidence of the open state of English politics and of Aberdeen's uncertainty about his own direction. He thought briefly of standing for Pitt's own Cambridge University seat, arguing that, as peers were allowed to vote in university constituencies, they should be allowed to sit for them, but he accepted the advice from Cambridge that this was impossible. It is unlikely that he would have won the seat. By a curious quirk of fate his future adversary, Palmerston, did, as an Irish peer, contest the seat but he was heavily defeated by Henry Petty, the future Lord Lansdowne.[12]

On 28 January, his twenty-second birthday, Aberdeen took stock of his life in the manner of the times.

My prospects are miserably changed since last year. Lord Melville, and Mr Pitt, my only friends, both gone. Had Mr P. lived I should certainly in the course of the summer have got my English peerage, as he promised Lord Melville I should be the first created. I must now depend on myself, but I am determined never to renounce the principles Mr Pitt has taught me, or to become dependant on Government. I pray God to grant me abilities and honour to steer through all difficulties.[13]

But the maintenance of independence was not easy. Early in February, Lord Grenville formed the 'Ministry of All the Talents', with Charles James Fox as Foreign Secretary. The government obviously saw Aberdeen as a potentially promising recruit, now that Pitt was dead. On 10 February, Aberdeen dined at the Duchess of Gordon's, in company with the Duke of Bedford, Lord Lauderdale, Richard Sheridan and Richard Fitzpatrick, all Whigs. He noted, 'Lauderdale was very civil and gracious to me.' Lauderdale was, at this time, about half-way through the transformation which was to take him from being 'Citizen Maitland' and one of the founders of the 'Friends of the People' in 1792, to the die-hard anti-reformer of 1831, but he was a very talented election manager – perhaps more talented than Melville who had for so long organised the Scottish interest for Pitt. The next day Aberdeen was sounded out again by Lord Cassilis, who hinted that he might be included in the 'government list' for the next election of the sixteen representative Scottish peers. Aberdeen 'talked in general terms and told him I would answer tomorrow', and that evening he 'supped at Devonshire House with Lauderdale'. But, by the next day, he had decided that he was in danger of being deceived and recorded in his journal,

Returned the following answer to Ld. Cassilis, being convinced his overtures were from a cabal entirely in the Prince's interest:

> Berkeley Square,
> Feby 12, 1806.
>
> My dear Lord,
>
> I return you the list of the Scots Peers: I have only to repeat that I should be most happy to support the sixteen candidates who are best entitled either by Rank, Fortune or Ability, to expect a seat in the House of Lords. I think it is the duty of every peer so to act, who has at heart the dignity of our Body, without reference to political opinions. With regard to myself, I return you my warmest thanks for your promise of support, and as I before stated, from my general sentiments respecting the present government, there can certainly be no reason why on their part it shd. be necessary to exclude me from a list of favoured candidates.'

Aberdeen, while declining the overture, had conspicuously refused to burn his boats and on 15 February he approached Grenville direct. He wished first to ask him about rumours of the creation of United Kingdom peerages, which might create vacancies among the Scottish representatives. Grenville assured him that no such vacancies were likely. Aberdeen told Grenville that Pitt had intended to offer him an 'English peerage' and although he must now abandon that hope, he intended to offer himself as a Scottish representative peer at the next general election. He added, 'that in the prosecution of that object I should, as far as possible, be directed by the Spirit of Mr Pitt's Policy: and that in talking so I trusted it was not to an enemy'. Grenville too did not wish to burn his boats and politely replied, 'Certainly not; no man can respect his memory more than myself.'[14]

Aberdeen was now involved in discussions with both Castlereagh and Canning about the best tactics for Pitt's old supporters to adopt. He recorded, 'I had much conversation with Castlereagh about the best line for the opposition to take – we agreed that it was necessary to begin with moderation; but to meet frequently in order to keep together; for without violent measures in public something is necessary to cement the party out of the House.' He had already dined with Canning on 13 February and he dined with him and others at White's on 11 March, when 'it was determined that we should have frequent dinners, and extend the nature of the Company as much as possible'. On the 26 March, after listening to the debate on Melville's impeachment, about twenty-five of them including Hawkesbury, later Lord Liverpool, Castlereagh, Canning and Abercorn again dined together at White's. Aberdeen noted, 'Sat next Canning, who was remarkably pleasant.'[15] Canning was related to Melville

by marriage and this period marked the beginning of the complex, and sometimes rather strained, relations between Aberdeen and Canning.

Aberdeen could not, however, play any real part in politics until he had
secured his election to the House of Lords and for that he had to wait for the
general election of the autumn of 1806. On 29 October, Lord Spencer sent
Lord Leven and other Scottish peers a list of sixteen names for whom their
support would be 'very desirable for Government and peculiarly gratifying to
me individually'. Leven, who was not prepared to give a blanket assurance,
replied, 'The list enclosed I have found to my surprise is not much less public
here than the Almanack'.[16] The production of the 'government list' was
regarded by their opponents in 1806, as exceptionally blatant and struck an
old sore spot. Partly as a result, the 1806 election was one of the most fiercely
contested in the history of Scottish peerage elections. After the Act of Union,
the government had rarely had any trouble in getting their men elected and
it was generally accepted that opposition candidates had little chance. In 1733,
however, there had been a vigorous protest from a group of discontented peers,
the second Earl of Aberdeen among them, complaining that the nomination
of sixteen peers – the so-called 'King's List' – was 'contrary both to the letter
and spirit of the twenty-second Article of the Treaty of Union'. The protest
was unsuccessful at the time but the peers were becoming less docile. 1774
was the last time the King's List was carried in its entirety. Despite Dundas's
careful management, from about 1780 onwards the elections were genuinely
contested and family ties and personal associations came to count for as much
as political allegiance.[17]

Aberdeen plunged into a strenuous campaign, urged on by Melville (with
the impeachment now safely behind him) and Abercorn, who was extremely
anxious for his son-in-law to succeed. Together they initiated Aberdeen into
the mysteries of 'exchanging' lists, that is, promising to support another peer's
candidates, in return for a similar promise. Abercorn, however, became disillusioned with Melville's supposed skills as an election manager and certainly
Melville made rather heavy weather of working out tactics with Aberdeen. He
wrote to him on 21 November that he had been 'ruminating':

It is clear that if there are only two Candidates, the one having any thing above the
half of the whole voters must prevail, but I am puzzled to unravel what may be the
result in the case of a number of candidates. In the 1802 [election] there were only
nineteen or to speak more accurately eighteen. There were only 59 voted but Lord
Elphinstone lost the election with 7 in number more than half of all that voted . . . It
seems very clear that no man ought to vote for any one who does not exchange with
them, and they should throw away their votes so as they may not benefit them by their
Strength. It ought likewise if possible to be stated to electing Peers who are not themselves candidates, that they would greatly contribute to the success of those about
whom they are most interested, if they likewise would rather throw away their votes
than give them to rival candidates.

This last was a crucial point and Melville returned to it on a number of
occasions.[18]

Both Melville and Abercorn reproached Aberdeen for spending too much time at Haddo (where he was still concerned about the progress of Catherine's pregnancy after the feared miscarriage in October), instead of removing himself to Edinburgh, where the real action was. The reproach was on the whole unjustified. Aberdeen was very anxious to be elected and exerted himself hard to secure all the support he could. It was a gruelling task for one who disliked asking favours. Many Scottish peers enormously enjoyed their elections and refused to commit themselves until the last moment, not only to secure political advantages but also, it would seem, to wring the last drop of flavour from the excitement and intrigues.

From some, Aberdeen had great difficulty in extracting straight answers. Lord Kinnaird, for example, told him,

I can have no hesitation in saying that laying party considerations aside, I sincerely wish you success. My own situation as Candidate puts me under some difficulties as to voting for you: but to speak fairly to you after *some particular persons* shall be secure; I mean to assist you, *if you want assistance* – I am told however that you will not need any, and in that case you *must not ask it of me*. I need not say that this letter is strictly *confidential*, for altho' I am bound to no list whatever, nor have I indeed seen any, I might be teazed by applications without end. I hope I have spoken *plain*. *Some Friends I must secure* if possible. Therefore I cannot assist you *if your success sh. interfere with theirs. If it does not*, I will vote for you.[19]

As a man on the government list, Kinnaird was in a genuinely difficult position but the same excuse did not apply to others. Lord Morton must have been peculiarly irritating, telling Aberdeen on 29 November, 'Although I did not chuse to come under any engagements, early during the present contest, nor to inform any person of my intentions, on the subject of voting, with whose intentions I was not acquainted, I can assure your Lordship that at the Time, when I had the pleasure of seeing you at Dalmahoy, your name was in my List.' Cathcart too refused to be pinned down. 'Cathcart', Aberdeen told Abercorn, 'in a speech of an hour told me he would not decide before the Election.'[20]

Some refusals of support were more hurtful than others; on 14 November, Aberdeen told Abercorn, 'The Interference of Government is really intolerable, in as much as they have used their utmost endeavours not only to make individuals desert their friends, but even to break the most solemn promises; in one quarter they have succeeded but too well, and where I least expected it.' According to a later letter the deserter was Lord Erroll, who 'is my neighbour, and was my very intimate friend.'[21]

By late November Aberdeen was gloomy. He wrote to Abercorn,

The state of my affairs continues very doubtful, having met with so many reverses. I thought the D. of Argyle sure, Lord Bute the same, the D. of Queensberry, Lord Hyndford and others; however it may still go well, notwithstanding the great attack is made against me and Lord Dalhousie. I have exchanged votes with fourteen – Strathmore, Kellie, Haddington, Dalhousie, Elgin, Leven, Balcarras, Aboyne, Aberdeen [sic], Glasgow, Forbes, Blantyre, Napier and Reay; all of those are to have your vote except the last. I have also proposed to exchange with Cathcart and Somerville, the first palavered, and the other said nothing. You have been active, but I must mention a few names, in case you should be able to discover any means of getting at them.

Lothian, Eglinton, Dysart, Portmore, Mansfield, D. of Leeds, Torphichen, Belhaven, Fairfax, Elibank.

He added, 'All our friends, candidates, are in very low spirits as to their success.'[22]

All kinds of skulduggery were going on. Aberdeen's close friend, Lord Binning, the son of Lord Haddington, wrote, 'As to Lauderdale's meditated attack on my Father's Peerage (if indeed the whole is anything more than an idle Edin[h]. story) it is too ridiculous not to laugh at. It happens unfortunately for him to be one of the most indubitable titles in Scotland.'[23] Binning had other advice for Aberdeen too. He wrote,

My Father saith that thou art wooden or Blockheaded. He strongly advised you and Aboyne not to go together to Torphichen – but to *go separately*. But he says he does not believe it would have avail'd you. He touch'd with him on your subject; but got no encouragement. I would not however have you despair as he is a very odd strange surly fish. Elibank we know of. Rollo we are glad of. Caithness we have hopes of. Dundonald is wavering again I find – but I hope not essentially. My Father has Dunmore's vote; Elgin has refus'd him. Galloway & Home we are sure of. Arbuthnot has been sulky & never answer'd the Justice Clerk's letter desiring him to vote for my Genitor. Have you heard of him? Do you know anything of Belhaven? Have you got Hyndford? My father has. Mair is as yet dubious. I think two or three of you gentlemen at least will come in . . .[24]

By 25 November Aberdeen had taken up residence in Edinburgh at Dumbreck's Hotel but he seems to have been in a considerable state of disorganisation. He wrote to Abercorn that he believed he had now secured 34 or 35 votes but he had just lost his list and as 'there is not such a thing as a Scots Almanack in Edinburgh', he could not immediately find a list of the peerage in order to draw up a new one. He was also at cross purposes with Abercorn, whose proxy he was holding, but the accuracy of whose list he doubted.[25] Even before he received this exasperating letter, Abercorn was in despair about his son-in-law's prospects; 'I really believe (indeed am convinced)', he wrote, 'that you are endangering, perhaps losing, your Election, merely for want of management & concert . . . But how is it possible that you can make the best use of my Proxy in exchanging and bartering votes, when instead of being at Head Quarters & looking about you, you are perpetually on the road bobbing about between Edin[h]. & Haddo?' He feared further desertions, vowing that if the Duke of Argyll did not vote for Aberdeen, 'it will be a breach of Friendship that to the end of time I will never forgive.'[26]

Interestingly, Aberdeen was not disconcerted by this blast from the formidable Abercorn and few things illustrate their relationship better than the complete insouciance with which Aberdeen replied, 'I forgive all your scurrilities and abuse on account of the distance at which you are.' He explained that he had in fact been very active, 'I have got Torphichen and Cathcart after many magnificent speeches has at last exchanged.' He had secured Breadalbane 'through another quarter, viz. his wife.' He thought he had Dundonald 'but there is no trusting him.' He feared he had lost Argyll, Rollo and Arbuthnot but he had got Morton, whom Abercorn had accused him of neglecting. Their friends were to meet in Edinburgh on 2 December to concert tactics. 'The true mode of rendering their votes really efficient', he had decided 'would be only to support eight of us opposed by government.'[27] Abercorn was given to euphoria as well as despair. At one time he wildly prophesied that Aberdeen would top the poll and, after the reproaches of 26 November, he was writing as if Aberdeen had already won, 'Huzza! Aberdeen for ever'.[28]

Even the excitement of a Scottish peerage election had to come to an end eventually and at noon on Thursday, 4 December 1806, thirty four peers assembled at Holyroodhouse for the voting. Others had appointed proxies or sent 'signed lists'. The proceedings were entirely formal. No speeches were allowed and there was little pomp. This lack of ceremony and discussion was quite deliberate. In the eighteenth century British governments had had good reason to fear that this periodic meeting of the Scottish peers might have become a political forum. Despite the muted atmosphere, the 1806 election was 'one of the keenest contests that ever took place'. It went on until the unusually late hour of 5.30 p.m. and the spectators' seats were filled 'early in the forenoon'.[29]

Abercorn's prophecy was not fulfilled. Aberdeen did not top the poll. He scraped home with 43 votes. Of the successful candidates only Kinnaird, about whose willingness to stand there had been some doubt, scored less. But, given the odds against him, it was a remarkable performance for an untried man of twenty-two. *The Times* commented, 'All those chosen, with the single exception of Lord ABERDEEN, were supported by the Earl of LAUDERDALE and his friends.' Aberdeen's own political friends, Haddington, Dalhousie, Aboyne and Napier all failed. Aberdeen himself believed that, after some early civility, the government particularly campaigned against him but it seems rather that they had not despaired of him as a recruit and had indicated to their supporters that, if they were unwilling to support the whole government list, Aberdeen was the independent the ministry would find least objectionable. Certainly some government men voted for him.[30]

Aberdeen lost no time in plunging into Scottish politics. During the election campaign, Lord Grenville, supported by Lord Selkirk, had put forward the suggestion that the sixteen representative peers should be elected for life and that all other Scottish peers, like Irish peers, should be eligible to sit in the Commons. Aberdeen spoke against this proposal at a large meeting of Scottish peers held in Edinburgh, the day after the election. He had already told Abercorn on 28 November, 'I reprobated in toto, the idea of any change.' In view of his interest, only a few months earlier, in representing Cambridge University, his attitude is a little surprising. Abercorn was horrified at the idea, telling Aberdeen that he did not think even Parliament had the power to alter the terms of the Act of Union and deploring 'the degradation of our Peerage as making Commoners of even those who would be base enough to make themselves so.'[31] By this time Aberdeen seems to have been passing in various subtle ways from the influence of Pitt, which had led him to regard public service and public office as the highest occupation of a gentleman, to the influence of

Abercorn. Abercorn, while he believed that of course Aberdeen must have a seat in the Lords, saw politics as a rather despicable trade, and office as a bore which the true gentleman would try to avoid.

The election of 1806 was in itself a traumatic experience for Aberdeen. He had to fight two more Scottish peerage elections, those of June 1807 and November 1812. On each occasion he was on the government list and was elected without difficulty. In 1807, when the Duke of Portland was in office, he increased his vote to 48 and in 1812, after Lord Liverpool had assumed office, he actually topped the poll with 51 votes. In spite of this, he never overcame his dislike of peerage elections and his desire for an 'English' peerage, which would relieve him from them, became almost obsessional.

The general election of 1806 was a contentious one in many ways. Aberdeen told Melville, 'I hear there are forty Petitions in the House of Commons. Sheridan, it is said, means to take the Chiltern Hundreds, as he dare not stand a Scrutiny . . . It is not merely Bribery of which he is accused, but subornation of Perjury, viz., giving a man a guinea for his vote, and then if he would vote a second time, two Guineas, and so on in proportion.' Sheridan was, of course, a personal, not a political, friend and Aberdeen saw no reason why they should not add to the government's embarrassment. He suggested raising the question of the government's 'interference' in the Scottish peerage election in the Lords, but Melville, who had good reasons for not wishing to see too close an enquiry into government 'management' of elections, dissuaded him.[32]

Aberdeen took his seat in the House of Lords on the Tory benches on 17 December 1806.[33] The next hurdle was his maiden speech. That, unfortunately, proved a disaster. The Ministry of All the Talents had decided to bring forward the measure for the abolition of the Slave Trade, on which they were united but the opposition divided. Aberdeen himself favoured the measure and had carefully prepared a judicious speech[34] but in the event he lost his nerve and failed to deliver it. Whittington wrote to reproach him, 'What a soldier & afraid! Why did you not let off your well digested matter? The result of so many opinions & much mature deliberation. I was greatly disappointed by the papers both of Saturday & Tuesday, no subject in the world could have been more admirably adapted for your debut.' Whittington knew exactly how to needle his friend and went on to assure him that what he had prepared would have had an excellent effect, not only in London, but also in Aberdeen and among 'the whole circle of heritors who wish to look up to you as their chief in Aberdeenshire'. He reminded him of some 'sage words' of 'old Crombie', "Lord Huntley", says he, "has now got the start of Ld. A. – but Ld. A. has a fine game in his hands; great expectations are formed of his character & talents & depend upon it, for I know the people, that *one good speech* from Ld. A. in the House of Lords will give him more friends in the north than *twenty dinners* of Lord Huntly" – you really must screw up your courage & shew them, what we your companions all know, that you can speak with great vigour & effect.' He could only suggest that Aberdeen must now speak on the Catholic Bill but that would be a formidable task because it was 'the most difficult measure of internal policy that has ever been proposed.'[35]

99

Despite a feeble attempt by Aberdeen to persuade Whittington that he had simply postponed his speech for another day[36] – an excuse he was to use on other later occasions – the incident revealed Aberdeen's Achilles' heel in politics. He was terrified of speaking in the House of Lords. In over fifty years in politics, many of them in high office, he never became accustomed to the House. His affliction is all the stranger since he had been familiar with parliament from his boyhood; he knew and was on friendly terms with most of his fellow peers, and he was capable of making perfectly competent speeches in other surroundings. In his life time, he made a few good speeches in the Lords but usually he was the despair of the Hansard writers, as well as of his colleagues, being inaudible and difficult to follow.[37] Quite early in his career, political friends began to say that Aberdeen would be a considerable asset to any government, if only he could speak; perhaps, as he was an intrepid traveller and a good linguist, diplomacy might be more his line? J. W. W. Ward, later Lord Dudley, summed up the dilemma when he wrote to a friend in 1811, 'To be an Ambassador is splendid at seven and twenty, but were he to speak often in the House of Lords, as he did the other day, a still more brilliant career would be open to him at home. His Party is not overstocked with talents, particularly in that House, so that he could hardly fail, if they continued in power, to rise to some very considerable station.'[38]

At first Aberdeen devoted his attention to Scottish matters. During its short remaining lifetime the Ministry of All the Talents caused considerable alarm in the Scottish ranks. Whittington commented caustically that they seemed 'never to have come to a single decision on foreign politics, but to have entirely employed themselves on parish business'.[39] In two months they had proposed to alter the Scottish judicature, the Scottish clergy, the poor laws, the tenure of landed property and the test laws, apart from Wyndham's 'revolution' in the army and the volunteer system, and St Vincent's new code of naval regulations. The first measure in particular, which would have altered the structure of the Court of Session, roused all the old Scottish fears about interference from England. The Lord Justice Clerk, John Hope wrote on 6 March that if Grenville persisted with his Bill in the face of the opinions he had received, 'it will be such an insult to this Country, that I shall feel myself justified in endeavouring to rouse it from one end to the other'. The Heads of the Bar were all against it.[40] Melville thought it a 'Rash and dangerous project originating in the vanity and levity of a few individuals', who did not know the country. This was another topic on which Melville thought that Aberdeen might well have made his maiden speech. Aberdeen took a keen interest in the question and amassed many papers on it but, before the government could press the matter, it fell on the Catholic question.[41]

The ministry had been compelled to abandon their intention to relax the legislation which forbade Catholics to hold senior appointments in the army but had declined to give the king the assurances he sought that they would not raise the matter again. Aberdeen gave his own version of events to Whittington, which was no doubt the received version of his own circle:

The immediate cause of all this, although arising out of the Catholic Question, is very different from what you have detailed in the Papers. They have made a shameful attempt to Bully the King, whose case is very good. He has shown much spirit and determination; the ministers are surprised beyond measure, never having conceived it possible for the King to resist them. Sheridan says he has heard of people dashing their heads against a stone Wall, but never of anyone before who built one for that purpose. It is hoped there will be no occasion for a dissolution, but if there should be, it is determined to appeal to the people. I think the Government [of Portland] will be good, and well formed. I cannot however say that it will make any difference to me except giving me a seat on the fire side of the House of Lords, instead of the cold Opposition Bench.[42]

Aberdeen finally made his maiden speech on 13 April, arguing that the King had not acted at all unconstitutionally in demanding assurances about their future conduct from his ministers.[43] It was not a good speech. The argument was often obscure. But it made his party loyalty quite clear. He seems to have been offered a Lordship at the Treasury or Admiralty, a normal starting place for a young politician, which Palmerston accepted with alacrity at this time, but Aberdeen did not, perhaps advised by Aberdeen that it was too junior for him. Abercorn himself refused the Lord Lieutenancy of Ireland.[44]

Aberdeen was then offered the Russian embassy. He told Whittington, 'This you must allow is arduous and I think I should prefer a mission of less importance. Unfortunately Constantinople, which I should like better than any place in Europe, is now shut up. But all is a matter for mature deliberation, and as I write in confidence, you will of course not mention the circumstances to anyone whatever.' Whittington replied urging him to take it, '. . . why not establish your reputation at the grandest theatre! It will require all your energies but you certainly have it in your power to do.anything. Where have you *really* exerted yourself & not succeeded?'[45]

Aberdeen, however, decided that he would sooner succeed his old friend, William Drummond, when he returned from Sicily. He approached Canning, who had taken the Foreign Office, through Melville.[46] Canning was at first entirely happy to agree. He was unsure exactly when Drummond would return but promised him, 'Your succession to Mr. D. whenever he comes home, I consider as fixed *on my part* at least & subject only to your own decision.'[47] Drummond himself wrote describing the situation in Sicily and saying that he would rejoice if Aberdeen took his place.[48] Aberdeen's son was under the impression that his father eventually refused the embassy to Sicily, as he had refused that to Russia, but this was not exactly the case. Canning in fact virtually withdrew the offer in November 1807. Sicily had by now become a very important pawn in the struggle with France and he was not satisfied with Drummond's handling of the situation. In view of his earlier categorical promise, Canning had to approach the matter delicately; technically he left the decision to Aberdeen but he made it clear that he wanted a man of experience, 'a character established by long service' in Sicily. 'You will, I am sure,' he wrote, 'think it no disparagement of yourself that there is only the quality of experience to be found wanting in you.' In the circumstances, Aberdeen had no alternative but gracefully to withdraw his claims. 'I think you are already persuaded', he told Canning 'that it is no vulgar avidity of Employment or Place which has ever led me to apply to you . . . I should consider it as wholly unpardonable in me to presume on that kindness, at the expense of what you felt to be your duty.' He entreated him to act 'as it appears to you best'.[49]

Surprisingly, Canning renewed his offer in September 1808. This time Aberdeen was wary and asked for precise information about the relative jurisdictions of the Minister and the local Commander-in-Chief and of the degree to which Britain was involved in the complicated internal affairs of Sicily. But he seems to have wanted the appointment and assured Canning that he would not discredit him despite the novelty of the work. Canning took a very long time to reply and eventually, in November, Aberdeen withdrew his tentative acceptance but he made it clear that he was still available if Constantinople should be on offer. He told Canning:

Since my return from that country, for four years the state of the Turkish Empire has been my chief study. A constant intercourse has been kept up with various parts of it, and nothing has been neglected by me which might contribute to furnish a true picture of that singular country, its inhabitants and government; which it is unnecessary for me to say here are so little known in this part of the world.[50]

Despite the lack of experience which had cost him the Sicilian appointment, Aberdeen still had the entrée into the very highest political circles and was treated with a remarkable degree of respect. At the time of the famous duel between Castlereagh and Canning in 1809, Castlereagh wrote to Aberdeen, justifying his challenge to Canning and sending copies of their correspondence to support his case. When Aberdeen replied in frank terms, criticising him for his 'peremptory' action and pointing out that Canning had not been alone in his criticisms of Castlereagh's conduct and doubting whether he was the 'properest object' for Castlereagh's resentment, Castlereagh answered very meekly, promising to explain verbally circumstances he could not well put in a letter.[51] Although it is clear that Castlereagh was using Aberdeen as a means of communication with other members of the party, it is still a remarkable correspondence between a senior cabinet minister and a relative recruit and helps to explain their very egalitarian attitude to each other in 1813–4.

That Aberdeen was out of office between 1806 and his appointment to Vienna in 1813, was largely a matter of his own choice. In 1811 the then Foreign Secretary, Lord Wellesley, suggested to Aberdeen that he might go to Constantinople or Washington, but Aberdeen declined.[52] He was absorbed in his family, his estates and multifarious other activities. When his old friend, Robert Walpole, returned from Egypt in 1807, he told Aberdeen that he would be glad to know whether he was now 'totally literary or totally political, or something of both'.[53] In fact, Aberdeen had not entirely made up his mind in which direction he wished his life to run. Pitt was now gone and Abercorn was an ambivalent influence so far as a public career was concerned. On one subject Abercorn was a consistently negative influence: he did not much wish his son-in-law to take up an overseas appointment. There were good practical reasons for this. Overseas appointments, even to embassies, were fraught with danger in the early nineteenth century. Aberdeen still did not have a son and, if he should die without one, the position of Catherine and her daughters would be a very unhappy one. It was probably not coincidence that it was in 1808, when Aberdeen was considering diplomatic appointments, that serious discussions began again about drawing up a proper marriage contract, which had been postponed in 1805, but they were never brought to fruition.[54]

NOTES

1. Add. MSS 43229, Whittington to Aberdeen, 27 Jan. 1805.
2. Gurney Papers, RQC 334/2, Aberdeen to Gurney, 'Saturday 10th [Sept. 1802]'.
3. Gurney Papers, RQC 334/4, Aberdeen to Gurney, 9 Mar. 1802.
4. HH 1/19, Aberdeen to Foster, 20 Nov. 1804, 20 Nov. 1805 (copies).
5. Add. MSS 43229, Drummond to Aberdeen, 24 Apr. 1804.
6. Lady Elizabeth Foster to Augustus Foster, 5, 10 Apr., n.d. 13 July 1805; Augustus Foster to Lady Elizabeth Foster, 30 July 1805, Vere Foster, pp. 210–2, 215–6. 230, 232–3; cf. Lady Bessborough to Lady Caroline Lamb, Bessborough, p. 134.
7. Add. MSS 43229, Duke of Gordon to Aberdeen, 20 June 1806, Aberdeen to Kellie, 9 Aug. 1806, Kellie to Aberdeen, 16 Aug. 1806, Stuart Wortley to Aberdeen, 29 Sept. 1806, 'Saturday [Oct. 1806]', Aberdeen to Alex. Brodie, 12 Nov. 1806.
8. Augustus Foster to Lady Elizabeth Foster, 2 June 1805, Vere Foster, p. 225.
9. Add. MSS 43229, Aberdeen to Whittington, 24 Jan. 1806. As the letter remains in Aberdeen's papers perhaps Aberdeen decided it was too emotional and did not send it.
10. Add. MSS 43229, Aberdeen to Whittington, Berkeley Square, 'Monday'; Add. MSS 43227, Lady Melville to Aberdeen, 29 Jan. 1806.
11. The Journal is in Add. MSS 43337. There are extensive extracts in Balfour, vol. 1, pp. 47–51.
12. Add. MSS 43337, Journal, 25, 26 Jan., 8 Feb. 1806.
13. Add. MSS 43337, Journal, 28 Jan. 1806.
14. Add. MSS 43337, Journal, 10, 11, 12, 15 Feb. 1806.
15. Add. MSS 43337, Journal, 20 Feb., 11, 26 Mar. 1806.
16. SRO, GD 26/13/198, Spencer to Leven, 29 Oct. 1806, Leven to Spencer, 5/6 Nov. 1806.
17. J. Ferguson, *The Sixteen Peers of Scotland*, esp. pp. 36, 75–89.
18. Add. MSS 43225, Abercorn to Aberdeen, 26 Nov. 1806; Add. MSS 43227, Melville to Aberdeen, 18, 21 Nov. 1806.
19. Add. MSS 43229, Kinnaird to Aberdeen, 25 Nov. 1806.
20. Add. MSS 43229, Morton to Aberdeen, 29 Nov. 1806; Add. MSS 43225, Aberdeen to Abercorn, 14 Nov. 1806.
21. Add. MSS 43225, Aberdeen to Abercorn, 14, 25 Nov. 1806.
22. Add. MSS 43225, Aberdeen to Abercorn, 21 Nov. 1806.
23. Add. MSS 43229, Binning to Aberdeen, 28 Nov. 1806.

24. Add. MSS 43229, Binning to Aberdeen, 28 Nov. 1806.
25. Add. MSS 43225, Aberdeen to Abercorn, 25 Nov. 1806.
26. Add. MSS 43225, Abercorn to Aberdeen, 26 Nov. 1806.
27. Add. MSS 43225, Aberdeen to Abercorn, 28 Nov., 1 Dec. 1806.
28. Add. MSS 43225, Abercorn to Aberdeen, 28, 29 Nov. 1806.
29. Ferguson, pp. 19, 36.
30. *The Times*, 9 Dec. 1806; Add. MSS 43225, Aberdeen to Abercorn, 14, 25 Nov. 1806; SRO, GD 26/13/198/11, 15, Leven's lists.
31. A Letter to the Peers of Scotland by the Earl of Selkirk' in SRO, GD 26/13/198; Add. MSS 43225, Aberdeen to Abercorn, 28 Nov., 6 Dec. 1806, Abercorn to Aberdeen, 2 Dec. 1806.
32. Add. MSS 43227, Aberdeen to Melville, 21 Dec. 1806, Melville to Aberdeen, 28 Dec. 1806.
33. *House of Lords Journal*, 17 Dec. 1806.
34. His notes are in Add. MSS 43229, under date 5 Feb. 1807.
35. Add. MSS 43229, Whittington to Aberdeen, 19 Mar. 1807.
36. Add. MSS 43229, Aberdeen to Whittington, 21 Mar. 1807.
37. There are few speakers of whom *Hansard* can have had to record, 'The Earl of Aberdeen said a few words', *Hansard*, XV, 9, (23 Jan. 1810).
38. Add. MSS 43230, Ward to Edward Copleston, later Bishop of Llandaff, 13 Feb. 1811. Aberdeen had just moved the Address in reply to the Royal Speech, *Hansard*, XVIII, 1148–55 (12 Feb. 1811).
39. Add. MSS 43229, Whittington to Aberdeen, 25 Mar. 1807.
40. Add. MSS 43229, Hope to Robert, 6 Mar. 1807, Hope to Aberdeen, 7 Mar. 1807.
41. Add. MSS 43227, Melville to Aberdeen, 7 Feb. encl. Islay Campbell to Melville, 7 Feb. 1807, and following papers.
42. Add. MSS 43229, Aberdeen to Whittington, 21 Mar. 1807.
43. *Hansard*, IX, 352–4.
44. Add. MSS 43229, Whittington to Aberdeen, 25 Mar. 1807, Aberdeen to Whittington, 26 Mar. 1807.
45. Add. MSS 43229, Aberdeen to Whittington, 26 Mar. 1807, Whittington to Aberdeen, 28 Mar. 1807.
46. Canning Papers, Bundle 31, Melville to Canning, 6 Apr. 1807, encl. Aberdeen to Melville, 6 Apr. 1807.
47. Add. MSS 43229, Canning to Aberdeen, 27 Apr. 1807.
48. Add. MSS 43229, Drummond to Aberdeen, 28, 29 July 1807.
49. Stanmore, p. 17; Add. MSS 43229, Canning to Aberdeen, 8 Nov. 1807, Aberdeen to Canning, 14 Nov. 1807.
50. Add. MSS 43229, Canning to Aberdeen, 7 Sept., 10 Oct., 11 Nov. 1808; Canning Papers, Bundle 53, Aberdeen to Canning, 11 Sept., 3 Oct., 9 Nov. 1808; cf. Add. MSS 43225, Aberdeen to Abercorn, 16 Oct. 1808.
51. Add. MSS 43230, Castlereagh to Aberdeen, 30 Sept. 1809 and enclosures, 2 Oct. 1809.
52. Add. MSS 43230, Ward to Copleston, 13, 20 Feb., 4 Mar. 1811. It was suggested that Copleston should accompany Aberdeen if he went to Constantinople.
53. Add. MSS 43229, Walpole to Aberdeen, 10 Apr. 1807.
54. Add. MSS 43227, Melville to Aberdeen, 15 Nov. 1808.

CHAPTER SEVEN

Acceptance of the Vienna Embassy

In one way Aberdeen may have felt that his lack of a job between 1806 and 1813 was frustrating. Four of his brothers were in the thick of the war against Napoleon, while he was a mere spectator. He took the keenest interest in their activities and demanded full accounts in letters. Alexander, in particular, obliged him by keeping what amounted to a day to day journal of the war in the Peninsula.

These first hand accounts played an important part in influencing Aberdeen's views on the strategy of the war. In 1808 Alexander had taken part in the Copenhagen expedition, when Britain made a pre—emptive strike to prevent the Danish fleet from falling into French hands. The attack on neutral Denmark was severely criticised but Aberdeen made one of his few effective speeches in the Lords, defending the expedition and arguing that 'self-protection was a leading principle of the law of nations'.[1]

Initially, Aberdeen shared Melville's doubts about the wisdom of extending the war to Spain. Melville had protested to Castlereagh in June 1808 that an expedition to gain control of the Spanish, French or Russian fleets, then in Spanish ports, would be reasonable enough but he thought the government had been seriously misled, if they had embarked on a land campaign 'tempted by any general speculations of a disaffection in the minds of the Spaniards against either their own Government, or the Government of France erected there'. Aberdeen continued to have a poor opinion of Spanish reliability, although he came to think more kindly of the Portuguese.[2]

Alexander took part in most of the major engagements of the Peninsula war and, because of his linguistic skills, he was employed by Wellesley on a number of important missions to the French. He was therefore well placed to give his brother a great deal of confidential information. He did so for a long time without scruple, partly, it seems, with the deliberate intention of influencing decisions in London. 'I think', he wrote in November 1808, 'Ministers deserve to be turned out if this army is sacrificed. Why in God's name did they not send a man of Rank & Talents to know the real state & situation of things before they committed themselves?'[3] Sir John Moore, the then commander, was no hero to Alexander: 'Sir John Moore, ought to be hung,' he wrote heatedly in January 1809, 'his conduct has been infamous.' And, in a longer complaint from Corunna, he inveighed against 'the shameful conduct of Sir John Moore against whom the whole Army talks loudly. By God since we have joined him his Acts have been one continual scene of imbecility & folly.' He had failed to destroy the bridges behind the retreating army and had worn out his men with immense marches. The evacuation should have been from Vigo but, at the last moment, it had been switched to Corunna, where there were no ships.[4]

Alexander could also be fairly indiscreet with military information. In July 1810 he sent Aberdeen a return of the French forces in Spain found among intercepted papers, although on this occasion he did warn his brother to be careful.[5] Alexander did not hesitate to criticise politicians at home, especially when they did not send the desired reinforcements. He told Aberdeen, early in 1811, 'I think Canning has taken a miserable part & will outdo himself' and 'I very much fear we shall soon have a peace if the Prince is regent. In my connections with the French they always hope for such an event taking place with a change in our Government.'[6] In July 1811 Aberdeen asked him questions about the quality of some of his brother officers in Spain, including Castlereagh's half-brother, Charles Stewart, with whom Aberdeen himself was subsequently to serve. Alexander replied that Stewart 'is a most gallant fellow, but perfectly mad, & if anything as a General officer worse than Cole'. (He had previously given his opinion that Cole had '*very, very* moderate talents indeed – quite lost & confused in the field.') After this candour, Alexander turned obstinate, virtually accusing his brother of being indiscreet with the information he was supplying and refusing to provide any more. This led to a brief quarrel between the two brothers, both of whom were quick-tempered, Aberdeen informing Alexander that if he was not prepared to tell him more than he could learn from the press, he was 'very indifferent' whether he wrote at all.[7] Alexander explained reasonably enough the need for discretion. 'Lord W.', he said, 'often expatiates to me upon the impropriety of Officers letter writing, and believes that things have been made publick which he wished not, by some of those about him writing to their Friends.' Alexander believed that, apart from Wellington's secretary, he was the man most in the general's confidence and he warned his brother of Wellington's implacable nature.[8] Alexander continued to write freely of military matters but Aberdeen did not embarrass him by further requests for character sketches of individuals.

Although Aberdeen took the closest possible interest in the progress of the war and in public affairs in general at this time, he rarely spoke. He scored a modest success when he moved the Address in reply to the Royal Speech (strictly the Lords Commissioners' Speech) in February 1811, and he spoke on the Catholic question in January 1812. He told Alexander, 'I spoke for about 40 minutes and was very well satisfied with myself and had every reason to be so with what others said of me.'[9]

But these years were overshadowed by the great tragedy of Aberdeen's life, the death of Catherine. At the end of November 1810 she had given birth, a month prematurely, to the long-desired son, who died within an hour. At the time there seemed to be no explanation and both Catherine and Aberdeen put a brave face on the matter. Aberdeen wrote to Alexander, 'She bears it . . . with the greatest composure, and is getting well even faster than on any other occasion.'[10] Alexander replied comfortingly that they had plenty of time for more sons. So it seemed at first, especially when Aberdeen could write and tell his brother a month later that Catherine was 'quite recovered' and at Bentley Priory, where they had been 'very gay'.[11] In the spring of 1811 they were planning to open the new salons at Argyll House but, in April, Catherine became ill with congestion of the lungs. It still did not seem to be serious and, at the end of the month, Aberdeen was able to tell his brother that she was 'nearly recovered' and, although her illness had delayed the opening of Argyll House, she would probably be quite well in a few days. Catherine was not one to be defeated and eventually they held their party to open the house.[12]

In June they were shocked by the sudden death of Melville, while on a visit to Edinburgh. Aberdeen took what comfort he could from the fact that the post-mortem examination showed that his heart was badly diseased and that, if he had lived, he would have been a mental and physical wreck.[13]

Aberdeen and Catherine too were about to set out for Scotland but Aberdeen told his brother, 'Lady A. has been very unwell, and it is quite possible her health may prevent us from going so soon. She is a great deal better, but by no means well.' A few days later he added, '. . . we do not very well know what is the matter with her'.[14] They went to Tunbridge Wells but Catherine did not improve. Aberdeen told Alexander, 'Her cough is slight and she has no pain whatever; but she is weak and has a very high pulse.'[15] In fact the congestion of the lungs in April had marked the onset of pulmonary tuberculosis.

Aberdeen suggested that they went to Lisbon for the winter. It was a bold suggestion in the middle of the Napoleonic wars but the warm climate might have given Catherine hope of recovery, or at least a reprieve. Catherine, however, perhaps sensing the hopelessness of her condition despite her husband's determined optimism and insistence that she was 'improving', refused to leave her children.[16] They thought of wintering in Devon, and then, for a time, took a house in the Isle of Wight but eventually the doctors recommended that the invalid be brought back to Argyll House. Aberdeen frantically consulted every doctor who seemed to promise any hope of improvement. He told Alexander, 'Baillie, Pemberton and Knighton attend regularly – what medicine can do will be done – I pray God the result may repay our cares.'[17] Unhappily, the medical science of the day probably aggravated rather than alleviated Catherine's condition. Doctors were obsessed by the need to keep tubercular patients in an even temperature and therefore confined them indoors – one of the advantages of Argyll House was that 'the air can be so well regulated as to be of the same temperature the whole day long'.[18] They regularly bled the already weakened patient. Aberdeen himself stayed constantly by her side and, as he told Alexander, 'when not actually occupied with her, it is not easy for me to think of anything else'.[19]

It was at the end of October that Aberdeen faced the fact, which he feared must long have been apparent to others, that Catherine was not going to get better. He wrote a distraught letter to William Howley, admitting that he could no longer think clearly. Yet, he remained always the rational man who was trying to understand what was happening to him. He asked Howley searching questions about why evil was permitted. Should he, he asked, regard this visitation as the result of general laws 'and are these cases of individual misery permitted in the completion of the general good; or ought they to be considered as special dispensations of the divine power?' He still could not give up hope. 'Still', he wrote, 'there is nothing which absolutely compels me to throw away all hope – penitence, humiliation and prayer may avert the dreadful blow.'[20] Howley, racked with sympathy, returned a long and laboured reply, counselling the need for resignation but offering practical advice too. Aberdeen must not despair but, above all, he must not give way because he feared that there would be yet darker times to face before the end.[21]

Aberdeen replied in an even more distressed letter, accepting the need for resignation but lamenting his own lack of faith. He wrote,

The true cause of the frightful and overwhelming nature of the impressions which this makes on my mind, is I fear (what I have before lamented to you) a want of an active and lively belief in the truths of revelation. It is true, my prayers are in the words of the gospel, all its contents are *admitted*, but they make no impression, or at least a faint one, upon me. All events are contemplated with a view to natural religion only – Could I, from a rooted trust in the truth of revelation, feel *sure* of her being translated to Heaven, as I ought to do, my situation would be comparatively happy; but at present it is only some general feeling which tells me that virtue and innocence like hers must lead to bliss.

He now had little hope of human remedy. He went on,

In her presence I have never betrayed the horrors of my mind – your advice shall be followed – what care and affection can do shall be done – the evil of the moment shall be sufficient – the rest may be committed to Heaven. Your exhortation will not have the less effect, from your not having pretended to diminish the difficulties of my task – but you do me more than justice; with a mind disorganized as mine is, there is no strength, no manliness, little resignation.

He feared even Howley could not fully comprehend. Only 'he who beholds the object of his admiration and love, gradually wasting before him, who thinks he hears for the last time sentiments of wisdom and virtue, and the exercise of innocent gaiety – who knows that even the kisses which she lavishes on her children are numbered', could understand.[22]

Catherine fought to the end. Perhaps she tried to keep the fatal knowledge to herself even as her husband was doing. Only twenty-four hours before she died she was discussing the new novel, *Sense and Sensibility*, and speculating on the identity of the author with what Aberdeen called, 'that playful fancy, which I shall never see again'. It was, he said, the last book which gave her pleasure.[23]

She died on 29 February 1812, and, in the words of his youngest son, 'the sunshine went out of his life for ever'. For the rest of his life he wore mourning for her and, for a year after her death, he kept a journal in Latin of her constant appearances to him. Stanmore published a few extracts from the journal, 'Vidi', 'Vidi, sed obscuriorem', 'Verissima dulcissima imago', 'Tota nocta vidi, ut in vita', 'Verissima tristissima imago'.[24]

His close relations with Howley continued. He went to stay with Howley and his large family in Oxford immediately after Catherine's death and the two men travelled in Scotland together later in the same year. Aberdeen was very fond of the Howley children and stood godfather to his namesake, George, who unhappily died in 1820.[25]

Howley seems to have been the only man to whom Aberdeen could really talk. He not only continued to discuss religion and theology with him. Some months after Catherine's death one of the two deer, which had so enchanted her when she first came to Haddo, was savaged by dogs and had to be destroyed. Aberdeen admitted to Howley that the incident had distressed him beyond measure and Howley replied with warm sympathy.[26]

There were practical questions to be settled too. Aberdeen had three mother-less little girls to provide for. In the spring of 1812 he took them to Baronscourt. He was grateful to Lady Abercorn for her assistance, not least because he was conscious that she was Lord Abercorn's third wife and strictly speaking only the childrens' step–grandmother. A governess had to be found. He consulted Howley and, more surprisingly, he consulted his theatrical friends, particularly the Kembles. In fact, Howley too was a devotee of the theatre and the advice overlapped to a great extent. Mrs Baillie recommended a lady of forty-five, whom Aberdeen rejected as too old, emphasising that his girls needed someone young and lively. Mrs Kemble recommended a Miss Atkinson, who had been governess to Mrs Siddons' daughter. Howley gave it as his opinion that 'theatrical manners and ideas . . . cannot be deemed infectious, if they are not caught in a cottage with Mrs Siddons'. It was true that Miss Siddons was a girl of 'unpleasant manners' but that might not be the governess's fault.[27] In the end, a Miss Holloway was appointed, whom the girls seem to have liked well enough, although their elders tended to judge her to be incompetent. The children had now outgrown their nurses but Aberdeen told Howley that he would always retain Mrs Gale in his service even if she had nothing to do. It was the least he could in return for her 'unremitting and tender care' of Catherine. Mrs Gale stayed on to become the closest confidante of the three girls, to whom most of their surviving letters are addressed.[28]

In 1812 Aberdeen seems to have been torn between a feeling that his life was over and that nothing, except the care of his children, could matter again and a restless desire to seek relief by throwing himself into work and activity. Some of his friends even complained of his 'unceasing conversation', so unlike his usual taciturnity.[29]

In October 1812 he was invited to become the Governor of the Ionian Islands which the fortunes of war had recently brought into British hands. His love of Greece was still strong and he gave the offer serious consideration, but in the end he declined it.[30]

In 1813 he began to keep a journal again.[31] It was little more than an engagement diary but it gives a clear picture of his life at this time. He was once again going out into society and was a regular patron of the theatre and opera. In May he sat for Nollekens to make a bust. He was assiduous in his duties to the Society of Antiquaries and the British Museum. He attended various sales and exhibitions. On 1 May he was present at the Royal Academy dinner and proposed a toast. He was particularly active in organising the commemorative exhibition for Sir Joshua Reynolds and after the great dinner on 8 May, attended by two hundred people including the Prince Regent, he found himself, rather unexpectedly, acting as master of ceremonies at the 'British Gallery', where the pictures were displayed by lamplight.

He was reading extensively. Much of his reading centred on current events, especially the war between France and Russia. In March he read, ' "Retraite des Francais", a short Pamphlet published at Petersburgh. Said to be authentic, but containing an account of distresses scarcely credible'. The same month he read *Le Progres de la Puissance Russe* and ' "The Book" – an Investigation and defence of the Conduct of the Princess of Wales in 1806'. He also read Mrs More on female education – concern for his small daughters continually mingled with serious affairs of state. He recorded his walks and visits with six–year–old Jane as solemnly as he did his official engagements.

He was also assiduous in his attendance at the House of Lords. The great question of the day was the renewal of the East India Company's Charter and Aberdeen sat day after day on the India Committee, as well as attending the debates in the House. He interested himself in a Bill which his friend, Lord Harrowby, had introduced to improve the salaries of Anglican curates, to try to curb the evils of non-residence. He still did not speak frequently in the Lords but, in a House where many noble lords never spoke at all his name occurs with fair regularity. He was, in effect, advertising that he was available for public service. His social engagements give the same impression, and he rarely dined alone. Either a distinguished company assembled at Argyll House or Aberdeen went out to dine at one of the other great London houses. Sometimes his companions were best known for literary and artistic reasons, Sir Walter Scott, Thomas Lawrence, Sir Benjamin West, Payne Knight and others, but more often they were politicians. On 23 March he was at a very intimate dinner at the Prime Minister's. He noted, 'Dined with Liverpool; no person but Ly. Liverpool and Harrowby. Much talk, agreeable.' He was on particularly close terms with the Castlereaghs, regularly frequenting Lady Castlereagh's supper parties and escorting Lady Castlereagh and Castlereagh's brother, Sir Charles Stewart, temporarily in London, to places of interest. He also went frequently to Chiswick and resumed his old friendship with Lady [Georgiana] Morpeth and her sister, Lady Harriet Cavendish, now Lady Leveson-Gower. Augustus Foster too was in London and one of the circle.

This friendship with the Cavendishes was now personal rather than political. Aberdeen had decided that he must remarry. He still had no heir and it was not satisfactory to leave his daughters to the care of governesses. Lady Abercorn had taken charge of them for some time and Lady Maria, who had helped to nurse her sister through her last illness, had also been a stalwart support but permanent arrangements must be made. His letters to Maria were so affectionate that a later generation has sometimes thought that, if this had been after the Dead Wife's Sister's Act, the best solution would have been for the bereaved husband to have married the bereaved sister, but this was not possible in 1813 and, in any case, there is some evidence that Maria's affections were bestowed elsewhere.[32]

Maria was his staunchest ally in seeking a new wife. He was first attracted by Anne Cavendish, the daughter of Lord and Lady George Cavendish and the cousin of Georgiana and Harriet, but his suit was vetoed by Lord and Lady George. Stanmore believed that their objections were political and perhaps that is what his father told him but it seems rather that they thought some kind of scandal attached to Aberdeen. To be the grandson of the third Earl of Aberdeen and the son-in-law of Lord Abercorn cannot have been a reassuring pedigree for the parents of a marriageable daughter but it is not clear of what they thought Aberdeen guilty. He himself took the philosophical view that he would have to live it down.[33] It may have related to his friendship with Georgiana and Harriet. There is one letter from Aberdeen to his brother, Robert, of which the most obvious meaning is that Georgiana had been his mistress, although he hastened to assure his brother that this was not the interpretation he must put on it. It contained the curious sentence: 'You must observe that for many years, a connection had subsisted between me and Ly. Georgiana which you are to consider as of the *tenderest possible* description; although I do not mean you to understand that it has been created by that cause which most cements friendship between a man and a woman; in its effects, however, it is the same.'[34] He and Georgiana had certainly enjoyed a mildly flirtatious relationship in his bachelor days. He had addressed poems to her and called on Whittington for assistance when his own powers of invention gave out.[35] Any serious liaison, however, would have had to have continued during his marriage to Catherine and this seems psychologically almost impossible. His disclaimer to Robert was probably true but the closeness of his relationship with Georgiana may well have been known and the cause of suspicion. Again, in the eyes of the Cavendish family, he had practically jilted Harriet in order to marry Catherine in the summer of 1805. They cannot have been reassured by the fact that, while courting Anne Cavendish, he was also considering Lord Harrowby's daughter, Susan, as a possible wife.[36] They may have feared that Anne would be left for Susan, as Harriet had been left for Catherine.

Aberdeen, although fond of both Anne and Susan, was not in love with either of them. Despite Aberdeen's own disclaimers,[37] the Cavendishes were right in thinking that essentially he was looking for a suitable wife for reasons of convenience. There survives, among the papers at Haddo, a description by Aberdeen of a wife, which has been tentatively identified as a description of his first wife but it seems much too cool and, in any case, does not fit Catherine's character. It is more likely that it dates from his search for a second wife.[38]

Aberdeen's affairs became very tangled. The Duke of Devonshire was more sympathetic than Lord and Lady George and in July 1813 he invited him to supper at Devonshire House after the opera. Aberdeen found himself sharing a small table with Anne Cavendish, 'Lady H.' (who could be either Lady Holland or Lady Hardwicke), his own brother Robert, and Lady Harrowby. He and Anne carried on an animated conversation, in which Anne apparently took the initiative, as Aberdeen subsequently told Maria, 'charming and catechising me in an unusual manner'. The whole conversation had been carried on 'almost in a whisper' and Anne seemed 'to wish not to be heard'. The Duke had seen them together and 'appeared delighted'. Aberdeen was puzzled. He could not believe that Anne was a coquette. Perhaps her family was relenting. He protested vigorously to Maria that he was not seeking a simple *marriage de convenance*. Although he could never forget his ideal love for his first wife, he was quite capable of offering 'ardent and pure' affection to Anne.

He protested with a certain egoism, 'Do I not sacrifice, or at least impair, the attachment of the best friends I have had [the Harrowbys] on her account?' and give up 'a person [Susan] whose innocence of character, whose amiable qualities, whose regard for myself, whose beauty, all conspire to make me love her?' It is understandable that Susan's mother, Lady Harrowby, had watched Aberdeen during the supper party, 'in such a manner as would have frozen me at another time'. Despite this interlude, Aberdeen was discouraged. He told Maria, 'I owe it to myself not to encourage a pursuit which is to lead only to disappointment and vexation.'[39] His ill success was hurtful to his pride, as well as wounding to his affections and it was almost certainly one factor in his decision to accept the Vienna embassy.

A more substantial reason was his continuing desire for a United Kingdom peerage. The 1812 Scottish peerage election, coming while he was still grieving for Catherine, re-awakened all his old distaste. He several times approached friends like Harrowby, then Lord President of the Council, for help in securing a British peerage. He harped on the fact that Pitt had promised it, had even told Lord Abercorn, 'I will take care of him as if he was my own son'. He protested that people in Scotland were puzzled as to why it had not been done. He came of an ancient and wealthy family, long ennobled. 'With respect to myself individually', he went on, 'I will not affect a modesty which I do not feel, and will confess that I do not envy the talents or acquirements of a vast majority of the Peers on either side of the House.'[40] Harrowby regretted that he could do little to help and advised Aberdeen to go direct to Liverpool. Aberdeen's relations with Liverpool were a little ambivalent and the stupid muddle over his election as a Trustee of the British Museum had not reassured him. He found a direct approach to Liverpool embarrassing and, in any case, it was delicately conveyed to him that Liverpool was faced by many claims and it would be difficult to give Aberdeen precedence, unless he had some clearly established case.[41] A successful foreign mission in time of war would constitute a strong claim. It was probably in this connection that the Ionian Islands appointment was first mentioned.[42] A special mission to Vienna to re-open the diplomatic relations which had been severed since 1809 would be equally suitable. This domestic dimension helps to explain why Aberdeen was so determined that, if he undertook this mission, his part should be clearly visible and that any credit should be attributed to him and to no one else. If he was ever inclined to forget it himself, Lord Abercorn was always there to remind him and to warn him, not without reason, that there were plenty in England who, for political reasons, would wish to denigrate him. But the 'special mission' was to turn into a major undertaking, which not only occupied a year of his life but also fundamentally influenced the whole of the rest of his career.

In 1812 Napoleon's great Russian campaign had failed, defeated by the scorched earth policy and the Russian winter. Robert, returning across Russia from Teheran, had actually seen the burnt-out ruins of Moscow.[43] Of the 600,000 men Napoleon had committed to the Russian campaign, only about 100,000 escaped. But Napoleon was far from finally defeated. He had returned to Paris in December 1812 and, by the spring of 1813, he had raised a new army of over 200,000 men from France and her satellites. Much of Europe remained more or less loyal to him. He controlled the Low Countries, the Confederation of the Rhine, Italy and the Illyrian Provinces, which Austria had been forced to cede to France in 1809. Neither the King of Prussia, Frederick William III, nor the Emperor of Austria, Francis I, was in any hurry to take up arms against Napoleon. Frederick William remembered too vividly the disasters of 1806, as a result of which Prussia had lost all her territories west of the Elbe and her share of Poland. Francis was probably not greatly influenced by his new dynastic tie with France, resulting from the marriage of his daughter, Marie Louise, to Napoleon in 1810 but he too feared the probable consequences of another defeat at French hands. Even if he contrived to be on the winning side, he was not much less nervous of Russia and Prussia than of France.

When Napoleon embarked on his Russian campaign in 1812, he had been sufficiently master of Europe to compel Austria and Prussia to ally with him and provide him with troops. The Prussian contribution had always been a reluctant one. Prussia had suffered severely from French exactions and, at the beginning of 1813, the Prussian peasantry fell eagerly on the retreating French army. It was the commander of the Prussian contingent, which was supposedly co-operating with the French, General Yorck, who forced Frederick William's hand by concluding his own convention of neutrality with the Russians at Tauroggen in December 1812. The Prussian war party, led by the exiled patriot Stein, who was now advising the Tsar, Alexander I, and already dreaming of a united Germany, forced the pace. On 27 February 1813, Prussia and Russia concluded the Treaty of Kalisch, in which Alexander promised that Prussia should receive back all the territories she had lost since 1806. Prussia declared war on France on 17 March.

At last the British government could see the possibility of a new coalition against Napoleon and this had become urgent to them. Britain had been continuously at war since the breakdown of the Peace of Amiens in 1803, and by 1811 the British economy was severely disrupted. Napoleon's Continental System, aimed at placing Britain in a state of blockade in relation to the rest of the continent, had been more successful than the government cared to admit, although the continent had suffered too. The economic hardship had led to a spate of potentially revolutionary outbreaks, particularly in the north and the midlands.[44] Although the situation was better in 1813 than it had been the previous year, there was still cause for alarm.

Unfortunately, Britain was not in a strong position to influence continental events. Her strength at sea did not greatly impress the three Eastern powers, Russia, Prussia and Austria, except in so far as Britain's definition of her 'maritime rights', principally that of stopping and searching neutral vessels, had seriously irritated the Russians. British eyes were fixed on the Peninsular War, but the British army there did not seem particularly important to the continental powers (despite its success in pinning down large numbers of French troops), until Wellington's victory at Vitoria in June 1813 opened up the possibility of an invasion of France from the south. Britain had no army in central Europe, where it seemed the decisive battles must be fought. There remained Britain's traditional role as the paymaster of coalitions but, as a result of the economic disruption, she was experiencing real difficulty in raising the necessary ready cash even to support Wellington in the Peninsula, let alone to finance a new continental alliance.

At the diplomatic level, Britain had almost lost touch with the continent during the years of Napoleon's supremacy. Diplomatic relations had been suspended with Russia and Prussia in 1807, with Austria in 1809 and with Sweden, then still an important military power, in 1810. Napoleon's invasion of Russia in June 1812 altered the picture. In July Castlereagh sent Lord Cathcart, a seasoned soldier, who had fought in the American War of Independence as well as in the Napoleonic Wars, as British Ambassador to the Tsar. It also became possible to resume relations with Sweden when Napoleon's former marshal, Bernadotte, now Crown Prince of Sweden, quarrelled with his old master, when Napoleon occupied Swedish Pomerania and refused to back Bernadotte's ambition to wrest Norway from Denmark. In April 1812, Sweden and Russia made common cause, Sweden agreeing to cede Finland to Russia in return for Russian support on Norway, but Bernadotte made no military move during the winter of 1812–13. Prussia's changed position finally forced the Swedes into action. By the Treaty of Stockholm with Britain of 3 March 1813 they agreed to supply 30,000 troops against the French in return for a subsidy and the promise of British help to obtain Norway.

As soon as he heard of Prussia's declaration of war, Castlereagh hastened to resume diplomatic relations and sent his own half-brother, Sir Charles Stewart. Stewart, like Cathcart, was a soldier and a novice in diplomacy. It had originally been intended that he should be only 'military commissioner' and subordinate in diplomacy to Cathcart but the protocol proved to be too difficult to arrange and he was fully accredited as Ambassador to Prussia, although he was also appointed military commissioner to both Prussia and Sweden. Stewart, a man of thirty-five and already a major-general, had served as adjutant general to Wellington in the Peninsula. Alexander's strictures on him were justified. He was a gallant but impetuous cavalry officer and Wellington prudently refused to give him general command of the cavalry in the Peninsula. He always saw himself as a soldier rather than a diplomat and spent much of the summer of 1813 actually fighting in the field. This had its disadvantages because, when

Stewart was wanted for negotiations, he tended to be on the battlefield, or in bed recovering from his wounds.

Castlereagh undertook a major re-appraisal of British policy in April 1813, in the light of the new and much more hopeful state of affairs. He revived Pitt's programme of 19 January 1805, which had spelled out Britain's war aims during the Third Coalition. Castlereagh had helped to draft this in 1805, and it remained the basis of his policy from 1813–15. Pitt had hoped that France might be reduced to her pre-revolutionary limits, effectual barriers set up against further French encroachments and a permanent alliance formed between the allies to guarantee the peace treaties. More specifically, he wanted to see the French evacuate Germany and Italy, the independence of the United Provinces and Switzerland re–established, the Kingdom of Sardinia restored, and security provided for Naples. Further, he hoped that France might be compelled to evacuate the whole of the Low Countries and the territories she had occupied on the left bank of the Rhine. This, however, constituted Pitt's maximum programme and he was well aware that military events or the disposition of Britain's allies might compel him to settle for less. This caution was repeated to Cathcart by Castlereagh in April 1813.[45] It was painfully clear in 1813, as in 1805, that the fragile new coalition might not hold together at all. There was also in 1813 a very real danger that the three Eastern Powers might conclude what was then termed a 'continental peace' with Napoleon, relating only to central Europe and totally ignoring Britain's special interests at sea, in the Peninsula, or in the Low Countries.

It was recognised in London that Austria held the key to the situation but there was also a profound distrust of Austria's Foreign Minister, Count Metternich, and his apparent duplicity. From an Austrian point of view, Metternich was playing a brilliant but dangerous game. Just as no Prussian could forget 1806, no Austrian could forget the defeats of 1809. In any case his watchword was 'equilibrium'. He did not wish to see the complete triumph either of France or of Russia and Prussia. What he wanted was a negotiated peace in which Austria played the part of mediator and, in so doing, controlled the situation at least in central Europe. As early as February 1813, Metternich sent envoys to all the belligerents to sound out the possibilities. Baron von Wessenberg came to London and was given a poor reception by the government and the press. The government distrusted a mediator who was still in alliance with the enemy. They doubted whether Wessenberg was fully in Metternich's confidence. In accordance with the usual practice of the times, they intercepted his despatches and found that he was frequently left without instructions and seemed himself to be quite 'defeatist'.[46] If real negotiations were to be opened it was important for an English representative to go to Vienna.

Castlereagh's relations with Aberdeen were very close in the spring of 1813. They frequently dined together and Aberdeen twice stayed with the Castlereaghs at their home at North Cray.[47] On 12 April Castlereagh gave Aberdeen a large number of Foreign Office papers which Aberdeen spent the next few days reading. It is on 25 April, the day after his second visit to North Cray, that the single word 'Vienna' appears in his diary. A week later, on 3 May,

Aberdeen told Abercorn that Castlereagh had proposed that he should undertake a mission to the Austrian Emperor and that he, Aberdeen, had 'rather indicated a consent to the proposal'. At the same time he avowed mixed feelings about the offer. On the one hand he was disinclined to leave the country and his children. On the other hand he understood that the mission would be a short one, not more than six months, and it might be too important to refuse.[48]

For once Abercorn did not raise his customary objections, although the financial provision for the children was once again causing difficulty. Aberdeen had discovered 'to his mortification' that his estate was even more encumbered than he had supposed and that the only provision he could make for his daughters was £4,000 on an estate to which the entail did not apply. He had therefore entered into an agreement with his brother, William, that he would pay him £1,000 a year for the rest of his life, if William would undertake to pay Aberdeen's children £13,000 within a year of their father's death. With the £10,000 which it had been agreed would come to them on Abercorn's death, this would give them £9,000 each, which was not so much as he would wish but would place them out of 'real distress'. Unfortunately he could not execute a deed relating to the £10,000 until it had been properly registered. It was three years since Abercorn's solicitor had told him that he had sent to Ireland for that purpose but he seemed 'a strange sort of person' and Aberdeen could get nothing positive from him.[49]

It may have been for that purpose that Aberdeen went to Ireland in June 1813. He had told Abercorn that if he did not accept Castlereagh's offer he intended to go to Ireland but Castlereagh still seems to have been expecting his acceptance at that time. On 23 May Aberdeen dined at Castlereagh's with the Prince of Orange, Wessenberg, Baron Jacobi, the Prussian Minister in London, Count Münster, the representative of Hanover, and a number of British cabinet ministers, including Harrowby, Bathurst and Liverpool himself. Frederick Lamb, the younger brother of William Lamb, who was to accompany him to Vienna was also there. A similar party with the addition of Count Lieven, the Russian Ambassador, assembled on 4 June, just before Aberdeen left for Ireland.[50]

The mission hung fire for some weeks. Stanmore suggests that Aberdeen declined to go unless he was authorised to promise Austria money, but the documents are ambiguous on this. It is true that Wessenberg received a cold reply to Metternich's suggestion that Austria might offer armed mediation if she received British subsidies. The British government wanted a firmer undertaking than this before they would expend money on Austria – they were already fully extended elsewhere – but on 30 June Castlereagh instructed Cathcart to open direct communications with Metternich and authorised him to place £500,000 at the disposal of the Austrian government if their army actually engaged in hostilities.[51]

Britain had already concluded subsidy treaties with Prussia and Russia at Reichenbach on 14 and 15 June. In return, the two powers promised not to make peace without Britain and, by implication, to keep her informed as to negotiations. In fact the three Eastern Powers were already pursuing a course from which Britain was effectively excluded. The spring campaign of 1813 had not gone well for the allies. Napoleon had defeated a combined Russian and Prussian force at Lützen on 2 May and a Russian force at Bautzen on 20 May, and had established himself at Dresden, the capital of Saxony, whose king had allied himself with the French. Napoleon, however, had suffered heavy losses and, not fully appreciating the weakness and disunity of his enemies, agreed to an armistice, signed at Plestwitz on 4 June. For Napoleon it was a gamble to give him time to organise and reinforce his army. Metternich had taken the initiative in securing the armistice. He now pressed forward with his intended mediation. He reached agreement with Russia and Prussia at Reichenbach on 24 June (the formal treaty was signed on the 27 June) that Austria would offer France peace based on four points: the dissolution of the Duchy of Warsaw, the enlargement of Prussia, the restitution of the Illyrian Provinces to Austria and the re-establishment of the Hanseatic towns. If Napoleon declined these terms the offer would be withdrawn and Austria would join the allies in the war against France. This was a clear offer of a 'continental peace'. England's interests were nowhere considered and the British representatives at Reichenbach, Cathcart and Stewart, were neither consulted nor even informed. It is important to remember the British exclusion from Reichenbach in considering the role Aberdeen was to play in the later negotiations at Frankfort.

Metternich went to Dresden to convey these terms to Napoleon himself. Napoleon's first reaction was to bluster and to refuse the terms outright. After their first interview, Metternich asked the Austrian commander-in-chief, Prince Schwarzenberg, how long it would take to put the Austrian army on a war footing. He was told three weeks.[52] Metternich thereupon set out to secure an extension of the armistice. Napoleon too wanted time and on 30 June he agreed that a conference should be held at Prague. The armistice was extended until 10 August. The conference met on 15 July but broke up without agreement. On 12 August Austria declared war on France.

It was against this background that Castlereagh decided early in July that the presence of a British representative in Vienna had become urgent. Aberdeen had returned to Scotland and Castlereagh took advantage of the fact that his brother, Robert, was on his way to Haddo to press for a definite answer. He was sorry, he told Aberdeen, that Robert 'seems to think your disposition to have undergone some Change'. He would not hold Aberdeen to his offer if he had decided it was impossible but 'If you could reconcile yourself to an Excursion on the Chance of finding things ripe, I should wish to put the execution of our views into your hands.' He admitted that everything was still uncertain but he denied the Austrian complaints that they had been denied pecuniary support. He warned Aberdeen, 'If you determined upon going, I think Time of Importance.'[53]

Aberdeen again consulted Abercorn but the tone of his letter makes it clear that he had made up his mind. '. . . it is probable', he wrote 'that I shall now be obliged to go, for the urgency of Castlereagh himself, as well as the entreaties of the other ministers are so great that it would be affectation to refuse.' He was determined not to play second fiddle to Cathcart. He told Abercorn,

'The two points in which I intend to insist are, 1st. Whatever may be my nominal diplomatick rank, if any, I must be on a footing of perfect equality with Lord Cathcart, or any Ambassador whatever. – 2nd. In the event of a Congress, I must be on a footing of perfect equality with any English negociator with whom I may be joined.' He also wanted guarantees that his mission would not be prolonged beyond a few months and that he might come home when he wished. Even so, the thought of his children almost made him change his mind. He wrote, 'They are pretty well, Alice not perfectly; when I think of this it is indeed a pang to leave them scarcely to be endured.'[54] Abercorn, who had never himself held a diplomatic appointment, replied at length with advice, much of it bad, to which Aberdeen unfortunately seems to have paid some attention. He told him that he was perfectly right to insist that he would be *Nulli Secundus* and counselled him:

An undisguised personal & national Haughtiness (with a sweet sauce of studied unremitting, ceremonious, *condescending* politeness & attention) is much more advantageous than is supposed or grasped. Much more is lost than gained by manoeuvring & going round about, & pretending to insist upon more than the real object, for fear of getting less . . . But an Ambassador with an established character of straitforwardness, of never receding himself from his real purpose, & disdaining to cajole or be cajoled, will nine times out of ten [succeed].[55]

More interesting than Abercorn's sudden desire to play Polonius is the implication throughout the letter that, unless Aberdeen makes his position very secure, he will be over–reached or left in the lurch, not by his foreign protagonists, but by his political friends at home. The same fear seems to have affected Aberdeen, especially when his mission did not run smoothly.

Castlereagh has been criticised for appointing a young and untried man to such an important post at so critical a time. Nevertheless, it was not such a strange appointment as it seemed to later generations. It was a young man's world. Aberdeen was nearly thirty when he went to Vienna. Canning had been Foreign Secretary at thirty-seven. In 1813 Metternich himself was not yet forty. Aberdeen had travelled widely and proved his capacity to rough it in strange places, a not unimportant consideration in an ambassador following an army in a disordered Europe. Castlereagh had a very limited choice. The British diplomatic service had practically disintegrated since 1809, but, in any case, Vienna was not an appointment for a career diplomat. The Austrian court expected a man of high rank, fully in the confidence of his government. Aberdeen moved naturally, if rather stiffly, in the highest society, and was the friend and confidant of cabinet ministers. Some historians have been scandalised by his tendency to discuss matters on equal terms with Castlereagh and even at times to lecture his chief, but these were in fact the terms which they were on. Aberdeen frequently said in his private letters (he was punctilious in his public despatches) that he would speak just as if he were talking to Castlereagh in his own sitting room as they had often done in the past. Castlereagh, who had meekly accepted Aberdeen's criticisms at the time of the duel with Canning, seems to have taken Aberdeen's comments in the spirit in which they were meant and encouraged Aberdeen to continue to speak freely, even when he could not agree with him.

Other criticisms too have been exaggerated. Too much has been made of an isolated remark by Metternich's secretary, Gentz, that Aberdeen was 'not fully master of the French language'.[56] It is no doubt true that Aberdeen did not speak it with the facility of Metternich, for whom it was virtually his first language, but it is absurd to imply as some historians have done that Aberdeen 'could not speak French'. He read it fluently, as his earlier controversies with French scholars demonstrated. He was a good linguist, interested in language, and had taken pains ever since 1802 to improve his knowledge. All in all his was essentially an eighteenth-century appointment, which only came to look idiosyncratic with the development of the career diplomat later in the nineteenth century.

Aberdeen's situation would have been easier if he had been given more professional support among his assistants. The job of Secretary of Embassy was offered to Stratford Canning, but he turned it down on the grounds that it would be a step backwards in the service since he had already held the rank of Minister Plenipotentiary in Constantinople. At the time his cousin, George Canning, thought he had made a mistake.[57] The appointment went to Frederick Lamb. Although, as Lord Beauvale, he later became a fairly successful career diplomat, he was then completely inexperienced. The only true professional was David Morier, appointed as Aberdeen's private secretary, and described by him as 'a treasure'.[58] For part of the time, Aberdeen also had the assistance of his own brother Robert, who had at least some limited experience in Teheran.

Aberdeen's embassy to Austria was the most important single formative influence of his political career. He met the leading continental statesmen of the time and, on the whole, assessed them shrewdly. He was not a naive young man, as he has so often been portrayed, although like most men he was not impervious to flattery and courteous attention from important people. He recognised Metternich's stature and did not hesitate to learn statecraft from him although he also perceived his weaknesses, especially his vanity. He never lost sight of the fact that the flattery was directed at the British representative who might be able to conjure up large subsidies rather than at the Earl of Aberdeen, although he liked to reassure himself that he was doing a good job when the situation in Germany seemed black and he was having trouble convincing London that matters looked very different in Teplitz or Frankfort than they did from England. Above all, it was during this embassy that he came to take a continental, rather than a purely British, view of European problems. It was a quality which he shared with Castlereagh and a dimension which was lacking in both Canning and Palmerston, although Aberdeen would never have denied (any more than Castlereagh would have done) that a British minister's first duty was to his own country.

NOTES

1. *Hansard*, X, 15–6 (21 Jan. 1808).
2. Add. MSS 43227, Melville to Castlereagh, 8 June 1808; Add. MSS 43223, Aberdeen to Alexander, 30 Apr. 1811.
3. Add. MSS 43223, Alexander to Aberdeen, 17 Nov. 1808.
4. Add. MSS 43223, Alexander to Aberdeen, 14 Jan. 1809 (2 letters).
5. Add. MSS 43223, Alexander to Aberdeen, 18 July 1810.
6. Add. MSS 43223, Alexander to Aberdeen, 26 Jan., 2 Feb. 1811.
7. Add. MSS 43224, Aberdeen to Alexander, 14 July, 10 Oct. 1811; Alexander to Aberdeen, 8 Aug. 1811.
8. Add. MSS 43224, Alexander to Aberdeen, 27 Nov. 1811.
9. *Hansard*, XVIII, 1148–55 (12 Feb. 1811); *Hansard*, XXI, 418–21 (31 Jan. 1812); Add. MSS 43224, Aberdeen to Alexander, 4 Feb. 1812.
10. Add. MSS 43223, Aberdeen to Alexander, 1 Dec. 1810.
11. Add. MSS 43223, Alexander to Aberdeen, 8 Dec. 1810; Aberdeen to Alexander, 1 Jan. 1811.
12. Add. MSS 43223, Aberdeen to Alexander, 13 Mar., 30 Apr., 4 June 1811.
13. Add. MSS 43223, Aberdeen to Alexander, 4 June 1811.
14. Add. MSS 43223, Aberdeen to Alexander, 4, 8 June 1811.
15. Add. MSS 43224, Aberdeen to Alexander, 14 July 1811.
16. Add. MSS 43224, Aberdeen to Alexander, 14 July, 26 Aug. 1811.
17. Add. MSS 43224, Aberdeen to Alexander, 31 Dec. 1811.
18. Add. MSS 43224, Aberdeen to Alexander, 23 Nov. 1811.
19. Add. MSS 43224, Aberdeen to Alexander, 10 Oct. 1811.
20. Howley Papers, 2186A, Aberdeen to Howley, 31 Oct. 1811.
21. Add. MSS 43195, Howley to Aberdeen, 4 Nov. 1811.
22. Howley Papers, 2186A, Aberdeen to Howley, 8 Nov. 1811.
23. Howley Papers, 2186A, Aberdeen to Howley, 12 May 1812.
24. Stanmore, pp. 18–9.
25. Howley Papers, 2186A, Aberdeen to Howley, 12, 29 Apr., 2, 15, 22 June, 26 July 1812, 6 Sept. 1820; Add. MSS 43195, Howley to Aberdeen, 4 Sept. 1820.
26. Howley Papers, 2186A, Aberdeen to Howley, 15 June, 22 Oct. 1812; Add. MSS 43195, Howley to Aberdeen, n.d. Oct. 1812.
27. Howley Papers, 2186A, Aberdeen to Howley, 28, 29 Apr., 12 May, 15 June, 8 July 1812; Add. MSS 43195, Howley to Aberdeen, 1, 9, 21 June 1812.
28. Howley Papers, 2186A, Aberdeen to Howley, 'Tuesday' [Dec. 1812]. Their letters to her are in HH 1/14.
29. Bessborough, p. 230.
30. Add. MSS 43230, Castlereagh to Aberdeen, 8 Oct. 1812, Bathurst to Aberdeen, 9, 24 Oct, 1812, Liverpool to Aberdeen, 'Thursday', n.d. 1812.
31. The journal which is in Add. MSS 43338 ran from 13 Mar. to 11 June 1813.
32. Her name had been variously linked with that of Lord Henry Petty and Lord Henry Paget, *Morning Post*, 26 July 1805. About this time she had a serious quarrel with her father (apparently about an affair of the heart) which Aberdeen managed to resolve, see below p. 157.
33. HH 1/28, Aberdeen to Maria, 25 Oct. 1813.
34. Add. MSS 43209, Aberdeen to Robert, 9 June 1814.
35. Add. MSS 43229, Whittington to Aberdeen, 12 Apr. 1805; Add. MSS 43227, Aberdeen to Lady Melville, 6 May 1805.

36. Add. MSS 43209, Aberdeen to Robert, 9, 25 June 1814.
37. HH 1/28, Aberdeen to Maria, 29 July 1814.
38. HH1/32, n.d.
39. HH 1/28, Aberdeen to Maria, 29 July 1814
40. Harrowby MSS, vol. XIV, ff. 3–4, Aberdeen to Harrowby, 24 Aug. 1812, ff. 7–10, Aberdeen to Harrowby, 1 Oct. 1812.
41. Add. MSS 43230, Harrowby to Aberdeen, 23 Sept. 1812.
42. Add. MSS 43230, Harrowby to Aberdeen, 26 Nov. 1812.
43. Add. MSS 43209, Robert to Aberdeen, 16 Jan. 1813.
44. Aberdeen himself commented to Howley that he thought the disturbances in the manufacturing districts were the effect of an extensive plot of insurrection and riot, Howley Papers, 2186A, Aberdeen to Howley, 12 May 1812.
45. The relevant documents are printed in Webster, *British Diplomacy*, pp. 1, 389–94.
46. FO 7/105, Metternich to Castlereagh, 3, 8 Feb. 1813, Castlereagh to Metternich, 9 Apr. 1813; Add. MSS 43073, Castlereagh to Aberdeen, 30 Aug. 1813, 'Most Private'.
47. Add. MSS 43338, Journal esp. 16, 19, 22, 23, 24 Mar., 10, 12, 15, 17, 18, 24, 28 Apr., 1, 4, 6, 8, 23 May, 4, 9 June 1813.
48. Add. MSS 43225, Aberdeen to Abercorn, 3 May 1813.
49. HH 1/29, Aberdeen to Abercorn, 22 Feb. 1813.
50. Add. MSS 43338, Journal, 23 May, 4 June 1813.
51. Stanmore, proofs, quoted Iremonger, p. 41.
52. Metternich, *Autobiographie*, pp. 146–55.
53. Add. MSS 43073, Castlereagh to Aberdeen, 8 July 1813.
54. Add. MSS 43225, Aberdeen to Abercorn, 16 July 1813.
55. Add. MSS 43225, Abercorn to Aberdeen, 22 July 1813.
56. '. . . des Franzoschen nicht recht mächtig', quoted Webster, *Castlereagh 1812–1815*, p. 156. A few days later Gentz took back most of his criticisms of Aberdeen.
57. Lane-Poole, vol. 1, p. 202.
58. Add. MSS 43075, Aberdeen to Castlereagh, 29 Oct. 1813.

CHAPTER EIGHT

Teplitz and Leipzig

Aberdeen was ready to leave for Vienna at the beginning of August 1813. His general instructions are dated 3 August and even in this formal document some clauses are revealing. He was to 'confirm and improve the good understanding' between the two courts, and, as far as possible 'penetrate into those councils and designs of the Emperor which may have any influence on the affairs of Our Kingdom and on the public Tranquillity'. In particular, he was to find out any steps 'that may be taken for extending the duration or altering the terms of any Treaty, or other engagements now subsisting, for renewing former alliances, or for forming new connexions between the Court of Vienna and any other of the Courts of Europe, particularly those of Petersburg and Berlin, or any other Powers of the North'. If possible he was to get accurate copies of all treaties and engagements lately entered into.[1] These instructions show how completely Britain had become excluded from the councils of the other European powers. Aberdeen's first task, and it was a difficult one, was simply to re-establish a British diplomatic presence. He has seldom been given the credit for the extent to which he succeeded.

His detailed instructions, dated 6 August,[2] show how much uncertainty surrounded the whole mission. He was to go to allied headquarters on his way to Vienna and try to find out the actual state of affairs from Cathcart and Stewart. Castlereagh did not know whether the discussions then going on at Prague would end in the renewal of hostilities or in negotiations 'of a more formal, and possibly more extended nature'. Because of the uncertainty about the Austrian position, Aberdeen was furnished with alternative credentials as Minister Plenipotentiary or as Ambassador, and authorised to tell the Emperor, if necessary, that he had come on a 'special mission', comparable to that of Wessenberg in London, which did not imply a formal re-opening of diplomatic relations. To complicate matters further, his Secretary of Embassy, Frederick Lamb, was furnished with powers as Minister Plenipotentiary to be used if Aberdeen left, or even in some circumstances if Aberdeen remained. If he found that Austria had 'separated' herself from the allies, Aberdeen was to suspend his journey and await instructions.

His instructions on Britain's war aims were equally open and subject to contingencies. He was told 'the Basis of a general Peace . . . ought in the judgement of Her Majesty's Government to confine France at least within the Pyrenees, the Alps and the Rhine', if the other Great Powers would fight for this but:

If . . . the Powers most immediately interested should determine rather than encounter the Risks of a more protracted Struggle, to trust for their Security to a more imperfect Arrangement, it has never been the Practice of the British Government to attempt to dictate to other States a perseverance in War, which they did not themselves recognize to be essential to their own as well as to the common safety.

For the details of what would be acceptable, Aberdeen was referred to Castlereagh's despatch of 5 July to Cathcart.[3] In this, Castlereagh retained the Pittite distinction between the points on which Britain was inviolably pledged, those on which she would wish to insist if possible, and those which were merely desirable. In the first category, Britain was pledged to the restoration of Spain, Portugal and Sicily to their legitimate sovereigns, and by her recent agreements with Sweden. In the second, she was ready to insist with her allies on the 'foundation of some Counterpoise in the centre of Europe to the Power of France' to be brought about by the restoration of the power of the Prussian and Austrian monarchies. Britain would co–operate with her allies in requiring the liberation of Holland and its re-establishment as an independent Power. She also wished to see the 'absolute restoration' of Hanover – in which, of course, the Prince Regent had a strong interest. The restoration of the rest of Germany and of Switzerland and Italy came under the third and least precise heading. If Austria joined the allies, Castlereagh had good hopes that the objectives outlined in this despatch might be attained. Above all, Aberdeen was to 'direct your Endeavours at all times to preserve an Union of Interest and Councils amongst the Allies'. This was often the hardest part of his task.

Castlereagh also furnished Aberdeen with additional instructions relating to Italy, in which Austria was likely to feel a particular interest.[4] She had effectively renounced any interest in recovering the former Austrian Netherlands and was expected to take compensation in Italy. This was quite agreeable to Castlereagh, especially if it meant that Austrian influence would drive out French. He told Aberdeen: 'The Prince Regent will see with the Greatest satisfaction the House of Austria assume its ancient Preponderance in the North of Italy.' The Tyrol should be restored to Austria, and to this end Aberdeen should encourage the insurrection there. Castlereagh was quite ready to sacrifice the ancient republic of Venice, so lamented by Wordsworth, and now in French hands, and he instructed Aberdeen: 'His Royal Highness is especially desirous of seeing the important Position of Venice placed in his Imperial Majesty's Hands.' The King of Sardinia and the Pope were to be restored to their former dominions. Naples was a much more difficult problem. It might be felt that Britain was pledged to place it in the hands of the King of Sicily, but at present it was ruled by Napoleon's brother-in-law, Joachim Murat. Murat had commanded Napoleon's cavalry in Russia and indeed assumed command of the remnant of the Grande Armée after Napoleon returned to Paris, but there now seemed a reasonable chance that he might be persuaded to desert Napoleon, as Bernadotte had already done. There was the additional complication (or opportunity), well known to Aberdeen, that Murat's wife, Caroline Bonaparte, Napoleon's youngest sister, had been Metternich's mistress.[5] Aberdeen was very confidentially instructed that, although the best solution would be for Murat to surrender Naples to the Sicilian Bourbons and take compensation elsewhere in Italy, he might, if it were absolutely necessary, sign a convention with the Austrians allowing Murat to retain Naples while promising compensation elsewhere to the Sicilian royal family.

Aberdeen left London for Yarmouth on 6 August. His general instructions had contained a formal caution that he should 'on no account communicate with your private friends on public affairs', an injunction which he observed more scrupulously than many diplomats of the period. He risked offending Abercorn, who expected to be kept informed, by sending him no information and merely asking Castlereagh to pass on all that he thought proper. He was cautious even in writing to Harrowby, a cabinet minister, again leaving it to Castlereagh to give him 'political' information.[6] But he seems to have felt a compulsion, in his new and strange surroundings, to write to someone about the war and his personal experiences. He wrote mainly to Harrowby and his sister-in-law, Lady Maria Hamilton. The result is an unusually full account of his mission. Sometimes he wrote about literary and historical matters, as if in relief from the discomforts and horrors by which he was surrounded.

The mission was a strenuous and even dangerous one. The last British envoy to Vienna, Benjamin Bathurst, had been murdered in 1809, whether by the French or by common brigands had never been satisfactorily established.[7] Much of Europe was still occupied by Napoleon's forces, and Aberdeen's first problem was to reach allied headquarters. The only route open was through Sweden. He left Yarmouth with Frederick Lamb and David Morier on a British warship, H.M.S. *Cydnus*, on 10 August and arrived at Gothenberg on 14 August. The journey through Sweden was pleasant enough. The roads were good and he told Maria how he had travelled in a carriage, 'drawn by half a dozen little long-tailed ponies that put one in mind of Cinderella and her *attelage*.' Perhaps the last information was meant for his children who were now staying at the Priory. When he arrived at the southern Swedish port of Ystad he learnt that Austria had at last declared war. He told Maria, 'This relieves me of much difficulty, but much yet remains.'[8]

At Ystad, Aberdeen could not find an English ship and eventually took passage on a Swedish packet for Stralsund. They ran into a gale and for twenty-four hours 'the sea was very high, and the vessel laboured much'. Aberdeen was always a bad sailor and, perhaps remembering Royston, he resigned himself to his mission ending then and there but on the evening of Friday, 20 August, they arrived at Stralsund, 'a wretched place'. They were now quite near the fighting. Aberdeen was impressed by the warlike spirit of the Prussians and their unanimous hostility to the French but the war news was very confused. They arrived in Berlin at 7 a.m. on Monday, 23 August, to discover that a French force under Oudinot was advancing on the city. Cannon fire could be clearly heard and the streets were full of soldiers and messengers arriving and departing. Aberdeen responded with almost schoolboy excitement. He could not resist a classical allusion in his account to Maria. 'I never before,' he wrote 'witnessed a scene of such powerful interest; it put me in mind of the state of Athens on the approach of Philip to Cheronea.' He would have liked to have stayed and seen the battle. His first duty, however, was to reach allied head-quarters and General L'Estocq, the commandant of Berlin, warned him that by the next day his route through Frankfort-on-Oder might be cut. Aberdeen therefore decided to set out at once with Lamb, leaving the rest of his staff and the baggage (the latter must have been extensive since it required twenty-four horses) to follow behind. Aberdeen and Lamb reached Frankfort at two o'clock the following morning and pressed on at the same pace. Travelling day and night had its hazards and the following night Aberdeen's carriage overturned. He suffered concussion and, rightly or wrongly, blamed that accident for the severe headaches he was to suffer all his life. They were still in real danger from the French. An enemy force had been burning villages within three miles of one place where they stopped to change horses. Despite more gloomy warnings from the military that their road was cut, Aberdeen and Lamb arrived at Breslau late on Thursday, 26 August, and were able to go to bed for the first time since leaving Stralsund being, as Aberdeen admitted, 'completely worn out.'[9]

The next day they set out for Prague, again travelling day and night. The roads were very bad and once more their carriage overturned. This time they had to wait for four hours in the rain before any assistance could be procured. Aberdeen told Maria, 'We had then to sit in our wet things for the rest of the night. We have more than once spent the day without other food than some dry bread.' At Prague, Aberdeen learnt that the Austrian Emperor was either at Lann or Teplitz. He also learnt that Bernadotte had saved Berlin by defeating Oudinot at Gross Beeren on 23 August, but that the major allied assault on Dresden on 26–27 August, had failed.[10]

The journey to Teplitz, which they reached either late on 2 September, or more probably, early the following day, was harrowing. For the first time Aberdeen saw war in a very different light from the excitement of Berlin. 'The whole road from Prague to this place', he wrote to Maria, 'was covered with waggons full of wounded, dead and dying. The shock, and disgust, and pity produced by such scenes are beyond what I could have supposed possible at a distance. There are near two thousand men round this town. There is much splendour, and much animation in the sight, yet the scenes of distress and misery have sunk deeper in my mind. I have been quite haunted by them.'[11]

The little town of Teplitz (the modern Teplice) was the temporary head-quarters of the allied armies, although the French were still encamped only a few miles away. Aberdeen told Maria, 'Every morning we pack up everything, ready to start, in case they attack the town.'[12] The Emperor of Austria, the Tsar of Russia and the King of Prussia were there in person with their military and civilian advisers, as well as a dozen lesser princes. The British party was quartered in the same house as the Duke of Oldenburg and Prince Eugene of Wurtemburg but Aberdeen described their accommodation as 'wretched'. The town was grossly overcrowded and few necessities were to be had either in Teplitz or in Prague. Aberdeen, who had not been expecting anything like this, had left London quite unprepared and told Maria ruefully, 'I cannot expect to fare well.'[13] Instead of a mission to Vienna, with a brief stop at army headquarters, he now had to join the Emperor on campaign with all its attendant hardships. Even the Emperor had been sleeping on straw. Aberdeen told Castlereagh bluntly, 'I never expected to be in such a scrape.' He was taken ill within a few days of arriving at Teplitz with some kind of dysentery and had to return briefly to Prague.[14] He described his miseries most fully to Harrowby:

I must tell you that all my gloomy apprehensions have been verified . . . I have been very unwell, although now somewhat better, but the wonder is how we exist at all in this vile hole, with scarcely anything to eat, and that of the worst kind. Surrounded by such multitudes of the living and the dead, human and brute, the air is pestilential. Novice as I am in the scenes of destruction the continual sight of the poor wounded wretches of all nations is quite horrible and haunts me day and night. Walking the other evening in a sort of shrubbery belonging to a house in the town, I stumbled over a great heap of arms and legs which had been thrown out of a summer house in which they had been cut off . . . However, I do not deny that there is a great deal very striking. These fine armies, with all their pride, pomp and circumstance. The Emperors and Princes assembled give a lustre which might prevent many from seeing anything else.[15]

It was against this background of discomfort, danger and outright horror that Aberdeen had to organise his mission. He did it with remarkable efficiency which betrayed no signs of amateurism. Castlereagh told him subsequently, 'Your Dispatches are those of an old Stager in the Line',[16] and it was a deserved compliment. Later, as Foreign Secretary himself, Aberdeen would have been delighted (and often surprised) to have received such full, workmanlike, literate and legible despatches as he sent off from Teplitz from 5 September onwards, punctiliously answering all Castlereagh's questions and enclosing a great deal of military intelligence, often gleaned from captured documents. The intelligence side of the British embassy worked very well and filled in many gaps in London's knowledge. The high standard was maintained later in the campaign when despatches often had to be composed on horseback and when Aberdeen had very little clerical assistance.[17] Some of the credit undoubtedly goes to the professional expertise of his secretary, David Morier, but the overall direction was his own.

Before formally presenting himself to the Austrians, Aberdeen, as instructed, discussed the situation with his colleagues, Lord Cathcart and Charles Stewart, both present in Teplitz. Stewart was about to leave to join Bernadotte but was detained by a wound which he had received at the battle of Kulm a few days earlier. Aberdeen was able to reassure Castlereagh about his brother's condition and expressed his sincere regret at his impending departure to both Castlereagh and Maria. He liked the wild Irishman, but preserved a discreet silence about his opinion of Cathcart, who had already irritated him by making difficulties about sharing clerical assistance.[18] During these first few days in Teplitz, Aberdeen also met another extraordinary Englishman, General Sir Robert

Wilson.[19] Wilson was technically the British military adviser to Turkey but, as soon as the war broke out between France and Russia in 1812, he obtained his ambassador's permission to go on a mission to Russia, where he had already served in 1806. Cathcart saw him as a rival and had good reason to complain of Wilson's indiscretions in his dealings with Russian friends and in his letters to opposition leaders at home. He refused to accord him any official position, but Wilson remained with the Russian army.[20] He struck up a friendship with Stewart, who was something of a bird of a feather, but on Aberdeen's arrival he saw a better opportunity. Aberdeen was not deceived as to Wilson's character. He subsequently called him 'a madman',[21] but he took a liking to him. Wilson shared his passion for classical archaeology and he too had searched for the site of Troy.[22] Aberdeen recognised him as a very good and very shrewd soldier. Perhaps it was not difficult for him to persuade Aberdeen that he had been badly treated by Cathcart. As early as 6 September, Aberdeen was writing privately to Castlereagh suggesting that Wilson be given an official appointment as the British military agent with the Austrian army. Prince Schwarzenberg held him in high esteem, and Lord Burghersh, who had been promised the appointment, could be accommodated elsewhere.[23] The Wilson affair was to cause endless complication during Aberdeen's mission but that was still in the future in early September.

Aberdeen presented his credentials on 5 September. Since Austria had now broken with France there was no difficulty about receiving him as Ambassador. Aberdeen promptly wrote privately to Castlereagh asking that he might be immediately gazetted as ambassador and made a Privy Councillor, as was customary. Aberdeen's concern about his status was partly a matter of personal dignity – and he was to show himself very touchy about this during the next few months – but it also reflected a shrewd assessment that in foreign eyes his status and his influence with his own government were linked.[24] For all his personal regard for Stewart, Aberdeen cannot have been under any illusions about the ineffectiveness of Cathcart and Stewart as ambassadors. Gentz once called tham 'real caricatures of Ambassadors'[25] and they raised feelings alternately of mirth and exasperation among the continental professionals.

For Aberdeen, the critical question was what kind of relations he could establish with Austria. The Emperor, Francis I, was gracious to him at their first interview and Aberdeen found him agreeable.[26] More importantly he found he could get on with Metternich who, besides being a consummate diplomat, was also a cultured man who shared Aberdeen's interest in the opera and in collecting *objets d'art*. During the rough campaigning of 1813–14 they forged a friendship which lasted for the rest of their lives. Aberdeen told Maria, 'The great thing which has been most satisfactory is the liking that Metternich has taken to me', and later, 'Metternich is more and more my friend.' On another occasion he told her of the comic incident when the Austrian Foreign Minister and the British Ambassador had been benighted together in the Thuringian forest and had had to take refuge in a hay loft.[27] It has always been suspected that the inexperienced Aberdeen fell under the spell of the wily Metternich and became in some measure his mouthpiece, even with his own government. There is little doubt that Aberdeen was sometimes over–reached by Metternich, as were many far more experienced men, but he was no fool. His letters to Castlereagh often contain a note of caution and of warning. On 23 September, complaining of the 'lenteurs' of the Austrian cabinet, he told Castlereagh that he still had some confidence in Metternich personally 'yet it may be, after all that he is only a most consummate actor'.[28]

Aberdeen came to champion the Austrian cause for quite legitimate reasons. The government in London regarded the Russians, who had been fighting the French since 1812, as their established and dependable ally, who must be given priority of consideration in any arrangements. In contrast, they saw the Austrians as late and doubtful adherents to the allied cause who might yet defect. To Aberdeen the situation looked quite different. The Austrians had now burnt their boats. If Napoleon was again victorious their position would be much worse than in 1809. The Austrians above all must fight to the end and could therefore be trusted. The Russians on the other hand were deeply divided. Many of the generals felt that now the French had been expelled from Russian soil, Russia had no real interest in continuing the war. So far, the Tsar, Alexander I, was in favour of going on fighting, but he was a strange and unpredictable man who might at any moment listen to the peace party. Aberdeen further argued that the future security and stability of Europe would depend far more on Austria than on Russia, so a clear understanding with her must be the first priority. He and Castlereagh argued the matter in their despatches and private letters for the rest of 1813, a dialogue impeded by the slowness and uncertainty of communications which meant that events had often made comments out of date before they were received.

Aberdeen had not been in Teplitz many days before he saw the dangers both of a divided military command and of the total break up of the coalition. He told Castlereagh in a private letter on 7 September that, although Schwarzenberg had been appointed commander-in-chief, his authority was purely nominal. 'The vigour of every measure is paralysed, the wisdom of every proposition is almost rendered abortive, by the delay which is necessary to procure the approbation of the different Sovereigns and their advisers.' One solution would be for the Tsar Alexander to assume overall command; another for all the sovereigns to withdraw and leave Schwarzenberg, or someone else, in actual command, although Cathcart thought the departure of Alexander would signal the end of the coalition. As it was, each army was virtually acting independently and each had a different plan of campaign. The Austrians wanted to advance on Wurtemberg and Bavaria, the Russians to attack Saxony.[29] Any illusions he might have had about the greatness of the men with whom he was now associated quickly evaporated. He told Harrowby:

I have found *my own* Emperor much more sensible than I expected. The Emperor of Russia agreeable and rather clever, but *shewing off*. The King of Prussia, most judicious, perfectly right-headed, and a truly interesting character, deficient in nothing but in confidence. The Heroes we read of at a distance with respect, dwindle into minor figures at a near approach. Barclay de Tolly dull and stupid to the last degree. Wittgenstein not an uncommon person. Old Platoff, striking, but a barbarian. Schwartzenberg, an excellent, gentlemanlike agreeable·man but no genius . . . It really appears to me that Stewart is a superior man to them all.[30]

Aberdeen, however, had his own instructions to fulfil, to try to find out what was going on between the allies and to cement the renewal of diplomatic relations with Austria by the conclusion of a subsidy treaty. He opened his negotiations with Metternich on 7 September with a deliberate show of frankness, communicating to him the substance of Castlereagh's despatch of 5 July, which set out the British war aims. In return Metternich showed him a copy of the new treaty about to be signed between Austria, Russia and Prussia. This provided for the dissolution of the Confederation of the Rhine and the restoration of Austrian and Prussian power to what it had been in 1806. It guaranteed the restoration of Hanover, but did not mention Spain or Holland.[31]

Such a treaty could not satisfy Britain. Stewart had left Teplitz but his very efficient Secretary of Embassy, George Jackson, protested to the Prussian Foreign Minister, Baron Hardenberg. Hardenberg replied that the treaty was only intended to be a general treaty of alliance and that Britain must take up those points which particularly interested her, herself. Stewart cautioned Aberdeen in a letter from Prague that he must make sure that Spain, Holland and Britain's obligations to Sweden were included in any treaty of alliance between Britain and Austria.[32] Aberdeen replied that he was not authorised to negotiate a general treaty, only a subsidy treaty, but he did take up these points with Metternich. Metternich was bland about Spain, Portugal, Sicily and even Sweden, although he pointed out that any promise to give Norway to Sweden would probably wreck the Austrian attempts to conclude an agreement with Denmark. On Holland he was a little more specific. He recognised that the Rhine frontier would not give Britain all the security she wanted, but made the reasonable point that more could be demanded only if the military situation permitted.[33] Aberdeen was not satisfied although he did not share Stewart's suspicion that secret negotiations were already going on between the French and the other allies. But he was aware that the three resident sovereigns were surrounded by every kind of intrigue and cabal, and that the three allied armies were 'full of mutual discontent and recriminations'.[34] This was the more alarming because Bonaparte now seemed to be resuming the initiative. He wrote to Harrowby, on 23 September:

We have been kept on the alert for this last week by a cannonading every morning, sometimes very near us; and musketry within two or three English miles. At night the French Bivouac made a beautiful fireworks. Buonaparte was here himself several times, but it seems they are all retired at least for the present. B. was distinctly seen by many of the army: and one evening had his horse shot under him. Our army is in position; a fine sight, but the weather is very rainy, and they are perfectly exposed.[35]

He told Castlereagh the same day: 'No one knows what to make of his [Bonaparte's] present movements. It is certain that he was down here himself with 90,000 men — too few to beat us, and too many for a reconnaissance. A Battle seems yet to be expected.' It was not reassuring that Metternich thought that, if the battle took place in the open country, Napoleon would win.

Aberdeen feared that if the allies were defeated, the whole coalition would quickly fall to pieces.[36]

The battle did not take place and the sovereigns and their advisers remained penned up in Teplitz. The Austrians were now hopeful that they could secure the alliance of Bavaria and anxious also to secure Denmark. Relations between Aberdeen and Cathcart were deteriorating. Cathcart insisted on detaining the messenger by whom Aberdeen wanted to send off the important details of the new treaty between Austria and Russia. Aberdeen, much provoked, told Castlereagh in a private letter that he was sending off his despatch by the Prussian messenger leaving that night 'for it does not signify if they do open it [since the Prussians already knew the details]'.[37]

The conclusion even of the subsidy treaty hung fire until the beginning of October, partly because Aberdeen was instructed to press the Austrians to include commercial clauses for the benefit of British trade, to which the Austrians were unwilling to agree. The treaty was only actually signed on 9 October, although at Metternich's request it was dated 3 October, which was when the terms were effectively settled. It provided for a British subsidy to Austria of one million pounds, although this included the £500,000 which Cathcart had already disbursed in August.[38]

While the negotiations for the subsidy treaty were grinding on, Aberdeen tried to concert British and Austrian policy on Italy and Germany. Metternich refused to be drawn on his general plans for Italy, beyond saying that the Austrians wanted the River Mincio as the Austrian frontier, which would have given them the Italian Tyrol and Venetia.[39] Murat was a more immediate problem. The allies, who had expected Murat to defect as Bernadotte had done, were disconcerted to find that he had joined Napoleon in Dresden. They suspected that Napoleon had got him there by a trick but he had apparently thrown in his lot with Napoleon again and taken command of his cavalry. But at the same time Murat opened secret negotiations with Metternich and Metternich believed that they could ultimately win him over. In these circumstances Aberdeen was reluctantly persuaded to furnish Metternich with a written statement of the British government's views, including the admission that they would not rule out the possibility of Murat retaining Naples. Aberdeen has been criticised for thus going to the extreme limit of his instructions within a fortnight of arriving at Teplitz, but it can reasonably be argued that, if Murat was to be persuaded to join the allies, the bait had to be spread immediately. No useful purpose could have been served by delay. Castlereagh approved his action.[40]

Germany was an even more complex problem than Italy. Castlereagh had given Aberdeen only the vaguest of instructions. He told him on 21 September: 'I rather wish to keep clear of the German Internal Politics as much as possible, and only to interfere in extraordinary Cases.'[41] He knew that he was ignorant of the real situation and he feared the conflicting claims of Austria, Prussia and, perhaps, of other allies. Metternich assured Aberdeen during their early discussions that Austria had no desire to restore the Holy Roman Empire and this left the future organisation of Germany uncomfortably open. Of most immediate concern was the position of Bavaria and Saxony who were still allied to France. The King of Saxony was impervious to allied blandishments but Bavaria joined the allies by the Treaty of Ried of 8 October The allies recognised the sovereign rights of the King of Bavaria who returned the German Tyrol, which he had acquired in 1805, to Austria. Aberdeen was cheered by the Treaty of Ried, which he impressed on Castlereagh had been achieved by Austria, and hoped that other states of the Confederation would follow Bavaria's example and render Napoleon's position so untenable that he would be compelled to retreat to the Rhine.[42]

The recognition of the sovereignty of the King of Bavaria cut across the plans for the re-organisation of Germany which were then being advocated by the Prussian patriot, Stein, who had been forced to flee to Russia in 1812, and was now an adviser to the Tsar Alexander. Stein hoped that the lands recaptured from Napoleon would not be automatically returned to their former rulers but would be temporarily administered by a 'Council for Germany' and all decisions postponed until after the war. Both Castlereagh and Aberdeen were aware of new possibilities and new dangers. As he passed through northern Germany on his way to Teplitz, Aberdeen had been greatly impressed by the national spirit of the Prussians and their enthusiastic hostility to the French. He wrote on 27 August: 'This patriotic spirit in Germany is quite new, and must produce the best results.'[43] Castlereagh, who is not usually thought of as an exponent of national aspirations, appears in his private correspondence with Aberdeen as an enthusiast for mobilising the people against Napoleon. He told Aberdeen on 29 September that he should 'work Metternich up to embark *the Nation* in the contest – an armed People is a better security, than a Family Connection with an ambitious Neighbour . . . Why not imitate Prussia in rousing their whole Population?'[44]

Aberdeen's views, however, had undergone a considerable change. He wrote on 1 October that Castlereagh would be aware of the 'revolutionary plan of Stein and his friends' by which the lesser states of Germany were to be 'new modelled' and two confederations established under the protection of Austria and Prussia. The Austrians were entirely against this.

Instead of imitating Bonaparte, we ought to pursue a conduct directly opposite, and avoid everything of a revolutionary tendency. Let us restore everything to the right owners; make what terms and conditions you please, but the principle of restitution should never be lost sight of. There is a spirit in the North of Germany which is dangerous. *The Friends of Virtue* ought to be attended to. It is impossible to say what may arise from this discontented and restless disposition – but it is clear that we ought to put down as much as possible the mischievous effects produced by these speculating philosophers and politicians.[45]

This high Toryism sounds more like Metternich than Aberdeen, but Aberdeen understood what was behind Metternich's virulent hostility to Stein. Stein's relations with the Tsar seemed suspicious and his reform plans could as well be a machiavellian Russian plot as a patriotic proposal. Aberdeen had written to Castlereagh as early as 14 September: 'Suspicion of Russia is beginning, and the plan of Stein, of giving Saxony to Prussia with the consent of Russia is alarming to Austria, who looks to Russian aggrandisement in Poland as the consequence.'[46] He had here put his finger very accurately on the great controversy which was to divide the allies at the Congress of Vienna.

One small matter bedevilled the early days of Aberdeen's embassy. By his despatch of 13 July, Castlereagh had authorised Cathcart to tell the Tsar that Britain was now ready to accept Austrian mediation. The despatch only arrived as the conference at Prague was about to break up and Austria was preparing to fulfil her commitment to join the allies. In the circumstances, the Tsar asked that Austria should not be told of the British decision. Aberdeen became increasingly embarrassed at this concealment which accorded badly with his professed policy of complete frankness and, despite reservations on Cathcart's part, eventually told Metternich the whole story. Metternich expressed surprise but professed to understand the Russian motives – as no doubt he did. Aberdeen, who was conscious that he had separated himself from Cathcart on this, was relieved to find that Castlereagh too had come to the conclusion that the matter could no longer be concealed. Russia, Sweden and Spain knew of the British decision and it was likely to become public when Parliament re–assembled on 4 November.[47]

. The imminent meeting of Parliament had another, more important, effect on Castlereagh's plans. He now hoped that a general treaty of alliance could be signed between the allies before Parliament met. This was Castlereagh's great project for a grand alliance against Napoleon. It was to be signed by Britain, Russia, Austria, Prussia and Sweden, and invitations to adhere were to be extended to Spain, Portugal and Sicily. It would incorporate the British war aims, although Castlereagh conceded that the details must still wait on military events. Britain had been excluded from the Treaty of Teplitz of 9 September, and her interests neglected. Now, hopefully, she would be at the centre of the new coalition. Cathcart was to take the initiative in getting these negotiations underway. The choice of Cathcart was the natural one. Russia was still a more important and reliable ally in Castlereagh's eyes than either Prussia or Austria. But Castlereagh knew that his decision would be very unwelcome to Aberdeen.

Castlereagh sent official instructions to Cathcart on 18 September.[48] To Aberdeen he sent copies not only of the official despatches but also of his private letter to Cathcart, explaining why it was important that the first overtures should be made to Russia, and why he feared that Austria might still hesitate. He wrote in soothing and encouraging terms to Aberdeen himself: 'You will find from the Dispatches I now send you that there is yet something left to exercise your Talents upon in Austria. *You* will have the labouring Oar in the negociation, and if you succeed in placing the Key Stone in the Arch which is to sustain us hereafter you will not feel that your labour has been thrown away.' He discreetly backed Aberdeen's policy of entering into confidential relations with Metternich. He had already heard from his brother all Metternich's protestations about his difficulties and his laments that he was distrusted in England. Castlereagh suggested that it might be as well to appear to take

Metternich at his own valuation. 'I am inclined to think it best to make a Hero of Him, and by giving him a Reputation, to excite him to sustain it.'[49]

Castlereagh's important despatches on the projected new alliance did not reach the ambassadors until 18 October. By then the allied armies had at last moved against Napoleon. They now had four armies in being, the army of Bohemia, under Schwarzenberg, the army of the north under Bernadotte, the army of Silesia under Blucher and the newly formed army of Poland under Bennigsen. They heavily outnumbered Napoleon and there had been truth in Metternich's taunt to Napoleon at Dresden that the new French levies were unseasoned boys but the same was true of the allies. The French still had two great advantages, a unified command and the magic of Napoleon's name. The allied generals were willing enough to engage Napoleon's marshals – Barclay de Tolly had defeated Vandamme at Kulm, and Bernadotte and the Prussian, Bülow, successfully ambushed Ney at Dennewitz – but they all dreaded a confrontation with the Emperor himself. Aberdeen saw no reason to revise his low opinion of the generals or his anxiety about the tensions between them. Physically, conditions were becoming steadily worse. Both armies were suffering severely from the weather. It was cold and rained incessantly. The troops had no shelter and only green wood to burn. The countryside had been exhausted of provisions. Aberdeen wrote to Maria: 'Many of the troops are young recruits, who fall fast under this cruel trial.'[50]

Napoleon's reconnaissance at Teplitz had been part of his general regrouping of his forces west of the Elbe which culminated in his setting up his forward base at Leipzig on the river Elster. The Tsar and the Emperor Francis left Teplitz on 5 October. They fixed their new headquarters in the small town of Comotau where Aberdeen found Francis's partiality for him rather inconvenient. The diplomatic corps had been assigned quarters in the larger town of Saatz [Zatec] and Aberdeen had been given a good lodging in a picturesque old house but Francis insisted that Aberdeen, alone of the foreign diplomats, should stay with him in Comotau. Aberdeen had to exchange his comfortable house for 'a room just built, the walls not dry, and without any fireplace'. On 15 October he followed Francis to Marienberg where things were, if anything, worse. He wrote, 'In this town nothing is to be found but potatoes and black bread'. He was conscious that they were now in enemy territory, although the Saxons seemed friendly enough.[51] He was more worried by the undisciplined behaviour of the Russian troops. When he had first seen Tartars, on the way to Prague, he had been charmed by their picturesque appearance, telling his sister-in-law, 'They have the Chinese face, and are exactly like the fellows one sees painted on tea-boxes'.[52] But at Teplitz he had written, 'Crowds of Cossacks prowl around', and told Maria that, if one was rash enough to walk in the woods alone, 'there is some chance of being run through with the spear of a Cossack, or shot by one of the innumerable quantity of people who are always firing off muskets. The other day, as Wilson and I were walking, a ball came close between us.'[53] Matters were now much worse and he admitted to Maria, 'They [the Russians] contrived to keep those horrible robbers, the Monguls, quiet, while they were in Prussia and Bohemia, by telling them they were still in

Russia, and promising them full liberty to plunder when once they had passed the frontier. Brutes as they are, they latterly began to suspect the deceit, and now the poor Saxons suffer for it.'[54] But bad as conditions were, Aberdeen was cheered by the thought that decisive action was at last at hand.

The battle of Leipzig began on 16 October when part of Schwarzenberg's army under Barclay de Tolly attacked the French. In terms of the numbers involved it was the greatest battle of the Napoleonic wars. The French in all committed nearly 200,000 men, the allies over 360,000. Despite the numerical superiority of the allies it took them three days to gain a very narrow victory. The French threw back Barclay de Tolly's initial attack and might have routed them but for a determined assault by Blucher from the north. Aberdeen, who as a non-combatant was behind the lines at Zwickau, heard alarming reports of the ill success of the first day's fighting. He rode forward to Altenburg in an attempt to get better information.[55] Little fighting took place on the 17th, a Sunday. Napoleon tried to re-group his forces but the allies received substantial reinforcements when Bennigsen and Bernadotte, whose dilatory tactics had so far roused both the despair and the suspicions of his allies, arrived with their armies. The allies attacked in force in all sectors the following day. The French resisted with heroic determination for nine hours, but in the evening Napoleon ordered a phased withdrawal. He might have retreated in good order but for a fatal misunderstanding by a French engineer who prematurely blew up a vital bridge across the Elster. The last stages of the withdrawal became a panic-stricken rout. Marshal Poniatowski drowned while trying to swim the river and it was erroneously reported that Marshal Macdonald had met the same fate. Some even believed that Napoleon himself had perished.[56]

Aberdeen experienced very mixed feelings about the battle of Leipzig. On the one hand he exulted in the victory. He wrote officially to Castlereagh, in quite uncharacteristic terms, 'The deliverance of Europe appears to be at hand', and suggested that 'our feelings of exultation as Englishmen' might be enhanced by 'the reflection that this event will be mainly attributable to the unshaken constancy and perseverance of Great Britain'. He added – although it seems unlikely – that this view was shared by men of all nationalities. No doubt in the excitement and relief of victory everyone was congratulating every one else. Aberdeen left it to the military men to report the details of the battle itself but he added some general information. The booty taken in the city had been immense. The principal gates had all been blocked by carriages, baggage wagons and equipages of every description as people tried to escape. The King of Saxony, who was still in the city, had tried to capitulate to the allies but his attempt to ingratiate himself had been coldly received. More sombrely, thousands of bodies had been taken from the river, and the streets were heaped with the dead and wounded.[57]

Allied casualties too had been high and exultation gave way to horror as Aberdeen came to realise the cost of victory in human terms. He wrote to Maria of the entrance to Leipzig:

For three or four miles the ground is covered with bodies of men and horses, many

not dead. Wretches wounded unable to crawl, crying for water amidst heaps of putre-
fying bodies. Their screams are heard at an immense distance, and still ring in my
ears. The living as well as the dead are stripped by the barbarous peasantry, who have
not sufficient charity to put the miserable wretches out of their pain. Our victory is
most complete. It must be owned that a victory is a fine thing, but one should be at
a distance.[58]

The battle of Leipzig was marked by one incident, the importance of which
has tended to be exaggerated by Aberdeen's biographers as far as it affected
Aberdeen personally, although it was linked with an important chain of developments. The Austrian general, Merfeldt, had been captured by the French on
16 October. During the lull in the fighting the following day, Napoleon had
a long interview with Merfeldt, during which, apart from trying to pump him
on allied strategy, he outlined a peace proposal.[59] He was prepared to make
extensive concessions and withdraw from Germany, Holland, Spain and perhaps Italy, if Britain would return the captured French colonies and restore the
freedom of the seas.[60] The proposal was a clear attempt to divide the allies.
Merfeldt was then paroled and asked to convey the offer to Metternich. On his
way back, the next day, Merfeldt first met Schwarzenberg who was on the
field of battle accompanied by Sir Robert Wilson. Merfeldt detailed the proposals to Schwarzenberg. Wilson heard, or perhaps overheard – his account
seems deliberately ambiguous on this point – Merfeldt's message. Wilson
immediately wrote an account of what he had heard and sent his ADC, Captain
Charles, with it to Aberdeen, so that the British might know what was in the
wind. Aberdeen, however, was ten miles back at Altenburg and Captain
Charles first encountered Sir Charles Stewart, who was as usual on the battle
field.[61] It was not perhaps so unreasonable as Lord Stanmore implies for Captain
Charles to deliver his message to Stewart.[62] The important thing after all was
to get the message to London, and, as things turned out, it was fortunate that
he did so since Stewart's messenger arrived in London well ahead of Aberdeen's.[63] It was more questionable for the captain, satisfied that his mission
was accomplished, to gallop off back into the battle without making any further
attempt to find Aberdeen.[64] The message duly reached London, although the
'reward' which Stewart is supposed to have reaped seems to have amounted only
to a formal expression of thanks from the Prince Regent conveyed through
Castlereagh.[65] The really aggrieved party was Wilson, who was very anxious
to establish his credit with the British government and whose (admittedly very
important) contribution came to be completely overlooked. It chanced that
Wilson's family asked Aberdeen's family for permission to use old papers relating to the incident in connection with a biography of Wilson, about the time
of the death of the fourth Earl and this may have established it in Stanmore's
mind as a rather more weighty matter than it really was.[66] Aberdeen was mildly
annoyed with Stewart for not putting him in the picture when the two men
met in Leipzig, but Stewart may genuinely have believed that by that time
Aberdeen would know more than he did. He had told his brother, 'I have
received this . . . information accidentally. You will have it probably from
Lord Aberdeen in the same words with more accurate intelligence, however as

I hope it will get to England first, I have detailed what has come to my knowledge.'[67]

Wilson was becoming a serious embarrassment between Aberdeen and Castlereagh. Aberdeen had whole-heartedly taken Wilson's side and repeatedly wrote to Castlereagh on his behalf. Castlereagh took the matter lightly at first, telling Aberdeen that he knew Wilson to be active, intelligent and brave but he was 'always playing a game'. He knew he was a 'pet' of Aberdeen's 'friend Charles' (i.e. Castlereagh's brother), 'but he is a military coxcomb'. He could not displace Burghersh who had already sailed, but if Aberdeen still wanted Wilson when Burghersh was 'fairly established', a place could be found for him.[68] A little later he was writing much more sharply that Wilson was 'a dangerous Coxcomb'. He would prefer him to leave altogether but if he was dismissed he might stay on as a 'Spectator and Military Journalist' and do more harm. It would therefore be better to send him to Italy and let him report directly to Castlereagh.[69] Aberdeen in turn became seriously annoyed that Castlereagh persisted in ignoring his advice and was almost inclined to treat the matter as one of confidence. He went on pleading Wilson's case long after there was anything to be gained by it.[70] In the end Wilson had to take his departure for Italy. Burghersh in turn protested that Aberdeen had tried to exclude him. Aberdeen denied this.[71] Aberdeen was probably right in thinking that Wilson, for all his eccentricities, was more useful than the inexperienced Burghersh.

Aberdeen did not easily forget old friends. In 1821 Wilson was dismissed from the army for his part in turning the funeral of Queen Caroline into a public demonstration of sympathy for her against her husband, George IV.[72] Aberdeen supported Peel in getting Wilson restored to the Army List in 1830 and backed his appointment as Governor of Gibraltar in 1841.[73]

NOTES

1. FO 7/101, Castlereagh to Aberdeen, General Instructions, 3 Aug. 1813.
2. FO 7/101, Castlereagh to Aberdeen, No. 2, 6 Aug. 1813; Castlereagh Papers, D3030/3554/1–2, Castlereagh to Lamb, 6 Aug. 1813.
3. FO 65/83, Castlereagh to Cathcart, No. 42, 5 July 1813.
4. FO 7/101, Castlereagh to Aberdeen, No. 3, 6 Aug. 1813, 'Most secret & separate', 6 Aug. 1813.
5. Add. MSS 43075, Aberdeen to Castlereagh, 8 Nov. 1813.
6. Add. MSS 43074, Aberdeen to Castlereagh, 23 Sept. 1813; Add. MSS 43225, Abercorn to Aberdeen, 5 Dec. 1813; Harrowby MSS, vol. XIV, f. 11, Aberdeen to Harrowby, 23 Sept. 1813.
7. Bindoff, *British Diplomatic Representatives*, p. 13.
8. Add. MSS 43225, Aberdeen to Maria, Ystadt, 19 Aug. 1813.
9. Add. MSS 43225, Aberdeen to Maria, Breslau, 27 Aug. 1813.
10. Add. MSS 43225, Aberdeen to Maria, Prague, 1 Sept. 1813, continuation of previous letter.
11. Add. MSS 43225, Aberdeen to Maria, Teplitz, 4 Sept. 1813, continuation.

12. Add. MSS 43225, Aberdeen to Maria, 19 Sept. 1813.

13. Add. MSS 43225, Aberdeen to Maria, 1, 4 Sept. 1813.

14. Add. MSS 43073, Aberdeen to Castlereagh, 14 Sept. 1813.

15. Harrowby MSS, vol. XIV, ff. 11–4, Aberdeen to Harrowby, 23 Sept. 1813.

16. Add. MSS 43075, Castlereagh to Aberdeen, n.d. Nov. 1813.

17. Add. MSS 43074, Aberdeen to Castlereagh, 9 Oct. 1813.

18. FO 7/102, Aberdeen to Castlereagh, No. 1, 5 Sept. 1813; Add. MSS 43073, Aberdeen to Castlereagh, 6 Sept. 1813.

19. There is a recent biography of Wilson by M. Glover, although he seems unduly prejudiced against Aberdeen, cf. pp. 140–1.

20. Glover, pp. 93–4, 99–131.

21. 'My old friend Sir Rob. Wilson has got into a bad scrape [for helping the Comte de Lavalette to escape Bourbon vengeance]; it is not unlike what I should have expected from such a madman.', HH 1/29, Aberdeen to Abercorn, 31 Jan. 1816.

22. Wilson, *Private Diary*, vol. 1, pp. 82–107, 369–83.

23. Add. MSS 43073, Aberdeen to Castlereagh, 6 Sept. 1813.

24. FO 7/102, Aberdeen to Castlereagh, No. 1, 5 Sept. 1813; Add. MSS 43073, Aberdeen to Castlereagh, 6 Sept. 1813.

25. Quoted Webster, *The Foreign Policy of Castlereagh 1812–15*, p. 47.

26. FO 7/102, Aberdeen to Castlereagh, No. 1, 5 Sept. 1813; Add. MSS 43225, Aberdeen to Maria, 6 Sept., 10 Oct. 1813.

27. FO 7/102, Aberdeen to Castlereagh, No. 2, 12 Sept. 1813; Add. MSS 43225, Aberdeen to Maria, 19, 29 Sept., 27 Oct. 1813.

28. Add. MSS 43074, Aberdeen to Castlereagh, 23 Sept. 1813.

29. Add. MSS 43073, Aberdeen to Castlereagh, 7 Sept. 1813.

30. Harrowby MSS, vol. XIV, ff. 11–4, Aberdeen to Harrowby, 23 Sept. 1813.

31. FO 7/102, Aberdeen to Castlereagh, No. 2, 13 Sept. 1813.

32. FO 64/89, Jackson to Stewart, 17/18 Sept. 1813; Add. MSS 43074, Stewart to Aberdeen, 20 Sept. 1813.

33. Add. MSS 43074, Aberdeen to Stewart, 21 Sept. 1813; FO 7/102, Aberdeen to Castlereagh, No. 11, 29 Sept. 1813.

34. Add. MSS 43074, Aberdeen to Castlereagh, 23 Sept. 1813.

35. Harrowby MSS, vol. XIV, ff. 11–4, Aberdeen to Harrowby, 23 Sept. 1813.

36. Add. MSS 43074, Aberdeen to Castlereagh, 23/25 Sept. 1813.

37. FO 7/102, Aberdeen to Castlereagh, No. 7, 24 Sept, No. 9, 25 Sept. 1813; Add. MSS 43074, Aberdeen to Castlereagh, 29 Sept. 1813 (2 letters, 'Private' and 'Most Private').

38. FO 7/102, Aberdeen to Castlereagh, No. 3, 13 Sept, No. 15, 9 Oct. 1813; Add. MSS 43074, Aberdeen to Castlereagh, 10 Oct. 1813; B.F.S.P. vol. 1, pp. 104–5.

39. FO 7/102, Aberdeen to Castlereagh, No. 7, 24 Sept. 1813.

40. FO 7/102, Aberdeen to Castlereagh No. 4, 14 Sept. 1813, encl. Aberdeen to Metternich; FO 7/101, Castlereagh to Aberdeen, 15 Oct. 1813, 'Private & Confidential'.

41. Add. MSS 43074, Castlereagh to Aberdeen, 21 Sept. 1813, original (copy in FO 7/101).

42. FO 7/102, Aberdeen to Castlereagh, No. 2, 12 Sept., No. 7, 24 Sept. 1813; Add. MSS 43074, Aberdeen to Castlereagh, 10 Oct. 1813.

43. Add. MSS 43225, Aberdeen to Maria, 27 Aug. 1813.

44. Add. MSS 43074, Castlereagh to Aberdeen, 29 Sept. 1813.

45. Add. MSS 43074, Aberdeen to Castlereagh, 1 Oct. 1813.

46. Add. MSS 43073, Aberdeen to Castlereagh, 14 Sept. 1813.

47. FO 65/83, Castlereagh to Cathcart, No. 45, 13 July 1813; FO 7/102, Aberdeen to Castlereagh, No. 2, 12 Sept. 1813, No. 6, 23 Sept. 1813; Add. MSS 43074, Castlereagh to Aberdeen, 21 Sept. 1813.

48. FO 65/83, Castlereagh to Cathcart, No. 65, 18 Sept. 1813.

49. Add. MSS 43074, Castlereagh to Aberdeen, 21 Sept. 1813 (copy in FO 7/101).

50. Add. MSS 43225, Aberdeen to Maria, 19 Sept, 8 Oct. 1813.

51. Add. MSS 43225, Aberdeen to Maria, 8, 15 Oct. 1813.

52. Add. MSS 43225, Aberdeen to Maria, 1 Sept. 1813.

53. Add. MSS 43225, Aberdeen to Maria, 1 Oct. 1813.

54. Add. MSS 43225, Aberdeen to Maria, 15 Oct. 1813.

55. Add. MSS 43225, Aberdeen to Maria, 16, 17, 18, 19 Oct. 1813.

56. Add. MSS 43225, Aberdeen to Maria, 20 Oct. 1813.

57. FO 7/102, Aberdeen to Castlereagh, No. 18, 22 Oct. 1813.

58. Add. MSS 43225, Aberdeen to Maria, 22 Oct. 1813.

59. Add. MSS 43074, 'Précis d'un entretien du Genl. Comte de Merveldt avec l'Empereur Napoleon, 17 Oct. 1813', with draft of Aberdeen's, No. 18, 22 Oct. 1813.

60. According to a part of the draft of No. 18 in Add. MSS 43074 (which does not appear in FO 7/102) Napoleon said, 'How is it possible that I can submit to their extravagant pretensions of maritime rights? How can Europe submit to them?'

61. Wilson Papers, Add. MSS 30107, two copies of Wilson to Aberdeen, 'In the Field in front of Wachau', 18 Oct. 1813, marked 'Report of Ct. Merveldt's Conversation with Buonaparte . . . Sent to Lord Aberdeen from the field of battle but Charles not finding him gave it to Stewart . . .'

62. Stanmore, pp. 32–3.

63. Stewart's messenger arrived on 2 Nov. (FO 64/86, Castlereagh to Stewart, 5 Nov. 1813), Aberdeen's on 20 Nov. 1813.

64. Wilson Papers, Add. MSS 30107, Capt. Charles to Wilson, 21 Oct. 1813.

65. FO 64/86, Castlereagh to Stewart, No. 72, 30 Nov. 1813.

66. R. Wilson, *Private Diary*, vol. 1, p. xix.

67. Add. MSS 43075, Aberdeen to Stewart, 5 Nov. 1813; FO 64/90, Stewart to Castlereagh, No. 117, 'Secret', 19 Oct. 1813.

68. Add. MSS 43073, Aberdeen to Castlereagh, 6 Sept. 1813; Add. MSS 43074, Castlereagh to Aberdeen, 29 Sept. 1813.

69. Add. MSS 43074, Castlereagh to Aberdeen, 15 Oct. 1813.

70. Add. MSS 43075, Aberdeen to Castlereagh, 11 Nov., 17 Nov. 1813, 'Most Private', Castlereagh to Aberdeen, 30 Nov. 1813.

71. Castlereagh Papers, D3030/3584, Berghersh to Castlereagh, 9 Nov., /3586, 10 Nov., /3588, 12 Nov., /3611, 11 Dec. 1813, /3598, Castlereagh to Berghersh, 30 Nov. 1813; Add. MSS 43075, Aberdeen to Castlereagh, 9 Dec. 1813.

72. Glover, pp. 166–79.

73. Aberdeen arranged for Wilson to be Governor of Gibraltar when he was Colonial Secretary in 1835, but lost office before this could be implemented. In 1841 he reminded the new Colonial Secretary, Lord Stanley, of this arrangement and Stanley honoured it, Derby Papers, 135/7, Aberdeen to Stanley, 12 Nov. 1841.

CHAPTER NINE

The Frankfort proposals

Of more significance than his irritation about the treatment of Wilson was Aberdeen's indignation at the subordinate role assigned to him in the negotiations for the great new alliance. Castlereagh's long delayed instructions of 18 September finally reached the ambassadors during the closing stages of the battle of Leipzig. Aberdeen poured out his frustrations to Castlereagh in a private letter four days later. 'You must give me more to do; *your labouring oar* is not work enough', he wrote. He was probably right in thinking that the best moment to have opened the project would have been during the euphoria after the battle when all the allied leaders were still together 'and God knows when we may meet again'. Cathcart, however, had procrastinated as usual. He wrote indignantly: 'He only broached the subject in conversation but did not follow it up – Stewart and I were at him for an hour but we could not get him to move.' He questioned the wisdom of still giving priority to Russia. It could not fail to give offence to the Austrians who had now brought 300,000 men into the field and would soon bring 100,000 more, apart from the 60,000 they had requested from Hungary. He begged Castlereagh to remember that Metternich 'who moves this great machine, is himself much actuated by personal vanity' and added 'Do not suppose me arrogant when I think that I have considerable personal influence with Metternich.' His feelings then burst through quite nakedly:

Why do you name me second in the full powers? My rank as Ambassador being equal with Cathcart, and my private rank higher, even if we should as a matter of domestic arrangement among ourselves open the matter to the Emperor Alexander first, why should my name not stand first in the Instrument? I always take precedent of him, and even the Emperor Alexander placed me at his right hand the other day when we dined with him . . . you may not be aware how much these things signify to me. If we are meant to be equal, my standing first is a matter of course. But his being named first is quite out of the natural order.

At the end of the letter Aberdeen tried to return to a more judicial assessment of the situation. 'We are excellent friends', he assured Castlereagh, 'but he [Cathcart] will not communicate much. I have tried a great deal but there is

139

no reciprocity. Stewart and I have no secrets from each other. He is here, quite well, and adored by the Swedes and Prussians.'[1]

Aberdeen reiterated his views in other private letters over the next few days as they passed over bad roads through the Thuringian Forest. The Tsar was being extremely difficult and wanting to assume command of the army, although Schwarzenberg thought his conduct at Leipzig very injudicious. He had also caused offence by handing over the Saxons who had changed sides to Bernadotte, although they wished to surrender to the Austrians. The Saxons were now refusing to serve because they feared that Alexander really meant to hand them to the Prussians as part of a scheme to transfer Saxony to Prussia. The Russian army itself was 'clamorous for peace'. All this was clearly designed to persuade Castlereagh that Austria, not Russia, was the reliable ally and should be cultivated, but the information was essentially correct. Aberdeen emphasised his own favoured position. The Emperor Francis 'has insisted on my dining and supping with him *every day* and desires me to do it through the whole campaign'. Pembroke, who had led the mission to Austria in 1807, would tell Castlereagh what a 'revolution' this was in Francis's habits.[2]

Aberdeen returned to the attack in a letter from Smalkalden on 29 October, marked 'Private. For yourself alone.' Despite the continued discomforts of the · campaign and the difficulties of running his office on the march, he was now very optimistic about the war. 'Everything goes on well,' he reported, 'we shall with tolerable good luck, be on the Rhine very soon', but the rapid progress of military events made agreement between the allies urgent and he could not conceal his total distruct of Cathcart and his passionate desire to take charge of the negotiations himself. He complained, 'with respect to the general Alliance, Cathcart whom I saw this morning, has done nothing.'[3]

This was not entirely true. Cathcart, after allowing himself to be put off at Leipzig and Weimar, had managed to have an interview with the Tsar at Ansbatt on 26 October. The Tsar had already been warned of the impending British proposals by his ambassador in London, Count Lieven, and he was ready with counter suggestions for further British subsidies and a discussion of the maritime rights question, especially in the context of the American war. Castlereagh had already indicated to Cathcart that while a form of words could be found to deal with the first, there could be no question of embarking on the second. Cathcart had given in to the Tsar's desire that Sweden should not be one of the original signatories of any alliance treaty, although she might be invited to accede later, but little progress had been made on any other point. Cathcart himself conceded in his report to Castlereagh that since the Austrians, unlike the Russians, did not have strong views on maritime rights and related questions, Metternich would have to play a key role in resolving the difficulties in the way of an alliance. He added that the Tsar 'approved entirely of my removing any restraint upon the communications which Lord Aberdeen and Sir Charles Stewart are ready to make to their respective Courts'. It was exactly this kind of dependence on Cathcart – which could hardly have arisen in a normal diplomatic situation – that Aberdeen found so galling.[4]

In his letter of 29 October, Aberdeen bluntly suggested to Castlereagh that he be put in charge of the negotiations. He told him:

It is necessary that you should now look to the question of peace, as well as of war. As I wish to have no desire or anything else concealed from you, I fairly confess that I look with a degree of anxiety to be employed on this occasion which I can scarcely express. I do not know if it is presumptious in me, but with your instructions I shall not fear. What may be your opinions I will not guess, but it is the mutual confidence both of Austria and Russia which makes me bold in putting this forward. Metternich told me in so many words, that if you appointed me to this Congress that he would be ready to give me the Austrian Full Powers as well as my own. I do not know if Cathcart stands in the way, and certainly I do not wish to act unfairly, but what I should tell you, if unoccupied, I may say now. Nesselrode particularly approved of my being the only person informed of what is now proposed to be done in the way of overture in reply to Napoleon's appeal to Austria through Merfeldt at the battle of Leipzig. He, although not very wise himself, has the most perfect contempt for Cathcart, and frequently expresses it. He says it is impossible to communicate with such an *idiot* – and that he is the Emperor's footman etc. etc. This is very strong, and whether merited or not, shows that C. has not succeeded in obtaining the respect of the Russian Cabinet. Indeed I am informed that the Emperor's language is much the same. But Stewart can give you an account of this and for fear you should think I have an interested motive I forbear.

If Castlereagh could not see his way to putting the negotiations entirely in Aberdeen's hands, he asked him at least to unite him with Cathcart on equal terms.[5] This letter certainly reads as if Aberdeen had drunk deeply at the well of Austrian flattery. Both Metternich and Nesselrode had had no difficulty in identifying the basic weakness of the British diplomatic position, the profound distrust between Aberdeen and Cathcart, although their exasperation with Cathcart's shortcomings was genuine.

In his letter, Aberdeen had referred to the 'overtures' to be made in response to Napoleon's approaches during the battle of Leipzig and for the next few weeks these quite overshadowed any treaty of alliance such as Castlereagh desired. The Allies saw a chance to open secret negotiations with Napoleon through the French minister at Weimar, the Baron St Aignan, Caulaincourt's brother-in-law,[6] who had been captured during the fighting. Aberdeen warned Castlereagh of this in a despatch of 29 October. He assured him, 'All written communications with Bonaparte will at present be avoided.' St Aignan was 'to repeat the proposal of the grand geographical features of the Rhine, the Alps and the Pyrenees, as the limits of the French Empire. If Bonaparte accepts this as a basis, the Allies are willing to assemble a Congress and commence negotiations. If he refuses to treat, the most vigorous hostility will be pursued on our arrival at the Rhine . . .' Aberdeen had discussed at length with Metternich what this offer of the so-called 'natural frontiers' really meant. There was no difficulty about the Pyrenees. There they would simply maintain the status quo. On the Rhine and the Alps, Metternich agreed that they must insist on the absolute independence of Holland and Italy but he felt 'the precise line which should denote the Frontiers of France towards these Countries could not be laid down without difficulty and inconvenience at the present moment, and must to a certain degree be necessarily influenced by the relative position of the Belligerents at the moment of negociation.' It must be remembered that at this time Napoleon was still in complete control of the Low Countries and largely in control of Italy, except the Tyrol, where Aberdeen was very anxious to further the insurrection. He doubted whether Lombardy, Tuscany and Genoa would ally themselves with any enthusiasm to the Austrian cause.[7] In other words, even an offer of the 'natural frontiers' meant asking Napoleon to surrender many areas which were still in his hands and which the Allies' chances of capturing were, at best, prospective and at worst, doubtful.

Aberdeen added a postscript to this despatch on 31 October to warn Castlereagh that Merfeldt might be sent to conduct negotiations with Napoleon. He feared that if Castlereagh learnt this from any other source he might suspect that Austria was once again on the point of defecting. He hoped that, if serious negotiations ensued, Napoleon might allow a messenger to go direct to London through Holland. Communications with England were particularly difficult at this point. The Allies had held Hamburg briefly in the spring of 1813 and this had temporarily opened up an easy channel but the French had recaptured the city on 30 May. The British continually urged Bernadotte to try to retake it but he made no move. Once the Baltic was frozen – and winter set in early in 1813 – communications would be a major problem. Aberdeen was thus left very isolated at the vital moment of the opening of negotiations. He had no dependable colleague on the spot and he could not readily consult his home government.

Allied headquarters now moved to Frankfort–on–Main. Francis and Alexander made a triumphal entry there on 6 November. The journey from Leipzig to Frankfort had been traumatic despite the beautiful country through which they passed. Some of it was wild and dangerous without proper roads or bridges, but other parts reminded Aberdeen of the gentle scenery round Berry Pomeroy in Devon. He was delighted by the vines which grew over the cottages and which were cultivated in neat terraces on the hill sides, as in Italy, but he could not rejoice over the beauties of nature with the hideous signs of war still all around. They were following the route of the retreating French army and every minute or two they passed a body; 'these poor wretches had dropped down from fatigue, some actually in the middle of the road, and the people had not taken the trouble to remove them to the side, although they had all been not only carefully searched for anything of value they might have had, but the bodies were stripped of every vestige of clothing.' But the sight he found most affecting of all was some young children dancing with glee round their burning homes, only conscious of the excitement of the moment, and oblivious of the fact that the fire 'consumed the whole property of their parents and condemned them to cold and hunger'. It was after this experience that he wrote to Maria: 'The cause prospers, and I pray God we may be near to a termination of these horrors.'[8]

Aberdeen had ridden all the way on horseback, usually in company with

Metternich and other leading men, including Merfeldt. They had contrived to dine together in the evenings although their lodgings had been primitive. One night Aberdeen passed at the local butcher's, thankful for the frost since, although he nearly froze without a fire it made the smell bearable. Another night he had the only intact room in the devastated house of the local pastor. Hanau, where the Bavarians had engaged the French, was 'a charnel-house'. By comparison, Frankfort was a haven of comfort where Aberdeen had 'an excellent house'. The people prudently gave the Emperor Francis a tumultuous welcome and the allied leaders began to relax. Huge ceremonial dinners were held and every morning 'we have grand military parades and reviews'.[9] But the serious diplomacy went on behind the scenes.

St Aignan, their chosen intermediary, arrived in Frankfort on 8 November and had a preliminary interview with Metternich. No time was to be wasted. It was suggested that St Aignan should set out for Napoleon's headquarters the next day. Metternich, Nesselrode and Aberdeen met to discuss what proposals he should take. Aberdeen's attitude was cautious, even pessimistic. He reported to Castlereagh that Nesselrode had wished to state the terms as high as possible at first and reduce them if necessary in the course of negotiation. Aberdeen had opposed this on the grounds that it was first necessary to get Napoleon to the negotiating table and he was not convinced that Napoleon was yet sufficiently reduced to treat at all. Aberdeen suggested that they state 'the terms as low as possible, and firmly adhere to them'. For reasons of his own, this suggestion was entirely agreeable to Metternich and he supported Aberdeen. They agreed that 'the specific line of the French frontier towards Holland and Piedmont should be open to discussion, taking care to make the independence of Italy and Holland conditions of Peace sine quibus non.'[10]

In a private letter, a week earlier, Aberdeen had specifically asked Castlereagh what he would be prepared to accept as the Dutch frontier. At that time it had even seemed possible that Louis Bonaparte would have to be left as King of Holland. The Allies had been relying on Bernadotte to open the campaign in the Low Countries but Bernadotte was once again procrastinating. Aberdeen had no faith in him, and had called him 'a Jacobin quack' to Abercorn.[11] He knew that Bernadotte was intensely suspicious of the allied attempts to win over Denmark and feared that England's promise that he should have Norway, which had never been popular with the other Allies, might be jettisoned. Bernadotte preferred to keep his army intact to attack Denmark, rather than Holland, if necessary. Strangely, Castlereagh forgot to answer Aberdeen's question[12] but, in any case, no answer could have arrived in time to influence the Frankfort negotiations. Aberdeen in fact had no up-to-date instructions. The last communication he had received was a note from the undersecretary, Hamilton, dated 12 October, acknowledging his first four despatches from Teplitz and Prague. He complained bitterly to Castlereagh in his private letter of 9 November, that he had not heard from him for 'a century'. He did not receive Castlereagh's long private letter of 15 October, approving his conduct over Murat, but deploring Metternich's continued preference for 'negociation', rather than 'exertion', until 11 November.[13]

Metternich and Nesselrode saw St Aignan on the evening of 9 November, immediately before his departure, and Aberdeen told Castlereagh: 'They requested me to join them, as if by accident, in the course of their meeting, which I accordingly did.'[14] In a sense this put Aberdeen in a false position from the beginning. Technically, he was not a party to the negotiations. Indeed, Nesselrode's position was somewhat obscure since the message conveyed through St Aignan was really an answer to Napoleon's message through Merfeldt, which had been directed specifically to his father–in–law, Fráncis I. Possibly Aberdeen should have refused to be put in such an equivocal position, but it was not an easy decision. Britain had been totally excluded from the vital negotiations between the continental allies at Reichenbach and Teplitz, and Aberdeen had been sent out with very specific instructions to 'penetrate the councils' of Austria. He could and did comfort himself with the (perhaps unrealistic) belief that the proceedings were informal and exploratory and not binding on anyone.

He told Castlereagh, 'M. St Aignan reduced to writing but in an informal manner, the Substance of the conversation.'[15] Much of it seemed entirely satisfactory to Aberdeen. St Aignan was to declare to Napoleon, in the most positive manner, 'the utter impossibility of a Continental Peace'; only a general pacification could be admitted. Thus, Britain's first nightmare, of being left to fight on alone, was dispelled. Aberdeen then summarised his understanding of the terms to be offered:

Among the conditions sine quibus non, were stated, the adoption by Bonaparte of the natural limits of France; meaning generally, the Alps, the Rhine and the Pyrenees. The absolute independence of Germany, and the renunciation of every Species of constitutional influence on the part of France; not meaning thereby the natural and indispensable influence which every powerful State must exercise over its weaker neighbours. The restoration of Ferdinand VII and the ancient Dynasty to the throne of Spain. The existence of States, absolutely independent, between the Austrian and French Frontiers towards Italy. The absolute independence of Holland; but the precise line of Frontier as well as form of Government to be subject to negociation.

But, if it was to be a general peace, maritime questions could not be altogether avoided. Napoleon had told Merfeldt at Leipzig that he did not believe England wanted peace but that if she would restore the French colonies he would restore Hanover. He resisted the idea of reconstituting Holland, saying that it no longer existed and, if it were isolated, it would be dependent on England. He had declared passionately that he would not dishonour himself and, in particular, he would never consent to limit his ships of the line to thirty, as he believed England wanted.[16] All this was bound to be the subject of discussion at Frankfort. Aberdeen denied that Britain had ever proposed such a limitation on the French fleet. Castlereagh had, it is true, said that England was prepared to make 'great sacrifices', by which he meant return the French colonies if it would aid a general settlement.[17] Aberdeen told Castlereagh, 'M. de St Aignan noted also that England was ready to make great sacrifices in order to obtain peace for Europe, that She did not interfere with the freedom of commerce or with those maritime rights to which France could with justice pretend.' This was getting on to dangerous ground and Aberdeen 'particularly cautioned him against supposing that any possible Consideration would induce Great Britain to abandon a particle of what She felt to belong to her maritime Code, from which in no case could she ever recede'. He assured Castlereagh that there was no question of an armistice while the discussions proceeded, but that if Napoleon accepted these as bases for discussion, a place on the right bank of the Rhine might be made neutral and a congress assembled.

Aberdeen had originally understood that St Aignan would take only a verbal communication to Napoleon,[18] and during the next few days he saw with increasing unease the Frenchman's *aide-memoire* assume a quasi-official status. He only sent a copy to Castlereagh on 16 November, assuring him that he would have done so before had he not believed that the note had been made for St Aignan's use only and no copy left with Metternich.[19] He had reason for his dismay because St Aignan had worded the document with the skill of a Talleyrand, pleading all the time that he must make the offer as palatable as possible to Napoleon, who would be very much minded to reject it. He began fairly enough by recording the Allies' intention to make only 'une paix générale' and not, as they had intended at Prague, 'une paix continentale'. But the Allies' insistence that Napoleon must not claim anything beyond France's natural limits became subtly transformed to the recognition that the Alps, the Rhine and the Pyrenees were France's natural limits, which she had a right to claim. The intended French renunciation of 'every species of constitutional influence' in Germany became a much narrower renunciation of 'souveraineté' there. Neither Germany nor Italy was to be subject to France 'ou de toute autre Puissance Préponderante'. The stipulation that the Dutch frontier and form of government should be the subject of further negotiations, became a proviso that the *état* of Holland should be the object of negotiations, providing only that it was to be independent. Finally, there came the notorious sentence, 'Que l'Angleterre était prête à faire les plus grands Sacrifices pour la paix sur ces bases, et à reconnaître la liberté du commerce, et de la navigation à laquelle la France a droit de prétendre.'[20] The ambiguity of the reference to Britain's recognition of the liberty of trade and navigation which France had the right to claim is obvious. It could mean either that Britain recognised those rights which France did claim, or that Britain would recognise only those rights to which she, Britain, accepted that France was entitled. Aberdeen had understood it in the latter sense but any attempt to resolve the meaning would, in itself, open the way for Britain's maritime rights being discussed at any future peace conference.

It has commonly been supposed that Aberdeen's imperfect knowledge of French led him into grave error, but the truth may be more complex. He did spot the ambiguity in St Aignan's text, and protested (according to his despatch to Castlereagh of 9 November) that Britain would not surrender 'a particle' of her maritime code.[21] Metternich, whose knowledge of French was certainly impeccable, allowed equally serious ambiguities to pass without comment in clauses affecting Austrian interests. The first reason for Metternich's complaisance was that (as at Dresden, in June) he saw the proposals as a lure to get Napoleon to the conference table, where they could be radically amended. But Metternich also had another motive. He knew that Napoleon was at last beginning to lose the confidence of his own people and that even the generals were asking themselves whether his judgement was failing. Metternich was anxious to issue a 'Declaration' in which he would appeal to the French people over Napoleon's head, assuring them that the Allies were offering generous terms and that only Napoleon's vanity and obstinacy stood between them and an honourable peace. Nesselrode and Aberdeen persuaded Metternich that such a move would be premature at the beginning of November but he returned to the project at the end of the month. His proposed declaration contained the words 'Les Puissances confirment à l'Empire français une étendue de territoire que n'a jamais connue la France sous ses Rois.' In other words, Metternich did not scrutinise the St Aignan memorandum too closely because it was never intended as more than an opening gambit.[22]

Aberdeen was aware of the complex manoeuvres which were going on round him but his unease increased, and with reason. The intention no doubt was to over–reach Napoleon but Britain might well be over–reached too. None of the continental powers felt the slightest sympathy with her on the maritime rights question. The French Foreign Minister, the duc de Bassano, replied to Metternich on 16 November. He noted that England, as well as the continental powers, was now prepared to join in a congress – this was new information to the French who had not known of England's acceptance of Metternich's mediation at the time of the Prague conference – and suggested Mannheim as the venue. He made no reference to the specific proposals conveyed by St Aignan but expressed general approval of the idea of a peace 'sur la base de l'indépendance de toutes les nations, tant sous le point de vue continental, que sous le point de vue maritime' and added, disturbingly for Aberdeen, 'Sa Majesté conçoit un heureux augure du rapport qu'a fait M. de St Aignan de ce qui a été dit par le Ministre d'Angleterre'. Metternich replied that Mannheim would be an acceptable venue but first Napoleon must give some indication that he was prepared to treat on the bases suggested to St Aignan.[23]

Aberdeen told Castlereagh, on forwarding a copy of St Aignan's *aide-memoire* on 16 November, that he had refrained from asking for an alteration in the passage relating to England because he had feared to give it additional status by making it an agreed statement instead of simply St Aignan's notes. Castlereagh subsequently told him that he had acted correctly in this.[24] But on reading Bassano's reply, Aberdeen decided that he must make a formal statement. He told Castlereagh, 'It is probable that Bonaparte may endeavour to entangle us in the question of maritime rights; and in the event of the failure of any negociation, to throw the whole odium of the prolongation of the war upon England.' On 27 November he sent a note to Metternich pointing out that, when he arrived at Metternich's rooms, he had been confronted by a 'Minute non-officielle d'une conversation confidentielle' and that he had immediately protested, in the presence of Metternich and Nesselrode, that the words relating to England could be misinterpreted. Britain would certainly concede to France the liberty of navigation and commerce she had the *right* to claim 'mais que la question entr'Elles roulait précisement sur la Nature de ce Droit.' Britain would never submit her maritime code to a congress called to discuss quite different matters. The 'sacrifices' Britain was prepared to make for the general good related solely to the return of the captured colonies. There had never been any question of Britain demanding the limitation of the French fleet. He concluded that Britain sincerely desired peace and that he had only been moved to make this statement to prevent 'tout malentendu'.[25]

Castlereagh's first reaction on receiving Aberdeen's despatches of 8 and 9 November and his private letters of 9 and 10 November recounting the St Aignan negotiations was one of approval, although he thought that any delay on the French side would be tantamount to rejection.[26] In a private letter of the same date he expressed his growing confidence in Metternich and his regret that the slowness of communications led to misunderstandings:

I hope my Correspondence has latterly satisfied you that we do Justice both to your Exertions and the Conduct of your Court. When we write, we both naturally take our Tone from the Circumstances not as then existing, but as known to us. Thus when I was fretting about the Elbe and the apprehended indecision of Austria, the Allies were laying the solid foundation of all subsequent Glory, and Metternich performing Miracles both in Negociations and in his armaments.

Castlereagh felt that Metternich 'has behaved in the most loyal manner to us, since we became friends', and Aberdeen could assure him 'There is no preference in any Quarter which ought to give him Umbrage.'[27]

When Castlereagh received the text of St Aignan's memorandum on 6 December he was much less happy. He saw the spectre of maritime rights being raised in a very dangerous form and instructed Aberdeen to make a formal written protest and sent a 'sketch' of the note he wished Aberdeen to deliver to Metternich and Nesselrode. The key passage '. . . the British Government must decline being a party in a general Congress to any Negotiation on the Maritime Code' did not differ much from that in the note Aberdeen had already presented to Metternich, but Castlereagh still insisted upon it being delivered because he felt it necessary to give Napoleon due notice 'that it is not the intention of the Allies to suffer the question of Peace to be complicated with any revision of the Maritime code, which must rest as heretofore upon the general Law of Nations, except in so far as that Law may from time to time be modified by special conventions between particular States.'[28]

Aberdeen had taken a considerable risk in entering into the St Aignan negotiations without consulting Cathcart and Stewart. So far as Stewart was concerned, it was not his fault. Stewart had gone north to join Bernadotte and Aberdeen had expressed genuine regret at not finding him in Frankfort but he had easily allowed the Russians to persuade him not to include Cathcart. On the evening of 9 November Aberdeen had dined with the Tsar and Nesselrode had taken him aside before dinner to pour out their complaints about Cathcart. He told him that he was 'a person with whom it was difficult to communicate the subjects of importance; and, in fact, in civil terms, gave me to understand that they [the Tsar and Nesselrode] both thought him an old woman.' Unfortunately, this was music in Aberdeen's ears, although he was embarrassed when Nesselrode asked him whether he thought any communication should be made to Cathcart about St Aignan's mission. Aberdeen eventually replied that he could see no objection to such a communication. He apologised to Castlereagh for speaking so freely and asked him not to 'commit these letters to the inspection of the Office'. (Castlereagh did not.) Nesselrode in fact told Cathcart of St Aignan's mission on the evening of 9 November, but too late to affect the outcome. It is not surprising that Cathcart should have complained to Castlereagh: 'There is certainly no communication whatsoever that I have kept back from either Lord Aberdeen or Sir Charles on points not exclusively belonging to Russia. But although the former has always communicated everything I have asked for, such communications have not always been early or spontaneous, and scarcely in a single instance in the way of consultation . . .'[29]

Cathcart, however, took his exclusion from the St Aignan negotiations in remarkably good part. Aberdeen does not seem to have consulted him directly until he showed him his note of 27 November to Metternich. Cathcart then read to him part of Castlereagh's private letter of 27 September, recounting Castlereagh's conversation with Count Lieven on a possible alliance treaty, which as Cathcart pointed out, 'is the only document which treats of the principle of not discussing maritime points between England and France, if any such shall occur in a general negotiation'. In this letter, Castlereagh had expressed himself vehemently to the effect that maritime rights were an inadmissible topic of discussion, that the French would only introduce it for sinister purposes and that Cathcart must be on his guard against any covert introduction of the subject.[30] This makes any assessment of Aberdeen's culpability in opening a possible door for such a discussion all the more difficult. Aberdeen had not himself received any instructions on the subject and he had continually complained of being left without instructions on important points. Cathcart does not seem to have communicated the contents of the letter of 27 September to him until 27 November. On the other hand, if he had consulted Cathcart at the outset of the St Aignan discussions he would presumably have been put in possession of his government's views. Rather surprisingly, his relations with Cathcart began to improve after the St Aignan affair.

In contrast, his relations with Stewart at least temporarily deteriorated. When Stewart heard of the proposals he was sharply critical of the fact that they made no specific mention of three of the four points on which Britain was firmly pledged; Sicily, Portugal and – the one about which Stewart cared most – Sweden. He wrote indignantly to both Aberdeen and Castlereagh.[31] Aberdeen refused to engage in a direct controversy with him, but he explained to Castlereagh that the 'unofficial conversations with St Aignan' had never been intended to cover all the bases for peace. Many things had not been mentioned, including the Duchy of Warsaw, as well as Norway. It is clear, however, that Aberdeen was not sympathetic to Swedish aspirations. He asked Castlereagh how he really felt about the matter and warned him that, although so far he had insisted on the need to adhere to engagements already made 'it is quite impossible to pretend to hold up the character of the Prince Royal [Bernadotte], whose quackery is in every mouth'.[32] Interestingly, Castlereagh defended Aberdeen quite warmly in his reply to his brother, entirely accepting Aberdeen's explanation that it would have been impossible and inappropriate to have entered into details in the St Aignan conversations and pointing out that practically everything remained to be settled, including the Duchy of Warsaw, Hanover, the size of Austria and of Prussia, Sicily and Portugal. Although Castlereagh promised that Britain would support Sweden on Norway, he counselled his brother to say as little as possible for fear of making Denmark more 'obstinate'.[33]

At the same time, Castlereagh did furnish Aberdeen with much more specific instructions on Britain's war aims and tactics. The note which he instructed Aberdeen to present to Metternich, to clarify the British position on the St Aignan talks, not only emphasised the inadmissibility of the maritime rights question, but also denied that France had any natural right to the Alps, Pyrenees and Rhine as her frontier; although it might be convenient to take these as a base for negotiation 'subject to certain essential Modifications and Exceptions'. While declining to go into details, Castlereagh drew particular attention to 'the omission in that part of the Memorandum which relates to the Independence of Holland, of an express Claim to an adequate Barrier, on the necessity of which the British Government has never failed to insist.' He also disliked the terms of Metternich's proposed 'Declaration of Frankfort' to the French people because it disclaimed any intention to take French territory and it would be unusual and impolitic to suggest that the French would be immune from 'the ordinary consequences of an unsuccessful War'. On the particular question of Holland, a number of possibilities were still open but the key was Antwerp.

I must particularly entreat you to keep your attention upon Antwerp, the destruction of that arsenal is essential to our Safety. To leave it in the hands of France is little short of imposing upon Gt Britain the Charge of a perpetual War Establishment. [The continental Powers owe this to Britain.] Press this as a primary object of their operations. [Offer in return] *Credit Bills*, which they can now realize as advantageously on the Continent, as a Bill upon the Treasury.[34]

The stiffening tone of Castlereagh's despatches has sometimes been interpreted as a tacit rebuke to Aberdeen for weakness during the St Aignan conversations but this is to wrench them out of their context. The real change was in the war situation. Castlereagh was not speaking the truth when he said that Britain had 'never failed to insist' on a barrier for Holland, although he may have judged it politic to tell his continental allies so. His instructions to Aberdeen in August had made it clear that what could be obtained would depend on the military situation and the disposition of the Allies. Only in the first week of November did the British Cabinet make up its mind that the Rhine would not be an acceptable frontier in the Low Countries and Castlereagh's instructions of 5 November on this did not reach Aberdeen until 1 December.[35] That Castlereagh was still well aware that military fortunes would supply the final arbiter is demonstrated by his advice to Aberdeen that he should, without interfering with the general plan of campaign, urge the desirability of securing the territories which were important to Britain, since it was always much easier in negotiations to retain than to secure territories.[36]

The news of the victory at Leipzig had been received with great rejoicing in Britain, where it had too easily been assumed that the war was as good won.[37] On 15 November (six days after the conversation with St Aignan) the Dutch rose against the French. Castlereagh wrote candidly to Aberdeen on 30 November, 'You will not be surprized to learn after such a Tide of success, that this Nation is likely to view with disfavour any Peace, which does not confine France strictly within her ancient Limits; indeed Peace with Buonaparte on any Terms will be far from popular.' Despite this, the government 'are not inclined to go out of our Way, to interfere in the Internal Govt. of France, however much we might desire to see it placed in more pacifick hands'. They would not wish to encourage their Allies to make 'imperfect arrangements', although they might have to submit to them. He acknowledged that, if the coalition fell apart, it would be impossible to re–assemble it.[38]

Despite his willingness to participate in an attempt to secure a negotiated peace, Aberdeen cannot be accused of lack of zeal in trying to further the prosecution of the war. On 2 December (before he received Castlereagh's hint about the 'bills of credit') he authorised the expenditure of £25,000 of secret service money to buy arms to help the insurrection in Holland. He was also anxious to aid the patriotic movements in the Tyrol, Dalmatia and Switzerland, and Castlereagh authorised him to make advances up to £100,000, but warned him that he must do it on his own responsibility since, if it were known that he had authority to draw for the purpose 'you would be torn to pieces'.[39]

Castlereagh was still urging the necessity of recruiting the forces of nationalism on the allied side. He told Aberdeen on 15 October, 'The people are now the only Barrier. They are against France, and this is the Shield above all others that a State should determine to interpose for its protection which is so wholly destitute as Austria of a defensible Frontier.' Aberdeen by this time had also decided that Metternich was too timid in trusting the people. He replied to Castlereagh on 16 November:

I confess that Prince Metternich appears to me to have too great a dread of *disorganization*. Finding the people ready to support the Government, he has not had recourse to any measures by which an enthusiastic Spirit and independent movement may be excited among them. He is, I think, too anxious to make the Government the sole Source of action, and indeed has not sufficient respect for the unassisted and spontaneous exertions of the general body of the people. Any general movement of this kind he deprecates as tending to disorganize the State of Society; and declares that it is from the experience of the war of 1809 that he deprecates a recurrence to similar measures.[40]

Two thumbnail sketches of Metternich which he sent Castlereagh about this time suggest that he was by no means completely under his spell. He told Castlereagh on 10 November, the day after the St Aignan conversations:

I do not mean to deny that he [Metternich] was drawn into the war in a great measure against his intentions . . . He is a vain man: and when he found that he could not be the pacificator of Europe, he set his glory on being Her deliverer. This, with a sincere love of his country, even to the indulgence of absurd prejudices, is the principal motive by which he is governed. This motive will lead him to do more, than if he acted from considerations of prudence, and the result of calculation. Metternich is not a clever man, but he is tolerably well informed. He is very agreeable in society, and in transacting business; without any stiffness or formality . . .[41]

He returned to the same theme two days later, pointing out that Metternich was 'a good Austrian' and must be expected to have an Austrian, as well as a European game to play, and admitting, 'He may perhaps like the appearance of negociation a little too much'; but 'To enter into the war with most insufficient means, to deliver himself, even if successful into the hands of Russia and Prussia, could not be wise in the Minister of this weakened, but still mighty empire.' For the present he was convinced that Metternich was trustworthy and 'the main support of warlike measures'.[42] Aberdeen still distrusted Russian constancy, telling Castlereagh that the Tsar 'was the only man in his army who has a particle of zeal for the cause, and if he cools the whole is destroyed'. Barclay de Tolly was prone to talk of returning to Russia for the most trifling cause, such as a bad lodging. His chief adviser, Nesselrode, was a mediocre man. In Aberdeen's opinion, 'He has chosen Nesselrode, a very good man, but of moderate talents in order to prevent the possibility of its being supposed that he is governed by him.' In the circumstances, it was as well that both the Tsar and Nesselrode were inclined to let themselves be advised by Metternich. This interpretation was to some extent confirmed by Cathcart.[43]

In his letter of 12 November, Aberdeen reproached Castlereagh for not really understanding the continental situation. 'My dear Castlereagh,' he wrote, 'with all your wisdom, judgement and experience, which are as great as possible, and which I respect sincerely, I think you have so much of the Englishman as not quite to be aware of the real value of Foreign modes of acting'. Such a remark between friends would be unexceptional, although it has been questioned whether it could, with propriety, be addressed by an ambassador to his Foreign Secretary even in a private letter. But Aberdeen was soon to have a taste of 'foreign modes of acting' which was disconcerting in the extreme.

On 5 December, Metternich received a new reply from the French, accepting the Frankfort terms and asking that negotiations might begin. The three British ambassadors were not immediately informed. Instead the three continental powers entrusted Pozzo di Borgo, a dissident Corsican in the service of Russia, with special instructions to their respective representatives in London. Stewart, furious at the concealment, took matters into his own hands and obtained a copy of the French reply from 'a particular Friend' on Metternich's staff. He then sent it home with his Secretary of Embassy, Jackson, by the newly opened route through Holland in an attempt to beat Pozzo di Borgo to London. He told his brother, a little cynically, that he was astonished Aberdeen had not been informed, since Aberdeen believed that he had the 'implicit confidence' of the Austrians.[44] Cathcart shrugged the matter off, saying that a twenty–four hour delay in communication was 'allowable'. Aberdeen, however, as he told

Castlereagh, 'thought from the footing I was on with Metternich that I had the right to expect a more speedy communication. He challenged Metternich, who 'defended himself by saying that the three Cabinets were perfectly united but that the three English ministers were not: that the Emperor of Russia had chosen Pozzo to be the bearer of this communication and of their views on the subject before it was imparted to us, in order that it might be fairly before you without our conflicting statements.' Metternich then made the embarrassing proposal that he would have no secrets from Aberdeen if Aberdeen promised not to tell his colleagues. Aberdeen very properly declined. He told Castlereagh quite bluntly that he did not find Metternich's explanation convincing. On the other hand, he thought that Stewart had reacted too strongly. He told Castlereagh, Metternich 'complains bitterly of Stewart having robbed his office' and had sent six or seven people, whom he suspected of complicity, back to Vienna as a consequence.[45]

The French reply, signed by the duc de Vicenza (Caulaincourt) who had replaced Bassano as French Foreign Minister, had been couched in very general terms but had referred especially to 'l'integrité de toutes les Nations dans leurs limites naturelles' and to the 'sacrifices' which Britain had said she was prepared to make in order to arrive at a general peace. Metternich in his reply did no more than promise to bring the French communication to the attention of his allies.[46] By January the Allies had agreed that the progress of the war had rendered the Franfort bases obsolete. But just as the bases were abandoned they came to public attention.

Napoleon communicated them to the French Senate on 27 December, and they were naturally widely reported in the British press.[47] The French government had made a good deal of play of the fact that a British representative had been present. As the *Courier* put it to its readers: 'The English Ambassador, Lord Aberdeen was present at this conference. Observe this last fact, Senators, it is important.'[48] The overtures were very unpopular in Britain, where people were already convinced that Napolean was defeated and negotiations unnecessary. The Courier proclaimed 'The War Faction has proved to be the wise Faction.'[49] When it became known that maritime rights had been discussed, Aberdeen became the target of sharp criticism. *The Times* suggested that for France to ask Britain to give up her maritime rights was like the burglar asking the householder to draw the teeth of his guard dog.[50]

His role in the Frankfort proposals has always been the aspect of Aberdeen's mission to Austria which has attracted most criticism. Some but not all of it is fair. He was out–classed by Metternich as a diplomat, and he allowed foreign statesmen to see and play upon his quarrels with Cathcart. On the other hand, Aberdeen has been made a scapegoat for what was essentially a weakness in the British diplomatic position at this time. Britain had no military presence in Germany where the great issues of the Napoleonic wars were being decided. There was nothing that he, or anyone else, could have done to have prevented Russia and Austria, with or without Prussia and Sweden, from concluding a peace with France, if they had been so minded. Napoleon tried, skilfully, to persuade the continental Powers that Britain alone was intransigent and would be an obstacle to a reasonable peace. Not one of the continental Powers sympathised with Britain on the maritime rights issue or cared much about Antwerp. There was always a real danger that the coalition itself would fall to pieces. Aberdeen knew that the Frankfort proposals were really bait either for Napoleon, or for the generals who might overthrow Napoleon. In the end Britain was able to demand very much more but that was because the Allies were able to drive Napoleon back across the Rhine (which was by no means certain in the autumn of 1813), and because by the spring of 1814, Wellington's army was on French soil.

NOTES

1. Add. MSS 43074, Aberdeen to Castlereagh, 22 Oct. 1813.
2. Add. MSS 43074, Aberdeen to Castlereagh, 27 Oct. 1813.
3. Add. MSS 43074, Aberdeen to Castlereagh, 29 Oct. 1813.
4. FO Supp. 343, Castlereagh to Cathcart, 27 Sept. 1813, Private, Cathcart to Castlereagh, 30 Oct. 1813, Private. Stewart too protested, FO 64/90, Stewart to Castlereagh, No. 118, 21 Oct. 1813.
5 Add. MSS 43074, Aberdeen to Castlereagh, 29 Oct. 1813.
6. Caulaincourt, the duc de Vicenza, became French Foreign Minister in November 1813.
7. FO 7/102, Aberdeen to Castlereagh, No. 23, 29 Oct. 1813, Most Secret.
8. Add. MSS 43225, Aberdeen to Maria, 27 Oct., 1, 2, 3, 4 Nov. 1813.
9. Add. MSS 43225, Aberdeen to Maria, 2, 3, 5, 7, 11, 15 Nov. 1813, Aberdeen to Abercorn, 15 Nov. 1813; Add. MSS 43075, Aberdeen to Stewart, 5 Nov. 1813.
10. FO 7/102, Aberdeen to Castlereagh, No. 27, 8 Nov. 1813, Most Secret.
11. Add. MSS 43075, Aberdeen to Castlereagh, 30 Oct. 1813; Add. MSS 43225, Aberdeen to Abercorn, 15 Nov. 1813.
12. Add. MSS 43075, Castlereagh to Aberdeen, 30 Nov. 1813.
13. Add. MSS 43075, Aberdeen to Castlereagh, 9 Nov. 1813, 'Private – For yourself alone'.
14. FO 7/102, Aberdeen to Castlereagh, No. 31, 9 Nov. 1813, Most Secret.
15. FO 7/102, Aberdeen to Castlereagh, No. 31, 9 Nov. 1813, Most Secret.
16. Add. MSS 43075, 'Précis d'un entretien du Genl Comte de Merveldt avec l'Empereur Napoleon, 17 Oct. 1813'.
17. F.O.65/83, Castlereagh to Cathcart, No, 46, 13 July 1813.
18. FO 7/102, Aberdeen to Castlereagh, No. 23, 29 Oct. 1813, Most Secret.
19. FO 7/103, Aberdeen to Castlereagh, No. 39, 16 Nov. 1813, Most Secret.
20. 'Notes de M. de St Aignan', enclosed in No. 39.
21. FO 7/102, Aberdeen to Castlereagh, No. 31, 9 Nov. 1813, Most Secret.
22. FO 7/102, Aberdeen to Castlereagh, No. 23, 29 Oct. 1813, Most Secret, esp. postscript of 31 Oct., No. 27, 8 Nov. 1813, Most Secret; FO 7/103, Aberdeen to Castlereagh, No. 39, 16 Nov., Most Secret, No. 50, 4 Dec., No. 52, 9 Dec. 1813; Add MSS 43075, Aberdeen to Castlereagh, 12 Nov. 1813.
23. FO 7/103, Aberdeen to Castlereagh, No. 47, 28 Nov. 1813, 'Secret', encl. Bassano to Metternich, 16 Nov. 1813 and Metternich to Bassano, 25 Nov. 1813.

24. FO 7/103, Aberdeen to Castlereagh, No. 39, 16 Nov. 1813, Most Secret; FO 7/101, Castlereagh to Aberdeen, No. 44, 7 Dec. 1813, (the original, received by Aberdeen is in Add. MSS 43075).

25. FO 7/103, Aberdeen to Castlereagh, No. 47, 28 Nov. 1813, 'Secret' encl. Aberdeen to Metternich, 27 Nov. 1813, and Metternich to Aberdeen 28 Nov. 1813.

26. FO 7/101, Castlereagh to Aberdeen, No. 38, 30 Nov. 1813. (Original in Add. MSS 43075.)

27. Add. MS6 43075, Castlereagh to Aberdeen, 30 Nov. 1813.

28. FO 7/101, Castlereagh to Aberdeen, No. 44, 7 Dec., No. 45, 10 Dec. 1813; FO 7/103, Aberdeen to Castlereagh, No. 59, 24 Dec. 1813; Add. MSS 43075, Castlereagh to Aberdeen, 7 Dec. 1813.

29. Add. MSS 43075, Aberdeen to Castlereagh, 8 Nov., 9 Nov. 1813, 'Private – for yourself alone'; FO Supp. 343, Cathcart to Castlereagh, 4 Dec. 1813, Private.

30. FO, Supp. 343, Cathcart to Castlereagh, 28 Nov. 1813, Private and Confidential; Castlereagh sent Aberdeen a copy of his letter of 27 Sept. on 7 Dec., FO 7/101, Castlereagh to Aberdeen, No. 44.

31. FO 7/103, Aberdeen to Castlereagh, No. 50, 4 Dec. 1813 encl. Stewart to Aberdeen, 4 Dec. 1813; FO 64/91, Stewart to Castlereagh, No. 149, 28 Nov. 1813.

32. Add. MSS 43075, Aberdeen to Castlereagh, 17 Nov., 25 Nov. 1813; FO 7/103, Aberdeen to Castlereagh, No. 47, 28 Nov. 1813, Secret.

33. FO 64/86, Castlereagh to Stewart, No. 82, 17 Dec. 1813.

34. FO 7/101, Castlereagh to Aberdeen, No. 44, 7 Dec. 1813 and encls; Add. MSS 43075, Castlereagh to Aberdeen, 30 Nov., 7 Dec. 1813, Private and Secret.

35. FO 7/101, Castlereagh to Aberdeen, No. 26, No. 33, 5 Nov. 1813.

36. Add. MSS 43075, Castlereagh to Aberdeen, 30 Nov. 1813.

37. Stewart's despatches from the field of Leipzig reached London on 2 Nov. 1813 (brought by Mr Solly, who probably slipped through the enemy lines and got out through Hamburg) just in time for the Prince Regent's Speech at the opening of Parliament. FO 64/86, Castlereagh to Stewart, No. 61, 5 Nov. 1813.

38. Add. MSS 43075, Castlereagh to Aberdeen, 30 Nov. 1813.

39. FO 7/103, Aberdeen to Castlereagh, No. 48, 2 Dec. 1813, Secret and Confidential; Add. MSS 43075, Castlereagh to Aberdeen, n.d. Nov. 1813.

40. Add. MSS 43075, Castlereagh to Aberdeen, 15 Oct. 1813; FO 7/103, Aberdeen to Castlereagh, No. 40, 16 Nov. 1813.

41. Add. MSS 43075, Aberdeen to Castlereagh, 10 Nov. 1813.

42. Add. MSS 43075, Aberdeen to Castlereagh, 12 Nov. 1813.

43. Add. MSS 43075, Aberdeen to Castlereagh, 10 Nov. 1813; FO, Supp. 343, Cathcart to Castlereagh, 28 Nov. 1813, Private & Confidential.

44. FO 64/90, Stewart to Castlereagh, No. 158, 4 Dec. 1813, No. 166, 8 Dec. 1813.

45. Add. MSS 43075, Aberdeen to Castlereagh, 9 Dec. 1813.

46. FO 7/103, Aberdeen to Castlereagh, No. 53, 9 Dec. 1813 and encls.

47. *The Times*, 3, 5, 6, 10, 13 Jan.; *The Courier*, 4, 6 Jan.; *Morning Post*, 3, 10 Jan.; *Morning Herald*, 5, 7 Jan.; *Morning Chronicle*, 6 Jan.; *Sun*, 6, 7, 8 Jan. 1813.

48. *The Courier*, 6 Jan. 1813.

49. *The Courier*, 4 Jan. 1813.

50. *The Times*, 3 Jan. 1813.

CHAPTER TEN

Frankfort to Paris

The Frankfort proposals came to nothing but there still remained the scheme for the grand alliance. Cathcart had at last removed the curbs on his colleagues discussing the question with their own courts. By 25 November Aberdeen believed that he had succeeded in persuading both the Austrians and the Russians. He wrote to Castlereagh that Metternich had just returned from an interview with the Tsar and 'The Treaty of general Alliance will *positively be made forthwith*. The difficulties have not been few or slight, but M. has made a point of bringing your unjust suspicions of Austria to shame. Now, pray observe, these are not fine words but *facts*, and pretty important too. I wait for your amende honourable [sic].' The Tsar wanted the treaty executed in London but Aberdeen could see no objection to that. The Tsar was about to send Pozzo di Borgo to London to explain the situation. Only one minor difficulty seemed to remain. The continental powers wanted more precise information on which French colonies Britain was prepared to use as bargaining counters. Aberdeen drafted an additional article to the effect that Britain would make her conquests, except those deemed 'necessary for the safety and prosperity of [His Majesty's dominions]' available as a resource to ameliorate a general peace.[1] The Russians, however, continued to make difficulties.

Cathcart and Stewart objected to the transfer of negotiations to London. Cathcart wrote to Castlereagh, acknowledging how much Aberdeen had achieved, but stating his reservations:

Lord Aberdeen had made great progress in so far as to have got Prince Metternich to recommend it, and he states that the Emperor would accede to a proposition to sign in England; but this would only be to revert to the answer first given to me, which was to include the Project in a new Treaty of concert and subsidy, it being supposed that a negotiation for an object devised by the British Government carried on in London might lead to increase the portion of supply for the Continent.[2]

Aberdeen was not at first too disturbed by this objection, telling Castlereagh that he hoped Metternich might be able to persuade the Tsar to change his mind. On 28 November Aberdeen made up his mind to return to England to consult Castlereagh and he actually asked Castlereagh to have a frigate ready to meet him and Pozzo at Cuxhaven or Bremen, both now in allied hands.[3]

When Aberdeen made his decision he still believed that things were going very well. But he also felt that he had been abroad long enough, perhaps too long. It had been understood from the beginning that his was a 'special mission' to reopen relations with Austria after the long interruption and that he would stay only a short time. This was why Frederick Lamb had been furnished with contingent powers as minister plenipotentiary. Lamb, who had found the squalor of life at allied headquarters unbearable, had gone on to Vienna and was pressing to have his powers as minister plenipotentiary activated. He argued, correctly, that there were precedents for having an ambassador and a minister plenipotentiary accredited at the same time, although the only recent example of this, at Constantinople in the time of Lord Elgin, had been an almost unmitigated disaster.[4]

In one of his earlier letters to Maria, that of 19 September, Aberdeen still hoped to be home within a few weeks. He regretted the slowness with which his negotiations with Austria were then progressing because 'the Baltic will not be passable after November, and will be very unpleasant then.'[5] What might have been a brief ceremonial mission had turned into six months of danger, discomfort and very hard work. He felt cut off from the London political world. He told Castlereagh on 12 November, 'Parliament has met, and although I am not a regular performer, that is the scene after all.' It could be argued that, once the Anglo-Austrian treaty was concluded at the beginning of October, Aberdeen had, as it were, fulfilled his contract. He warned Castlereagh in the same letter of 12 November, 'If we are to have negociations, and you chuse me to stay, I will do my best, and with the utmost pleasure: but if war continues, I almost think of home.' On 24 November he told Castlereagh that he had much to say to him and 'If the war continues without negociation, I must beg to avail myself of the permission you gave me and return to England: at all events in the first instance as if on leave of absence, to prevent you having more trouble than necessary. If there should be negotiations and you have other hands to employ, I must equally beg to go home.'[6]

There were also pressing domestic reasons why Aberdeen wished to return home. He had never been happy at leaving his motherless children to the care of others and they had never been out of his thoughts. His real feelings come through very vividly in his frequent letters to them. Before he left Yarmouth in August he wrote to Jane in a large, clear script suitable for a six-year-old to read. 'I am going on a long long journey, and it will be some time before I see you again; but I hope none of you will forget me, but that you will all continue to love me as much as ever. I am sure you will all be very good; and when I return, it will give me the greatest pleasure to find you all as good as when I left you. God bless you all my sweetest loves.' Almost immediately after his arrival at Teplitz he wrote again to Jane, 'Although I am very far from you, I hope you do not forget me. I think of you and Caro and Alice a hundred times a day. I am not able to say when I shall see you again, but I hope it will not be very long.' He asked her to write to him and tell him all that she and her sisters were doing. Before he left Teplitz he begged Jane, 'Do not forget me my dearest loves, for I hope it will not be very long before I see you again.

I am going soon to a place where I will try to find something pretty to send you.' The 'pretty thing' was duly sent from Comotau by his brother, Robert, who returned to London with despatches. He wrote sadly, 'I wish very much that it was in my power to go home and see you my sweet loves, but I must wait for a long while before I can set out.' Significantly, he wrote from Frankfort on 28 November, 'I hope it will not be very long before I have the happiness of seeing you all again'. He assured them that he had their picture, which their grandmother had sent, near him as he wrote. He thought it very like Jane and Caro 'who I find must be much improved. Alice looks like a comical little *quiz*.'[7]

There had also been an unexpected development in his personal affairs. When he left London he had resigned himself to the fact that her parents appeared to be irrevocably opposed to a marriage between Anne Cavendish and himself.

While abroad he tried hard to forget Anne and told Maria that he had succeeded 'to a certain degree'. In some ways it was easier because amid the dangers and horrors of the campaign, he began again to dream of Catherine and it was his children who filled his thoughts. But just after the battle of Leipzig he received new letters from Maria which raised his hopes again. At first he resolved to treat the matter very coolly. He told Maria, 'I will . . . not commit follies, nor do anything unbecoming.' He could not forbear to express his indignation that the Cavendishes should treat him so disdainfully. His situation was 'very distinguished. I have met with quite enough praises to turn a stouter brain . . . Events of importance unparalleled are passing through my hands.' A few days later his resolution was weakening. He wrote again to Maria, 'Only let this rise into a reasonable hope and I fly to England . . . The business which occupies me is urgent and may continue to be so, and I know that my presence is earnestly desired but what is all this compared with the hope on which I feed, a prospect of domestic happiness.' Maria's later communications were less encouraging and Aberdeen began to feel a rising anger. 'Lady G's absurdity is striking', he wrote on 31 October, 'and to be sure it is humiliating to think one is at the mercy of such motives. Indeed I have drawn myself into a situation in which I never thought it possible that I could be, and which I ought certainly to get out of as soon as possible.'[8]

In the end, it was not to be the hope of marrying Anne but grave news about Maria herself that hardened his resolution to come home quickly. Maria was a volatile young woman and Aberdeen, just before he left, had been instrumental in settling a serious quarrel between Maria and her father. In his letters to both of them he frequently expressed his satisfaction that they were reconciled and begged them to keep the peace between them. He did not take Maria's first casual references to her own health very seriously, advising her in an elder brotherly fashion to exert herself to overcome 'that state of nervous irritability' to which she was prone. It was all the greater shock when he learnt from Lord Abercorn that she too had succumbed to tuberculosis and that her situation was desperate.

In October Abercorn had written to reassure him that his eldest son, Lord Hamilton, who had also been ill, was wonderfully recovered and that he and

Maria had gone to Brighton to improve their health. Early in December Abercorn broke the news, 'But alas my dear A. you must prepare yourself for the chance of never seeing poor Maria again. Before she went . . . to Brighton I really thought her looks strength & spirits held out a fair prospect of convalescence. But she has returned, too evidently within very few Stages of her last. I will not for both our sakes enter further upon the subject.' This letter reached Aberdeen on 22 December. Two days later he wrote to Harrowby in very emotional terms, revealing how Maria's peril had torn open all the wounds of the still recent death of his wife. Private reasons, he told him, made him anxious to go home; '. . . the alarming account of Lady Maria's health is a motive of action stronger than all others. If it be true that she is not destined to survive more than a few months, I solemnly declare to you that I had rather be the means of contributing to her happiness and tranquillity during the dreadful time than preserve the crown on the Emperor's head.' He begged Harrowby to look at the matter as a friend and not as a member of the government: 'See the person nearest in blood, worthy in every respect to be the sister of the most perfect being whom God in his power ever created − see her reduced to the state in which she is, and then, following the dictates of your own heart, tell me what on earth can stand in competition with her claims on my love and attention.'[9]

To extricate himself honourably was not, however, easy. He felt that he had been unnecessarily snubbed by Castlereagh over the Wilson affair. Aberdeen's championing of Wilson, which he carried on long after there was any sense in doing so, arose not only from his genuine feeling that Wilson had been badly treated but also from his own fear that Burghersh would be yet another personal rival.[10] There is no question that Aberdeen did want to return from his mission crowned with success nor that he feared that political intrigues might rob him of his just deserts. The question of the United Kingdom peerage, which had been one of the mainsprings of his original acceptance, rose to his mind several times. He asked Abercorn early in December whether he knew anything of supposed new creations of which he had heard rumours, adding 'I hope there is little chance of my being forgotten after all that has passed.'

Abercorn replied that he knew nothing of the creation of new peers. He assumed that Aberdeen could not be passed over but 'if there appear a Batch without you, I will go to Ld Liverpool & give him a proper rattle.'[11] Abercorn was encouraging Aberdeen in his discontent. As early as October he wrote, 'I told Bathurst yesterday that you never intended to be upon the footing of a Diplomatic Resident. I shall take an opportunity to say the same to Castlereagh.' Abercorn was extremely angry with Castlereagh for not showing him Aberdeen's official letters, complaining of unkindness, disrespect and ingratitude which 'I never shall forgive'. Abercorn too had noted that Aberdeen's name stood second in the 'Full Powers' and cautioned him not to play 'second fiddle to Lord Cathcart & the Russion Government'.[12] Aberdeen tried to pacify his father-in-law by assuring him that it had only been intended as a compliment to the Tsar. In fact, a rather startled Castlereagh had assured Aberdeen that the order had no significance at all. The superscription had been written

by a Foreign Office clerk and he, Castlereagh, had never even seen it.[13] Abercorn was still suspicious and cautioned his son-in-law, 'Only do not be the
Journeyman of Castlereagh who though I have always thought him essentially
fair & honourable towards those employed by him, has it not in him to have
any feeling or consideration for you individually or your honour, interest or
situation or in fact for anything but himself & his Administration & strength
of Government.' He thought that, if the government was anxious for Aberdeen
to remain at his post, he might even stipulate for a peerage to put him on an
equal footing with Cathcart.[14]

On one point Abercorn's reaction greatly disappointed his son-in-law. The
Austrian Emperor had determined to mark his approval of Aberdeen by conferring on him the Order of St Stephen. Aberdeen was delighted since both
Cathcart and Stewart already had foreign orders. Aberdeen knew that it would
be impossible for him to accept it – Stewart and Cathcart had only been allowed
to retain theirs by the convenient fiction that they were for military services
to an ally for which special dispensations from the usual prohibition might be
given. He told Castlereagh that he would of course decline it, although it was
one of the great orders of Europe, but, dropping a broad hint, he looked for
his reward only at home. Abercorn, however, assured him crushingly that it
was not an order worn by the great nobility. It was more like the Order of the
Bath than of the Garter and was not so high as the Order given to Wellington,
although Aberdeen was Wellington's superior by birth.[15]

The likely effect on his own future career was certainly a factor in Aberdeen's
decisions during his mission but, unlike his father-in-law, he was not completely obsessed by it. No one, either then or later, ever doubted either his
integrity or his strong sense of duty. At the beginning of December he was
a sorely puzzled man, anxious to go home for personal reasons and very uncertain about his best course of action on public grounds. He had patched up his
relations with Stewart and Burghersh, although he told Harrowby rather ruefully that Stewart was 'a little quick [in temper]'. Burghersh, with whom he
had been at Harrow, was 'a good natured fellow'.[16]

He did not go home with Pozzo di Borgo as he had planned and the basic
reason for that was that he detected that things were going wrong or, as he
put it to Castlereagh, there was still 'work for him to do'.[17] There were still
difficulties about the alliance treaty. Even Metternich did not want the article
on Norway included unless the negotiations with Denmark failed. The Russians
were still pressing for precision about the colonies. On 9 December Aberdeen
had an 'animated' interview with Nesselrode and Metternich, in which it
became apparent that, while still expressing the utmost good will, neither
Power had any immediate intention of signing the treaty. Aberdeen argued in
vain that it was essential to conclude such a treaty before entering into negotiations with Napoleon and that such evidence of solidarity between the Allies
would be worth more than 'a victory of the most splendid description'. Aberdeen was irritated in the midst of these negotiations by what was undoubtedly
a gaffe on the part of the British government. In the Speech from the Throne
at the opening of Parliament, Russia had been warmly praised for her exertions

while Austria had been put on a par with Bavaria. The Austrians had naturally been much offended when they learnt of it and Aberdeen complained bitterly to Castlereagh that the Austrian army was now larger than the Russian and a few more instances of that kind 'will go far to loosen the very foundations of the coalition'.[18]

The three continental allies were becoming increasingly irritated by the divisions between the three British ambassadors, who rarely spoke with one voice, and their doubts as to which, if any, of them would eventually be supported by his home government. Pozzo di Borgo carried instructions to the Austrian, Russian and Prussian representatives in London to ask the British government to clarify the situation and to beg them to nominate one man who might be regarded as speaking officially for London. Both Nesselrode and Metternich assured Aberdeen that they had suggested that he should be put in charge of the negotiations. Aberdeen entirely believed this and told both Abercorn and Harrowby of it. He wrote to Abercorn on 11 December:

The overtures of France have now led to such a state of things as to demand some person may be specially charged with their management. The Austrian and Russian Govts. have united, without my knowledge, to demand me as that person. I confess that the importance of the charge, the incalculable benefits it may confer on the whole world incline me strongly to covet this employment. I have learnt less to distrust myself, and although you may think it great arrogance, I have no fears about giving satisfaction. If, however, any other person should be named, which is very probable, considering my inexperience, and the activity of jobbers at home, I instantly go to England.[19]

According to Sir Charles Webster, Metternich deceived Aberdeen about the nature of the communication he had sent to Wessenberg and he had in fact asked for some new and more senior man, perhaps George Canning or Lord Wellesley, to take charge of the negotiations.[20] The references Sir Charles gives are less than conclusive and, in fact, Metternich's despatch to Wessenberg named nobody. He wrote,

Un premier point et un des plus essentiels . . . est celui que le Gouvernement britannique nomme un *seul* ministre qui soit chargé de prendre connaissance des questions relatives à une future négociation. Le Triumvirat que nous avons à notre quartier général n'est pas fait pour avancer la besogne, et les puissances remarquent journellement davantage une grande divergence dans les idées mêmes des trois ambassadeurs. Le moins que nous puissions exiger, c'est l'Angleterre ait *un* representant qui ait le droit de parler sur *une* chose.[21]

The papers of the senior British ministers concerned, Liverpool, Castlereagh, Harrowby and Bathurst make no mention of Canning or Wellesley. If Webster was right, it suggests that Metternich knew little of British politics. His quarrels with Canning came later but their ideas were never compatible and Wellesley had been one of the least effective Foreign Secretaries Britain had had.

The decision that Castlereagh should go out himself was taken at a long Cabinet meeting on 20 December.[22] Whatever the merits or demerits of the three British ambassadors it was clear that Britain was seriously underrepresented at allied headquarters. The other three Great Powers were represented by both their heads of state and their chief ministers. It was, in modern parlance, a kind of standing summit conference. Each continental Power could take immediate and binding decisions. The three British ambassadors could not do that any more than could the representatives of the other three Powers in London, with whom Castlereagh virtually refused to discuss the outstanding questions. With peace negotiations apparently imminent, the weight of British representation had to be increased immediately.

Castlereagh broke the news to Aberdeen in an official despatch on 21 December. He explained to him in a private letter the following day that the march of events was so rapid that it was impossible to keep pace with them by instructions from home. If it were practicable 'the Government itself should repair to headquarters.' (This was not mere hyperbole; even the Foreign Secretary in person would not have the power of decision, enjoyed by the other governments at headquarters.) He summed up tactfully, but entirely justly, what had been the weakness in the British position so far. He told Aberdeen, 'If I could have foreseen the great questions that were impending, I should certainly have thrown the three Ministers who were at headquarters into a species of commission, and have required them to consider and decide upon subjects of general policy in their collective capacity, transacting the inferior details in their distinct capacities. What has been wanting was a central authority.'[23]

Aberdeen had told both Abercorn and Harrowby that, if anyone else was named as the negotiator, he would leave immediately but Castlereagh's decision to come in person created a rather different situation. He told Abercorn that he must at least stay and greet him although he was pessimistic about Castlereagh's chances of success; 'if he comes with all the partialities and prejudices long cherished in England, his presence will be most pernicious.' His letter to Harrowby was more circumspectly worded. It had given him, he said, 'sincere pleasure' to learn that Castlereagh was coming because 'independently of the great public benefits to be derived from it . . . it enables me to remain long enough to be of some use to him in whatever he may undertake connected with the interests of Austria.'[24]

Aberdeen had confided to Abercorn a little earlier that another reason why he looked to come home was that he found it difficult to face 'the intolerable inconvenience of travelling about from place to place', which was about to begin again.[25] The comparatively comfortable interlude at Frankfort was nearly over. Despite the possibility of negotiations the allied armies were beginning to move into position for a spring offensive. The original plan of attack, involving over half a million men, was that Bernadotte should attack northern France through the Low Countries; Blücher would watch the Rhine fortresses; the *grande armée* under Schwarzenberg would attack through Switzerland; the army of Italy, under Bellegarde, would try to enter France from the south and, if possible, link up with Wellington, coming up from Spain. Bernadotte was still proving completely unreliable. Abercorn wrote, 'Bernadotte is Bernadotte still.'[26] The Tsar had developed conscientious scruples about violating Swiss neutrality. He was only partially comforted when the Swiss, like the Dutch, rose and invited the allied armies to come to their assistance.[27]

Even more alarmingly, the Tsar now wanted to proclaim Bernadotte, Emperor of France. So far the official line of all the Powers had been that they were contemplating a negotiated peace with Napoleon although, since Leipzig, they had all, including Britain, begun to consider the possibility of a Bourbon restoration and to calculate whether an appeal to the French royalists would be effective or merely serve to unite most Frenchmen against them. At this stage the British Cabinet, supported by Wellington, had decided that an alliance with the royalists would be too dangerous a gamble. The Tsar's new idea was described by Aberdeen as a mad project and he had been told by Metternich that, although Francis would agree to the restoration of the Bourbons if necessary, he would never let his daughter be turned adrift to give place to Mme Bernadotte.[28]

As he accompanied the Emperor and the Austrian *grande armée* south to Darmstadt, Heidelberg, Carlsruhe, Freybourg, and eventually Basle, Aberdeen was pessimistic both about the chances of military success and the stability of the coalition. He told Abercorn that the army movements seemed random, 'made more for the sake of doing something than with any definite view'. The state of the coalition worried him even more. He wrote:

The diversity of opinion among us is truly alarming. Success kept us tolerably well together; but the real difficulties of the enterprise before us are now the means of producing all the feelings of rancour, and jealousy and Envy which have been smothered. The Coalition is beginning to have the decrepitude of age, and the evils inherent in its very existence are felt daily. The hope of a negociation will excite them to one last vigorous exertion; but depend on it, we shall not see another campaign. If we are obstinate, the Continental Powers will leave us.[29]

He was relieved by the comparative moderation of the British Government's views although they had 'very properly extended' as a result of the earlier military successes. The revolution in Holland was a 'masterstroke' which 'gives us a stand in negociations to which I scarcely ventured to look'. He assured Abercorn that his opinions 'are not those of a croker – I never have been one'. At Teplitz he had expected their speedy arrival at the Rhine but now he saw all the difficulties. In subsequent letters he repeated his anxieties about the divisions of the Allies, the precarious situation of the armies, and the desirability of securing a negotiated peace if at all possible.[30]

The journey up the Rhine was, however, less traumatic than the earlier journey across Germany in the wake of fighting armies and Aberdeen's usual curiosity about the country through which he was passing reasserted itself. He wrote long accounts to Abercorn and Harrowby as well as to Maria. Abercorn's letter of 21 December had given a less pessimistic account of the invalid than his earlier one and Aberdeen had received a cheerful letter from Maria herself written in the middle of December. He refused to consider her case hopeless and even persuaded himself that a crisis had been reached and passed and she might now be expected to improve.[31] He was still writing to her almost every day, amused to compare his impression of Germany with those of Mme de Stael who was currently holding court in London. A few days after leaving Frankfort he told Maria that he had come to Heidelberg, through 'delightful country' and 'On every eminence where there ought to be a castle, we always observed a ruin of some kind . . .' He sent her an engraving of Heidelberg castle, 'Magnificent from its preservation, and beautiful from its destruction . . .' Carlsruhe was 'like an immense toy; the palace is a central point, from which the streets diverge like the sticks of a fan. It is a town such as children would build, if they had the means.' He had decided that he liked the Germans better on acquaintance. 'In the sort of life I have led, it has been my chance to be the guest of all ranks, from the highest to the lowest, one night sleeping in a palace, another in a cottage. I have been generally a forced guest, it is true, and might, therefore, have found the worst side apparent. I have, on the contrary, always been struck with the goodness, the bonhomie, the honesty of all ranks.'[32]

Castlereagh arrived at Basle on 18 January. The Tsar had already left for the advanced headquarters at Langres and, although he left polite messages for Castlereagh, Aberdeen suspected that he had gone because there were a number of questions which he found it inconvenient to discuss with Castlereagh just then, including the future government of France.[33]

Castlereagh was very reluctant to allow Aberdeen to take his departure. He never at any time expressed the criticisms of Aberdeen's handling of affairs, which have occurred to historians, and there is no reason to suppose that his silence was merely politic. He saw for himself the extreme difficulty of conducting negotiations at allied headquarters. The confidential relations which Aberdeen had established with Metternich, Nesselrode and others, were useful. He had a detailed knowledge of the negotiations up to date and he was undoubtedly a conscientious and hard-working man. Castlereagh had every reason to try to keep him as his assistant and Aberdeen, despite the vocal opposition of Abercorn, gradually thawed.

He told Harrowby, a few days after Castlereagh's arrival, that he would stay as long as Castlereagh wished although he did not suppose that there would be much left for him to do. A week later he wrote to Abercorn in very different terms from his letter of 29 December, in which he had criticised Castlereagh's insularity. Now he said, 'Castlereagh's presence will do much good, and indeed has already, for the spirit of Party runs very high among the Continental Courts, which he is able to moderate and sometimes to extinguish.' Castlereagh treated him with 'sufficient confidence, although with less than Metternich, for I learn more from M. of what passes between them than from Castlereagh himself.' But 'compared with others [Cathcart and Stewart] I cannot complain'.[34]

Abercorn was furious at Aberdeen's decision to remain and wrote to warn him, 'I can only lament from the bottom of my heart that Ld Cas.'s cool head & cold blood have been too successful with you, & that your high reputation must I fear be in some degree a sacrifice to them!' He regretted that he had not been there to advise him. He 'dreaded' the impending negotiations with the French. 'Nothing will make them go down here, & all the odium will be vented upon the Negociators . . . I think peace with Bonaparte while there remains a chance of the allies holding together, political suicide.' Abercorn, contemplating Wellington's successes in the south of France, was even prepared to fight without the Austrians if necessary. He added that he knew Aberdeen would not agree.[35]

Aberdeen's assessment of the situation was indeed very different. Writing on French soil at Langres, with the Austrian advanced posts already at Troyes, he was very conscious that, although the French were too war-weary to resist much at present, it would take very little to rouse their patriotic feelings. He said bluntly that, if they had to retreat now, he believed they would be shot at in every village. Although a strong party wanted to go to Paris and, although he thought it possible that the French would accept the restoration of the Bourbons, if it was the best way to ensure tranquillity, he believed that hardly any Frenchmen were in favour of it and he considered negotiations with Napoleon to be by far the most prudent course if Napoleon would accept reasonable terms.[36]

Negotiations were in fact about to begin at Chatillon—sur—Seine, in response to Caulaincourt's reply of 6 January. Castlereagh persuaded Metternish that the Frankfort terms and the offer made in the Declaration of 1 December relating to the 'natural frontiers' were now cancelled by the progress of the war. He had some success in getting his allies to accept the proposals in his own instructions from the British Cabinet (which he had in fact drawn up himself) as the basis of negotiations. These embodied most of the points in Castlereagh's despatch to Cathcart of 5 July 1813.

The Foreign Ministers of the Powers had, however, decided not to appear as principals themselves at Chatillon and Aberdeen saw the chance to assume the role of negotiator, which he had coveted from the beginning. Castlereagh's considered decision therefore came as an unpleasant shock. Aberdeen, Cathcart and Stewart were to be joint plenipotentiaries. Castlereagh explained this on the grounds that to do otherwise would be to slight Russia and Prussia. Aberdeen believed that he had been forced to do it by the jealousy of Cathcart and Stewart but, in fact, he was mistaken in this suspicion. Both his fellow plenipotentiaries were once again in the field and very reluctant to give up the excitement of a good battle for the boredom of the conference table.[37]

Castlereagh had accorded Aberdeen a certain primacy. Aberdeen told Abercorn, 'I am to be the official person: to make all reports, to be the sole *mouth piece*, and generally, the negociator, with the assistance of a sort of Cabinet formed by Cathcart and Stewart. I think this a very bad arrangement and very disagreeable, but under the circumstances in which I am placed, I have thought it better to accept.' The proposal had been put to him very civilly and with 'the most flattering expressions' but 'The affair is not more pleasant from the nature of my Colleagues. Cathcart is a man of very moderate talents, but stiff, pedantic and difficult. I rate Stewart's talents higher, but he is shatterbrained [sic], obstinate, and wrongheaded.' He tried to impress upon Abercorn that he was still admitted to the highest circles, telling him that there were frequent conferences between Castlereagh, himself, Metternich, Stadion, Hardenberg, Razumovsky and Nesselrode. He concluded, 'I know you will not like the manner in which this business is settled; but without an absolute rupture with Castlereagh and the Govt I could do nothing else. Au reste, I think there is scarcely any hope of peace, and this does not make the business more agreeable.' Abercorn retorted angrily, 'As to rupture with Govt. it certainly would not have followed. Rupture with Ld. Cas. I should have much prefer'd to playing into his & his Brother's hands. But he would have taken care enough to steer clear of rupture for his own sake. As it is you identify yourself with him, & he does not identify himself with you.'[38]

The Chatillon Conference formally opened on 5 February and was not finally dissolved until 19 March when it had been far outstripped by the events of the war. Aberdeen had described Chatillon to Abercorn on 30 January as 'a wretched spot'. It was at present in allied hands but the situation might change. Officially Chatillon was neutralised for the conference but it was extremely insecure and the mayor of the little town lived in constant fear that one of the plenipotentiaries would be assassinated. Aberdeen had no illusions about what being on enemy territory meant. 'We are now waging a *Spanish war*', he wrote on 1 March, 'with the difference of having to deal with a more intelligent and active population.'[39]

Technically, Castlereagh had appointed Aberdeen as President of the commission of ambassadors representing Britain at the Chatillon Conference. He was scrupulous in forwarding Aberdeen's reports to the Foreign Office with expressions of approval[40] although, alone of the Foreign Ministers of the Great Powers, he was present in Chatillon himself for part of the time of the conference. He regularly attended the private meetings of the allied representatives, although he was not present at the formal sessions with Caulaincourt. Castlereagh had been long enough at headquarters to have realised that the divisions between the British ambassadors had been a source of scandal, and amusement, to the other Powers. In his confidential instructions to them of 2 February he warned them that, if they allowed their differences of opinion to show, it would 'weaken the useful influence of their government'. He dropped a broad hint that, if they could not agree, they would be superseded. He would not like, he said, 'the necessity of transferring to another that confidence which I desire to preserve to those with whom I have had the satisfaction to act through a long course of arduous and important service' and he would like them 'to have the reputation of bringing it [the negotiation] to a close'.[41] In fact the ambassadors kept the peace. Aberdeen did his best to bring the negotiations to a successful conclusion, although he does not seem to have had the naive belief in ultimate success which Stadion attributed to him. On the contrary, he was privately pessimistic.[42]

The first formal session was held on 5 February. Stadion was appointed to act as spokesman for all the Allies. Aberdeen was surprised by the reasonableness of the French at that first meeting. He reported that either Bonaparte must be more reduced in the means of resistance than they supposed, or he was anxious to impress the French people with his moderation.[43] Caulaincourt still adopted a very reasonable tone at the second meeting on 9 February. He was informed at the outset, on Castlereagh's insistence, that there could be no question of discussing maritime rights and he acquiesced in this without difficulty. On other points, notably that of the 'natural frontiers', he attempted repeatedly to return to St Aignan's memorandum, insisting at one point that it was an agreed document since there was a correction on it in Metternich's handwriting – thus confirming Aberdeen's wisdom in refusing to reword it at the time. Eventually the Plenipotentiaries 'rejected the authority of the minute as private and unofficial'.[44]

The Conference was dominated by military events. After a very limited allied victory at La Rothière on 1 February, the Tsar wanted to end negotiations and march straight for Paris. The coalition was near to dissolution. Ironically, what saved it was the French victories at Montmirail on 11 February, and at Montereau on 18 February. Far from the way to Paris being open, the Allies were now in retreat and in some danger of being swept out of France altogether.

It was Castlereagh who steadied the coalition. He did a great deal more than steady it: on 1 March he persuaded Austria, Russia and Prussia to sign the Treaty of Chaumont which brought the Grand Alliance into being. It was remarkably close to what Pitt had envisaged in 1805. Not only did the four Great Powers pledge themselves to fight until their objectives were attained, they also agreed that the alliance should remain in being for twenty years to counter any French attempts to undo the peace settlement, which provided the germ for the whole Congress System. In return Castlereagh had to pledge a financial contribution from Britain considerably in excess of what had been agreed by the Cabinet. But this, of course, was the difference between a Foreign Secretary negotiating and an ambassador negotiating.

The military tide turned while the Chatillon negotiations were still deadlocked. On 9 March Blücher defeated Napoleon at Laon. Wellington was now advancing rapidly from the south and on 12 March he entered Bordeaux. This time the way to Paris really was open. The Chatillon Conference met on the afternoon of 13 March when the Allies asked Caulaincourt for a straight acceptance or rejection of their proposals. Caulaincourt again offered the Frankfort proposals as a *centre-projet*. The Conference adjourned and was finally dissolved on 19 March.[45]

Aberdeen wrote to Abercorn the following day to tell him of the final breakdown. Although he rejoiced at the improving military situation, he thought the Allies had been 'clumsy' in their negotiations. For himself, 'I have gone through this negociation better than I expected.' He would not have chosen to have acted with Cathcart and Stewart but 'by good temper and discretion they may both be managed'. 'It has been altogether', he wrote, 'a school from which much good may be derived, but though the discipline has been salutary it has not been agreeable.'[46]

He intended to join Castlereagh at Bar-sur-Seine the next day and travel home with him in about a fortnight. He acknowledged that Castlereagh's presence had been of great service. He told Abercorn, 'I do not know that Castlereagh himself has done much more than might be expected from a British Minister in his situation. At the same time there is a soundness and *right headedness* about him which has had great effect, and indeed most deservedly. He has seen things as they are, and is in a condition to think and act with more propriety than any other Minister before him.' He returned to the subject of Castlereagh in a letter from Dijon on 29 March. 'Castlereagh', he said, 'is a strange personage. I do not know what to make of him. He is by way of being very civil and kind to me, but he is quite unfathomable. His presence here as English minister must of course throw me a good deal in the background, and notwithstanding many personal grounds of satisfaction, must give rise to unpleasant feelings.' Abercorn might be wondering why Aberdeen did not put an end to the situation by coming home but, he admitted, 'I do not wish to confirm the newspaper speculations [that he was being superseded for conceding too much at Frankfort] by a conduct which might contribute to this effect. Besides, if we are to be in Paris in a short time, it may be as well to sail with the stream, and having accompanied the Emperor from the beginning of the campaign, to remain with him to the end.' The next natural opportunity to go home would be with Castlereagh, whom he now expected to remain until 18 or 20 April.[47]

Abercorn was not prepared to hear any good of Castlereagh. He was on excellent terms with Bathurst, who was acting as Foreign Secretary during Castlereagh's absence, and he told his son-in-law, 'Since Ld Cas. has been out of the way I have been so confidently trusted that I believe I know everything that is to be known.' He assured Aberdeen that the newspapers and politicians had let him alone of late; 'The circumstances of your interview with St Aignan I have long known, & all discussion of them we will reserve for conversation.'[48]

Aberdeen's return was to be delayed even longer than he expected but he was able to give Abercorn increasingly cheerful news. Paris fell on 31 March. Aberdeen learnt of the capitulation at Dijon on 4 April. He was holding a large dinner for 'all the principal persons of all the allied nations'. They all wore the white cockade and Aberdeen himself gave the first toast to Louis XVIII – even though he suspected that there was very little real support for the Bourbons in France. On 8 April Aberdeen could write to Abercorn, 'The great work is at last accomplished.' Everyone had now deserted Bonaparte, if only because they wanted peace.[49] Bonarparte abdicated on 11 April.

Even now Aberdeen could not get away. He told Abercorn on 18 April that Castlereagh would probably stay another month to 'settle everything' and Castlereagh insisted that he stay with him.[50] Aberdeen therefore accompanied Castlereagh to Paris and assisted him in the negotiations which led to the first Treaty of Paris of 30 May 1814.

Perhaps because he was longing to get away, Aberdeen found Paris tedious, the society boring and the French extremely dislikable. He told Abercorn that he was exasperated by the 'profligacy and baseness of this despicable people', and Harrowby that, although he was sorry for the King, 'the great mass of the nation can do nothing better than destroy each other. You will be surprised at my rancour, but you must see this vile people in their present state before you can comprehend that the feeling is natural.' He lost his temper with Marshal Ney who, at a dinner in the presence of Wellington and the victorious generals of the Rhine, entertained Aberdeen 'by proofs of the ease with which the expedition to England would have succeeded'. Aberdeen answered him sharply and commented grimly, 'I do not think he is likely to return to the subject.' He was glad to see his brother Alexander, who arrived with Wellington, and enjoyed meeting Mme de Stael at Talleyrand's, but he found society, even that at Lady Castlereagh's suppers, 'stupid'.[51] Generally, his letters are those of a querulous man who was just beginning to react to the long strain through which he had been.

On public matters he was pessimistic. He thought Talleyrand, now Louis XVIII's Foreign Minister, wanted to drag out the negotiations. There was little enthusiasm for the Bourbons and the army was still attached to Napoleon. In the Vendée, on the contrary, people had risen for the restoration of property. He comforted himself that instability in France might be the best guarantee of peace but, with so many disputes unresolved, 'I consider war in Europe as certain in the course of two years, although the source may not as usual be found in this capital.[52]

The first Treaty of Paris only settled the outstanding questions between France and the Allies – much of the work of drawing the new boundaries of Europe was left for the Congress of Vienna, which did not meet until November 1814. France was reduced to the frontiers of 1789, with some modest additions won in the early days of the Revolution. She abandoned her claim to the 'natural frontiers' by relinquishing territory on the left bank of the Rhine and in Savoy. In return Britain returned most of her colonies. France was also to be allowed to keep the numerous art treasures which she had looted, mainly from Italy, during the Napoleonic wars. Aberdeen particularly interested himself in this last provision. He told Harrowby:

I have been strenuous in recommending the preservation here of the pictures and statues – principally as a lover of art, for they would infallibly be destroyed by a journey into Italy. They have suffered much in being transported here, although done with the greatest care and expense which a Great Emperor could bestow – but I hope the question is decided. I am sure it would do more to discredit the French Govt than anything in the world. The cession of the Netherlands and Antwerp is not felt as such a national disgrace as the surrender of these trophies would be. The name of the Bourbons would be inseparably connected with the last degree of humiliation. You will think me zealous, but at present I am a little interested in their preservation for when not engaged at a conference, my time is spent almost entirely in the Louvre. Were it not for the inexhaustible stores of art collected here, Paris would be intolerable.[53]

He urged Harrowby to come and see them. Was there perhaps a sneaking motive at the back of his mind that these treasures would be much more accessible in Paris than scattered over Europe?

Aberdeen left Paris the day after the treaty was signed. According to his son's account, he brought the treaty home with him in his own carriage. This may be so, although Aberdeen expected his old friend, Frederick Robinson, who had come out as an aide to Castlereagh the previous December, to convey it and, according to the press, Castlereagh's private secretary, Joseph Planta, brought it.[54] Aberdeen had told Abercorn that he did not really understand why Castlereagh had asked him to stay on at all when the negotiations were all in Castlereagh's hands. Apart from the fact that Aberdeen was a conscientious and useful assistant, Castlereagh may have felt that he was fulfilling his implied promise of 2 February that those who had borne the heat and burden of the early negotiations should have the 'reputation' of being there at the conclusion. On 16 July he was granted his long–desired British peerage as Viscount Gordon of Aberdeen.

Ironically, the bestowal of an honour on Aberdeen at that point was not altogether easy for the government. A few months earlier he had been in grave danger of becoming the scapegoat for the disappointed hopes of his countrymen. The British had been fighting Napoleon for a long time. They were determined that 'Boney' was going to be crushed. After Leipzig and Vitoria they were quite unrealistically convinced that the war was won. A compromise peace had become anathema to them: only a fool or a traitor would suggest it. Cabinet ministers who believed, at least until March 1814,[55] that a negotiated peace was inevitable realised that they were taking their lives into their hands – perhaps literally – by advising it. At an early stage of the Chatillon Conference when it seemed possible that Caulaincourt would accept the allied terms, Castlereagh wrote to Aberdeen, 'My dear Aberdeen, we must sign. Certainly we must sign. We shall be stoned when we get back to England, but we must sign.' As late as 11 March, Harrowby wrote: 'We shall all swing together whenever your signature at Chatillon, or elsewhere, brings us to the gallows, for nothing but "no peace with Bonaparte" is to be heard from the Land's End to Berwick.'[56]

NOTES

1. Add. MSS 43075, Aberdeen to Castlereagh, 25 Nov. 1813.
2. FO Supp. 343, Cathcart to Castlereagh, 28 Nov. 1813, Private and Confidential.
3. Add. MSS 43075, Aberdeen to Castlereagh, 28 Nov. 1813.
4. Add. MSS 43074, Lamb to Castlereagh, 12 Oct. 1813; Add. MSS 43075, Aberdeen to Castlereagh, 29 Oct. 1813 'Private. For yourself alone.'
5. Add. MSS 43225, Aberdeen to Maria, 19 Sept. 1813.
6. Add. MSS 43075, Aberdeen to Castlereagh, 12, 24 Nov. 1813.
7. HH 1/30, Aberdeen to Jane, 10 Aug., 7, 19 Sept., 12 Oct., 28 Nov. 1813.
8. Add. MSS 43225, Aberdeen to Maria, 19 Sept. 1813; HH 1/28, Aberdeen to Maria, 22, 25, 31 Oct. 1813.
9. Add. MSS 43225, Aberdeen to Maria, 15 Nov., 18 Dec. 1813; Abercorn to Aberdeen, 15 Oct., 5 Dec. 1813, Aberdeen to Abercorn, 15 Nov., 29 Dec. 1813; HH 1/28, Aberdeen to Maria, 29 July, 22 Oct. 1813; Harrowby MSS, vol. XIV, ff. 19–22, Aberdeen to Harrowby, 24 Dec. 1813.
10. Add. MSS 43075, Aberdeen to Castlereagh, 11 Nov. 1813.
11. Add. MSS 43225, Aberdeen to Abercorn, 4 Dec. 1813, Abercorn to Aberdeen, 21 Dec. 1813.

12. Add. MSS 43225, Abercorn to Aberdeen, 15 Oct., 5 Dec. 1813.
13. Add. MSS 43225, Aberdeen to Abercorn, 4 Dec. 1813; Add. MSS 43075, castlereagh to Aberdeen, 30 Nov. 1813.
14. Add. MSS 43225, Abercorn to Aberdeen, 21 Dec. 1813.
15. Add. MSS 43075, Aberdeen to Castlereagh, 5 Dec. 1813; Add. MSS 43225, Aberdeen to Abercorn, 4 Dec. 1813, 9 Jan. 1814, Abercorn to Aberdeen 21 Dec. 1813.
16. Harrowby MSS, vol. XIV, ff. 15–8, Aberdeen to Harrowby, 6 Dec. 1813; Add. MSS 43075, Aberdeen to Castlereagh, 9 Dec. 1813.
17. Add. MSS 43075, Aberdeen to Castlereagh, 5 Dec. 1813.
18. F0 7/103, Aberdeen to Castlereagh, No. 51, 5 Dec. 1813, Most Secret, No. 53, 9 Dec. 1813; Add. MSS 43075, Aberdeen to Castlereagh, 5, 9 Dec. 1813.
19. Add. MSS 43225, Aberdeen to Abercorn, 11 Dec. 1813; cf. Harrowby MSS, vol. XIV, ff. 19–22, Aberdeen to Harrowby, 24 Dec. 1813.
20. *Castlereagh, 1812–1815*, p. 177.
21. Haus-, Hof-u. Staatsarchiv, Metternich to Wessenberg, 6 Dec. 1813 'Par M. le Pozzo di Borgo'.
22. *Castlereagh, 1812–1815*, p. 188.
23. FO 7/101, Castlereagh to Aberdeen, No. 52, 21 Dec. 1813; Add. MSSS 43076, Castlereagh to Aberdeen, 22 Dec. 1813.
24. Add. MSS 43226, Aberdeen to Abercorn, 6 Jan. 1814; Harrowby MSS, vol. XIV, ff. 23–4, Aberdeen to Harrowby, 17 Jan. 1814.
25. Add. MSS 43225, Aberdeen to Abercorn, 11 Dec. 1813.
26. Add. MSS 43225, Abercorn to Aberdeen, 5 Dec. 1813.
27. FO 7/103, Aberdeen to Castlereagh, No. 62, 25 Dec., No. 63, 30 Dec. 1813; Add. MSS 43075, Aberdeen to Castlereagh, 5 Dec. 1813; Add. MSS 43225, Aberdeen to Abercorn, 19, 29 Dec. 1813.
28. Harrowby MSS, vol. XIV, ff. 23–4, Aberdeen to Harrowby, 17 Jan. 1814; Liverpool Papers, Add. MSS 38191, Castlereagh to Liverpool, 30 Dec. 1813; Bathurst MSS, Loan 57/7, Castlereagh to Bathurst, 30 Dec. 1813, Aberdeen to Bathurst, 20 Jan. 1814.
29. Add. MSS 43225, Aberdeen to Abercorn, 11 Dec. 1813.
30. Add. MSS 43225, Aberdeen to Abercorn, 11, 19 Dec. 1813.
31. Add. MSS 43225, Aberdeen to Abercorn, 29 Dec. 1813, 6 Jan. 1814.
32. Add. MSS 43225, Aberdeen to Maria, 15 Dec. 1813.
33. Harrowby MSS, vol. XIV, ff. 23–4, Aberdeen to Harrowby, 17 Jan. 1814.
34. Harrowby MSS, vol. XIV, ff. 25–30, Aberdeen to Harrowby, 21 Jan. 1814; Add. MSS 43225, Aberdeen to Abercorn, 29 Jan. 1814.
35. Add. MSS 43225, Abercorn to Aberdeen, 13 Feb. 1814.
36. Add. MSS 43225, Aberdeen to Abercorn, 29 Jan. 1814.
37. Add. MSS 43225, Aberdeen to Abercorn, 30 Jan. 1814; *Castlereagh 1812–1815*, pp. 208–9.
38. Add. MSS 43225, Aberdeen to Abercorn, 30 Jan. 1814; Abercorn to Aberdeen, 13 Feb. 1814.
39. Add. MSS 43225, Aberdeen to Abercorn, 1 Mar. 1814; Harrowby MSS, vol. XIV, ff. 29–30, Aberdeen to Harrowby, 1 Mar. 1814.
40. FO 7/107, Reports on Chatillon Conference, No. 1, 5 Feb. – No. 15, 19 Mar. 1814.
41. FO 92/2 Castlereagh to British Plenipotentiaries, No. 2, 2 Feb. 1814, Confidential.

42. Add. MSS 43225, Aberdeen to Abercorn, 30 Jan., 1, 6 Mar. 1814
43. FO 7/107, Report No. 1, 5 Feb. 1814.
44. FO 7/107, Report No. 3, 7 Feb., No. 4, 9 Feb. 1814.
45. FO 7/107, Report No. 11, 13 Mar., No. 15, 19 Mar. 1814.
46. Add. MSS 43225, Aberdeen to Abercorn, 20 Mar. 1814.
47. Add. MSS 43225, Aberdeen to Abercorn, 20, 29 Mar. 1814.
48. Add. MSS 43225, Abercorn to Aberdeen, 5 Mar. 1814.
49. Add. MSS 43225, Aberdeen to Abercorn, 4, 8 Apr. 1814.
50. Add. MSS 43225, Aberdeen to Abercorn, 18 Apr., 9 May 1814.
51. Add. MSS 43225, Aberdeen to Abercorn, 9, 10 May 1814; Harrowby MSS, vol. XIV, ff. 31–5, Aberdeen to Harrowby, 15 May 1814. He wrote to Jane on 15 May that he would soon be home and that Uncles Robert and Alexander were with him, HH 1/30, 15 May 1814.
52. Add. MSS 43225, Aberdeen to Abercorn, 9 May 1814.
53. Harrowby MSS, vol. XIV, ff. 31–5, Aberdeen to Harrowby, 15 May 1814.
54. Stanmore, p. 65; Harrowby MSS, vol XIV, ff. 31–5, Aberdeen to Harrowby, 15 May 1814; *London Gazette*, 2 June 1814, quoted in most newspapers.
55. As late as January 1814 Harrowby reminded Bathurst that the Allies 'have not actually obtained the possession of all they demanded in the terms loosely stated to St Aignan', Bathurst Papers, Loan 57/7, Harrowby to Bathurst, 16 Jan. 1814.
56. Stanmore, pp. 62–3; Add. MSS 43230, Harrowby to Aberdeen, 11 Mar. 1814; Add. MSS 49326, A. Gordon to Waterfield, 20 Jan. 1871.

CHAPTER ELEVEN

Return to private life

It was a sad homecoming. Maria had died on 21 January. Aberdeen heard the news just before the Chatillon Conference opened. William Howley wrote on 12 February to offer his sympathy and tell him that Abercorn was 'overwhelmed' by grief.[1] As usual, Howley counselled Christian resignation and Aberdeen told Harrowby that this was the only course. He had earlier written to Abercorn, 'Unless we are the sport of a blind chance, there must be wisdom, there must be goodness, and there must be mercy.'[2] While Aberdeen had been abroad Howley had been appointed Bishop of London. Although pleased at his friend's promotion, Aberdeen had expressed misgivings to Harrowby that he might not be 'worldly' enough for that particular bishopric.[3]

The tale of private tragedies was not yet done. Abercorn had several times written to express anxiety, not only about Maria, but also about his son and heir, Lord Hamilton. At the end of April he wrote, 'My son is in so hopeless a state, that without being utterly out of the world, I can hardly be said to live in it.' When he arrived back in London early in June 1814, Aberdeen found that Argyll House was not yet ready for him and went to call on Lord Harrowby in Grosvenor Square, where he was met with the news that Hamilton had just died.[4]

It was, however, some time before Aberdeen could turn his attention entirely to private matters. The Tsar of Russia and the King of Prussia had come to London. Aberdeen was disappointed that the Emperor Francis had not come too. He had found Francis an intelligent and cultivated man and had hoped that his presence in London would correct the caricature of him which had been presented in the English press.[5] But Metternich came and Aberdeen lodged him at Argyll House. He told his brother Robert ruefully, 'They occupy my four drawing rooms in addition to their bedrooms. Metternich has all his Secretaries, his whole Chancellerie established etc., many servants whom I keep. In short, if it were not that I am determined to go through with it handsomely I should be out of all patience.' He knew Metternich very well and he added sardonically that he was introducing him to everyone and 'he succeeds very well, especially with the women'.[6]

Metternich urged him to stay on as British Ambassador to Vienna and Castlereagh too wished him to return to Vienna and act as his assistant at the forthcoming conference, as he had previously done at Chatillon and Paris. Aberdeen refused, although he would have been willing to undertake a purely ceremonial visit to take the Order of the Garter to the Emperor. He was heartily sick of diplomatic intrigues, both domestic and foreign. He received some private information about the progress of the Congress of Vienna – he discreetly scratched out the name of his informant even in his private letter to Abercorn. He was sharply critical of what was being done and told Abercorn, 'Some most infamous projects are on foot, which I fear there is little chance of baffling.' The reference is probably to the plans to give the Tsar control of Poland and compensate Prussia at the expense of the King of Saxony, since Aberdeen went on to say that the 'atrocious policy' of the Allies was giving France the chance to assume 'wise, just and moderate language' and to appear almost as the mediator. He was also cynical about the British support for the Bourbons 'for whom we robbed the King of Sardinia [of part of Savoy]', who were now accusing the Allies of being as hostile to them as Bonaparte or the revolutionaries.[7]

Aberdeen was anxious to attend to his own affairs. There was still the difficult question of a second marriage to be settled. After the half–overtures to renew his offer to Anne Cavendish, which he had received while abroad, it had been agreed by all parties that he should return entirely free and with no commitments. His principal confidant was now his brother Robert, and his letters make clear that he simultaneously pursued his suit with Anne Cavendish and with Susan Ryder in a way which could only have aroused the distrust of all concerned, if they knew what was happening, as apparently they did. While abroad he had frequently sent messages to Susan and her mother, through Lord Harrowby, and on his return told Robert, 'On seeing Ly S. I was a good deal struck with her improved appearance, but more delighted with the sweetness and purity which she has preserved. I have seen a good deal of her, indeed every day, and although she is still a child, I have every reason to be satisfied with her mind and acquirement.' At the same time he had good reason for saying to Robert, 'Nothing can be more awkward than my situation.'

Soon after his arrival in London he had supped at Devonshire House and seen Anne for the first time since his return. He told Robert, 'I was afraid there would have been a *regular scene*.' After a few minutes he had felt it necessary to go up to Anne to ask her how she was, 'She turned as pale as death and did not answer a word.' Aberdeen was 'a good deal alarmed' and turned to talk to Lady Georgiana. After a few minutes Anne recovered sufficiently 'to join in some common place conversation about the Emperor etc.' He remained talking with them for about a quarter of an hour and then took Georgiana into supper. The following night there was a small party at Lady Jersey's. He and Georgiana sat together and 'she gradually contrived to introduce the subject; and though she in a certain degree veiled her expressions, she gave me clearly to understand that the acquiescence of A. in her family's rejection of the marriage had always been a great sacrifice, that latterly it had made her miserable, and that the family had entirely changed, especially Lord G. who was now as anxious as he had been adverse.' Aberdeen confessed that he had been trying to forget the whole affair and to consider it as at an end:

Ly Georgiana begged me to do nothing rashly – alluded to Ly S. – but only begged that nothing might be hurried, and that I should only make myself certain of what would suit me best . . . Is not this a terrible affair? I do not know what to do – but in the meantime I shall take Lady Georgiana's advice and do nothing hastily. Without making myself particular with either, I shall go on with both as I see them, and then decide on the best view I can take of the whole affair.[8]

This uncomfortable state of affairs went on for several months. Aberdeen could not avoid meeting Anne frequently at social gatherings, nor indeed does he seem to have tried to do so. He told Robert later, 'I afterwards went to Lansdowne's and saw A. I spoke as usual, and although at first her constraint was great it wore off.' Robert rather disapproved and Aberdeen assured him 'I have avoided any particular attention, such as giving her my arm etc.' He had had further conversations with Georgiana and Lord and Lady George 'are now both very civil'. At the same time he was seeing a good deal of Susan and told Robert, 'She is certainly delightful in every respect.'[9] He had consulted Lord and Lady Abercorn and Abercorn introduced yet another candidate, warmly recommending a marriage with 'Ly G. B.' – presumably Lady [Louisa] Georgiana Bathurst, the daughter of the third Earl Bathurst. Contrary to Stanmore's account, Abercorn did not try to prevent the Cavendish marriage. On the contrary he told Aberdeen that, although he did not know Anne Cavendish personally, he would approve such a marriage if Aberdeen was unwilling to consider 'Lady G. B.' Surprisingly, it was Susan Ryder to whom Abercorn took strong exception. He did not like Harrowby and persuaded Aberdeen to consider such a marriage 'out of the question'. Aberdeen himself had some reservations because of Susan's youth. In any case, his return to Bentley Priory had aroused vivid memories of his first wife and he told Robert, 'It is too soon yet to venture to touch wounds which exhibit no sympton of healing.' Aberdeen was reduced to a state of painful embarrassment and admitted to Robert that his initial agreement to take the Garter to 'old Franz' was 'partly to get out of the way'.[10]

One reason why he began to hesitate in his courtship of Anne Cavendish was a growing doubt about her health, although he also flattered himself that she was pining for him. He told Robert on various occasions, 'She does not look at all well', 'A's looks are sufficient indication of what she feels', and 'Anne is in a *desperate way*'. In the autumn Aberdeen escaped to Haddo with his children and the following spring he told Robert that he hardly ever saw Anne these days.[11] Ironically, his fears about her health – not altogether unreasonable if she was to bear him sons and be a mother to his existing children – were totally unfounded. She eventually married a younger son of the Duke of Grafton, bore him four children and outlived Aberdeen by many years.

His marriage plans having come to nothing, Aberdeen turned back to the management of his estates, which he had neglected, not only while he was abroad, but since the shock of Catherine's death. He wrote to Abercorn from Haddo in September 1814, to tell him of the improvements he was having done indoors, including new provision for his library, but he admitted that Abercorn was right and he would have to go 'softly'. His finances were not in good order; for the last three years he had neither looked into his affairs nor had it done for him. He seems to have suffered a reaction from the strains and privations he had undergone on the continent. His health was not good and he suffered incessant headaches. He was still not entirely reconciled to his Scottish estates and longed for Bentley Priory which, he told Abercorn, 'will always have more charms for me than any other place in the world'.[12]

When he returned to London it became apparent that Abercorn now had entirely new plans for his son-in-law. Why should he not marry his son, Lord Hamilton's, widow, the former Harriet Douglas? Harriet was considered a beauty, although it was perhaps a pity that Aberdeen's opinion of her, expressed to his brother Alexander in 1810, was that she was 'certainly one of the most stupid persons I ever met with'.[13] Such a marriage would be almost entirely for Lord Abercorn's benefit. His health was beginning to fail and it seemed more than likely that he would die before his grandson and heir, James, came of age. James was Aberdeen's godson and Abercorn knew what a devoted father Aberdeen was. If Aberdeen was seeking a marriage of convenience, what better solution could there be than that Harriet should become the step-mother of Aberdeen's three little girls and he the step-father of her two sons and one daughter? Both would remain within the circle of Bentley Priory. Harriet seems to have fallen in with the plan with enthusiasm. Aberdeen took a good deal more persuading and even Harriet's son, Lord Stanmore, does not try to disguise the fact that he was overborne by Abercorn's determination, although a shrewd and friendly observer, Mrs George Lamb, thought at the time that they had fallen in love if only from shared misery. She wrote to Augustus Foster to say that she supposed he knew of Aberdeen's impending marriage: '. . . .two miserable creatures. He says, What else have we to do? The truth is, she is beautiful, and he is very much in love with her.'[14]

The marriage took place at Stanmore in July 1815, as soon as Harriet's year of mourning for her husband was up. It was an uneven marriage. Sexually it was successful, and not only because Harriet bore Aberdeen the desired sons, four of them, as well as a daughter. When they were apart Aberdeen wrote her constant love letters and, for the time, spoke in fairly explicit terms of his longing for her in bed. But Stanmore greatly understates the case when he says that Harriet was not the 'intellectual equal' of Catherine.[15] Aberdeen was never able to enjoy the meeting of minds with Harriet which he had always had with his first wife. As they grew older he seems to have sought that intellectual companionship with Catherine's daughters. Harriet was increasingly infuriated. Her position from the beginning was difficult. Although she had entered into the marriage with her eyes open, to be married to a man who constantly and openly mourns for his first wife cannot be easy for any woman. Harriet certainly did not have the character to transcend the situation but to seek to revenge herself, as she eventually did, on Catherine's children, was petty.

The marriage seemed happy enough at first even though it was celebrated against the background of further tragedy. A month earlier Alexander had been killed at Waterloo. Aberdeen, together with his brothers and his sister, Alicia, caused a monument to be erected to him on the field of Waterloo and built a replica at home at Haddo. Aberdeen and Harriet went to Haddo in the autumn after their marriage and entertained some company, including the Kembles, although Aberdeen himself seems to have been ill again. The winter was a hard one and the visit to Haddo was not a comfortable one. Ominously, Aberdeen told Abercorn that they would shorten their visit next year and would not leave England until the end of October so that they could pass the whole summer at the Priory.[16] Harriet's reaction to Haddo was quite different from Catherine's. She disliked it and soon resolved to spend as little time there as possible.

But all this seemed totally unimportant beside the fact that, at last, on 26 September 1816, Aberdeen had a healthy son and heir who lived. The child was named George John James for his father and Lord Abercorn. Harriet bore Aberdeen a second son, Alexander, at Haddo on 10 December 1817. It had been intended that the birth should take place in London and an obstetrician had to be hastily procured from Aberdeen. The boy himself did not suffer. Like the uncle after whom he was named, he became a soldier and proved to be the most robust of Aberdeen's sons, but Harriet was alarmed and recovered slowly from the birth.[17] Nevertheless, she bore another child, a daughter, Frances, before the end of 1818.

During the early years of Aberdeen's second marriage, Abercorn began to fail. Aberdeen wrote regularly both about public affairs and literature, perhaps to try to entertain his father-in-law. In November 1817 he expressed the view that the death of the Prince Regent's only daughter, Charlotte, was a private rather than a public calamity but Abercorn disagreed. He thought Charlotte's husband (later Leopold I of the Belgians), the 'most right headed man in this Country' and feared that when the Prince Regent succeeded to the throne, the Royal Dukes would all hold opposition courts and keep 'Court & Parliament & Nation in perpetual hot water'. Despite his declining health, Abercorn was still building at Bentley Priory and he complained, late in 1817, 'that Prince of a Jack Ass Wilkins made the Walls so inadequate . . . that it is ascertained that I have for some months been sleeping in some danger.' The whole storey would have to be pulled down. Aberdeen's last letter to Abercorn was a critique of their old friend, Sir Walter Scott's, latest novel, *Rob Roy*.[18] Abercorn died on 18 January 1818.

Abercorn's death left Aberdeen many new responsibilities. His step–son, James, was only six years old and, until he came of age, Aberdeen had to administer his estates in both Scotland and Ireland. He was also effectively for the next fifteen years, master of Bentley Priory. It became his principal residence, so much so that the older children of his second marriage scarcely knew Haddo as children.[19] Abercorn left Aberdeen substantial sums of money in his Will, for which Aberdeen was duly grateful and he consulted Hudson Gurney on the propriety of quartering the Abercorn coat of arms with his own to symbolise the union of the two families. Gurney advised him that this would be irregular and suggested that instead Aberdeen should incorporate the Abercorn antelope as one of the supporters of his own arms. But Aberdeen pointed out that, as his existing supporters were a knight and a lawyer, he would have to have two antelopes because one would look strange 'with the man in a wig for his neighbour'. Nothing came of the suggestion to change the arms but Aberdeen incorporated the name Hamilton with his own to become officially, Hamilton-Gordon.[20]

The care of his own and the Abercorn estates occupied a great deal of Aberdeen's time during the next ten years. The golden years of the Napoleonic wars were over for British farmers and difficult times lay ahead. In December 1815 he told Abercorn that there was increasing distress in Aberdeenshire, although they had not yet suffered the outrages which had occurred in Ireland. He had not yet experienced a 'deficiency' of rents, although he feared he might in the next half-year. He approved the new Corn Law, which forbade the import of corn until the price stood at eighty shillings a quarter and thought it would do good in Ireland.[21] The year 1817 saw a bad harvest. In the middle of October it was only half in and the late corn had been destroyed by frost. By December rents were badly in arrears, although he told Abercorn that land was till in demand.[22] His long-term optimism seemed borne out by the good harvest of 1818 and he wrote jubilantly to Hudson Gurney that it had been a 'glorious year' for the north of Scotland. 'Our farmers are paying up arrears. Their *Cattle* is in great demand, and corn at a fair price. We are exporting *potatoes* and *turnips* in large quantities (the Aberdeen fruit). We are even sending Hay to the Haymarket.'[23] The improvement was not maintained; 1819 was another bad year, marked by widespread disorders.

In 1821 Aberdeen carefully reviewed the state of his property with Crombie. He was still plagued by inherited debts. He told Harriet that he did not know the whole amount of his debts but in the last three years he had paid off £10,000 although he added ruefully, 'It is astonishing how much we spend in different ways, of which we have little idea.' So far as the estate was concerned, 'The present gross rental of the estate is above £21,000 a year, and it will this year be raised to 22,000. There are pretty heavy arrears existing, nearly seven thousand pounds; but he [Crombie] expects some time or other to get the whole of it. I am beginning to renew some of the leases which I let in 1804, but in consequence of the state of the time, if I can prevent any diminution, it will be well enough.'[24]

Aberdeen undertook a similar thorough review with Crombie again in the autumn of 1822. He told Harriet that Crombie would stay for a few days, 'to examine in detail the state of arrears, and make proportional abatement on each. Crombie told me that he thought all the farms I let in the years 1802, 3, 4 and 5 will give rather an increase of rent when out of lease. Those in 1806, 7, 8 and 9 will barely maintain their rent with great difficulty; and those let in 1810, 11, 12, 13 and 14 must be reduced.' He had a thousand tenants to review and, after long sessions with Crombie, he came to the conclusion that matters were even worse than he had supposed. 'The state of the Tenantry', he wrote to Harriet, 'is certainly bad, and I fear getting worse. The appearance of things is greatly changed: formerly they crowded here to me to obtain new leases, and to take farms at any price; yesterday I supposed there were not fewer than sixty who came and insisted on reductions as they were utterly unable to pay. I fear we shall lose the arrear which is due.'[25]

Despite the diminution in his income Aberdeen pressed on with improvements on the estate and at Haddo House and Argyll House. He was still planting trees as enthusiastically as ever and clothing the whole Formartine (Gight) region in woodland. It became one of his favourite haunts, despite local superstitions for, as he told Harriet, 'The people of the country think the place unlucky.'[26] He had romantic ideas of building a tower there. The tower was eventually built but its foundations must have been unsound for it subsequently fell in a gale.[27] Argyll House had been renovated at almost ruinous cost in 1811 but, after Catherine's death, Aberdeen doubted if he could bear to live there. He almost sold it – the Duke of Wellington was one prospective purchaser – but he could only have done so at a subsantial loss and was dissuaded. In 1819 he was again having major works done there and he told Harriet, who was in Brighton, 'This house is detestable, the smell of mortar, bricks, paint and rubbish is quite intolerable.'[28]

Rather sadly, many of the improvements at Haddo were made in an attempt to persuade Harriet to live there at least part of the year with him. He told her in August 1822 that the plantations were wonderfully grown and the garden looked well; 'We might enjoy a residence here for some time.'[29] Harriet was adamant. She much preferred London and Brighton and resolutely refused to come north. Harriet's objections were not altogether without foundation. The journey was still a long and difficult one and the Abercorn family consistently considered an expedition to Aberdeenshire a much more formidable undertaking than one to their Irish estates in County Tyrone. In the 1820s Aberdeen got into the habit of sending his household by sea and became such a good customer of the shipping company that they sought his permission to name their new ship the *Earl of Aberdeen*. However, his own dislike of the sea was so great that he always took the land route, although he frequently arrived unwell because of the jolting of the carriage.

Harriet, often pregnant in the early days of the marriage and suffering ill–defined aches and pains throughout the 1820s, simply refused to subject herself to such discomforts. Harriet wallowed in ill health, in stark contrast to the gallant Catherine who had fought bravely to the end of her short life, but her ills may well not have been imaginary. She too died of tuberculosis in 1833 and her discomforts, depressions and almost hysterical irritability during the previous ten years may have been early and unrecognised symptoms of the disease. But she was plainly a very difficult woman to live with and her unfortunate husband alternated between sympathy and exasperation.

Their early years were comparatively harmonious and Harriet did not then exhibit the resentment of Catherine's children she was to show later. There is a letter from Alice to her father, dated in a later hand '1813' but obviously later, recounting a hilarious afternoon which the two families spent together trying to ride some recalcitrant donkeys, which suggests nothing but good relations.[30] These years were shadowed by the long illness and death of Aberdeen's second daughter, Caroline. Caroline, who seems to have been attacked by tuberculosis in the spine, was confined to bed at Argyll House while her two sisters were brought up mainly at the Priory. Harriet urged them to write to Caroline every day by 'the cart', which regularly took goods and messages from one house to the other, but begged them not to write about her garden because she longed so to see it and could not.[31] Jane, who was a downright child, eventually asked her stepmother whether her sister would ever recover. Harriet replied in careful and sympathetic language:

As to what you ask my dear Jane about poor Caro – it is difficult for me to answer you – you know that all things are possible to God – and that if it is his will he may still permit her to recover even after this lingering and dangerous illness – but the probabilities I am forced to say appear against it – for her weakness is so great that that alone without any other illness to make her situation very dangerous [sic]. I know it must be impossible for you to think of this without feeling very unhappy – but I must earnestly beg you not to dwell upon the subject more than you can help – for two reasons – that whatever God orders is for the best tho' we cannot see why – and that the thing that would make Papa and me more unhappy under this misfortune would be seeing you look ill and unhappy. Bless you my dearest Jane.[32]

Caroline died in July 1818.

Unfortunately, the good relations and understanding did not last and in 1819 Aberdeen and Harriet began to spend time apart. She remained at the Priory, pleading ill health, while he fulfilled various engagements. In the spring he went to a house party at the Duke of Bedford's at Woburn Abbey and in September to Lord Ashburnham's in Sussex for the shooting, followed by another house party at the Bathursts' home at Cirencester, at which the Granvilles were also present. In July he wrote bracingly to Harriet, 'I hope you feel comfortable today, as I do not like the thought of your being so low and nervous, especially as you have no good reason. Patience is difficult but I feel satisfied that it is all which is required.' In September he was a little more sympathetic, telling her, 'I am sorry you are so dismal and so uncomfortable' and promising that he would not go to Scotland unless she felt up to it.[33]

They had spent the summer at Brighton in a rented house, 'that wretched House' as Aberdeen termed it, which he feared had had disastrous results for the health of his two surviving daughters.[34] While he plainly thought that Harriet was suffering from hypochondria and must be jollied into exertion, he was extremely worried about Jane and Alice. He wrote to Harriet, still at Brighton, from Argyll House, that Jane had a high fever and a very bad throat. 'There are very large *Apthae* in her throat', he said, 'which [the doctor] showed me.' He feared that if they developed into an ulcer there was no telling what the result might be.[35] Jane, who seemed at that time to be the most robust of Aberdeen's daughters, recovered but Alice's health gave prolonged anxiety. She too suffered from a bad throat and fever and from persistent weakness. Aberdeen told Harriet that Alice was asking for her, and occasionally threw in references to his own health, but Harriet turned a deaf ear. Aberdeen consulted doctor after doctor and himself turned nurse in a way quite extraordinary for a nineteenth–century father. He took his children's pulses, noted their symptoms and dosed them with all manner of medicines which, unhappily, probably did more harm than good.[36]

The pattern of 1819 was repeated in 1820. They again took a house in Brighton, West Cliff House. Both Harriet and Alice were ill and the doctors could no longer conceal that they feared that Alice might have pulmonary tuberculosis. Aberdeen sensibly suggested that he should take her to a warmer climate but, as with her mother, the doctors preferred to keep her in an even temperature by confining her to the house. Draconian measures were mooted such as not allowing her out of doors between November and April and sealing the windows of her bedroom so that no draughts could enter. She was spared the frequent bleeding to which her mother had been subjected but she was dosed with calomel (chloride of mercury) and other fearsome medicines. Amazingly, Alice survived and even made partial recovery.[37]

In 1821 Aberdeen went to Haddo alone and established a pattern which lasted for several years. His bachelor brothers and neighbours, like Charles Gordon of Cluny, joined him for the shooting. Shooting was a sport which Aberdeen, like Peel, always enjoyed. His preservation of pheasants and partridges on the Haddo estate was now proving highly successful and there was deer stalking as a variation. Aberdeen kept the tables of his family and friends well supplied. Usually his offerings were very welcome but sometimes the slowness of transport proved too much. Lord Ashburnham had to admit 'the game on which you meant I should feast was on its arrival in London already like brave Percy – food for worms'.[38] Aberdeen's account of these shooting parties is in marked contrast to the formal style of entertaining which was later developed at Haddo. The young men seem to have roughed it a good deal. Aberdeen told Harriet indignantly that he was not overeating – he was not tempted to, he had a very bad cook.[39] His brothers were not always good company. John could be 'sulky' and William 'in a good humour but dullish'. Charles's poor shooting was a standing joke and Aberdeen sent Harriet regular bulletins on whether Charles had 'bagged his bird'. When Charles took up the flute, his brother, who had a sensitive ear for music, was sorely tried. Charles played in his bedroom but the sound penetrated very distinctly into his brother's library. Aberdeen, however, assured Harriet that he 'would not for the world' hint that his 'delicate notes' were not agreeable.[40] When Aberdeen was not shooting he led, as he told Harriet 'a very methodical life', rising at eight, dining at six-thirty and retiring to bed at eleven-thirty and filling in most of the day with inspections of the estate and consultations with his head gardener and head forester. Like Gladstone he seems to have enjoyed chopping down trees and sometimes joined his men in thinning the plantations, which were now growing rapidly.[41]

This time Harriet had been left with the children and Aberdeen's letters are full of anxious enquiries about his step-children, Claud and Harriet, as well as about his own children. Caroline was still in his mind and he expressed his thankfulness for Alice's recovery and that he would be spared witnessing in her case the sufferings he had seen in Caroline three years ago and 'which are not easily forgotten'. Harriet was reading plays with the older children and Aberdeen advised her that almost all modern authors were 'moral' but those of the last age, like Congreve and Vanbrugh, were 'by no means so'. He doubted if they would understand *The Critic*. He still refused to take Harriet's 'aches and pains' very seriously. He was determined that the next year she should join him at Haddo. On leaving Haddo himself he was overcome by a strange depression. 'I always feel a little dismal on leaving this place,' he wrote, 'from a sort of indistinct presentiment that I may not see it again; but this of course is nonsense.' The melancholy stayed with him all the way back to London.[42]

Harriet did not accompany him to Haddo the next year and their marriage reached a crisis. Harriet became obsessed with the idea that Jane bullied James and Claud and that if she, Harriet, died, Jane would have charge of the younger children and mistreat them. She insisted on a formal promise from her husband that Jane should never have such a position. Aberdeen felt obliged to comply, although he rated childish quarrels at their true value, assuring her that they would soon be outgrown and forgotten. He pointed out to Harriet that he might be the one who died first and, whereas he had always treated her sons as if they were his own, he would leave Jane to the care of a step-mother who had made plain her dislike and treated the girl somewhat harshly.[43]

Harriet continued to demand that Aberdeen should prove that he loved her until he was reduced to near despair. He wrote to her, 'You ask if I think of you when I go to bed in our room. I have told you dearest that I always do . . . I think if I were sure of finding you there tonight that I should go with about the thousand times more pleasure' and, on another occasion, 'When I say, with all the concentrated energy of which human nature is capable that I *love*, I know not how to add more, for everything else is comparatively weak.' Nothing seemed to satisfy Harriet and Aberdeen sought relief in physical exertion, chopping down trees and going for long walks across his estate, seven hours without stopping as he told her once.[44]

To anyone less prejudiced than Harriet their surviving letters make it hard to see how anyone could have disliked Jane and Alice. The longest series is one of thirty-six letters to Mrs Gale, their former nurse, the majority written by Alice. They extend from 1818, or perhaps earlier, to Alice's death in 1829. Unfortunately many of them are undated and some have no address, which makes it difficult to fit them into any sequence, but they radiate the same love of life and generosity of spirit which is so striking in Catherine's early letters. The girls led busy lives with lessons from various masters in drawing, music and languages; they visited the opera, the theatre and other entertainments; they chatted about the plants in their garden and about Jane's pet bird; but running like a dark thread through all of them are constant references to ill health, a 'cold', a 'cough', a 'sore throat'. Almost invariably they made light of their own condition, insisting that they were 'better' or 'almost well' and enquiring anxiously about other members of the family. No great anxiety was felt about Jane's health although, with hindsight, it is easy to conclude that the swollen glands in her neck from which she suffered were probably tubercular, and in 1824 she began to go out into society. She wrote to Mrs Gale that she was going to the opera and had recently dined at Lord Wicklow's, where Lady Charlemont knew her at once because she was so like her father. In July she was rather proud to go to a concert at Lady Melville's by herself because her parents had a dinner engagement, and told Mrs Gale that she would be going to the Priory on the Saturday. On the letter there is a sad note in pencil, 'Lady Jane went to the Priory as here proposed & the next week expired after two days illness the greater part of which she was in convulsions. How caused it never was ascertained. She died July 1824 anno aetatis 18.'[45]

According to Stanmore Jane's unexpected death shocked Harriet into sharing her husband's anxiety about the sole surviving daughter of his first marriage. But contemporary letters do not bear this out. Aberdeen determined to do all he could to save Alice. He decided that a winter in the south of France would do her more good than another winter confined to their London house and in December 1824 he set off with Alice for Nice. Alice kept a journal of their travels, very much in her father's manner, and in excellent French.[46] Aberdeen had expended much time and trouble to make his daughters fluent in French and Italian, sometimes writing to them in those languages himself.[47] They followed much the same route as Aberdeen and Whittington had taken in 1802 and the whole journal illustrates the closeness of father and daughter. Among Alice's often acute observations of the people, the towns and the countryside, the phrase 'Papa me dit' constantly re-echoes. Although she was far from well, she never lost her sense of humour. She found the smell of French towns trying and, at Lyons, her father went to purchase some sal volatile for her. To her glee the apothecary supposed that he wished to drink it, having heard fearsome stories of Englishmen's capacity to consume spirits. They arrived at Nice on 6 January, where they were subsequently joined by John, Charles and Harriet, who had travelled out with an inordinate train of baggage and servants. They remained at Nice until March. Aberdeen pottered about botanising and keeping notes on the plants.[48]

Aberdeen and Harriet planned an extension of their journey into Italy. He told Gurney in March that the following month they hoped to go to Genoa along the Cornice 'which is much improved I hear since we crossed it, but still something of a feat for a woman'. They would then go to Milan where he would be glad to see the Austrian Emperor and 'to judge with my own senses, what is the condition of the people'. They would return to Paris by way of Turin, Mont Cenis and Lyons. Predictably, Harriet declined to accompany him but Aberdeen left for Genoa as planned. He seems, however, to have cut his expedition short. He never arrived in Florence where Lord Ashburnham was expecting him.[49] It is, unfortunately, impossible to know how far he carried out his intention of assessing the Italian situation for himself.

On the whole the winter on the Mediterranean had been a success. Alice was greatly improved and Aberdeen, who had been beginning to show signs of strain himself, could report that he was 'very well'.[50] It was decided to repeat the experiment the next year, although unhappily Alice was again worse. Aberdeen wrote to Gurney, 'I repeat my sad journey of last year, and unfortunately under circumstances of increased urgency.'[51] He was ill himself and their departure was delayed. Once again he and Alice travelled alone together, arriving at Nice on 19 December. This time the journey had been an uncomfortable one.[52] Harriet had been unable to make up her mind whether to endure the fatigues of the journey and, in the end, she not only refused to come but pettishly demanded that her husband return to her side since she too was ill. Aberdeen was in a dilemma. Alice had her governess, Miss Holloway, with her but Aberdeen considered her 'more helpless than a child'. Robert stayed briefly but had to go on to Vienna where he was now Secretary of Embassy. Alice was seriously ill with chest symptoms and a persistent swelling of her legs which probably denoted heart failure. To leave her unprotected in a foreign country seemed unthinkable but he was now genuinely concerned about Harriet. As he told Gurney, whatever he did would be 'a choice of sacrifices'.[53] He remained in Nice until 10 February, by which time he had a promise from John that he would come out. He made a fairly leisurely return home, spending a week in Paris, where he dined with the Bedfords and the Hollands who were there, discussed politics with the Ambassador, Lord Granville and attended a reception given by Lady Granville, the former Lady Harriet Cavendish.[54]

Alice's health improved as the spring arrived and she wrote cheerfully to Mrs Gale that their rented house was called Maison Avigdor and was near the beach where they had made a nice gravel walk called '*the English walk*'. She was sorry papa had gone but he wrote often and she was very well, her cough gone and her legs less swollen. She was busy with lessons from Italian, drawing and botany masters. She was well enough to go out riding on a donkey twice a day and had been to Villafranca.[55]

The improvement in Alice's health was maintained until the autumn of 1827 when, on returning to the Priory from Scotland, where she had seemed very well, she was taken seriously ill again.[56] Once again she made an apparent recovery but by the spring of 1829 she was losing strength fast. In March she was still sufficiently interested in what was going on round her to ask Mrs Gale to send her atlas but she apologised for not writing because she was too tired. On 4 April she wrote a shaky note in pencil to thank Mrs Gale for some flowers, again apologising and explaining, 'My hand is so unsteady, I can hardly write.'[57] She died on 29 April in her father's arms where, as Stanmore records, 'for hours previously she had lain'. By this time Aberdeen was in office as Foreign Secretary and 'for some days afterwards he shut himself up at the Foreign Office absolutely alone'. He found it impossible to communicate with others in his grief. To old friends like Hudson Gurney, telling them the bare facts of his daughter's illness, he could only say that he could write no more.[58]

Between 1814 and 1828, Aberdeen had held no political office. He had made it clear in the summer of 1814 that he did not wish to continue with a diplomatic career and he did not take advantage of his now secure seat in the Lords to play a prominent part in domestic politics. The increasing responsibilities, problems and anxieties of his private life provide the most obvious explanation for this. During the earlier part of the period too he was actively engaged in many other activities which were in some ways more congenial to him, the

Antiquaries, the Dilettanti, the Elgin Marbles controversy, the British Museum and the Royal Society. And yet there is always an undercurrent in his letters, not only of a lively interest in public affairs, but of a half-concealed desire to play an active role. When the opportunity came to take high office with his friends in 1828 he took it, although private problems still pressed. There must therefore be some further reason for his political eclipse between 1814 and 1828.

It may be relevant that he was on bad terms with the Prince Regent, who became George IV in 1820. Exactly why is not clear. The Prince was a rake but Aberdeen got on well with other rakes. He may have found it harder to forgive the Prince's clumsy attempts to flirt with Catherine to which Stanmore alludes.[59] He disapproved of George's actions at the time of the Queen's Affair in 1820. He thought it likely that Caroline was guilty of most of the charges against her but to publicly parade them could only bring all monarchy into disrepute. He wrote bluntly to Gurney, 'What a strange situation the Queen's Bill [to dissolve her marriage to George] is in! The truth proved by Witnesses unworthy of credit, and those Witnesses impeached by others no better than themselves! Yet I presume no man of common sense can doubt what the real facts of the case are.' But he condemned the 'folly and absurdity' of the ministry in the matter. 'If the Bill does not pass,' he commented, 'as I suppose it will not, and perhaps ought not, we shall fix the Queen firmly on her throne, having first satisfactorily proved her infamous and proclaimed her infamy throughout Europe, which she had not quite succeeded in doing herself.'[60] The Bill passed the Lords by a small majority but its chances of getting through the Commons looked so bad that the government dropped it. Aberdeen himself abstained from either speaking or voting. The antipathy between George and Aberdeen was well known in 1828. Lord Ellenborough remarked that, although George had gone out of his way to conciliate Aberdeen, Aberdeen made no secret of his dislike and distrust. Palmerston noted that the King was 'very cold' to Aberdeen.[61]

Perhaps more important than his estrangement from the Prince was the fact that Aberdeen's own political views were by no means settled at this time. His first marriage had drawn him more clearly into Tory circles than his association with Pitt and Dundas had done, but those who met him were frequently surprised by how radical his views on particular issues were. Sir Robert Wilson, that inveterate Whig, had written in his journal soon after their first meeting in 1813:

By principles Aberdeen belongs to *us*. He is a Liberal politician, and a man of high independent spirit, with a very reasoning mind, in which there is no inextirpable prejudice. I should have thought Lord Grey and he would have been inseparables; and they would have been if accident had favoured nature and brought them more in communication.[62]

Wilson may have been wrong in thinking that Aberdeen would necessarily have agreed with Lord Grey but he was right in identifying his 'independent spirit'. He had a completely cross-bench mind, approaching each problem with an attempt to make a fresh assessment of possible solutions. His conclusions were frequently not those of his friends or political colleagues and what may have been a strength in the man was certainly a weakness in a politician.

Many of his friends continued to be to his left politically, although he did not necessarily agree with all their ideas. In 1811 he promised to help Hudson Gurney with his parliamentary ambitions, although Gurney had mildly embarrassed him by giving him a reputation for 'Jacobinism'. When Gurney was returned at the 1812 election he sent him rather teasing congratulations:

Of course, you would make a quartetto with Burdett Warburton and Cobbett, had these latter worthies succeeded in getting in: as it is I expect to see you a good deal at the Baronet's service. I should not be surprised, however, if when you saw a little 'dessous des cartes', you took quite a contrary turn. If you have a mind to try a revolutionary experiment – à la bonne heure – but if not, you will in time perhaps recollect, that Kings, Lords, and Aristocratical Commons, are as necessary evils, as unprincipled journalists, or jacobin attorneys. However, I know you are truly an honest and an independent man, and your line is therefore interesting. With respect to Burdett, I have met him occasionally in very private society, and have heard him talk a good deal. He is plausible, mild and gentlemanlike, but when pushed, the man is profoundly ignorant.[63]

In 1820, at the time of the Queen's affair, he wrote to Gurney that he had heard that 'my old friend Wilson is your oracle' and 'if you stick to your leader you will have an active time of it'. He supposed Gurney had a commission in the army of 200,000 men whom Wilson had told him some time ago 'was ready, in and about London to carry into effect a summary and radical reform whenever it was ordered to do so'. When this was done he 'as a quiet, pacifick and obedient subject' would solicit Gurney's influence with his general. Aberdeen always declined to be thrown into a panic by the unrest of the post-war years.[64]

His real attitude to reform is summarised in his reply to Gurney as early as 1812 when Gurney asked him for his opinion of the constitutional reforms which Bentinck, another Whiggish reformer, was trying to force on Sicily. He wrote:

You ask me about Sicily – some of the things which have been done, appear to me clearly good, but some are rather doubtful. To talk of giving the British constitution, is quite nonsense: you must first create the people, the state of society, the whole system to which the British Constitution is adapted. Give the people more liberty as you see they can make good use of it – break the power of the nobles – destroy commercial monopoly – introduce justice in taxation – banish venality and corruption from the judicature – all by specific measures as fast as you please but to give them a fine sounding name, will not carry much real good along with it.[65]

The attachment to the idea of practical reforms, the distrust of high-sounding promises, and the belief that reform must come when the time was ripe for it, remained with him all his life and was to surface most clearly during his premiership. But it left him rather puzzled as to how to act after 1815.

Nevertheless he attended parliament regularly, behaved as a government supporter and played a more active role behind the scenes than his infrequent speeches in the Chamber might suggest. When he did speak it was usually on foreign or Scottish affairs. He frequently seems to have come in for reasons of personal loyalty to defend a friend.

In 1815 he came to Castlereagh's defence at the time of Napoleon's escape from Elba. The opposition condemned Castlereagh for having weakly allowed the Tsar to dictate the Treaty of Fontainebleau, which had given Napoleon his miniature kingdom. Castlereagh, said Aberdeen, had hastened to Paris with all possible speed and, although he could not prevent the treaty being concluded, he had insisted upon modifications in very difficult circumstances when every moment was precious. This was an exact statement of the truth,[66] although it was not perhaps quite the defence Castlereagh would have chosen for himself. This scrupulous desire to keep the record straight, when political considerations might have dictated reticence, remained with him all his life and was very conspicuous at the time of the Crimean war.

But his speeches in the Lords in 1816 do not bear out the traditional picture of a man who was so horrified by war in 1813–14 that he saw war itself as intolerable. In March he supported the government in opposing the Duke of Bedford's attack on the size of the military establishment. Britain, he said, could not confine herself to an insular situation. Peace depended on a cordial union between all the great European powers. There was still a threat from France. Britain must play her part in maintaining the balance of power. 'Justice', he remarked significantly, 'was armed.'[67]

A few weeks later he supported the government in rejecting the Duke of Buckingham's motion for an enquiry into the state of Ireland. Aberdeen agreed that something must be done for Ireland although he maintained that parts of the north were more tranquil and prosperous than many parts of England. He thought the revenue laws should be reformed and he favoured Catholic Emancipation, although he warned that Emancipation was no panacea. In an earlier speech he had pressed the need for education in Ireland, drawing on his knowledge of the contrast between County Tyrone and Aberdeenshire. His declaration in favour of Catholic Emancipation offended many of his friends.[68]

Aberdeen's support for the government in 1817 seems to have become a little half-hearted. 1816 was a year of bad harvests and the winter of 1816–17 saw the notorious Spa Fields riot. Aberdeen spoke in support of the Seditious Meetings Bill, which gave the government greater control of public meetings, but only after a long and careful study of the problem. Necessity alone could justify such a measure, he argued, but the government had made a case. The distress was real but to permit anarchy and bloodshed would make the situation worse, not better. He poured scorn on the idea that there was any kind of international conspiracy of the right. Unlike the opposition he could see no connection between events in Britain and Austrian actions in Italy.[69]

The disturbances of 1816–17 were repeated in 1819, culminating in Peterloo and the Six Acts. Aberdeen again took a moderate position. He wrote to Gurney, who was abroad, that he thought that the suspension of Habeas Corpus would be inappropriate, as well as extremely unpopular. Discontent would not disappear until the distress was alleviated but he did not think that that could be achieved by legislation. Of Peterloo he wrote:

The business at Manchester has been unfortunate, the precipitation of the magistrates, although pardonable, has produced unfortunate effects. For now the matter, instead of being left to the ordinary tribunals, seems to be taken up by the opposition as a party question . . . But these Whig Patriots are much mistaken if they think that Mr. Hunt and his friends will accept of their qualified support any longer than it may coincide with their own projects . . . and their objects [are] so obviously destructive of everything like security of property that the immense majority of those who have anything to lose must be unanimous.

He supposed that Gurney was often asked about 'the progress of the Revolution' in England. Many Englishmen expected it too, but 'this is a notion which I can never for an instant entertain; nor even if our difficulties were ten times greater should I see cause to apprehend anything more than momentary disorder and excess.'[70]

Aberdeen in this period took a considerable interest in economic questions and, in February 1819, he was elected as one of the thirteen members of the 'Secret Committee' of the House of Lords, which was to enquire into the resumption of cash payments by the Bank of England – since 1797 the issue of gold coins had been suspended in favour of paper money. Other members of the committee included Harrowby, its chairman, Bathurst and Liverpool. A comparable House of Commons committee included Sir Robert Peel. The Lords committee started taking evidence on 8 February and sat until April. They examined a large number of witnesses, including David Ricardo, and amassed a good deal of written evidence and statistics. His letters show that Aberdeen took an active part in the work of the committee. They reported in May in favour of a phased return to payments in gold. Although they admitted the great practical difficulties they took it as their guiding principle that there should be a return to a 'metallic standard' as soon as possible. They also touched on the specialised question of the relationship of gold and silver coinage, on which Aberdeen was regarded as something of an expert because of his investigations into the coinage of the ancient world.[71] Aberdeen continued to take an interest in the currency problem, which, for all its highly technical nature, was one of the most important issues of the 1820s. The only occasion when he clashed with Liverpool in the Lords was when he objected to the proposal to abolish small denomination notes in Scotland, as was already being done in England. Aberdeen drew attention to the fact that the Scottish banking system was different from, and more stable than, the English.[72] This dislike of English interference in Scottish affairs was to surface more than once in Aberdeen's political career.

It seems probable that Aberdeen was offered an appointment when Liverpool's ministry was reconstituted in 1822. He subsequently wrote to Harriet, 'My dearest you tell me not to regret having missed the tide, which, taken at its height, might have led to fortune. This does not weigh permanently with me. They are only passing regrets of little consequence.'[73] It is possible that Canning offered him the Under-Secretaryship at the Foreign Office in September. He first offered it to Aberdeen's close friend, Lord Binning. Binning declined but on 10 October he wrote a cryptic letter to Canning: 'If the

Doubter's Doubts are at an end by Post time tomorrow, send or make Backhouse send a line direct to the Priory, Stanmore. A friend of his & mine has [been] busy giving him advice that if followed will lead to his acceptance of the proposal.' It is, however, also possible that Aberdeen was the 'friend' who was bringing pressure to bear on Ward, who also declined the job.[74]

Aberdeen could not, however, avoid playing a role when George IV paid his royal visit to Edinburgh in 1822. The whole occasion was stage-managed by Sir Walter Scott. Aberdeen did not try to conceal in his letters to Harriet that he regarded much of it as pure comedy. George's insistence on wearing a kilt (and flesh-coloured tights) struck most contemporary Scotsmen as ridiculous. The kilt was a Highland, not a Lowland, garment and smacked more than a little of 'barbarism'. Aberdeen thought it preposterous and described how at the Levée on 17 August, 'The King himself was in Highland dress, which was absurd enough, as although it is a compliment to one part of the country, it is by no means so the rest; and I suppose he is the first King of Scotland who ever wore it, at least since the times of actual barbarism.' A number of peers appeared in the kilt, to which Aberdeen remarked they had as far as he knew no right, but he determinedly put on breeches. He was equally scathing about the idea of a Peers' Ball. He commented, 'The Peers may unite to support a Throne, or upset a King, but to unite to give a Ball!!!' – although it was a pity he said it to Lord Rosebery before he realised that he was the moving spirit. Some events, such as the grand procession on the 23rd, Aberdeen had to admit went very well. Aberdeen had to read an address from King's College, Aberdeen, because the Chancellor, the Duke of Gordon, was ill. The grand city dinner on the 26th was almost the final straw. Every toast was drunk 'three times three' and Aberdeen complained that he was forced to drink more than a bottle of claret himself.[75]

It was while in Edinburgh that he learnt of Castlereagh's dramatic suicide. He told Harriet that it had cast a 'horrible gloom' over them all because 'with all his imperfections, he was a thorough gentleman, and a most efficient minister'. Although he had seen little of him recently, 'it is quite impossible to forget former intimacy and kindness'. He was the last man of whom he would have expected such an action 'for his coolness and self possession were most remarkable, but it shews that no man is exempt from this calamity'. He found Harriet's later accounts, in which she presumably recounted the gossip, 'very curious'. He had no idea that Castlereagh's mind had been affected for so long and now understood why he had not answered his letters. Harriet attended the funeral in his stead.[76]

During the 1820s Aberdeen spoke mainly on Scottish affairs, except for the occasional intervention on foreign policy. The strait-jacket imposed by Scottish entails, which had proved so inconvenient to Aberdeen himself, was coming to be generally regarded as intolerable. A House of Lords appellate decision which prevented the heir at entail from raising money against future rents – as Aberdeen himself had wished to do in 1810 – still further aggravated the situation. The first measure to relax the strict law of entail was passed in 1821, but it was the second measure, that of 1824, which Aberdeen himself introduced into the Lords, which lay particularly close to his heart. This gave the heir at entail power to commit approximately one-third of the revenues of his estate to provide a life-rent for his wife and to make provision for his lawful children to the equivalent of one year's rent for each child. This, with the proviso that not more than two-thirds of the income of an estate could be committed in this way, was accepted. Aberdeen himself saw quite clearly that the changes he proposed were likely to result eventually in the end of the entail system altogether and he told his friend, John Hope, the Dean of the Faculty of Advocate, that he rejoiced in the prospect. He wrote:

The feudal system has perished, and what remains of it is destined to ultimate extinction . . . provided it is not affected by means of revolution or of measures, inflicting suffering and loss upon multitudes of harmless individuals, can it [the extinction] be regarded as evil? Few will deny that the changes in the position of the great and of the people, which have steadily advanced in the last few centuries, have been attended with advantage . . . Personally, I am much of Gibbon's opinion, that primogeniture is an 'insolent prerogative'; but I am sure that its abolition would at this moment produce mischiefs not to be counterbalanced by any corresponding advantage. It may not always be so. But I must stop, or you will think Hudson Gurney quite justified in styling me 'a Jacobin'.[77]

He was rather glad that his colleagues in the House had not appreciated the probable implications of his measure, otherwise he doubted whether it would have passed.

The previous year Aberdeen had wished to abolish appeals from the Scottish courts to the House of Lords. He argued that the Act of Union had not allowed for such appeals and that the House could very properly decline to hear them. He reminded them that Scots law was not a 'rude and barbarous system', but based on the practice of the most civilised nation in antiquity and he hinted politely that English lawyers had not shown themselves very good at understanding it.[78] Liverpool managed to shelve the whole question for future study, although it had been the embarrassment of too many appeals, which had given Aberdeen the chance to raise the matter.

Aberdeen's interventions on foreign affairs are interesting. His position generally was conservative but he could show occasional flashes of radicalism in foreign, as in domestic affairs. The most striking example of that was his initial support for the cause of Greek nationalism, which is dealt with in the next chapter. For the rest he argued for the *status quo*, but the *status quo* with justice, although he was influenced by his confidence in Austria and a tendency to defend his friends, British or foreign. He rather reluctantly defended Austrian actions against the popular movements in Italy in 1821, pleading that the House should not automatically assume that justice was on the side of the weaker party.[79] He was angered by Ellenborough's suggestion that Britain should offer her mediation and, if it were refused, allow British 'volunteers' to go to Naples. Aberdeen took his stand on Castlereagh's great State Paper of 5 May 1820, which Canning was also to adopt as his own, to deprecate interference in the affairs of other states. Aberdeen, who called it 'one of the wisest and most judicious papers ever issued from the Foreign Office', was one of the first to recognise its critical importance in the evolution of British foreign policy.[80]

Aberdeen also came to Austria's aid in 1824, when Lord Holland attacked the Bill to accept £2,500,000 in full payment of Britain's loans to Austria in 1795 and 1797. He defended Francis and Metternich, pointed out that the loans were mainly to secure British objectives, such as the recovery of the Netherlands from France, and drew on his own experience of 1813 to show that, although the loans were nominally for six millions, exchange difficulties had ensured that Austria would have received little more than three millions in practice.[81]

He clashed again with Ellenborough in 1823, when Ellenborough condemned the French intervention in Spain in support of King Ferdinand VII, and the ineptness of British government policy. Aberdeen defended Wellington's conduct at the Congress of Verona the previous year. He had no sympathy for the French action but he insisted that, in this instance, neutrality was the right policy for Britain. If Wellington had adopted a menacing tone Britain would now be ridiculous and isolated.[82]

Aberdeen's speeches were always brief but they were cogent and effective. He was still a close friend of many leading politicians and it was generally accepted that it was only a matter of time before he would join a ministry.

NOTES

1. Add. MSS 43195, Howley to Aberdeen, 1 Feb. 1814; Howley Papers 2186A, Aberdeen to Howley, 16 Feb. 1814. Robert, who was at the Hague, got a message to his brother, Bathurst Papers, 57/7, Clancarty to Bathurst, 26 Jan. 1814.
2. Harrowby MSS vol. xiv, ff. 29–30, Aberdeen to Harrowby, 1 Mar. 1814; Add. MSS 43225, Aberdeen to Abercorn, 29 Dec. 1813.
3. Harrowby MSS vol. xiv, ff. 11–14, Aberdeen to Harrowby, 23 Sept. 1813.
4. Add. MSS 43225, Abercorn to Aberdeen, 28 Apr. 1814; Stanmore, p. 66.
5. Add. MSS 43225, Aberdeen to Abercorn, 18 Apr., 9 May 1814.
6. Add. MSS 43209, Aberdeen to Robert, 9 June 1814.
7. Add. MSS 43209, Aberdeen to Robert, 25 June 1814; HH 1/29, Aberdeen to Abercorn, 15 Oct., 6 Nov. 1814.
8. Add. MSS 43209, Aberdeen to Robert, 9 June 1814.
9. Add. MSS 43209, Aberdeen to Robert, 10, 25 June 1814.
10. Stanmore (proofs) p. 51, quoted Iremonger, p. 95; Add. MSS 43209, Aberdeen to Robert, 25 June, 5 July, 11 Aug. 1814.
11. Add. MSS 43209, Aberdeen to Robert, 10, 25 June, 5 July 1814, 13 May 1815.
12. HH 1/29, Aberdeen to Abercorn, 4, 17 Sept., 15 Oct. 1814.
13. Add.MSS 43223, Aberdeen to Alexander, 17 Nov. 1810.
14. Stanmore, p. 66; Vere Foster, p. 405.
15. Stanmore, p. 67.
16. HH 1/29, Aberdeen to Abercorn, 17 Oct. 1815, 31 Jan. 1816.
17. HH 1/29, Aberdeen to Abercorn, 10, 21 Dec. 1817, 4 Jan. 1818.

18. HH 1/29, Aberdeen to Abercorn, 26 Nov. 1817, Abercorn to Aberdeen, 10 Dec. 1817, Add. MSS Aberdeen to Abercorn, 18 January 1818.
19. Stanmore, p. 67; Elliott, p. 1.
20. Gurney Papers RQC 334/38, Aberdeen to Gurney, 29 Aug. /39, 21 Sept., /40, 19 Oct. 1818.
21. HH 1/29, Aberdeen to Abercorn, 15 Dec. 1815.
22. HH 1/29, Aberdeen to Abercorn, 18 Oct., 21 Dec. 1817.
23. Gurney Papers, RQC 334/39, Aberdeen to Gurney, 21 Sept. 1818.
24. HH 1/30, Aberdeen to Harriet, 26 Sept. 1821.
25. HH 1/30, Aberdeen to Harriet, 31 Aug., 8, 16, 17 Sept. 1822.
26. HH 1/30, Aberdeen to Harriet, 27 Sept. 1821, 7 Sept. 1822.
27. HH 1/30, Aberdeen to Harriet, 27, 29 Sept., 5, 6, 12 Oct. 1821, 3, 4 Sept. 1822, HH 1/29, Aberdeen to Lady Haddo, 26 Jan., 6 Feb., 27 June 1847.
28. Add. MSS 43224, Aberdeen to Alexander, 8 Oct. 1812; HH 1/30, Aberdeen to Harriet, 'Thursday' [1819].
29. HH 1/30, Aberdeen to Harriet, 29 Aug. 1822.
30. HH 1/21, Alice to Aberdeen, n.d. The children were still on excellent terms much later, cf. HH 1/28, Abercorn (James) to Aberdeen, 13 Oct. 1824, telling a rather similar story.
31. Add. MSS J. P. Kemble to Aberdeen, 6 July 1818; HH 1/30, Aberdeen to Jane, 'Tuesday', Harriet to Jane, 16 June, Harriet to Jane n.d. [1818] 'poor Caro is worse . . . I am afraid she will never be really strong again.'
32. HH 1/30, Harriet to Jane, n.d. Mrs Iremonger was misled, possibly by the very dubious dating, into thinking that this letter referred to Jane's own illness, in which case it would have been, as she supposed, a very strange and insensitive letter.
33. HH 1/30, Aberdeen to Harriet, 5 Apr., 'Monday', 'Tuesday' (all from Woburn), 1 July, 4, 11, 13 Sept. 1819.
34. HH 1/30, Aberdeen to Harriet, 'Tuesday', numbered '24'.
35. HH 1/30, Aberdeen to Harriet, 'Tuesday', numbered '24'.
36. HH 1/30, e.g. 'Thursday', 'Thursday night' (both from the Priory), 'Saturday', 'Tuesday ½ past 5' (both from Argyll House).
37. HH 1/30, Aberdeen to Harriet, 'Tuesday', numbered '24', 'Tuesday morning', Argyll House [1819], 20, 21 Sept., 18, 20, 29 Oct., 'Wednesday 6 o'clock', Priory, 'Monday, 22nd', Argyll House [1820].
38. Add. MSS 43230, Ashburnham to Aberdeen, 25 Nov. 1818.
39. HH 1/30, Aberdeen to Harriet, 3 Oct. 1821, 8 Sept. 1822.
40. HH 1/30, Aberdeen to Harriet, 25 Sept. 1821, 1, 11, 17 Sept. 1822.
41. HH 1/30, Aberdeen to Harriet, 21, 23 Sept., 2 Oct. 1821, 1, 10 Sept. 1822.
42. HH 1/30, Aberdeen to Harriet, 28, 29 Sept., 2, 5, 7, 9, 22 Oct. 1821.
43. HH 1/30, Aberdeen to Harriet, 30 Aug., 9, 20 Sept. 1822.
44. HH 1/30, Aberdeen to Harriet, 3, 4, 6 Sept. 1822.
45. The letters are in HH 1/14.
46. Stanmore, p. 69. Alice's journal is in Add. MSS 43348. There are further accounts in her letters to Mrs Gale, HH 1/14.
47. HH 1/30, e.g, there is a delightful letter to Jane of 4 Mar. 1820, beginning 'Madame' and thanking her in French for a gift of violets, cf. Aberdeen to Jane, 3 Sept. 1822, encouraging her to continue her study of Italian.
48. HH 1/30, Aberdeen to Harriet, 7, 10, 11, 15, 26, 31 Jan. 1825. His botanical notebooks are in Add. MSS 43349.

49. Gurney Papers, RQC 334/53, Aberdeen to Gurney, 21 Mar. 1825; Add. MSS 43231, Ashburnham to Aberdeen. 1, 13 June 1825; HH 1/14, Alice to Mrs Gale, Avignon, 20 Apr. [1825]
50. Gurney Papers, RQC 334/53, Aberdeen to Gurney, 21 Mar. 1825.
51. Gurney Papers, RQC 334/54 Aberdeen to Gurney, 10 Nov. 1825.
52. HH 1/14, Alice to Mrs Gale, 19 Dec. 1825.
53. Gurney Papers, RQC 334/55, Aberdeen to Gurney, 30 Dec. 1825, HH 1/30, Aberdeen to Harriet, 13 Dec. 1825, 24, 26, 29, 31 Jan., 3, 5, 7, 9, 12, 15 Feb. 1826.
54. HH 1/30, Aberdeen to Harriet, 24 Feb. 1826.
55. HH 1/14, Alice to Mrs Gale, 3 Mar. 1836.
56. Gurney Papers, RQC 334/56, Aberdeen to Gurney, 6 Nov. 1827.
57. HH 1/14, Alice to Mrs Gale, 21 Mar., 4 Apr. 1829.
58. Stanmore, p. 107; Gurney Papers RQC 334/58, Aberdeen to Gurney, 30 Dec. 1827, /61, 9 Dec. 1829.
59. Stanmore, pp. 14–5.
60. Gurney Papers, RQC 334/48, Aberdeen to Gurney, 16 Oct. 1820.
61. Ellenborough, *Political Diary*, vol. 1, p. 173 (22 July 1828); Bulwer, vol. 1, p. 285, Palmerston's Journal, 12 June 1828.
62. Wilson, *Private Diary*, vol. 2, p. 238 (28 Nov. 1813).
63. Gurney Papers RQC 334/28, Aberdeen to Gurney, 16 Jan. 1810, /30, 7 Jan. 1811, /33, 21 Oct. 1812.
64. Gurney Papers RQC 334/48, Aberdeen to Gurney, 16 Oct. 1820.
65. Gurney Papers, RQC 334/33, Aberdeen to Gurney, 21 Oct. 1812.
66. *Hansard*, 579–80 (12 Apr. 1815); cf Aberdeen's contemporary accounts to Abercorn, Add. MSS 43225, 8, 18 Apr. 1814.
67. *Hansard*, XXXIII, 168–70, (12 Mar. 1816).
68. *Hansard*, XXXIII, 821–2, 170 (2 Apr. 12 Mar. 1816); Add. MSS 43225, f. 157, Aberdeen to Harriet, 'Monday' [?1816].
69. *Hansard*, XXV, 1263–5 (25 Mar. 1817).
70. Gurney Papers, RQC 334/43, Aberdeen to Gurney, 13 Oct. 1819.
71. PP, III (1819) 363; Add. MSS 43230, Harrowby to Aberdeen, n.d. [May 1819]; Harrowby MSS, vol. xiv, ff. 5–6, Aberdeen to Harrowby, 'Sunday night' [21 May 1819]; Add. MSS 43225, Aberdeen to Harriet, 'Tuesday' [April 1819].
72. *Hansard*, XIV, 1393 (17 Mar. 1826).
73. Add. MSS 43225, Aberdeen to Harriet, 19 Aug. 1822.
74. Canning Papers, 66, Canning to Binning, 14 Sept. 1822, Binning to Canning, 17 Sept., 10 Oct. 1822, Canning to Ward, 20 Sept. 1822.
75. Add. MSS 43225, Aberdeen to Harriet, 10, 13, 14, 16, 17, 19, 23, 24, 25 Aug. 1822.
76. Add. MSS 43225, Aberdeen to Harriet, 16, 17, 18, 20, 23 Aug. 1822.
77. Aberdeen's drafts are in Add. MSS 43231, ff. 92–9; *Hansard*, XI, 959 (1 June 1824); PP I (1824) 437, 443; Add. MSS 43202, Aberdeen to Hope, June 1824.
78. *Hansard*, IX, 1328 (30 June 1823).
79. *Hansard*, IV, 1056 (2 Mar. 1821). He admitted to Harriet that it was 'up hill work' to defend Austria, Add. MSS 43225, f. 156, 'Tuesday'.
80. *Hansard*, IV, 1472 (27 Mar. 1821).
81. *Hansard*, X, 883 (11 Mar. 1824).
82. *Hansard*, VIII, 1220 (24 Apr. 1823).

CHAPTER TWELVE

Wellington's government

In February 1827 Liverpool suffered a paralytic stroke which brought his long administration to an end. After extremely complex manoeuvres, Canning reconstituted the government.[1] Two stories circulated among the London gossips, one that Canning had asked Aberdeen to join his Cabinet and he had refused, and the other that Aberdeen was so angry that he had not been made an offer that he opposed the government. Stanmore believed the first[2] but neither the Aberdeen nor the Canning Papers give a clear answer. Canning may have sounded Aberdeen out through their mutual friend, Binning, but relations between Aberdeen and Canning had long been ambivalent. The Sicilian offer of 1808 had ended in a near quarrel and Canning had been sharply critical of Aberdeen's conduct in 1813.[3] If Canning did make him an offer in 1822, Aberdeen turned it down. Even when Aberdeen wanted Canning to serve on a committee to erect a memorial to John Kemble in Westminster Abbey in 1823, he approached him through Binning, although he spoke in the most flattering terms of him as 'the most cultivated statesman of the age'.[4]

Aberdeen's friend, J. W. Ward, now Lord Dudley, did accept the Foreign Office in 1827, although his reason for doing so was extraordinary. He told Aberdeen that he had taken it until the end of the session although he knew it was beyond him because he had a 'curiosity . . . to have a peep at official life. In three months I cannot do *much* harm to the publick, or to myself'. He added, 'I hope you are not going into opposition, tho' considering who are gone out, I am not sanguine as to the support the new govt. is to receive from you.'[5] The allusion was to the Duke of Wellington and Sir Robert Peel, with whom Aberdeen was becoming increasingly associated, and Dudley had probably put his finger on the real reason why Aberdeen would not have wished to have joined Canning, even if he received an invitation. In May Aberdeen made it quite clear in the Lords that he could give the government only qualified support. Rather surprisingly, he put it on the grounds of Catholic Emancipation. He had voted with the minority in favour of Sir Francis Burdett's measure in 1825. He accepted, he said, that Liverpool could not make it government policy because his Cabinet was divided but Canning's colleagues were all 'Catholics' and it was hypocritical for them to continue to make it an open question.[6]

Canning died in August and his government was succeeded by the short-lived ministry of Aberdeen's old friend, Frederick Robinson, now Viscount Goderich. Aberdeen was rightly sceptical about Goderich's staying-power. He wrote to Gurney, 'Robinson is doubtless a most excellent, honest, fair and straightforward fellow. Having known him for thirty years, I cannot well be deceived in his character; but with all his merits, I confess that I never expected to see him in his present situation.' He had, he thought, 'an oddish jumble of colleagues'.[7] Goderich in fact resigned without meeting Parliament. Politics now seemed to be in a state of complete deadlock. Aberdeen at first expected Goderich to be succeeded by an administration 'essentially Whig' and was much amused when, as he told Gurney 'It is clear that they must be at a great loss for a Minister, for a man accosted me in the street, and not only asked me if I was not to be Premier, but said he thought I should make the best!!!'[8]

The King sent for the Duke of Wellington. He was expected to try to re-form Liverpool's administration, which had shed its more conservative members when Canning became Prime Minister, but, to their indignation, most of the ultras were not asked back and many Canningites were retained. Some even thought that the Whig leader, Lord Grey, would be asked to join but, apart from the King's objections, Wellington had no intention of trying to manage a coalition as broadly based as that. Even the absorption of the Canningites proved, in the end, impossible, although Aberdeen thought that their leader, William Huskisson, was a very able man.[9] A rising young politician, Edward Law, Lord Ellenborough, who had become Lord Privy Seal, recorded their tussles with glee. At their first Cabinet meeting they exhibited all the politeness of men who had just fought a duel. A little later, in April, the Lord Chancellor, Lord Lyndhurst, remarked to him, 'We should have no Cabinets after dinner. We all drink too much wine and are not civil to each other.'[10] The quarrel, which had provoked Lyndhurst's comment, had been about the Foreign Enlistment Bill but it could equally well have been about the Corn duty, the Test and Corporation Act, or the disfranchisement of Penrhyn and East Retford for corruption – all burning issues of the day. In May the Canningites resigned.

Wellington had written to Aberdeen, who was at Bentley Priory, on 15 January, inviting him to join the ministry and assuring him that the Catholic question would still remain 'open', with every minister free to express his views publicly. Aberdeen immediately expressed his willingness to join the admin-istration on those terms and came to London the next day to see the Duke.[11] The first possibility was that Aberdeen would become Lord Lieutenant of Ire-land in place of Lord Anglesey.[12] As a moderate 'Catholic', with first–hand knowledge of Ireland through his administration of the Abercorn estates he seemed an ideal choice but Anglesey chose not to resign. The next possibility was the Foreign Office but, unexpectedly, Dudley too elected to remain and as his retention was considered important by his fellow Canningites, he could not be displaced. In the end Aberdeen became Chancellor of the Duchy of Lancaster with the understanding that he would assist Dudley at the Foreign

Office. Dudley accepted his help willingly enough and put up with the unsolicited advice of Lord Ellenborough.

When the Canningites resigned in May, Aberdeen succeeded Dudley at the Foreign Office according to the previous understanding. Ellenborough was furious. He passionately coveted the Foreign Office himself.[13] Ironically, he complained of Aberdeen's lack of experience, although his own experience was limited to being married to Lord Castlereagh's sister and having visited Vienna during the famous Congress. He convinced himself that Wellington really wished to have him as Foreign Secretary but had been compelled, for quite unexplained reasons, to put up with Aberdeen. Nothing in the Wellington Papers bears this out. They show clearly that Wellington trusted Aberdeen and distrusted Ellenborough as a rash and unreliable man.

Ellenborough's almost obsessive jealousy would be of no significance but for the fact that he kept a very detailed diary, which was published as early as 1881, and has always been regarded as an invaluable source of information on Wellington's administration. From May 1828 onwards he kept up a constant stream of vituperation against Aberdeen's handling of foreign affairs, which only began to slacken in 1829 when Ellenborough himself became absorbed in Indian affairs. Sometimes his criticisms find their mark. Aberdeen in his despatches, he said, 'fell into the same fault he had imputed to Dudley, that of writing an essay', and this is true. Aberdeen was inclined to write a scholarly analysis of a situation, rather than a directive to action. But many of Ellenborough's criticisms were based on the simple principle that Aberdeen must be wrong and he alternately accused him of weakness and rashness. In a famous passage he complained, 'It is thus, by little errors, that Aberdeen will let down the diplomacy of the country.' A few days earlier he had written, 'I had some conversation with the Duke on the subject of our diplomacy, and he agreed with me in thinking it a nullity. Why, then, did he make Aberdeen———?' Again, he wrote, 'Had some conversation with Arbuthnot. Told him I was sure the Duke would not be able to keep Aberdeen. That he would find nothing was done very ill, but nothing well, and our diplomacy was let down.'[14] When these comments were published, after the Crimean War, they accorded so well with the popular view of Aberdeen's weakness that they were easily accepted as objective assessments.

Aberdeen was doubly unlucky in that the other important book relating to this period, which was published in the 1880s, was Lane-Poole's *Life* of Stratford Canning. A substantial part of the first volume was devoted to a study of Canning's mission to Turkey and Greece, which ended with his angry resignation and his replacement in 1829, by Aberdeen's brother, Robert. Canning had a genuine grievance against Aberdeen, the validity of which Aberdeen privately acknowledged, although he could never do so publicly. Lane-Poole presented the case for Canning's defence which inevitably cast Aberdeen as the villain. Lane-Poole's account, taken with Ellenborough's, all seemed to add up to the picture of a man whose weakness and almost predetermined failure could and should have been obvious from the beginning. This was certainly not the view of the contemporaries but, because no detailed study of the foreign policy of the Wellington administration has ever been published, the partiality of Ellenborough's and Canning's accounts has not been tested and they have remained a virtually unquestioned part of the myth.

Looking back, Aberdeen saw the early months of 1828, when he held only the honorific office of Chancellor of the Duchy of Lancaster, as the lull before the storm. Here there is no reason to doubt Ellenborough's story that Aberdeen gave his Chancellor's robes to his successor with the proviso only that he would claim them back if he ever had the 'good luck' to return to that office.[15] The lull was only relative. In domestic affairs it was an uncomfortable and strained interlude.

At this time Ellenborough and Aberdeen were friendly and Ellenborough throws light on Aberdeen's attitude. On 22 January, after going together to Royal Lodge, Windsor, to receive their seals of office, they went to dine with the Duke at Apsley House. The meal was not cordial and Ellenborough recorded, 'Aberdeen . . . observed, as well as myself, the extreme coldness of our new allies. He does not like our position at all.'[16]

The first serious domestic embarrassment came when Lord John Russell introduced a motion into the Commons to repeal the Test and Corporation Acts, which obliged the holders of certain offices to take communion according to the rites of the Church of England. On the evening of 20 February, after. a Cabinet dinner at Lord Dudley's, Aberdeen, Ellenborough, Huskisson and Charles Grant remained behind after their colleagues had left and discussed whether the repeal should be adopted as a government measure.[17] It was not a clear–cut issue. Dissenters had been protected from the operation of the Acts for many years by the passage of annual Indemnity Acts and some feared that repeal would only obscure and delay the larger question of Catholic Emancipation. The Cabinet decided on 25 February to oppose Russell's measure but the following day, to the Duke's great indignation, the government was beaten in the Commons, largely by the defection of their own friends. The government made the best of a bad job and adopted the measure itself.

The next crisis, over the sliding scale on corn, almost broke up the government altogether. Aberdeen and some others originally supported the Duke in wanting to keep the duty high but Wellington miscalculated his strength. First Huskisson and then Grant pressed for modifications. Aberdeen, together with Peel and Bathurst, advised a compromise and became annoyed by the Duke's intransigence. Aberdeen was convinced that the government would fall but in the end the Duke accepted the compromise proposal. Aberdeen made a gallant but ineffective attempt to raise the duty on oats.[18]

It was the dispute over the re-allocation of the seats of Penrhyn and East Retford which drove out the Canningites and led to Aberdeen's succession to the Foreign Office. The remaining Cabinet ministers were rather relieved to see the Canningites, Dudley, Palmerston, Huskisson, Grant and Herries, go. Ellenborough recorded of the next Cabinet meeting, 'We all seemed to feel comfortable at being so few.'[19] Ellenborough spoke quite openly to Aberdeen of his own disappointment. Aberdeen made a soothing answer and even spoke of the Foreign Office being rather 'a bore'. Ellenborough got the impression – the wish perhaps being father to the thought – that Aberdeen did not mean to stay at the Foreign Office but to transfer quickly to a non-departmental office like Lord Privy Seal. It was Harriet who disillusioned him by revealing that Aberdeen had lent the Foreign Secretary's official residence to Sir George Murray, the new Colonial Secretary, since they meant to remain at Argyll House. Ellenborough realised 'should I succeed, it would be very awkward for me to put him out'.[20]

The Cabinet reshuffle raised one major question in an unexpected and acute form, Catholic Emancipation. William Vesey Fitzgerald became President of the Board of Trade and, according to the law of the period, had to seek re-election. Fitzgerald sat for County Clare and no particular difficulty was anticipated, but Daniel O'Connell took advantage of the fact that although a practising Catholic could not sit in the House of Commons (because of the oaths requiring him to renounce the Pope and Catholic doctrines), there was nothing to stop him standing for election. O'Connell won the election. Both Wellington and Peel had been 'Protestants', that is to say opposed to Emancipation, but faced with a real possibility of civil war in Ireland, Wellington opted for the lesser evil and introduced the Catholic Emancipation measure.

The question posed no problem of conscience for Aberdeen. He had been publicly committed to Emancipation since 1816. But he agreed with his Cabinet colleagues that it must be accompanied with a further restriction of the Irish franchise and the county franchise was raised to £10. Ellenborough thought his agreement was reluctant[21] but Aberdeen had been in favour of some such measure in 1825. He had written to Gurney at the time he supported Burdett's Catholic Relief Bill that the Irish Catholics were very susceptible to pressure. 'Your Irish Catholics', he said, 'are a sad race.' Emancipation would have to be accompanied by the abolition of the forty-shilling freeholder and the raising of the franchise to £5 or £10. He added, 'Universal suffrage might do nearly as well, but the present system is the worst that could possibly be devised.'[22] This apparent paradox in fact represented Aberdeen's considered opinion for many years about the British as well as the Irish franchise. The existing franchise secured the worst of all possible worlds. It did not confine the franchise to those who were too independent to be easily bribed or intimidated, nor did it extend it to so many that bribery and intimidation became impracticable.

Aberdeen supported the Duke in his battle for Catholic Emancipation but throughout this period he stuck fairly closely to his last, which was foreign affairs. There was more than enough there to occupy any man – a war between Russia and Turkey which seemed likely to signal the final collapse of the Ottoman Empire, civil war in the Iberian Peninsula where Britain had long-standing trading and strategic interests, the French intervention in Algeria, the French and Belgian revolutions of 1830 and even disputes with the United States which foreshadowed the more acute problems of the 1840s.

The Near-Eastern crisis had begun seven years earlier with the Greek risings of 1821. It was to result in the creation of a small independent Greek state in the Morea and the islands in 1830, but it was far from clear in the early days of the revolts that this was the probable, or even the intended, outcome. Few things were worse understood in the west than Greek objectives in the 1820s. Aberdeen, with his first-hand knowledge of the area, probably came a little nearer the truth than many.

The Ottoman Empire had replaced the Byzantine as the dominant power in the region in the fifteenth century. The harsh, but not altogether unjust, judgement of a modern historian, to which Aberdeen would probably have subscribed, was that 'the Turkish empire had never been more than a settlement of military nomads, without political originality or civilized traditions, in the ruins of the fallen power of Byzantium'.[23] The weakness of the Ottoman empire had been revealed to Europe by its lack of success against the Russians in the wars of 1768–74 and 1787–92. From that time, the possibility of a Russian take-over of the Ottoman empire existed and was generally judged to be unacceptable by the rest of Europe. But what was the alternative? By the end of the nineteenth century, men like Gladstone would advocate the creation of independent national states. But this was not the solution that occurred to men, including the oppressed Christians of the Ottoman empire, at the beginning of the century. They looked to the revival of a 'Greek' empire. It must be remembered that the test of being 'Greek' was not ethnic, or even linguistic; it was religious, being a member of the Greek Orthodox Church. Greeks were spread all over the Ottoman Empire. They controlled most of its trade and they held vital positions in its administration. The Ottoman Empire seemed unable to reform itself and the idea of an energetic and organised group within the empire taking over the empty shell was by no means an impossible one. The first impulse came from what might be called the Greeks of the dispersion, merchants who were heading often lucrative and successful enterprises from Russian and French ports. Some of them formed secret societies, of which the most famous was the *Philike Hetaireia*, founded in Odessa in 1814. The idea that a modern Greek state would be a resurrection of ancient Greece, the Greece of Homer and Pericles, was almost entirely a western concept, immediately attractive to men educated in the classics and made popular by a few gifted writers like Byron, but it would have had very little meaning for most of the men actually concerned with the early days of the Greek revolt.

The Greek opportunity seemed to arrive when Ali Pasha of Janina rebelled against the Sultan and pinned down a considerable number of Turkish troops in northern Greece. The *Philike Hetaireia* engineered a rising in Moldavia and Wallachia, under Alexander Hypselantes. That the Danube, rather than Greece, should have been chosen for the initial attempt illustrates the point that this was an empirewide rebellion and not primarily concerned with setting up a Greek national state. But it was ill-chosen. The rising was put down and Hypselantes fled to Austria.

The Turkish authorities were understandably nervous and in the spring of 1821 they ordered the Greeks of the Morea to hand in their weapons. The Greeks rose and the insurrection soon degenerated into a frenzy of killing. As a modern historian, William St Clair, grimly puts it, 'The Turks of Greece left few traces.'[24] In a very short time the Greeks of the Morea massacred in the region of 20,000 Turks in the countryside and in the Turkish quarters of the towns, mostly families who had lived there for generations and who, in all but the critical matter of religion, were indistinguishable from the Greeks themselves. The Turks quickly exacted a savage revenge, although not on the main perpetrators of the outrages. The Greek Patriarch, Gregorios, was hanged in Constantinople on Easter Day. Prominent Greeks were put to death all over the empire and Moslems were encouraged to attack the Greek communities not only in Constantinople, but also in Smyrna, Rhodes, Cyprus and elsewhere. The Turkish massacres of the Greeks, particularly in Constantinople and Smyrna, were much more visible to western observers than the Greek massacre of the Turks of the Morea had been but it was not until after the Turkish massacre of the Greeks on the island of Chios in 1822 that there was a general public reaction in favour of the Greeks in England.

Earlier, in the autumn of 1821, a rather obscure classical scholar, Dr Lemprière, appealed for subscriptions to provide financial help for the Greeks. 'Athenian' Aberdeen was an obvious man to approach and Aberdeen willingly contributed. Perhaps he remembered how he had written in his journal eighteen years before, 'It was among the barren Rocks and Shores of Attica, that I first learnt that Patriotism was inherent in every bosom and the produce of every soil – that not the sword, nor even the lapse of slow consuming time can destroy the vital spark of that patriotic flame which glows in the breasts of all mankind.'[25] His subscription received some publicity and horrified his friends in the government. They saw the Greek revolt as part of a general pattern of revolutionary outbreaks which had already manifested itself in Italy, Spain and Germany. Many of the 'volunteers' who went to Greece had taken part in these risings and established governments saw them almost as a kind of 'Rent-a-mob'.[26] It is true that most of them were very little use to the Greeks when they got there. Even more, the government was concerned with the dangerous international implications of the outbreak of serious troubles in a sensitive area, and they feared that the Tsar, who had already shown a disturbing eagerness to intervene everywhere as the saviour of conservative Europe, would have yet another excuse to move.

His close friend, Bathurst, who was then Colonial Secretary, took it upon himself to curb Aberdeen's enthusiasm. He appealed to him on two grounds. First, the British government had declared itself neutral and for a government supporter to come out so openly for one side was a kind of censure on the government, which the opposition would exploit. He reminded him that the Greek cause was supported by 'every Jacobin' in France and England. This alone might not have convinced Aberdeen, who was used to being called 'a Jacobin' by now. But he could hardly ignore the other grave evidence which Bathurst placed before him. The government was not so ignorant as the general public of the Greek share of the atrocities. They had an excellent 'listening post' in the Ionian Islands, which they had retained in 1815. Bathurst very confidentially sent to Aberdeen reports of the horrifying events which followed the surrender of Tripolitsa, the Turkish headquarters in the Morea, to the Greeks. Although the Turks thought they had surrendered under safe conduct:

a dreadful slaughter commencing, many thousands were massacred indiscriminately. But the most terrific of all scenes was reserved for the following day, when about 3,000 souls, chiefly women and children, were conducted out of the town and from the camp where they had been staying for two days and led to a sort of gorge outside the town, where they were all stripped naked and most horribly butchered: the bellies of the pregnant women were ripped open, their bodies dreadfully mangled, their heads struck off and placed on the bodies of dogs, whilst the dogs' heads were placed on theirs, and also on their private parts.

In addition, the Jewish inhabitants of Tripolitsa, a considerable colony of men, women and children, were tortured to make them reveal their wealth, and many of them burnt alive. The testimony was the more convincing because it came from Thomas Gordon of Cairncross, a neighbour of Aberdeen's, who had been one of the first Britons to go out to aid the Greek cause. He had fled to Corfu. 'Will you', asked Bathurst, 'subscribe to a cause you see your namesake and countryman has abandoned as too disgraceful to belong to?'[27]

It was almost gilding the lily also to warn Aberdeen that the Greeks of the Morea 'have no steady notions whatever of any future principle or government, their thoughts running wholely and solely on plunder and savage revenge' and that none of the funds collected to help the Greek cause had reached their intended destination. They had all 'stuck fast to some other hands'. Aberdeen was shaken and even offered to act as an intermediary to warn other potential sympathisers, including Lord Lansdowne, that things were not all they seemed.[28] Aberdeen did not join the London Greek Committee, established in March 1823, which was to send Byron to Greece. In fact, the London Committee generally attracted men on the political left – the Benthamite influence was strong – and conservative England remained very cautious about the Greek cause.

The government strove for neutrality. Castlereagh aligned himself with the Austrians, who also feared Russian intervention. Towards the end of November 1821 he drafted a despatch to the British Ambassador in St Petersburg, meant for the Tsar's eyes, in which he counselled Alexander not to give his support to the Greek rebels. Alexander was in a dilemma. On the one hand, he was now the embodiment of the Holy Alliance, committed to the suppression of all rebellions against lawful sovereigns; on the other, he was the champion of the Greek Christians against the oppression of the Moslem Turks. Both Castlereagh and Metternich hoped that this indecision would prevent him from taking any action at all.

Castlereagh consulted Aberdeen about this despatch since Aberdeen was both an expert on Greece and familiar with Alexander's character. Up to a point Aberdeen agreed with Castlereagh and even reinforced his arguments. Since the Tsar saw himself as the 'preserver of tranquillity in Europe', he suggested that they should warn him that, if he became embroiled in the Levant, this might provide the opportunity for revolutionary outbreaks in the West. Castlereagh was struck by this argument and incorporated it in his despatch. But after this, Aberdeen parted company with Castlereagh. He was pessimistic about the chances of restraining the Tsar and felt that it would be difficult to oppose him. He feared that the Tsar would intervene mainly to further Russian ambitions, but:

The existence of the Greek Insurrection would give an entirely new character to a Turkish war. It would no longer be a dispute between Governments for frontiers or provinces, but the cause itself would be in a measure sanctified . . . The attempt of any Government in Europe to support the Turkish power for the avowed purpose of riveting the chains of their unhappy Christian subjects would scarcely be tolerated.

Aberdeen did not cherish romantic illusions about the Greeks as the heirs of ancient Greece. He said bluntly, 'when we hear of the descendants of the ancient Greeks, we hear of that which has little reality. The Christian population of Greece is a bastard and mongrel breed derived from many sources – Romans, Sclavonians, Gauls, Catalans, Venetians, and others.' But, at the same time, they were Christians, quickwitted, and anxious to improve their lot. Recently, there had been a considerable increase in both wealth and education. In western Europe this would tend to 'modify the most arbitrary power' but the dead hand of the Turks had prevented any natural evolution. It was not reasonable to suppose, as Castlereagh suggested, that they would be willing to wait for 'Time and Providence' to improve their lot. 'Having personally witnessed their condition', Aberdeen wrote, 'I can have no hesitation in thinking them fully justified in using every possible means to shake off the horrible yoke under which they groan.' There would, he admitted, be cause for alarm if the Greeks gained their freedom with Russian help and the cause 'was made subservient to the aggrandisement of this already colossal power'. For this very reason he thought that Britain should play a part in bringing about a settlement.[29]

This was not what Castlereagh wished to hear and he made it clear that he had no intention of joining in any scheme for the regeneration of Greece. His reply was rather sarcastic. He would, he said, prefer to follow the instructions of a 'Friend and Philosopher' on such subjects than those of a 'mongrel minister' in St Petersburg, who was intent on subverting the Turkish Empire, but Aberdeen would not be surprised to hear that he did not intend to employ his time in Downing Street in 'such portentous Experiments, especially in an Age, when half the World is at Sea in search of the means of self-government'.[30] The 'mongrel minister' was Count Capodistrias, born in Corfu in 1776, who had entered the Russian service in 1807. He had been at the Tsar's headquarters after the battle of Leipzig and Aberdeen had come to know him during the complicated negotiations with Switzerland, for which Capodistrias had been responsible. Britain had some reason to be grateful to Capodistrias because he had strongly advocated that the Ionian Islands should remain under British protection after 1815 but, in the 1820s, this came to be tinged with the suspicion that Capodistrias meant to use the islands as the nucleus of a free Greece. From 1816 until 1822 he acted as joint Russian Foreign Minister with Nesselrode but, in the latter year, he resigned because of Alexander's refusal to support the Greeks. He returned to Greece in January 1822 and was to be an important figure there during Aberdeen's tenure of the Foreign Office.

Canning, for all his supposed sympathy with national movements, was as pragmatic in his approach as Castlereagh had been but, in 1823, he was compelled to recognise the Greeks as belligerents in order to protect British shipping in the area. The Greeks were encouraged by this to ask for British protection in the summer of 1825. By this time their situation had deteriorated. The Sultan, Mahmud II, had reluctantly called for the help of his powerful vassal, Mehemet Ali, Pasha of Egypt. Mehemet Ali had despatched his son, Ibrahim, who had quickly subdued Crete and, in February 1825, landed on the mainland. The first British response was not encouraging. The government reaffirmed their neutrality and their prohibition (not always obeyed) of British subjects taking part in the war. The Greeks then made overtures to the Russians. Canning saw an opportunity to deliver a body blow to the Congress System by concluding a bilateral agreement with Russia and, more importantly, to limit Russia's freedom of action by binding her to a previous agreement with Britain. The Duke of Wellington was despatched to St Petersburg nominally to congratulate the new Tsar, Nicholas I, on his accession, but really to open a negotiation. The choice of envoy did not suggest enthusiasm for the Greek cause. Wellington believed that the stability of Europe demanded the preservation intact of the Turkish empire and, if this involved the sacrifice of the Greeks, that was a regrettable necessity of policy.

The outcome was the Protocol of St Petersburg of April 1826, by which the two Powers were to offer their mediation to the Porte. They proposed that Greece should remain a dependency of the Porte, paying an annual tribute, but that the Greeks should have control, with certain reservations, of their internal government. To prevent future collisions of interest the Greeks should buy out all Turkish property 'on the Continent of Greece, or in the Islands'. Wellington showed himself anything but an alert diplomatist in allowing the insertion of the third article. This bound Britain and Russia, whether or not the Turks accepted their mediation, to consider these terms 'as the basis of any reconciliation to be effected by their intervention, whether in concert or separately, between the Porte and the Greeks'. While binding Russia to work for a particular solution of the Greek problem, it also gave a certain sanction to (undefined) separate intervention by Russia. France subsequently joined Britain and Russia and the terms of the St Petersburg Protocol were incorporated in the Treaty of London of July 1827.

In the summer of 1827 it seemed possible that the Greek question would be settled in Turkey's favour by military events. Ibrahim had subdued the Morea and, although the rumours that he meant to replace the Greek by a Moslem population were probably unfounded, it was known that he was subjecting the Greeks to a harsh and punitive regime. In these circumstances the Treaty of London went much further than the Protocol in demanding an immediate armistice – the deadline was eventually set for 7 September – and providing that, if either combatant refused the armistice, the three allies would prevent further collisions, although without resorting to hostilities. How this miracle was to be achieved was not spelt out and responsibility for interpreting basically contradictory instructions was shifted to the admiral in charge of the

British fleet in the area, Admiral Codrington. Codrington sought the opinion of the British Ambassador in Constantinople, Stratford Canning. Canning advised him in a phrase he was to come to regret that, although he must avoid hostilities if possible, in the last resort, 'when all other means are exhausted', he must enforce his instructions 'by cannon-shot'.[31] Ibrahim was not co-operative and the probably predictable result, after a series of misunderstandings, was that a combined Anglo-Franco-Russian squadron destroyed the Turkish and Egyptian fleets in Navarino Bay on 20 October 1827. By then George Canning, the author of the policy, was dead. It was Wellington's administration that had to deal with the consequences.

NOTES

1. This is examined in detail in A. Aspinall, 'The Coalition Ministries of 1827, 1, Canning's Ministry', *E. H. R.*, 42 (1927), pp. 201–26 and in *The Formation of Canning's Ministry, February–August 1827*, Camden Society, 3rd ser., vol. 59.
2. Stanmore, p. 75.
3. He had eventually told Stratford Canning that he was glad he had not accompanied Aberdeen 'who seems to have been unequal to his situation, – probably from thinking himself *imo supra*', Lane-Poole, vol. 1, p. 202.
4. Canning Papers, 90, Aberdeen to Binning, 18 Mar. 1823.
5. Add. MSS 43231, Dudley to Aberdeen, 23 Apr. 1827.
6. *Hansard*, XIII, 767 (17 May 1825), XVII, 854 (17 May 1827).
7. Gurney Papers, RQC 334/57, Aberdeen to Gurney, 23 Sept. 1827.
8. Gurney Papers, RQC 334/58, Aberdeen to Gurney, 30 Dec. 1827.
9. Gurney Papers, RQC 334/57, Aberdeen to Gurney, 23 Sept. 1827.
10. Ellenborough, *Political Diary*, vol. 1, p. 6 (24 Jan.), p. 76 (3 Apr. 1828).
11. Add. MSS 43056, Wellington to Aberdeen, 15 Jan. 1828; Wellington, *Correspondence*, vol. 4, Aberdeen to Wellington, 15 Jan. 1828.
12. Palmerston to Lady Cowper, 13 Jan. 1828, quoted Ziegler, p. 97; cf. Ellenborough, vol. 1, p. 129 (29 May 1828).
13. Ellenborough, vol. 1, pp. 125–8 (28 May), 128–30 (29 May 1828).
14. Ellenborough, vol. 1, pp. 146 (14 June), 216 (8 Sept.), 212 (6 Sept.), 213 (7 Sept. 1828); cf. pp. 135 (3 June), 152 (24 June), 169–70 (19 July), 202–3 (22 Aug.), 207–8 (5 Sept.), 235 (3 Oct.), 244 (24 Oct. 1828).
15. Ellenborough, vol. 1, p. 213 (7 Sept. 1828).
16. Ellenborough, vol. 1, pp. 1–3 (22 Jan. 1828).
17. Ellenborough, vol. 1, p. 35.
18. Ellenborough, vol. 1, pp. 52–7 (10–14 Mar.), 66–7 (24 Mar.), 73 (30 Mar. 1828).
19. Ellenborough, vol. 1, p. 133 (31 May 1828).
20. Ellenborough, vol. 1, pp. 129 (29 May), 131 (30 May), 149 (18 June 1828).
21. Ellenborough, vol. 1, p. 358 (24 Feb. 1829).
22. Gurney Papers, RQC 334/53, Aberdeen to Gurney, 21 Mar. 1825.
23. E. L. Woodward, *The Age of Reform*, p. 202.
24. W. St Clair, *That Greece might still be free*, p. 1. Of the many books on the Greek

War of Independence, St Clair's is the most useful in making clear the factors that Aberdeen had to take into consideration.

25. D. Dakin, *British and American Philhellenes*, p. 42; Aberdeen's 1803 Journal, 26 Apr. 1803.
26. St Clair, p. 32.
27. Add. MSS 43031, Bathurst to Aberdeen, 25 Dec. 1821. Gordon's report is in CO 136/1085. He returned to fight for the Greeks in 1826, after being assured that the situation was now quite different. He omitted any mention of the atrocities in his *History of the Greek Revolution* but the 1821 reports are published in W. H. Humphreys (ed. Sture Linner), *First Journal of the Greek War of Independence*, pp. 74–8, 137–44.
28. Add. MSS 43231, Bathurst to Aberdeen, 27 Dec. 1821.
29. Add. MSS 43231, ff. 20–3, Aberdeen to Castlereagh, n.d.
30. Add. MSS 43231, Castlereagh to Aberdeen, 4 Dec. 1821.
31. Lane-Poole, vol. 1, p. 449.

The Eastern Crisis, 1828–1830

The first problem in discussing Aberdeen's foreign policy between 1828 and 1830 is to determine how far that policy was his own. Ellenborough had commented in February 1828, when Dudley was still at the Foreign Office, 'I am not sure I should like to be Foreign Secretary, and have so much of the business taken out of my hands as is taken out of Dudley's by the Duke.'[1] The Cabinet, too, discussed outgoing despatches in considerable detail and sometimes made substantial alterations. Ellenborough quickly realised that Aberdeen was not such a malleable man as Dudley and he eventually found an effective counter to Cabinet interference by never having anything ready in writing in time for Cabinet meetings so that they could only offer general comments.[2] The Duke was a different matter. He expected to exercise a very tight supervision over foreign affairs which, more than domestic affairs, he regarded as his own domain. He wrote inordinately long memoranda on every subject of importance and often amended Aberdeen's despatches in detail. Palmerston thought that during the five months they sat together in the Cabinet, from January to May 1828, Aberdeen consistently sided with the Duke on foreign questions against the Canningites.[3] Publicly he may have done so, and in general terms they were in agreement, but from the beginning there were differences of nuance. Later, Ellenborough, a hostile but sometimes astute witness, realised that about half-way through the ministry Aberdeen suddenly became much more independent of the Duke in his opinions and policy.[4]

The Eastern Question was the most pressing problem. His colleagues were aware that from the beginning Aberdeen had reservations about the Treaty of London of 1827 although, on the face of it, it was in line with the policy he had himself advocated in 1821, co–operation between Britain and Russia to secure the freedom of Greece. Bathurst understood that his objections were on practical points, such as the removal of the Turkish population from an autonomous Greece, and he suggested that Wellington should put him in possession of the facts, presumably that the massacres of 1821 had ensured that there were now very few Turks to remove.[5]

Wellington was intent on maintaining the integrity of the Turkish Empire and distancing himself from the policy of Canning which had led to Navarino, although Palmerston and the other Canningites took the retention of Dudley at the Foreign Office as a pledge that the Treaty of London would be carried out. The first test came over the draft of the King's Speech. Wellington prevailed in his determination that the battle of Navarino should be described as an 'untoward event', even though the King would have preferred 'unlooked for' and Peel thought that 'untoward', with its implication of condemnation, would 'bring us into a scrape'. In the foreign policy debate of 11 February Ellenborough even called Canning 'a dangerous minister'. It was a strong phrase and Aberdeen at first privately demurred although, according to Ellenborough, he eventually agreed.[6]

The Russians, however, were pressing for yet stronger measures against the Turks. An ambassadorial conference had been meeting intermittently in London, under Dudley's chairmanship, since August 1827 to consider the implementation of the Treaty of London. In January 1828 the Russian Ambassador, Prince Lieven, suggested the occupation of the Danubian Principalities of Moldavia and Wallachia, a blockade of the Greek coast to intercept Turkish supplies, a blockade of the Bosphorus and the Dardanelles, and a march on Constantinople 'to dictate peace under the walls of the Seraglio'. The French too were pressing for a military expedition to the Morea to defeat Ibrahim and save the Greeks. The situation seemed to be getting out of hand and, at a Cabinet meeting on 9 March, Wellington produced his proposals for a settlement. The autonomous state of Greece should be confined to the Morea and certain named islands; the Porte should select its ruler, possibly from names submitted by the Greeks; the Greeks should pay the Turks an annual tribute of £200,000; they should also pay a lump sum (£1,500,000 according to Palmerston, £2,500,000 according to Ellenborough) as compensation for Turkish property in the Morea; and finally, Greece should be bound to follow Turkey in peace and war. The restricted boundaries were not acceptable to the Canningites, and even Peel said bluntly that he would prefer independence to this kind of suzerainty. Everyone agreed that the proposed tribute was too high. Aberdeen drew on his local knowledge to say that the whole tribute of the Morea could traditionally be carried on twelve mules. Only Ellenborough and Bathurst were, according to Palmerston, 'for cutting down the Greeks in every way'.[7]

The Ambassadors' Conference met again on 12 March but nothing was agreed except that the allied admirals should continue to blockade the Greek coast from the Gulf of Volo to the mouth of the Aspropotamos to prevent supplies reaching the Turkish forces. In fact the Conference had been overtaken by events because Lieven, acting on a despatch from Nesselrode, informed his colleagues that Russia was about to declare war on Turkey for reasons which were technically, but not in reality, unconnected with the Greek problem. The Turks' anger at the battle of Navarino had led to the precipitate withdrawal of the British, French and Russian Ambassadors from Constantinople and the Turks had also repudiated the Convention of Akkerman, which they had signed with Russia in 1826. The immediate cause of the Russo-Turkish war was Turkish interference with Russian shipping in the Bosphorus in contravention of the Treaty of Akkerman. Lieven put it to his colleagues that the Protocol of St Petersburg had allowed for separate action, if necessary, and that, if Britain and France would agree to the proposals Russia had put forward in January they could still act together; otherwise Russia would have to act – in a phrase which caused much difficulty – according to 'ses intérêts et convenances'.[8]

This immediately raised the question of whether the Treaty of London should be considered as at an end. The sittings of the Ambassadors' Conference were suspended. Aberdeen wrote Wellington a lengthy memorandum on the subject in which he did not try to disguise his dislike of the complicated position in which he felt that Canning's diplomacy had trapped them. Strictly speaking, he believed, Russia by becoming a belligerent had disqualified herself as a mediator and the Treaty might properly be considered dissolved. On the other hand, it might be against Britain's interests to consider the Treaty abrogated since it did bind Russia and France to certain objectives. What he really feared was that Britain and France would be dragged at Russia's heels to secure objects which were more Russian than European or Greek. He advocated an under-standing with France, particularly on how far Russia might be allowed to go, and saw as particularly sinister Nesselrode's reference to the fact that Turkey was not a party to the Vienna Settlement. His memorandum is undoubtedly open to Ellenborough's stricture of being an essay, rather than a clear statement of what should be done.[9] But Aberdeen, in common with most of his col-leagues, had not made up his mind as to the best course of action. Only the Duke felt convinced that this was an excellent opportunity for abandoning the Treaty altogether and he could not carry the Cabinet with him, especially when they received assurances through the French, that the Russians still wished to co-operate and still felt bound to their allies on Greece.

Historians have always been aware that Wellington's attitude became less intransigent after Aberdeen replaced Dudley at the Foreign Office in May but they have hesitated to ascribe this to the influence of the new Foreign Secretary, preferring to explain it on the grounds that the Duke became less obstinate when Canningite pressure was removed. In this they have followed Palmerston, who wrote rather indignantly in his Journal, 'A great and decided change took place about this time in the measures of the Government as to the Greek ques-tion; and many of the things which we had in vain been urging day after day, and which had been pronounced either improper or impossible, were now found possible and right.' There seems no good reason for ruling out Aberdeen's per-sonal influence. He was still, as Bathurst saw, 'a great Greek'[10], although much must also be attributed to developments in the international situation.

The London Conference resumed its sitting on 15 June. Crawley, in his *The Question of Greek Independence, 1821–1833*, finds it difficult to attribute this to Aberdeen since Aberdeen had been opposed to the resumption of the Confer-ences in May.[11] But the memorandum in question, that of 2 May, seems to be one of Aberdeen's 'essays', in which he looked at all possibilities. It is true that he saw great difficulties in renewing the Conferences and even envisaged an allied fleet arriving at Constantinople to find 'the city in flames under the bombardment of a Russian fleet, or occupied by Russian troops, and the Sultan himself a fugitive in Asia'. But he said specifically that if the changes in the Russian attitude, reported by the French, proved to be correct, it would 'unquestionably be proper to renew the conferences', at least for the purposes of 'confidential communication' and that, if the Russians abandoned their character as belligerents in the Mediterranean, joint instructions could again be given.[12]

The convenient fiction that Russia was at war with Turkey in the Black Sea but neutral in the Mediterranean was adopted. The way for this was opened by Nesselrode's despatch to Lieven of 17/29 April, in which he expressed a wish to continue co-operation with Britain and France and softened the earlier Russian declaration that she would act according to her own interests. Aberdeen replied to this on 6 June in his first important diplomatic communication, which was discussed at the Cabinet meetings of 31 May and 4 June. In it he insisted that the Greek question must be kept entirely separate from Russia's other grievances against Turkey and that the accomplishment of the Treaty of London must not be made dependent on the outcome of a war to which Britain was not a party. He also took the opportunity to remind the Tsar that, although the Sultan was not a party to the Treaties of Vienna and Paris, 'no material alteration could be affected in the condition, strength and character of a great Power' without altering the balance of Europe.[13]

Two other important decisions were taken immediately upon Aberdeen's assumption of office, to send Lord Heytesbury as Ambassador to Russia and to send Stratford Canning back to the eastern Mediterranean. Since 1826 Britain had had only a *chargé d'affaires* in St Petersburg, latterly Palmerston's own brother, William Temple. Palmerston believed that the decision to send Heytesbury to the Tsar's headquarters in the field was prompted by an Austrian decision to do the same. Metternich now seemed to be trying to upstage the European liberals by advocating an independent Greece – on rather the same grounds as Peel, that it would be preferable to an ill-defined autonomy.[14] Heytesbury was instructed to go out by way of Vienna but, despite continuing suspicions that Aberdeen would be 'too Austrian' in his policy, he does not seem to have had much more faith in Austria than in any other potential continental ally. Lord Cowley, the British Ambassador in Vienna, had just reported that the Austrian army was in great disarray and Aberdeen warned Heytesbury that her policy would probably be 'timid and calculating'. French policy would follow an 'uncertain and tortuous course', according to which party currently had the upper hand in Paris. Prussia would probably support Russia. The important thing, therefore, was to influence the young Tsar Nicholas. He might be tempted to embark on a career of 'youthful conquests' but Heytesbury should impress upon him that a character for probity and good faith towards allies was just as important. Heytesbury was not to protest against Russia claiming reasonable reparations for injuries from the Porte, but in the event of 'territorial aggrandizement', or any disposition to retain fortresses upon the Bosphorus, he was to 'adopt the gravest tone of remonstrance consistent with abstaining from all language of menace' and immediately seek further instructions from his government.[15]

Stratford Canning had arrived in London early in January after the ambassadors' hasty withdrawal from Constantinople. Canning knew that his views diverged from those of the Duke; in particular he had urged the need for an Anglo-French expedition to the Morea, or at the very least British support for a French expedition. It seemed unlikely that he would be sent back to the East. He was too closely identified with the policy of his cousin, George Canning, which Wellington increasingly regarded as an embarrassment. It is not clear how far Aberdeen personally was responsible for the decision to send him out again. It was obviously risky to employ a strong-minded man whose views were known to run ahead of his government's.[16]

Aberdeen sent Canning his instructions on 2 July, based on the decisions of the London Conference which had met the same day. Canning was to proceed, with his Russian and French colleagues, to Corfu or some other convenient location. Since the contingency envisaged in the Treaty of London, of the Turks refusing and the Greeks accepting allied mediation, had now arrived, the plenipotentiaries could properly open communications with the Greeks. In particular, they should find out what the Greeks wanted on the difficult question of the frontier. Any frontier should include a 'fair proportion' of the Greeks who had been in actual insurrection. It should be clearly defined and defensible. The Aberdeen who had once considered publishing an atlas of the Morea in collaboration with Gell can perhaps be heard speaking in the comment that it should not be difficult to find such a frontier in a country of 'deep ravines' and 'abrupt ridges of mountains'.

Four possible lines were suggested by the Conference; the first, from north of the Gulf of Volo to the mouth of the Aspropotamos, which Aberdeen admitted was suggested more because it included the whole coast blockaded by the order of 15 October 1827 than for any other reason; the second, from the Pass of Thermopylae to the Gulf of Corinth, following the ridge of Mount Aeta and including the mountains of the Parnassus group; the third to include Attica and Megara, by following the well-defined ridges of Parnes and Cithoeron; and the fourth, and most restricted, to limit Greece to the Morea, although including the mountain passes which commanded the approach to the Isthmus from the north. The boundary should certainly include a large proportion of the islands, not only in the immediate vicinity of the Morea but also the ancient Cyclades. It was proposed to include nearly all the islands between 36° and 39° north and between continental Greece and 26° east, but excluding Euboea (Negropont), which was almost entirely Turkish in population and had taken no part in the insurrection. The plenipotentiaries would also have to decide on a reasonable amount of annual tribute, bearing in mind the exhausted state of the country, and on compensation for the Turkish property in the ceded districts. They should also concert with the Greeks as to what remaining control the Sultan should have, in such a manner as to reconcile practical independence for the Greeks in internal matters with reasonable security for the Turks.[17] These instructions were extremely wide and Stratford Canning had good reason for claiming later that they authorised him in everything he did.

One fundamental problem was that, while transferring negotiations to the three allied ambassadors nominally accredited to Constantinople (who eventually met on the little island of Poros, off the east coast of Greece, and not at Corfu), the London Conference remained in being and continued to take decisions. A yawning gap soon opened up between the decisions taken in London and the decisions taken at Poros. The Austrians quickly saw the problem and expressed the view that matters should be settled in London. Aberdeen replied that he would have preferred it too but he could not persuade the Russians and French to agree.[18]

The final change of policy immediately after Aberdeen came into office was that the Duke, who in March had been suggesting that the despatch of a French force to the Morea would be a *casus belli* between Britain and France, now consented to it. Agreement was reached on this at the London Conference on 19 July. Aberdeen reminded the British Ambassador in Paris, Lord Stuart de Rothesay, that the agreement was that the French would retire as soon as 'the Mussulmans' did and not, as the French Foreign Minister, La Ferronays, seemed to wish to imply, only when the Treaty of London was carried out, which might take a long time. He also warned Stratford Canning that, although the French were entitled to stay there until all the Turco-Egyptian troops had withdrawn, and not just the Egyptian force under Ibrahim, yet they must always remember that the object of the Treaty of London was to separate the belligerents and not to conquer territory for the Greeks. It was an apposite warning, because the French were soon to show themselves much more enthusiastic for the Greek cause than the British government.[19]

Heytesbury was to prove a good ambassador but his merits were not quickly appreciated in London. He arrived at the Russian headquarters at Odessa early in August. He was soon converted to the view that the Tsar did not have territorial ambitions. The Tsar had asked him 'What neighbour could suit me so well as the Turks? What could Russia gain by the destruction of the Ottoman throne?' Modern research has confirmed that this was an accurate statement of Russian opinion[20] but it was received with great scepticism by the Duke of Wellington. Wellington was particularly irritated because the Tsar had drawn a distinction between the views of George IV, who was inclined to believe the Tsar's protestations, and those of Wellington who was consumed by suspicion of Russia. The fact that the distinction was accurate only made matters worse. Wellington insisted that Aberdeen should rebuke Heytesbury for having allowed the Tsar to say such a thing to him.[21] Wellington's suspicions seemed to be confirmed by the fact that the Russians, despite their formal declaration of neutrality in the Mediterranean, were now proposing to blockade the Dardanelles and even for this purpose to use Admiral Heyden's fleet, which was supposed to be acting jointly with the British fleet under Codrington and the French fleet under de Rigny in the Greek question. Heytesbury was later to explain that the Tsar had ordered the measure without much consideration because a French merchant in Odessa had persuaded him that it would compel the Turks to sue for peace within six weeks. This did not make it any less embarrassing. The British had insisted, despite Russian protests, on making

210

a public reference to Russian neutrality in the Mediterranean in the King's Speech to explain the resumption of the London Conferences, and British ships had sailed on the strength of government assurances that there were no hostilities in the area. Aberdeen spoke stiffly to Lieven and sent Heytesbury instructions to try to secure exemption from the blockade for all ships which cleared from British ports before 1 October, or Mediterranean ports before 30 October. He was to tell the Tsar that, in the last extremity, British warships would protect British commerce in the Mediterranean. This would almost certainly have meant war with Russia but the Russians gave way and granted the desired indemnity.[22]

Another blockade was also to cause Aberdeen great anxiety. He wrote ruefully to Hudson Gurney, 'We are the blockade (quasi blockhead) administration.'[23] This was the allied blockade of Crete. The Sultan had promised that Mehemet Ali should have Crete for his assistance against the Greeks and Ibrahim had occupied it in 1824. His rule had been harsh and, according to some reports, the population had been reduced by half. Crete had, after some hesitation, been included in the allied blockade of the autumn of 1827, and a new insurrection began there about the same time. The Greeks were very anxious that Crete should be included in any new Greece but the British government was not prepared to support so bold a step. In view of the changed situation on the mainland, they wished to abandon the blockade of Crete, which had originally been justified on the grounds of preventing fresh supplies reaching Ibrahim. The ambassadors at Poros wanted to continue the blockade and the question caused sharp exchanges between Aberdeen and Stratford Canning. Canning argued that to withdraw the blockade would be to encourage the Turks to indulge in further massacres of the Greek population. The argument disturbed Aberdeen but he could only suggest that the Sultan should be warned that any such action might result in European intervention.[24]

The whole question now really turned upon the future boundaries of a Greek state. Ibrahim had been induced to leave the Morea. The story of his departure is an interesting one and one which hardly shows Aberdeen as averse to machiavellian tactics if they would serve a desired end. Wellington was determined that Codrington should be recalled. It was scarcely possible to recall him for his part in the battle of Navarino and, early in May, Wellington persuaded the Cabinet that he should be recalled for dereliction of duty in allowing Ibrahim to send some captive Greek women and children to Egypt. That Aberdeen's heart was not entirely in it may be gauged from the fact that he allowed Ellenborough to draft the despatch and always tried to disassociate himself from the affair.[25] Codrington did not take the matter lying down and kept up a constant bombardment of despatches to prove that he had never disobeyed his instructions.[26] The French sympathised and connived with him in scoring one last triumph. Mehemet Ali was now anxious to disengage Ibrahim from the Morea before he came into conflict with the French expeditionary force under General Maison. Mehemet Ali was a protegé of the French and heavily dependent on French military advisers. Indeed, the French found themselves in 1828 in the curious position of supplying technical assistance and advisers to both sides in the Graeco-Egyptian conflict. Mehemet Ali, however, did not want to offend the Sultan by voluntarily withdrawing his forces from Greece. A stratagem was therefore resorted to. Codrington agreed with Mehemet Ali by the Convention of Alexandria of 9 August that an Egyptian fleet should set sail for Greece, ostensibly carrying supplies but really taking back the Greek prisoners. It should be intercepted by an Anglo-French fleet and conducted by what Aberdeen subsequently called 'douce violence' to Navarino, where the prisoners would be disembarked, Ibraham's army embarked, and the fleet escorted back to Alexandria. Wellington was horrified when he learnt of the plan. All was fair in war, he commented, but they were not supposed to be at war. Aberdeen was not shocked. It seemed a convenient solution to a difficult problem, including the practical one of where they were going to get the ships to transport Ibrahim's army. He pointed out that the only person to be deceived would be the Sultan and obviously regarded that prospect with equanimity. The only thing he feared was that Mehemet Ali might be deceiving the allies, not his suzerain.[27] The plan was carried out, despite some protests from Ibrahim.

Once Ibrahim had withdrawn, the remaining Moslem forces in the Morea put up only a token resistance to the French. Nevertheless, the extent of country under Greek control was much less than it had been three years earlier. The Turks had recaptured Athens and Attica. Maison, with some encouragement from the French War Office, which was not entirely in step with the French Foreign Office, was anxious to advance north of the Gulf of Corinth and, above all, to take Athens. Aberdeen, under pressure from Wellington, persuaded the French to forbid Maison to undertake more extended operations.[28]

The London Conference resolved on 16 November that the Morea and the Cyclades should be placed under the protection of the three Powers, until agreement was reached with the Sultan. By the Protocol of the Conference this was to be done 'without prejudicing the definitive limits'[29] but Wellington at least had made up his mind that this was to be the final limit. General Richard Church, a British soldier but in the employment of the Greek government that had been established in 1827 under the presidency of Capodistrias, was waging a successful campaign in western Greece and Wellington warned Aberdeen in September that Britain must be careful not to help the Greeks to wage war outside the Morea. Capodistrias himself was suspect in British eyes since it seemed more than likely that he was still 'Russian' in his sympathies and Wellington was hostile to his requests for financial as well as military assistance. He stated his views forcefully in a letter to Aberdeen on 2 November:

In respect to Greece, I would confine the limits to the Peloponnese if possible or as near as possible to the Isthmus of Corinth. I think that as Capodistrias says that he cannot go on without foreign assistance, he renders it less expedient to give to Greece an extended frontier. Indeed there never was such a humbug as the Greek affair altogether.

He thanked God that it never had cost Britain a shilling 'and never shall'. The gulf between Aberdeen's and Wellington's thinking is illustrated by the fact that as early as September Aberdeen was arguing that, if the Turks kept Negropont (Euboea), Greece could not be strong.[30]

Meanwhile the three ambassadors at Poros were, as instructed by their governments, deliberating on the future frontiers of Greece. The Russian and French Ambassadors were in favour of generous frontiers and sympathetic to Capodistrias's plea that, as the Porte had rejected allied mediation and shown no disposition to recognise the existence of Greece, she must be given defensible frontiers. Their instructions of 2 July also emphasized this. As an individual Stratford Canning held very similar views. The ambassadors' recommendations were embodied in a Protocol of 12 December 1828. This would have given the Greeks a frontier from the Gulf of Arta to the Gulf of Volo and would have included Crete, Samos and Euboea in the new Greek state. They recommended that Greece should still be under the suzerainty of Turkey, paying an annual tribute of £60,000 but that it should be constituted as an hereditary monarchy, the allied powers to nominate the monarch.[31]

The Poros Protocol was received in London on 2 January. On 30 January Aberdeen replied in a despatch which Stratford Canning, reasonably enough, regarded as a stinging rebuke. Aberdeen told him that his reasoning on the frontier was founded on false assumptions. The Treaty of London did not contemplate an independent Greece, still less a Greece which was intended to be a counterpoise to Turkish power. All that was required was that the Greek and Turkish populations should be separated and for that a frontier running from Lepanto to Aegina would be sufficient. The British government had made it quite clear that they did not favour the inclusion of Crete. Aberdeen concluded that he did full justice to the difficulties of Canning's situation but he must conform strictly to his instructions. Aberdeen had already rebuked Canning for his dilatoriness in obeying his instructions to raise the blockade of Crete.[32] Stratford Canning's response was to return home and resign his post.

Aberdeen's strictures were less than fair. It is true that his despatch of 18 November, following the London Conference decisions of 16 November, should have warned Canning that the British government's thinking was now more restrictive than it had been in July. In that despatch Aberdeen had emphasised that the objective of the Treaty of London was pacification, not the formation of a strong Greek state, and that the objectives of the Treaty would be attained by a Greece confined to the Morea and the islands. But Canning did not receive this despatch until the Poros negotiations were well advanced and he had already put forward proposals based on his instructions of 2 July.[33]

The truth was that the restrictive policy towards Greece was that of Wellington, not of Aberdeen.[34] His colleagues were well aware that Aberdeen still 'hankered after Athens'. His private letters encouraged Canning to get the best possible deal for the Greeks. He wrote on 26 July:

I fear that if we succeed in expelling Ibrahim, the limits of Greece will practically be defined by the state of possession. This would not carry us beyond the isthmus. There will be time enough to think of this when we see how our Egyptian friends are likely to be disposed of . . . It would not be possible for us to undertake fresh operations, which by no stretch of ingenuity we could possibly call *neutral* for the recovery of Attica and the neighbouring provinces. If, after all we are compelled to give up Athens, it will be a cruel sacrifice, but I foresee the possibility of such being the case.

He expressed similar sentiments in a letter of 11 September when he regretted that they would have to confine the French activities to the Morea.[35]

Aberdeen did not have the same feelings about Crete. He told Canning quite plainly on 20 September and 2 October that he should not 'meddle' with Crete because they could not afford to see such an important island, commanding the whole Levant, fall into the hands of a hostile power. Wellington feared that Crete would provide Russia with naval stations in the Mediterranean. Both Aberdeen and Wellington thought that, even if an independent Greece was not under Russian control, she might be hostile to Britain because she would be jealous of the British possession of the Ionian Islands.[36]

Aberdeen was, however, plainly uneasy that he might have misled Canning. His despatch of 20 December, rebuking Canning for allowing the continuation of the Cretan blockade, was accompanied by a private letter couched in very different terms. No doubt, he said, Canning had had good reasons for acting as he had done. He was sorry he had had to express the government's disapproval but he hoped it would not be ' painful' to Canning's feelings. Canning replied from Naples (the Poros conference having ended), 'My situation towards the Government is one of extreme difficulty not to say of painful mortification.' Although Aberdeen's letter precluded him from thinking that there was any deliberate intention of humiliating him, there seemed to be some doubt about the honesty of his intentions. If that was so, said Canning, 'I have but one answer to make; recall me.'[37]

Aberdeen's private letter which accompanied his despatch of 30 January was rather stiffer in tone. The time had come for 'frank explanations'. Canning's proceedings at Poros had been 'very embarrassing' and not consistent with the known views of his government. At the same time he did not wish to replace him with anyone else and there had been no diminution in his personal regard.[38] Canning had not confined his protestations to private letters but had written a very angry despatch of 17 January, in which he had accused Aberdeen of 'taunting' him and, by implication, of not caring about Turkish atrocities in Crete.

Aberdeen tried to persuade him to withdraw the offending paragraph, telling him, 'The publick despatches which have passed between us lately, have not been such as I could have wished either to write or to receive. It will never do for us to be skirmishing in publick while we embrace in private'. Canning did not respond to this attempt to introduce a lighter note. He replied asking Aberdeen to withdraw some expressions in his despatch. The correspondence now became acrimonious. Aberdeen replied that, if Canning had asked him to do so privately at the outset, he would have complied but he could not do so now. His predecessors would not have continued a private correspondence in the circumstances but he would make allowance for a 'certain infirmity of temper, and a morbid sensibility much to be lamented'. It was not exactly conciliatory but, after the intervention of Joseph Planta, the Under-Secretary, Canning calmed down sufficiently to withdraw the offending paragraph. Aberdeen then withdrew his own expressions which had upset Canning.[39]

In the midst of this row, Canning told Aberdeen that he could not continue to conduct negotiations if they were not to be on the basis of the Poros recommendations, to which he was personally committed. Aberdeen received this 'conditional resignation' with some relief and lost no time in appointing his brother, Robert, to succeed Canning.[40] At the same time Aberdeen still had a distinct feeling of guilt towards Canning. He secured the K.C.B. for him and promised him another diplomatic appointment, if he wanted it – although the Duke thought they were well rid of him.[41] Perhaps it was a lingering feeling that he should have supported Canning in 1828–29 that made it so difficult for Aberdeen to deal with him in 1853.

Aberdeen had allowed his views to be overborne by the Duke but it soon became apparent that it was Wellington who was out of touch with the realities of the situation. Ibrahim's withdrawal, the victories of Maison and Church, the attitude of the French government and the Russo-Turkish war, even though the Russians were checked in their 1828 campaign, made Wellington's restrictive policy obsolete. When the Duke's policy finally collapsed in the face of the Russian victories of 1829, it gave Aberdeen's policy a chance to assert itself.

The return of the Russian Ambassador to Constantinople was obviously impossible so long as the war continued but, as early as the autumn of 1828, the possibility began to be canvassed that the British and French Ambassadors might return to Turkey and begin discussions about the Greek settlement. Wellington had long been dissatisfied with Martignac's government in France, which he believed to be too pro-Greek, and actively supported his supercession by the man who had been French Ambassador in London since 1823, the ill-fated Prince de Polignac. The Duke was disappointed in his hopes. Polignac pursued much the same policy towards Greece as his predecessor.[42] England found herself outnumbered two to one at the London Conference. Agreement of a kind was reached at the meeting of 22 March. The British and French Ambassadors were to return to Constantinople and negotiate with the Sultan in the name of all three allies on the general basis of the Poros report. Some modifications were made to the report, notably that Samos and Crete were to be excluded. The future government of Greece was to be in the hands of a prince to be chosen by the Powers.[43] The Tsar was becoming very disturbed by the growth of anarchy and republicanism in Greece and saw an hereditary monarchy there as the only safeguard.[44] Stratford Canning had offered his resignation mainly because he felt that he could not honourably negotiate except on the Poros terms and he was correspondingly indignant when he discovered that the basis of the negotiation was to be the Poros report.[45] The memoranda which the three Powers deposited with the Protocol of 22 March illustrate, however, that the terms meant different things to the different Powers and that the British government (i.e. the Duke) were looking for the minimum of concessions to the Greek cause.[46]

Aberdeen's private letter to his brother, Robert, suggests that he had not learnt as much as he might have done from his misunderstandings with Canning. He admitted privately that, in accepting the Protocol of 22 March, Britain had 'receded' from her previous opinion. He thought that the Morea and the islands would be sufficient, if under the guarantee of the Powers, for Greek security but he admitted that, for sentimental reasons, he would like Attica included. He added, with what sounds like private satisfaction, that the French government, under pressure from public opinion, would probably *insist* on the inclusion of Attica. The reference to a 'guarantee' was also a sweeping one. Although the use of the word went back to the Protocol of St Petersburg of 1826, negotiated by the Duke himself, a guarantee of any state was an onerous responsibility which the British government usually tried to avoid and Britain had by no means decided exactly what responsibilities she was prepared to undertake in 1829. Aberdeen's letter to Robert also indicates, as does the British memorandum attached to the Protocol of 22 March, that Britain had reservations about the desirability of an hereditary monarchy. The problem was, who was to be monarch?[47]

Wellington's anxiety about the Greek settlement was fuelled not only by fears of the establishment of a Russian satellite, or even bases, in the Eastern Mediterranean, but also by the threat he apprehended to the British possession of Corfu and the Ionian Islands. Sir Frederick Adams, the British High Commissioner in the islands, had actually suggested that some of them should be transferred to a new Greek state. Aberdeen, without taking the suggestion very seriously, thought that there would be no harm in transferring Cephalonia, Zante and Cerigo. Wellington, on the contrary, insisted that the frontiers of Greece ought to be drawn so as to keep any new Greek state at a distance from the islands. The Ionian Islands were an important 'listening post' and espionage centre for the British in the Eastern Mediterranean. The foreign post which regularly passed through the islands was detained under the quarantine regulations and routinely opened. This was one reason why British intelligence about the area was generally good.[48]

When Sir Robert Gordon arrived in Constantinople it was not long before he became a thorough partisan of the Turks, at least in their dealings with Russia. Many of his suggestions were forceful to the point of recklessness. Aberdeen would certainly have rebuked, perhaps recalled Stratford Canning, for similar proposals but he regarded his brother's views more indulgently, praising him to George IV and defending him when necessary to the Duke, although of necessity rejecting his wilder suggestions. By the summer of 1829 the situation was becoming very dangerous. The Russian campaign of 1829 had gone much better than that of 1828. In June Silistria fell to the Russians and the British government was not much consoled by secret information from the Rothschilds that the Pasha had been bribed to surrender. By 21 July the Russians were across the Balkan Mountains. Aberdeen, who had been on a brief visit to Tunbridge Wells, returned to London a few days later to find the Lievens confident that the Russians could get to Constantinople.[49] Neither Wellington nor Aberdeen was sure at this time what the Russians really wanted. Heytesbury still insisted that they did not have territorial ambitions but there were exceptions to this. The Russians had taken the two important ports of Anapa and Poti on the eastern shores of the Black Sea and by July even Wellington thought that it would be better for Turkey to surrender them than to continue the war. As long ago as the previous December, Metternich had suggested a conference and, although sceptical of its success, Wellington was prepared to consider an Anglo–French mediation between Russia and Turkey.[50]

By 10 August Wellington was taking an extremely gloomy view of the situation. Everything had gone wrong. The policy of 1826, which had been designed to prevent a Russo-Turkish collision had led to one. The French as well as the Russians had established their influence in Greece. The Ionian Islands were threatened. Revolutionary ideas were spreading. Unless the Turks made regrettable concessions, the Russians would be in Constantinople in a few weeks. At the least the British squadron in the Mediterranean should be strengthened. Even Aberdeen began to feel that the Greek treaty was an embarrassment since it made them a sort of party to a war, the results of which they deplored. Wellington was in favour of a firm bid to enlist the French against the Russians. He commented, 'It pledges us to nothing'; no one could expect them to go to war single-handed to prevent Russia from taking possession of Constantinople while Europe looked on. The French were unresponsive. On 26 August there were rumours in London that Constantinople had already fallen.[51]

It was during this crisis that Aberdeen really asserted his independence from Wellington. Ellenborough had seen it coming some months earlier at the time of the Protocol of 22 March. He noted in his journal, 'Il commence à s'émanciper, and everything will go on worse' and, a week or two later, 'I am sorry to see he does not communicate beforehand now with the Duke.'[52] Aberdeen had no doubts that, if the Russians reached Constantinople, 'A new epoch is about to arrive.' The Austrian Ambassador came to see him to try to find out British intentions, remarking that Britain could afford to be 'comparatively at ease' but it was becoming a matter of life and death to Austria. Aberdeen was carefully non-committal but the Duke was still fighting a rear-guard action on Greece.[53]

On the evening of 26 August, Aberdeen received despatches from his brother Robert, who seemed hopeful of a settlement on Greece. Nevertheless, Aberdeen doubted whether, after the sacrifices he had made, the Tsar could afford to be moderate. William Temple, who had recently returned from St Petersburg, had suggested a few days earlier that there was much unrest in Russia and this might make the Tsar cautious. Aberdeen thought, on the contrary, it would make him anxious for spectacular successes in foreign affairs.[54] The next day, the 27th, Aberdeen saw Lieven and Count Matuscewitz, who had come to London as the Tsar's special representative nominally with instructions on Greek affairs, but in reality because relations between the Duke and the Lievens had become so bad that rational discussion had become almost impossible.[55] As a result of these talks Aberdeen concluded that the Russians might accept the Morea plus Attica. The French would probably agree.[56]

The next day the Duke replied in a letter which came near to being a rebuke

217

of Aberdeen himself. As he saw it the British and French Ambassadors had been sent to Constantinople to make propositions on the basis of the Treaty of London. The Sultan had made a counter-proposal, which the Ambassadors judged to be inadmissible, and themselves suggested to their own governments that the three Courts should recognise and guarantee the independence of the Morea, without leaving to the Sultan any of the guarantees under the Treaty of London. Aberdeen had summoned a meeting of the London Conference to deliberate on this, before he received a copy of the Sultan's counter-proposals. Neither the French nor the Russian Ambassador was in a position to give a firm opinion. It now appeared that the Sultan was prepared to treat under the terms of the Treaty of London. As soon as they heard of this the Russian representatives came to Aberdeen and wanted to take up the Ambassadors' proposals. Wellington insisted that, if the Sultan was prepared to negotiate on the basis of the Treaty of London, they must agree to do so. He instructed Aberdeen to summon the Cabinet for Sunday or Monday.[57]

Aberdeen duly summoned the Cabinet for Monday afternoon but he told the Duke firmly that his letter was founded on misapprehensions and more than hinted that Wellington's policy was becoming unrealistic. The reality was that the Russians were on the point of defeating the Turks. Lieven and Matuscewitz made their last proposal, not because they had heard that the Sultan had accepted the Treaty of London, but because they had learnt that General Diebitsch was advancing without opposition on Constantinople and that the Greek affair might be included in a Russo-Turkish peace treaty. They knew that Britain had always wished to keep the two questions separate and were now proposing that agreement should be reached in London on Greece before a peace treaty was concluded. 'Very likely', Aberdeen admitted, 'they may have some underhand view in making their proposal; but if we could agree upon the terms I do not think that it would be without its advantages.' 'Should the Sultan and the Turkish government be utterly destroyed,' he pointed out, '. . . the Greek Treaty [i.e. the Treaty of London] can no longer exist; although we shall still have on our hands the disposal of these, as well as the other provinces of the empire.' If Diebitsch dictated peace terms, which included a Greek settlement which was not to Britain's liking, there would be very little she could do about it.[58]

There was much force in Aberdeen's arguments and Wellington was compelled to accept the logic of the situation. If the Tsar really wanted peace, he argued, Diebitsch should halt. But if he did not, Constantinople was at his mercy. If Diebitsch got to Constantinople and Admiral Heyden controlled the Dardanelles, 'there is an end of the Greek affair, and to the Turkish Empire in Europe . . . The world must then be reconstructed.' The best grounds for that would be Anglo-French co-operation. Wellington now began to toy with the idea of a complete reconstruction. The Power which had Constantinople, the Bosphorus and the Dardanelles, must also have the mouths of the Danube but that Power must not be Russia. 'We must reconstruct a Greek Empire, and give it Prince Frederick of Orange, or Prince Charles of Prussia.'[59] Here again is an excellent illustration that in this period, as Metternich complained,

'Greek' could mean a territory, a race, a language or a religion.

Wellington's hope for Anglo-French co-operation was itself rather unrealistic in the light of the private information Aberdeen was getting from his ambassadors. Heytesbury wrote that France and Russia were now very intimate and Robert told his brother that the French were intriguing against the British at Constantinople.[60] Aberdeen had to write to his brother to caution him to be very careful what he put in despatches and to confine his 'reflexions' to his private letters. He admitted that the new French government was no more 'English' than the last and that, indeed, Polignac was anxious to live down newspaper taunts about his 'English origins'. He told his brother, rather ruefully, than his last intelligence – that the Porte would now accept the Treaty of London – had come just in time to stop them agreeing to the independence of Greece without the Sultan's consent, although he thought himself that that would be the best solution, not least for the Porte.[61]

Gordon now determined on moves that bear a great similarity to the opening of the Crimean War. He told his brother in a private letter of 29 August that Constantinople was at the Russian mercy. If the responsibility had not been too great he would have liked to have ordered Sir Pultney Malcolm, Codrington's successor, to bring the British fleet up to defend the entrance to the Bosphorus. As it was he had asked him to come to Tenedos, from whence he could pass the Dardanelles at a moment's notice. The ostensible reason would be to protect British lives and property. He hoped that this demonstration would have a salutary effect on the Russians. By 10 September Gordon had realised that, if the Castles fell, the British fleet would be in danger of being trapped in the Bosphorus. To be effective it would have to go into the Black Sea.[62]

Aberdeen replied regretting that he thought this impractical. It was a manoeuvre which could only safely be carried out with a strong fleet. The seven sail of the line they had available would be 'in a sort of rat-trap' at Constantinople. If Robert had ordered them up, he must send them down the Dardanelles again in 'a natural and easy manner'. He added that 'Knowing Constantinople as I do', he understood his brother's fears for the Christian population but he feared the presence of a British fleet might aggravate the dangers without impressing the Russians. In fact Robert did not order the fleet up but he made clear in a further private letter that his intention would have been to have prevented the fall of Constantinople, rather than to have taken off British refugees. He flattered himself that the 'menaced approach' of the British fleet did play its part in halting the Russians and added with curious foresight of future dilemmas that, if Britain ever did go to war with Russia, she must take care to have a fleet north of the Dardanelles. Aberdeen told him roundly that his reasoning was 'good for nothing'. Wellington agreed that they would simply have been in a 'rat–trap' but Aberdeen added significantly that, if they could have sent a fleet into the Black Sea at an earlier stage, the Russians might never have crossed the Balkan Mountains at all but it had been out of the question then.[63]

The Russians stopped short of Constantinople and signed the Peace of

Adrianople with the Turks on 14 September. The British had been in the dark about their intentions up to the last. Heytesbury, on Aberdeen's instructions, had asked Nesselrode for information on the Russian war aims on 27 August. Nesselrode had been reluctant to reply. Heytesbury suspected that they wanted to see how much Diebitsch could achieve first. But Nesselrode agreed to give him a general idea verbally. They wanted only, he said, the execution of the Treaty of Akkermann and other ancient treaties and free navigation of the Bosphorus. They did not want an inch of territory in Europe except perhaps a small island at the mouth of the Danube. There must be an indemnity but he would not indicate the amount. Pressed by Heytesbury, Nesselrode admitted they meant to keep Anapa and Poti and a few other points necessary for the security of Georgia. Nesselrode said he hoped a march on Constantinople would not be necessary but, as Heytesbury put it, 'at the moment I am writing either a peace is signed, or the Cossacks are bivouacking in the seraglio.'[64]

The terms of the Treaty of Adrianople conformed fairly closely to those which Nesselrode had indicated to Heytesbury in August. Russia made no territorial gains in Europe, apart from a small area at the mouth of the Danube, but she did retain substantial portions of the east coast of the Black Sea. The Turks were to pay a sizeable indemnity and the Russians were to remain in occupation of Moldavia and Wallachia until it was paid. The two Principalities were eventually to be returned to Turkey but the Turks promised to introduce a new system of government there, of which Russia would be the guarantor. The Convention of Akkermann was re–affirmed and Russian merchants were guaranteed complete freedom in the Black Sea and the Straits. Despite the modesty of its actual terms the Treaty of Adrianople represented an important advance in Russian influence in the Near East and the Russians in fact refrained from demanding more stringent terms because they feared that they might precipitate the collapse of the Ottoman Empire with all its attendant dangers.

The details of the Treaty were very slow to reach London. The government's first information came from unofficial reports from Vienna and from the Rothschilds. Wellington's first reaction was one of complete pessimism. He decided that it was all up with the Turkish Empire and that Britain would have to abandon the line she had so far maintained on Greece. He wrote to Aberdeen on 4 October, when they still had little more than rumour to go on:

It will be absurd to think of bolstering up the Turkish Power in Europe. It is gone in fact: and the Tranquillity of the World . . . along with it. I am not quite certain that what will exist will not be worse than the immediate annihilation of the Turkish Power. It does not appear to me to be possible to make out of the Greek Affair any substitute for the Turkish Power; or anything of which use could be made hereafter in case of its entire annihilation and destruction. All I wish is to get out of the Greek affair without loss of Honour; and without imminent Risk for the safety of the Ionian Islands.

A week later he wrote a very long memorandum in which he castigated the supposed 'moderation' of the terms and pronounced it to be the death–blow to Ottoman independence. He thought it would have been better if the Russians had entered Constantinople and the Turkish Empire been dissolved. They must now prepare for that eventuality. The Five Powers must agree that any future disposition of the Turkish dominions must be made by a conference. In the meantime they must remonstrate strongly with the Tsar on the terms of Adrianople.[65]

Aberdeen's reaction was more moderate and realistic than the Duke's but he too saw the possibility that the final dissolution of the Turkish Empire might not be long delayed. He told Robert on 10 November that they must re–think their whole policy on Turkey which was now clearly at Russia's mercy. It was very possible that there would be a revolt within the Ottoman Empire which would overthrow the Sultan. Russia and Austria might well agree on a partition as they had done with Poland, only a generation earlier. He hoped it might just be possible to persuade the other European Powers to join in a general guarantee of Turkey, similar to that which the Tsar Alexander himself had suggested in 1814.[66]

Aberdeen very reluctantly acquiesced in the Duke's insistence that they must send a comprehensive protest against the terms of the Treaty of Adrianople. He delayed the despatch until the end of October, until he had received an official copy of the Treaty from Lieven, perhaps hoping that the Duke might think better of it. It was a swingeing attack on the settlement. Russian gains on the east coast of the Black Sea would enable Russia to control Asia Minor and open the way to either Constantinople or Teheran at will. Moldavia and Wallachia would become virtually independent of the Sultan and, together with associated concessions to Servia and Greece, would complete a hostile ring against Turkey. The right of Russian merchant vessels to pass through the Bosphorus without even a check on their identity was scarcely compatible with sovereignty. The indemnity was a grave burden and might lead to an insurrection in Turkey. Heytesbury was to read the despatch to Nesselrode. With it went a private letter from Aberdeen which was much more representative of his own feelings. Heytesbury was to communicate the despatch with 'caution and explanations' so as not to produce an 'unpleasant effect'. The British government had had to put their views on record for the sake of their own consistency but they had no 'hostile tendency' towards Russia. He suggested taking up Alexander's idea of a general guarantee.[67]

The communication of the despatch had all the bad effects Aberdeen feared. Heytesbury reported that he had never seen Nesselrode 'so much moved by anything'. Nesselrode commented shrewdly enough that he supposed it was really meant for the British Parliament and, in that case, Russia would have to reply. Nesselrode had, in fact, tried to stop Heytesbury communicating it at all but the British Ambassador had to tell him that his instructions were positive. In a private letter Heytesbury told Aberdeen that the despatch had made the worst possible impression, especially as it contrasted with the French attitude which had congratulated the Tsar on his moderation and magnanimity. Heytesbury had not dared to mention the guarantee because he knew that any proposal from England would be unfavourably regarded. It was not reassuring for the British government also to learn from Heytesbury that the French had raised the possibility of the partition of the Ottoman Empire possibly in return for France acquiring her 'natural frontiers', although the Russians had been unresponsive.[68]

In the circumstances, it seems extraordinary that the Duke was still fighting a rearguard action for his negative views on Greece and, to some extent, still compelled Aberdeen to go along with him. In July Aberdeen had put forward a suggestion, which Wellington ignored, that northern Greece might be made into a separate autonomous state, if it was thought undesirable to join it with the Morea.[69] In a region of small principalities, this was by no means such an absurd proposal as some historians, following the Duke, have supposed. At the London Conference on 25 September there was 'a stormy discussion of two hours'. The Russian and French representatives were 'outrageous' at the memorandum which Aberdeen read to them relating the whole history since the Treaty of London of 1827 and analysing whether the Sultan had now accepted its terms. Aberdeen had to agree to modify it but in reality the whole discussion had become absolute.[70] Aberdeen had another rather heated discussion with the Russian representatives on 29 September. He protested at the idea of General Diebitsch enforcing the Protocol of 22 March on the Turks. He hinted that the other Powers had always meant the Protocol, which with minor modifications embodied the Poros terms, to be an ultimatum. The Russians replied with the suspicion, justified so far as the Duke was concerned, that the British had never really supported it. It was now Aberdeen who suggested to the Duke that they had better have a Cabinet meeting.[71] In his heart he was moving closer to his diplomatic colleagues and away from the Duke. He might not have gone so far as Heytesbury who suggested that, if the dissolution of the Ottoman Empire was at hand, they had better support 'the natural pretenders to the succession (the Greeks, in short)', but he believed that the Russians now saw the Greeks less as clients and more as potential rivals, and he would have liked to have seen Greece taken out of any possible area of partition. He told his brother that they must now look at the Greek question in quite a different light. It must be independent and the extension of the frontier would be a good thing. Only recently, even Aberdeen had seen the choice as lying between a small 'independent' Greece and a larger Greece still under Turkish suzerainty.[72]

He expounded his views in a private letter to his brother on 21 November. The Sultan would still be given the choice between the Protocol of 22 March, that is suzerainty, and Greek independence within defined limits, but the Powers now favoured the latter alternative. He wrote:

You know that I am no Greek, and that to preserve the Porte substantially entire was my great wish. But the instance that the Russians arrived at Adrianople, and when we saw of what the Turkish Empire was composed, I changed my views, and determined to lay the foundation, if possible, of making something out of Greece . . . the real fact is, that I now look to establish a solid power in Greece, with which we may form a natural connection; and which, if necessary, we may cordially support in future.

This letter accompanied an official despatch, approved by Wellington and the Cabinet, in which the fall of the Turkish Power was openly discussed. 'We may', wrote Aberdeen,

perhaps be tempted to suspect that the hour long since predicted is about to arrive, and that, independently of all foreign or hostile impulse, this clumsy fabric of barbarous power will speedily crumble to pieces from its own inherent causes of decay . . . We may still attempt to avert the period of its final dissolution, and may possibly for a time succeed; but whenever this feeble and precarious dominion shall cease, we ought not to occupy ourselves in vain efforts to restore its existence. Our object ought rather to be to find the means of supplying its place in a manner the most beneficial to the interests of civilisation and of peace.

They could not be blind to 'the detestable character of Turkish tyranny' and when it fell there could be no 'attempt to restore a Mohammadan authority in Europe'. When the dissolution came they should make sure that there existed 'in the Greek State a substitute whose interests we should naturally be called on to support in preference to the pretensions of all others'.[73]

Everything now turned on the selection of a Prince to govern Greece. This problem was to tax the ingenuity of the Powers for three years and was not to be solved during Aberdeen's time at the Foreign Office. When the Tsar first suggested an hereditary prince in December 1828, he named four possible candidates: Leopold of Saxe-Coburg, the bereaved husband of George IV's daughter, Charlotte; Prince Frederick of Orange; Prince Gustavus of Sweden; and Prince Philip of Hesse-Homburg.[74] In the course of 1829 the list lengthened to include, among others, Prince John of Saxony, Prince Charles of Bavaria, the Archduke Maximilian and Prince Charles of Mecklenburg. Aberdeen believed that any Catholic prince would be unacceptable to the Greeks. He warned the Duke, 'I know the Greeks well enough to be certain, unless they are greatly changed, that they would as soon have a Turkish Prince as a Roman Catholick', although they might 'tolerate' a Protestant as being a fellow enemy of the Catholics.[75]

Leopold's name had been suggested by the Greeks themselves as early as 1825 and Stratford Canning had raised the possibility again towards the end of 1828 but the British government had never been enthusiastic despite his connection with the British royal house. But the real opponent of the idea was George IV, who was determined that Leopold should not have the Greek throne. Indeed he had promised the King of Prussia, through the Duke of Cumberland, that he would support the claims of Charles of Mecklenburg, the brother of the Duchess of Cumberland and of the late Queen of Prussia. The matter blew up into a ministerial crisis which nearly brought down Wellington's government in January 1830.

Early in December 1829 the ministers learnt of the King of Prussia's approach to George. Wellington condemned it as 'most irregular' although Aberdeen, after making enquiries, reported, 'The case is not quite so bad as you suppose, although it is quite bad enough.' Strictly speaking, the offending letter had been from an unidentified German to the Duchess of Cumberland, although it was clearly intended for the King's eyes. Aberdeen agreed that something must be done and he nobly offered to go down to Windsor himself the next day, telling Wellington, 'The business is far from agreeable certainly, but it is not fair that everything of this kind should fall upon you.' He obtained the King's permission to write to the British Minister in Prussia, civilly declining any support for Charles of Mecklenburg. The Duchess of Cumberland, understandably, complained bitterly that this was inconsistent with the King's earlier promises.[76]

In fact by 8 January, Britain, France and Russia had agreed that Leopold was the only possible candidate. George IV was still the stumbling block. Ellenborough was convinced that he was using the issue to get rid of Wellington's government. In any case, Wellington saw it as a test of his authority and was determined not to give way. Aberdeen was despatched again to Windsor on 12 January to tell the King that the Cabinet was agreed. He had an interview with George, lasting an hour and a half, which was not made easier by the fact that the King was both agitated and ill and had taken 100 drops of laudanum to steel himself for the interview. George made himself unpleasant, taunting Aberdeen with the rumours that Leopold was about to marry a daughter of the Duke of Orleans (the future King Louis Philippe) and insisting that Leopold 'should not carry English money [his royal pension] out of the country'. However, Aberdeen's opinion, as communicated to Ellenborough at a Cabinet dinner at Argyll House the following night, was that 'it is a *real* quarrel – not a plot to get rid of us – the King thoroughly hates Prince Leopold.' Wellington went down to see George himself the next day. The King was still ill and irritable but a few days later, on 19 January, he reluctantly gave his consent. The immediate crisis was over.[77]

On 3 February 1830 the Conference of London prematurely congratulated itself that it had completed its 'long and arduous negotiation'.[78] Leopold was to be offered the crown of an independent kingdom, guaranteed by the three Powers. The frontier was to be on the Aspropatomos–Zeitoun line, including Euboea, but not Samos or Crete. Leopold, however, was only prepared to accept the crown on conditions. He wanted a large loan, guaranteed by the Powers; allied troops, at least until a Greek army could be properly organised; the cession of Crete; and a firm indication that the Greeks wanted him as their sovereign. Crete was regarded as non-negotiable. Rather surprisingly, neither Aberdeen nor Wellington saw any objection to the demand for troops, although they were agreed that Britain should provide money for German or Swiss mercenaries, rather than British soldiers.[79] The loan proved more difficult but, on 1 May, the British government guaranteed their share of the £1,500,000 loan. The loan was to be a thorn in the side of successive British governments because the Greeks never met their obligations. Leopold, however, was still hesitating. On 21 May he formally declined the throne, nominally on the grounds that he had not received an unequivocal invitation from the Greeks. The outbreak of the July Revolution in France further delayed negotiations and when Wellington's ministry fell in November, the Greek question was still not finally settled.

Stratford Canning said that the Greeks owed their independence to France and that, if it had depended on Aberdeen, they would have had a long wait.[80] This is true in so far as Aberdeen was curbed by Wellington and the rest of the Cabinet. It is not true of Aberdeen's own views. In 1829 he embarked on the same mental journey as Gladstone and Salisbury were to take after him, accepting that the preservation of the Ottoman Empire, although it might be worth attempting for a time, could only be a short–term expedient and that thought must be given to what would follow it. In 1830 he came to accept that so far as Greece was concerned, and Gladstone was later to believe this of the whole Balkans, the creation of a strong independent state was the best security against both anarchy and foreign intervention. It was doubly ironic that a quarter of a century later he should be compelled to go to war to save an empire he already believed to be doomed.

NOTES

1. Ellenborough, vol. 1, pp. 41–2 (25 Feb. 1828).
2. Ellenborough, vol. 1, pp. 125–6 (28 May 1828), vol. 2, p. 57 (24 June 1829), p. 113 (11 Oct. 1829).
3. Bulwer, vol. 1, Palmerston's Journal, e.g. p. 246–7 (2 Apr. 1828).
4. Ellenborough, vol. 1, p. 394 (14 Mar. 1829), vol. 2, p. 2 (1 Apr. 1829).
5. Palmerston to W. Temple, 8 May 1828, Bulwer, vol. 1, p. 225; Bathurst to Wellington, 6 Jan. 1828, Wellington, *Corr.*, vol. 4, p. 181.
6. Ellenborough, vol. 1, pp. 6–9 (24–26 Jan.), pp. 28, 31 (11, 12 Feb. 1828).
7. Ellenborough, vol. 1, p. 49 (9 Mar. 1828); Bulwer, vol. 1, pp. 229–31, Palmerston's Journal (9 Mar. 1828).
8. PP, XXXII (1830) 19–41, Protocols of Conference and enclosures.
9. Aberdeen to Wellington, 17 Mar. 1828, Wellington, *Corr.*, vol. 5, pp. 312–5.
10. Bulwer, vol. 1, pp. 287–8, Palmerston's Journal (Dec. 1828); Wellington, *Corr.*, vol. 4. p. 181.
11. Crawley, p. 111. Although published over fifty years ago, this is still the best diplomatic history of the war in English.
12. The memorandum was sent to Bathurst, Bathurst to Wellington, 2 May 1828 and encls., Wellington, *Corr.*, vol. 4, pp. 419–22.
13. FO 65/176, Aberdeen to Prince Lieven, 6 June 1828; Ellenborough, vol. 1, p. 133 (31 May), p. 137 (4 June 1828).
14. Bulwer, vol. 1, p. 289, Palmerston's Journal.
15. Add. MSS 43114, Aberdeen to Heytesbury, No. 4, 13 June 1828.
16. Lane-Poole, vol. 1, pp. 458, 460–1.
17. FO 78/164, Aberdeen to Stratford Canning, No. 5, 2 July 1828; PP, XXXII (1830) 74–6.
18. FO 7/206, Cowley to Aberdeen, No. 115, 12 July 1828; FO 7/203, Aberdeen to Cowley, No. 11, 5 Aug. 1828.
19. PP XXXII (1830) 80–82; Bulwer, vol. 1, p. 289; FO 27/378, Aberdeen to Stuart de Rothesay, No. 27, 22 Aug. 1828; FO 78/164, Aberdeen to Stratford Canning, No. 22, 11 Sept. 1828.
20. FO 65/173 Heytesbury to Aberdeen, No. 7, 11 Aug. 1828; R. J. Kerner,

'Russia's new policy in the Near East after the Peace of Adrianople', *Cambridge Historical Journal*, 5 (1937), pp. 280–90.

21. FO 65/173, Heytesbury to Aberdeen, No. 7, 11 Aug. 1828; FO 65/173, Aberdeen to Heytesbury, No. 15, 19 Sept. 1828; Wellington, Memorandum, 8 Sept. 1828, Wellington, *Corr.*, vol. 5, pp. 31–3.

22. FO 65/173, Heytesbury to Aberdeen, No. 15, 28 Aug. 1828; FO 65/173, Aberdeen to Heytesbury, 2 Oct. 1828, Separate & Conf.; FO 65/176, Aberdeen to Prince Lieven, 30 Sept. 1828; Add. MSS 43089, Heytesbury to Aberdeen, 14 Dec. 1828.

23. Gurney Papers, RQC 334/59, Aberdeen to Gurney, 4 Oct. 1828.

24. FO 78/164, Aberdeen to Stratford Canning, No. 29, 2 Oct. 1828, 28 Oct. 1828; FO 78/167, 168, Stratford Canning to Aberdeen, No. 49, 10 Oct., No. 73, 10 Dec. 1828; Add. MSS 43056, Aberdeen to Wellington, 3, 22 Oct. 1828.

25. Ellenborough, vol. 1, p. 106 (14 May 1828), p. 135 (3 June), pp. 137–8 (4 June), p. 158 (8 July 1828).

26. They are printed *in extenso* in Wellington, *Corr.*, vol. 7.

27. Add. MSS 43056, Wellington to Aberdeen, 21, 24 Aug., Aberdeen to Wellington, 23, 26 Aug. 1828.

28. Add. MSS 43056–7, Wellington to Aberdeen, 4, 15, 23 Sept., 4, 5, 6 Nov., Aberdeen to Wellington. 12, 22 Sept., 3, 4, 5 Nov. 1828.

29. PP, XXXII (1830) 100–1.

30. Add. MSS 43056–7, Wellington to Aberdeen, 17 Aug., 15 Sept., 24 Oct., 2 Nov., Wellington's Memoranda, 10, 16 Nov., Aberdeen to Wellington, 22 Sept. 1828.

31. PP, XXXII (1830) 637–43.

32. FO 78/178, Aberdeen to Stratford Canning, No. 2, 30 Jan. 1829.

33. FO 78/164, Aberdeen to Stratford Canning, No. 37, No. 38, 18 Nov. 1828. His accompanying private letter told Canning that he should 'cooperate cheerfully in the execution of what you may not abstractedly approve', Stratford Canning Papers, FO 352/20, Part B, Aberdeen to Canning, 18 Nov. 1828.

34. Aberdeen's own first reaction was neutral, Aberdeen to Wellington, 2 Jan. 1829, but Wellington had been lashing himself into a fury since the middle of December, e.g. 14 Dec. 1828, 'Memorandum upon reading Mr S. Canning's Dispatches', Add. MSS 43057.

35. Stratford Canning Papers, FO 352/20, Part B. Aberdeen to Canning, 26 July, 11 Sept, 1828.

36. Stratford Canning Papers, FO 352/20, Part B, Aberdeen to Canning, 20 Sept., 2 Oct. 1828. Add. MSS 43057, Wellington to Aberdeen, 2 Nov. 1828, Wellington, Memorandum, 14 Dec. 1828.

37. FO 78/164, Aberdeen to Stratford Canning, No. 40, 20 Dec. 1828; Add. MSS 43090, Aberdeen to Stratford Canning, 20 Dec. 1828, Stratford Canning to Aberdeen, 17 Jan. 1829.

38. Stratford Canning Papers, FO 352/20, Part B, Aberdeen to Canning, 30 Jan. 1829.

39. Add. MSS 43090, Stratford Canning to Aberdeen. No. 2, 17 Jan. 1829 includes the words:

I hoped also to be excused for submitting, in vindication of my claim to the ordinary feelings of humanity, that your Lordship, when taunting me with "complacency" in calculating the number of troops necessary to effect the evacuation of Candia by the Turks, appears to impute to me a sentiment which I am scarcely more capable of applying to that contingency, than to any speculation founded on the number of victims sacrificed in the late massacre at Canea, however I may have erred as to the degree of importance which I attached to the deplorable occurrence.

marked 'Passage withdrawn by Mr Stratford Canning'. It accordingly does not appear in the Despatch preserved in the Foreign Office; Aberdeen to Canning, 3 Feb, 12 Mar., 9 Apr., Canning to Aberdeen, 21 Feb., 26 Mar. 1829.

40. Stratford Canning Papers, FO 352/20, Part B, Aberdeen to Canning, 28 Mar. 1829.

41. Stratford Canning Papers, FO 352/20, Part B, Aberdeen to Canning, 28 Mar. 1829; Add. MSS 43090, Aberdeen to Canning, 30 Apr. 1829.

42. Add. MSS 43056, Wellington to Aberdeen, 22 Sept. 1828; Add. MSS 43210, Aberdeen to Robert, 2 Sept. 1829.

43. PP XXXII (1830) 107–10.

44. Add. MSS 43089, Heytesbury to Aberdeen, 27 Dec. 1828.

45. Lane-Poole, vol. 1 pp. 489–90.

46. PP, XXXII (1830) 110–28.

47. Add. MSS 43210, Aberdeen to Robert, 9 Apr. 1829.

48. Add. MSS 43057, Aberdeen to Wellington, 5 Jan. 1829; St Clair, pp. 132–3.

49. Add. MSS 43057, Aberdeen to Wellington, 28 July 1829; Add. MSS 43083, Stuart de Rothesay to Aberdeen, 14 Aug. 1829.

50. Add. MSS 43057, Wellington to Aberdeen, 18 Dec. 1828, 29 July 1829; FO 65/179, 180, Heytesbury to Aberdeen No. 1, 2 Jan., No. 87, 4 Aug. 1829 E.

51. Add. MSS 53057, Wellington to Aberdeen, 10, 24 Aug., Aberdeen to Wellington, 26 Aug. 1829; Add. MSS 43083, Aberdeen to Stuart de Rothesay, 21 Aug. 1829.

52. Ellenborough, vol. 1, p. 394 (14 Mar.), vol. 2, p. 2 (1 Apr. 1829).

53. Add. MSS 43057, Aberdeen to Wellington, 24, 25 Aug. 1829.

54. Add. MSS 43057, Aberdeen to Wellington, 20, 26 Aug. 1829.

55. The deterioration of the relations between Wellington and the Lievens is traced in H. Arbuthnot, *The Journal of Mrs Arbuthnot*.

56. Add. MSS 43057, Wellington to Aberdeen, 27 Aug. 1829.

57. Add. MSS 43057, Wellington to Aberdeen, 28 Aug. 1829.

58. Add. MSS 43057, Aberdeen to Wellington, 29 Aug. 1829.

59. Add. MSS 43057, Wellington to Aberdeen, 11 Sept. 1829.

60. Add. MSS 43089, Heytesbury to Aberdeen, 13 Aug. 1829; Add. MSS 43210, Robert to Aberdeen, 8 Aug. 1829.

61. Add. MSS 43210, Aberdeen to Robert, 2 Sept. 1829.

62. Add. MSS 43210, Robert to Aberdeen, 29 Aug. 10 Sept. 1829.

63. Add. MSS 43210, Aberdeen to Robert, 3 Oct., 8 Dec., Robert to Aberdeen, 30 Oct. 1829.

64. FO 65/181, Heytesbury to Aberdeen, No. 112, 11 Sept. 1829. Add. MSS 43089, Heytesbury to Aberdeen, 11 Sept. 1829.

65. Add. MSS 43058, Aberdeen to Wellington, 5 Oct., Wellington to Aberdeen, 4, 11 Oct. 1829 encl. memo of 10 Oct.

66. Add. MSS 43210, Aberdeen to Robert, 10 Nov. 1829.

67. FO 65/178, Aberdeen to Heytesbury, No. 22, 31 Oct. 1829; Add. MSS 43089, Aberdeen to Heytesbury, 7 Nov. 1829; Ellenborough, vol. 2, p. 113 (11 Oct.), p. 115 (14 Oct. 1829).

68. FO 65/181, Heytesbury to Aberdeen, No. 150, 25 Nov. 1829; Add. MSS 43089, Heytesbury to Aberdeen, 27 Nov. 1829.
69. Add. MSS 43057, Aberdeen to Wellington, 19 July 1829.
70. Add. MSS 43057, Aberdeen to Wellington, 25 Sept. 1829.
71. Add. MSS 43057, Aberdeen to Wellington, 29 Sept. 1829.
72. Add. MSS 43089, Heytesbury to Aberdeen, 30 Sept. 1829; Add. MSS 43210, Aberdeen to Robert, 10 Nov. 1829.
73. Add. MSS 43210, Aberdeen to Robert, 21 Nov. 1829.
74. Add. MSS 43089, Heytesbury to Aberdeen, 27 Dec. 1828.
75. Add. MSS 43058, Aberdeen to Wellington, 28 Nov. 1829.
76. Add. MSS 43058, Wellington to Aberdeen, 8 Dec., Aberdeen to Wellington, 9 Dec. 1829; Ellenborough, vol. 2, pp. 164–5 (11 Jan. 1830).
77. Ellenborough, vol. 2, pp. 160–1, 166–71, 174, (8, 12, 13, 15, 20 Jan. 1830). The Princess Lieven gave a highly inaccurate account of Leopold's candidature in her Diary (ed. H. Temperley, pp. 135–54). Her hostility to Aberdeen at this time is probably due to her inability to influence him against Wellington, cf. Arbuthnot, vol. 2, pp. 315, 323 (12 Nov. 1829, 5 Jan. 1830).
78. PP, XXXII (1830) 134.
79. Add. MSS 43058, Aberdeen to Wellington, 16 Feb., Wellington to Aberdeen, 16 Feb., Wellington, Memorandum, 17 Feb. 1830.
80. Lane-Poole, vol. 1, pp. 463–4.

CHAPTER FOURTEEN

Reaction and revolution, 1828–1830

The Eastern Crisis dominated the foreign policy of the Wellington administration but was not the only problem it faced. In western Europe the British government was confronted by the possible breakdown of the peace settlements at the end of the Napoleonic wars, to which both Wellington and Aberdeen were committed. Anglo-French disputes spilled over into Africa, and American questions assumed a new significance.

The most persistent problem in western Europe was Portugal. The story went back to 1807, when the Portuguese royal family fled to their great colony of Brazil to escape French domination. The King, John VI, did not return to Portugal until 1821, by which time a revolutionary junta in Lisbon, influenced by the Spanish rising of 1820, had proclaimed a new constitution to which John, on his return, took an oath of loyalty. John had left his elder son, Pedro, as Regent of Brazil but Pedro, under pressure from the forces, which all over South America were seeking to break free from European control, proclaimed himself 'constitutional emperor' of an independent Brazil in 1822.

The Powers of the Holy Alliance authorised France at the Congress of Verona in 1822 to put down what they saw as the dangerous revolution in Spain but Canning's influence was sufficient to prevent any extension of the intervention to Portugal. Britain's claim to a 'special relationship' with Portugal derived nominally from the treaty of 1373, several times re-affirmed, by which Britain promised to defend the integrity of the Portuguese dominions, but more immediately from the sentimental feelings in Britain about the scenes of Wellington's triumphs during the Peninsular war, and from Britain's economic and strategic interests in the area. But a counter-revolution began in Portugal itself in 1823, led by John's younger son, Miguel. John himself had to flee for refuge to a British warship.

Canning contrived to restore some stability to the situation in 1825 through the British Minister in Lisbon, Sir William A'Court (later Lord Heytesbury), and a special envoy to Rio de Janeiro, Sir Charles Stuart (later Lord Stuart de Rothesay). A settlement was reached by which Miguel went into exile in Vienna and John recognised the independence of Brazil. The following year John VI died. Pedro succeeded him as King of Portugal but, deciding that it was not practicable any longer for one man to govern both Portugal and Brazil, he abdicated his rights to the Portuguese throne in favour of his seven-year-old daughter, Donna Maria da Gloria. At the same time he proclaimed a new Portuguese constitution, the Charter, to take the place of the 1820 constitution, which John had been forced to abrogate during the troubles of 1823–24.

Many in Portugal, particularly among the peasantry, the Church and the army, believed that with Pedro's abdication, the throne had rightfully passed to Miguel. They disliked the Charter and sought help from the absolutist government of Ferdinand VII in Spain to make Miguel their King. The constitutionalists appealed to Canning for help on the basis of treaty obligations, ancient and recent. Canning persuaded the Cabinet to respond with alacrity. Within a matter of days a fleet and 5000 British troops were on their way to Portugal. The Spaniards hastily retreated and Miguel once again withdrew. Canning's reputation as the champion of liberalism and nationalism rested in large part on his response to the Portuguese crisis and the famous speeches in which he defended it. 'We go to plant the standard of England on the well-known heights of Lisbon', he told the Commons. 'Where that standard is planted, foreign dominion shall not come.'[1] It is not, therefore, surprising that Aberdeen's reluctance to become involved in Portuguese affairs and his refusal to accept that Miguel was wholly in the wrong, identified him with Wellington as an arch-conservative and the enemy of liberal-national causes.

The public had little understanding of either Canning or Aberdeen's position. Canning in fact had very limited sympathy with the Portuguese constitutionalists, whom he once described as 'rascally ragamuffins'[2] but he calculated that British interests required active measures in the face of probable intervention by other Powers. But Aberdeen did react differently to the Greek and the Portuguese problems. He saw the Greeks as a people striving to be free from alien tyranny and he believed that they should be supported as far as such support was compatible with the overriding need for European stability. He saw the Portuguese struggle as a purely domestic one which the Portuguese should be left to decide for themselves. He doubted whether, morally, there was much to choose between the two sides. The important thing he believed was to return to Castlereagh's sensible doctrine of 'no interference in the affairs of other Powers'.[3]

In any case, the situation which had faced Canning in 1826 had changed when Wellington came into office. Pedro, who acknowledged that his brother had some rights in the matter, agreed that the disputed succession should be resolved by a marriage between Miguel and Maria, as soon as Maria was old enough. Marriages between uncle and niece, although they required a papal dispensation, were almost commonplace in the tangled royal history of the Iberian peninsula. No difficulty was anticipated there. In the meantime Miguel should act as Regent for his infant niece and future bride. On his return to Portugal in February 1828 Miguel took the oath to the Charter.

This last information came as a relief to Wellington's government, who feared that otherwise they would be subjected to parliamentary criticism for the line they were taking. Heytesbury had left Lisbon in January 1828 and the new British Minister was Aberdeen's old friend and colleague, Federick Lamb. He had actually travelled to Lisbon with Miguel, who had returned to Portugal by way of Paris and London, where he had made himself agreeable and negotiated loans. Since the immediate crisis seemed to be over, it was agreed, before Aberdeen replaced Dudley at the Foreign Office, that the British troops should be withdrawn from Portugal.

Unfortunately, Miguel had scarcely returned to Portugal before he began to show his real hand. Supported by his mother, Queen Carlotta, he determined to assert his own right to the crown. He dissolved the Chamber which had been summoned under the new Constitution and recalled the ancient Portuguese Cortes. In June he persuaded them to proclaim him King. The constitutionalists, led by Saldanha, who had been the Portuguese Prime Minister from 1826 to 1827, tried to make a stand at Oporto but were easily defeated and Saldanha was forced to fly to England. The absolutists began to take reprisals against their enemies throughout Portugal. Canning's policy was in ruins and, once they had left the Wellington government, the Canningites, led by Palmerston, delivered thunderous attacks on government policy in Portugal.

The first problem the government had to face was whether to proceed with the withdrawal of the remaining British forces. Most had already left when Miguel dissolved the Chamber in March but Lamb, who quickly became a partisan of the Constitutionalists, decided to detain the remaining 3000. At a Cabinet meeting on 18 March Huskisson made a strong plea for the continuation of what he understood to be the Canningites' policy, namely the fulfilment of a British pledge of support to the constitutionalists. The majority of the Cabinet, however, declined to recognise that there ever had been such a pledge.[4] They were also understandably nervous that the British troops in Portugal were now too few to be effective and feared that the retention of British forces in Portugal would seem to justify the French in retaining fortresses in Spain. On the other hand, they could not completely ignore Lamb's opinion that British lives and property were in danger. They compromised by agreeing to keep a British battleship in the Tagus and a small force of marines at Fort St Julian so long as the ship should remain. In April it was decided that even these should be withdrawn. As soon as the Canningites had left the ministry Wellington made his views clear to Aberdeen. If British subjects insisted on residing at Lisbon or Oporto, when the country was 'in a state of revolution', they must do so at their own risk. 'Inform them', he told Aberdeen, 'that the King's ships will remain in the Tagus and the Douro five days after the receipt of your letters; and such of them as think proper may come away in those ships. But they must not look to the constant presence of his Majesty's ships in the Tagus for their protection.'[5]

Lamb's own position had become one of acute embarrassment. He had been accredited to Miguel as Regent and if Miguel now assumed the crown Lamb's powers expired and it could be argued that he should leave Lisbon. Aberdeen, however, pleaded for caution. It was easier to recall an envoy than to re-instate him 'with credit'.[6] It would be most unfortunate if Britain recalled her representative and the other Powers did not. Britain would then lose any chance of influencing events. Wellington was prepared to be cautious in withdrawing British representation but he was deeply dissatisfied with Lamb. He complained that Lamb had fallen completely into the hands of the constitutionalist party and had written despatches to Dudley, which verged on the improper in their insistence on British government action. Wellington wrote firmly to Aberdeen on 7 July, 'It is quite obvious that from the commencement of his embassy, Sir Frederick Lamb has taken an erroneous view of the relative situation of this country and Portugal. We are not the protectors of Portugal. Portugal is not a dependency of this country either *de jure* or *de facto*, or in principle, or by a construction of our treaty, or in practice.' Wellington wanted to recall Lamb for his 'offensive letters'.[7]

Lamb had certainly treated Dudley with scant respect. He had written to him in a despatch in April that since he could hardly expect Dudley to waste his 'valuable time' referring to past despatches, he would review all the orders which had been given to him and demonstrate that he had executed them, and proceeded to do so, at least to his own satisfaction.[8] He returned to the attack in a private letter at the beginning of June, before he knew that Aberdeen had succeeded Dudley. Could they deny, he asked, 'speaking as gentlemen and upon our consciences', that it was largely Britain who was responsible for the Charter, which had only failed to achieve tranquillity because of Miguel's 'misconduct'? It was the arrival of British forces which had induced many Portuguese to support the Charter. Could they now honourably leave them to the vengeance of their enemies?[9]

Aberdeen was uneasy and not only, as Ellenborough supposed, because 'Lamb is a friend of his'.[10] He did not like the way Miguel was behaving. He was certainly in breach of his engagements and, as he told Lamb in one of his first despatches, Miguel's opponents seemed to be loyal to Pedro and there did not seem to be a 'revolutionary and democratick spirit at work under the mask of loyalty'.[11] Wellington was supported by Ellenborough, Melville and Bathurst in his desire to recall Lamb but Peel, Goulburn, Murray and Herries joined Aberdeen in demurring. In the end they compromised. Aberdeen should write to Lamb telling him that he deserved to be recalled but that they would not do so at present for fear the government's policy should be misunderstood.[12]

The official despatch was severe, speaking of Lamb's 'impertinence' and deploring his 'temper of mind' but with it went a private letter in which Aberdeen told Lamb that he sent the despatch with great regret. 'You will understand', he said, 'that although I am the executioner, the Cabinet has been unanimous upon the subject.' He feared that his colleagues had got the impression that Lamb was hostile to the government but he thought himself that Lamb had spoken in haste under the strain of circumstances and implored him, 'If this should be the case, for God's sake say so.'[13] Wellington in fact cautioned Aberdeen to answer all Lamb's points in detail in case they had to answer the charges in Parliament. Lamb, however, had made up his mind. He told Aberdeen on 9 June, '. . . if I receive from you any other instructions than that of imposing the law upon the Infant [Miguel], I shall answer by my resignation, provided only that the Oporto people do not carry their point by themselves.' A little later he told him, 'We are covered with disgrace.'[14] He left Lisbon on 5 July.

The British government's embarrassments were only just beginning. Pedro had sent Donna Maria back to Portugal to take up her inheritance but, on arriving at Gibraltar, she learnt of her uncle's *coup d'état*, which seemed to have been accepted by most of the country. Her advisers decided to bring her to England and she arrived at Falmouth in the middle of September 1828. This was exactly the kind of involvement the Duke was determined to avoid and he wrote to Aberdeen, 'The arrival of this young Queen in England is the work of an intrigue, and is intended to give and will give us a good deal of trouble.' Interested parties would try to establish that Britain was responsible for the Portuguese constitution and had obligations to support Maria. Wellington insisted that their obligations to Portugal related only to external aggression and in no way compelled them to support one branch of the House of Braganza against another.[15] This was the line which Aberdeen was to take in the Lords against strong opposition criticism, led by Lord Holland.[16] In his instructions to Lord Strangford, on his special mission to Brazil, he went even further and advised Pedro that, in view of the general support for Miguel in Portugal, he should be acknowledged as King, on condition of his completing the marriage with Maria and that all acts should be done in their joint names.[17] Meanwhile Maria was hospitably received in London and by George IV at Windsor.

The Marquis de Barbacena, who accompanied Maria, asked for British intervention in Maria's cause and was refused, but there was more danger of British neutrality being breached by clandestine means. The constitutionalists, who had made a brief stand for Maria in Oporto in June 1828 under General Saldanha, were given temporary asylum in Britain, on the understanding that they would go on to Brazil. By September, however, the British government was becoming uneasy at their activities at Plymouth, where they were reported to be drilling in military formations and receiving reinforcements of German mercenaries.[18] In October Barbacena made a bad tactical error by asking the Duke of Wellington for a British naval escort to take his force safely to Terceira, the only island in the Azores where the garrison was still holding out for Maria. Wellington replied curtly, saying he knew of no 'Portuguese Troops' in Britain, only of individual refugees who were behaving very badly.[19] A month later Aberdeen told Itabayana, the Brazilian envoy, that the Portuguese soldiers round Plymouth must disperse, but Count Palmella, the former Portuguese Prime Minister, also a refugee in Britain, assured Wellington that they would sooner go straight to Brazil. Wellington immediately offered them a naval escort – an offer which Palmella hastily declined.[20] Saldanha and his men sailed from Plymouth on 6 January for Terceira, not Brazil. They were unarmed but the British had been persuaded – deceived in Wellington's view – to allow a consignment of arms to sail for Brazil which, it was now clear, was intended to rendezvous with Saldanha's men. Captain Walpole of H.M.S. *Ranger* was ordered to stop Saldanha's force reaching the Azores. On 16 January he prevented them from landing at Porto Praya, on Terceira. Shots were fired and one Portuguese killed. Under protest the Portuguese put back to a French port.[21]

The government was fiercely attacked in Parliament and Lord Clanricarde tabled an angry motion of censure. Aberdeen made a long and fairly effective speech, arguing that while some maintained that Britain should have supported Maria as the 'legitimate sovereign' of Portugal and others that they should have acknowledged Miguel, whom the Portuguese had almost unanimously chosen, they had preferred the course of strict legal neutrality. Clanricarde's motion was easily defeated by 95 votes (31–126).[22]

By 1830 the question had really become whether formal recognition of Miguel could be delayed much longer. Miguel was now *de facto* king and all effective resistance seemed to have ceased. The Speech from the Throne in February 1830 hinted at the resumption of diplomatic relations. Aberdeen, when challenged by Holland and Clanricarde, said that, although nothing would be done without the knowledge of the House, he considered 'the recognition as a question of time only'.[23] There was a rather unpleasant exchange between Aberdeen and Holland later in the debate when Aberdeen, on being further pressed, said the government would not ask for Holland's advice and Holland retorted that that did not surprise him since Aberdeen never consulted Parliament or anyone else.[24] It was the kind of ill-tempered exchange into which Aberdeen was sometimes led, particularly when acutely embarrassed, which damaged his relations with the House.

Aberdeen was well aware that recognition would be very unpopular. Maria's visit to Britain had generated a good deal of sympathy for the young queen while Miguel was being portrayed as a monster of depravity. The *Annual Register* for 1829 devoted ten pages to a catalogue of his crimes, beginning, 'A disposition, the slave of violent passion, and insensible to the workings of ordinary humanity, was aggravated by the consciousness that the throne, which he had seized, was not secure.'[25] Although Aberdeen assured the House that the reports were exaggerated and repeated that it was no concern of Britain's which Braganza brother had the better claim to the Portuguese throne,[26] he was angered by Miguel's treatment both of his fellow countrymen and of English residents in Portugal. He emphasized that there could be no question of recognition until Miguel granted an amnesty to his political opponents and restored the lands which he had been so freely confiscating.[27] The matter was still unresolved when Wellington's government fell from power in November.

Just before the fall of the ministry, a similar situation seemed to be developing in Spain. Ferdinand VII was still childless when his third wife died in 1829 and it was generally expected that Ferdinand would be succeeded by his brother, Carlos. Ferdinand, however, immediately married again and his fourth wife, Maria Christina of Naples, gave birth to a daughter, Isabella, in October 1830. But in the eyes of many Spaniards women were excluded from the succession. A disputed succession might therefore be expected in Spain as well as in Portugal.

Aberdeen's successor at the Foreign Office, Palmerston, was first to establish his reputation as a liberal in foreign affairs by his effective support for Maria in Portugal and Isabella in Spain in the 1830s. The matter came to be represented to the British public as a simple struggle between constitutional parties, supporting the young queens, and absolutist parties, supporting their respective uncles, Miguel and Carlos. If Palmerston was plainly the liberal, Aberdeen was equally plainly the reactionary because he had not supported Maria. The foundations of a legend were laid in Portugal but the legend overlooked many important points. No one, least of all Aberdeen, doubted that Miguel and Carlos sympathised with the absolutist position and governed harshly and badly when in power. What was more in doubt was whether the 'constitutionalists', who surrounded Maria and Isabella, were any less self-seeking, or governed any better, or any more even-handedly. Aberdeen certainly doubted it. But, in any case, the situation was different in 1828–30, from that which developed between 1831 and 1834. In 1830 Miguel was the *de facto* ruler of Portugal, with no serious challenger in sight. After Pedro's expulsion from Brazil in 1831 and his return to Portugal to assert his daughter's claims, a situation of civil war once again existed and it was difficult, if not impossible, for Britain to avoid taking sides. It is true that in Portugal Aberdeen re-asserted Castlereagh's doctrine of non-intervention in the affairs of other states, and Palmerston Canning's doctrine of intervention to prevent the intervention of other Powers, but in totally different circumstances.

Wellington had good reason to expect to be regarded as the expert on Portuguese affairs and, for the most part, Aberdeen accepted his claim without question, asked for his advice and even saw him take personal charge of affairs, notably the Terceira affair,[28] without demur. Wellington also saw himself as an expert on France and here Aberdeen was less docile in following his lead, although both men were agreed in regarding any instability in France as a particularly serious threat to European peace. It was particularly unfortunate that the British government did not have an ambassador in Paris whom they felt they could trust. Lord Granville had, after some hesitation, resigned his appointment on the change of ministry and George IV had promised the embassy to Lord Stuart de Rothesay one day at Ascot. Neither Wellington nor Aberdeen wanted Stuart but Wellington concluded that it was not worth another quarrel with the King. Instead he grumbled perpetually about Stuart and his 'wretchedly bad' information.[29]

Wellington's conservatism was nowhere more marked than in his attitude to France. He complained bitterly to Aberdeen in September 1828, 'We may rely upon it that the Liberal opinion is now the favourite one in France. We, and I in particular, are out of fashion because I am not a Liberal. The meaning of liberality in France is war . . . war and bullying and boasting are essential.' The ministers of Charles X would do whatever the population demanded and Charles himself would do whatever he thought necessary to keep possession of the throne. Wellington blamed his own country for this, complaining 'This state of things is certainly the result of our Liberal regime. We have put the word in fashion.'[30] He was pleased when in the summer of 1829, Martignac's moderate, but sometimes ineffective, ministry was replaced by the ultras, led by Polignac, the former French Ambassador in London.

Other men were more shrewd in their assessment. The Russian Ambassador in Paris, the wily old Corsican, Pozzo di Borgo, immediately saw the dangers. Stuart sent home a very garbled version of his views but Aberdeen ascertained the truth from Lieven. Pozzo thought that Polignac would never be able to control the Chambers and 'Should the ministers, conscious of their weakness in the Chambers, attempt to govern by Ordonnances and by force, he considers the revolution as certain.' Pozzo believed that the leading liberals were ready to act and that the change of dynasty would be carried through without difficulty or bloodshed.[31] It was a remarkable display of prescience in August 1829 but it was to be a year before the British Cabinet appreciated the truth of it.

It was the French intervention in Algiers which cost Charles X Wellington's sympathy. On the face of it the French had justification for their action. It requires a considerable mental effort to remember that only a few years before Victoria ascended the throne, the Mediterranean sea was still preyed upon by pirates. Aberdeen himself had encountered them in the Aegean in 1803, and Britain had mounted a punitive expedition against Algiers in 1816. Smaller nations regularly paid protection money to escape their attentions but, when the nuisance became intolerable, more powerful nations usually mounted punitive expeditions against their more notorious bases. The other Powers accepted that French shipping had suffered injury in the 1820s from Barbary pirates, operating from the coastline under the nominal control of the Bey of Algiers. The problem about the usual style of punitive raid was that the pirates simply regrouped and resumed their operations from some other point. Only a more general and sustained attack was likely to be effective.

The French decision to undertake such an operation in 1830 was, however, regarded with grave suspicion by the other Powers. The French already had an army operating in Greece. Were Napoleonic ideas of making the Mediterranean 'a French lake' being revived? French intrigues with their protegé, Mehemet Ali, added fuel to the flame. They suggested that Mehemet Ali should carry out the intervention on their behalf and should then remain in control of Algeria himself. (This might also reconcile him to the loss of the Morea and Crete.) Metternich assured Lord Cowley that he was in possession of (intercepted) despatches from Guilleminot, the French Ambassador to Turkey, to Polignac, which even envisaged the involvement of Russia and the United States 'both of which Powers are, he [Guilleminot] observes, desirous of having establishments in the Mediterranean.'[32] Aberdeen was at first sceptical of these intelligence reports but towards the end of January 1830 the French Ambassador in London confirmed that his government had been negotiating with Mehemet Ali. Wellington was convinced that the Russians were encouraging the French designs on Algiers. Aberdeen protested to the French that the Sultan, as Algiers's suzerain, had the first right to be consulted although he admitted to his brother, Robert, that the Algerian coast was in a barbarous condition.[33]

On 19 February Aberdeen defined the British position to Lord Stuart de Rothesay. The French had a right to 'reparations' for the 'provocations and insults' they had suffered but he hoped the Sultan would bring the Bey to 'a sense of reality'. The British could not object to a mere punitive expedition but he hoped the French would not leave a garrison on the coast or try to claim any exclusive influence. If Mehemet Ali was to become involved, hostilities should not spread to Tripoli or Tunis. The British government had already decided that, so far as they were concerned, Tunis was a more sensitive area than Algiers. Stuart saw Polignac on 25 February when Polignac gave him verbally the assurances he sought. He told him that the expedition was now resolved upon and that the French would insist on the Bey abolishing piracy and slavery but that they had no intention of forming a colony or leaving a garrison and that, as soon as satisfactory arrangements were made, the French troops would leave.[34]

During the next few months Aberdeen tried repeatedly and unsuccessfully to get these verbal promises put into writing. Polignac continually evaded the issue, complained that Britain only wanted these assurances for 'parliamentary' purposes and protested that his own parliamentary difficulties were greater than the British ones. He promised Stuart that satisfactory explanations would be sent through Laval but they were not. Aberdeen began to doubt the reliability of Stuart's information until Stuart was stung into replying that Aberdeen must know the French government well enough to know that he could not be 'rendered responsible for the falsehood of the assurances I receive, or the failure of Monsieur de Polignac's promises'.[35]

Aberdeen and Wellington were seriously alarmed by the size of the French expedition and by French hints that they intended to obtain 'securities' of an unspecified nature for the future. As early as 18 April, Wellington hinted that Charles X's conduct was such that it might release other Powers from any obligation to support the restored Bourbons. He wrote to Aberdeen:

. . . the Prince de Polignac appears to have made a strange mistake in thinking that we can allow France to seek safety from domestic troubles in foreign conquests, even on the coast of Africa. Neither Bonaparte nor the Directory behaved worse than the French Government have in this case . . . The French Government are quite mistaken in supposing that any of the quarrels between Bonaparte and Europe were to be attributed to their fears of revolutionary principles. They were apprehensive of his conquests, and they therefore leagued against him.

Aberdeen conveyed these sentiments to Stuart a few days later and warned him that Britain could not watch with indifference when 'a French army, the most numerous it is believed which in modern times has ever crossed the sea, is about to undertake the conquest of a territory which, from its geographical position, has always been considered of the highest importance'. A little later he told Stuart, 'The affair, in truth, begins to wear a sinister appearance.'[36]

In one sense it was Charles X for whom the Algerian adventure was to prove fatal. The French expedition sailed on 25 May. News of the fall of Algiers reached Paris on 9 July. It was apparently this success which encouraged Charles X to proceed with his *coup* against the Chambers. Aberdeen scolded Stuart for not giving his government any warning of this event. This was not strictly true. Stuart had warned his government on 16 July, when it became clear that the French elections had not gone in favour of the government, that the ministry might use their majority to alter the election law and curb the freedom of the press. His despatch of 23 July was, however, misleading. He thought the government was collecting troops in the Paris area but he did not believe that they meditated a *coup*. He was wrong on both counts. He certainly did not anticipate the four ordonnances of 26 July, dissolving the Chamber, reducing the electorate and suppressing the freedom of the press – but neither did anyone else in Paris.[37]

During the next few days the British government was hampered by lack of official information. The revolutionaries obstructed the despatch of diplomatic messengers from Paris. Interestingly, Aberdeen was in close touch with the House of Rothschild who had, more than once in the recent past, supplied the Foreign Office with information from their own excellent courier network. The Rothschild couriers were still getting out of Paris and Aberdeen privately instructed Stuart to use them.[38]

Aberdeen received Stuart's despatch telling him of the *coup* and expressing fears of future violence on 29 July. He instructed him to maintain a 'complete reserve' on the question of the ordonnances. If Polignac wanted to know the British government's reaction he must enquire through his ambassador in London.[39] This was obviously a holding position until the government had time to assess the situation. Stuart's next despatches, received on 3 August, told him that there had been some resort to violence. The students of the École Polytechnique had occupied the Hôtel de Ville and he understood that two regiments of the line had gone over to the insurgents. He did not think the King disposed to make concessions and the assembled Deputies regarded themselves as the only legal authority. On the other hand he thought only a few of them were republicans and, if the King abdicated, most wanted the Duke of Orleans to be Regent for the King's infant grandson, the Duke of Bordeaux.[40] So far, British public opinion was taking the crisis very quietly. Aberdeen told Stuart that the City was not alarmed and the effect on the funds was slight because it was expected that a change of ministry would solve the matter. Aberdeen himself thought that it would go further than that and the question would be 'whether a monarchy under any form will be permitted to exist, or whether we shall again see a republic' but he too expected a speedy settlement. He tried to instill a little more energy into Stuart. 'This is a time'. he wrote, 'when a little exertion may reasonably be expected.' Probably he meant by way of keeping his government informed but he was to be startled by Stuart's interpretation of that advice.[41]

Stuart constituted himself the ally and protector of the Bourbons. In the end he almost saw himself playing Flora Macdonald to Charles X's or at least the Duke of Bordeaux's, Charles Stuart. In a cypher despatch which he sent by Rothschild's agent, Contini, he told Aberdeen that he had received a message from Orleans, asking whether he should come to Paris. Stuart had replied that Orleans could not honourably accept the offer made to him (whether of the Crown or the Regency is not clear) and that his elevation would not be acceptable to the Powers who were parties to the treaties putting the Bourbons on the throne.[42] This was scarcely consistent with his assertion to Aberdeen that he had done as the Foreign Secretary wished and expressed no opinion.[43] He was more cautious when Charles X himself asked the advice of the Ambassadors of the Great Powers. Stuart met his Austrian, Russian and Prussian colleagues and they agreed that they could tender no advice, beyond counselling the King to provide for his own safety. On 3 August Stuart and his Russian colleague went publicly to the Palais Royal, where Orleans had arrived despite Stuart's advice, to express anxiety as to Charles's personal safety. Even this met with Aberdeen's disapproval. He told Stuart privately that such interference might do more harm than good and he must refrain from all action or expressions of opinion.[44]

Much worse was to follow. On 3 August Charles agreed to abdicate and it appeared to be arranged that he would leave from Cherbourg, together with his young grandson, but Stuart told Aberdeen in a private letter that he hoped that when the bearer of the letter (apparently an unofficial messenger) returned to Cherbourg he would bring advice to Charles that Bordeaux must stay in France to maintain the principle of legitimacy, even if it put Bordeaux's life at risk. Moreover, Charles X was in urgent need of money. Although the Rothschilds were supposed to have sent him 600,000 francs in gold, he feared it would not reach him before he embarked.[45] A Mr Ivers, whom Stuart told Aberdeen he had 'confidentially' employed for two years, informed Stuart that the King wanted 150,000 francs at his immediate disposal. Stuart asked Aberdeen to entrust Ivers with that sum, which would be repaid from the two million francs belonging to the King at Coutts Bank. Charles was now convinced that his enemies were conspiring to send him to America and begged the British government to send two vessels to Cherbourg to escort him to Jersey or some other safe place.[46]

Aberdeen's first reaction to this tangled story was mild, if sceptical. He thought it most unlikely the King was being 'kidnapped' and sent to America. The American government would not connive at it and, in any case, Britain could hardly intervene forcibly. Nor could the British government take the responsibility of advising what should be done about Bordeaux. As Rothschild had sent money to Cherbourg, he did not see how Charles could still be in need but, if he was, Stuart had authority to raise it.[47]

Before Stuart received this reply he plunged much deeper into intrigues. A 'person' had come from Rambouillet, asking him on the King's behalf to endorse a draft on Messrs Coutts for 600,000 francs and asking Stuart to keep them informed of events in Paris, especially anything touching Bordeaux's right of succession. Stuart gallantly replied that he would at every risk comply with the King's wishes. When Bérard's motion for the exclusion of the royal family came before the Chambers, Stuart despatched an attaché, Colonel Craddock,[48] to tell Charles what Orleans had said about Bordeaux to Stuart and the Russian Ambassador. Craddock arrived at Merleroult late on 7 August and had to rouse the King from his bed. Charles was still lingering on his journey, hoping for an improvement in his fortunes, but he was reluctant to agree to Craddock's suggestion that he leave Bordeaux in France. Bordeaux's mother was convinced he would be poisoned if he were separated from his family and, if Orleans declined the charge, there was no trustworthy person with whom he could leave the boy. Craddock held out hopes of an English man-of-war and money to meet Charles at Cherbourg and, reported Craddock, the King 'shook my hand violently when I told him of it'. Stuart communicated an edited version of these transactions to Orleans.[49]

Wellington exploded with anger when Stuart's private letters arrived reporting all this, partly at Stuart's indiscretion but even more at the obscurity of his account which left his government in the dark on many vital points. He covered Stuart's letters with furious comments. He could not, he complained, make out whether Stuart had actually endorsed the bill for Coutts. 'Is it now in circulation with his name on the back of it?' Stuart had told Charles X but not his own government what Orleans had actually said about Bordeaux. Above all, Stuart had no right to tell Orleans that a British warship was going to Cherbourg, particularly as the British government had decided against it. Wellington had no illusions as to how disastrous the whole episode could be. He admitted that he had originally favoured Bordeaux's succession himself but circumstances had changed. He wrote:

We will suppose that the King follows this advice and leaves in France his grandson; and that there should be a party in his favour in consequence and a civil war. Who will be responsible for it? We may swear ourselves black in the face but nobody will believe that we did not order Lord Stuart to take these measures purposely to create this civil war. But supposing, what is more likely, that this Prince should be poisoned or murdered! We shall be eternally disgraced!!!

Stuart must be recalled before he further compromised his government.[50]

Aberdeen took the matter more calmly than the Duke. Indeed, it is hard to resist the conclusion that his own romantic Jacobitism stirred a little. He had to admit that Stuart 'has gone much further in the way of interference than we imagined' but he was sure that, now he had received his instructions, he would be 'more on his guard' and 'as cautious in his conduct and in his speech also as his nature will permit.'[51] He did complain to Stuart of his 'meagre and obscure' reports and even sent him copies of his letters with the Duke's comments on them. But, at the same time, he urged Stuart to further 'exertions', although it might be argued that Stuart had been exerting himself much too much already. His principal fear was that the matter might leak out. 'You will see', he wrote, 'that if this matter should be pressed, it may lead to consequences unpleasant to yourself. I cannot say, personally, that I blame you; because I am myself sufficiently a friend to legitimacy to have desired to see the Duc de Bordeaux succeed to the crown.'[52] Stuart regarded this hint that he might be publicly disavowed as verging on the ungentlemanly. He pointed out that he had suppressed all mention of these transactions in his official despatches and he presumed his private letters were not liable to be 'brought forward'. In fact the matter did not leak out and no trace of it survives in the Foreign Office files.[53]

Charles X finally arrived at Portsmouth on 17 August. He would have liked to have gone to Jersey but the British government judged this to be provocatively near to the French coast. Instead he went to Dorset but there were rumours that he was in danger of being kidnapped by French agents. More seriously, he was being dunned by his creditors and in some danger of being arrested for debt. It seemed wise to pack him off to Scotland, where he would be out of English jurisdiction. Holyrood House was put at his disposal, despite some grumbles from the new King, William IV, who complained that he wished to go there himself.[54]

The British government had been deliberately tepid in their reception because, now the legitimist cause was lost, they had to decide how to adjust their relations with whatever government emerged in France. Stanmore says that it was Aberdeen who persuaded Wellington that it was essential to recognise the July Monarchy, under Orleans, who assumed the title of King Louis Philippe.[55] It is certainly true that Aberdeen and Wellington took the decision themselves without consulting either the Cabinet or their European allies, but Wellington, for all his conservatism, was a realist and the surviving documents suggest that they reached the same opinion virtually simultaneously. Wellington wrote to Aberdeen on 12 August that he expected to hear soon whether Orleans had accepted the Crown and:

We can then decide whether we will act without assembling the Cabinet, or without waiting for the opinion of any of our allies. There are some bitter pills to swallow; the cockade; the apparently verbal, but, in fact, real and essential, alterations of the Charter; the act of placing it under the *sauvegarde* of the National Guard; the tone assumed by La Fayette. However, the best chance is to swallow them all . . . I believe that there is not a Power in Europe who will not be relieved from a load of anxiety when it will be known that we have recognized the new Government.[56]

It was Wellington who drew up the elaborate statement of their position for communication to other Powers. The basis of his argument was that by the treaties of 1815, reaffirmed at Aix-la-Chapelle in 1818, the Powers only promised to uphold a French monarch who was both legitimate and constitutional. By the July ordonnances, Charles had behaved unconstitutionally and so had relieved the Allies of any duty towards him. It was true the Allies still had the right to consult their own interests as to whether intervention was called for. Wellington was gloomy about the dangers. Charles's opponents were the enemies of Britain and of Europe. 'What has happened is the revolution acted over again by many of the same characters; the use of the same means, the same symbols, and the adoption of nearly the same measures.' Either civil war or foreign war was possible and the 'Liberal party, in every country in Europe' would act under French protection. But, at the end of the day, Wellington believed that the acceptance of Orleans offered the best hope of peace. Aberdeen replied entirely concurring in his arguments. Technically, he believed, they would have been justified in invoking the Concert of Europe against the overthrow of the Bourbons but, in practice, there was nothing to be gained by such a course. Regrettably, they had no choice but 'to recognise what Lafayette truly calls "the best kind of Republic" '.[57]

Both Aberdeen and Wellington were moved principally by the desire to

preserve the peace of Europe and to prevent either French aggression or a wild-
fire of revolution spreading through the continent. In immediate practical
terms, Greece and Portugal were still unresolved. Aberdeen wrote to Stuart to
find out what he could of the new Prime Minister, Molé. He knew Molé
slightly himself and admitted that he 'gave me a favourable impression of his
honesty and good intentions'. He told Stuart that he took it for granted that
Molé was 'an ultraliberal' but 'in foreign affairs, is he likely to lean to England
or to Russia?'[58] Stuart's reply was not altogether reassuring. Molé was a friend
of Lansdowne, Holland and other leading members of the opposition but, in
international affairs, he was likely to be favourable to Russia.[59] On Greece the
French continued the policy of their predecessors but on Portugal they showed
a disposition to support Maria and Aberdeen wrote to Stuart to emphasise that,
in his opinion, Miguel would have to be recognised in the end.[60]

More immediately, there seemed to be a danger that the French revolution
would provoke a new insurrection in Spain and that men and supplies would
be smuggled over the border. Indeed, the French government used the border
situation to put pressure on the Spaniards to recognise Louis Philippe and
Aberdeen told Heytesbury in a private letter that he regarded the French conduct as 'scandalous'.[61] It was all the more embarrassing because Spanish radicals
had also taken refuge in Britain. Aberdeen promised William IV that, although
under the then alien law it was impossible to exclude them, the government
would try to see that they did not get any money.[62] The whole of Europe
seemed to be ripe for revolution. Aberdeen told his brother, Robert, that Germany was in an extraordinary state with insurrections, for ill-defined causes,
breaking out everywhere, in such places as Brunswick, Hesse, Saxony and
Hamburg. Italy was not in a much better case with trouble likely in Piedmont
and Rome.[63]

It was, however, Belgium which provided the most severe test for British
statesmanship. Holland and Belgium had been united by the Allies in 1814,
when it became clear that Austria had no intention of resuming responsibility
for the old Austrian Netherlands. It was not such an absurd union as European
Liberals were later inclined to claim. It was true that there were linguistic and
religious differences in the now-united Netherlands, but so there were in Switzerland and the differences did not (and do not) correspond with the frontier
between Holland and Belgium. Economically, the union seemed to make sense.
Belgium was comparatively industrialised, Holland an agrarian country with
a great carrying trade. Access to the Dutch empire overseas could be a boon
to Belgian industry. It was the clumsy and prejudiced policy of the Dutch
King, William I, which made the union unworkable. But the Netherlands was
an extremely sensitive strategic area. The Allies' main purpose in uniting Holland and Belgium had been to provide a strong and effective barrier on France's
northern border and consequently, nothing that happened there could be a
matter of indifference to the other great Powers of Europe.

The British Ambassador in The Hague was Sir Charles Bagot, formerly British Minister in the United States and Ambassador in Russia and later Governor-
General of Canada. Wellington lost his temper with Bagot, as he had done

with Stuart de Rothesay, and complained that Britain was 'ill-served' in the Netherlands. Bagot committed some indiscretions, notably Sir Howard Douglas's mission to Antwerp, but he was a very different man from Stuart de Rothesay and kept his government well informed. Like Stuart, he conveyed the most important information to Aberdeen by private letter.[64]

Bagot was, however, in The Hague and he was completely taken by surprise by the outbreak in Brussels on 25 August. Only the previous day he had written to Aberdeen to say that, although there was some press agitation in the south and although the government was taking precautions about the frontier with France, he did not expect serious trouble.[65] Neither Bagot nor Aberdeen was at first sure whether they were witnessing a riot or a revolution. The outbreak began at the Opera House where *La Muette* was being performed. It was customary to applaud the references to Liberty in the opera but this time agitation spread to the streets. Bagot told Aberdeen that there seemed to be no 'distinct political cry'. Only the dregs of the population were so far involved and they seemed bent on mere mischief and pillage. Of the 'respectable bourgeoisie' 3,000 had been issued with arms as a precaution.[66] By 28 August Bagot had changed his opinion. There was, he said, no doubt that it was a revolution, although so far it was confined to Brussels. It was difficult to know what the 'armed Bourgeoisie' wanted, whether they sought independence, union with France, or something else. The States General were to be convoked to The Hague and the Prince of Orange had asked him whether they could count on British assistance in the case of a *casus foederis* arising. Bagot, being a more discreet man than Stuart, replied that only his government could answer that.[67] In the next few days he reported that the disturbances had spread to Antwerp, Liège, Louvain, Namur and Bruges.[68] Stuart de Rothesay sent an express despatch from Paris to say that Molé had called on him to tell him that the maintenance of the Belgian connection with Holland now seemed doubtful. The French insisted that the rebels' objectives were local and France was not concerned but they could not remain 'silent spectators'. They would like to cooperate with Britain and they also proposed to consult Prussia but they would await a British answer first.[69]

When he received these communications, Aberdeen sent them on to Wellington, who was at Stratfieldsaye, admitting his perplexity. He told Bagot, 'Your revolution, or whatever it may be called, is a most incomprehensible affair.' The convocation of the States General seemed to be a judicious move but he could not say whether a *casus foederis* had arisen; at the moment there seemed no intention to separate.[70] This was the question to which Wellington addressed himself. He did not think that either the Eight Articles of 1814, which set up the joint kingdom, or the Treaty of Vienna itself, constituted a guarantee. The status of France was a problem. She had not been a party to the Eight Articles but the matter had been dealt with in the secret articles of the First Treaty of Paris. It was therefore impossible to exclude France from any allied concert on the question. For the rest he was, like Aberdeen, inclined to wait and see how events developed.[71]

From the British government's point of view the situation deteriorated.

Insurrection became more widespread. The Dutch government could neither assemble enough troops to regain control, nor raise enough money to finance operations. The first Dutch appeal to Britain was for a loan of £500,000 from Baring or Rothschild, to be guaranteed by the British government. Aberdeen told Bagot that he regretted that they could not comply with the request because they could not be sure of having it approved by Parliament.[72]

At first it seemed that a compromise might be reached. The Prince of Orange went to Brussels and, since he did not have enough troops to 'overawe' the city, took the considerable risk of entering it alone. Aberdeen approved of his conduct, although neither Bagot nor Wellington did.[73] Some degree of autonomy for the south would not necessarily have constituted a risk but the Prince of Orange's conduct became increasingly an object of suspicion to the British government. In October Bagot wrote privately, 'God knows what the Prince is really doing at Antwerp' and Aberdeen wrote to Heytesbury that Orange was not helping matters by 'throwing himself into the arms' of his Belgian advisers.[74]

As early as 9 September Aberdeen judged the situation to be very serious. The States General were to consider the possibility of 'separation'. It was not clear what was meant by 'separation' but, if it satisfied the insurrectionists 'it will be equivalent to a junction with France'. If finances and the army were separately administered, 'what becomes of the engagements of the King to protect the frontier?' In one sense it was ridiculous to negotiate with France about this. 'The frontier was manifestly constituted against France: is France to deliberate upon the condition of that which is intended to be a protection against herself?' On the other hand the question was clearly a 'European' one and France could reasonably assert her right to be consulted. He concluded quite flatly, 'I take for granted that no party in this country would acquiesce in the separation of the Netherlands from Holland, if such separation was to be of the character we apprehend.' His letters to both Wellington and his brother, Robert, make it clear that at this time he thought the Belgian question a very probable and proper reason for war with France.[75]

Aberdeen was influenced in his reactions by his experiences in 1813–14 and the discussions which had then taken place on Britain's vital interests in the Netherlands. At the end of October, when the chances of the Dutch king regaining control of the south seemed negligible, he still hoped that he might retain Antwerp. Aberdeen's firm rejection of separation early in September must of course be read with his own proviso, separation 'of the character we apprehend'. On 3 October he told Stuart de Rothesay that Britain would not object to separation 'if it can be effected consistently with the security of other States, which regard the independence of the Netherlands, and the maintenance of an efficient barrier on the southern frontier, as essential to their own protection, and to the tranquillity of Europe.'[76]

On 16 October the Dutch Minister of Foreign Affairs saw the representatives of Britain, Austria, Russia and Prussia and formally asked for a Congress to effect a mediation between the two parts of the kingdom. He asked Britain to invite France. The Dutch wanted it to meet immediately, preferably at The

Hague, and to try first to secure an armistice. The Russian and Prussian Ministers agreed, subject to receiving the necessary instructions. The previous day the French had suggested a conference in Paris. Metternich was also hankering after a conference, although one concerned with wider matters than the Netherlands. Aberdeen had written to Robert in September, 'Our friend Metternich is now again beginning to be in all his glory. We shall have conferences without end, which, however, I have strongly objected to for the present.' A conference limited to the Belgian question was a rather different proposition.[77]

Both Aberdeen and Wellington objected to the idea of a conference in Paris and there were difficulties about a venue in the Netherlands as well. Since it was now feared that the troubles might spread to the north, no place could be considered quite secure, but, more immediately, there would be the problem of whether a representative of Belgium, as well as of Holland, should be admitted. Wellington believed that this problem could be avoided in London. The French held out against the proposal that the conference should meet in London mainly, Stuart de Rothesay believed, because the new French Ambassador in London was Talleyrand and his opponents did not wish to see him distinguish himself. Aberdeen, who had learnt of the appointment with a mixture of amusement and amazement, replied rather tartly that, since Talleyrand had helped to frame the original treaties, he seemed a most suitable person to conduct the negotiations.[78] The matter was becoming urgent and the other Powers acquiesced in the choice of London for the meeting.

Palmerston was to score what has usually been considered his greatest triumph in the conduct of foreign affairs, in his skiful handling of the London conference on Belgium which was to remain in session for the next nine years; but it was Aberdeen who, after Wellington had formally opened the first meeting on 4 November, presided at the early sessions.[79] With both the Greek and the Belgian conferences meeting there, London had become to an unusual degree the centre of European diplomacy. It is not surprising that, during the next decade, Metternich tried to shift that centre to some place in Germany or Austria where it would be more under his control, or that Palmerston strongly resisted the move.[80] London's prominence in 1830 was partly fortuitous, and partly due to the exceptional prestige of the Duke of Wellington as an international statesman. Aberdeen's role could only be subordinate to the Duke, but it still placed him in a crucial position at the heart of European diplomacy. Added to the experience of 1813-14 it made him an exceptionally experienced man, *au fait* with all the often contradictory currents which were running, familiar with both the problems and the men. No man was more aware of the difficulties inherent in conference diplomacy but he continued to believe that ambassadorial conferences were a useful diplomatic device, which offered a reasonable chance of substituting negotiation for conflict.

European problems occupied most of Aberdeen's time at the Foreign Office but the American continent contributed its share. It was still not certain that Spain would finally acquiesce in the loss of her American empire. In February 1830 Aberdeen was alarmed by a report that Spain meant to send an expedition to Mexico from her remaining colony of Cuba. He warned Henry Addington, the British Minister in Madrid, that such an attempt could have disastrous consequences. It might lead to a rising in Cuba itself which would give the United States an excuse to intervene. In view of Cuba's crucial strategic importance in the Caribbean, such intervention would be very unwelcome to Britain.[81]

Britain had other potential quarrels with the United States. The Treaty of Versailles of 1783, at the end of the American war of Independence, had described the boundary between the United States and the remaining colonies of British North America in words, but no map had been annexed to the Treaty. The exact line of the boundary between Maine and New Brunswick had been in dispute ever since. Negotiations on the question had begun in 1794 and, in 1827, during Canning's administration, it had been agreed that the matter should be referred to the arbitration of some European sovereign. Wellington had not liked the idea but it was difficult to go back on it. The matter had become the more urgent because the Americans were now objecting strongly to the British exercising jurisdiction in the disputed area, although the British replied that they had always exercised authority in the area in question. It could only be a matter of time before a major international incident occurred. The King of the Netherlands was asked to examine the available documents and to determine the intentions of the treaty-makers of 1783. In the autumn of 1829 Aberdeen was busy collecting the material for the arbitration. He determined to put the matter into the hands of Stratford Canning, 'who thoroughly understands the subject', from the time when he had been British Minister in Washington from 1820 to 1823. This attempt to make an *amende honorable* to Canning did not meet with Wellington's approval. He replied scathingly, 'I think the Case is too serious for S. Canning. He made out a Case for Mr Canning on the Principalities most ingeniously. But it was false from beginning to End.'[82] On this occasion Aberdeen ignored Wellington's advice and used Canning to prepare a British memorandum on the subject. The King of the Netherlands, however, came to the conclusion that it was impossible to arrive at the original intention of the treaty of 1783. The evidence was too confused, and the maps too inaccurate. Instead, in 1831, he suggested a compromise line, which in turn, was rejected by the United States.

South America was also troublesome. The 'United Provinces of the River Plate' were in fact so disunited that, at times, Britain was uncertain whom to address as the legitimate government. Nevertheless, on 10 June 1829 the Buenos Aires government proclaimed Louis Vernet, a Hamburg merchant, Governor of the Falkland (Malvinas) Islands. Aberdeen, prompted by Sir George Murray at the War Office, addressed an official protest to Buenos Aires, pointing out that this was a breach of British sovereignty, which had been acknowledged as recently as 1771 by Spain.[83] But it was left to Grey's government, with Palmerston at the Foreign Office, to enforce the claim with a British naval detachment in January 1833. The question returned to haunt Aberdeen, when he was next in office as Colonial Secretary in 1834–5. Wellington, now Foreign Secretary, asked for his advice on the Argentine protest about the British action. Aberdeen was sceptical of the Argentine claim that they had been in 'notorious and tranquil possession for more than half a century up to the moment when we were dislodged by force on the 5th of Jany. 1833', despite their appeal to Blackstone's doctrine, 'Occupancy is the true ground and foundation of all property'. At the same time he was unconvinced by enthusiasts' assertions that the Falklands would be as important for the Pacific trade round Cape Horn as the Cape of Good Hope was for Indian trade. The question of whether it would be 'expedient' to go on occupying the Falkland Islands was still unresolved when Aberdeen retired from the Colonial Office. It was again left to Palmerston to continue to assert British claims by sending out 'two or three Families of Fishermen from the Shetland or Orkney Islands'.[84]

NOTES

1. *Hansard*, 2nd ser., XVI, 369 (12 Dec. 1826).
2. Bagot, vol. 2, p. 183.
3. See also his reply to Lord Holland, *Hansard*, 2nd ser., XIX, 1725–6 (16 July 1828).
4. Ellenborough, vol. 1, pp. 62–3.
5. Add. MSS 43056, Wellington to Aberdeen, 20 July 1828.
6. Add. MSS 43056, Aberdeen to Wellington, 10 May 1828.
7. Add. MSS 43056, Wellington to Aberdeen, 7 July 1828; Ellenborough, vol. 1, p. 152 (24 June 1828).
8. FO 63/332, Lamb to Dudley, No. 62, 23 Apr. 1828.
9. Add. MSS 43088, Lamb to Dudley, 3 June 1828.
10. Ellenborough, vol. 1, p. 154 (25 June 1828).
11. FO 63/331, Aberdeen to Lamb, No. 3, 5 June 1828.
12. Ellenborough, vol. 1, p. 152 (24 June 1828).
13. FO 63/331, Aberdeen to Lamb, Separate, 28 June 1828; Add. MSS 43088, Aberdeen to Lamb, 25 Sept. 1828.
14. Add. MSS 43056, Wellington to Aberdeen, 7 July 1828; Add. MSS 43088, Lamb to Aberdeen, 9, 21 June 1828.
15. Wellington, Memorandum, 19 Sept. 1828, Wellington *Corr.*, vol. V, pp. 63–4.
16. *Hansard*, 2nd ser., XIX, 1724–7.
17. Add. MSS 43081, Aberdeen to Strangford, No. 2, 19 Aug. 1828.
18. Add. MSS 43056, Wellington to Aberdeen, 2, 5, 23 Sept. 1828.
19. Barbacena to Wellington, 15 Oct. 1828, Wellington to Barbacena, 18 Oct. 1828, PP, XXVI (1829) 93–5.
20. Wellington to Palmella, 20, 27 Nov. 1828, Palmella to Wellington, 3 Dec. 1828, PP, XXVI (1829) 96–9.
21. Palmella to Wellington, 20 Dec. 1828. 2 Jan. 1829, Wellington to Palmella, 23, 30 Dec. 1828, Admiralty to Capt. Walpole, 12 Dec. 1828, Walpole to Admiralty, 14 Feb. 1828, PP, XXVI (1829) 105–23.
22. *Hansard*, 2nd ser., XXIII, 737–49 (23 Mar. 1830).
23. *Hansard*, 2nd ser., XXII, 42 (4 Feb. 1830).
24. *Ibid.* 44–5.

25. *Annual Register* (1829) pp. 174–84.
26. *Hansard*, 2nd ser., XXII 44–5.
27. Add. MSS 43085, Aberdeen to Stuart, 28 Sept. 1830.
28. Wellington dealt directly with both Barbacena and Palmella, see letters published in PP, XXVI (1829) 13, 'Papers respecting the Relations between Great Britain and Portugal 1826–29'.
29. Ellenborough, vol. 1, pp. 145, 148 (13, 15 June 1828); Add. MSS 43058–9, Aberdeen to Wellington, 23 Nov. 1829, Wellington to Aberdeen, 31 Aug., 7 Sept. 1830.
30. Add. MSS 43056, Wellington to Aberdeen, 22 Sept. 1828.
31. Add. MSS 43057, Aberdeen to Wellington, 24 Aug. 1829.
32. FO 7/221, Cowley to Aberdeen, No. 3, 3 Jan. 1830.
33. Add. MSS 43210, Aberdeen to Robert, 25 Jan. 1830.
34. FO 27/405, Aberdeen to Stuart, No. 9, 19 Feb. 1830; FO 27/407, Stuart to Aberdeen, No. 82, 26 Feb. 1830.
35. Add. MSS 43084, Stuart to Aberdeen, 8, 22 Mar., 24 Apr., 14 May 1830, Aberdeen to Stuart, 12, 19 Mar., 21 Apr., 4, 11 May 1830.
36. Add. MSS 43058, Wellington to Aberdeen, 18 18 Apr. 1830; FO 27/405, Aberdeen to Stuart, No. 23, 21 Apr. 1830; Add. MSS 43084, Aberdeen to Stuart, 4 May 1830.
37. FO 27/405, Aberdeen to Stuart, No. 39, 30 July 1830; FO 27/411, Stuart to Aberdeen, No. 344, 16 July, No. 355, 23 July 1830.
38. FO 27/411, Stuart to Aberdeen, 29 July 1830; Add. MSS 43085, Aberdeen to Stuart, 31 July 1830.
39. FO 27/411, Stuart to Aberdeen, No. 362, 26 July 1830; FO 27/405, Aberdeen to Stuart, No. 39, 30 July 1830.
40. FO 27/411, Stuart to Aberdeen, No. 364, 28 July, Nos 365, 366, 367, 29 July 1830.
41. Add. MSS 43085, Aberdeen to Stuart, 31 July 1830.
42. FO 27/411, Stuart to Aberdeen, No. 370, 30 July 1830 (This was received 1.30 a.m. 2 Aug.).
43. FO 27/412, Stuart to Aberdeen, No. 379, 2 Aug. 1830.
44. FO 27/412, Stuart to Aberdeen, No. 387, 3 Aug. 1830; Add. MSS 43085, Aberdeen to Stuart, 6 Aug. 1830.
45. Add. MSS 43085, Stuart to Aberdeen, 5 Aug. 1830 (3 letters). The Duke, ever practical, said 600,000 francs in gold could never be sent by carriage, it would break the springs, Add. MSS 43059, Wellington to Aberdeen, 15 Aug. 1830.
46. Add.MSS. 43085, Stuart to Aberdeen, 5 Aug. 1830 (2nd and 3rd letters).
47. Add. MSS 43085, Aberdeen to Stuart, 8 Aug. 1830.
48. Craddock, who later preferred to spell his name Caradoc, was an extraordinary character, who turned up in most of the world's trouble–spots. He succeeded his father as Lord Howden in 1839, *D.N.B.* IX, 29.
49. Add. MSS 43085, Stuart to Aberdeen, 9 Aug. 1830 (2 letters) encl. Craddock to Stuart, 9 Aug. 1830.
50. Add. MSS 43085, Comments on Stuart to Aberdeen, 9 Aug. 1830; Add. MSS 43059, Wellington to Aberdeen, 13, 16 Aug. 1830.
51. Wellington Papers, Aberdeen to Wellington, 12 Aug. 1830.
52. Add. MSS 43085, Aberdeen to Stuart, 11 Aug. 1830; NLS, MS 6245, Aberdeen to Stuart, 19 Aug. 1830 (copy in 43085 dated 20 Aug.).

53. Add. MSS 43085, Stuart to Aberdeen, 23 Aug. 1830. Traces were left in the Wellington Papers and some relevant letters were published in the Wellington *Corr.*, vol. VII, but the full story only survives in the Aberdeen and Stuart de Rothesay Papers.

54. Add. MSS 43085, Aberdeen to Stuart, 19 Aug. 1830; Add. MSS 43040, Sir Herbert Taylor to Aberdeen, 1 Sept. 1830, Aberdeen to Taylor, 7 Sept. 1830; Wellington to Aberdeen, 8, 9 Sept. 1830, Aberdeen to Wellington, 20 Sept. 1830, Wellington to Peel, 9 Sept. 1830, Wellington, *Corr.* vol. VII, pp. 248–9, 251, 271–2; Ellenborough, vol. 2, pp. 378, 380.

55. Stanmore, pp. 100–1.

56. Add. MSS 43059, Wellington to Aberdeen, 12 Aug. 1830.

57. Add. MSS 43059, Wellington to Aberdeen, 14 Aug. 1830 (2 letters) encl. Memorandum by Wellington, 14 Aug. 1830; Wellington Papers, Aberdeen to Wellington, 16 Aug. 1830.

58. Add. MSS 43085, Aberdeen to Stuart, 17 Aug. 1830.

59. Add. MSS 43085, Stuart to Aberdeen, 20 Aug. 1830.

60. Add. MSS 43085, Aberdeen to Stuart, 28 Sept. 1830.

61. Add. MSS 43089, Aberdeen to Heytesbury, 17 Oct. 1830.

62. Add. MSS 43040, Aberdeen to Sir Herbert Taylor, 7 Sept. 1830.

63. Add. MSS 43210, Aberdeen to Robert, 20 Sept. 1830.

64. Add. MSS 43059, Wellington to Aberdeen, 19 Oct. 1830. Bagot sent Douglas, in great secrecy, to discover the state of the defences at Antwerp and along the French frontier but news of his mission leaked out and caused a sensation, Add. MSS 43087, Bagot to Aberdeen, 29 Oct., 6, 8 Nov. 1830.

65. Add. MSS 43087, Bagot to Aberdeen, 24 Aug. 1830.

66. Add. MSS 43087, Bagot to Aberdeen, 27 Aug. 1830.

67. Add. MSS 43087, Bagot to Aberdeen, 28 Aug. 1830.

68. Add. MSS 43087, Bagot to Aberdeen, 30 Aug. 1830.

69. FO 27/413, Stuart to Aberdeen, No. 462, 31 Aug. 1830.

70. Add. MSS 43059, Aberdeen to Wellington, 2 Sept. 1830; Add. MSS 43087, Aberdeen to Bagot, 3 Sept. 1830.

71. Add. MSS 43059, Wellington to Aberdeen, 3 Sept. 1830 encl. memorandum.

72. Add. MSS 43087, Aberdeen to Bagot, 9 Sept., 15 Oct. 1830.

73. Add. MSS 43087, Bagot to Aberdeen, 3 Sept. 1830, Aberdeen to Bagot, 9 Sept. 1830; Add. MSS 43059, Wellington to Aberdeen, 8 Sept. 1830.

74. Add. MSS 43087, Bagot to Aberdeen, 13 Oct. 1830; Add. MSS 43089, Aberdeen to Heytesbury, 17 Oct. 1830.

75. Add. MSS 43059, Aberdeen to Wellington, 9 Sept. 1830.

76. FO 27/405, Aberdeen to Stuart, No. 55, 3 Oct. 1830; Add MSS 43087, Aberdeen to Bagot, 26 Oct. 1830.

77. FO 37/170, Bagot to Aberdeen, 16 Oct. 1830; Add MSS 43210, Aberdeen to Robert, 20 Sept. 1830.

78. Add. MSS 43059, Wellington to Aberdeen, 19 Oct. 1830 encl. memorandum; Add. MSS 43085, Stuart to Aberdeen, 22 Oct. 1830, Aberdeen to Stuart, 22 Oct. 1830; Add. MSS 43059, Aberdeen to Wellington, 13 Sept. 1830.

79. PP, XLII (1833) 1.

80. For discussion of this see Webster, 'Palmerston, Metternich and the European system', *Proceedings of the British Academy*, XX (1934).

81. Aberdeen *Corr.*, BP 12/2, Aberdeen to Addington, 17 Feb. 1830.

82. Add. MSS 43058, Aberdeen to Wellington, 20 Oct. 1829, Wellington to Aberdeen, 21 Oct. 1829.

83. Add. MSS. 43233, Aberdeen to Murray, 4 Aug 1892; FO 6/499, Aberdeen to Parish, No 5, 8 Aug 1892; FO 6/27, f16, 'Draft of official Note to be presented by Mr. Parish'.

84. CO 78/2, FO to CO, 2 Feb 1835, Parish to Palmerston (copy), 1 July 1834, CO to Admiralty, 18 Feb 1835, FO to CO, 30 Apr, 29 May 1835.

CHAPTER FIFTEEN

A Conservative at home

Wellington's government resigned in the middle of November 1830, after a comparatively minor defeat in the Commons. Two months earlier Aberdeen had written to his brother, Robert, that he was 'at single anchor'. He admitted that for a number of reasons, mainly personal, he would be glad to leave office but that there were also many things that he would regret.[1]

Wellington's ministry had not looked to be in imminent danger of falling in the summer of 1830. George IV had died on 26 June and his successor, William IV, was better disposed towards the ministry than his brother had been. George's death necessitated a general election but Wellington at first thought that the news of the revolution in France would rally all the conservative and property-owning classes in Britain to the support of the government. In fact, the party managers believed that the government had gained seventeen seats and that they could count, more or less, on 368 votes in the Commons against 234 for the opposition. The weakness of the calculation lay in the fact that the commitment of many of those 368 to the ministry was very loose indeed.

On 2 November 1830 the Lords debated the Address in reply to the King's Speech. At that time there seemed no certainty that 1830 would not turn out to be another 1789 in Europe. The revolution had already spread beyond France and equally there was no certainty that it would not spread to Britain. Already, in the summer of 1830, there had been serious rick-burnings in Kent and Sussex. Farm machinery was being broken by bands claiming to operate under the direction of the mysterious 'Captain Swing'. The Cabinet were warned that there would be attempts against their lives and that of the King when the King attended the Lord Mayor's banquet on 9 November.[2] Some men, including Lord Brougham and Lord John Russell, had already come to the conclusion that the only way to stave off revolution was reform, and more particularly parliamentary reform. In Europe Wellington had supported Aberdeen in adopting a very pragmatic approach. In Britain he resolved to take a much tougher and more uncompromising line.

In the Lords that veteran reformer, Lord Grey, wound up the debate for the Opposition by suggesting that reform was the best antidote to the prevailing distress, although admitting that he was not bound to any particular reform scheme. Wellington took up this point in his reply to say that he too knew of no measure which anyone could say would be better than the existing parliamentary system. Then, either by deliberate intent or carried away by the apparent approval of the House, he went on to deliver an encomium on the perfection of the British constitution, to deny that anyone wanted change, and to make it quite clear that he would resolutely oppose even the most limited reform. There are several versions of what exactly happened next but that given by Aberdeen's son is as convincing as any. When the Duke sat down he turned to Aberdeen, sitting beside him, and said, '"I have not said too much, have I?" Lord Aberdeen put his chin forward, with a gesture habitual to him when much moved, and only replied: *"You'll hear of it!"* After leaving the House he was asked what the Duke had said. He said that we were going out, was the reply.'[3] The government was probably relieved to be able to resign after the defeat on the Civil List on 15 November because the following day Brougham was to propose a radical motion on parliamentary reform in the Commons. The government expected to be defeated on it and the reform gauntlet would have been thrown down with a vengeance.

Aberdeen told his son many years later that, if the Duke had consulted him, he could and would have stopped him speaking as he did.[4] Aberdeen respected Wellington's judgement but he respected that of William Pitt more and he believed that Pitt had died still committed in principle to Parliamentary reform, although compelled to concede that it must be indefinitely postponed during the French wars. Parliamentary reform, however, meant different things to different people. To Pitt it meant primarily redistribution and Aberdeen too seems to have interpreted it mainly in this sense in 1830. The absurdity of Old Sarum having two members when Manchester had none was too obvious to be defensible. The widening of the franchise was another and more debatable question. Those few boroughs which had a wide franchise, the so-called scot-and-lot and potwalloper boroughs, were notorious centres of corruption and intimidation.

Lord Grey's Whig government introduced their first Reform Bill into the Commons in March 1831. Sixty boroughs with fewer than 2,000 inhabitants were to lose both their members; forty-seven more with between 2,000 and 4,000 inhabitants were to retain only one member. Eleven hitherto unrepresented boroughs, including Manchester and Birmingham, gained two members; twenty-one others, one. Twenty-seven English and Welsh counties gained additional members. In the boroughs, in addition to existing voters, occupiers of houses worth at least £10 a year were to have the vote. In the counties the £10 copyholders and £50 long-leaseholders gained the vote beside the forty-shilling freeholders. The Bill passed its second reading but was defeated in committee in April. Grey persuaded the King to dissolve Parliament and the government was returned with an increased majority. The Cabinet considered raising the borough qualification or modifying the disfranchising schedule but in the end they reintroduced the Bill in June substantially unchanged. It passed the Commons but was rejected by the Lords on 8 October.

Aberdeen had been in favour of moderate reform but he did not regard the Whig measure of 1831 as moderate. He wrote to Alexander Crombie in June 1831 regretting that the ministers had not had the courage to introduce the changes in the second Bill which they themselves knew to be necessary. 'The fact is', he complained, 'that the question of Reform is no longer in the hands of the Government. Ministers are at the mercy of a Revolutionary faction, by whom alone they are kept in office; and to whose dictation, if they desire to preserve their places, they must yield obedience.' He still hoped the measure might be defeated or 'materially improved'.[5] He voted with the majority against the Bill in the Lords in October.

As he travelled north to Haddo after the prorogation, Aberdeen wondered what he would find. Riots had broken out in many parts of the country. Nottingham castle, belonging to the Duke of Newcastle, a leading anti-reformer, had been burnt down. In Derby a mob had attacked the houses of opponents of the Bill and tried to storm the county gaol to release those who had been arrested. Bristol was in the hands of the rioters for three days and the Mansion House, the Bishop's palace, three gaols and the Customs House were among the buildings destroyed. In all three cities troops restored order with difficulty and some loss of life. The situation seemed to be truly revolutionary and Aberdeen wrote to Crombie:

I shall be very anxious to learn what effect may be produced in Aberdeen by the rejection of the Reform Bill. With such feeble means of preserving the publick peace, the situation of the town may be alarming in the event of any great excitement. I do not think it likely that anything serious will happen in London; but in some of the great manufacturing towns mischief is to be feared. In Derby great excesses have already been committed.[6]

He found the country north of the border less excited than he expected. He wrote to the Duke of Wellington on 5 November, after he had arrived at Haddo:

In this part of the country the people are not only indifferent but decidedly opposed to it [Reform]; and I would readily engage to produce a petition, signed by three-fourths of the farmers who have votes, against the bill. Such is the case in this and the adjoining county. My own tenantry, who are a numerous body of near nine hundred, have made the most unusual demonstrations of satisfaction and good-will. Even in the town of Aberdeen they are beginning to get tired of the question; for the last meeting gave evidence of increasing indifference. It was not attended by twenty persons who would have the votes as ten-pound householders, although four or five thousand of the populace were present.

He castigated the government for having called into existence a revolutionary spirit, which would not otherwise have existed, and which they could in no way control. He added grimly, 'The events at Bristol show what we are to 'expect' and he feared 'the means of resistance possessed by property alone would not be great.' His own tenantry continued to be friendly and he told Gurney on his return to London in December that he did not find that 'my character of an Anti-Reformer had made me odious in my own neighbourhood'.[7]

But he still believed the situation to be basically a revolutionary one and that the government had embarked on a course which could only result in the destruction of all established institutions. He told Gurney:

I suppose our new Government and Constitution will be completed in the course of the ensuing year. The Duration of the constitution, when made, cannot be long. The house of Lords, as such, will first fall, and indeed ought not to exist. I strongly suspect too that the authority of the Crown, and perhaps the Kingly character itself, are destined to speedy destruction.

Ministers were 'floundering' from one difficulty to another at home and abroad. He thought that Gurney, who was always prophesying disaster, was at last right and that there would be a financial smash and a continental war.[8]

The government introduced a third version of the Reform Bill into the Commons in December. This time it embodied more substantial concessions. The number of boroughs to be completely or partially disfranchised was reduced. The county franchise was extended to £10 long–leaseholders and £50 tenants–at–will. The government began to put pressure on the King to promise to create additional peers if the House of Lords still proved obstinate. The Bill passed its second reading in the Lords in April but on 7 May Lord Lyndhurst persuaded the House to adopt what was essentially a delaying motion. When William refused to create fifty peers, the government resigned on 9 May.

By now, however, everyone except a handful of die-hards was convinced that some reform measure was imperative. Aberdeen himself thought the third Bill 'in some respects to be better; in others, worse than the old'. The important thing was to prevent the mass creation of peers. He was active in organising an Address from a number of peers to the King, begging him not to consent to the additional creations. 'The great object now', he told Crombie, asking him to get the Duke of Gordon's signature, 'is to endeavour to confirm the King in his disinclination to create Peers for the purpose of carrying the Bill.'[9]

But Aberdeen was not averse to compromise. The Bishops were the particular target of radical wrath for having secured a majority against the Bill in the Lords in October 1831, but in fact Aberdeen's old friend, William Howley, who was now Archbishop of Canterbury, had tried very hard to obtain a behind–the–scenes compromise. He had sent his proposals to Aberdeen who had passed them on to Peel. But Peel had been pessimistic, believing that the government was now committed to its whole Bill and could not compromise. The negotiations came to nothing.[10]

By the spring of 1832 Aberdeen's real sympathies may well have lain with the group known (not very flatteringly) as the 'Waverers', led by his own close friends, the veteran Harrowby and Binning, now Lord Haddington, seventeen of whom voted for the second reading of the Bill on 14 April. Wellington had been sharply critical of the Waverers in February and Aberdeen himself did not vote at all in the critical division of 14 April – although his abstention may have been due to illness. He wrote to Crombie shortly afterwards, apologising for not answering letters and explaining that he had been quite seriously ill (possibly with influenza) and would not be allowed out for some time. On the other hand he may well have been among those peers who 'while wanting Harrowby to win, also wanted [from loyalty to the Duke] not to vote for him'. [11]

Early in May Aberdeen made detailed comments on some amendments suggested by Croker. He strongly favoured the idea that the household franchise should depend less on the value of the property than on length of residence. He told Wellington, 'I apprehend that the best possible test of respectability in the lower orders consists in a fixed residence, whether of one or of three years.' It would also make it possible to substitute payment of the poor rate over the stipulated period for 'registration' as the test of eligibility to vote. Aberdeen was deeply suspicious of the registration procedures, complaining, 'The busy, discontented, and political part of the community will take care to get their names formally registered. The quiet portion of the community, who attend to their own affairs and not those of the State, will either not register at all, or be guilty of some remissness that will technically defeat the vote.' [12] He was certainly correct in foreseeing that registration procedures would provide a field-day for election agents over the next few years.

When Grey resigned on 9 May, the King sent for Wellington. Wellington, ever the realist, was prepared to try to carry a compromise measure. As he told Lord Falmouth, they were going to have a Reform Act in any case, the only question now was whether it would be with or without sixty additional peers. Aberdeen and several other former ministers were prepared to join him in the attempt but Peel was adamant that it was for the Whigs to carry the Bill. [13]

Peel's refusal was fatal to Wellington's hopes. The country now seemed genuinely close to revolution. Grey came back into office on 18 May with the King's promise to create peers if necessary. There was now no serious alternative to Grey's measure and Aberdeen again abstained from voting on 4 June when only 22 die-hard peers voted against the final reading of the third Reform Bill. [14]

It dealt only with England and Wales. Scotland was the subject of a separate measure, introduced into the Commons in March 1831 and finally passed by the Lords in July 1832. Only Scottish members and Scottish peers took much interest in it. They complained, with reason, that the original draft showed how little Westminster lawyers understood of the Scottish system. They had not realised that Scottish leases tended to be much longer or that Scottish rents were still often paid in kind — tables had to be drawn up of money equivalents. [15]

The differences, however, were much more profound than that. The Scottish electoral system was enshrined in the Act of Union of 1707. In the burghs, members were elected by the town councils. In the counties the franchise had originally been based, as in England, on the forty-shilling freeholder but, whereas in England changes in the value of money had meant that the forty-shilling freeholders had come to constitute quite a wide electorate, in Scotland the vote remained tied to certain properties which had had the franchise at certain periods. It was possible by the Scottish system of 'superiorities' (a relic of feudal law) to retain the right to vote, independently of the actual possession of the property, and the franchise had come to acquire a monetary value of its own in any sale of property. As a result, Scotland 'resembled one vast, rotten borough'.[16] In 1831 she returned forty-five M.P.s to Westminster but, out of a population of nearly two and a half million, only four and a half thousand had the vote.

Even die-hards found it difficult to defend this system and the most popular argument against reform was that the Scots were so unaccustomed to representative government that its sudden introduction would cause disorder. Some, like Aberdeen himself on his visit to Haddo in the autumn of 1831, felt that there was no demand for it. Aberdeen's friend, Haddington, played an active part in trying to get modifications in the Scottish Bill. He pleaded unsuccessfully in 1832 for representation for the Scottish universities, and Aberdeen supported him when he asked that those who had lost 'property' because they could no longer sell the right to vote with their land, should be compensated.[17] The House of Lords was unsympathetic and, in fact, all interest in the details of the Scottish Bill had petered out when the main measure for England and Wales passed.

The English and Welsh electorate increased by something between 50 and 80 per cent,[18] that of Scotland by 1,500 per cent. At a stroke the Scottish electorate rose from 4,500 to 65,000, that of the Scottish counties from 3,000 to 33,000. The Aberdeenshire electorate increased *pro rata* from 182 in 1831 to over 2,000 in 1833. Aberdeen would have been less than human if his thoughts had not turned first to how this massive expansion of the electorate would affect his own interests. His brother, William, had represented the county since 1818 and, as early as June 1831, he asked Crombie to calculate the effects of the proposed reforms and 'prepare accordingly'.[19] The election which followed the passage of the Great Reform Act proved that it was possible to keep 'Captain William' there but that it was going to be very much more expensive to do so. Crombie died, to Aberdeen's great sorrow,[20] in November 1832 but his successor, James Brebner, kept very careful accounts of the election expenses.[21]

The election cost Aberdeen £5,686. 2s. 7d. Brebner's accounts began with a modest sum of £1. 10s. 6d. paid to Arthur Duff for music at the Committee Dinner on 22 December 1832 and continued with £50 paid to various charities, including £10 to the Shipwrecked Seamen's Fund and £10 to the Infirmary and Lunatic Asylum. Many of the items were, at least on the face of it, entirely unexceptional, for example, £100 to John Davidson and Co., Printers, presumably for posters and other election literature, miscellaneous sums to various poll clerks (an expense which candidates were expected to bear), and several hundred pounds for horses, presumably to get electors to the poll. Others are more difficult to interpret; for example, £1 on 9 March, 'Paid John Main Savock allowance for expenses at Registration'; £20. 5s. 6d. on 25 March, 'Paid Mr Gordon of Cairnbulg for his expenses about Registration'; £2. 2s. 0d. on 11 May, 'Paid Charles McKenzie for expense about election'; or £5. 5s. 0d. on 31 May, 'Paid Joseph Robertson for trouble about Election'. Apart from these small sums it is not clear what Messrs Adam and Anderson supplied in return for £853. 6s. 0d or Mr Farquhar for £455. 7s. 9½d. Brebner was very apologetic for the amount of money he had had to expend for 'the Captain's' election. 'These expenses I am sorry to say are very heavy', he wrote, 'but I trust that there will be no occasion for such a heavy expenditure in future.'[22]

It was the more irritating because the unexpected expenditure had put Aberdeen's account in the red for the year. Without the election, Aberdeen's receipts had been £21,154. 6s. 11d; his disbursements, £18,070. 17s. 5½d. After the election expenses had been met there was an adverse balance of £2,602. 13s. 1½d. and, as Brebner warned Aberdeen, there would be interest charges on the deficit, which had presumably been met by loans.[23] £5,000 was a large item in an annual budget of £21,000 and it is perhaps understandable that Aberdeen commented sourly to Peel, 'In this County my brother is safe, if we can bring the voters to the poll, and successfully resist violence and intimidation. But the expense of the whole affair is ruinous; and I do not see very clearly in what respect the member will be more independent than when elected by two hundred gentlemen.'[24]

'Bringing the voters to the poll' meant partly wrestling with the intricacies of registration but Aberdeen's fears of intimidation were amply fulfilled. Even Henry Cockburn who drew up the Scottish Reform Bill admitted that Scottish mobs were dangerous, '. . . they never joke; and they throw stones'.[25] Aberdeen had every reason to appreciate that. He wrote to Wellington the day after the poll closed, 'There has been a good deal of intimidation, and some violence. One of my younger brothers [Charles] had his leg broken by a mob, who attacked him and some of his friends with large stones. The fracture so made is a serious one.'[26] For some time Aberdeen's family letters carried regular bulletins on the slow healing of Charles's leg. But William won the election by 1182 votes to 1102.

Aberdeen had to face two further elections in 1835 and 1837, and, although he tried to put a good face on the matter, he found the expense nearly ruinous. He told Hudson Gurney in 1834 'elections are pleasures which recur rather too frequently', and Princess Lieven in 1837 '. . . the expense is enormous; and two contests in three years are enough to ruin a man of moderate fortune. I may be able to bear it; but it would be out of the power of many to do so.' It was, he thought, no advertisement for the advantages of popular representation.[27]

Aberdeen could, however, count on a genuine reservoir of goodwill on his own estates. Haddo provided an excellent example of the workings of the so-called 'politics of deference', or, in more neutral language, of tenants' belief that the agricultural interest stood or fell together and that it was not only the right, but the duty, of the landowner's family to represent that interest at Westminster. In 1837 he had to meet what he called to his eldest son 'a sharp contest' and, to Princess Lieven, 'a vexatious opposition' in the county.[28] The opposition concealed their intention of fielding a candidate until the night before nominations closed, when they put up Sir Thomas Burnett. The Conservatives then found that every district in the county was full of their opponents' agents, busy registering voters, and that, as Aberdeen put it 'every post horse had been engaged against us'. The Haddo farmers, however, feeling more in common with Captain William than with the Aberdeen lawyers, rallied round to offer horses and other assistance. William emerged with an increased majority of over 500. Aberdeen still commented to his son, 'This is all very triumphant; but it is enormously expensive; and as I have had to stand two contests in three years, without receiving the assistance of a single shilling, I can very ill afford it.'[29] The Aberdeenshire voters were loyal but they expected their views to be taken into account. When Aberdeen decided that it was time for William to give up the seat to Lord Haddo, William was not very willing to do so, although his brother argued that the bargain had always been that Aberdeen would finance his brother in the seat only until he wanted it for his son. (In fact the original bargain had been that Aberdeen would finance William in return for a promise to look after Catherine and her daughters if Aberdeen died without a direct heir.)[30] It was soon made clear to Aberdeen that the electors regarded William as their member and would take a poor view of having him set aside for a young and untried man.[31]

Finding a seat for Haddo was a problem. As soon as Haddo came of age in 1837, although he was travelling abroad and not much interested in Parliament, his father set out to buy him a seat. If he had been asked to justify his actions he would no doubt have replied in the conventional conservative terms of the period, that it was a man's independence when he got to Parliament which counted, not how many voters had put him there, and that rotten boroughs had been excellent nurseries for talented young men. Canning, Castlereagh and many other great statesmen had arrived by that route. Probably he did not find it necessary to justify it, even to himself. He was doing his best for his family in the usual manner of the eighteenth– or early nineteenth–century aristocrat. He approached F. R. Bonham, the Conservative party manager, to find a suitable seat and, in 1838, entered into negotiations to secure the notorious borough of Penrhyn, where a by-election was expected. When the expected vacancy did not occur Haddo thankfully escaped abroad again. In the autumn of 1839 Bonham suggested Honiton in Devon as a possible seat and Aberdeen promised him that Haddo would be available by the Easter of 1840. Aberdeen would have liked Haddo to have had a county seat but dared not risk such a contest when his party was out of office. Expense was a major consideration. He had warned Haddo in 1838 not to buy antiques in Rome, 'for I assure you, that money matters are becoming very serious'. Honiton was expensive but, at first, it seemed a safe seat and Aberdeen told Bonham, 'I should much prefer the *certain seat*, at an expense not exceeding two thousand pounds, to the chances of a contest on more reasonable terms.' When, however, Bonham's local agent, a solicitor named Neale, wanted £1000 guaranteed even in the event of failure, Aberdeen jibbed. He told Bonham, 'I approve of the terms of £2500 for the seat but I do not approve of the payment of £1000 in the event of failure.' For £1000 he could have 'a chance of success' in twenty places. The arrangement fell through and Haddo was not accommodated with a seat until 1853.[32]

Aberdeen might have found another justification for this manipulation of the supposedly 'reformed' parliament in that for some years he honestly believed that the constitution was doomed and that they were fighting a rearguard action against revolution. He had told Gurney in December 1831 that he did not believe that the House of Lords and the monarchy could long survive the democratisation of the Commons.[33] Aberdeen, like some other conservatives, was too logical, or at least premature, in his assumption that once the Commons came to be regarded as the voice of the whole people and not just as the representatives of certain interests in the nation, there would be no place for other institutions in the state. He commented to Wellington in December 1832: 'The country is thoroughly revolutionised in heart, and we must depend on the good pleasure of the leaders of the revolution for semblance of a government.'[34]

His comments to his intimate friends on public affairs during the next few critical years are revealing. They range from the frankly, sometimes scurrilously, partisan to courageous and independent attempts to think through the new issues before the country. The 1835 elections were 'villainous' and there were no 'moderate men' left in Parliament. Daniel O'Connell was an 'Irish Savage' who was intimidating the government and trying to subvert Scotland.[35] At the same time he was not prepared to dismiss all the Whig reforms out of hand. He read widely and some of his thinking bore fruit when he was Prime Minister twenty years later. He was particularly interested in penal reform, which he discussed at length with Gurney. The problem, as he saw it, was that imprisonment, like transportation, was bound to be unequal in its effects. For the 'quiet, domestick man', transportation could be worse than a death sentence; for the young and sanguine, it could be almost an adventure. The punishment of death was 'dreadful' and for lesser offences they had not yet found a punishment which was severe without being cruel.[36] He saw some good in the Benthamite reform of the Poor Law and thought that there was an element of 'real reform' in that other Benthamite measure, the Municipal Corporations Act.[37] He jibbed, however, at its extension to Scotland and joined Haddington in protesting that, once again, London had failed to understand the complexities of the Scottish situation, in particular the close connection between local government and the Church in Scotland.[38]

He had other reasons for not wishing to see the House of Lords oppose the Municipal Corporations Bill. As he told Princess Lieven, they should avoid incurring 'odium'.[39] He spelt out his views even more clearly to Gurney. 'After all,' he said, 'the fellow [Daniel O'Connell] is not far wrong: for it seems clear, that an independent H. of Lords cannot long exist with a reformed House of Commons.' A few weeks later he prophesied, 'We shall find it impossible to act with independence in the face of a Reformed House of Commons. As yet we have done nothing very unpopular, and have therefore not yet exposed our weakness. If we mean to live, and see good days, we must act with the utmost prudence and circumspection.' He explained this 'softly, softly' approach even more clearly to Princess Lieven when she complained of the failure of the Upper House to protest at British policy in Spain. 'Our strength', he wrote, 'is the cause of our embarrassment. We could carry any vote we pleased: but I fear it would not put a stop to the course which has been adopted by the Government. It would provoke a species of collision with the House of Commons, and tend perhaps to give an additional popularity to a cause, about which the country in general is at present tolerably indifferent.'[40]

Such a clash on a domestic issue on which the country felt strongly would have been much more dangerous. Unfortunately, the two issues which aroused most feeling in the early 1830s were Ireland and the Church, and they were at their most sensitive when they were combined in an Irish Church question. Any attack on the Church touched exposed nerves in the House of Lords, not only because some members were genuinely committed churchmen, but also because it all seemed to be part of one pattern of a general attack on property and established institutions. Matters came to a head in 1834 when the Whig government, at Lord John Russell's instigation, introduced a Bill to abolish a number of Irish bishoprics and impose new taxes on the Irish Church. This was too much for some of the Anglicans in the Cabinet and the Earl of Ripon, Lord Stanley, Sir James Graham and the Duke of Richmond resigned. It was from this group, together with Goulburn and some of the younger men in the Commons, like Sidney Herbert and William Gladstone, that Peel began to fashion the leadership of the new Conservative Party. Peel's stature as a party leader was just beginning to become apparent. Aberdeen remained close to the Duke of Wellington on foreign affairs but on domestic affairs he began to move very close to Peel. Still at heart the disciple of William Pitt, he was very happy to throw in his lot with a group that promised reform without revolution.

Although out of office throughout most of the 1830s, because his party was out of office, Aberdeen remained keenly interested in public affairs. He did not, as in the period 1814–28, partially withdraw from them. But domestic questions claimed a good deal of his attention. In October 1832 his elder step-son, Lord Abercorn, married Lady Louisa Russell, the daughter of the Duke of Bedford. Aberdeen felt some anxiety about the marriage, commenting, 'Abercorn is very young, and not only in years' but adding tolerantly that youth was impatient.[41] His anxiety was not on political grounds. Social contacts always crossed party boundaries and Aberdeen assured Wellington that he need not fear that the Russells would make a Whig out of Abercorn.[42] Abercorn indeed proved a much more rigid Tory than Aberdeen himself. Aberdeen had always been an occasional visitor at Woburn, although his opinion of the family was not of the highest. He once told his son, 'Of the gentleman Russells, I cannot say very much, in the way of polish at least.'[43] But the Abercorn marriage cemented his contacts with the Russells and perhaps played its own small part in bringing about the coalition twenty years later.

Aberdeen still had private griefs to endure. In December 1829 Harriet gave birth to his youngest son, Arthur – a third son, Douglas, had been born in the spring of 1824. Harriet never really recovered her strength and she died in August 1833. As usual it was to Howley that Aberdeen turned. 'I can truly say', he wrote, 'that I have felt thankful for the termination of those sufferings which I had so long witnessed.' But it was difficult to be resigned. 'Although I have been severely schooled by misfortune', he said, 'I have still much to learn. It is only when that faith and confidence in those great truths, to which

I now yield assent, becomes a lively and operating principle, that I can hope to experience their blessed effects. At present, I am like him who exclaimed, "Lord, I believe – help Thou my unbelief"'. He told him that he would like to come, with his step-daughter, Harriet, to spend a few days with the Howleys at Addington.[44] Peel invited him to Drayton, assuring him that he should not be disturbed by other company but Aberdeen declined, telling Peel that in the 'unreasonableness of grief' he was sorry that Lady Aberdeen could not know of Peel's regard but he would not intrude on Peel 'with details, and lamentations, which may more suitably be repressed'.[45] As usual, he found it almost impossible to express his grief. He took refuge at Haddo, although he admitted to Gurney that he did not know whether he had done well to come. Many circumstances made it 'intolerably painful' but everywhere would be the same. Gurney was one of the few people he would like to see because he had some idea of 'the amount of my loss', although no one could tell 'in what manner it has pressed most heavily upon me'.[46] Perhaps he was racked by guilt for the years of misunderstanding, although they had been far more Harriet's fault than his own.

The following year the only daughter of his second marriage, Frances, died. She had been in poor health for several years and Aberdeen had nursed her as devotedly as he had done the children of his first marriage. She was buried at Stanmore but Aberdeen could not bear to be present at her funeral. He told Gurney that he had only two consolations, that her mother had been spared the final pain of her death and that, when he himself died, he would not leave her 'in a state of helplessness, requiring such care and attention, as I should feel she could never hope to receive from anyone but me'.[47] The feeling that his own death might be imminent never quite left him again.[48] He suffered a further bereavement in the autumn of 1835 when his brother, Charles, died suddenly of a cerebral haemorrhage in Geneva on his way to rejoin his regiment at Corfu.

Princess Lieven told François Guizot in 1837, 'Quoiqu'il vous ressemble en fait d'infortunes, et les siennes surpassent toutes les autres, c'est un sujet qui lui fait horreur-il renferme tout, et son visage d'Otello va fort bien avec ce mouvement d'épouvante sombre par lequel il repousse toute allusion à ses malheurs.'[49] Aberdeen's liaison with Princess Lieven, if indeed it ever occurred, must have dated from about this period or a little earlier. She had generally been highly critical of him when he was Foreign Secretary from 1828 to 1830, mainly because he refused to take her side in her quarrels with the Duke of Wellington, and she had repaid him by writing scurrilous, and generally untrue, things about him in her diary and in her letters to Lord Grey and to Lady Cowper, later Lady Palmerston.[50] Even at this period she admitted that she found him amusing and they seem to have been on good terms at Tunbridge Wells in the summer of 1829. Aberdeen accompanied the Lievens on a visit to see Bridge House, Lord Abergavenny's home, but as the invitation had only been to the Russian embassy, Aberdeen, whose old gifts as a comedy actor had obviously not deserted him, passed himself off as a Russian for two hours.[51] But Aberdeen seems to have been slightly surprised when he received a letter from Princess Lieven in the autumn of 1832. He replied politely and thus began a long correspondence in which they swopped political gossip for the next twenty years.[52]

In June 1837 the Princess became the mistress of François Guizot, who was already well known both as a scholar and as a conservative politician. A few weeks later she visited England. According to her letters to Guizot she felt that she must in honour tell Aberdeen that she had found another to protect her. She wrote, 'Il l'a reçu en véritable Anglais; quelques mots sans suite, un serrement de main plus fort que de coutume et il m'a quittée . . .' He returned the next day, fearing that the Princess might have misunderstood his silence. He asked leave to speak to her in English lest she misunderstand what he said. He told her that he was glad that she had found consolation and begged her not to forget him. 'Et puis il me déclare que sa voiture de voyage est à ma porte, qu'il part pour les montagnes en Écosse et qu'il ne me demande qu'une chose, c'est de baiser ma main pour la première fois de sa vie.'[53] It is an affecting scene, Aberdeen kissing her hand and rushing away to his Scottish mountains. A little later he expressed a most earnest wish to become the friend of Guizot.[54] It is an odd reaction for a man who has been supplanted – unless, of course, Aberdeen was privately thinking, 'Thank God, she has found someone else.'. Princess Lieven was, however, a terrible liar and Aberdeen's later congratulations to her on her histrionic gifts may have been more ironic than they at first appear.[55] Certainly London gossip dubbed her his mistress and Aberdeen seems to have thought it wise to put his youngest son in the picture before introducing him to her when she was in exile in London in 1848–49.[56]

Apart from demanding women, Aberdeen had plenty of trouble with wayward sons in these years. Arthur proved to be a delicate child and his father lavished every care on him. Arthur was probably the only one of Aberdeen's sons who inherited his father's intelligence but, as the journals he kept as an adolescent show, he was intensely jealous of anyone who threatened to supplant him in his father's affections. He kept up constant feuds with two of his brothers, Alexander and Douglas (particularly Alexander) and with Aberdeen's favourite daughter–in–law, Mary. Alexander was the antithesis of the delicate, rather aesthetic Arthur. A tough, robust boy he grew up to be a very good soldier and, to his father's great pleasure, became equerry to Prince Albert. But a soldier's life could not be without its dangers and in 1838 his father had to see him depart for Canada with his regiment to put down the rebellions, just as later he had to endure knowing that his son was in the Crimea throughout the war. In 1838 Aberdeen wrote to Haddo that Alexander was about to embark and that he was pleased but his father was not.[57]

If Alexander always determined to be a soldier, Douglas always determined to be a clergyman. The only problem was that Aberdeen could not conceal, even from himself, that his third son was stupid. He wrote to Christopher Wordsworth, the then Headmaster of Harrow, apologising for his son's 'deficiencies'.[58] Fortunately, Howley was prepared to give Douglas his patronage in his career but Aberdeen felt compelled to remind his friend that although his son's conduct had never given him a moment's anxiety he could not pretend that his mental gifts were other than 'moderate'.[59] Douglas was eventually found a comfortable living at Stanmore, where the family built a new church, and where his rectory provided a convenient meeting place after Abercorn's extravagance had compelled him to part with Bentley Priory.

Aberdeen's real anxiety, however, centred on George, Lord Haddo, his eldest son. George, like Arthur, was judged too delicate to be sent to Harrow and was educated by private tutors. Aberdeen had well–founded doubts as to how well George, who had not been to a public school, would cope with life at Cambridge.[60] He went up a rather earnest and indeed pathologically shy young man but achieved some modest academic success in his first year. Aberdeen wrote that he had been moved almost to tears because he could not share his pleasure with Haddo's mother.[61] But the delights of Cambridge proved too seductive and soon Aberdeen, who was generous in the money he sent his son, was rebuking him for extravagance and indolence. He had already expressed disappointment that his son had been negligent in learning French, warning him, 'In the present state of society, it is perhaps the most valuable and most necessary of all acquirements.' Haddo, bored by the classics, suggested taking up geology or estate management. Aberdeen told him rather tartly that the study of geology was in its infancy and that he and Brebner could teach him all he needed to know about estate management. It was not necessary for him, like Peter the Great, to become 'a ship's carpenter'.[62]

Aberdeen's irritation is partly explained by the fact that his son had contrived to embarrass him politically. Haddo not only refused to join the Pitt Club but also wrote an article in an undergraduate newspaper criticising it. The story was taken up with glee by the *Globe*, the *Chronicle* and the 'Aberdeen Radicals'.[63] Haddo contrived to fail his second-year examinations but set off happily for a tour of Scotland. His father, pointing out that books in a trunk would not impart their contents to his head, reminded him that 'a *second* failure would really be deplorable'. Haddo managed to scrape a pass degree but forget to tell his father who wrote in exasperation that, as the names of candidates who had not attained honours were not given in the newspapers, he had been left completely in the dark about his son's fate.[64]

Haddo then left for Constantinople, taking with him his father's journal of his travels. Aberdeen constantly complained that his son rarely wrote and never kept him informed of his movements, apparently forgetting that he too had disappeared for months in much more dangerous country to the consternation of his friends.[65] While he was abroad, Aberdeen celebrated his coming of age in due style. A thousand people were dined in a huge marquee, lit by two chandeliers. Aberdeen made a speech, although he had to 'bellow like a bull' to make himself heard. The band of the Aberdeenshire Militia played; there were fireworks; and a balloon, twelve feet in circumference, was sent up. The celebrations seem to have marked the final healing of the breach with the third Earl's illegitimate descendants, several of whom appeared on the platform with Aberdeen.[66]

Aberdeen, who a few years earlier had been worried because his son was so gauche with women,[67] now began to fear that he would make an unsuitable marriage. He told him in December 1838 that Abercorn had said that Haddo went to Windsor to 'obtain the sight of a young lady. That is all very well, *as a Lark*' but he expected to be consulted before his son entered into any serious commitment.[68] He hoped that Haddo would find a bride both wealthy enough to ease the always precariously balanced finances of the family and sufficiently well connected to add further lustre to the family's position. While Haddo was on his eastern travels his father was alarmed by a rumour that he was paying court to the daughter of Sir Edmund Lyons, the British envoy in Athens. Although Sir Edmund's family was respectable enough, his daughter did not meet either criterion and Aberdeen wrote to rebuke his son. Haddo replied cheerfully that Miss Lyons was engaged not to him but to the future Duke of Norfolk.[69]

When Haddo did decide to marry, he did it as impulsively as his father had always feared he would, although Aberdeen was relieved to learn that his choice was not totally unsuitable. Aberdeen suddenly received a letter from his son in September 1840, telling him that he intended to marry the daughter of Mr Baillie of Jerviswood. Slightly dazed, Aberdeen replied that his son did things so unlike everyone else that he did not know whether to take the letter seriously or which of the two Baillie sisters he meant. He understood that Mary was an excellent person and Grizel very beautiful, although very young. He reminded his son that he had expected to be consulted but added magnanimously that he was prepared to love either Miss Baillie when he learnt which was to be his daughter-in-law.[70]

When he learnt that Mary was Haddo's choice he wrote her a very kindly letter of welcome. The Baillies were closely related to Aberdeen's old friend, the Earl of Haddington; indeed, Mary's brother eventually succeeded to the title. They were also a wealthy family, although very little of the family fortune seems to have come to Mary and she and Haddo spent their early married life in comparative poverty. Haddo was impatient that the marriage should take place at once but his father restrained him, pointing out that there were many business matters to be settled first. He sent Brebner to Edinburgh to take care of them. He told Haddo that he had guaranteed a sum of £10,000 to the younger children so that there was no need for them to insure their lives and 'As to the contingencies connected with the jointure, as it is my intention *to die first*, there is no occasion to take much trouble about the matter.'[71] The light-hearted remark was to seem grim enough a few years later when it seemed almost certain that Haddo would predecease his father.

Aberdeen was not unsympathetic to his son's desire for a speedy marriage and promised to arrive at Taymouth Castle, the home of the bride's eldest sister, Lady Breadalbane, on 3 November. He told them that he would like a free day to see them both and the marriage could then take place on Thursday, 5 November, as in Scotland, 'it is not otherwise appropriated to squibs and crackers'. If it could not be on the Thursday, it must be on the Saturday 'as Friday is an unlucky day all the world over'. The marriage duly took place at Taymouth on 5 November and the celebrations when the young people returned to Haddo rivalled those when George came of age. Aberdeen warned

Mary what to expect. Two or three hundred mounted tenants would meet them to escort them to the house. At 3 p.m. there would be a dinner in the marquee for seven hundred people at which George must be prepared to make a speech and drink toasts.[72]

Despite some disappointment, Aberdeen had made up his mind to welcome his son's wife in the place of the daughters whom he had lost. He told Gurney, 'There might have been more rank, and more money; but there could not be better people, or a more respectable family. I am perfectly satisfied with his choice, and am quite prepared to be in love with my daughter.'[73] Other people, including his youngest son, Arthur, found her cold and aloof and difficult to get on with but Aberdeen immediately took to her. He wrote, 'She is quite charming . . . I never expected to like any one so well again.'[74] Mary for her part was nervous of meeting her austere father-in-law, but, like other people, she was astonished by the contrast between his public reputation and his actual kindness. The bond of affection between father and daughter-in-law grew steadily over the years and she soon became his closest political confidante among the younger members of the family.[75]

NOTES

1. Add. MSS 43210, Aberdeen to Robert, 20 Sept. 1830.
2. For a modern account see E. J. Hobsbawm and G. Rudé, *Captain Swing:* for contemporary reaction see Ellenborough, *Diary*, esp. vol. 2, pp. 386–7, 415–27.
3. *Hansard*, 3rd ser., I, 52–3; Stanmore, p. 104; cf. M. Brock, *The Great Reform Act*, pp. 118, 353–4. Stanmore got his version of the story from Gladstone, Add. MSS 44319, Gladstone to A. Gordon, 21 Apr. 1861.
4. Stanmore, p. 104.
5. HH 4/6, Aberdeen to Crombie, 27 June 1831.
6. HH 4/6, Aberdeen to Cromhie, 21 Oct. 1831.
7. Add. MSS 43059, Aberdeen to Wellington, 5 Nov. 1831; Gurney Papers, RQC 334/63, Aberdeen to Gurney, 23 Dec. 1831.
8. Gurney Papers, RQC 334/63, Aberdeen to Gurney, 23 Dec. 1831.
9. HH 4/6, Aberdeen to Crombie, 18 Dec. 1831.
10. Howley's letter to Aberdeen is so faded as to be almost illegible, Add. MSS 43195, Howley to Aberdeen, n.d. Oct. 1831; Add. MSS 43061, Peel to Aberdeen, 14 Oct. 1831.
11. Brock, esp. pp. 276, 379; Add. MSS 43059, Wellington to Aberdeen, 18 Feb. 1832; HH 4/6, Aberdeen to Crombie, 27 Apr. 1832. Aberdeen's connection with the Waverers is further suggested by his letter to Wellington of 17 Feb. 1832 (Wellington Papers) in which he suggests that Howley show him the 'Wharncliffe correspondence'; Wharncliffe had been the Waverers' original leader.
12. Add. MSS 43059, Aberdeen to Wellington, 2 May 1832.
13. Wellington Papers, Wellington to the King, 12 May 8 p.m. 13 May 1 p.m., 14 May 6.30 p.m., 14 May 3 p.m., 15 May 1832, Wellington to Falmouth, 25 May 1832.
14. *Hansard*, 3rd ser., XIII, 349.

15. PP, II (1830–31) 261; III (1831–32) 443.
16. Gash, *Politics in the Age of Peel*, pp. 35–8; cf. description of the Scottish electoral system in Sinclair, vol. 1, pp. 88, 98.
17. *Hansard*, 3rd ser., XIV, 54.
18. The post-reform electorate was about 653,000; the pre–reform electorate has been variously computed at between 366,000 and 435,000.
19. HH 4/6, Aberdeen to Crombie, 27 June 1831; P P, VII (1820) 276.
20. Although Crombie had retired some months earlier, Aberdeen told Hudson Gurney that he did not know how he would manage without him, Gurney Papers, RQC 334/64, Aberdeen to Gurney, 22 Nov. 1832.
21. HH 4/7, 'State of Expenses incurred for Captain The Honble. William Gordon during the late Canvass & Aberdeenshire Election.'
22. HH 4/7, Brebner to Aberdeen, 29 June 1833.
23. HH 4/7, Brebner to Aberdeen, 29 June 1833; 'State of Cash received by James Brebner Advocate in Aberdeen on account of the Earl of Aberdeen. From November 1832 to 30th June 1833' and 'State of Disbursements ditto'.
24. Add. MSS 40312, Aberdeen to Peel, 4 Dec. 1832.
25. Quoted in Gash, *Politics in the Age of Peel*, p. 49.
26. Aberdeen to Wellington, 23 Dec. 1832, Wellington Corr., vol. VIII, p. 491.
27. Gurney Papers, RQC 334/78, Aberdeen to Gurney, 16 Dec. 1834; Aberdeen to Lieven, 9 Aug. 1837, Jones-Parry, vol. 1, p. 79.
28. HH 1/22, Aberdeen to Haddo, 12 Aug. 1837; Jones-Parry, vol. 1, p. 78.
29. HH 1/22, Aberdeen to Haddo, 12 Aug. 1837.
30. HH 1/29, Aberdeen to Lady Haddo, 28 Mar., 5 Apr. 1847.
31. HH 1/29, Aberdeen to Lady Haddo, 28 Mar. 1847.
32. HH 1/22, Aberdeen to Haddo, 23 Jan., 2 Apr., 24 Dec. 1838, 15 Jan., 26 Feb. 1839; HH 1/8, 9 Oct. 1839. The full story of the Honiton candidature is told in Gash, *Politics in the Age of Peel*, pp. 166–8.
33. Gurney Papers, RQC 334/63, Aberdeen to Gurney, 23 Dec. 1831.
34. Aberdeen to Wellington, 23 Dec. 1832, Wellington *Corr.*, vol. VIII, p. 491.
35. Gurney Papers, RQC 334/79, Aberdeen to Gurney, 27 Jan., /84, 19 Oct. 1835.
36. Gurney Papers, RQC 334/87, Aberdeen to Gurney, 19 Feb. 1836.
37. Gurney Papers, RQC 334/87, Aberdeen to Gurney, 19 Feb. 1836: Aberdeen to Lieven, 8 May 1835, Jones-Parry, vol. 1, p. 30.
38. *Hansard*, 3rd ser., XXX, 578 (17 Aug. 1835).
39. Aberdeen to Lieven, 8 May 1835, Jones-Parry, vol. 1, p. 30.
40. Gurney Papers, RQC 334/84, Aberdeen to Gurney, 19Oct./85, 27 Nov. 1835; Aberdeen to Lieven, 30 July, 8 Sept., 22 Oct. 1835, Jones–Parry, vol. 1, pp. 35, 38, 41.
41. Gurney Papers, RQC 334/64, Aberdeen to Gurney, 22 Nov. 1832.
42. Aberdeen to Wellington, 23 Aug. 1832, Wellington *Corr.*, vol. VIII, p. 392.
43. HH 1/32, Aberdeen to Haddo, 20 June 1834.
44. Howley Papers, 2186A, Aberdeen to Howley, 3 Sept. 1833.
45. Add. MSS 43061, Peel to Aberdeen, 22 Sept. 1833; Add. MSS 40312, Aberdeen to Peel, 1 Oct. 1833.
46. Gurney Papers, RQC 334/65, Aberdeen to Gurney, 10 Sept./66, 14 Oct. 1833.
47. HH 1/35, Aberdeen to Haddo, 21 Apr. 1834; Gurney Papers, RQC 334/76, Aberdeen to Gurney, 21 Apr. 1834.
48. When he accompanied the Queen to Germany in 1845 he had a premonition that he would not return and left a sealed letter for his daughter-in-law, begging her

to look after Arthur and telling her 'the last words of his mother are still sounding in my ears', HH 1/28, Aberdeen to Lady Haddo, 8 Aug. 1845.

49. Princess Lieven to Guizot, 13 July 1837, *Lettres* (ed. J. Naville), vol. 1, p. 27.
50. For example, 'a wretched minister' (Lieven *Diary*, ed. H. Temperley, p. 136); 'a poltroon' (*The Lieven-Palmerston Correspondence*, 1828–56, p. 15).
51. Princess Lieven to Grey, 11 Aug. 1829, *Correspondence of Princess Lieven and Earl Grey*, vol. 1, pp. 266–7.
52. Aberdeen to Lieven, 26 Sept. 1832, Jones-Parry, vol. 1, p. 3.
53. *Lettres* (ed. Naville), vol. 1, p. 6. Lieven to Guizot, 15, 16 July 1837, pp. 30, 31–2.
54. Aberdeen to Lieven, 9 Aug., 6 Oct. 1837, Jones-Parry, vol. 1, pp. 78, 82.
55. Aberdeen to Lieven, 5 Nov. 1850, Jones-Parry, vol. 2, pp. 524.
56. Add. MSS 49253, Stanmore Journal, 28 Jan. 1849.
57. HH 1/22, Aberdeen to Haddo, 23 Jan. 1838.
58. Wordsworth Papers, 2142, f. 199, Aberdeen to Wordsworth, 11 Aug. 1841.
59. Howley Papers, 2186A, Aberdeen to Howley, 14 Nov. 1946.
60. H 1/35, Aberdeen to Haddo, 8 Nov. 1834.
61. Elliott, *Memoirs of Lord Haddo*, pp. 3–4; HH 1/35, Aberdeen to Haddo, 22 Nov. 1834.
62. HH 1/35, Aberdeen to Haddo, 26 Oct. 1833, 3 Mar., 22 May, 20 Sept. 29 Nov. 1835.
63. HH 1/35, Aberdeen to Haddo, 29 Nov., 9 Dec. 1835.
64. HH 1/35, Aberdeen to Haddo, 7 Mar., 13 May, 13 July 1836, 22 Jan. 1837.
65. HH 1/35, Aberdeen to Haddo, 17 Mar. 1837; HH 1/22, 21 May, 12 Aug., 11, 25 Dec. 1838; HH 1/28, 30 May 1839; Gurney Papers, RQC 334/92, Aberdeen to Gurney, 10 Sept. 1837.
66. HH 1/22, Aberdeen to Haddo, 5 Oct. 1837; Add. MSS 43070, Aberdeen to Gladstone, 29 Sept. 1837. Gladstone, who had just been visiting Haddo, helped to plan the celebration.
67. HH 1/35, Aberdeen to Haddo, 20 June 1834.
68. HH 1/28, Aberdeen to Haddo, 5 Dec. 1838.
69. HH 1/22, Aberdeen to Haddo, 15 Jan., 26 Feb. 1839.
70. HH 1/28, Aberdeen to Haddo, 24 Sept. 1840.
71. HH 1/28, Aberdeen to Miss Baillie, 1 Oct. 1840, Aberdeen to Haddo, 9, 27 Oct. 1840.
72. HH 1/28, Aberdeen to Haddo, 27 Oct. 1840, Aberdeen to Lady Haddo, 20 Nov. 1840.
73. Gurney Papers, RQC 334/100, Aberdeen to Gurney, 3 Oct. 1840.
74. H 1/28, Aberdeen to (?) Lady Breadalbane, n.d. Nov. 1840. For further light on the strained relations between Mary and Arthur see J. B. Conacher, 'A visit to the Gladstones in 1894', *Victorian Studies*, 2 (1958–59), pp. 155–60.
75. Lady Haddo's own recollections, quoted Balfour, vol. 2, pp. 26–27. The letters between Aberdeen and Lady Haddo are all at Haddo, although some are included in the printed volumes of the Aberdeen *Correspondence* in the British Library.

CHAPTER SIXTEEN

A Conservative abroad

Aberdeen and Wellington were dismayed at losing power in November 1830, just when the Vienna Settlement seemed in greater danger than at any time in its existence. Stability, hardly won at Vienna in 1814–15, seemed to be the primary good which must take precedence over all other causes. Neither Aberdeen nor Wellington trusted their successors in office to achieve this. Apart from the distractions of the Reform Bill crisis, Grey always seemed to his opponents to underestimate the French danger and they expected no correction of Grey's weaknesses from the new Foreign Secretary, their former colleague, Lord Palmerston.

During Grey's administration Aberdeen and Wellington kept up a constant fire on foreign questions. Very often Aberdeen introduced the discussion and Wellington came in to support him. Aberdeen managed these set speeches well and his old fear of the Chamber seemed for the time to have left him. On one occasion even Grey felt compelled to congratulate him on his 'long and able address',[1] although on other occasions he complained of his 'long and desultory' speeches. He also revived the old charge that Aberdeen 'sneered' in his speeches,[2] although the offence must have been given by the manner rather than the substance of his speeches which read as moderate and courteous. Grey frequently complained that he had not been given due notice of questions, although in fact there was a good deal of consultation between the two front benches. But there was substance in Aberdeen's complaint that Grey's government was keeping Parliament starved of information and even failed to publish papers which were already available from continental sources. Aberdeen frequently asked for papers, for example, on Portugal and Belgium in 1831 and on Algiers in 1833.[3] This thirst for information rather contrasted with Aberdeen's own practice in office, although in fact he published a good deal.

Even in opposition he was most careful to observe the proprieties and to concede that treaty-making, for example, was a royal prerogative but in 1832 he took advantage of the fact that the King's Speech had promised the new Belgian treaty and so given the House official cognisance of it, in order to demand details.[4] Indeed Aberdeen constituted himself something of a guardian of diplomatic propriety and protested strongly when a treaty was signed and laid before the House only in French, the English version having only the status of a translation, although Grey proved on this occasion that there were precedents. For Grey and his government, the watchful and experienced scrutiny of Aberdeen and Wellington could be embarrassing and sometimes led to short-tempered exchanges.[5]

Aberdeen concentrated his fire on four main issues: Greece, Belgium, Portugal and Algiers. On Greece he was inhibited by the same private sympathy which he had shown when in office. In February 1831 he challenged Grey as to whether new negotiations were going on about the Greek frontiers and expressed unease at the abandonment of the agreement of 3 February 1830. When Grey admitted that new negotiations had begun, Aberdeen conceded that the previous agreement had never been regarded as immutable.[6] He was on stronger grounds when he criticised the Powers' choice of Otho of Bavaria to be the ruler of Greece. Otho, he complained, had never been considered a serious candidate when he was at the Foreign Office. He was still a minor and the last thing an insecure young state wanted was a Regency. He was a Roman Catholic which would make him unacceptable to many of his new subjects. Grey rebuked Aberdeen for making this public reference to Otho's unfitness but Aberdeen proved correct. Otho remained isolated from his people, surrounded by a small clique of Bavarian officers. Palmerston was compelled later to admit that the selection of Otho was 'the worst day's work he ever did'.[7]

On Belgium and Portugal the gravamen of Aberdeen's (and Wellington's) charges was the same. The maladroitness of the British government had allowed France, and a potentially revolutionary France at that, to seize the very advantages which Britain had fought so long and expensively to prevent her from obtaining during the Napoleonic Wars. This put Aberdeen in the position of defending both Don Miguel and the King of Holland, unpopular figures in Britain. In each case he insisted that he held no brief for Miguel or William I, although he thought the charges against them exaggerated and their opponents' record no better, but that the over–riding consideration ought to be British interests.

Portuguese affairs reached a new crisis in 1831 when a French squadron sailed to Lisbon, to seek redress for two French citizens who had been imprisoned, and seized the Portuguese fleet. It was the fear of the French capture of the Portuguese fleet which had first involved Britain in the Peninsula in 1807. The French action in 1831 interfered with British shipping. To make matters worse Don Pedro, expelled by his own people from Brazil, had come to London to seek money and other help to aid his daughter's cause in Portugal. The only part of Portugal still under Pedro's control was Terceira in the Azores and there a British ship, the Coquette, had been seized and forced to take part in a raid on the neighbouring island of St. George where, Aberdeen insisted, a massacre had been perpetrated.[8] Worse still, the British government was turning a blind eye to the fact that the Foreign Enlistment Act of 1819 was being openly flouted and men, including even British naval and army officers, were sailing from British ports to help Pedro to establish a bridgehead on the Portuguese mainland at Oporto. In June 1833 Aberdeen alleged that in the previous three months nearly 2000 Englishmen and 3000 foreigners (mainly Poles, Germans and French) had left British ports, or in a few cases French ports, for Portugal. In Gravesend the parish officers had actually become 'crimps to Don Pedro' by helping to recruit the able-bodied poor as mercenaries. He knew that the Whigs had no liking for the Foreign Enlistment Act but while it remained the law the government should enforce it. It would be a disgrace to the constitution 'if the Jews and jobbers of London [a reference to the loans to Don Pedro] could carry on war against a foreign nation – if they could levy troops and send them abroad unchecked to commit robbery and murder.'[9]

Both Aberdeen and Wellington insisted that Britain had treaty obligations to protect Portugal from outside assault of this kind. Aberdeen spoke of the French naval activities in the Tagus as a 'humiliation' for Britain and contended that since his expulsion from Brazil Don Pedro was a mere private citizen, levying a private war. He insisted that Miguel would have been formally recognised as the ruler of Portugal by the Wellington government before they left office but for the delays imposed by Pedro's insincere negotiations to reach an amicable settlement. He brought forward private information to demonstrate that Miguel's rule was not so oppressive as it was alleged to be and presented a petition from British shippers engaged in the Portuguese trade complaining that the British government's actions were ruining their trade and that they obtained far more ready redress of grievances from Miguel's government than from 'our liberal and constitutional friends'.[10] Aberdeen assured the House that he respected liberty as much as any man and he did not deny that the Portuguese government was despotic, but he saw no signs that the people at large wanted the constitution that the British government now seemed to want to force upon them. It reminded him, he said, of Squire Weston in *Tom Jones* when he wished to marry his daughter against her inclinations: ' "Rot her," said the Squire, "she shall be happy enough though I break her heart for it." ' He believed that Don Pedro and the 'constitutionalists' were more Anglophobe than the Miguellists. Above all, he feared that the support for Pedro would involve Portugal, which had attained some degree of stability, in a civil war which might well spread to the entire Peninsula with all that would imply in providing opportunities for French intervention.[11]

The fear of French intervention was the key to his attitude to Belgium as well. He accepted that the events of 1830 had left no real alternative to the 'separation' of Belgium from Holland, but there were many steps between administrative separation and complete independence, and the Whig government had jumped too easily to the conclusion that there was no alternative to complete independence, which was all too likely in practice to mean French domination. He deplored the way in which the King of Holland had been put in the dock and constantly reminded the House that he had been their 'ally'. In 1815 the Dutch had accepted the loss of the Cape of Good Hope and other colonies because they had been given Belgium. Belgium was now taken away without compensation. The London Conference had met at William's invitation and he had done his best to comply with its proposals for boundaries and armistices. It was the Belgians who had made difficulties but the sympathy and indulgence of the Conference had been continually extended to them. The French attitude was only too clear from their insistence that certain border fortresses must be dismantled. Leopold, who had not behaved well over Greece, was, because of his close connection with the French royal family, a dangerous choice as sovereign.[12] Aberdeen saw the most perilous moment as being that in the summer of 1831, when a French army entered Belgium to protect it from a Dutch counter-attack. The British government despatched a fleet, but whether to deter the Dutch or the French was far from clear. To Aberdeen, vividly remembering 1813, the world seemed to be going mad. He wrote that he fully expected that the government would contrive to get the country into a continental war.[13]

A year later, Aberdeen was even more pessimistic. He recalled that Gurney, still close to the Quaker pacificism of his roots, had sometimes accused him of being 'warlike' but he begged him to remember that:

when the D. of Wellington left office, not only was there no question of hostility with any Power on the face of the earth; but I assure you, on my word of honor, that our relations with every state were friendly and cordial, even with the Government of Louis Philippe himself. We might have blundered, but I venture to say that we should have stayed clear of War. This is a War, so odious and unnatural, that even now I have some difficulty in believing that it can possibly take place. But who can answer for the feelings of men under the dominion of passion? In this respect, Lord Grey is more like a child, than a man possessed of common sense.[14]

Further disturbing evidence of the restlessness of French ambitions seemed to be provided by the projected despatch of a French expedition to Ancona, in reply to Austrian action in going to the aid of the Pope against his own dissidents. Aberdeen complained that the appearance of the tricolour in Italy could only excite rebellion because it was looked on there as the 'standard of revolution and disorder'.[15] French intervention in Italy seemed the more sinister when combined with her continued presence in Algiers. Just after the Ancona crisis, Aberdeen reminded the House that the July Monarchy had promised to fulfil the engagements into which Charles, government had entered to withdraw from Algiers. When challenged on this, he asked Grey to produce the relevant papers, stressing the naval importance of Algiers and the danger of France trying to make the Mediterranean into a 'French lake'. Grey agreed in principle to do so but explained that it was difficult to produce Stuart de Rothesay's despatch of 18 August 1830, reporting a private conversation with Louis Philippe since, in the first place, Britain had not at that time formally recognised Louis Philippe's government and, secondly, since there had been no minister in attendance, the conversation could not have any official status. Aberdeen was forced to acquiesce in this, although without it there was no clear undertaking of withdrawal from Louis Philippe's government.[16]

During this debate Grey expressed regret at Aberdeen's severe animadversions on the policy of his government which, earlier in the debate, Aberdeen had called 'calamitous'. Aberdeen now rose to defend himself and explain the basis of his policy. 'His own hostility to the noble Earl and his Government', he said, 'was at times represented as passing the bonds of moderation.' It was true that he had been led into 'some warmth of language' when he felt that the honour and interests of the country were involved. He saw the main danger coming from France. If France was not England's natural enemy, she was certainly her natural rival. It might be true that, in order to preserve peace, it was necessary to prepare for war, but it was hard to interpret France's conduct in this light. In a great state, such preparation usually meant aggression. He distrusted Marshal Soult and suggested that France was getting all she wanted in Algiers, in Italy and in Portugal without war. He feared that Francophiles, like Grey and Lord Holland, the Chancellor of the Duchy of Lancaster, who frequently seconded Grey in these debates, were quite unable to appreciate the potential dangers.[17]

It was a trenchant statement of the conservative view of Europe which found many echoes in Aberdeen's correspondence with Princess Lieven. In 1833 he even welcomed the meeting of the Russian and Austrian Emperors at Münchengratz. He told the Princess:

The meeting of the Emperors gave me more satisfaction than any public event which has recently taken place, because it held out the prospect of arresting the progress of revolution in Europe; and by establishing a perfectly good understanding between the two princes, gave each of them additional means of preserving the general peace and safety. It is on the cordial and intimate union of the Northern Powers that the chance is afforded of preserving the tranquility and happiness of Europe against the disorganising and revolutionary policy of the present Governments of England and France.[18]

Aberdeen was an effective performer in the conservative cause early in the 1830s but by 1841, when he returned to the Foreign Office, he had modified his views in many important particulars.

In July 1834, Grey, tired and discouraged by the continuing difficulties in Ireland, gave up the premiership to Aberdeen's old friend, William Lamb, Lord Melbourne, who kept the Whig government in being until November, when he acquiesced readily in the King's dismissal of his ministers. But the Tories, as well as the Whigs, were by this time having their internal differences. Peel's refusal to support Wellington in his attempt to form a ministry in May 1832 led to a serious deterioration in the relations between the two men until, by the spring of 1834, they were barely on speaking terms. A Tory stalwart, Charles Arbuthnot, took it upon himself to appeal to Aberdeen, as the trusted friend of both men, to try to resolve the situation, pointing out the dire political consequences which would follow if the Tories were called upon to form a government while Wellington and Peel were estranged. Aberdeen decided that it was an occasion for plain speaking and he sent Arbuthnot's letter to Peel with the additional comments that, although he thought that Wellington bore the greater responsibility, he could not hold Peel 'blameless'. Peel preferred not to reply in writing and saw Aberdeen a few days later at Argyll House. Judging by the memorandum which Peel kept of the conversation he adopted a stiff line and reminded Aberdeen of a number of complaints which he had against the Duke, going back to the very embarrassing position in which he had been placed at the time of Catholic Emancipation.[19] Nevertheless, Aberdeen's intervention opened up a channel of communication and made it possible for Wellington not only to work with Peel when the Whig government retired but even to tell the King that it was Peel who must be Prime Minister.

Peel made his epic journey back from Italy and assumed office in December 1834. If Peel was to be Prime Minister, the only suitable appointment for Wellington was that of Foreign Secretary. This meant that another office had to be found for Aberdeen. Aberdeen was prepared to take whatever appointment would best help Peel and he was first proposed as Lord President of the Council or First Lord of the Admiralty but he finally took the Colonial Office.[20]

Strictly speaking he was Secretary of State for War and the Colonies and, although being Secretary of State for War was almost a sinecure in peacetime, it did make Aberdeen responsible for a very long, and sometimes confidential, pensions list which, combined with the considerable patronage exercised by the Secretary of State for the Colonies, he found the most irksome part of his new responsibilities. In March 1835 he had to tell Peel that the Secret Service money in his office only amounted to £3000 and that was already committed. He would put M. Guillemot on the pensions list, if Peel wished, but it might be awkward if the French found out since Guillemot had been active in the duchesse de Berri's attempt to raise La Vendée for her son, the duc de Bordeaux, in 1832.[21] According to Stanmore, the other reason why Aberdeen disliked the Colonial Office was that he was conscious that there were very genuine grievances in many British colonies but that the reformers' demands were so mixed up with 'faction and unreasonable pretensions' that redress was extremely difficult.[22] This was not an unfair statement of the position.

When Aberdeen went to the Colonial Office in December 1834, a number of colonial questions were in a delicate, even dangerous, state. The emancipation of all the slaves throughout the British empire had taken place on 1 August 1834, although freed slaves were still liable for several years more to work part of the time for their former masters as 'apprentices'. Many former slave owners were still bitter at the change, in spite of the fairly generous compensation which had been voted them by Parliament. It was still uncertain whether the former slaves would continue to provide labour for the plantations, as apprentices or as free labourers. Whether they would return to work after the Christmas break in 1834 was judged to be a critical test of the future smooth working of the system.[23]

In Lower Canada the provincial government was dangerously near to complete breakdown. In February 1834 the House of Assembly had passed the famous Ninety-Two Resolutions, severely criticising the government and demanding radical reforms. In the meantime they refused to vote supplies. The emancipation of the slaves was causing particular dissatisfaction in Cape Province, where the Boer farmers found it more difficult to claim their compensation than did the West Indian planters, who mostly had agents in London, and the situation was aggravated in December 1834 by a large scale 'Kaffir' invasion of the eastern frontier of the Cape.

Aberdeen had able assistants at the Colonial Office, notably the Permanent Under-Secretary, Robert Hay, and a future Under-Secretary, James Stephen. Stephen, a member of the Clapham Sect associated with William Wilberforce, had abandoned a lucrative career in law to work single-mindedly for the abolition of slavery in the British empire. A friendship, which lasted for the rest of their lives, grew up between Aberdeen and Stephen during Aberdeen's brief time at the Colonial Office.[24] As in his embassy to Vienna in 1813 some of the credit must go to Aberdeen's professional assistants but, again as in his earlier embassy, the immediate impression is of an energetic and conscientious man who set out to master the material and arrive at speedy conclusions on the outstanding questions. His task was not made easier by the fact that there had been a rapid succession of Colonial Secretaries during the Whig administration, first the Earl of Ripon, then Lord Stanley, then Thomas Spring Rice, and matters were further complicated by the fact that Spring Rice had removed many of the office papers. On the other hand he was not subjected to anything like such close scrutiny by the Cabinet as he had been when Foreign Secretary and was largely left to get on with running his Department as he chose.

Aberdeen had taken no part in the parliamentary proceedings for the abolition of slavery, which had coincided with Harriet's last illness, but in February 1835 he reminded the House that his very first vote in Parliament had been given in favour of the abolition of the slave trade and he promised that he would do his utmost to ensure the success of the recent measure.[25]

Lord Mulgrave, a former Governor of Jamaica, asked a number of searching questions about that island. Aberdeen replied that, as a token of their good faith, the government had retained Lord Sligo as Governor of the island although, no doubt, as a Whig he had expected to be recalled. Mulgrave complained that the planters were combining against the dissenting and evangelical missionaries who had supported the blacks. Aberdeen promised that they should receive all the protection of the law, although he feared that their zeal had sometimes outrun their discretion, but he felt that their main duty ought to be the education of the former slaves. He returned to this theme a little later when he told the House that he had been engaged in drawing up a general scheme for education throughout the colonies, although he warned his fellow peers that it would require much money to put it into practice, whether that money was raised by Parliament or from the colonies. Aberdeen was to press the point again some years later when he was out of office.[26] His belief that education was the real key to progress and prosperity was as strong in dealing with the non-white races in the colonies as it was in dealing with the depressed peasantry of Ireland.

With Sligo he had a long and detailed correspondence concerning the practical problems of Jamaica. He endorsed his views that disputes concerning the apprentice system must be resolved by special stipendiary magistrates, although the expense involved was considerable and, in some West Indian islands, it had been necessary to employ the ordinary resident magistrates but he checked Sligo's more extravagant requests and refused to increase the number of stipendiaries beyond sixty-one. He did, however, approve of Sligo's action in publishing their instructions to prove to the suspicious planters that they did not have orders to settle cases in the apprentices' favour.[27] Aberdeen took a determinedly optimistic line, telling both the Lords and Sligo that he was convinced that most of the sugar crop would be got in as usual and that the Negroes would 'gradually fall into habits of cheerful industry'.[28] He recognised the danger, pointed out to him by Sligo, that the freed slaves might migrate to the unsettled areas of the mountains and squat there rather than provide labour on the plantations and agreed that the first step must be to survey the uncultivated regions but, he asked cautiously, who would pay for the survey? Would the Assembly? He also authorised Sligo to allow the planters to go ahead in importing immigrant labour but he showed considerable concern that such immigrants should be fairly treated. It might be as well for the government to lay down a scale of graduated rents which the immigrants should be charged for their plots. Care should be taken that they were not exploited because they were ignorant of English law and perhaps even of the English language. The government should control the consumption of 'Spiritous Liquors' which had already been responsible for much death and misery on the island.[29]

Not all the problems of Jamaica were connected with the emancipation of the slaves. Jamaica, like other old British colonies, had its own assembly, which had long-established privileges of which the assembly was very jealous and which it sometimes abused. Aberdeen firmly backed Sligo in disallowing an Act passed by the Assembly to extend the period of compulsory labour by the apprentices beyond the time determined by Parliament, commenting that this would be a direct contradiction of the spirit of the law.[30] But generally he was cautious in dealing with the Assembly's claims and in considering the question of their powers felt compelled to grapple with all the fundamental questions which were then beginning to be raised concerning the relationship between the home government and colonial legislatures. In reply to Sligo's complaints that the Assembly was voting away sums of money without the concurrence of other branches of the legislature, that is to say the Governor and his Council, Aberdeen replied that, in that case, the Assembly was arrogating to itself a power which the House of Commons never claimed. At the same time he considered that one could not expect a complete parallel between the system at home and usages in the colonies, only a 'general coincidence' and, even more importantly, he doubted whether 'realistically' they could oppose it. It had already been sanctioned by long custom and the Assembly's reaction would probably be simply to hold up all supplies. If the government eventually had to give in, it would lead to other 'usurpations'. In the circumstances he could not advise Sligo to 'embark on such a discussion'.[31]

The administration of Cape Province, where there was as yet no elected Assembly, also required Aberdeen's detailed attention. Lord Stanley had required the Governor, Benjamin D'Urban, to draw up a scheme to reduce costs in the colony with the intention that the colony should defray its own civil expenses from its ordinary income and that the British government should be responsible only for its military establishment. The latter provision could not be avoided at such an important base as the Cape but the British government always felt strongly that its colonies should be self-sufficient in revenue and not draw on the British taxpayer. Aberdeen approved of most of D'Urban's voluminous proposals, although he added a few tart comments of his own; for example he hoped that the new Land Board would 'not lapse into a state of inactivity like the last' and might even provide proof of its existence by period-ically transmitting accounts of its proceedings.[32]

Full details of the 'irruption' of numerous tribes of Kaffirs into the eastern districts of the Cape the previous summer only reached Aberdeen in April. He approved D'Urban's energetic measures for the defence of the colony but expressed surprise at the invasion after D'Urban had received friendly assurances from the African tribes in the region. At such a distance, decisions had to be left to the discretion of the man on the spot but Aberdeen was careful to urge D'Urban in the direction of humanity. He relied on him, he said, 'for tem-pering the horrors of warfare in which the Colony has unavoidably become engaged, by all those considerations of humanity which it becomes the Servants of a civilised nation especially to bear in mind in avenging the assaults of ignorant Savages.'[33]

One decision was taken while Aberdeen was at the Colonial Office, the full significance of which was not to be apparent for another generation. He approved the treaty which D'Urban had concluded with Andries Waterboer, the chief of the Griquas. By it Waterboer undertook to keep order in his ter-ritory and to protect that section of the colony's borders. Aberdeen praised the arrangement highly as a model example of the policy the colony should pursue in its relations with native tribes.[34] The Griquas were in fact a community of mixed European and African descent (dating from the days when the Dutch of the Cape had not eschewed all relations with the Africans), who farmed and fought in European style. Their later importance derived from the fact that they had settled in the valley of the Orange River, near where the Kimberley diamond fields were to be sited and the 1834 treaty helped to establish the priority of British claims to the region.

More immediate problems related, as in the West Indies, to the abolition of slavery. Aberdeen put some pressure on D'Urban to try to obtain up-to-date estimates of the numbers of slaves in the colony at the time of emancipation, pointing out that the last statistics available dated from 1825 and that the Commissioners for Compensation required exact particulars.[35] If Aberdeen's policy of trying to establish compensation rights in the Cape had been followed up, the Boers might have been less aggrieved and less determined to 'trek' out of the colony the following year. At the same time his policy was bound to offend them in other ways. In March he informed D'Urban of a circular which had been sent to various colonial governors, consequent on a resolution of the House of Commons, asking the government to give such instructions as would 'secure to the Natives the due observance of Justice and the protection of their rights, promote the spread of civilization among them and lead them to the peaceful and voluntary reception of the Christian religion'. As passed by the Commons it was not strictly applicable to the Cape but Aberdeen sent it, as he told D'Urban, so that he might know the government's wishes. More specifically, he confirmed D'Urban's action in disallowing, on the advice of the judges, an Ordinance on vagrancy passed by the Legislative Council, agreeing that it would be in direct contravention of British policy since 1829. The Ordinance would have allowed an official to send any Hottentot, who appeared to be wandering about without means of support, to the public works until he could be contracted to an individual employer.[36] Since the famous 50th Ordinance of 1829 the British government had always firmly held to the position that the Hottentots were free men who could move about at will. The colonists, who regarded the peripatetic Hottentots as a nuisance, deeply resented the protection which the British government extended to them.

Aberdeen's attitude to the non-European races in the colonies with which he had to deal was, if sometimes paternalistic, responsible and humane. It was another European group, the French Canadians, who were to provide him with his severest test. Canada was then administered under William Pitt's Act of 1791, which had divided the old French colony on the St Lawrence, acquired by England in 1763 at the end of the Seven Years' War, into two parts. Upper Canada (the modern Ontario), was, by the 1830s, predominantly British in character and population. Lower Canada (the modern Quebec) was still substantially French, although there had been considerable British immigration into certain areas, notably the Eastern Townships. Both provinces were governed by a Governor, sent out from Britain, assisted by his Councils, and an elected Assembly. The French Canadians had not at first been familiar with, or enthusiastic for, British forms of representative government but they had soon learnt to manipulate them, with some helpful tuition from dissident English colonists. The Quebec Act of 1774 had guaranteed the privileged position of the Roman Catholic Church in the province and had retained the use of the French civil law, which included the French system of land tenure and commercial law. The British settlers who moved into the province found this very unsatisfactory. The French law in question was, of course, that of the *ancien régime*, not that of the Napoleonic Codes, and English colonists complained that it was like trying to conduct their business according to the Custom of Paris of the thirteenth century. On their side the French complained that the Governors always favoured their fellow countrymen and that French Canadians were never given their fair share of offices and appointments.

They soon found that the most effective means of bringing pressure on the colonial government was to withhold supplies, on which, among other things, official salaries depended. The situation was aggravated by a well-meant but badly considered Act of the British Parliament of 1831, passed while Ripon was Colonial Secretary, but associated with the name of his Under-Secretary, Lord Howick, the son of Lord Grey of the Reform Bill. By this Act the government had divested itself of the duties levied under the Quebec Revenue Act of 1774, without ensuring that the Assembly of Lower Canada would vote it a permanent Civil List in place of the lost revenue. The problems of Lower Canada had been moderately well known to the government and the Colonial Office since a select committee of the House of Commons, the Canada Committee, had investigated them in 1828 but in the early 1830s matters had gone from bad to worse. A combination of French Canadians, under Louis Papineau, and disaffected British colonists, led by a Scotsman, John Neilson, had refused to vote any supplies at all and the government had had to resort to dipping into the 'Military Chest' to pay immediate expenses, including salaries. In February 1834 the Assembly had passed the provocative Ninety-Two Resolutions. Round the main grievances there proliferated a whole forest of minor and local problems, such as whether the Seminary of St Sulpice owned the site of Montreal and could obstruct the building of wharves.[37]

If Peel's government had been in office long enough in 1834–35, they would have anticipated the strategy of Melbourne's government in 1838 when, following small-scale rebellions in both Upper and Lower Canada in 1837, they sent out Lord Durham to take overall charge and to report on the whole situation. The Governor-General in Canada in 1834 was Lord Aylmer who had been appointed by Sir George Murray, towards the end of Wellington's government. Aberdeen and Peel were reluctant to blame him for the deterioration of the situation in Canada, which they thought had been beyond his control, but they were agreed that he was now so unpopular that he had no chance of restoring the position. Aberdeen favoured transferring him to India so that he could be removed without apparent disapproval but no one else much liked the plan. There remained the problem of who could replace Aylmer. Aberdeen first approached Sir James Kempt, who had been the Governor of Lower Canada from September 1828 to October 1830 when the province had been relatively peaceful, but Kempt declined.[38] Aberdeen next tried Lord Elphinstone, who had a high reputation as an Indian administrator, although he admitted that he did not know him and that he believed him to be 'something of a Whig', but Peel proved to be right in supposing that Elphinstone, having already turned down 'a warm, comfortable offer of Secretary to the Board of Control', would be unlikely to be prepared to face a Canadian winter and a Canadian Assembly.[39] Aberdeen then made an even bolder suggestion. He proposed Lord Howick himself, the son of Lord Grey, who had inaugurated the conciliation policy in 1831. It would be, he told Peel, 'the best appointment they could make'. Unfortunately, at this point, Howick vehemently attacked the new government in the House and launched a particularly fierce onslaught on Aberdeen himself. Peel, reasonably enough, held that it would be quite impossible either for them to make the offer or for Howick to accept.[40] Lord Canterbury was persuaded to accept but subsequently withdrew on the grounds of family illness.[41] Eventually the choice fell on Lord Amherst, himself a former Governor-General of India. Aberdeen toyed with the idea of sending Canterbury or Amherst out as 'Commissioners' and associating Aylmer with them in their work but he decided that this was impracticable and that Aylmer would have to be recalled, however politically embarassing that might be after his policy had been supported by successive governments.[42]

While he was trying to find a man to take charge of the Canadian situation, Aberdeen studied the options available in some detail. In September 1834, James Stephen and Robert Hay had prepared a quite remarkably frank appraisal of what had gone wrong in Canada. Stephen summarised the history of the numerous disputes, especially the financial ones, and concluded that one of the chief causes of the failure to find a solution had been the continual changes at the Colonial Office. In seven years there had been seven Secretaries of State and the resulting 'indecision' and 'neglect' could hardly be exaggerated. Hay was even blunter. He thought Sir George Murray less culpable than Ripon or Stanley only because he had had to act on less information. Ripon had made a 'great error' in giving up the Quebec Revenue Act duties without the *certainty* of obtaining a Civil List in their place but Stanley had committed an equally grave error in 1833 by using the 'language of intimidation' when the government had staked its policy on conciliation. Hay argued that the government must act steadily either by coercion or conciliation but not try to combine the two. On the whole he favoured a firm policy, no further surrender of crown revenues, no further concession on the composition of the Legislative Council and the retention of control of the 'waste' (or unappropriated) lands in the colony, which would otherwise lead to a regular system of 'jobbing' in the hands of the Assembly.[43]

Another confidential Colonial Office memorandum of January 1835 suggested that there were four possible ways of dealing with the immediate crisis. They could accede to the Canadian demands and surrender the remaining crown revenues and agree to the election of the Legislative Council but, if Papineau was aiming at agitation and not the redress of real grievances, no good would come of further concessions. They might repeal the 'Howick Act', which gave the Assembly the right to appropriate the revenues. Stanley had meant to do this but had been prevented by his cabinet colleagues. The British Parliament might make up the financial deficiency. The writer commented, rather sardonically, that the objections to this were obvious but it would at least alert the Commons to the crisis. Finally they could continue to take money from the Military Chest. No comment was offered on this.

The writer then speculated on long-term solutions. The two provinces of Canada could be reunited. Stanley had thought that the time was not yet ripe for this but the annual immigration from Britain would render it more practicable later. Alternatively the more English part of Lower Canada, that is 'Lower provincial Montreal and the Townships on the Right Bank of the St Lawrence' could be separated from the rest. British capital would then be in large measure transferred from Quebec to Montreal, 'leaving the "Nation Canadianne" as a separate community'. Thirdly, there could be a federal union of all the British provinces of North America. The writer commented 'This is not a new idea.' It had been canvassed since 1822. The diversity of the provinces would make it difficult and it might be thought 'to savour too much of an invitation to independence'. He then said that in a confidential paper it was permissible to speculate that independence would come about 'at no distant period' in any case and they should 'provide accordingly'. In the immediate future, however, he faced the unpleasant possibilities that the Assembly might declare its sitting permanent or there might be a run on the Banks. A further 'Most confidential memorandum' of 21 March 1835 commented that the French Canadians could not be expected to feel any loyalty to the English royal family. France was the country 'of their Pride & their Love' but they knew that they could not return to her jurisdiction and their hatred for the United States was such that only the 'maddest' system of misrule could turn their thoughts in that direction. Among a number of specific suggestions offered in this memorandum were those of giving educated French Canadians a fair share of official situations, facilitating the education of Canadians in England, and giving Canada representatives in the Imperial Parliament.[44]

During his first weeks in office, Aberdeen had to grapple with the practical problems of authorising the payment of salaries while supplies were stopped, and accepting or disallowing numerous Acts passed by the Assembly, some of which were intentionally disruptive. Facilitating the grant of a Charter for McGill College must have been one of the few pleasanter duties of this period.[45] But meanwhile he was studying the situation and the papers put before him show that most of the solutions made famous in the Durham Report of 1839 were already being canvassed in 1834–5. His Instructions to Lord Amherst, which were ready at the beginning of April 1835, did not enter into long-term speculations but proposed a fresh start in which he tried to combine conciliation and firmness. Amherst was to be the Governor of both Upper and Lower Canada and 'His Majesty's High Commissioner for the investigation and adjustment of the grievances' of which the Assembly had complained. Immediately on his arrival in Lower Canada he was to convene an extraordinary session of the Legislature and explain his mission.[46]

In his substantive proposals, Aberdeen returned to the policy of Ripon, which he repeatedly defended, ignoring the interlude when Stanley had been at the Colonial Office. He offered to transfer the remaining hereditary and territorial revenues to the control of the Assembly in return for a Civil List which was to be granted, in the first instance, for seven years. He emphasised that the Assembly must continue to pay those pensions to which the government was 'in honour' committed. In transferring the revenues from the 'wild lands', the government did not, however, intend to surrender the right to dispose of these lands. In a passage which is full of the spirit of Edward Gibbon Wakefield and the Colonial Reformers, he defended Ripon's view that these lands should only be sold at a 'fair price' at public auction.

Aberdeen made it clear that if the Assembly were unwilling to accept these proposals, Amherst had no authority to alter any of their 'fundamental Principles'. The government meant to stand by the 1791 Act and he thought the more far-reaching demands represented popular agitation, not the considered view of the Assembly. In particular, he did not think that a Legislative Council, chosen by the Assembly, 'would adequately represent or convey the opinions of the Collective Society of the Province' but he was prepared to consider proposals for improving the Council, possibly by limiting the number of office holders who could sit in it, or even excluding them altogether. Perhaps all members of the Legislative Council should have 'a stake in the Soil of Canada'. He assured the French that there were no grounds for their fears of discrimination against their language and he was prepared to give what he termed 'authoritative sanction' to his assurances. He endorsed everything Ripon had said on the need to employ Frenchmen in public office and to provide a sound educational system. He concluded that his policy was based on a few simple principles. The government was determined to preserve the 1791 settlement but it was ready to transfer the control of all public revenues to the representatives of the people. They wished to end discrimination and promote prosperity.[47]

In the event Amherst did not go out to Canada. Peel's government fell and on 18 April Aberdeen was replaced at the Colonial Office by Charles Grant. The Whig government sent out a fact-finding commission under the Earl of Gosford with much less far-reaching powers than had been intended for Amherst. Any more radical settlement of the Canadian deadlock was postponed for another five years until after the famous mission of Lord Durham.

Aberdeen was called upon to defend his Canadian policy in the House of Lords a few weeks after he had lost office. He did so vigorously, maintaining that, after examining the situation carefully, the government had resolved on a policy of bold concessions. He was sorry the new government had not seen fit to endorse his policy and confirm Amherst's appointment.[48] Free from the restraints of office he proclaimed a very liberal view of the rights and responsibilities of colonial parliaments. 'Legislative Assemblies', he said, 'were not to be treated as children, and entirely directed from this country; but should be left to the enjoyment of the utmost freedom, consistent with the maintenance of the King's dominion.' He had expressed similar views about the rights of the Jamaica Assembly.[49]

Three years later he supported the sending of the Durham mission. He condemned the Canadian rebellions as unjustified and, characteristically, attributed them to ignorance and lack of education. 'A certain degree of information', he commented, 'was necessary for the proper exercise of political rights and privileges.' At the same time, he said, that he could not close his eyes to the fact that there would ultimately be separation between Britain and Canada, although he thought that that day might be long postponed.[50] In this Aberdeen showed a typical Peelite 'pessimist' view to the Empire. Eventually the colonies of settlement would all become independent, as the United States had done. In the meantime it was doubtful how much material advantage Britain actually derived from the possession of colonies. Nevertheless, she had duties and obligations to her colonies which could not be lightly cast aside and it was not for Britain to take the initiative in cutting the remaining ties.

This, broadly, was also the view of Aberdeen's most formidable permanent adviser, James Stephen, and it was to become the view of his political Under-Secretary, William Gladstone. It was at the Colonial Office in 1835 that Aberdeen and Gladstone first came into close contact. Gladstone was then aged twenty-five and had only been in Parliament for two years. Aberdeen had originally chosen Stuart Wortley as his Under-Secretary but Wortley had failed to secure his re-election to Parliament. Aberdeen then selected, presumably on Peel's recommendation, the young Gladstone whom, as he told Gurney, he had never seen although he was on friendly terms with his father.[51] Peel had appointed Gladstone a Lord of the Treasury and it was Peel who broke the news to Gladstone one afternoon late in January 1835 that he would like him to transfer to the Colonial Office. The offer, as Gladstone confessed to Aberdeen's youngest son many years later, rather dismayed him. He knew Aberdeen only by 'public rumour' and although he knew of his 'high character', he had also heard of him 'as a man of cold manners, and close and even haughty reserve'. He went to see his new chief 'in fear and trembling' and was amazed by his reception. He recalled:

It was dusk when I entered his room – the one on the first floor, with the bow – window looking to the Park – so that I saw his figure rather than his countenance. I do not recollect the matter of the conversation; but I well remember that, before I had been three minutes with him, all my apprehensions had melted away like snow in the sun; and I came away from that interview, conscious indeed – as who could fail to be conscious? – of his dignity, but of a dignity so tempered by a peculiar purity and gentleness, and even friendship, that I believe I thought more about the wonder of his being at that time so misunderstood by the outer world, than about the new duties and responsibilities of my new office.[52]

It was the beginning of a friendship which lasted until Aberdeen's death in 1860.

Stanmore's belief that his father found the Colonial Office 'highly distasteful' is not entirely borne out by his contemporary letters. It is true that he told Princess Lieven that he went there reluctantly because it cut him off from foreign affairs, 'the only official life for which I have any taste'. Wellington was later to remind him that he went to the Colonial Office, 'disliking it and its business', but added flatteringly that he succeeded in it so well 'that you are now the standard of our Colonial policy'. Lord Howick who, as Earl Grey, was to be a very successful Colonial Secretary himself, later publicly withdrew all his criticisms of 1835.[53] Aberdeen's own complaints to Gurney sound lighthearted. Gurney, he said, would be glad to hear that Heligoland was quiet because he could not say the same of any other colony. 'Hot water' seemed to be 'the favourite element' of colonial mankind and, if they liked it like that, he would not quarrel with them. On another occasion he promised to 'steal a few minutes from the attractions of negroes and Caffres' to visit Gurney, who had been ill. The impression is rather of a man who was enjoying himself than of one who was seriously disgruntled.[54]

Certainly Aberdeen showed all the makings of a very good Colonial Secretary. He saw clearly the nature of the real problems in Canada, South Africa and the West Indies. His views were liberal and humane and he set about applying them with firmness and tact. His tenure of the Colonial Office suggests what his later tenure of the premiership seems to confirm: that his real talent lay in presiding over the administration and implementation of a steady reform policy rather than in the necessarily adversarial politics of foreign policy. But this was never Aberdeen's own view. As soon as Peel's government resigned in April 1835 he returned to his watching brief on foreign affairs in the Lords.

He no longer attacked Whig foreign policy with the vigour and consistency he had done a few years earlier. The danger of general revolution, which had seemed so real in 1830–31, had now largely passed. Palmerston painstakingly worked out a settlement of the Low Countries, which included a guarantee of Belgian neutrality that was accepted by the Great Powers in the Treaty of London of May 1839. The Iberian Peninsula continued to give trouble, although the storm centre was now Spain rather than Portugal.

Ferdinand VII died in September 1833 and his infant daughter was proclaimed Queen, as Isabella II, with her mother, Maria Christina as Regent. Her accession was not accepted by Ferdinand's brother, Carlos, who maintained that the settlement at the end of the War of the Spanish Succession debarred women from the throne. Since Carlos was supported by the Church and the absolutists, Christina was forced into a mildly liberal stance, taking her ministries from the *Moderados* and *Progressistas*. Carlos found his main support in the Basque country where the inhabitants resented the centralising tendencies of the liberal ministries in Madrid.

In April 1834, Palmerston had persuaded the French government to sign the Treaty of Quadruple Alliance with the governments of Queen Christina in Spain and Queen Maria in Portugal, as a direct reply to the Münchengratz agreement of the three Eastern Powers. With English and French support the Carlists and Miguellists were defeated. Miguel left Portugal to go into exile in Rome and henceforth fighting in Portugal was confined to contests between rival 'liberal' forces. Carlos was made of sterner stuff. Having surrendered to a British Admiral and been brought to England he subsequently, to Palmerston's intense embarrassment, made his escape and slipped back to Spain where he once again raised the Basque country. His forces were not finally defeated until 1840.

Peel's government, while disliking the Quadruple Alliance, conceded when in office that a treaty freely entered into must be honoured. But Aberdeen never made any secret of his own views then or later that Britain would have done far better to have kept out of the matter and left the Spaniards and the Portuguese to settle their own differences.[55]

But towards the end of Melbourne's ministry Aberdeen found himself supporting Palmerston against his critics in his own Whig party. The occasion was a new crisis in the Eastern Question. In 1831 Mehemet Ali, irritated that he had not received all the rewards promised him by the Sultan for his intervention in Greece, sent his son, Ibrahim, to invade Syria. After the defeat of the Turkish army at Konieh in December 1832, the way to Constantinople itself seemed open. The Sultan, in a panic, appealed to the Great Powers of Europe to help him. Palmerston would have been prepared to have despatched a naval force to overawe Mehemet Ali but the rest of the Cabinet, feeling that they already had enough difficulties at home and abroad, refused to agree. Instead Sultan Mahmud turned to Russia, as one of his officials observed, as 'a drowning man clings to a serpent'. The result was the Treaty of Unkiar Skelessi of July 1833 by which the Russians promised Turkey military assistance, if necessary, in return for a Turkish promise to close the Dardanelles to foreign warships if Russia requested it. The exact terms of the Treaty were not known in London but it was viewed with extreme suspicion. Palmerston was only too anxious to have another opportunity to intervene and to ensure that Britain participated in the settlement. The chance came in 1839 when Mahmud, who had had time to re-organise his army, launched a counter-attack on Ibrahim in Syria. He had miscalculated. His army was defeated and Mahmud, who had been a sick man when he ordered the attack, died on 1 July 1839. His successor was a boy of sixteen, Abdul Mejid.

A dangerous collapse of the Ottoman Empire seemed to have begun and the Great Powers of Europe consulted one another. Agreement was delayed by the fact that France was still trying to secure the best possible deal for her protegé, Mehemet Ali. In July 1840 the other four Great Powers went ahead without her and concluded the Quadruple Treaty by which they agreed to coerce Mehemet Ali. If Mehemet Ali quickly came to terms he was to have Egypt as a hereditary pashalik and part of Syria for his lifetime, but, if he delayed, these favourable terms were to be withdrawn. The ancient rule which forbade the passage of all foreign warships through the Straits when the Porte was at peace was to be reinstated. The French were furious at this treatment of Mehemet Ali and even more so at the slight to themselves in that they were not parties to the Treaty. Louis Philippe's Prime Minister, Thiers, particularly blamed Palmerston for the whole transaction. War fever began to mount in France. Plans for building new fortifications round Paris were put into operation. Wild speeches were made, suggesting that France was ready to take on the whole of Europe and reverse the verdict of 1814. Eventually Louis Philippe took fright, dismissed Thiers and recalled François Guizot. Guizot succeeded in forming an administration and calming the situation down. Mehemet Ali was duly coerced and, after some fighting, persuaded to settle for the hereditary pashalik of Egypt. France's face was saved by the conclusion of a new Treaty, to which she was a party, the Straits Convention of 13 July 1841, which reiterated that the Straits were to remain closed to all foreign warships when the Porte was at peace, except certain light vessels allowed for foreign embassies. The significance of the exception was not to be apparent until the eve of the Crimean War.

Palmerston had been subjected to vigorous criticism within his own party for the role he had played during the Eastern crisis. The many Francophiles, who still looked to Holland House as their natural home, felt that his disregard of French susceptibilities had been totally unjustifiable. They did not scruple to tell their French friends how they felt and may even have contributed to the bellicosity of Paris by giving the impression that Palmerston stood alone. Palmerston's son-in-law, Lord Shaftesbury, recorded in disgust in his Journal:

The 'Bear' Ellice . . . urged Thiers to resist the policy of Palmerston, assuring him that the Cabinet would never meet any *real* French resistance . . . Lord Holland writes to Guizot, and tells him everything . . . The Duc de Broglie writes to Lord Lansdowne, and Lord Lansdowne writes to Broglie: can this be done without communication, on my Lord's part, of his misgivings, waverings, etc. etc., and all the mischievous puerilities of the English Cabinet? . . . The fact is there has been foul intrigue to replace Palmerston.

Charles Greville, the Clerk to the Privy Council, and his friend, Henry Reeve, also played a questionable role.[56]

In contrast Aberdeen, like most of his Tory colleagues, behaved with impeccable propriety during the Eastern crisis and even supported what Palmerston had done. Aberdeen explained his views at length to Princess Lieven. He wrote to her in August 1840, 'I rather think that Lord Palmerston will be able to make out a good case in justification of the course which he has adopted, although I perceive that some of my friends are of a different opinion.' He could not feel alarm, despite all the 'warlike demonstrations' because he did not believe that Louis Philippe would allow 'the personal feelings of M Thiers, or the national vanity of his people, to precipitate him into a position so dangerous to the existence of his dynasty, as a war with the great Powers of Europe; and for no real French objects, or essential interests'. When Guizot succeeded Thiers, Aberdeen repeated the same sentiments, perhaps hoping that Princess Lieven would pass them on to the new French Prime Minister, as indeed she did. They were, he said, anxiously awaiting the outcome of the meeting of the French Chambers on 5 November:

deciding, as they will, the fate of this country, and of the world, with respect to peace or war. I confess that I am very sanguine about the pacifick character of their conduct. Not that I have any profound respect for the wisdom of the French Chambers; but France has really no case at all to justify the burning of an ounce of gunpowder . . . The *fanfaron*, whom M. Guizot has succeeded, perhaps may not have intended to produce war; but by his levity and rashness he might have placed matters in such a state as to render it unavoidable. [M. Guizot must know that there was no 'hostile intention' in the Treaty of 15 July.[57]]

In reply, the Princess Lieven pleaded the French case and Aberdeen conceded that it would be very unfortunate if any personal incivility by the British Foreign Office – and 'We know very well they can be uncivil enough in that quarter, when they please' – was allowed to complicate what was otherwise an entirely justifiable course of action. When Aberdeen read the Queen's Speech on the opening of Parliament in January 1841 he wrote at once to Princess Lieven to express his regret that it had contained no conciliatory reference to the new French government and that, because he had been unavoidably detained in Scotland, he had not been in his place to comment on the omission. He learnt later that both Peel and Wellington had done so.[58]

When they returned to office in September 1841 the Conservative attitude to France was distinctly different from what it had been in the early 1830s. They had then thought it was merely a matter of time before a French monarchy, which was little more than a disguised republic, showed itself in its true colours and embarked on an aggressive policy which might provoke revolution all over Europe. It was therefore important to 'contain' France, particularly in vital strategic areas like the Low Countries and the Iberian Peninsula. By 1841 Aberdeen, even more than Peel and Wellington, believed that Louis Philippe genuinely wanted peace and stability in Europe and was probably strong enough to control his own wild men at home. Thiers, after all, had been dropped. His successor, Guizot, was particularly congenial to Aberdeen.

François Guizot was an unusual man for a leading French politician. He was a Protestant, itself rare among French statesmen, and had all the virtues traditionally associated with the Protestant minority, industry, seriousness, integrity and caution. His first career had been as an academic and even after he turned to politics he published a number of major historical works, some of them on English history. Princess Lieven never ceased to sing praises of Aberdeen and Guizot to each other, and when Guizot came to London as Ambassador in February 1840, Aberdeen went out of his way to cultivate his acquaintance.[59] Both were outwardly austere, but warm-hearted men. Each saw himself as a scholar who had been drawn into the political world by a sense of duty. They liked each other and they came to trust each other. When he returned to office Aberdeen was prepared to gamble his whole policy on the belief that British interests depended on keeping Louis Philippe and Guizot in power in France.

Palmerston left the Foreign Office on the fall of Melbourne's government in September 1841, in a spirit of resentment. People were already saying that he was a dangerous man who could not expect to hold the Foreign Office again, even if the Whigs returned to power. Palmerston did not see it like that. In his view his daring policies, in Europe, Asia and America were about to pay off. Now he must surrender them into the hands of a man who would probably wreck them all. His irritation fuelled his attacks and he was in no mood to repay Aberdeen for his support in 1840–41.

NOTES

1. *Hansard*, 3rd ser., IX, 862 (26 Jan. 1832).
2. *Hansard*, 3rd ser., XV, 107–8 (5 Feb. 1833).
3. *Hansard*, 3rd ser., II, 660 (18 Feb. 1831), V, 799 (5 Aug. 1831), 1016–24 (9 Aug. 1831), VI, 641, 1109 (26 Aug. 1831), IX, 320 (16 Dec. 1831), XIII, 1064–5 (28 June 1832), XVII, 900–3 (3 May 1833). Asking for papers was of course sometimes a device for bringing on a discussion.
4. *Hansard*, 3rd ser., 834–62 (26 Jan. 1832).
5. *Hansard*, 3rd ser., IX, 778 (21 Jan 1832), X, 11–14 (7 Feb. 1832).
6. *Hansard*, 3rd ser., II, 658–60, 729–30 (18, 21 Feb. 1831).
7. *Hansard*, 3rd ser., XIV, 514–5 (18 July 1832).
8. *Hansard*, 3rd ser., V, 786–99 (5 Aug. 1831).
9. *Hansard*, 3rd ser., XVIII, 268–78 (3 June 1833).
10. *Hansard*, 3rd ser., IV, 301–5 (24 June 1831), V, 312 (26 July 1831), 815–6 (5 Aug. 1831), 786–99 (5 Aug. 1831), VI, 1096–1109 (5 Sept. 1831); cf. Add. MSS 43236, f. 48, 'Petition of . . . Merchants, Shipowners, Manufacturers and others, concerned in the Portugal trade', n.d.
11. *Hansard*, 3rd ser., VI, 1098–9, 1107 (5 Sept. 1831).
12. *Hansard*, 3rd ser., IV, 296–301 (24 June 1831), V, 313 (26 July 1831), 1016–24 (9 Aug. 1831).

13. Gurney Papers, RQC 334/63, Aberdeen to Gurney, 23 Dec. 1831.
14. Gurney Papers, RQC 334/64, Aberdeen to Gurney, 22 Nov. 1832.
15. *Hansard*, 3rd ser., X, 726 (27 Feb. 1831).
16. *Hansard*, 3rd ser., XI, 112–9 (13 Mar. 1832), XIII, 516–9 (18 July 1832), XVII, 900–6 (3 May 1833).
17. *Hansard*, 3rd ser., XVII, 901, 905–6 (3 May 1833), VI, 1108 (5 Sept. 1831), XV, 102–3 (5 Feb. 1833).
18. Aberdeen to Lieven, 8 Nov. 1833, Jones-Parry, vol. 1, pp. 12–3.
19. Add. MSS 40312, Aberdeen to Peel, 5 May 1834, Peel's Memorandum, 10 May 1834. Aberdeen had previously tried to mediate on his own initiative in 1833, Aberdeen to Peel, 14 Feb. 1833.
20. Gurney Papers, RQC 334/78, Aberdeen to Gurney, 16 Dec. 1834; Add. MSS 40312, Peel to Aberdeen, 18 Dec. 1834.
21. Add. MSS 40312, Aberdeen to Peel, 26 Mar. 1835.
22. Stanmore, p. 110.
23. CO 137/197, ff. 4–12.
24. Stanmore, pp. 110–11.
25. *Hansard*, 3rd ser., XXVI, 419–21 (27 Feb. 1835); cf. CO 138/56, Aberdeen to Sligo, No. 7, 29 Dec. 1834, confirming his appointment.
26. *Hansard*, 3rd ser., XXVI, 416–21, 423 (27 Feb. 1835), XXXIX, 940 (11 Dec. 1838).
27. CO 138/56, Aberdeen to Sligo, No. 17, 1 Jan., No. 39, 2 Feb., No. 48, 13 Feb. 1835.
28. *Hansard*, 3rd ser., XXVI, 1054–5 (17 Mar. 1835); CO 138/56, Aberdeen to Sligo, No. 50, 15 Feb. 1835.
29. CO 138/56, Aberdeen to Sligo, No. 32, 24 Jan., No. 64, 16 Mar. 1835.
30. CO 138/56, Aberdeen to Sligo, No. 18, 1 Jan. 1835.
31. CO 138/56, Aberdeen to Sligo, No. 51, 16 Feb. 1835.
32. CO 49/26, Aberdeen to D'Urban, No. 36, 11 Apr. 1835.
33. CO 49/26, Aberdeen to D'Urban, No. 34, 11 Apr. 1835.
34. CO 49/26, Aberdeen to D'Urban, No. 37, 11 Apr. 1835.
35. CO 49/26, Aberdeen to D'Urban, No. 35, 11 Apr. 1835.
36. CO 49/26, Aberdeen to D'Urban, Separate, 11 Mar., Separate, 31 Mar. 1835.
37. CO 43/29, Aberdeen to Aylmer, No. 4, 1 Jan. 1835.
38. Add. MSS 43061, Peel to Aberdeen, 7, 11 Jan. 1835.
39. Add. MSS 40312, Aberdeen to Peel, 10, 12, 13 Jan. 1835; Add. MSS 43061, Peel to Aberdeen, 11 Jan. 1835.
40. Add. MSS 40312, Aberdeen to Peel, 10 Mar. 1835; Add. MSS 43061, Peel to Aberdeen, 11 Mar. 1835. Howick's language had been extreme, calling Aberdeen 'an enemy of mankind'.
41. Add. MSS 40312, Aberdeen to Peel, 18 Mar. 1835.
42. CO 43/30, Aberdeen to Aylmer, Private, 30 Mar. 1835.
43. Add. MSS 43236, CO Conf. Print No. 24, 'Minutes for Mr Spring Rice's consideration . . .'
44. Add. MSS 43236, ff. 223–5, 'Memorandum on Canadian Affairs', 31 Jan. 1835, Confidential.
45. CO 43/30, Aberdeen to Aylmer, No. 18, 12 Feb. 1835.
46. CO 43/30, Aberdeen to Amherst, No. 1, 2 Apr. 1835.
47. CO 43/30, Aberdeen to Amherst, No. 2, 2 Apr. 1835.
48. *Hansard*, 3rd ser., XXVIII, 716–21 (12 June 1835).

49. *Ibid.*, 719; CO 138/56, Aberdeen to Sligo, No. 51, 16 Feb. 1835.

50. *Hansard*, 3rd ser., XL, 648–63 (2 Feb. 1838). But he deplored Gibbon Wakefield's action in leaking Durham's Report to *The Times, Hansard*, 3rd ser., XLV, 436–7 (15 Feb. 1839).

51. Gurney Papers, RQC 334/79, Aberdeen to Gurney, 27 Jan. 1835; Add. MSS 44088, Aberdeen to Sir John Gladstone, 26 Jan. 1835.

52. Stanmore, p. 111.

53. Stanmore, pp. 110, 112, 116; Aberdeen to Lieven, 19 Dec. 1834, Jones-Parry, vol. 1, pp. 23–4.

54. Gurney Papers, RQC 334/79, Aberdeen to Gurney, 27 Jan. 1835, /81, 7 Mar. 1835.

55. *Hansard*, 3rd ser., XXXI, 322–4 (12 Feb. 1836), XXXII, 387–92 (18 Mar. 1836).

56. Shaftesbury's Journal, 12 Nov. 1840, quoted Hodder, vol. 1, p. 317.

57. Aberdeen to Lieven, 14, 31 Aug., 9 Nov. 1840, Jones-Parry, vol. 1, pp. 144, 146–7, 150–1. Aberdeen expressed similar views to Gurney, Gurney Papers RQC 334/100, 3 Oct., /101, 29 Oct. 1840.

58. Lieven to Aberdeen, 19 Aug., 26 Oct., 16 Nov. encl. Guizot to Lieven, 12 Dec. 1840, 28 Jan., 5 Feb. 1841, Jones-Parry, vol. 1, pp. 145–64.

59. Aberdeen to Lieven, 24 Apr., 31 Aug. 1840, Jones-Parry, vol. 1, pp. 139, 147–8.

1. Lord Aberdeen by Sir Thomas Lawrence. Exhibited at the Royal Academy 1808. Haddo House.

2. Lord Aberdeen's father, Lord Haddo, by Pompeo Batoni, 1775. Haddo House.

3(a) Haddo House. William Adam's elevation of the entrance front, showing the original horseshoe staircase, and the main entrance at first floor level.

(b) Haddo House as it is today. This includes some alterations and additions later than the fourth Earl's time.

(b) Harriet Douglas, Countess of Aberdeen. After a portrait by Sir Thomas Lawrence. Haddo House.

4(a) Catherine Hamilton, Countess of Aberdeen. After a portrait by Sir Thomas Lawrence. Haddo House.

5. Lord Aberdeen's daughters, Jane, Caroline and Alice, by George Hayter, 1815. Haddo House.

6. Buchan Ness by James Giles. The two small figures are Lord Aberdeen and his daughter-in-law, Lady Haddo.

7. Lord Aberdeen by John Partridge, 1846.

(b)   Aberdeen smoking the pipe of peace. *Punch*, 17 December 1853.

8(a)   What everybody thinks. *Young Palmerston, a sharp clever boy:* 'Oh, Crikey! What a Scotch mull of a Prime Minister!' [That may be, but it is not pretty to say so. – *Punch.*] *Punch* 8 October 1853.

DESTRUCTION of the TURKISH SQUADRON, and AWFUL MASSACRE of the TURKS at SINOPE by the RUSSIANS.

When five Turkish Vessels of superior force, with their Crews, were either blown up or sunk, and from 1000 to 5000 human lives wantonly and cruelly sacrificed by an overwhelming Russian force, consisting of Six ten of Battle Ships, Two Frigates and three Steamers

Sketched by an English Gentleman, resident at Sinope

London. Published 1st of May 1854 by Read & Co., 10. Johnson's Court Fleet St.

9. The destruction of the Turkish squadron at Sinope, November 1853.

10(a) The ministerial split. *Palmerston*: 'I'll just frighten them a little.' *Punch*, 31 Dec 1853.

(b) What it has come to. *Aberdeen*: 'I must let him go!' *Punch*, 18 February 1854

11. Lord Aberdeen in the uniform of Lord Lieutenant of Aberdeenshire. The portrait was presented as a compliment to the Earl by the Provost and Town Council of Aberdeen in October 1854.

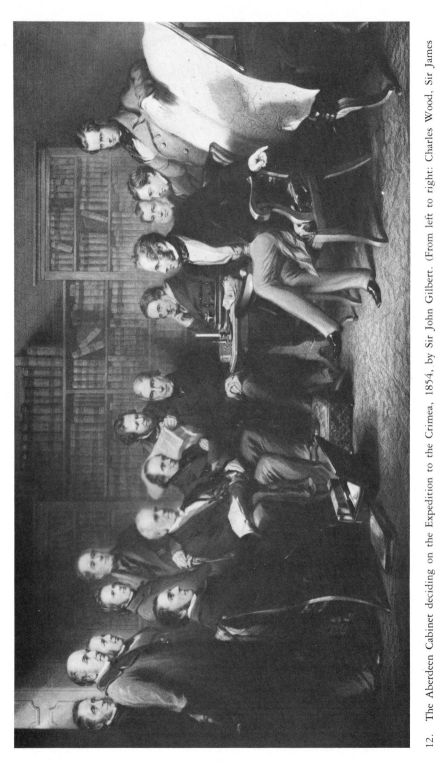

12. The Aberdeen Cabinet deciding on the Expedition to the Crimea, 1854, by Sir John Gilbert. (From left to right: Charles Wood, Sir James Graham, William Molesworth, W.E. Gladstone, Duke of Argyll, Lord Clarendon, Lord Lansdowne, Lord John Russell, Lord Granville, Lord Aberdeen, Lord Cranworth, Lord Palmerston, Sir George Grey, Sidney Herbert, Duke of Newcastle.)

13. The road from Balaclava to Sebastopol during wet weather.

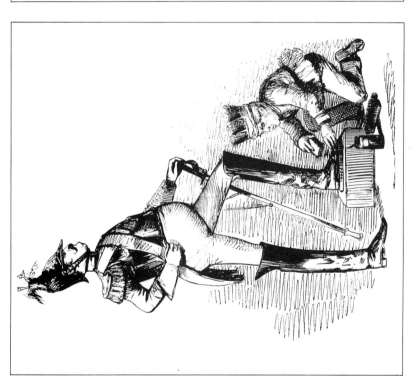

(b) 'You are requested not to speak to the man at the wheel.' *Punch*, 26 August 1854

14(a) Not a nice business. *Punch*, 1 July 1854.

(b)   Austria still plays on the Scotch fiddle. *Punch*, 2 December 1854.

15(a)   How to get rid of an old woman. *Punch*, 28 October 1854.

GEORGE GORDON,
4TH EARL OF ABERDEEN, K.T._K.G.
BORN JANUARY 28TH 1784,
DIED DECEMBER 14TH 1860.

AMBASSADOR,
SECRETARY OF STATE,
PRIME MINISTER.

Δικαιοτατος

AT GREAT STANMORE, MIDDLESEX,

16. Lord Aberdeen. Marble bust by Matthew Noble, 1854. Commissioned by William Gladstone and others.

A Scottish interlude

Although Aberdeen's attention was mainly occupied by Westminster politics in the 1830s, he did not neglect Scottish affairs, quite apart from keeping a watchful eye on legislation which affected Scotland. In 1838 he was persuaded by Wellington and Peel to assume the leadership of the Scottish Conservative party in succession to the Duke of Buccleuch.[1] He also remained an active Freemason and Freemasonry was always an influential force in Scotland. But the two institutions which absorbed most of his attention in this period were the universities and the Church.

He was elected Lord Rector of King's College, Aberdeen, in 1817 and succeeded the Duke of Gordon as its Chancellor. In 1826 he was appointed to the Royal Commission which was established to enquire into the state of the Scottish universities.[2] At its first meeting in Edinburgh on 31 August he was elected as its chairman and presided at all the early meetings in Edinburgh in September and October 1826.[3] He was not present when the Commission conducted its enquiries in Glasgow and St Andrews in January and July 1827 but he was again present and chaired the sessions when the Commission reached Aberdeen in September 1827.[4]

The Commission presented its Report in October 1830. The Report analysed the complex relationship between the universities and the Church in Scotland, pointing out that, although the universities were not ecclesiastical bodies, they were 'connected' with the established Church, 'the standards of which the Professors must acknowledge'. They drew attention to the considerable difference between Scottish and English universities. Scottish universities were designed for persons of all ranks and not especially for the aristocracy. They catered for students of all ages who could attend classes more or less at will. The Commissioners did not hesitate to make the most detailed recommendations, not only about the government of the universities, but also about the curriculum.[5]

Aberdeen presented them with a particular problem. There were two university institutions in the city, King's College, founded in 1495, and Marischal College, founded in 1593. The Commission came out strongly in favour of uniting the two. Their two main arguments were that it would make possible a great improvement in the medical school and it would solve the problem of

Marischal College's very dilapidated buildings. Earlier plans for union had failed but the Commission recommended that they follow the precedents set when St Leonard's and St Salvator's united to form the University of St Andrews. The detailed plans for the union were sensible and practical.[6]

A Bill for the union of the two Colleges was introduced into Parliament in 1835.[7] Aberdeen, although unwilling to oppose it, because it embodied the main recommendation of the Royal Commission, had many reservations about its details, which he felt had become tinged with party politics.[8] The Bill stirred up a hornet's nest. Petitions poured in and Aberdeen personally was lobbied from all sides.[9] On 28 June 1836, he warned the House that he proposed to introduce a number of amendments at the committee stage. The most important would guarantee that nothing in the Bill affected the rights of the established Church and would strictly limit the powers of the 'Boards of Visitors' who were being entrusted with the implementation of the union. A few days later the government decided to postpone the measure.[10] A fresh attempt was made to take up the question later in 1836 and a new Commission appointed to investigate the matter.[11] The union did not take place until 1860.

The connection between the universities and the Church always caused problems. It was not uncommon for appointments to professorships to be challenged on the grounds of the candidate's unsatisfactory theological views. Aberdeen was appealed to on a number of occasions but he usually politely declined to become involved and defended the university's right to make its own appointments.[12]

Aberdeen remained interested in Scottish university affairs but he resisted a suggestion in 1853 that the Scottish universities should return their own members to Parliament as Oxford and Cambridge did, arguing that Scottish graduates had no real corporate existence. He would prefer such a seat, he said, to go to the Faculty of Advocates, which did have such an existence.[13]

Aberdeen tried to perform one more service for Scottish learning. In 1854 he discussed with Gladstone the possibility of transforming the Advocates Library into something resembling a National Library, with access for the public.[14] The transformation finally took place in 1925 when the Faculty of Advocates presented the Library to the nation.

It was, however, the affairs of the Church which provided Aberdeen with his greatest problem in the 1830s and 1840s. Despite his personal preference for the Anglican Church, Aberdeen felt it to be important to show his solidarity with his tenants, who were virtually all Presbyterians. When at Haddo, he attended the parish church at Methlic every Sunday in some state. From 1818 to 1828 he even consented to represent the Presbytery of Ellon in the General Assembly of Scotland, although he cannot have been very active in his attendance since he was rarely in Scotland in May when the Assembly held its annual meetings.[15] Very much against his will he became caught up in the schism that split the Church of Scotland in the 1840s and led to the emergence of the 'Wee Frees'.[16]

In theory a minister was 'called' to his charge by his parishioners. In practice, by the middle of the nineteenth century, ministers were nominated by either lay or clerical patrons. Members of his future congregation had an ancient right to object to his appointment on grounds of unsoundness of life or doctrine and the local Presbytery then had the duty to investigate the truth of the charges, but in practice this right had fallen into complete desuetude. The more democratic spirit abroad in the 1830s, however, led to a more fundamental challenge to patrons' rights. A patron should not be allowed to 'intrude' a nominee, whom the parish did not want, even if there was no specific charge against him. In 1835 the General Assembly, led by the famous Dr Chalmers, passed the so-called Veto Act. The relevant clause read, 'The General Assembly declare, That it is a fundamental law of this Church, that no pastor shall be intruded on any Congregation contrary to the will of the people.' If 'the major part of the male heads of families, members of the vacant congregation, and in full communion with the Church, shall disapprove of the person in whose favour the call is proposed . . . such disapproval shall be deemed sufficient ground for the Presbytery rejecting such a person, and he shall be rejected accordingly.'[17]

The Act was tested when the parishioners of Auchterarder rejected a minister presented by Lord Kinnoull. He appealed to the civil courts. The Court of Session decided in his favour and the decision was upheld in 1838 by the House of Lords. Aberdeen had felt some sympathy with the idea of reactivating the Presbytery's ancient right to judge the fitness of a nominee. It was indefensible that an unfit man should be foisted on a reluctant parish. But the Veto Act was rather different. Aberdeen's reaction was rather like his reaction to the changes in the Irish franchise in 1829 when he said that he would have preferred universal suffrage to the existing situation. He would, he said, have no objection at all in principle to parishes simply electing their minister, although he thought the idea impracticable at that time since Parliament would never agree to it. But it was intolerable that a man who had been named by a patron should then be rejected by the parishioners without them having to state specific grounds, which could be tested by the Presbytery. There was no disgrace in losing an election but a man caught in this situation would be stigmatised for life with no means of redress.[18]

Aberdeen's attitude was hardened by a case which occurred in the parish of Methlic itself. The incumbent, the Rev. Ludovic Grant, who had been the minister for more than fifty years, died in 1839. Aberdeen, as patron, nominated a Mr James Whyte. Unfortunately, a rumour circulated round the parish that Whyte had been guilty of immorality in his youth. Aberdeen, true to his principles, asked the Presbytery to investigate and something like a full-scale trial was held in the church at Methlic. At the end of it the Presbytery pronounced Whyte to be entirely innocent and the lawyer, who had represented the complainants, expressed his agreement with the verdict.

Aberdeen naturally supposed that the matter was settled and that the parish would now accept Mr Whyte. He reckoned without the obstinacy of Scottish farmers. They told him that a minister who had a reputation for immorality (even if unfounded) would be of no use to them. To Aberdeen the whole matter now became a battle both for justice for Mr Whyte and his own influence with his people, particularly as he began to suspect that radical attorneys from

Aberdeen were stirring the pot. He met a hundred leading 'heads of families' but failed to convince them, although they professed every loyalty towards, and confidence in, Aberdeen himself. He decided to meet the challenge and summoned a meeting of all the two hundred and forty heads of families involved (over two hundred of whom had signed a paper opposing Whyte) in the parish church. He addressed them at length, reviewed the evidence in Whyte's favour and asked them to trust his judgement. To his enormous relief a few days later, when it became time for the formal 'call', no one opposed it and a large number followed Aberdeen himself in signing it. He told his friend, John Hope, the Dean of the Faculty of Advocates, 'Had I failed, considering the footing on which I have always stood with these people I really should not have known what to do or what to have felt.'[19]

Whyte apparently managed to win over his reluctant parishioners and remained on good terms with them until his death in 1881. But the general question did not resolve itself so easily. The Auchterarder case was followed by a similar dispute in Strathbogie which led to an open clash between the General Assembly and the civil courts. There now seemed to be no alternative to legislation and Aberdeen discussed the matter at great length with both Chalmers and John Hope.

Aberdeen wrote to Chalmers at the end of December 1839 telling him that when they last met in London he, Aberdeen, had had 'no strong prejudice' against the Veto Act and even less in favour of patronage but he had now modified his views on the Veto Act and believed it could not work. He hoped that the matter could be settled by an Act of the Assembly and that parliamentary action would be unnecessary. It would be deplorable if it became a party political matter. Chalmers replied that the demarcation between the civil and the ecclesiastical courts must be clearly defined. Otherwise there would be a disruption of Church and State.[20]

Under these pressures Aberdeen introduced a Bill into the Lords in May 1840 which would have restored to the Presbyteries the right to reject candidates for livings who were demonstrably unfit. The non–intrusionists in the General Assembly were not satisfied and wanted to amend the measure to make objections on the part of the majority of parishioners sufficient in themselves to secure the rejection of a candidate. This would, of course, have simply restored the Veto Act, which had been declared *ultra vires* by the courts, by another method. Stanmore blamed Chalmers, who tried to act as mediator, for saying one thing to Aberdeen and another to the non-intrusionists. His accusations called forth a reply from Chalmers' daughter publishing the correspondence between Aberdeen and her father in 1839–40, which does seem to prove that the position was very clearly stated on both sides.[21]

The difference was, however, fatal. As Aberdeen feared, the matter did become one of party politics. The majority of the General Assembly refused to support Aberdeen's Bill. Ironically, the Law Lords gave it as their opinion that it contained too many concessions to the Church. The Bill secured a second reading in the Lords on 16 June but Aberdeen privately consulted Melbourne and Lord John Russell and came to the conclusion that it would only pass the

292

Commons if he agreed to amendments which were unacceptable to him. He therefore withdrew the Bill.[22]

The Duke of Argyll, who supported the non–intrusionist party, then introduced a much more far-reaching measure but it perished with the fall of Melbourne's government in 1841. Peel's new government tried to revive Aberdeen's Bill which, it was arranged, should be introduced into the Commons by Sir George Sinclair. But the majority of the General Assembly was in no mood to settle for what it now regarded as half-measures. In 1842 it passed the 'Claim of Right' resolution, which, in effect, declared that legislation or court decisions which trespassed on the rights of the Church were themselves *ultra vires* and consequently null and void. In November the non–intrusionists pledged themselves to secede from the Established Church if the 'Claim of Right' was rejected. There was no possibility of any British government accepting it. Aberdeen's original Bill was passed in August 1843, but it had been overtaken by events. The great Disruption of the Church of Scotland had taken place at the General Assembly the previous May.[23]

Aberdeen's own exasperation may be gauged by the remark he made to Charlotte Canning when visiting Blair Atholl with Queen Victoria in 1844. Charlotte drew his attention to 'an odd log church . . . of the free variety'. Aberdeen said he would like to 'set it on fire'.[24]

The private strains of the 1830s began to tell on Aberdeen's health. At one time he had been inclined to laugh at Gurney's insistence that they were both getting old. He told him in December 1833, 'I see that my head is going grey, and that I am more sensible to various ailments, but essentially I feel as young as ever: too much so, I fear, a great deal.' Two years later he wrote, 'In some respects, I appear to myself to have lived a hundred years already; but in others, I am still young enough.' But in 1839 he suffered what was almost certainly a stress illness which he described in graphic detail to Gurney. He told him, 'I am returned from Scotland an altered man! I mean that you would scarcely know me. Without any illness, in the course of three or four weeks my hair became as white as snow, and then fell off altogether. Thus, I am perforce wigged. The change is made still more complete as my eye brows are as bare as any part of my forehead.'[25] The story got out and caused some mirth in London society. Lady Cowper told Princess Lieven that Aberdeen was 'very disfigured', even though he had bought a wig and dyed his whiskers, 'but there is no cure for the eyebrows and eyelashes'.[26] A year later Aberdeen wrote to Gurney that he had now got sciatica which made travelling difficult but 'my hair, some months ago, took to growing as suddenly as it fell off; and I accordingly threw my wig into the fire forthwith. I have now a venerable head, silver locks, a fair sprinkling of them, although not abundant. How I wish I could throw my Sciatica after my wig!'[27] This seems to have been the prelude to a general deterioration of his health when the headaches, to which he had always been subject, became so persistent and severe that they rendered the transaction of business difficult. When Aberdeen returned to office, although he may have had more freedom and more standing in the party, he did not have the health and energy he had had in the past.

By the late 1830s it was clear that the Conservatives' return to power could not be long delayed. They had steadily improved their position at each of the previous general elections. In 1833 they could barely muster 150 supporters in the Commons; 1835 saw the ministerial majority reduced to 60 and 1837 to 30. But Aberdeen agreed with other leading Conservatives that the experiment of 1834–35 had proved that they must bide their time and not take office again until they were sure of being able to command the House of Commons.[28] From 1836 onwards Aberdeen participated in a number of meetings of the Conservative leaders, some in London, some at Drayton, at which tactics were discussed. He was naturally among those whom Peel consulted in 1839–41, when the difficulties of the Melbourne administration seemed to be becoming insuperable.[29] Some of Aberdeen's comments in this period to outsiders like Princess Lieven, to the effect that he was not seeking office, should probably be read in the context that he did not wish his party to take office, rather than that he was tired of public life.[30]

The general election of 1837 was occasioned by the death of William IV. In the short run this strengthened the tottering Melbourne government, despite their electoral failures in some constituencies. William IV had been on bad terms with his ministers. The eighteen–year–old Queen Victoria was responsive to Melbourne's cynical and worldly charm. Aberdeen immediately perceived the political, and even constitutional dangers[31] inherent in the situation and the Bedchamber crisis of 1839 quickly proved that his fears were not groundless. On 7 May, Melbourne tendered his resignation to the Queen after a series of back-bench revolts. Victoria sent for Peel with the utmost reluctance and continued to take advice from Melbourne throughout the crisis. Peel felt compelled to ask for a mark of confidence in the form of some changes in the Queen's Household. The Queen was virtually surrounded by Whig ladies, some closely related to the outgoing ministers. Victoria, who went far beyond Melbourne's advice, refused to change any of her ladies to whom she felt an intense personal loyalty. The problem was complicated by the fact that there were no recent precedents for a change of ministry under a queen regnant. The King's household was always changed, but a queen consort's domestic arrangements had usually been considered unimportant. Peel refused to take office without the required mark of confidence and Melbourne returned. Many years later Victoria admitted that her inexperience had led her into a mistake but at the time she was triumphant. She had kept out Peel and retained her beloved Melbourne.

The Conservatives were not sorry to allow the situation to develop a little further before taking office but, in 1841, the issue could no longer be avoided. Finance had always been the weak point of the Melbourne administration and their problems began with the Budget and continued through the clash on the sugar duties. The ministry was defeated by one vote on a vote of confidence early on the morning of 5 June. Even then Melbourne decided to go to the country rather than resign immediately. The election left no further room for doubt. The Conservatives won a comfortable majority. In the first important division in the new House they defeated the government by 360 votes to 269.

Melbourne had no alternative but to resign and Peel began to form his second government on 30 August 1841. Wellington had suffered a stroke in 1840 and, although he had made a good recovery, it was agreed that he could no longer sustain departmental office. He came in as minister without portfolio and Aberdeen went to the Foreign Office.

Victoria awaited her new ministry with trepidation. Melbourne in his own way did his best to reassure her about his old friend, Aberdeen. He told her in September:

Lord Melbourne was always sure that when Your Majesty came to converse with Lord Aberdeen you would like and appreciate him. His principal fault is his temper, which is naturally very violent, but which he watches with great care & is generally successful in controlling.[32]

A few months later he wrote:

Palmerston dislikes Aberdeen & has a low opinion of him. He thinks him weak & timid & likely to let down the character & influence of the Country. Your Majesty knows that Lord Melbourne does not partake these opinions, certainly not at least to anything like the extent to which Palmerston carries them.[33]

Victoria was about the age that Aberdeen's youngest daughter, Frances, would have been if she had lived. Aberdeen had not forgotten his old skills as a courtier, which he had first displayed with the Emperor Francis and the Tsar Alexander in 1813. His attitude to his sovereign was always one of the deepest respect, but there was also a trace of the paternal in it. This showed most clearly in his concern for the Queen's comfort and well-being when he accompanied her on visits to France and Germany, but it also went deeper. It mingled with Wellington's sense that 'the King's government must be carried on'. Aberdeen's relationship with the Queen, although quite different from Melbourne's, became very close, and when he resigned as Prime Minister in 1855 she was as distressed as she had been at Melbourne's resignation.

NOTES

1. Stanmore, p. 116
2. PP, XXXI (1837) 43.
3. PP, XXXV (1837) 49–51.
4. PP, XXXVIII (1837) 31–2.
5. PP, III (1831) 115–99.
6. PP, III (1831) 131–4, 444–5, 479–94.
7. PP, IV (1835) 557–88.
8. *Hansard*, 3rd ser., XXXIV, 501–2 (14 June 1836).
9. Many of the petitions are in HH 8/2 and further correspondence on amendments Aberdeen was to propose is in NLS, MS 3868 and MS 2904.
10. *Hansard*, 3rd ser., XXXIV, 989–93 (28 June 1836).
11. *Hansard*, 3rd ser., XXXV, 757 (2 Aug. 1836).

12. For example, NLS, MS 3443, Aberdeen to Very Rev. Principal Lee, 2, 17 Apr. 1841; MS 11802 Aberdeen to Lord Minto, 2 Apr. 1841.

13. Russell Papers, PRO 30/22/11B, Aberdeen to Russell, 31 Dec. 1853.

14. NLS, MS 3581, Gladstone to Aberdeen, 16 May 1854, Aberdeen to Gladstone, 17 May 1854, 'Suggested to Dr Chalmers', n.d.

15. Stanmore, p. 129. This was presumably why Peel drew attention to Aberdeen as an example of a Presbyterian in the Cabinet at the time of the controversy over the Test Act although in fact Aberdeen would have found no difficulty in fulfilling the Act's requirements, *Hansard*, 2nd ser., XVIII, 755 (16 Feb. 1828).

16. Stanmore deals with the Disruption at length, pp. 121–51. Aberdeen's correspondence was voluminous. It is printed in full (591 pages of it) in one volume of the *Correspondence*, BP 12 (4).

17. *Acts of the General Assembly of the Church of Scotland 1638–1842*, p. 1044, 'Act commonly called the Veto Act', Sess. 9, May 29, 1835, Ch. IX.

18. Aberdeen to Chalmers, 31 Dec. 1839, *Correspondence between Dr. Chalmers and the Earl of Aberdeen*, pp. 16–20.

19. Stanmore, pp. 124–8; Aberdeen to John Hope, 5, 9, 12 Sept. 1839, *Correspondence*, BP 12 (4), pp. 17–20.

20. Aberdeen to Chalmers, 31 Dec. 1839, Chalmers to Aberdeen, 16 Jan. 1840, Chalmers, *Correspondence*, pp. 16–20, 24–9.

21. Stanmore, pp. 131–40; Chalmers, *The Correspondence between Dr Chalmers and the Earl of Aberdeen in the years 1839 and 1840*, esp. pp. 8–9.

22. Stanmore, pp. 141–2.

23. Stanmore, pp. 147–51.

24. V. Surtees, *Charlotte Canning*, p. 136 (14 Sept. 1844).

25. Gurney Papers, RQC 334/70, Aberdeen to Gurney, 14 Dec. 1833,/85, 27 Nov. 1835,/96, 7 Mar. 1839.

26. Lady Cowper to Princess Lieven, 21 Feb. 1839, *Lieven–Palmerston Correspondence*, pp. 163–4.

27. Gurney Papers, RQC 334/97, Aberdeen to Gurney, 5 Jan. 1840.

28. HH 1/35, Aberdeen to Haddo, 30 Apr. 1837; HH 1/28, Aberdeen to Haddo, 30 May 1839.

29. Gash, *Sir Robert Peel*, pp. 151, 159, 162, 201–3, 213, 222, 255.

30. For example, Aberdeen to Lieven, 27 Dec. 1837, 21 Jan., 7 Feb., 16 Sept. 1838, Jones-Parry, vol. 1, pp. 89, 95, 99, 112.

31. HH 1/22, Aberdeen to Haddo, 1 July 1837; Add. MSS 40312, Aberdeen to Peel, 11 Aug. 1838; Aberdeen to Lieven, 16 Sept. 1838, Jones–Parry, vol. 1, p. 113.

32. RA A4/11, Melbourne to Victoria, 20 Sept. 1841.

33. RA A4/47, Melbourne to Victoria, 17 Jan. 1842.

CHAPTER EIGHTEEN

Foreign Secretary again

Palmerston had left his successor at the Foreign Office a highly unpleasant legacy. Even before the Eastern crisis had matured in the summer of 1840, Aberdeen had written to Princess Lieven, 'In foreign affairs, we have enough on our hands; a war in China; a quasi war in Persia; a state of affairs in the Levant which does not promise a continuance of peace; an absurd squabble at Naples . . . In addition to all this, our relations with the United States are worse than ever.'[1] During the next five years, Aberdeen had to deal with crises in every part of the world.

In some ways his position was happier than it had been in 1828–30. The Cabinet no longer tried to write his despatches for him. He was no longer the junior partner to the masterful Duke of Wellington. It is true that Wellington, who had become a minister without portfolio in Peel's Cabinet, recovered his health more quickly and completely than was anticipated in 1840 and was soon looking over Aberdeen's shoulder and trying to correct and stiffen his policy on a number of issues. In particular the Duke had not changed his attitude to the French government as much as Aberdeen had done since 1830. He believed that Britain must rely upon her own strength to check France and distrusted Aberdeen's policy of growing co-operation. In the early days of the ministry this did not matter so much because Peel sided with Aberdeen against the Duke but eventually Peel too grew distrustful of France and Aberdeen's position deteriorated to the point where he wished to resign. Peel, however, was determined not to lose his experienced Foreign Secretary and personal friend and, generally speaking, he accorded Aberdeen as much confidence in his expertise in foreign affairs, as Aberdeen accorded Peel in domestic questions. The rest of the Cabinet, Sir James Graham at the Home Office, Lord Haddington at the Admiralty, the Earl of Ripon at the Board of Trade and Lord Stanley at the Colonial Office among them, were usually quite content to trust Aberdeen's judgement. His old tormentor, Lord Ellenborough, although originally appointed President of the Board of Control, was removed from the scene almost immediately in October 1841 when he became Viceroy of India.

Aberdeen might have expected to encounter problems with the Court, even greater than he had occasionally experienced with George IV when he was last at the Foreign Office. Victoria was still sore at the loss of Melbourne and resentful of the Conservatives for displacing him. The role of the Crown in the making of foreign policy was still not completely defined. Victoria undoubtedly held that the Crown was entitled to a voice in it and her hand was strengthened by her personal connections with other European royal families, which were reinforced by her marriage to Albert of Saxe-Coburg-Gotha in February 1840. But her marriage altered Victoria's views in many ways. Albert did not share her predilection for Melbourne. An earnest, hard-working, idealistic young man, although warmer-hearted and less humourless than contemporaries supposed him to be, he recognised a kindred spirit in Peel. Relations between the Court and the ministry improved slowly but steadily.

It is, however, symptomatic of the strain between monarch and ministry over the conduct of foreign affairs inherent in the situation in the middle of the nineteenth century that Aberdeen and Victoria quarrelled about the royal rights exactly as Palmerston and Victoria did, albeit more mildly. In January 1844, Victoria complained that despatches were often sent off before she had approved them. Aberdeen apologised and pleaded 'the press of business in the office'.[2] In October 1845 the Queen protested again in stronger terms. She wrote:

The Queen has observed that, for some time past, the *drafts* are sent to her from the Foreign Office when they are already gone, so that, if the Queen wished to make any observation or ask any explanations respecting them, it would be too late . . . They *used*, in affairs of importance, to be submitted for the Queen's approval; and signed by her, and the Queen wishes this not to fall into disuse, as she considers it of the greatest consequence to the Sovereign, and even her duty.

This time Aberdeen returned quite a sharp reply. The Queen, he said, had been 'misinformed'. He could testify from personal experience of the reigns of George IV and William IV that there had been no recent change in practice. He explained:

This practice has usually been to submit to Your Majesty the drafts of despatches at the same time that they are sent from this office. Should Your Majesty then be pleased to make any remark or objection, it would be immediately attended to by Lord Aberdeen, who would forthwith either make any necessary alterations, by additional instructions or he would humbly represent to Your Majesty the reasons which induce him to think that the interest of Your Majesty's service required an adherence to what had already been done.[3]

Victoria trusted Aberdeen sufficiently to accept his explanation. She was less willing to accept similar explanations from Palmerston. In practice, Aberdeen very seldom altered a despatch at the Queen's request.

Similarly, although he was punctilious in consulting her about diplomatic appointments, he rarely acted on her suggestions. She wished him, for example, to remove Sir Edward Disbrowe from The Hague because she thought him hostile to her uncle, Leopold of the Belgians. Aberdeen promised to do so as soon as a suitable vacancy arose but never found it convenient to do so.[4] In the autumn of 1843 Victoria was annoyed to see a press report that Lord William

Hervey was to become Secretary of Embassy in Paris. Victoria complained that she had not been consulted and would prefer Henry Wellesley. Aberdeen apologised profusely, blamed 'multiplicity of business' and assured her the newspaper had no authority for the statement.[5] Nevertheless, Hervey was appointed.

If Aberdeen managed the Court with ease, he had many other problems to face. It was still customary on a change of ministry to replace all senior diplomats abroad with supporters of the new government. Aberdeen did not have an impressive field from which to choose and he had to appoint several men with whom he already had every reason to be dissatisfied. Lord Granville came home from Paris to be replaced by Wellington's brother, Lord Cowley. Cowley was an experienced diplomat but, by now, deaf as a post. He embarrassed his government by mishearing several important conversations. The French found him 'bien sourd, bien lent, bien apoplectique'.[6] Aberdeen's brother, Robert, replaced Frederick Lamb, now Lord Beauvale, in Vienna and proved a moderately competent ambassador.[7] Despite his antics in Paris in 1830 Lord Stuart de Rothesay was sent to St Petersburg to replace Lord Clanricarde. He was now in failing health. As early as April 1842 Nesselrode called him 'un cadavre ambulant' and expected his death at any moment. In June 1843 he had a stroke which left him unable to conduct any business. He tried to conceal his condition and his resignation had to be forced early in 1844.[8] Lord Burghersh, the old school-friend of whom Aberdeen had had such a low opinion in 1813, went to Berlin in place of Lord William Russell. Russell was extremely angry at his recall – Aberdeen understood that it was because he did not want to leave his mistress – and he had to be soothed by his brother, Lord John Russell.[9] Finally, Sir Stratford Canning returned to Constantinople, replacing Lord Ponsonby, despite his quarrels with Aberdeen when he had been at that post before.

Guizot thought Aberdeen had made too few changes and complained, 'Lord Aberdeen est vraiment trop fidèle à l'heritage de Lord Palmerston.' Palmerston thought the opposite. He wrote to Russell in November 1842:

We had at all [the principal courts of Europe] men of talent, energy and enlightened views. The present government has substituted for those agents a set of dotards and fools. Those who have not lost their understanding by age and infirmity have escaped that loss by never having had any understanding to lose.

Allowing for some prejudice, it was not an unjust comment.[10]

Aberdeen was not very much better served at the Foreign Office itself. The organisation was antiquated and inefficient. The extraordinary system by which the countries of the world were divided between the Political Under-Secretary and the Permanent Under-Secretary, and each undertook alternate spells of duty, still prevailed. Aberdeen chose as his Political Under-Secretary, Viscount Canning, George Canning's son, on whose career he had kept a paternal eye since the death of the elder Canning. But the second Viscount had no diplomatic or administrative experience. Aberdeen was unlucky that the Permanent Under-Secretary, Backhouse, had to retire for health reasons soon after Aberdeen took office and his successor, H. U. Addington, although a diplomat of many years standing, had no experience in the Foreign Office itself. The work of the Office was rapidly increasing. In 1829 it had handled 10,760 out-going despatches; in 1849 it was to handle 30,735. With no mechanical aids, even senior officials were employed as mere copy clerks.[11] There were no specialised bureaux and scarcely anyone in the Office read German. Aberdeen once had to apologise for keeping a letter, communicated by the Prince Consort, for an abnormally long time because Mr Mellish, the only clerk who could translate German, was away.[12] This lack of organisation and shortage of staff threw a strain on men at all levels, most of all on the Foreign Secretary himself, who was still, in theory, expected to read every despatch which came in – an impossible task even in the 1840s. It helps to explain why Aberdeen sometimes went into negotiations ill-informed and badly prepared.

Being in the House of Lords Aberdeen was to some extent insulated from public criticism of his policy. It was Peel in the Commons who had to meet Palmerston's challenges and this contributed to Peel's more militant approach to policy. In the Lords Aberdeen had the support of many of the leading Whigs. Greville noted 'Throughout Aberdeen's foreign administration Clarendon has constantly acted in concert with him, and has made his position in the House of Lords a bed of roses. Never was there a Minister for Foreign Affairs who had such an easy time of it.'[13] Aberdeen even commanded the support of the unpredictable Brougham, and the Conservatives, who were woefully short of good speakers in the Lords, took care to humour Brougham in matters of patronage.[14] Aberdeen himself spoke frequently and competently enough, although he was still subject to the old charge of 'sneering'.[15] Aberdeen had frequently asked for papers when in opposition but in office he was sparing of producing them. He maintained, reasonably enough, that it was improper to give papers relating to negotiations in progress, even though the Americans sometimes departed from this convention. He did, however, sometimes volunteer papers to set the record straight, as he felt, in the face of misleading statements by foreign governments.[16]

If Aberdeen was lucky in the disposition of the House of Lords, he was even luckier in his relations with the press. His rival, Palmerston, certainly had a formidable weapon in the *Morning Chronicle,* which always supported him, but the solidly conservative papers, the *Morning Post,* the *Morning Herald* and the *Standard* had circulations which, taken together, exceeded that of the *Chronicle.*[17] Aberdeen's great stroke of luck came when the young editor of *The Times,* John Delane, while 'keeping no terms' with the Conservative administration as a whole, and even attacking Peel and Graham severely, offered his support to Aberdeen on foreign questions. Aberdeen responded by supplying Delane with information and, according to the practice of the times, supported Delane's brother's application for promotion in the Customs Service.[18]

Aberdeen played some small part in organising press campaigns in support of government policy, although the initiative was usually taken by others. Edward Everett, the former American Ambassador in London, obtained the insertion of articles in the *Examiner,* the *Edinburgh Review* and the *Quarterly* (the first two by Nassau Senior, the last by Croker) in favour of a compromise on the Oregon dispute. Aberdeen read the proofs of Senior's first article and supplied information to Croker.[19] He had less success in his attempts to get material inserted in the French press and in 1842 descended to the machiavellian tactic of trying to get a fake 'Memorial', supposedly from some British merchants in favour of a Franco-Belgian Customs Unions, published in the French press to arouse the suspicions of French merchants about the whole project.[20]

When the Conservatives took office in 1841, France was still estranged as a result of the Eastern crisis of 1840. Although the worst phase of that crisis had already passed tempers were still strained. The British suspected that the French were intriguing to increase their influence everywhere; round the shores of the Mediterranean, in the Levant, Greece, Spain and North Africa; and on the Rhine, in Belgium, and perhaps in Germany; as well as seeking naval and commercial stations in West Africa and the Pacific to the detriment of British interests. At the same time a series of incidents, some of them trivial in themselves, had brought Britain and the United States to the verge of war. The enmity of either France or the United States was an embarrassment to Britain. The simultaneous enmity of both was potentially dangerous. Three times during the Conservative administration Britain came close to war with the United States, in the autumn of 1841, the spring of 1845 and the spring of 1846. The temptation to Anglophobes in France to take advantage of Britain's difficulties was great. The Duke of Wellington prophesied that war with the United States 'will not be with that Power alone'[21] and British statesmen remembered 1778. Louis Philippe had no desire to embark on such a dangerous gamble but some French politicians were not so cautious and Lord Cowley sent home secret reports of French plans to capture British colonies in the event of an Anglo-American war.[22]

Three possible courses of action lay open to Aberdeen in September 1841. He could defy both France and the United States, confident that they had more to fear from a war than Britain did; he could seek alternative allies among the northern Powers; or he could try to restore amicable relations with France and the United States, or at least one of them, thus separating his two potential enemies.

The first was the course which Palmerston had pursued. He had remained calm throughout the Eastern crisis of 1840, rightly convinced that France would yield rather than go to war. He had been equally unbending in the face of American anger. The heir of Palmerston's policy in the Conservative Cabinet was the Duke of Wellington. He wrote to Peel at the time of the crises over Morocco and Tahiti in 1844:

The French Government in its present State, and with its Powerful Naval Force is not capable of maintaining its Relations of Amity and Peace! That Govt. can be kept in order only, by our certain and decided Naval superiority not only to their own; but to that supported by that of the United States.[23]

He repeated these views to Peel almost daily during the next eighteen months and in January 1845, after a brush with Aberdeen on the subject, wrote angrily:

It may be a very foolish opinion, but I think it better to rely upon our own means for our defence than upon the good faith and forbearance of France; and that if strong we are more likely to reap the benefit of such course to be adopted by our neighbours.[24]

A British diplomat in Paris, Henry Bulwer, wrote privately to Aberdeen that the best thing might be 'to frighten the King and his Government soundly – and to make them try to dam up the present current [of hostility of Britain] or to turn it, for which they have far more power than they wish to have us believe.'[25]

A policy of frightening the King and his government, or an American President and his government, had few attractions for Aberdeen and it is arguable that Britain was in sober fact ill–prepared for a major war in 1841 and that to avoid provocative conduct was realistic. Very little of the Royal Navy was ready for immediate service and, during the Eastern crisis the previous year, Britain had even had to denude her home ports of their guardships to send an effective force to the Mediterranean.[26] Britain was already at war in China and Afghanistan and her small professional army was fully extended.[27] Victory took longer to achieve than had been expected in China and the early campaigns in Afghanistan were disastrous. Ireland was in a constant state of unrest and the English manufacturing districts were disturbed. Foreign governments were well aware of these embarrassments. Both the French and the Austrian governments received detailed secret reports of the situation in Ireland and in Lancashire.[28] Bulwer told Aberdeen in April 1842:

We are supposed at this time to be in a scrape, and our crimes and misdemeanours are rated and felt almost exactly according to our difficulties. Had the last *accts*. from India brought us news of the taking of Caboul, or the surrender of Pekin your clear, calm and admirable statement to the Americans [on the right of search] would have been done justice to. As it is nobody will quote it, but to pervert it.[29]

Britain's friends abroad were greatly relieved to hear of the end of the Chinese war and Metternich wrote privately to Aberdeen to congratulate him.[30]

The second alternative, to seek allies against France and the United States among the northern Powers, was one which was more congenial to Aberdeen. It was in line with his earlier diplomatic experience of 1813–14 and 1828–30 and he pursued it to some extent. He always regarded Austria as Britain's most reliable ally but he had a low opinion of her material power. He once wrote to his brother in Vienna:

I look on Austria very much in the same light as Turkey, and as almost null in the scale of nations. They are pretty much in the state of helplessness and decrepitude, and almost equally incapable of any vigorous and enlightened policy.

Robert thought his brother's views exaggerated and told him that the country was well governed with a good army and sound finances and the fate of the empire was not, as Aberdeen seemed to think, 'appended' to the career of Metternich.[31] Aberdeen was disturbed by signs of a growing rapprochement between France and Austria. He told Robert in November 1842, 'I have seen a French tendency on the part of Metternich for some time past; and I see too, that we cannot rely upon him whenever anything like vigour and decision may be required.' Robert replied that Metternich was proud of his influence over Louis Philippe. 'It is grateful to him to be courted and consulted by the French Government, to be appealed to as an Arbiter and to be constantly told that through his influence and intervention France refrains from disturbing the peace of Europe.' But Metternich's real bias was towards England. 'I can positively affirm', concluded Gordon, 'that he looks with distrust to France and with confidence to England – in a word he is Austrian and that is to say anti-French.'[32]

Aberdeen himself was reassured when he accompanied the Queen to Germany in the summer of 1845 and met Metternich for the first time for twenty years, although he was still cautious about the amount of support which Britain might expect. He wrote to Peel, '. . . we may always be quite sure of Austria. They will throw their weight in our scale in any case of real emergency. We cannot expect much active co-operation nor will they ever take a lead but they are safe, and may be turned to good account.'[33]

On his side, Metternich was jealous of the growing understanding between Britain and France. He complained to Gordon after Victoria's visit to Louis Philippe at the Chateau d'Eu in the autumn of 1843 and Sir Robert reported:

Metternich does not attempt to disguise from me the regret and alarm with which he views the intimacy of relations that he believes to have been created at Eu betwixt France and England, and he says, but one feeling pervades the French and Italian courts on this subject. Ever mistrustful of the French, He dreads anything like identity of actions or of purpose betwixt the two powers which he says must disturb the peace of Europe and he listens but incredulously to my counter-declarations that the establishment of the most friendly relations is at least as justifiable for England as he has found it to be for Austria . . .[34]

A little later Robert told Aberdeen that Metternich was 'out of humour'. '. . . it is not', he said, 'that he has a fault to find with any of your acts, but his vanity is hurt by the apparent neglect with which He (your oldest friend) and his counsels have been treated.' In reply Aberdeen defended his policy of agreement with France although admitting that it was 'a difficult and dangerous policy' and he commented with pleasure on the visit of the Tsar to England in June 1844. 'I was delighted with this visit,' he said, 'Because although I highly value the *entente cordiale*, I am also desirous that it should be seen and known that we have more than one friend in the world.'[35]

Despite this declaration Aberdeen was cautious in his relations with Russia. In September 1841 the Russians were very anxious for a good understanding with Britain. Having successfully detached Britain from France over the Eastern Question in 1840, they hoped to keep the two western Powers apart. The Tsar Nicholas hated the parvenu French monarchy, which he regarded as the instrument of Jacobinism and, in September 1841, was even said to be looking forward to a new march on Paris.[36] He told Stuart de Rothesay that he was pleased by the change of government in Britain and would increase his efforts to maintain friendly relations. The Secretary of Embassy, Lord Bloomfield, had already reported that the Tsar's 'favourite idea' was a union between Britain and the northern Powers.[37] The Tsar had the whole-hearted support of his chief adviser on foreign affairs, Count Nesselrode, who was almost as old a friend of Aberdeen as was Metternich. Nesselrode, who led the so-called 'foreign party', in contradistinction to the Russian nationalist party, wanted closer relations with other European countries. Nesselrode himself was a cosmopolitan character. The son of a Catholic German father and a Protestant German mother, born in Lisbon in 1780, he had been baptised as an Anglican and – to the understandable astonishment of his Russian colleagues – practised that faith for the rest of his life. He proclaimed himself an Anglophile and his objective in sending his own protegé, Baron Brunnow, as his envoy in London in 1839 had been to seek a closer understanding. Brunnow, who had had his difficulties with Palmerston, was delighted when Aberdeen succeeded him, telling Nesselrode, 'What he says is solid, true, and carries the seal of integrity.'[38]

But Aberdeen remained politely non-committal in the face of the Russian overtures, even when the Russians expressed sympathy with British difficulties in China and Afghanistan. The Russians even assured the British government that they had restrained the Persians from taking advantage of the British defeats at Kabul and Kandahar, although Brunnow subsequently admitted that the disastrous Russian expedition to Khiva had been intended as a counterblow to the British campaign in Afghanistan.[39] Nevertheless, the Russians felt entitled to reproach the British for not showing the same understanding of Russian difficulties in Poland as the Russians were showing for the British position in Afghanistan and complained that the French were using Poland to upset 'l'heureuse union' between Britain and Russia.[40] In the Near East, Russia tried to persuade Aberdeen that Britain and Russia must continue to act together to prevent Mehemet Ali from trying to regain his position with French help. Here too Aberdeen was slow to respond to Russian overtures. The British and Russian envoys at Constantinople did act as joint mediators in the complicated and dangerous border dispute between Turkey and Persia but the initiative came from Stratford Canning rather than from London.[41]

The truth was that Aberdeen felt that Britain had as much to fear from Russia as from France in the Near East. Relations were strained in 1842–43 by a crisis in Serbia. In September 1842 the Serbs rose against their ruler Prince Michael Obrenovitch and substituted Prince Alexander Karageorgevitch. First reports suggested that this was a purely internal struggle and the Turks were prepared to confirm the Serbs' choice. The Russians, however, appealing to treaty rights which Aberdeen confessed he did not understand, demanded that the Turks should annul the election of Alexander.[42] Stratford Canning, who complained that he was left without instructions, encouraged the Porte to resist the Russian demands. The Austrians at first sympathised with the Turks but then switched their support to Russia. Aberdeen advised Canning that the Austrians were the European power most closely involved and, in view of their acquiescence, 'it would be madness for England and France to recommend resistance'.[43] The Russians forced a new election but, to their chagrin, Prince Alexander was re-elected. The incident was a minor one but interesting as foreshadowing some of the problems of the Crimean War. Aberdeen himself said that he was indifferent to what solution was found in Serbia and only anxious that a 'Serbian Question' should not be added to all their other 'Questions.'[44] But the incident did not improve Anglo-Russian relations.

A few months previously the Russians had tried to secure British co-operation in a more general European matter. In July 1842, the duc d'Orleans, the heir to the French throne, met his death in a carriage accident. His son, the comte de Paris, was a child of four. Since Louis Philippe was already approaching seventy it was clear that France might have to endure a long regency. The Russians expressed the fear that the revolutionaries would seize the change to overthrow the dynasty and, so that they should not be caught unawares as in 1830, the 'Cours Conservatives', Russia, Britain, Austria and Prussia, should come to a previous agreement on their policy. Austria and Prussia expressed some approval of the Tsar's idea but Aberdeen carefully avoided any direct reply.[45]

Prussia did not play any great part in Aberdeen's calculations. Prussia's prestige had not yet recovered from her defeats in the Napoleonic wars and her subsequent tutelage by Austria. The British government regarded Prussia as important in an economic context, as the leader of the German Zollverein whose fortunes they watched with interest, but they did not think of her as a political power of the first magnitude, or as a possible counter–weight to France or Russia.[46]

Aberdeen then had good reasons for not putting too much trust in a continuation of the embryonic policy of 1840, that is a coalition of the rest of Europe to check France. Austria was well-disposed but weak and not always completely reliable. Prussia was scarcely a Great Power. Russia was potentially as much a threat as France, and Aberdeen wanted to keep his hands free, especially in the Near East, to meet situations as they arose.

Essentially he favoured the old flexible balance of power system, which he had learnt from Castlereagh and which he had sometimes himself defended in the House of Lords. He deplored the fact that the three northern courts had broken off diplomatic relations with Spain and so left a naked power struggle between the British and French representatives who remained in Madrid. He similarly regretted that the Tsar had no diplomatic representative in Belgium and, during the crisis over the projected Franco-Belgian customs union, tried to get common action by Austria, Prussia and Russia. In Greece, Aberdeen concerted his policy with Austria as well as with Britain's fellow guarantors, France and Russia. In welcoming the possibility of pressing reforms on the Turks he reminded Stratford Canning that this policy could only be carried into 'salutary effect' by the concert of all the European Powers at Constantinople.[47] Aberdeen did not favour formal congresses, even at ambassadorial level, but he did favour the operation of an informal concert of the Great Powers on all dangerous and difficult issues.

This open system was incompatible with any kind of automatic coalition against France of the type which the Tsar seems occasionally to have favoured. Even if Austria and Prussia had been agreeable, which is doubtful, it would have made Britain too dependent on Russia and, in any case, it would have been of little help to Britain in resolving her overseas quarrels with France and America, which loomed so unusually large in this period. The Conservatives did not take Russia so seriously as a naval power, as their Whig predecessors[48] had done but, whether they were right or wrong in these calculations, Aberdeen was no doubt right in assuming that the continental powers would not take on any overseas commitments. Here Britain would have to fight her battles alone.

Aberdeen was therefore left with his third possible course of action – to try to restore amicable relations with both France and the United States or, failing that, with one of them. It was to this policy that Aberdeen committed himself. Relations with both Powers were so bad that it was clear that a high price might have to be paid. Aberdeen was helped by the fact that neither he nor most of his Cabinet colleagues cared very much about the details of many of the current disputes. Large concessions might therefore properly be made in pursuit of the ultimate goal of conciliation. Concessions were, however, likely to offend particular interests and provide opportunities for strenuous parliamentary attacks. The contrast was all the greater with Palmerston who managed at least to give the impression that he never made concessions. In these years Aberdeen was vulnerable on two counts. He does not seem to have studied questions with the same care that he showed in 1813–14 and 1828–30 and, as a result, he sometimes did not realise exactly what the issues at stake were. This may have been due to his state of health. He had taken office readily enough in 1841, but during the next few years the severe headaches, from which he had suffered most of his life, steadily worsened. In 1842 he offered Peel his resignation on grounds of ill health. As early as May 1842 he had written to his brother, Robert:

I am at last nearly knocked up, and doubt very much if I shall be able to go on. For the last six weeks or two months I have been tormented with a continual noise and confusion in the Head which has now become much worse, and is more like carrying about with me Niagara than anything else.[49]

Aberdeen had no illusions about what his health was doing to his capacity for business. He told Peel, 'Pain may be endured and even the knowledge of labouring under a mortal disease might be tolerated; but sensations which chiefly affect the power of application are more difficult to contend with . . .' But when Peel pronounced his resignation 'impossible', he acquiesced and soldiered on to the end of the ministry.[50]

Aberdeen had, however, another weakness, which Metternich had perceived in 1813 but which only really showed up in the 1840s. He found it very difficult to bluff, a technique at which Palmerston excelled. Palmerston himself, irritated by Aberdeen's policy, asserted that every state would give up three questions out of four rather than go to war for them, but it would be fatal to allow other Powers to know this in advance. Both France and the United States became aware that Aberdeen wanted a settlement and was usually indifferent to the details. Both took advantage of the fact.

When men looked back on Aberdeen's tenure of the Foreign Office a decade or so later, after the Crimean War, they found it easy enough to believe the charge that Palmerston had laid against him: that he was a weak man who consistently let his country down by being just 'under the mark'. But it must be said that this was not how it appeared at the time. It seemed then that Palmerston had left his country in a perilous state, with wars and rumours of wars in all parts of the world. When Aberdeen left office in 1846 the world was peaceful and Britain was on friendly terms with every other major Power. The policy of conciliation seemed to have worked. Very few felt that the price which had been paid had been too high.

NOTES

1. Aberdeen to Lieven, 24 Apr. 1840, Jones-Parry, vol. 1, p. 138. Britain had just ordered a blockade of Naples because the King had granted a monopoly on the Neapolitan sulphur mines to a mainly French group, which was supposed to violate the Anglo-Neapolitan commercial treaty of 1816.

2. Add. MSS 43043, Victoria to Aberdeen, 13 Jan. 1844; RA B8/13, Aberdeen to Victoria, 15 Jan. 1844.

3. Add. MSS 43043, Victoria to Aberdeen, 28 Oct. 1845; RA B9/150, Aberdeen to Victoria, 31 Oct. 1845.

4. Add. MSS 43042, Victoria to Aberdeen, 27 July, 13 Nov. 1842, Albert to Aberdeen, 11 Nov. 1842, Aberdeen to Victoria, 26 July, 14 Nov. 1842.

5. Add. MSS 43063, Peel to Aberdeen, 31 Oct., 2 Nov. 1843; Add. MSS 40454, Aberdeen to Peel, 1 Nov. 1843; Add. MSS 43043, Aberdeen to Victoria, 1 Nov. 1843, Victoria to Aberdeen, 2 Nov. 1843.

6. Guizot Papers, 42 AP 8, Guizot to Ste Aulaire, 23 Dec. 1841.

7. Although Aberdeen complained of his brother's extravagance and tried to persuade him to sell Balmoral, Add. MSS 43211, Aberdeen to Robert, 1 Sept. 1841, Robert to Aberdeen, 5 Sept. 1841.

8. Add. MSS 43142, Hamilton to Aberdeen, 6 Apr. 1842; Add. MSS 43144 Bloomfield to Aberdeen, 26 Sept., 26 Dec. 1843; Add. MSS 43044, Aberdeen to Victoria, 21 Feb. 1844.

9. Add. MSS 43066, Aberdeen to Russell, 8 Nov. 1841, Russell to Aberdeen, 10 Nov. 1841.

10. Guizot quoted Jones-Parry, *History*, XXIII (1938), p. 29; Bulwer, vol. 3, p. 114. Melbourne voiced more temperate criticisms, *Letters of Queen Victoria*, vol. 1, pp. 325–6, 333.

11. PP, XV (1850) 1, 'Report of Select Committee on Official Salaries'; PP, VI (1861) 1, 'Report of Select Committee on the Diplomatic Service'.

12. Add. MSS 43043, Aberdeen to Albert, 29 Mar. 1843.

13. Greville, *Memoirs* (ed. Wilson), vol. 2, p. 403.

14. Add. MSS 43063, Peel to Aberdeen, 14 Oct. 1843; correspondence with Brougham, mainly about patronage in this period, in Add. MSS 43193.

15. Greville, *Memoirs*, p. 412.

16. He only produced the Ashburton–Webster correspondence under pressure, *Hansard*, 3rd ser., LXVI, 203, LXVII, 1162, 1219, 1250, but he volunteered papers

to defend the British interpretation of Article VIII of the Ashburton–Webster Treaty to prove that Britain had not held back on the Oregon negotiations, PP, LXI (1843) 9; PP, LII (1846) 109; *Hansard*, 3rd ser., LXXXIV, 1112 (17 Mar. 1846).

17. In October 1841 the *Chronicle* sold 144,000 copies, the *Herald* 120,000, the *Post* 95,060, and the *Standard* 85,000. *The Times* outstripped them all, selling 425,000 copies in October 1841 and 625,000 in June 1842, PP, XXVI (1842) 561, 587, 'Stamp Duty Returns'.

18. *History of The Times*, vol. 2, Ch. 5 and appendix 2; Add. MSS 43062, Peel to Aberdeen, 28 Dec. 1842; Add. MSS 40453, Delane to Aberdeen, 22 July 1843.

19. *Examiner*, 26 Apr. 1845; *Edinburgh Review*, July 1845; *Quarterly Review*, March 1846. Add. MSS 43190, Croker to Aberdeen, 17, 19 Feb., 6, 21 Mar. 1846, Aberdeen to Croker, n.d. Mar. 1846. The matter is treated at length in F. Merk, 'British government propaganda and the Oregon Treaty', *American Historical Review*, XL (1934) pp. 38–62.

20. Add. MSS 43131, Aberdeen to Bulwer, 9 Dec. 1842 and encls., Bulwer to Aberdeen, 12 Dec. 1843.

21. Add. MSS 40461, Wellington to Peel, 8 Apr. 1845.

22. Add. MSS 43129, 'Rapport particulier' encl. in Cowley to Aberdeen, 31 Jan. 1842.

23. Add. MSS 40460, Wellington to Peel, 17 Aug. 1844.

24. Add. MSS 40461, Wellington to Peel, 7 Jan. 1845.

25. Add. MSS 43131, Bulwer to Aberdeen, 1 July 1842.

26. PP, XXVII (1842) 345, 'Returns relating to the Royal Navy'; Add. MSS 40461, Peel to Wellington, 9 Aug. 1845.

27. In 1841 Britain had 36,000 troops at home (12,000 in Ireland) and just over 64,000 abroad, PP, XXVII (1842) 36.

28. The comte de Jarnac sent Guizot detailed reports on Ireland and Lancashire, AAE., Angleterre, 658–666 *passim*. Cf. M. Hummelauer's secret report to the Austrian government on the situation in Ireland encl. in Aberdeen to Peel, 27 Apr. 1844, Add. MSS 40454.

29. Add. MSS 43131, Bulwer to Aberdeen, 8 Apr. 1842.

30. Add. MSS 43128, Metternich to Aberdeen, 24 Nov. 1842.

31. Add. MSS 43211, Aberdeen to Robert, 20 June 1844, Robert to Aberdeen, 18 Oct. 1844.

32. Add. MSS 43211, Aberdeen to Robert, 24 Nov. 1842, Robert to Aberdeen, 13 Dec. 1842.

33. Add. MSS 40455, Aberdeen to Peel, 20 Aug. 1845.

34. Add. MSS 43211, Robert to Aberdeen, 13 Sept., 13 Dec. 1843.

35. Add. MSS 43211, Robert to Aberdeen, 16 May 1844, Aberdeen to Robert, 20 June 1844.

36. FO 65/272, Bloomfield to Aberdeen, No. 61 Conf., 25 Sept. 1841.

37. FO 65/272–3, Bloomfield to Aberdeen, No. 72, 9 Oct. 1841, Stuart to Aberdeen, No. 11, 22 Nov. 1841.

38. Ingle, pp. 5–7, 121–7, 159.

39. FO 65/287, Nesselrode to Brunnow, 26 Feb./10 Mar. 1842 (comm. 14 Apr.); Add. MSS 40455, Aberdeen to Peel, 4 Oct. 1845.

40. Add. MSS 43144, Nesselrode to Brunnow, 18 July 1842.

41. FO 65/273, Stuart to Aberdeen, No. 12, 22 Nov. 1841; FO 65/287, Nesselrode to Brunnow, 15 Aug. 1842 (comm. 20 Sept.); FO 78/439, Aberdeen to Stratford

Canning, No. 7, 12 12 Nov. 1841; FO 78/476, Stratford Canning to Aberdeen, No. 58, 23 Mar., No. 121, 29 May, No. 236, 26 Nov. 1842.

42. FO 7/305, Crampton (Chargé in Vienna) to Aberdeen, No. 2, 10 Sept. 1842; FO 78/513, Aberdeen to Canning, No. 40, 20 Mar. 1843, No. 51, 6 Apr. 1843.

43. Aberdeen and Canning had a quarrel reminiscent of that of 1829; FO 78/480, Canning to Aberdeen, No. 200, 29 Sept., No. 213, 17 Oct. 1842;/515, No. 77, 18 Apr. 1843; FO 78/513, Aberdeen to Canning, No. 68, 20 May 1843; Add. MSS 43138, Aberdeen to Canning, 6 Apr., 9 May, 20 May 1843, Canning to Aberdeen, 17 June 1843.

44. Add. MSS 43138, Aberdeen to Canning, 24 Oct. 1842.

45. FO 65/282, Bloomfield to Aberdeen, No. 59, 27 Aug., No. 76, 24 Sept. 1842.

46. Peel did speak in the Commons on 27 Aug. 1841 of Germany as 'that magnificent country, which . . . burns with a spirit which would intimidate and overbear any invader' (*Hansard*, 3rd ser., LIX, 404–5) but this is rhetoric which is not reflected in the letters of the times. However, Aberdeen, vising Germany in 1845, was glad to find the Germans friendly to Britain and suspicious of France. Add. MSS 40455, Aberdeen to Peel, 1 Sept. 1845.

47. FO 72/571, Aberdeen to Aston, No. 23, 18 Nov. 1841; FO 10/95, Seymour to Aberdeen, No. 166, 6 Dec. 1842; FO 78/439, Aberdeen to Canning, No. 2, 3 Oct. 1841.

48. For the Whigs' preoccupation with the Russian fleet see Webster, *Palmerston*, vol. 2, pp. 563–7; cf. Bartlett, *Great Britain and Sea Power, 1815–1853*.

49. Add. MSS 43211, Aberdeen to Robert, 24 May 1842.

50. Add. MSS 40452, Aberdeen to Peel, 29 Sept., 1 Oct. 1842; Add. MSS 43062, Peel to Aberdeen, 30 Sept. 1842 'Most Private'.

CHAPTER NINETEEN

The Ashburton–Webster negotiations

American problems were the most urgent. Relations between Britain and the United States had been ambivalent since the war of American Independence. Some, like Macaulay, could speak of the Americans as kinsmen and of war between the two countries as fratricidal, but others held that American ambitions made war inevitable sooner or later. Aberdeen was never accused of the hostility to all things American which was attributed to Palmerston but he shared the prejudices of his class. When his friend, Augustus Foster, went to Washington in 1805, he wrote to him in fashionably scornful terms. 'Your Republic', he assured him, 'is certainly in her childhood, but she has nothing of infancy but its forwardness, and instead of strength and vigour of youth, she has nothing but its violence and ignorance.'[1] In 1846 William Gore Ouseley, the British Minister in Buenos Aires, who had previously served in Washington, assured Aberdeen that he could not from his 'Class, Gentleman's feelings and habits of thought fathom the depth of vulgar & ignoble principles and practices of my friends the Americans.'[2] The popular prejudices engendered by the great literary battle, the 'war of the quarterlies' of the 1820s, lingered on. Even Charles Dickens took a hand in his *American Notes* and *Martin Chuzzlewit*. In consequence the average Briton pictured the United States as a turbulent, loud-mouthed, rapacious democracy, while the average American despised the decadent, class–ridden monarchies of the old world.

Bad relations had been aggravated by the American financial crises of the 1830s. Three of the seven 'American Houses' in London, that is banks dealing largely with American business, had failed to meet their obligations and even the great firm of Baring Brothers only just weathered the storm. Several American states, including Pennsylvania, in which much British capital was invested, repudiated their debts.[3]

Deeper than British indignation at the American defaulter was British loathing of the American slave–owner. The Saints who, until 1833, had been absorbed in the struggle for abolition in the British colonies, now turned their attention to other countries. Their attitude was deeply resented in the Southern States, where few men believed that it was disinterested. The American slave-holders were convinced that the British West Indian planters, having been ruined by abolition, wanted to see it extended to the United States in order to end their competition. Some even believed that the British would be willing to provoke a slave rising.

It would have taxed the powers of any statesman to re-establish cordial relations in the face of such suspicions but, in addition to this generalised hostility, a number of disputes had suddenly become acute. These centred on the disputed north-east and north-west boundaries, the new state of Texas and the suppression of the slave trade.

Boundary questions, which had smouldered for years, flared into life because the idea that it was the 'Manifest Destiny' of the United States to rule the whole of the North American continent had begun to take hold of the American nation. *The Times* complained in 1845, 'The real principle for which the Americans are covertly contending implies no less than a progressive sovereignty or a gradual annexation, spreading from the Polar circles to the Tropics . . . With a whole continent to range over they become as captious in asserting doubtful claims as a mediatised Prince of the German Empire.'[4] These claims brought them to war with Mexico and to the verge of war with Britain, the other two Powers with interests on the North American continent.

By September 1841 the north-east boundary – between Maine on the one side and New Brunswick on the other – was in turmoil. The negotiations of 1828–31 had come to nothing. The King of the Netherlands, in his role of arbiter, had eventually proposed a compromise line, which the British would have reluctantly accepted but which the American Senate, under pressure from Maine, rejected.[5] Palmerston had proposed a fresh negotiation in 1840 but had refused to accept an American proposal that commissioners from Maine should be added to the negotiators. 'The British government', he said, 'negotiates with the Federal Government, and with that Government alone.'[6] The matter, however, could not be allowed to remain unsettled for much longer. Lumberjacks and others from both Maine and New Brunswick were penetrating into the disputed area and sometimes coming to blows.[7]

The boundary dispute was aggravated by incidents arising out of the Canadian rebellions of 1837. Some men in the United States bitterly resented the fact that a British colony remained on American soil and found it hard to believe that the Canadians did not wish to be 'liberated'. The federal government maintained a strictly correct attitude but the local authorities on the border sometimes turned a blind eye to gun-running and even raids across the border. The most serious incident was the *Caroline* affair. The *Caroline* was an American river steamer which was used to supply the Canadian rebels with arms. In December 1837 it was surprised and destroyed on the American side of the Niagara River by a Canadian force – although it did not plunge, blazing, over Niagara Falls as contemporary legend had it. An American called Amos Durfee was killed in the affray. In November 1840 a Canadian, Alexander McLeod, was arrested while doing business in New York State and charged with being concerned in the murder of Durfee. The international repercussions of his arrest were extremely serious. The American government had previously protested and Palmerston had prepared a statement, declaring that the destruction of the *Caroline* was an act of state for which the British government would take responsibility, but, as the Americans had not pressed the question, the statement was not communicated to John Forsyth, the American Secretary of State, until after McLeod's arrest. Forsyth refused to intervene in the case and Palmerston then ordered Henry Fox, the British Minister in Washington, to leave the United States at once if McLeod was executed.[8]

In March 1841 a new administration came into power in the United States. William Harrison and Daniel Webster replaced Martin Van Buren and John Forsyth as President and Secretary of State respectively. A month later Harrison died and was succeeded by his Vice-President, John Tyler. Webster sympathised with the British point of view and would have been willing to intervene on McLeod's behalf but he was prevented at every turn by the difficult question of States' Rights.

Immediately upon taking office, therefore, Aberdeen was faced by the possibility of a rupture of diplomatic relations, or even war, with the United States. Despite his hatred of war, Aberdeen was as firm as Palmerston upon a point where he felt that his country's honour was at stake. He wrote at once to Fox to assure him that British policy remained the same and, if McLeod was executed, he was to ask for his passports. Some extraordinary scenes ensued in Washington. President Tyler even threatened to prevent Fox from leaving.[9] Public excitement was such that the American authorities feared that, if McLeod were not convicted, he might be lynched. Meanwhile, Andrew Stevenson, the American Minister in London, described the British newspapers as 'filled with articles of the most extravagant and revolting violence' and told his government, 'There seems to be a general impression that war is inevitable'.[10] On 18 October, Peel, Aberdeen, Stanley, Graham and Haddington met to discuss the deployment of the British fleet in the event of war. Peel told Wellington later that day that they were resolved to take 'without delay' measures 'for the purpose of being prepared for the *possibility* of war'.[11]

At the same time Aberdeen took the opportunity to make a conciliatory gesture. In September 1841 some British soldiers had crossed the American frontier into Vermont to arrest an American citizen named Grogan, who had committed various crimes in Canada during the troubles of 1837–38. Aberdeen did not plead the excuse of 'hot pursuit' but immediately ordered Grogan's release.[12] The policy of firmness and conciliation paid off. McLeod stood his trial at Utica Assizes early in October but vital prosecution witnesses did not appear – it was suspected, but never proved, that the federal government was responsible for their absence – and McLeod was acquitted.[13]

Problems concerning the suppression of the slave trade had also reached boiling point in 1841. This was a particularly dangerous question because both the French and the Americans detested Britain's claim to 'police the seas'. It was connected with all the old controversy of 'maritime rights' and here the spectre of the war of 1812, rather than 1778, raised its head. Both Britain and the United States had independently declared the slave trade to be illegal in 1807. The Congress of Vienna had condemned it and, by 1825, all the major maritime Powers had outlawed it. To enforce the prohibition was more difficult. Only Britain was able and willing to keep a squadron on the West Coast of Africa to intercept slavers but, in the absence of specific international agreements, British cruisers had jurisdiction only over British ships. After 1815 Britain persuaded some of the lesser maritime Powers, notably Spain, Portugal and Brazil, to allow British warships to stop slavers flying their flags. The great maritime Powers, France and the United States, were much more cautious but in 1831, when the July Monarchy particularly needed British support, Britain and France signed a treaty allowing for a mutual right of search within certain defined areas.[14]

The American attitude was the biggest thorn in the side of the British antislavery movement. Although few American politicians would have defended the trade in public, it was generally connived at in the Southern States. By 1839 the United States was the only significant maritime Power outside the right of search arrangements and Spanish vessels in particular frequently covered themselves by using false American flags and papers. President Tyler himself admitted, 'that the American flag is grossly abused by the abandoned and profligate of other nations is but too probable', while the American Governor of Liberia said bluntly, 'The chief obstacle to the success of the very active measures pursued by the British government for the suppression of the slave trade on the coast, is the *American flag*.'[15]

In the 1830s the Whig government had tried to persuade all the great Powers of Europe to join in one right of search treaty in order to bring pressure to bear upon the Americans and to convince them that adherence to such a treaty meant no derogation of sovereignty. In 1838 Palmerston invited the Molé administration in France to join with Britain in initiating such a treaty. Unhappily the Eastern crisis intervened and, although Britain, Austria, Prussia and Russia signed the new treaty, France did not. Guizot, however, had no objections to the principles of the treaty and, as soon as the Conservatives came to power, he sent the French Ambassador in London, the comte de Ste Aulaire, authority to sign. The treaty was finally signed on 20 December 1841, but within weeks there was such an outcry in the French press that it was very doubtful whether the French government would be able to ratify it.[16]

The British government had tried to deal with the practical problems on the African coast, by drawing a distinction between the right of search proper and what they termed the 'right of visit'. By the latter they meant the right of a British captain to ascertain the true identity of a ship which he had good reason to believe was sailing under false colours in order to engage in the slave trade, if necessary by stopping her and going aboard to examine her papers. In 1840 two naval officers, Captain Tucker, R. N. and Lieutenant Paine of the U.S. Navy, serving on the African coast came to a working arrangement on their own initiative. They agreed that each should be authorised 'to detain all vessels under American colours found to be fully equipped for, and engaged in the Slave Trade'. If they proved to be American property, they should be handed over to an American cruiser, if they were Spanish, Portugese, Brazilian or English they should be handed over to a British cruiser. The British government hoped that this arrangement might become the basis of a general agreement but it was quickly disavowed by the United States. Its immediate effect was unfortunate since, on the strength of it, the British Africa squadron for the first time detained several slavers knowing them to be American.[17]

This led to an acrimonious exchange between Palmerston and Stevenson, the American Minister in London and himself a large slave proprietor, just before the Whig government fell. Stevenson told Palmerston 'these continued aggressions upon the vessels and commerce of the United States cannot longer be permitted.' Palmerston replied that Britain did not claim the right to search American vessels in time of peace but 'Her Majesty's Government do not mean thereby to say that a merchantman can exempt himself from search merely by hoisting a piece of bunting with the United States emblems and colours upon it.'[18] All the treaties for the suppression of the slave trade would become a dead letter. It was promptly reported in the United States that Palmerston had called the American flag 'a piece of bunting'.

The main question was exacerbated by a side issue. The *Creole* was an American ship engaged in the purely domestic slave trade between the Southern States, with which Britain had never claimed to interfere. In October 1841 she sailed for New Orleans from Virginia with 135 slaves aboard. During the voyage the slaves mutinied, killed a white passenger and took the ship into Nassau in the British Bahamas. The American Consul there asked the British authorities to secure the murderers and to ensure that the other slaves did not escape. The Bahamas government agreed to hold the actual murderers pending further enquiries but the rest of the slaves were set at liberty on the grounds that English law no longer recognised the state of slavery. Mutiny was rare, but American ships being driven into Bahamian ports by stress of weather was not, and this decision caused great alarm and anger in the United States.

There was a direct link between those Americans and those Frenchmen who resented what they saw as Britain's very high-handed attitude to the suppression of the slave trade. The moving spirit was General Cass, the American Minister in Paris, a slave-owner and a passionate Anglophobe. Cass was a potential Presidential candidate who thought that a strong line on the right of search issue was as good a way as any of recommending himself to the American electorate. He had written a vehement pamphlet on the subject[19] and he told *The Times* correspondent in Paris that any British attempt to search American ships would mean 'instantaneous War'.[20] He intrigued with various French leaders and, on his own responsibility, warned the French government that if they ratified the Quintuple Treaty of 20 December 1841, they would be in danger of being dragged into war with the United States. Daniel Webster apologetically told the British government that he disapproved of Cass's actions but domestic politics compelled him to sanction them.[21]

Neither the north-west boundary nor Texas presented such an immediate danger of conflict as did the north-east boundary and the slave trade issue but both obviously held the seeds of future trouble. In the west the boundary between the United States and British North America west of the Rocky Mountains was still undefined. In 1841 Mexico still owned the territory between the Rockies and the Pacific as far north as 42°, while the Russian claims north of

54° 40′ had been recognised by both the United States and Britain. The ownership of the land between had never been finally determined although, up to this time, the United States had never seriously claimed territory north of the forty-ninth parallel, nor Britain that south of the Columbia River. In 1818 the two countries had concluded a convention, providing for the joint occupancy of the disputed area for a period of ten years. This had been renewed in 1827 for an indefinite period and was still in force in 1841.[22]

The Americans had purchased certain historical claims from France in 1803 and from Spain in 1819, but Britain had rival historical claims, some of which had been recognised by Spain in the Nootka Sound Convention of 1790. Until the 1830s the British had been more active in the area, which was generally known as Oregon,[23] than the Americans. The Hudson's Bay Company had opened up the whole region for fur-trading and had planted agricultural settlements at Puget Sound and elsewhere. But in the 1840s the picture changed. American settlers began to flow in, some coming overland along the Oregon trail, some across the isthmus of Panama, others round Cape Horn. The land was less fertile than the mid-West but the settlers hoped to open up the Pacific trade routes. San Francisco, the only good harbour on the Pacific coast, was still in Mexican hands but at first exaggerated hopes were entertained of the Columbia River as a commercial outlet.[24]

In the South, Texas had broken away from the Mexican Empire in 1836 and formed an independent republic. Fearing a Mexican attempt to reconquer them, the Texans, many of whom were immigrants from the United States, asked to join the American Union but they were rebuffed by the northern and eastern states who were afraid that the adherence of Texas would shift the balance of power to the south. The Texans, therefore, had to stand on their own feet and, in 1837, despatched agents to all the leading Powers of Europe to secure commercial treaties and loans.

British interest in Texas was threefold. First, she hoped that an independent Texas would balance the power of the United States and bar the way to further United States' expansion into Central America or the West Indies, which might damage British trading interests in the Caribbean.[25] Secondly, Texas offered attractive trading possibilities. A number of able propagandists prophesied that Texas would become a great cotton-producing area, surpassing even Alabama, and being outside the United States' high tariff system, would free Britain from her dangerous dependence on United States cotton.[26] Thirdly, British abolitionists hoped that Texas might be persuaded to abolish slavery, in return for political and commercial concessions.[27] All three reasons for British interest were, unfortunately, peculiarly irritating to the Americans. A Texan envoy, General Hamilton, arrived in England in the spring of 1840 and three treaties were signed in November of that year. The first, a treaty of commerce and navigation, guaranteed 'most favoured nation' status to each country. The second offered British mediation between Texas and Mexico. The third, on which Palmerston had insisted, provided for a mutual right of search to suppress the slave trade. The Texans had reservations about the last and ratifications were not finally exchanged until June 1842. Britain had, however, particularly by the second treaty, committed herself to play some part in Texan affairs.[28]

Aberdeen, immediately on coming into office, grasped the American problem boldly. The McLeod case had frightened both governments. Unless outstanding problems were solved quickly, war seemed inevitable in the near future. Circumstances were not altogether unfavourable. President Tyler's new government was comparatively well disposed towards Britain and in particular his Secretary of State, Daniel Webster, was an Easterner committed to a policy of good relations with European states. Against this must be set the instability of the Tyler administration. Soon after taking office, Tyler quarrelled with his party about domestic legislation and, in September 1841, most of his cabinet resigned. Webster remained in office but his position was precarious and during the subsequent negotiations, British diplomats continually complained of the President's 'weakness' and of Webster's lack of real authority.

The possibility of a general settlement was canvassed in the autumn of 1841. The *New York Herald* of 15 October, suggested that a special minister, preferably Webster himself, be sent to London, but the American government preferred that negotiations should be in Washington and there were obvious advantages in conducting the discussions, especially on the boundaries, close to the scene of the disputes, where local evidence was available. Aberdeen soon came to the conclusion that nothing could be done through the existing British Minister in Washington, Henry Fox, since Fox disliked the Americans and was unpopular with them. There remained the possibility of sending a special envoy to Washington.[29]

It is clear that from the beginning Aberdeen had in mind a general settlement with the United States, which would remove the continual threat of war, and that he was indifferent to most of the details of the settlement. This was implicit in his choice of envoy. He chose Lord Ashburton, a member of the great banking firm of Baring Brothers, which had played a major part in financing the economic development of America and was still the leading 'American House' in London. Ashburton had much to commend him. He had excellent contacts in America, was married to an American wife and acquainted with many prominent American politicians, including Daniel Webster. He was a leading Conservative peer and a personal friend of Peel and Aberdeen. From the beginning of the Conservative administration he had constituted himself unofficial adviser and intermediary on American affairs. Against that must be set the fact that Ashburton was not a professional diplomat, used to international bargaining. He was an old man, rather reluctant to undertake the mission at all. He agreed to go only if Aberdeen could assure him that there was no 'indisposition to come to a settlement' on either side. The significance of his appointment was not lost on the public. Charles Greville recorded that, although it was 'much praised' at first, people soon had second thoughts and remembered Ashburton's reputation for irresolution, which age was not likely to have cured. Ashburton, however, understood well enough what Aberdeen had in mind. He interpreted the aim of his mission to be 'conciliation', the establishment of 'that better feeling which may prevent the present proneness to future misunderstandings', perhaps even to make 'a popular Treaty which would have exhibited us to the Disturbers at Paris as on terms of undisturbable amity with our Brethren in America'.[30]

Aberdeen's indifference to the details of the settlement is implicit too in the haste, and even carelessness, with which Ashburton's original instructions were drawn up, although there were good reasons for haste. Ashburton accepted the appointment on 22 December 1841 and it was immediately made known to the American Minister in London so that it should not seem to be the result of anything Tyler had said in his Annual Message to Congress, the text of which was daily expected.[31] Ashburton, who had received what he regarded as secret overtures from Webster even before he accepted the mission, and Aberdeen were both convinced that their best chance of success was a settlement with the existing American administration, which might break up at any moment. British politics made it desirable that Ashburton should set out before Parliament met in February. Finally, Ashburton himself – and perhaps Aberdeen sympathised – dreaded crossing the Atlantic and wanted to sail before the equinoctial gales.[32]

Ashburton was sent out to deal with five main points, the suppression of the slave trade, the *Creole* case, the north-east boundary, the *Caroline* incident, and the northwest boundary.

Until a few weeks before Ashburton sailed the slave trade question seemed to be the most urgent and dangerous issue but, towards the end of December, agreement appeared to have been reached in London on the most immediate problems connected with it. Aberdeen had been compelled to continue Palmerston's controversy with Andrew Stevenson. Aberdeen was more conciliatory in manner than Palmerston but his basic position was not very different. He told Stevenson that he wished to avoid 'any harshness or asperity of expression' for he understood 'the susceptibilities of national feeling' where questions of national honour were involved but he did not see how, in the face of Stevenson's own admissions that the American flag was being abused, Britain could relinquish the right of visit. He wrote:

. . . it can scarcely be maintained that Great Britain should be bound to permit her own subjects, with British vessels, and British capital, to carry on before the eyes of British officers, this detestable traffick in human beings . . . merely because they had the audacity to commit an additional offence by fraudulently usurping the American flag.[33]

A gleam of hope was provided by the recall of the uncompromising Stevenson and the appointment in his place of Edward Everett, a friend of Daniel Webster.[34] Everett was believed to have abolitionist sympathies and quickly came to be on excellent terms with Aberdeen. Soon after his arrival, on the day of the signature of the Quintuple Treaty, 20 December 1841, Aberdeen addressed an important note to him, renouncing the right of search, 'a purely belligerent right', but defending the right of visit, confined solely to the verification of the nationality of the vessel.

British cruisers, he said, had no instructions to intercept American ships. 'Such vessels must be permitted, if engaged in it, to enjoy a monopoly of this

unhallowed trade; but the British Government will never endure that the fraud-
ulent use of the American flag shall extend the iniquity to other nations by
whom it is abhorred.' If Stevenson's principles were carried to their logical
conclusion they would protect piracy as well as the slave trade. Contrary to
Stevenson's assertions, the Americans themselves used the right of visit to deal
with suspicious-looking vessels in the Gulf of Mexico. Aberdeen regretted that
the Americans had disapproved the Tucker–Paine arrangement of 1840. He
reminded them that the European Powers had just signed a right of search
agreement. 'This', he commented, 'is in truth a holy alliance, in which he
would have rejoiced to see the United States assume their proper place.' To
reassure the Americans he communicated the instructions then in force for
cruisers on the African coast and promised prompt compensation if a *bona fide*
American vessel was accidentally detained.[35]

This definitive statement of the British position was persuasive and conciliatory. It was difficult for the Americans to reject Aberdeen's arguments without openly condoning the abuse of their flag and it met any real grievances
about the molestation of their ships or delays in paying compensation. Everett
expressed himself well satisfied and Ashburton's impression on arriving in
America was that the question was settled. 'About the right or rather practice
of Visiting Webster professes himself satisfied with your last note and he thinks
the matter may there drop', he wrote.[36]

Unfortunately, the American government never returned any formal reply
to Aberdeen's note and ominous signs began to appear even while Ashburton
was still in America. The Americans had published the acrimonious correspondence between Palmerston and Stevenson and Aberdeen was disappointed
that Webster did not publish his latest note.[37] The truth was that American
opinion was so excited that the government dared not do anything which
seemed to acknowledge the right of visit.

This was not apparent when Ashburton set out on his mission and not much
emphasis was laid on the subject in his original instructions.[38] Ashburton,
however, gave the matter some thought and, while his ship was detained in
Yarmouth roads by bad weather, he composed a memorandum. He took up
a suggestion that General Cass had made that each British or American cruiser
should have aboard 'a person of the other nation who should alone visit and
authorise the capture' of ships of his own country. Peel reacted strongly against
this idea. 'The novelty of the principle', he wrote, 'a *foreign* controlling authority on board ship – is the startling objection.' Palmerston was later to ridicule
the same idea in Parliament, pointing out that what was granted to one maritime power would be claimed by others and soon each cruiser would become
'a veritable Noah's Ark' with naval officers in pairs.[39] When he got to America,
Ashburton found that the Americans had a rather more practicable suggestion
that British and American cruisers should 'hunt in couples'. Ashburton asked
for Aberdeen's instructions on this 'joint cruising' arrangement, as it came to
be called.[40]

Aberdeen was strongly in favour. If the Americans would not accept a mutual
right of search agreement, Britain would 'willingly accede' to a joint cruising

arrangement.[41] On 13 July Ashburton sent Aberdeen a draft communicated by President Tyler himself. This had two clauses. Each Power should maintain a squadron of at least 100 guns on the coast of Africa and they should act together diplomatically to suppress the slave markets which continued to flourish in Cuba and Brazil. Aberdeen was delighted and told Ashburton '. . . you are right in taking it for granted that you cannot go too far in that direction'. The two clauses were incorporated in the final treaty, although the squadrons were reduced to 80 guns. Ashburton did not regret the reduction since it was a minimum and more likely, he thought, to be met. More seriously, joint cruising arrangements were not spelt out. The Treaty only provided for the two squadrons to act 'in concert and co-operation . . . as exigencies may arise'.[42] Everything therefore really depended still on mutual goodwill.

Ashburton had wished to seek a more radical solution to the whole problem. In a despatch of 12 May he went to the root of the matter, the fact that the right of search and even the right of visit were indissolubly connected in American eyes with the question of impressment, the right which Britain still claimed in time of war to take her nationals off foreign ships and 'press' them into the British Navy. Ashburton told Aberdeen that Webster had raised the matter with him and, although he was not suggesting that the matter be mentioned in the Treaty, he would like Aberdeen's authority to address a note to Webster promising that the right would not be exercised in a future war if the Americans would promise in return that they would not take any British subject into their merchant service in time of war, unless he had at least five years' residence in the United States.

Ashburton pleaded his case strongly. 'Impressment,' he said, 'as a system, is an anomaly hardly bearable by our own people. To the foreigner it is undeniable tyranny, which can only be imposed upon him by force, and submitted to by him so long as that force continue.' Impressment had been the proximate cause of the war of 1812. America was now much stronger. Ashburton asked Aberdeen, 'Under these circumstances can Impressment ever be repeated?' Its first exercise would produce war. Was it not better, he asked, 'to surrender with a good grace a pretended right, while the surrender may bring you some credit, than to maintain what you will have no power to execute?'[43]

Aberdeen reacted with unusual sharpness. He told Ashburton officially that the objections to his suggestion were 'insurmountable'. It would be 'tantamount to an absolute and entire renunciation of the indefeasible right inherent in the British Crown to command the allegiance of its subjects, wherever found'. Privately he admitted that it would never be possible to exercise the right again in practice. A little later he told Ashburton that if the latter remained long enough in America he would not despair of coming to some arrangement 'but the subject is one of much delicacy in this Country and although public feeling may be a good deal modified, there is still much excitement connected with it. It is our Droit de Visite.'[44] This, of course, was absurd. The British public was not passionately attached to impressment. Ashburton's analysis was nearer the truth.

Ashburton and Webster in fact exchanged notes for publication with the

Treaty. Webster's was very long and ran through all the American objections to the practice. He concluded with a 'friendly warning' that the American government was resolved not to tolerate it in the future. Ashburton returned a very conciliatory answer, saying that the practice had not been used for many years 'and can not consistently with existing laws and regulations for manning Her Majesty's Navy be under present circumstances renewed'. He could not enter into the matter during the 'limited continuance' of his mission but he entertained 'the confident hope' that the matter would be satisfactorily settled in the future.[45] For all practical purposes Ashburton had conceded all Webster wanted and in so doing had considerably exceeded anything authorised in his official instructions, although what he did was in line with hints dropped in Aberdeen's private letters.

Ashburton had virtually conceded that the practice could never be resumed. Would it not have been better to have reaped the credit for a voluntary renunciation of the right? Aberdeen, usually a flexible negotiator, took an unexpectedly rigid line on formal renunciation. There was one substantial reason for this. It would have raised difficult and far-reaching questions of national allegiance. Ashburton explained this in his formal reply to Webster. He wrote:

America, receiving every year by thousands the emigrants of Europe, maintains the doctrine suitable to her condition of the right of transferring allegiance at will. The laws of Great Britain have maintained from all time the opposite doctrine. The duties of allegiance are held to be indefeasible . . .[46]

Aberdeen admitted privately that eventually the European nations would have to come to terms with this problem but Webster's original proposition that a five-years' residence in America should exempt a man from the obligation to serve his country in time of war looked too much like a tacit admission of the American doctrine of transferrable allegiance. Aberdeen may be forgiven for refusing to create a precedent on such an important point as a by-product of other negotiations. At the same time, Aberdeen had every reason to be personally nervous about any concession on maritime rights. He had not forgotten the furore which his acquiescence in an apparently reasonable sentence in St Aignan's memorandum of 1813 had raised.

The *Creole* case also proved difficult to adjust. Feeling in the United States was not improved by the trial and acquittal of the mutineers, nor by the fact that the British judge had been moved to comment on the 'natural and inalienable right' of persons held in bondage to regain their freedom. Ashburton complained sourly that he would have done better to avoid *obiter dicta* calculated to 'inflame half a continent'. Ashburton told Aberdeen that the *Creole* gave him 'more trouble than all the other questions taken together' and that he more than once feared that the whole negotiation would break down on it.[47]

The Americans would have liked a formal guarantee of the inviolability of their ships navigating the Bahamas Channel even if they were driven by bad weather or other cause into British ports. Instead Ashburton and Webster exchanged notes on the principles involved. Webster was prepared to concede that escaped slaves could not be reclaimed from British territory since British law did not recognise the state of slavery but, he contended, American ships in British waters were not 'within the exclusive jurisdiction of England' and consequently the British authorities should do nothing to alter 'existing rights of property between persons on board'. Without going so far as this, Ashburton was prepared to agree that there should be 'no officious interference'. Ashburton told Aberdeen frankly that Webster's statement was meant to preserve his own popularity in the South and his, Ashburton's, to evade any engagement.[48]

The *Creole* case had, however, one constructive result. The Americans admitted that, in the absence of an extradition treaty, Britain could not legally have handed over the *Creole* mutineers to them for trial. Aberdeen saw that an extradition treaty would cover some vexed cases on the Canadian border, such as that of Grogan. The two countries therefore signed an Extradition Convention on 2 August 1842 but it covered only murder and certain other serious offences. At Aberdeen's insistence it did not include 'mutiny and revolt' on board ships as, in itself, an extraditable offence.[49]

But in the end the north-east boundary dispute came to overshadow all other issues. After the failure of the King of the Netherlands' mediation, deadlock seemed to have been reached and Aberdeen pinned his hopes, not on any re–examination of the territory or of the words of the Treaty of 1783, which had already proved sterile, but on the negotiation of a simple compromise line. There may have been some justification for not wasting time in studying previous negotiations in detail but, in his haste to prepare Ashburton's instructions, Aberdeen overlooked some points of substance. He seems to have regarded the whole disputed territory as of equal – and dubious – value and have felt that a more or less fifty–fifty division should satisfy both parties. He had only two fixed points; the Madawaska Settlements on the St John's River should be retained because they were already under Canadian civil jurisdiction and the navigation of the St John should be safeguarded because of its importance to the Canadian timber trade. His original instructions did not mention what had always been Britain's two most important strategic objectives, the safeguarding of the only convenient land route from Halifax to Quebec and the banishment of the American frontier from the highlands just south of Quebec. Ashburton was authorised to accept any one of three propositions – the whole British claim (which no-one supposed was possible), a conventional line which would have given Britain the Madawaska Settlements and the navigable portion of the St John, or the King of the Netherlands' award, preferably with modifications.[50]

Aberdeen consulted few people and Wellington did not learn of these instructions until the evening of 8 February when Ashburton had already left London. The Duke was furious and sat up half the night writing three angry letters. The first demanded the recall of Ashburton's instructions. The second complained that the Duke had been given no notice of the question so his opinion, 'if I should be so foolish as to give any, is worth no more than that of any Chatterer or foolish Gossip about the Town'. But, having worked off his spleen, the Duke then wrote a third letter which showed a detailed knowledge of the question. He insisted, rather unrealistically, that they should still press the whole British claim, believing it to be justified, but he also explained why it was so important to secure the road and the highlands and why even the Dutch King's award was inadequate for this purpose.[51]

Aberdeen was badly shaken by the Duke's memorandum. He wrote at once to Ashburton, still detained by bad weather in Yarmouth Roads, telling him to await further instructions before entering into any negotiations. Ashburton was now nearly as irritated as Wellington and replied that he saw no chance of satisfying the Duke. He feared that the line which would suit them best would have to give way to 'views of expediency or policy in dealing with a troublesome people'.[52]

At this rather late stage Aberdeen began to consider the issue carefully. A memorandum was circulated to the Cabinet on 14 February, explaining that Ashburton's instructions had been prepared 'under great pressure, from want of time', enclosing a copy of Wellington's memorandum and warning the ministers that they would have 'at a very early date, to consider what modifications of the Instructions may be desirable'.[53] Aberdeen meanwhile had an elaborate précis prepared in the Foreign Office, detailing the previous negotiations.[54] He also consulted a number of military authorities, Sir James Kempt, who had been Governor-General of Canada, 1828–30, Sir Howard Douglas, Governor of New Brunswick, 1823–31, Lord Seaton, Lieutenant-Governor of Upper Canada, 1828–38 and Sir George Murray, the Master-General of the Ordnance. They were not unanimous in their opinion although none of them wanted to see the Americans north of the St John. Kempt, however, was sceptical about the value of the road from Fredericton along the north bank of the St John. It would, he thought, be exposed to attack and he wanted instead to develop a more northerly route.[55] The military opinions, therefore, still left some room for manoeuvre.

With all these enquiries going on, Aberdeen was still not ready with Ashburton's instructions early in March. In a letter apologising to him, he expressed his own views quite frankly:

for myself I must declare that if we shall at last be driven to quarrel with the United States, I sincerely pray that we may take our Stand on some great principle of National policy, or of humanity and justice, and that we not go to war [sic] for a few miles, more or less, of a miserable pine swamp.[56]

But when the instructions were finally ready at the end of March they had been strengthened a good deal in accordance with the views of Wellington and the military men. Aberdeen began by declaring 'it is the firm intention of Her Majesty to preserve the dominion of our North American Provinces.' The indispensable condition of this was the preservation of the line of communication between Halifax and Quebec. He now accepted the Duke's view that, as the Dutch King's Award had been rejected by the Americans, it had no 'obligatory character' and could only be accepted with modification. He detailed some possible modifications based on the military men's recommendations. Oddly enough the military men had no objection to ceding Rouse's Point on Lake Champlain, to which the Americans had a bad claim and which had usually been regarded as the key to the route to Montreal, in return for concessions on the Quebec Highlands. Aberdeen also raised the possibility of purchasing land to which the Americans had a good claim but which the British particularly desired.[57]

Neither Wellington nor Peel was completely satisfied by Aberdeen's new instructions. Peel wanted the old instructions put out of court altogether, lest they embarrass the British on some future occasion, and he thought the possibility of a money payment should be brought forward with 'great caution'. It looked like an admission of right and how embarrassing if the Americans said, 'Here are 2 millions of acres which the British Government require us to sell for *two shillings* an acre for the fee simple.' Appearances, he pointed out, would be very important when the matter came before the public on both sides of the Atlantic.[58]

Aberdeen was plainly out of tune with his colleagues and, not for the first time, he sent a private letter with his instructions which came very close to modifying them. Despite his assurances to the contrary to Wellington, it is clear that he still regarded the Dutch Award as the best settlement they were likely to get and that they would have to secure modifications in it by a money payment 'which, in the present state of American finances, ought not to be extravagant', or by concessions to allow the Americans to bring their timber down the St John.[59]

The long delay in sending his instructions had caused Ashburton embarrassment in Washington. He arrived without any instructions on the northeast boundary and his statement to this effect was initially greeted with delight by the Americans, who thought that he meant that he had been given a free hand. The Americans meanwhile returned to the proposal that Palmerston had rejected in 1840, that Commissioners from Maine and Massachusetts should be associated with Webster in the negotiations. Peel disliked the suggestion, although he was not prepared to veto it. Aberdeen actually welcomed it because he thought it represented the best chance of Maine accepting the settlement.[60] In this Aberdeen may have been more realistic than Peel or Palmerston. The British may have disliked the American federal division of authority but they had to live with it.

Before the Maine and Massachusetts Commissioners arrived, informal negotiations began between Ashburton and Webster, who, on a personal level, found it easy to do business. Ashburton was soon assuring Aberdeen of the importance of settling with the existing administration, which was dangerously weak. He was correspondingly angry when he received his new instructions of 31 March. He told Aberdeen frankly in a private letter:

My powers by your last letter place the whole of this negotiation in jeopardy . . . if you had read to me your present instructions before I left London I should have ventured . . . to give an opinion that it was inexpedient to send this mission.

A failure in Maine would probably lead to a failure on all points 'and a General failure . . . would leave relations with this ungovernable people in a much worse state than if no solemn attempt at settlement had ever been made.' He was 'strongly impressed with the dangers of letting the soldiers have their own way in this matter'. The letter was pervaded by the need for haste. Congress would not sit beyond the end of June and, finally, Ashburton could not stand the Washington climate much longer. He complained, 'Though we are not yet through. April the Thermometer is at 80 and my nerves give me warning.'[61]

Aberdeen complicated the issue himself by letting slip to the Texan, General Hamilton, a remark about the possibility of a money payment. The matter leaked to the American press and embarrassed Ashburton who had not yet mentioned the possibility to Webster.[62] Fortunately, Webster too was looking for compromises. He told Everett that he thought Britain's desire to retain her 'old and convenient communication between her two provinces . . . reasonable'. He was prepared to concede the Madawaska Settlements and, in return, suggested the free passage of American lumber down the St John.[63] Peel was impressed by Webster's latest suggestions, more particularly because he was exasperated by the renewed civil strife in Canada. He wrote to Aberdeen:

I think we must come to an agreement on the boundary . . . Let us keep Nova Scotia and New Brunswick — for their geographical position makes their sea-board of great importance to us – but the connection with the Canadas *against their will* – nay without the Cordial Cooperation of the predominant party in Canada – is a very onerous one . . .

If the Canadians were with them, honour would compel Britain to fight for them 'but if they are not with us . . . let us have a friendly separation while there is yet time.'[64]

Wellington had still to be persuaded but Aberdeen now had virtual *carte blanche* from Peel to try for a compromise settlement.[65] How difficult this was, is illustrated by the numerous drafts, ranging from the minatory to the yielding, which survive of Aberdeen's third and final instructions to Ashburton on the north-east boundary. These were not ready until 26 May. They again accepted the Dutch Award as 'a general Basis of Negotiation' and, on some points, embodied greater concessions even than the cancelled first instructions. Money payment was not mentioned but far-reaching concessions on navigation on the St John were envisaged.[66]

Despite the intransigence of the Maine Commissioners, general agreement was reached between Ashburton and Webster on 14 July. Maine and Massachusetts were finally won over by the promise of a money payment by the federal government. This was, with some impropriety, written into the final treaty, although it was made clear that the British government assumed no responsibility for it.[67]

The treaty on the north-east boundary was signed on 9 August. It did not follow precisely any of the proposals made by Aberdeen, although it was within the discretionary powers given to Ashburton. It did not secure for Britain the whole of the triangle of territory between the rivers St John, St Francis and St Lawrence, covering the Quebec highlands. Instead the boundary followed a zigzag course across them. Ashburton even had to surrender part of the Madawaska Settlements. On their side the Americans gained the boundary adjustments they wanted on the forty-fifth parallel at Rouse's Point and the inhabitants of Maine secured the right to convey their timber and agricultural produce, grown in the basin of the St John, down the river to the sea.[68]

Ashburton was well satisfied with his Treaty. He assured Aberdeen, 'You may rely that no better terms were obtainable.' He admitted that he had been fighting for details to which he did not attach much importance. A general settlement was the main thing 'and I am well pleased that we end by driving the Enemy off the crest of the Highlands so much coveted at the War Office.'[69] The British government was not quite so delighted. Peel thought that too much had been conceded on the navigation of the St John and even Aberdeen thought that the whole of the St Lawrence Highlands might have been secured 'with perseverance' and this would have been important in presenting the case to the public.[70] The government was now in fact becoming worried about the public reception of the Treaty and their pleasure was further marred by the mysterious affair of the maps, which formed a detective story in itself.

The most important map was the so-called 'red line' map, discovered by an American historian, Jared Sparkes, in the French Foreign Office archives. Sparkes believed it to be the map sent by Benjamin Franklin to the comte de Vergennes in December 1782, showing the boundary line agreed upon by the British and American Plenipotentiaries. The red line marked upon it corresponded, more or less exactly, with the British claim and, after some hesitation, Sparkes sent a copy to Webster. Webster took it seriously and used it to put pressure, first on the Commissioners from Maine and Massachusetts, and later on the Senate, to secure their acceptance of a compromise line.[71]

Webster was subsequently accused of sharp practice in not showing it to the British, and the British government let it be understood, although they never stated as much, that Ashburton first learnt of it on 9 August, the day the Treaty was signed.[72] This was not so. Ashburton wrote privately to Aberdeen on 9 and 13 August giving him details both of the red-line map and of another map, the so-called Steuben–Webster map, which also seemed to support the British case, but it is clear that Aberdeen already knew of them. Ashburton probably told him on 14 June. Ashburton's letter to Aberdeen of that date, as it now survives, ends with the cryptic first sentence of a postscript, 'My business is likely to move fast in about another fortnight.' Aberdeen in his reply of 2 July promised the utmost secrecy about the matters referred to in the postscript and assured Ashburton, 'you need not be afraid of employing the same means to a greater extent in any quarter where it may be necessary'. This reference to 'means' is explained in Ashburton's letter of 9 August in which he informed Aberdeen that he had served a bill on him for £2998, 1s. 0d. in respect of the Secret Service funds on which he was authorised to draw and told him 'The money I wrote about went to compensate Sparkes and to send him, on my first arrival to the Governors of Maine and Massachusetts.' Ashburton thought that 'without this stimulant Maine would never have yielded'.[73]

Both Aberdeen and Ashburton expressed their thankfulness that they had not known of the map 'officially' earlier. Ashburton wrote:

If I had known it before treating, in any way which would have permitted me to use it, we could not well have refrained from maintaining our undoubted right and yet we should never have got the Aroostook Valley without fighting for it. All the evidence of Angels would not have moved the Maine lumberers.[74]

Nevertheless, it was embarrassing when the opposition learnt of it.[75] In order to anticipate parliamentary criticisms Aberdeen made further enquiries in Paris through Henry Bulwer. Bulwer found Sparkes's map, although only after extraordinary difficulties, which made him think that General Cass must have bribed the subordinate staff at the French Foreign Office. Ironically, Bulwer came to the conclusion that the map was probably not Franklin's.[76] Aberdeen's enquiries resulted in the discovery of three other maps, purporting to show the line agreed in 1783. Two of these, one in the King's Library of the British Museum and another, drawn by Faden, George III's Geographer and found in Paris, favoured the American claims; a third, discovered in the State Paper Office, supported the British claim. The British Museum map proved useful when it became apparent that the Whig government had known of its existence and had gone to some pains to keep it from the Americans. This effectively spiked the Whigs' guns when they attacked Webster for concealing the red-line map and the Conservatives for being deceived about it.[77]

After investigating the maps, Aberdeen admitted privately to Bulwer that he had less faith in the justice of the British claim than he had had for ten years.[78] More recent and academic research has tended to confirm the American claims.[79] If that is so, the Conservative government got a better bargain than they suspected in 1842. At the time they believed in the justice of their claims, but even so, the bargain was not a bad one. Britain preserved her communications along the north bank of the St John and removed the American frontier further from Quebec. The Americans got the boundary adjustments they wanted on the forty-fifth parallel and the free navigation of the St John.

The *Caroline* case was comparatively easily settled. In his instructions of 8 February Aberdeen ordered Ashburton to represent the destruction of the *Caroline* as a regrettable but necessary act of self-defence, which was entirely the responsibility of the British government.[80] On his own responsibility, Ashburton expressed regret that 'some explanation and apology for this occurrence was not immediately made'. Webster formally replied that the question should be 'the topic of no further discussion between the two Governments'.[81] On their side the British government wanted an assurance that there would be no repetition of the McLeod case. A Bill to cover such cases was introduced into Congress and, despite Ashburton's fears that it would be lost in the turmoil of domestic politics, passed on 29 August.[82]

After some hesitation, all the important points of the settlement were combined in one document, which the Senate approved on 20 August. Ratifications were exchanged in London on 13 October.[83] British opinion accepted the Ashburton–Webster Treaty quietly. Aberdeen wrote to Ashburton on 26 September, 'The Treaty was at first either well, or silently received.' Charles Greville recorded: 'Everybody was alive to the inconvenience of having this question left open, and there was a universal desire to settle our various differences with America upon such terms as would conduce to the restoration of good humour and good will.'[84]

Palmerston alone tried to whip up feeling against the government for the 'Ashburton capitulation'. He had little success even with his own party. The Whig leaders, Russell, Clarendon, Lansdowne, Spencer and Bedford all approved the Treaty. Palmerston launched a vigorous campaign in the *Morning Chronicle* but it soon faded away. Greville commented, 'He ought to have felt the public pulse . . . It is now evident that he will not carry the public nor even his own party with him.' *The Times*, which was anti-American in tone and originally received the Treaty coolly, rallied to the government's defence.[85] Palmerston returned to the attack at the beginning of the parliamentary session of 1843. Peel made a crushing reply, pointing out that the negotiations had made no progress during the ten years Palmerston was in office, and that when the Conservatives came to power they found Britain and the United States trembling on the verge of war. Palmerston had the final humiliation of seeing the debate come to an ignominious end when the House was counted out for lack of a quorum.[86]

NOTES

1. NLS, MS 1808, Aberdeen to Foster, 4 Mar. 1805.
2. Add. MSS 43127, Ouseley to Aberdeen, 31 Jan. 1846.
3. Cf. William Wordsworth's 'Men of the Western World' and 'To the Pennsylvanians'.
4. *The Times*, 15 Dec. 1845.
5. *B.F.S.P.* vol. 18, pp. 1249–57.
6. FO 5/358, Palmerston to Fox, No. 23, 24 Aug. 1841.
7. PP, XXXIX (1837–38) 1, 123; XXXII (1840) 457, 631; LXI (1843) 95, 'Correspondence relating to the Boundary . . .'
8. FO 5/358, Palmerston to Fox, 18 Aug. 1841; *B.F.S.P.*, vol. 29, pp. 1129–39
9. FO 5/358, Aberdeen to Fox, No. 1, 14 Sept. 1841; FO 5/363, Fox to Aberdeen, No. 102, Secret, 1 Oct. 1841.
10. Soulsby, p. 52; Corey, pp. 55–64.
11. Add. MSS 40459, Peel to Wellington. For a general study of British defence policy in relation to North America see K. Bourne, *Britain and the Balance of Power in North America 1815–1908.*
12. FO 5/358, Aberdeen to Fox, No. 5, 3 Nov., No. 8, 18 Nov. 1841.
13. FO 5/363–4, Fox to Aberdeen, No. 114, 13 Oct., No. 118, 26 Oct. 1841.
14. The Treaty was amended in 1833, *B.F.S.P.* vol. 18, pp. 161–4, vol. 20, pp. 286–95
15. *Messages and Papers of the Presidents*, vol. 4, p. 1931; Foote, pp. 152, 218–22.
16. AAE., Angleterre 658, Guizot to Ste Aulaire, No. 49, 29 Nov. 1841; Guizot, *Mémoires*, vol. 5, pp. 297–300, vol. 6, pp. 130–57.
17. American slavers had been stopped by mistake before but never on purpose, *B.F.S.P.*, vol. 29, p. 624; FO 84/376, Aberdeen to Everett, 20 Dec. 1841; cf. Lawrence, *Visitation and Search* and Du Bois, *The Suppression of the African Slave Trade*, p. 165.
18. FO 84/376, Stevenson to Palmerston, 16 Apr. 1841, Palmerston to Stevenson, 27 Aug. 1841

19. 'An Examination of the questions now in discussion . . . concerning the Right of Search.' It was published anonymously but everyone knew the author, Add. MSS 43129, Cowley to Aberdeen, 31 Jan. 1842.
20. Add. MSS 43062, O'Reilly to Peel, 1 Jan. 1842.
21. Cass to Guizot, 13 Feb. 1842, Webster to Cass, 5 Apr. 1842, Cass to Webster, 15 Feb. 1842, Webster, *Official Papers,* pp. 170–83; Add. MSS 43123, Ashburton to Aberdeen, 29 May, 14 June 1842, Cass to Webster, 12 Mar. 1842; Add. MSS 43129, Cowley to Aberdeen, 16 Feb. 1842; AAE, Angleterre 658, Ste Aulaire to Guizot, No. 26, 22 Apr. 1842, Guizot to Ste Aulaire, No. 32, 8 Jan. 1842.
22. *B.F.S.P.*, vol. 6, p. 4, vol. 12, pp. 38, 595, vol. 14, pp. 975–6.
23. It was of course much more extensive than the modern state of Oregon.
24. Statement and Counter-Statement of American Plenipotentiaries, 3, 20 Sept. 1844, Statement of British Plenipotentiaries, 12 Sept. 1844, *B.F.S.P.*, vol. 34, pp. 64–83, 93–130; Sir Travers Twiss, *The Oregon Question examined.*
25. Britain again suspected that the United States was casting covetous eyes on Cuba. FO 72/597, Aberdeen to Aston, No. 94 Conf., 25 Oct. 1842.
26. Add. MSS 43126, C. Elliot to Aberdeen, 15 Sept., 2 Nov. 1842; Add. MSS 43062, C. Power to Peel, 20 June 1842; cf. W. Kennedy's *The Rise, Progress and Prospects of the Republic of Texas*, and Kennedy's letters in FO 75/2–3.
27. Add. MSS 43126, Elliot to Aberdeen, 15 Sept. 1842; E. D. Adams, *British Diplomatic Correspondence, Texas 1836–46*, pp. 13–4, 21–5, 37–8.
28. *B.F.S.P.*, vol. 29, pp. 80–96, vol. 30, pp. 1127–8.
29. Add. MSS 43061, Peel to Aberdeen, 31 Oct., 17 Nov. 1841.
30. Hidy, *The House of Baring in American Trade and Finance*, pp. 48 ff; Add. MSS 40486, Ashburton to Peel, 29 Aug. 1841; Add. MSS 43123, Ashburton to Aberdeen, n.d. Sept. 1841, 22 Dec. 1841, 29 May, 14, 29 June 1842; Greville, vol. 2, pp. 71–2.
31. Add. MSS 43123, Ashburton to Aberdeen, 22 Dec. 1841; Add MSS. 40453, Aberdeen to Peel, 23 Dec. 1841; Everett to Webster, 31 Dec. 1841, Webster, *Official Papers,* pp. 33–4.
32. Add. MSS 40486, Ashburton to Peel, 29 Aug. 1841; Add. MSS 43123, Ashburton to Aberdeen, 22, 28 Dec. 1841, 9 Jan. 1842; Add. MSS 40453, Aberdeen to Peel, 29 Dec. 1841; Add. MSS 43061, Peel to Aberdeen, 30 Dec. 1841.
33. FO 84/376, Aberdeen to Stevenson, 13 Oct. 1841.
34. Add. MSS 43123, Ashburton to Aberdeen, n. d. Sept. 1841, 'I advise you . . . to wait for the new man who has the confidence of the Govt. which is decidedly friendly to us.'
35. FO 84/376, Aberdeen to Everett, 20 Dec. 1841.
36. Everett to Webster, 28 Dec. 1841, Webster, *Official Papers,* pp. 140–1; Add. MSS 43123, Ashburton to Aberdeen, 13 July 1842.
37. Webster gave Ashburton the lame explanation 'the publication would leave you and me nothing to settle', Add. MSS 43123, Ashburton to Aberdeen, 26 Apr. 1842.
38. FO 5/378, Aberdeen to Ashburton, No. 2, 8 Feb. 1842. Aberdeen expressed the tentative hope that the United States would join the Quintuple Treaty.
39. Add. MSS 43123, Ashburton Memorandum, 10 Feb. 1842; Add. MSS 43062, Peel to Aberdeen, 21 Feb. 1842; *Hansard*, 3rd ser., LXXVII 119–20.
40. FO 5/379, Ashburton to Aberdeen, No. 2, 25 Apr., No. 6, 12 May 1842 encl. Report of American naval officers.
41. FO 84/423, Aberdeen to Ashburton, No. 5, 26 May 1842.

42. Add. MSS 43123, Ashburton to Aberdeen, 14 June, 13 July 1842, Aberdeen to Ashburton, 2 July 1842; FO 5/380, Ashburton to Aberdeen, No. 18, 9 Aug. 1842.
43. He repeated his arguments in a despatch and private letter of 29 May; FO 5/379, Ashburton to Aberdeen, No. 7, 12 May No. 8, 29 May 1842; Add MSS 43123, Ashburton to Aberdeen, 29 May 1842.
44. FO 5/378, Aberdeen to Ashburton, No. 9, 3 June 1842; Add. MSS 43123, Aberdeen to Ashburton, 3 June, 18 July 1842.
45. FO 5/380, Webster to Ashburton, 9 Aug. 1842, Ashburton to Webster, 9 Aug. 1842, Ashburton to Aberdeen, No. 21, 9 Aug. 1842.
46. FO 5/380, Ashburton to Webster, 9 Aug. 1842.
47. FO 5/379, Ashburton to Aberdeen, No. 6, 12 May, No. 20, 9 Aug. 1842; Add. MSS 43123, Ashburton to Aberdeen, 29 June, 28 July, 9 Aug. 1842; Add. MSS 43123, Ashburton to Aberdeen, 29 June, 28 July, 9 Aug. 1842.
48. FO 5/380, Ashburton to Aberdeen, No. 20, 9 Aug. 1842 and enclosures.
49. FO 5/379–80, Ashburton to Aberdeen, No. 2, 25 Apr., No. 5, 28 Apr.and encl. No. 12, 29 June, No. 18, 9 Aug. 1842; Add. MSS 43123, Aberdeen to Ashburton, 3 Mar., 3 June 1842.
50. FO 5/378, Aberdeen to Ashburton, No. 2, 8 Feb. 1842.
51. Add. MSS 43060, Wellington to Aberdeen, 8 Feb. 1842 (3 letters).
52. Add. MSS 43123, Aberdeen to Ashburton, 9 Feb. 1842, Ashburton to Aberdeen, 10 Feb. 1842.
53. Add. MSS 43123, Memorandum, 14 Feb. 1842.
54. Add. MSS 43123, 'Memorandum on the North East Boundary'; Add. MSS 43062, 'Abstract of Boundary Correspondence'.
55. Add. MSS 43123, Aberdeen to Kempt etc., 24 Feb. 1842; from Kempt, 1 Mar., from Douglas, 7 Mar., from Seaton, 8 Mar., from Murray, 6 May 1842.
56. Add. MSS 43123, Aberdeen to Ashburton, 3 Mar. 1842.
57. FO 5/378, Aberdeen to Ashburton, No. 6, 31 Mar. 1842. On Rouse's point cf. Webster, *Official Papers*, pp. 43, 263–6.
58. Add. MSS 43060, Wellington to Aberdeen, 22 Mar. 1842; Add. MSS 43062, Peel to Aberdeen, 'Sunday morning', n.d. Mar. 1842.
59. Add. MSS 43060, Aberdeen to Wellington, 22, 23 Mar. 1842; Add. MSS 43123, Aberdeen to Ashburton, 1 Apr. 1842.
60. Add. MSS 43062, Peel to Aberdeen, 27 Mar. 1842; Add. MSS 43123, Aberdeen to Ashburton, 1 Apr. 1842.
61. Add. MSS 43123, Ashburton to Aberdeen, 26 Apr. 1842.
62. Add. MSS 43123, Ashburton to Aberdeen, 12 May 1842 and encls., Aberdeen to Ashburton, 3 June 1842.
63. Add. MSS 43123, Everett to Aberdeen, 14 May 1842 encl. Webster to Everett, 25 Apr. 1842.
64. Add. MSS 43062, Peel to Aberdeen, 16 May 1842.
65. Add. MSS 43160, Aberdeen to Wellington, 22 May 1842, Wellington to Aberdeen, 24 May 1842.
66. FO 5/378, Draft, 26 May 1842; Add. MSS 43123, Drafts, n.d. May 1842; FO 5/378, Aberdeen to Ashburton, No. 8, 26 May 1842; Add. MSS 43123, Aberdeen to Ashburton, 16, 20, 26 May 1842.
67. Add. MSS 43123, Ashburton to Aberdeen, 26 Apr., 14 June, 13, 28 July 1842; FO 5/379–80, Ashburton to Aberdeen, No. 10, 29 June, No. 17, 9 Aug. 1842.
68. FO 5/380, Ashburton to Aberdeen, No. 15, 28 July, No. 17, 9 Aug. 1842.

69. Add. MSS 43123, Ashburton to Aberdeen, 28 July 1842.

70. Add. MSS 43062, Peel to Aberdeen, 2 Oct. 1842 'Most Private'; Add. MSS 43123, Aberdeen to Ashburton, 26 Sept. 1842.

71. Add. MSS 43123, Ashburton to Aberdeen, 9, 13 Aug. 1842; cf. Winsor pp. 17–21, Miller, *Treaties and other international acts of the United States of America*, vol. 4, pp. 404–6.

72. *Hansard*, 3rd ser., LXVII, 1247–51.

73. Add. MSS 43123, Ashburton to Aberdeen, 14 June, 9, 13 Aug. 1842, Aberdeen to Ashburton, 2 July 1842.

74. Add. MSS 43123, Ashburton to Aberdeen, 9 Aug. 1842; Add. MSS 40453, Aberdeen to Peel, 17 Jan. 1843.

75. In January 1843 Ashburton wrote, 'I have reason to believe it [the secret] has reached Broadlands where the great statesman [Palmerston] has said that he has got *something* to blow the capitulation out of the water.' Add. MSS 43123, Ashburton to Aberdeen, 21 Jan. 1843.

76. Add. MSS 43131, Bulwer to Aberdeen, 13, 17, 18, 20, 24, 26, 27, (2) Feb., 6 Mar. 1843.

77. Add. MSS 43131, Bulwer to Aberdeen, 17, 18, 19 Feb. 1843, Aberdeen to Bulwer, 3 Mar. 1843; FO 5/340, Panizzi to Palmerston, 29 Mar., 1 Apr. 1839, Palmerston to the Trustees of the British Museum, 1 Apr. 1839; *Hansard*, 3rd ser., LXVI, 1226–8, LXVII, 1249. Greville's story that the State Paper map was sent to Ashburton during the negotiations (Greville, vol. 2, pp. 101–3) is wrong. It was found in Feb. 1843.

78. Add. MSS 43131, Aberdeen to Bulwer, 3 Mar. 1843.

79. See in particular W. Ganong, 'Monograph on the evolution of the boundaries of the Province of New Brunswick', *Trans. Royal Society of Canada*, 1901–02, pp. 140–447.

80. FO 5/378, Aberdeen to Ashburton, No. 2, 8 Feb. 1842.

81. FO 5/380, Ashburton to Aberdeen, No. 14, 28 July 1842 and encls.; Add. MSS 43123, Ashburton to Aberdeen, 28 July 1842.

82. FO 5/380, Ashburton to Aberdeen, No. 24, 31 Aug. 1842.

83. FO 5/380, Ashburton to Aberdeen, No. 23, 13 Aug., No. 24, 31 Aug. 1842; FO 5/376, Aberdeen to Fox, No. 25, 18 Oct. 1842.

84. Add. MSS 43123, Aberdeen to Ashburton, 26 Sept. 1842; Greville, vol. 2, p. 109.

85. Greville, vol. 2, pp. 105–6, 109–11, 130–1; Bulwer, vol. 3, pp. 113–8; Russell, *Later Correspondence*, vol. 1, pp. 58–62; *Morning Chronicle*, 19–27 Sept 1842; *The Times*, 24 Aug – 23 Sept. 1842.

86. *Hansard*, 3rd ser., LXVII, 1162–1252, 1313, (21, 22, Mar. 1843).

CHAPTER TWENTY

The Oregon Crisis

Peel had declared in his reply to Palmerston that, for very small sacrifices, Britain had achieved a 'permanent and satisfactory peace'.[1] Was he right?

The north-east boundary settlement ultimately proved satisfactory to both parties. The *Caroline* and *Creole* cases were finally laid to rest and the extradition arrangements proved their worth. The slave trade clauses had a less happy sequel. The Americans assumed that the joint cruising arrangements would entirely supersede the right of visit, but the British had never envisaged giving up the right of investigating the *bona fides* of Spanish or other slavers who ran up the Stars and Stripes on the approach of a British cruiser. The matter became the subject of acrimonious dispute again in the winter of 1842–3, and Aberdeen, rather weakly, conceded that a ship flying the American colours should be visited only when suspicion amounted to certainty. In return, Webster promised that he would not defend a proven slaver.[2] In fact only one American ship, the *Roderick Dhu*, was visited between 1842 and 1846. More seriously, the Americans never maintained the squadron they had promised on the West African coast.

Peel was wrong when he told the House that a 'permanent' peace had been achieved. Ashburton was extremely angry when he realised that the Americans had not responded as he expected to his conciliatory mission. He told Aberdeen that in private life one would 'avoid further communication' in the face of such duplicity, but admitted that this was not practicable when dealing with '20 million of restless people'.[3] Both Ashburton and Aberdeen had to face the fact that, however good their personal relations with Webster or Everett, international relations were conducted according to rules different from those which obtained in private life. The American public remained suspicious and sometimes hostile, and within three years Britain and the United States were again on the verge of war as a result of the one major question which the Ashburton negotiations had left unresolved, the Oregon boundary.

The continued strain in Anglo-American relations manifested itself first over the question of Texas. Mexico and Texas were still in a state of war and, by Hamilton's second treaty, Britain had committed herself to proffer her good offices to both parties but Britain became more directly involved as the result of a naval incident which foreshadowed the much more famous *Alabama* case.

The Mexicans, acting through the British firm of Lizardi and Company, ordered two war-steamers, the *Guadeloupe* to be built at Liverpool and the *Montezuma* at London. To make matters worse the Mexicans wanted crews as well as ships and signed on two Royal Naval captains and a number of British sailors.[4] The matter came to the attention of the British government when Lizardi and Company requested permission to arm the vessels. Aberdeen hesitated before replying and Ashbel Smith, the Texan chargé in London, formally protested and asked the British government to detain the ships. Aberdeen, however, was impressed by the argument that it would be unfair to deny help to Mexico when Texas was clearly receiving help from the United States. After consulting the Admiralty, he informed Thomas Murphy, the Mexican agent in London, correctly, if rather casuistically, that it was illegal for private ships to be armed in British ports but that there could be no objection if the two vessels carried the arms as cargo and mounted them later.[5] During these discussions the *Guadeloupe* slipped away from Liverpool on 4 July 1842. According to Ashbel Smith she was 'fully armed and equipped as a vessel of war, manned with a war complement of British seamen, commanded by Capt. Charlewood of the British Navy'. Smith protested strongly and Cobden raised the matter in the Commons. The *Montezuma* was detained for some weeks at London but, after Murphy protested that he had followed Aberdeen's instructions and shipped her arms as cargo, she was allowed to sail in September. Smith's continual expostulations elicited only the promise that the British naval officers on board the *Guadeloupe* would be ordered to leave her on pain of being dismissed the service.[6] There was an extraordinary incident in the summer of 1843 when the British crew of the *Guadeloupe* hoisted the British flag before engaging a Texan squadron, protesting that they would fight under no flag but their own.[7] But for the fact that the two ships saw little action and the Texans had their own reasons for avoiding official complaints, the affair could have become more serious than the *Alabama*.

The Americans saw Aberdeen's attitude as biased in favour of the Mexicans. In fact, at this time Aberdeen was seriously exasperated by the Mexican government's arbitrary fiscal policy and their cavalier treatment of foreigners. What Aberdeen really wanted to see was an independent Texas, recognised by both Mexico and the United States. He instructed Richard Pakenham, the British Minister to Mexico, to urge the Mexicans to recognise Texas since they could never hope to win it back against the opposition of the United States. Although Aberdeen pointed out the advantages of Texas as a buffer state, the Mexicans received the suggestion coldly.[8]

In August 1842 the Texans proposed a triple mediation by Britain, the United States and France. The French took up the suggestion with Britain but Aberdeen thought it had little chance of success when the relations of Mexico with the United States were so bad. A truce was secured in the summer of 1843. In July 1843, Aberdeen, under pressure from the World Convention of the British and Foreign Anti-Slavery Society, meeting in London, suggested to the British chargé in Mexico, Percy Doyle, that Mexico should make abolition a condition of recognising Texan independence. Brougham raised the subject in the Lords. Aberdeen refused information but assured the House that he was not indifferent and that the government would press the matter 'by means of urging the negotiations, as well as by every other means in their power'.[9]

British interest and Aberdeen's deliberately guarded language created the wildest suspicions in the United States. The American press threatened that any British interference would 'rouse the whole American people to arms like one vast nest of hornets'. The government asked for explanations. This led eventually to the famous Pakenham–Calhoun correspondence of 1844 between Richard Pakenham, then British Minister in Washington, and the Secretary of State, John Calhoun. Calhoun said bluntly that Britain could do what she liked in her own colonies but when she declared her aim to be world-wide abolition, other nations must take measures for their own safety. To insist on abolition in Texas would make that country hostile to the United States and give Britain opportunities to intervene in the Southern States. Edward Everett, however, assured his government that British objectives in Texas were commercial rather than abolitionist. 'Her Texan policy', he wrote, 'was to build up a power independent of the United States who could raise enough cotton to supply the world.'[10]

Britain's supposed commercial ambitions in Texas were only slightly less distasteful to the United States than a crusade for the abolition of slavery would have been. The agitation against Britain was therefore easily and skilfully exploited to renew United States' interest in annexation. American feeling was deeply divided but President Tyler, as a Southerner who had already quarrelled with his own party, had everything to gain by a bold stroke. Without directly mentioning annexation, his Annual Message of December 1843 spoke of American interest in Texas and warned against foreign interference. For the next twelve months Aberdeen tried to persuade the French to consider an Anglo-French guarantee to the Texans. At one point he went very far indeed, suggesting to the Mexican agent, Thomas Murphy, that Britain 'irait jusqu'aux dernières extremités pour soutenir sa [i.e. Texan] résolution contre annexation'. The French, however, were wary of anything which might embroil them with the United States and the Mexicans refused to accept the necessary pre-condition of themselves recognising Texas.[11]

The United States, however, paid little attention to British or French opinion. Resolutions in favour of annexation passed through Congress in February 1845 and received the Presidential assent on 1 March. The European Powers could now only rely on Texan feeling, which they believed to be still hostile to annexation. The British agent, Charles Elliot, and his French colleague, Dubois de Saligny, hastened to Washington-on-the-Brazos, the temporary capital of Texas, in order to arrive there before Major Donnelson and the American proposals. They persuaded the Texans not to accept these proposals for ninety days, while Elliot went to Vera Cruz in a final effort to induce the Mexicans to recognise Texan independence.[12] Elliott succeeded but it was too late. The Texan Congress voted in favour of annexation in June and agreement was finally reached with the United States in November.[13]

Aberdeen's policy had been based on the assumption that the Texans did not want to be annexed. He was now embarrassed and anxious to extricate himself from an awkward situation. He applauded Elliot's energy but expressed fears that his journey to Mexico would make 'English agency appear too active, and too hostile to the United States'. He was convinced that the question was not serious enough to 'lead to any collision or serious difference between this country and the United States'.[14] As Mexico and the United States drifted towards war Aberdeen refused to mediate, although he was urged to do so by Charles Bankhead, the new British Minister in Mexico.[15] The Mexicans, in despair, even offered to cede California to Britain, if she would protect it from American attack. Lord Ellenborough, now returned from India and installed as First Lord of the Admiralty, was enthusiastic, holding San Francisco to be 'the key of the N.W. Coast of America'. There were some British settlers in California and the magnitude of the offer tempted even Aberdeen for a few days. But Peel was cold and more prudent counsels prevailed.[16] Matters were allowed to take their course and at the end of the Mexican war the United States gained California, as well as confirmation of her position in Texas.

In the last resort Britain backed down to the United States over Texas because American interests there were immediate and her government determined. British interests were marginal and her government disinclined to jeopardise their general policy for them. Much the same was true of the last great dispute of this period between Britain and America, the Oregon question. There was a direct link between the Texan and the Oregon issues in American domestic politics. Democrats from the north and west, who saw the annexation of Texas as a victory for the slave-owning Southern States, wanted Oregon to restore the balance. Manifest Destiny fever was gaining strength. 'Nature and nature's God', said a writer in the *Southern Quarterly Review*, 'seem to have decreed Oregon as our heritage.' 'Independent of any parchment or paper title', wrote Governor Reynolds of Illinois, 'Oregon is bound to compose part of this confederacy.'[17] At the Democratic Party Convention in Baltimore in May 1844, Texas and Oregon were linked together. The Convention declared '. . . the re-occupation of Oregon and the re-annexation of Texas at the earliest practicable period are great American measures, which this convention recommends to the candid support of the Democracy of the Union.'[18] By 1845 there were 5,000 American settlers in Oregon compared with about 700 Britons, but most of them were still south of the Columbia River. Nevertheless, in 1843 the Cincinnati Convention of the Democratic Party had passed a resolution that, 'The right of the United States to the Oregon territory, from 42° to 54° 40 north latitude, is unquestionable.' This represented a formidable extension of the American claim because the United States had never before seriously claimed the territory north of the forty-ninth parallel.[19]

Ashburton and Webster had dropped the Oregon issue in 1842 lest it compromise the settlement of what then seemed more urgent questions. Aberdeen later made several attempts to resume negotiations, either through Henry Fox in Washington or Edward Everett in London, and he was indignant when President Tyler implied in his Annual Messages of 1842 and 1843 that it was the British who were hanging back.[20] He did, however, miss one important opportunity when, unexpectedly, in October 1843 the Americans agreed to send full powers to treat to Everett. Aberdeen had just decided to recall Henry Fox and transfer Richard Pakenham from Mexico to Washington with special powers to negotiate and he told the Americans that his new diplomatic arrangements made it desirable that the Oregon negotiations should take place in Washington.[21] The further delay was unfortunate because time was not on Britain's side.

Aberdeen sent Pakenham his instructions in December 1843. He revived a proposal, previously made in 1826, that the boundary should run along the forty-ninth parallel from the Rockies to the north-east branch of the Columbia River (sometimes called McGillivray's River), then down the centre of that river and of the Columbia River proper to the Pacific Ocean. The Americans were offered the further inducement of free ports north of that line but Aberdeen's despatch closed with a warning that Britain was prepared to defend her rights.[22]

Pakenham did not arrive in Washington until 19 February and negotiations were further delayed by the death of the American Secretary of State, Abel Upshur, who was killed in an explosion aboard the US warship *Princeton*. His successor, John Calhoun, did not enter upon his duties for some weeks. In the meantime, Aberdeen had become convinced that they had no hope of achieving the settlement proposed in his despatch. On 4 March he wrote to Pakenham privately, telling him to try, without committing his government, to get a proposal from the Americans for the forty-ninth parallel to be the boundary to the Pacific, with safeguards for Vancouver Island, which was already settled, free navigation on the Columbia and free ports, this time on the American side of the frontier.[23] When this failed Pakenham was instructed to propose arbitration.[24]

But by this time the Tyler administration was in no position to take any decisive step. In November an almost unknown Westerner, James K. Polk of Tennessee, was elected President in the Democratic interest. Polk was a rabid product of 'Manifest Destiny', limited, partisan and extremely determined. As a Westerner he was deeply interested in the Oregon issue and never for a moment doubted the righteousness of his cause. He had won the election on the bellicose slogan '54° 40' or fight'.

Peel was convinced that threats must be answered by threats. He told Aberdeen, 'An additional frigate at the mouth of the Columbia, and a small artillery force on shore, would aid most materially the resident British settlers.'[25] Aberdeen too felt that only firmness would save the day. After a belligerent Inaugural Speech by Polk, Clarendon asked Aberdeen a question in the Lords by arrangement, which gave the Foreign Secretary a chance to state the British position. He appealed for calm. The 1827 Convention could not be terminated without a year's notice and he still hoped for successful negotiations, but he continued:

No man ever filled the high situation which I have the honour unworthily to hold, who felt more ardently desirous than I do to preserve to the country the blessings of peace, or who would make greater sacrifices, consistent with propriety, to maintain it . . . But our honour is a substantial property that we can never neglect . . . we possess rights which, in our opinion, are clear and unquestionable; and, by the blessing of God, and with your support, these rights we are fully prepared to maintain.

It was practically the only occasion in his life when Aberdeen sat down amidst 'loud and general applause'.[26]

The British government took a number of military precautions. Ships were detached from the Pacific fleet to visit the west coast of America. The Colonial Office and the Admiralty were asked about the defence of the Great Lakes and Sir George Simpson of the Hudson Bay Company prepared a memorandum on the defence of Oregon.[27] The issues of war or peace now depended on the Americans and they were not quite so bellicose as their speeches suggested. The new Secretary of State, James Buchanan, told Pakenham that he thought a solution could be found on 'the principle of giving and taking'. Pakenham thought Buchanan probably meant to propose 'the parallel of 49 to the Sea, as a Boundary, leaving to Great Britain the entire possession of Van Couver's Island with an agreement for the free Navigation of the Columbia River'.[28]

Aberdeen replied to Pakenham in a despatch and a private letter of 18 April. The despatch instructed Pakenham, if Buchanan did make this proposal, to put forward as a counterproposal that 'in addition to the Terms already offered by us [in Aberdeen's despatches of December 1843], we are prepared to allow all the Ports within the disputed Territory south of 49° North Latitude, whether on the mainland or on Vancouver's Island, to be made perpetually free Ports' but warned him 'Beyond this degree of compromise, Her Majesty's Government could not consent to go.' That Aberdeen did not really regard this as Britain's last word is proved by the accompanying private letter. In this he told Pakenham that he would not regard Buchanan's expected proposal as 'perfectly inadmissable . . . by some modification it might be accepted'.[29] Not for the first time, Aberdeen had transmitted his real views by a private letter which was difficult to reconcile with his public despatch. Unfortunately, Pakenham (like Stratford Canning in 1829) was left confused as to what course of policy he was really expected to pursue.

Pakenham had also raised the possibility of the Americans accepting arbitration, if one of the Great Powers of Europe would propose it. Aberdeen, acting on this hint, sounded out the French government. Guizot was willing, even eager, to co-operate. He wrote to Ste Aulaire:

N'hésitez pas à entrer dans le sens de lord Aberdeen s'il vous témoigne de nouveau le désire que nous prenions quelque part à l'arrangement de la question de l'Oregon . . . Malgré les embarras du role d'arbitre, il nous conviendrait ici . . . car la guerre entre l'Angleterre et les États Unis serait un grand mal pour tout le monde, et pour nous plus que personne.[30]

The Americans, however, preferred to continue with direct negotiations and on 16 July Buchanan communicated proposals to Pakenham, slightly less favourable than Pakenham had expected. Buchanan proposed a division of the territory along the forty-ninth parallel, 'from the Rocky Mountains to the Pacific Ocean', with free ports on the southern tip of Vancouver Island. Pakenham thought that they fell so far short of the 'ultimatum' in Aberdeen's despatch of 18 April that he rejected them without reference to his government. The British government learnt of this in the middle of August, while Aberdeen was in Germany with the Queen.[31]

Peel was critical of Pakenham's action but it was some time before the British government realised the full implications. They were most anxious to stand well in the eyes of the rest of the world, and particularly of France, in the event of a rupture with the United States. The Americans now took full advantage of the opportunity to make the British seem unreasonable. On 30 August Buchanan formally withdrew the proposal with many expressions of righteous indignation at the way Pakenham had treated it and Polk insisted that they were no longer bound by any compromise proposals and should hold out for 54° 40'.[32]

Aberdeen felt compelled to disavow Pakenham's action. He did so officially by a despatch of 3 October, with which he sent a private letter advising Pakenham to see Buchanan and offer to withdraw his note of rejection, in the hope that Buchanan would withdraw his reply.[33] These communications distressed Pakenham who replied privately at great length, demonstrating that Buchanan's proposals fell far short of anything he was authorised to accept by Aberdeen's despatches – or even by his private letters, which Aberdeen had himself regarded as representing extreme concessions. Pakenham concluded with a passionate plea to be recalled since, having misunderstood Aberdeen in such an important matter, he no longer had any confidence in his own judgement. 'For God's sake', he wrote, 'remove me from this country, in which nothing but pain and mortification can henceforth attend my course.' Aberdeen, perhaps uneasily aware that his own letters had contributed to the misunderstanding, refused to do anything of the kind and told Peel that he would 'pacify Pakenham' – an odd phrase in the circumstances.[34]

The American government was now divided about its policy but President Polk kept up a facade of complete intransigence. In his Annual Message, delivered on 2 December 1845, he recommended Congress to give notice of the termination of the 1827 Convention and spoke of the 'extraordinary and wholly inadmissible demands of the British Government'. Britain was still concerned about international reaction. The possibility of a Franco-American combination still troubled them. Croker wrote in panic to Aberdeen, 'For God's sake, end it; for if anything were to happen to *Louis Philippe*, we shall have an American war immediately, and a French one just after, a rebellion in Ireland, real starvation in the manufacturing districts, and a twenty per-cent complication in the shape of Income Tax.'[35]

In fact the French government remained friendly throughout the crisis and French co-operation at this time was the most tangible diplomatic fruit of the entente with France for which Aberdeen had sacrificed so much in other directions. Even so Guizot was extremely cautious in what he said in public. Henry Reeve, who was in Paris, assured Aberdeen that Guizot would come out openly in British support. In the event he only declared France's intention of remaining completely neutral. Even this made the American Minister in Paris, William King, accuse him of 'servile complaisance towards England' and similar views, expressed through the French Minister in Washington, Alphonse Pageot, had, according to Pageot, 'a sobering effect'.[36]

On the face of it things were at their most dangerous at the beginning of 1846. Pakenham had had no success in persuading Buchanan to withdraw the letters they had exchanged the previous summer. Aberdeen again offered arbitration and the Americans again refused it. An impasse seemed to have been reached.

But a number of things combined to sober American opinion still further. The first was the realisation that the British meant what they said. Britain substantially increased her military and naval budgets for the year 1846–47.[37] When Louis McLane, the new American Minister in London, raised the matter with Aberdeen, the Foreign Secretary told him that, in view of the Americans' attitude, he would 'feel it his duty to withdraw the opposition he had hitherto uniformly made to the adoption of measures, founded upon the contingency of war with the United States'. McLane understood that this would mean the immediate preparation of thirty sail of the line, as well as steamers and other warships.[38] McLane's despatch caused a sensation in Washington but it would have been less effective but for other pressures. War with Mexico was now imminent. The American army was far from prepared. The Secretary for War reported to the President that they had only one regiment available to garrison the 2,000 miles of frontier from Maine to Lake Superior. The Easterners had always opposed a war with Britain which would ruin their commerce, while the Southerners, once they had gained Texas, lost interest in Oregon, despite the bargain struck at Baltimore. Polk had at last to admit that James Buchanan, who had been urging caution, was right. The American people would not fight for the land north of the forty-ninth parallel. Within a few days of the receipt of McLane's despatch Polk agreed that a new proposition, slightly more favourable than the American offer of the previous July, should be sent to London.[39]

Aberdeen was informed of the changing climate of opinion in America by a number of private correspondents, including Edward Everett, who had now returned to Boston. Everett, however, warned him that 'the 49th degree for the mainland, and you to have the island' was the most any administration could agree to.[40] When the Senate on 16 April, while endorsing the President's request for a termination of the 1827 Convention, practically invited a resumption of negotiations, Aberdeen immediately sent a draft convention to Pakenham. This proposed that the boundary should run along the forty-ninth parallel but with a deviation to leave the whole of Vancouver Island to Britain. The navigation of the Columbia River from the forty-ninth parallel to the sea was to be 'free and open to the Hudson's Bay Company and to all British subjects trading with the same'. The property rights of the Hudson's Bay Company and of other British subjects south of the forty-ninth parallel were to be safeguarded.[41]

Pakenham communicated this proposition to Buchanan officially on 6 June. The Senate agreed to the British proposals on 12 June. The Treaty was signed on the 15th and ratified by the Senate on the 18th.[42] This sudden haste, after years of intransigence, was mainly due to the Mexican war but it also owed something to the fear that the British Conservative government would fall and Aberdeen be succeeded by Palmerston. It is possible that the British repeal of the Corn Laws did something to soften American feeling. Everett encouraged Aberdeen in his belief that this would be so and this led to a curious incident. His son's testimony leaves no doubt that Aberdeen gave premature information to Delane, which Delane immediately published in *The Times*, early in December 1845, of the Conservative government's intention to repeal the Corn Laws. Charles Greville certainly believed that this was done with the intention of influencing American opinion and Aberdeen wrote to Everett a little later that he thought it would have a good influence in the Western states which 'although the most warlike, are also the most agricultural'.[43]

The news of the signing of the Treaty arrived in London on the morning of 29 June, just in time for Peel to announce it in his final speech as Prime Minister. He dwelt with pleasure on the fact that the two governments had 'by moderation, by mutual compromise, averted the dreadful calamity of war, between two nations of kindred origin and common language, the breaking out of which might have involved the civilised world in general conflict'.[44] Congratulations poured in from many quarters and the opposition made no attempt to attack the Oregon Treaty as they had attacked the Ashburton–Webster Treaty. Palmerston, who had whipped up the criticism in 1842, knew that, if he was to succeed Aberdeen as Foreign Secretary, he must moderate his tone. Moreover, a clever propaganda campaign, organised by Edward Everett and an American business man, Joshua Bates, had convinced the British public, which knew little about Oregon, that the forty-ninth parallel would be a very fair settlement.[45]

In fact, Britain made greater concessions in Oregon than on the north-east boundary. Since the area really in dispute was not that between 42° N and 54° 40′ N – that was an artifically whipped-up election cry in which many Americans did not themselves believe – but that between the Columbia River and 49° N, Britain had conceded almost everything that was at stake. There were two reasons for this. The first was that the United States had settlers ready to pour into the area whereas the British did not. At a time when Canada was disaffected and separatist theories had a wide currency, the British government was not interested in extending British territory in North America. Considerations of prestige alone prevented them from abandoning the Oregon territory altogether. The outbursts of Jingoism in America during 1844–66 actually made a settlement more difficult because the British government felt unable to make concessions whilst patently under pressure, even when it had little objection to the substance of the concessions. Peel pointed out that a single month of Anglo-American war would have been 'more costly than the value of the whole territory',[46] but even Aberdeen had no doubt the national honour was a 'substantial property' for which they must, in the last resort, fight.

The second reason why the British came to terms was that, whereas to the United States, North American issues were the only ones which really mattered, to Britain they were only one part of a global pattern of conflicts. Aberdeen was prepared to yield on individual issues in order to achieve his overall objective of security for British interests, based on general harmony. British public opinion did not care greatly about American issues. His policy was to be more severely tested in Europe.

NOTES

1. *Hansard*, 3rd ser., LXVII, 1242–7 (21 Mar. 1843)
2. *Messages and Papers of the Presidents*, vol. 5, pp. 2048–9; Add. MSS 43123, Ashburton to Aberdeen, 1, 6 Jan. 1843; *Hansard*, 3rd ser., LXVI, 88–91 (2 Feb. 1843); FO 5/390, Aberdeen to Fox, No. 2, 18 Jan. 1843; Add. MSS 43123, Webster to Everett, 27 Apr. 1843; Webster to Everett, 28 Mar. 1843, Everett to Webster, 27 Apr. 1843, Curtis, *Life of Daniel Webster*, vol. 2, pp. 165–6.
3. Add. MSS 43123, Ashburton to Aberdeen, 21 Jan. 1843.
4. Garrison, *Diplomatic Correspondence of the Republic of Texas*, vol. 3, pp. 960–1003, 1015–7; FO 75/4, Aberdeen to Elliot, No. 10, 16 July 1842.
5. FO 50/157, Aberdeen to Murphy, 11 May 1842, 31 May 1842 (not sent until 15 July 1842); FO 75/5, Smith to Aberdeen, 14 June 1842; Garrison, vol. 3, pp. 960–2, 972–4, 997–9, 1030–1.
6. FO 75/5, Smith to Aberdeen, 14, 19 Sept., 10, 19 Oct., 12 Dec. 1842, Aberdeen to Smith, 16 July, 27 Sept., 8 Nov. 1842; FO 50/157, Aberdeen to Murphy, 22, 23 Aug. 1842, Murphy to Aberdeen, 17, 20 Aug. 1842; *Hansard*, 3rd ser., LXV 964 (2 Aug. 1842).
7. FO 50/163, Doyle to Aberdeen, No. 59, 29 Aug. 1843.
8. FO 50/152, Aberdeen to Pakenham, No. 26, 1 July, No. 34, 15 July 1842; FO 50/154–5, Pakenham to Aberdeen, No. 80, 29 Aug. 1842, No. 90, 29 Sept. 1842.
9. FO 27/646, Aberdeen to Cowley, No. 147, 15 Oct. 1842; *The Times*, 21 June 1843; FO 50/160, Aberdeen to Doyle, No. 19, 31 July 1843; *Hansard*, 3rd ser., LXXI, 915–8.
10. Washington, *Madisonian*, 24 June 1843; FO 5/404, Pakenham to Aberdeen, No. 36, 28 Apr. 1844; Senate Executive Documents 28 Cong. 1 Sess. vol. 27, Doc 341; PP, LXIV (1847–8) 125, 'Correspondence . . . relative to the General Abolition of Slavery in Texas and throughout the World'.
11. FO 27/689, Aberdeen to Cowley, No. 16, 12 Jan., No. 60, 1 Mar. 1844; Add. MSS 43154, Murphy's Memorandum (in French with English corrections) encl. in Aberdeen to Pakenham, No. 24, 3 June 1844.
12. FO 75/13, Elliot to Aberdeen, No. 14, 22 Mar., Secret, 2 Apr. 1845; Add. MSS 43126, Elliot to Aberdeen, 24 Mar., 3 Apr. 1845.
13. Add. MSS 43126, Elliot to Aberdeen, 23 May 1845; FO 75/13, Elliot to Aberdeen, No. 16, 30 May, No. 17, 12 June, No. 31, 14 Nov., Secret, 26 Nov. 1845.

14. Add. MSS 40455, Aberdeen to Peel, 11 May 1845; Add. MSS 43045, Aberdeen to Victoria, 27 Mar. 1845; FO 75/13, Aberdeen to Elliot, No. 10, 3 July 1845.
15. FO 50/164, Bankhead to Aberdeen, 30 Oct. 1845; Add. MSS 43065, Peel to Aberdeen, 14 Nov. 1845.
16. FO 50/185, Bankhead to Aberdeen, No. 78, 30 July 1845; Add. MSS 43198, Ellenborough to Aberdeen, 16 May 1846; Add. MSS 40455, Aberdeen to Peel, 23, 25 Sept., 3 Oct. 1845; Add. MSS 43064, Peel to Aberdeen, 24 Sept. 1845.
17. Quoted in Weinberg, *Manifest Destiny*, p. 140.
18. FO 5/405, Pakenham to Aberdeen, No. 54, 29 May 1844; Jacobs, pp. 197–208.
19. FO 5/392, Fox to Aberdeen, No. 97, 28 July 1843; Jacobs, pp. 169–76.
20. Add. MSS 43123, Ashburton to Aberdeen, 1, 6 Jan. 1843; Add. MSS 40453, Aberdeen to Peel, 13 Oct. 1842, 10 Jan. 1843; FO 5/376, Aberdeen to Fox, No. 25, 18 Oct. 1842, No. 2, 18 Jan., No. 35, 18 Aug. 1843; FO 5/391, Fox to Aberdeen, No. 20 Conf. 24 Feb. 1843.
21. Add. MSS 43123, Everett to Aberdeen, 1 Nov. 1843; Everett to Upshur, Conf., 2 Nov. 1843, Miller, vol. 5, pp. 22–4.
22. FO 5/390, Aberdeen to Pakenham, No. 10, 28 Dec. 1843.
23. Add. MSS 43123, Aberdeen to Pakenham, 4 Mar. 1844.
24. FO 5/403, Aberdeen to Pakenham, No. 45, 1 Nov. 1844.
25. Add. MSS 43064, Peel to Aberdeen, 23 Feb. 1845.
26. *Hansard*, 3rd ser., LXXIX, 115–24 (4 Apr. 1845)
27. Add. MSS 40461, Wellington to Aberdeen, 8 Apr. 1845; Add. MSS 43123, Aberdeen to Pakenham, 2 Apr. 1845; FO 5/540, Addington to Admiralty, 5, 8 Mar. 1845, to Colonial Office, 3 Apr. 1845, Simpson's Memorandum, 29 Mar. 1845; FO 5/457 *passim*, reports of Lieuts. Warre and Vavasour.
28. FO 5/425, Pakenham to Aberdeen, No. 40, 29 Mar. 1845.
29. FO 5/423, Aberdeen to Pakenham, No. 22, 18 Apr. 1845; Add. MSS 43123, Aberdeen to Pakenham, 18 Apr. 1845.
30. Guizot Papers 42 AP 8, Guizot to Ste Aulaire, 19 May 1845.
31. FO 5/426, Pakenham to Aberdeen, No. 87, 29 July 1845 encl. Buchanan to Pakenham, 12 July 1845; Add. MSS 43064, Peel to Aberdeen, 19 Aug. 1845.
32. FO 5/428, Pakenham to Aberdeen, No. 95, 13 Sept. 1845 encl. Buchanan to Pakenham, 30 Aug. 1845; Polk, *Diary*, vol. 1, pp. 1–12.
33. FO 5/423, Aberdeen to Pakenham, No. 64, 3 Oct. 1845; Add. MSS 43123, Aberdeen to Pakenham, 3 Oct. 1845.
34. Add. MSS 43123, Pakenham to Aberdeen, 28 Oct., 29 Dec. 1845; Aberdeen to Pakenham, 3 Dec. 1845; Add. MSS 40455, Aberdeen to Peel, 21 Nov. 1845.
35. Add. MSS 43239, Croker to Aberdeen, 13 May 1846.
36. Add. MSS 43245, Reeves to Aberdeen, 26 Dec. 1845, 4, 6, 19, 14, 22, 24 Jan. 1846; Cowley, *Diary*, pp. 298–9; AAE, États Unis 102, Guizot to Pageot, No. 29, 27 Jan. 1846, Pageot to Guizot, No. 114, 26 Feb. 1846.
37. PP, XXVI (1846) 40, 183.
38. McLane to Buchanan, 3 Feb. 1846, Miller, vol. 5, pp. 57–9.
39. Buchanan to McLane, 26 Feb. 1846, Miller, vol. 5, pp. 60–2; Polk, *Diary*, vol. 1, pp. 241–53; Executive Documents, 29 Cong., 1 Sess., vol. 1, p. 193.
40. Add. MSS 43123, Everett to Aberdeen, 15 Nov., 10 Dec. 1845, 28 Jan., 15 June 1846.
41. FO 5/445, Aberdeen to Pakenham, Nos 18 and 19, 18 May 1846.
42. FO 5/449, Pakenham to Aberdeen, No. 68, 7 June, No. 77, 13 June, No. 79, 23 June 1846; Add. MSS 43123, Pakenham to Aberdeen, 7, 13 June 1846.

43. Stanmore, *Sidney Herbert*, vol. 1, pp. 61–3; *The Times*, 4 Dec. 1845; Greville, vol. 2, p. 310; Add. MSS 43123, Aberdeen to Everett, 3 Jan. 1846.

44. *Hansard*, 3rd ser., LXXXVII, 1049–53 (29 June 1846).

45. See pp. 300–1.

46. *Hansard*, 3rd ser., LXXXVII, 1052.

CHAPTER TWENTY-ONE

Britain's 'natural rival'

A settlement with the United States was imperative but to propose the re-establishment of an understanding with France was unexpected policy from a Conservative Foreign Secretary. Alliance with France was traditionally a Whig, not a Tory, policy. Aberdeen himself had disapproved of the close relations between France and Britain in the early 1830s and had expressed his views both in Parliament and to Princess Lieven. As late as February 1840, he complained that, if the Portendic case (a quarrel arising out of a French blockade on the west coast of Africa) was the result of the Whigs' much vaunted French alliance, 'that alliance bore bitter fruit, as far . . . as the commerce and prosperity of the country were concerned'.[1]

Although Aberdeen's suspicions of France lessened as the revolutionary fears generated by 1830 were not fulfilled, no Conservative leader had ever advocated too close a connection with France. The attack on Palmerston's Eastern policy was led by radicals and Whigs, not by Conservatives. In January 1841 Peel deprecated 'an intimate alliance of an exclusive nature between this country and France', and Wellington commented, 'He had heard a good deal . . . of the alliance between England and France . . . He knew, however, of no alliance other than a good understanding between the two countries when consulting on several points of general interest to Europe.'[2]

Aberdeen shared these views and spelt them out carefully to the French charge, Bourquenay, during their first formal interview. He told him:

J'ai blamé, dans le Ministère Whig, la politique qui s'intitulait elle-meme, il y a quelques annees, politique de l'alliance française, au detriment et à l'exclusion des autres grandes Puissances de l'Europe; mais des rapports affecteux, sincères, droits avec son Gouvernement, mais un travail commun avec Elle pour le maintien de la paix de l'Europe pour la surveillance des grands interêts Européens; voilà ce que je proclame utile, nécessaire; voila ce dont on peut faire ouvertement la base de sa politique.[3]

Guizot was equally cautious. He wrote to the new French Ambassador Ste Aulaire, a little later, 'Nos relations avec l'Angleterre ne sont plus celles d'une alliance spéciale, intime: mais elles n'en peuvent, elles n'en doivent pas moins rester pacifiques, bienveillantes, amicales.'[4]

Both Aberdeen and Peel were conscious of the desirability of keeping the pacific and comparatively Anglophile ministry of Guizot in office but it was at first doubtful whether this would be possible. The French government was virtually paralysed in the winter of 1841–42 by its weakness in the Chambers, and in the summer of 1842 Guizot, against the advice of Louis Philippe, determined to put his fortunes to the test in a general election. The results were ambiguous. Henry Bulwer wrote to Aberdeen on 1 July, 'I can hardly think Guizot, tho' the Chamber will be conservative, can stand. As it is he is crippled; & is the responsible agent for a policy wch. if what he says be true, is not his own.' Ten days later he wrote again:

I should personally very much regret Guizot's resignation – but he is so unpopular, and the prejudice agst. him so strong, & the foolish suspicion that he is over English so current that I am not certain whether his [?secession] is not the next best thing to his obtaining, which seems more than unlikely, greater real power.[5]

Against all the odds, Guizot retained power until 1848, but his pleas to the British government that they must do nothing to undermine his already precarious position were all too successful.

It was in fact Peel who opened the way for the French to make overtures for the resumption of closer relations. In August 1842, Peel, stung by Palmerston's comprehensive criticisms of the Conservatives' foreign policy and his taunts that they were feeding on the 'broken meats left in the larder' by the previous administration, replied with a vigorous speech which put the blame for the estrangement from France squarely on Palmerston's shoulders. Every British interest in the Near East, he said, could have been maintained without disturbing their relations with France and their present difficulties were 'the consequence of that alienation, of that state of irritable feeling, which either through the fault or the misfortune of the noble Lord have been the consequences of his policy.'[6] In the heat of the moment, Peel went beyond anything the Conservatives had said before and the speech caused a sensation in France. A fortnight later, Guizot told Lord Cowley, the British Ambassador, that when he assumed office he had three objectives, to re-establish France's relations with the other Great Powers, to build up a strong party in the Chamber of Deputies and to restore cordial intimacy with Britain. Only the third task remained and must now be undertaken.[7]

There were many minor matters in which Britain and France could give practical expression to their desire for renewed co-operation. Negotiations for a fisheries convention, an extradition treaty and a postal convention were taken up with a new vigour and all brought to a successful conclusion in the early months of 1843. But there were other more fundamental matters which were not so easily resolved.

The Eastern Question was comparatively quiescent during the early 1840s. The French made no real effort to restore the fortunes of their protegé, Mehemet Ali, after the Powers had expelled him from Syria but no one could calculate the ultimate effect of Mehemet Ali's rebellion on the already precarious authority of the Sultan. Aberdeen still adhered to Wellington's policy of trying to preserve the Ottoman empire. He told Stratford Canning, 'The policy of Great Britain in the Levant has long been distinguished by a sincere desire to support the Turkish Power; and to avert the dissolution of the Empire either from the effects of internal convulsion or of Foreign aggression.'⁸ Aberdeen authorised Canning to support any reforms which seemed likely to increase the stability of the Turkish Empire but he was to avoid 'a busy, meddling policy'.⁹ Aberdeen hoped that both Guizot and Metternich would support him in this policy. His hopes were, on the whole, fulfilled and there was no great international contest for influence in the Ottoman Empire in this period.

This was not, however, the case in one former province of the Turkish Empire. Greece became the scene of a serious Anglo-French struggle. Otho had proved to be as unsatisfactory a king as Aberdeen had predicted. He made no attempt to implement the promises of constitutional government made by the three guarantor Powers, Britain, France and Russia, in 1830. His nominal ministers had little power and he surrounded himself with a small clique of Bavarian friends. Greek administration and finance sank into chaos. Just before Aberdeen came into office there was one brief attempt to establish an efficient, constitutional government under a moderate Greek politician, Mavrocordato, who was generally regarded as pro-British but, finding he had no support from the King, Mavrocordato resigned in August 1841. His successor, Christides, was associated with the French party and the British Minister at Athens, Sir Edmund Lyons, did not hesitate to say that the change had been brought about by French intrigues. The French denied this and Aberdeen was inclined to believe them, cautioning Lyons to act with complete impartiality in Greek politics.¹⁰

A new Anglo-French contest also seemed likely to arise in Spain. The Carlists had had to acknowledge defeat in 1839, but the triumphant constitutionalists were themselves divided. In October 1840, Queen Isabella's mother, Queen Christina, the leader of the Moderado party, resigned the Regency and withdrew to France, where she was very well received. Seven months later, in May 1841, the Cortes elected Espartero, Duke de la Victoria, the leader of the Progressistas party, Regent during the remainder of Isabella's minority. The government of Espartero, which was believed to be liberally inclined in trade matters as well as comparatively progressive in internal affairs, was approved by Palmerston, but soon after Aberdeen came into office a new crisis occurred. In October 1841, there was a widespread rising in the northern provinces and an attack on the royal palace in Madrid, designed to overthrow Espartero and restore Queen Christina to the Regency. The British government, including Aberdeen, believed that the insurrection had been countenanced, if not aided, by France. They were not reassured when the French government increased their troops on the Spanish border from 25,000 to 45,000 men and sent two sail of the line to Barcelona.¹¹

Privately, Peel rather sympathised with the Moderados but Aberdeen said without hesitation that he would support Espartero, if he provided the best guarantee of Spanish independence.¹² The French denied having anything to do with the insurrection and insisted that their troop movements were purely precautionary. Aberdeen did not believe them. He told Arthur Aston, the British Minister in Madrid, that the French government's known sympathy for Christina 'will leave a strong suspicion in the minds of all impartial men, that they cannot have been entirely strangers to the Plot'.[13] But he thought it best to take the French denials at their face value and leave them to prove their words. By this means he persuaded the French to remove a number of Spanish exiles and trouble-makers from the frontier. At the same time he advised the Spaniards to avoid all provocation and, in particular, to drop their request that the French should expel Christina.[14]

The notorious Spanish marriage question, the choice of a husband for the youthful Queen Isabella, then eleven years of age, and her still younger sister, the Infanta Luisa Fernanda was already under discussion. Louis Philippe had several times denied that he wished any of his sons to marry Isabella but, during the first flush of Christinos successes in October 1841, the possibility of Isabella marrying the duc d'Aumâle began to be openly canvassed in Paris.[15] This was perfectly well known in England. Aberdeen, meeting Palmerston one day, bet him half a crown that such a marriage would not take place.[16] After the defeat of the Christinos, Louis Philippe repeated his renunciation of his sons' claims but insisted that Isabella must marry a descendant of Philip V. He wished also, specifically to exclude a German prince.[17] The British government replied that they had no objection to a Bourbon but saw no reason why Isabella's choice should be·limited to one. Aberdeen insisted that Isabella's husband must be the free choice of the Spanish nation. If that condition were fulfilled he would not even rule out the younger sons of Louis Philippe, although he was gratified to learn that Espartero favoured a German prince.[18] The question was thus still completely open in October 1841, with no engagements yet entered into on either side.

The increasing French interest in Greece and Spain looked the more sinister when combined with French activity on the other side of the Mediterranean. Aberdeen had reminded the Lords in 1833 that Napoleon's ambition had been to make the Mediterranean 'a French lake' and the British government looked with disapproval on the growing French influence in North Africa. Probably the July Monarchy would have been only too glad to have withdrawn from Algeria but they dared not relinquish what their Bourbon predecessors had acquired; so, by the 1840s, they had been drawn into a full scale military campaign to subdue the hinterland. Britain had never recognised the French position there and the British consul in Algiers still held his exequatur from the Porte, although most of the other consuls held theirs from the King of the French.

An awkward diplomatic incident occurred soon after Aberdeen took office. Ste Aulaire, the new French Ambassador, reported to Guizot that Aberdeen had said 'Je regarde . . . votre position à Alger comme un fait accompli, contre lequel je n'ai plus à élever aucun objection.' During a critical debate in the French Chambers, Guizot read Ste Aulaire's despatch. Aberdeen angrily protested that he had not used the words *fait accompli*. What he had actually said was that he had 'no further observations to make' and 'It does not follow that objections, although not expressed, may not be entertained'. The matter continued to be hotly debated in the Chambers and in Parliament until both Aberdeen and Louis Philippe began to fear it would seriously impair relations. Eventually Ste Aulaire accepted Aberdeen's wording, although insisting that it was a distinction without a difference.[19]

Privately, the British government admitted that the French position in Algeria was a *fait accompli* and they would not have been so intransigent in public if they had not feared that it might be extended into Tunis and Morocco. The Bey of Tunis was still nominally a vassal of the Sultan, although the latter had long since ceased to exercise any real authority there. In August 1841, an obscure quarrel arose between the Sultan and the Bey, and the French professed to believe that a fleet then fitting out at Constantinople was intended for an attack on Tunis. The French insisted that they would not tolerate Turkish troops on the Algerian border. They reinforced their Levant squadron and ordered its commander to prevent the Turkish fleet reaching Tunis, by force if necessary. Bulwer told Aberdeen privately, 'The principal subject of foreign interest to the King at this moment is Tunis.'[20] Peel was in favour of a strong line. He wrote to Aberdeen:

It is manifest they [the French] wish to establish themselves in Tunis in some way or other either by force after having got up a Quarrell, or by means of gradual encroachment. I think the sooner we come to an understanding on this point with the Bey and with the French the better.

He suggested increasing the British naval forces in the Mediterranean.[21] Aberdeen warned the French government that Britain viewed the situation seriously and instructed Stratford Canning to use his influence to settle the quarrel between the Sultan and the Bey.[22]

The British felt even more strongly about Morocco. The French advance in Algeria under General, later Marshal, Bugeaud, was strenuously resisted by Abd–el–Kader whom, even Bugeaud admitted, was no mere rebel leader but the personification of the Arab cause whose word commanded instant obedience from all the local tribes. But Abd–el–Kader was unable to defeat a well equipped French army and he was forced to take refuge in the desert region on the Moroccan border from which he conducted a successful guerrilla warfare, with some help from across the border.[23] The French military authorities wanted to take vigorous action against the Moroccans but the British were determined that France should not dominate Morocco with its key strategic position at the western end of the Mediterranean.

Like the Mediterranean, the Low Countries were an ancient field of Anglo-French rivalry. The French had never entirely relinquished their dream of the Rhine frontier. After the final settlement of the Belgian question in 1839, when the Great Powers joined in a guarantee of the independence and neutrality of the new state, it seemed that the French, having failed to gain the Low Countries by military and political means, were now trying to dominate them by economic means. The possibility of a Franco-Belgian Customs Union was intermittently discussed by the two governments from 1836 onwards.[24] For

Belgium the attractions were economic. She was a comparatively industrialised state with an urgent need for markets. The separation from Holland and the Dutch empire had left her isolated in the midst of a highly protectionist continent. An arrangement with either France or the German Zollverein seemed imperative. France stood to gain little economically and any arrangement was likely to be unpopular with the French manufacturers. Guizot admitted in retrospect that the French motives were entirely political.[25]

The Belgians were galvanised into action by a large increase in the French linen duties in June 1842. They feared that half of their 3-400,000 linen workers would be thrown out of work and the following month they signed a Convention with France by which they were exempted from the new duties in return for concessions on wines and silks and a promise to levy the new duties on linen entering Belgium from abroad. The British government was alarmed at the implications and Aberdeen wrote to Hamilton Seymour, the British Minister in Brussels, that the guarantor Powers might have to take it into 'serious consideration'[26] but he did not elicit much response from the other Powers and the Belgians bought the Prussians off by extending the reductions on French wines and silks to Prussian products.

Events took a more serious turn in the autumn of 1842. Leopold, who was an enthusiast for the scheme, visited Louis Philippe at St Cloud and found him a ready listener. A *projet de traité* was drawn up, which envisaged the abolition of customs posts on the frontier, the assimilation of the flags of the two merchant marines, the inclusion of Belgium in the French tobacco monopoly and the admission of French inspectors into Belgium.[27] Although the details of this far-reaching project were not known in London, Aberdeen feared that a scheme would be 'smuggled through by the two kings' and Cowley's 'secret reporters' told him that Guizot favoured the project and would take steps to get rid of those members of his Cabinet who opposed it.[28]

Aberdeen now tried to enlist the support of the other Great Powers but again he got a poor response. The Austrians hinted that Britain was only trying to stop a commercial treaty distasteful to herself. Sir Robert Gordon had a little more success with the Prussian Chancellor, Von Bülow, whom he met at a watering place in Germany. Gordon found Bülow 'strongly impressed with the idea that France would inevitably before long carry out her intention of coming to the Rhine and he wished to provide against this by a previous European concert'.[29] On 28 October, Aberdeen sent a circular despatch to Vienna, Berlin and St Petersburg, asking for such a concert but even the Prussians, although willing to protest, doubted if the scheme was contrary to any international agreement as Aberdeen maintained.[30]

At Prince Albert's suggestion, both he and Aberdeen wrote direct appeals to Leopold, arguing that a Customs Union was incompatible with Belgian independence.[31] Leopold replied in a very able letter which shook Aberdeen by pointing out Belgium's real difficulties and playing on the rival fear of revolution. 'We possess no colonies', he said 'and nearly all markets in and out of Europe are closed against us.' He dreaded the consequences of a depression in Belgium:

This Country has the most democratic form of Government in Europe, when one considers besides the habits of comfort of the inhabitants which are the natural consequences of an old and hitherto prosperous civilisation one must be struck that such a Country is less than any other calculated to bear 'de la misère materielle'.

He thought, in any case, that opposition from the French manufacturers would make the scheme impracticable.[32]

It was upon this opposition that the British government was now principally relying, and they began a press campaign. Peel proposed two or three leading articles in *The Times* suggesting that 'after the abolition of the French Customs Houses English Capital, English Workmen & English Machinery will be transplanted to Belgium in order to take advantage of free intercourse with France'. Leading articles along these lines appeared in *The Times* on 23 and 24 November 1842. It was at this point that Aberdeen sent the fake 'Memorial' to Bulwer, in which a group of English capitalists were supposed to ask the British government not to oppose the scheme. Bulwer thought it too risky and it was not used.[33]

The most dangerous moment came as a result of Lord Cowley's deafness. To prevent any misunderstanding Aberdeen instructed him to explain the British position 'very fully' to Guizot. Guizot received Cowley coldly and, according to the Ambassador, said he could not discuss the matter 'because it was his intention in the approaching Session to bring the whole question under the consideration of the Chamber of Deputies'. Aberdeen naturally interpreted this to mean that Guizot was about to put a proposal before the Chambers. He decided that the moment had come for strong language. He communicated his fears to Neumann, the Russian, and Bunsen, the Prussian representatives. To Neumann's great alarm he talked openly of war and told him 'Nous sommes surs de la Prusse et nous esperons que la Russie nous joindra.'[34]

It became apparent a few days later that Guizot had only said he would have to reply to questions in the Chamber. Bulwer, upon whom Aberdeen was beginning to rely instead of Cowley, was convinced that Guizot was not in favour of the scheme and that the French manufacturers would not countenance it.[35] Aberdeen, perhaps feeling that he had over-reacted, now substantially modified his views. He had been impressed by Leopold's letter and conceded that it was unrealistic to expect Belgium to abstain from all commercial arrangements with her neighbours. He wrote to Peel, 'To prevent them from having the market of France, without offering them that of Germany is scarcely reasonable.' So long as Belgium did not enter into such exclusive relations with one Power as to prevent herself from making similar arrangements with other Powers, he had probably been mistaken in thinking that Belgium was in danger of breaching her own neutrality. Peel counselled caution. 'We must', he said, 'be very careful not to let Belgium know the precise construction we put upon her power to make Treaties . . . or she will be inclined to make use – and a liberal use – of the Latitude allowed her.'[36]

Aberdeen, however, had now made up his mind to allow the storm to blow itself out. As the British grew calmer, the Prussians grew more excited. Von Bülow proposed a meeting of the four Powers in London to determine by what measures Belgian neutrality would be considered violated. Aberdeen now thought the proposal 'most objectionable' and Peel thought it would make the withdrawal of the project by France 'humiliating and impossible'.[37] In fact the Franco-Belgian negotiations broke down and Belgium turned instead to the Zollverein with whom she concluded a treaty in September 1844. An ordinary commercial treaty between France and Belgium in December 1845 caused the Powers no alarm. The Rhine frontier was safe for the time being.

The Mediterranean and the Low Countries were ancient fields of Anglo-French conflict but in the 1840s those conflicts extended to many overseas areas. Tension on the west coast of Africa was largely connected with the suppression of the slave trade, although it was also provoked by trading disputes. The French had finally signed the Quintuple Treaty, allowing for a mutual right of search of suspected slavers among all the Great Powers of Europe on 20 December 1841, but there was such a widespread outcry in France that Guizot told the British government that he dared not ratify it until the Chambers had debated the question. The French government narrowly escaped defeat when it was debated on 24 January. Cowley dined at the Tuileries that night and, when the message that the government had survived arrived, Louis Philippe said to him, 'Thank God'.[38] The other Powers exchanged ratifications on 19 February and the Protocol was left open for the adhesion of France. Guizot insisted for some months that France would ratify eventually but Bulwer described feeling in France as 'pathological'.[39] In August, Guizot suggested that it would be better if the Protocol were formally closed. Otherwise the matter would remain before the public and he would find it increasingly difficult to defend even the Treaties of 1831 and 1833, which were still in force.[40] In October, he formally proposed the closure, and this led to sharp exchanges between Aberdeen and Peel. Peel thought the French suggestions, and particularly the hints about the earlier Treaties, 'monstrous' and was disinclined to do anything to help Guizot out of his difficulties. Aberdeen pleaded that the closing of the Protocol was 'a piece of diplomatick pedantry'; Guizot's difficulties were real and the other Great Powers would think the preservation of his government more important than the closing of the Protocol. Peel, now supported by Wellington, objected to almost every proposal that was put forward for effecting the closure. Aberdeen, in a moment of exasperation, told Ste Aulaire, 'M. Guizot, ni vous, ne saurez jamais la dixième partie des peines que cette malheureuse affaire m'a données.'[41] But the protocol was formally closed on 9 November at a meeting at the Foreign Office.

French public opinion was, however, now thoroughly excited and Guizot warned the British government that he would be under pressure either to evade the earlier Treaties or to open negotiations for their abolition. Aberdeen spoke firmly to Ste Aulaire of the dangers of using technical objections to make the Treaties inoperative. 'I did not see', he told Peel, 'what else we could do but exercise the Search without Warrants. This of course would lead to War very speedily.'[42]

The following month there was an even more remarkable development. Guizot took Bulwer aside and warned him confidentially that Ste Aulaire was about to make a proposal to Aberdeen about the 1831 and 1833 Treaties which Aberdeen 'should reject . . . in the strongest manner, and without genéing himself in the least'.[43] Bulwer assumed that the French Cabinet was divided and, in the end, Ste Aulaire made no proposition. Peel was angry and caustic. He supposed Ste Aulaire had refused to take part in a 'discreditable farce' and he thought that Guizot's suggestion to Bulwer would be 'a clear case of impeachment against him'.[44] The whole question was allowed to die down, although there was one final attempt to link the right of search with the negotiations for a commercial treaty.[45]

French sensitivity about the West Africa Squadron was in part connected with trading quarrels. The most serious of a number of incidents was the Portendic case when, in 1835, the French had detained several British vessels during a blockade of Portendic on the Senegalese coast. Aberdeen, while still in opposition, had called it 'one of the most flagrant outrages that had ever been committed on our flag, and on the commerce of the country'.[46] The French eventually agreed, in April 1840, to the setting up of a joint Commission to settle the question but they dared not ask the Chambers for money to pay compensation. Aberdeen directed Bulwer to press the matter again in January 1842. By July, Peel had lost his temper. He wrote to Aberdeen that Britain would be justified 'in taking the Law into her own hands. and procuring by force, that is by the seizure of French Property, an Equivalent compensation for the losses of her subjects'.[47] Only the sudden death of the duc d'Orleans, which stilled diplomatic controversy for some weeks, prevented a serious breach. The matter was eventually referred to the arbitration of the King of Prussia who ruled, in November 1843, that the blockade was legal but that the British ships were entitled to compensation because they had not been warned of it. Financial details were referred to a liquidation commission.

British complaints of French encroachments in Africa were paralleled in the Pacific. The *cause célèbre* of the Tahiti incident, which brought Britain and France to the verge of war in 1844, was only part of the general Anglo-French rivalry in the Pacific. By 1840 the future possibilities of Pacific trade were, if anything, exaggerated. The sudden interest in the Pacific islands was partly the result of the opening up of the China trade. For forty years the European nations had been trying to break into the Chinese monopoly. Now Britain, at the cost of war, seemed likely to succeed. The possibility of a canal across the isthmus of Panama was already being canvassed and as steamers slowly began to replace sailing vessels, it was realised that ships would need coaling stations and comparatively elaborate dockyard facilities.

The war with China came to an end with the Treaty of Nanking in 1842. Britain acquired the island of Hong Kong and trading rights at five so-called 'treaty ports', as well as a favourable tariff agreement.[48] The British made it clear that they had no wish to retain any monopoly of these rights and, two years later, France and the United States signed comparable trading treaties with the Chinese government. British acquiescence in this was entirely consistent with the free trade convictions of the Peel government. Both in China and in the Pacific islands Britain held to what later came to be called the 'Open

Door' policy, trade freely open to the merchants of all nations with as few political commitments as possible. The attitude of the United States' government did not differ materially from the British. Under the July Monarchy, however, France was poised for a much more forward policy in the Pacific. The *Moniteur* of 25 April 1843, lamenting the lack of French bases in the Pacific, described Polynesia as 'un vaste champ ouvert aux conquêtes du commerce et de la civilisation'. The Pacific as a free field for all was one thing. Polynesia dominated by France was another. The British attitude was summed up in a leading article in *The Times* of 26 August 1843, which contemporaries believed to be officially inspired. It commented:

As colonial possessions, or even as naval stations, we have more than once exposed the absurdity of the attempt to found European establishments in these islands . . . In their independent condition, the islands of the Pacific were useful to all nations, and dangerous to none; and all that was needed was to respect that independence and to leave them alone.

Unfortunately, being 'left alone' was exactly what was not happening in the 1840s.

Up to this time, the French had been unlucky in the contest for influence in the Pacific. A French fleet had arrived in Botany Bay in 1788 just too late to prevent Captain Phillip's expedition from taking possession of New South Wales for England. The distractions of the French Revolution and the defeat of the French navy at Trafalgar practically drove the French flag from the Pacific. By the time the French again showed an interest in the region, Britain had extended her sovereignty over the whole of Australia and in 1840 she annexed New Zealand as well. Although there were well established British trading and missionary interests there, the annexation of New Zealand was particularly resented in some quarters in France, where a company had recently been formed in Nantes and Bordeaux, with the semi-official blessing of the French government, with the intention of founding a French colony there. In 1841, (and again in 1842) Aberdeen was alarmed by rumours that the French were contemplating expeditions to New Zealand or Australia and he instructed Cowley to keep 'a watchful eye' on the situation.[49]

The French government had in fact decided that it would be impracticable to challenge the British position but there were other islands in the Pacific. In 1841, Captain, later Admiral, Dupetit Thouars was sent out to take possession of the Marquesa Islands which he had previously recommended as a naval base and penal colony. There was no intentional challenge to Britain in this, as she had no interests in the Marquesas. Unfortunately, after taking possession of the Marquesas in June 1842, Dupetit Thouars decided that they were inadequate for the French purposes and began to cast covetous eyes on the Society Islands, of which Tahiti was the chief.[50]

Tahiti had already established itself as a storm centre of Anglo-French rivalry. A prosperous and fertile island, it had been unofficially 'colonised' by the London Missionary Society, which had been sending missionaries there since 1797. The Tahitians had asked to be taken under British protection in 1822 and 1826, but as Britain was then averse to the extension of political responsibilities in the Pacific they had received friendly but non-committal replies. However, Aberdeen, when at the Foreign Office in 1829, had recommended that British warships should call there more often.[51] The real trouble began with the arrival of French Roman Catholic missionaries in the 1830s. The Protestants regarded the Catholic attempt to break in where they had already established a mission field as 'unreasonable, ungentlemanly and unchristianlike'.[52] Two French priests, Fathers Carret and Laval, were forcibly expelled from the island in 1836. The *Venus*, under Dupetit Thouars, was sent to Tahiti in 1838 to demand an apology, compensation and a promise that Frenchmen would be permitted unrestricted access to the island. The Tahitians had no choice but to comply. The following year they had to submit to another French visitation which demanded that sites be provided for Catholic churches, on pain of the destruction of the Protestant church and other buildings. The London Missionary Society complained to Palmerston, who was angry but still declined to undertake the responsibility of a protectorate.[53]

George Pritchard, the leading missionary on the island who had also acted as British Consul, came to London in the winter of 1841–42 and saw Aberdeen. He tried to persuade him, among other things, of the strategic importance of Tahiti for the new steam routes to New South Wales. 'Tahiti', he said, 'will become a place of the utmost importance, as it lies in the direct track, and must from its position necessarily become the depot for coals, stores, or a station for other purposes.' This interview and other reports from the Far East made some impression on Aberdeen. Although he renounced any desire to establish 'paramount influence' in the area, he insisted on the need to maintain the independence of the native rulers and asked the Admiralty to send ships more regularly.[54]

In South America the British and the French at first tried to co-operate. The trouble centre there was the River Plate where the independent states of Buenos Aires and Monte Video had established themselves in the wreckage of the Spanish empire. Britain enjoyed a position of unquestioned commercial predominance in Buenos Aires whose development had been largely financed by the Baring Brothers. Monte Video on the other hand was the centre of French trade in South America. In 1838 the French blockaded Buenos Aires, following a quarrel with its ruler, General Rosas. The immediate quarrel between Rosas and the French was settled in October 1840, but in the meantime the French had secured the overthrow of the President of Monte Video, General Oribe, for failing to aid them. As soon as the French naval force was withdrawn, Oribe, now with the help of Rosas, tried to regain his capital. Monte Video was besieged and European commerce disrupted. An attempt by Guizot and Palmerston in the summer of 1841 to arrange a joint mediation had only ended in recriminations.[55]

In February 1842 the Monte Videans appealed for British help, and Aberdeen, accepting rather uncritically that Rosas was the aggressor, suggested to the French that they made joint representations. In the summer of 1842 he learnt of a series of atrocities which had been committed under Rosas' at least nominal jurisdiction, and he pressed upon the French 'the urgent necessity of some immediate and energetic steps'.[56] In September, Guizot decided that the

Plate would be a suitable field for a spectacular demonstration of Anglo-French co-operation. He told Cowley that the fighting must be ended and British and French subjects protected. For this 'an imposing force' would be necessary. This went beyond anything the British had in mind and Aberdeen told Peel 'Being rather shy of French co-operation, to such an extent as they would probably desire, I propose not to give immediate effect to the proposal of active or coercive measures.'[57] Early in December, Rosas won a major victory at Arroya Grande and the way to Monte Video lay open. Aberdeen had told J. H. Mandeville, the British Minister in Buenos Aires, of his conversations with the French and Mandeville, in conjunction with his French colleague, Baron de Lurde, went beyond their instructions by calling on the Argentinians to withdraw within their own territory, telling them that a powerful naval force was on its way from Europe. Mandeville and Lurde's despatches, reporting their actions, were received with dismay in London and Paris three months later.[58] Whatever their intentions in September 1842 – and they were very imprecise – the British and French governments quickly turned against the idea of armed intervention. The first Anglo-French intervention in the affairs of the River Plate petered out miserably, again leaving behind an atmosphere of recrimination and misunderstanding.

The attempt to demonstrate Anglo-French reconcilation to the world by means of a commercial treaty also ran into the sands. Negotiations for such a treaty had been suspended during the Eastern crisis. Aberdeen tried to take them up again as early as October 1841, but Guizot pleaded that he must wait until after the elections of 1842.[59] The French public was deeply divided. The wine-growing interest wanted a treaty but the textile manufacturers strongly opposed it. Guizot was convinced that a favourable election result depended on his pacifying the northern manufacturing districts, and he was compelled to increase the French linen duties in June 1842. Aberdeen felt that this would make it difficult for Britain to re-open negotiations, although Bulwer was unimpressed and told Aberdeen that France needed British yarn and 'it comes as before & is smuggled at Dunkirk'.[60] Formal negotiations were resumed in January 1843, but Guizot was inundated by delegations and petitions. Even a more modest proposal to lower the duties only on French silks and English cottons was unacceptable to the French manufacturers. Although he would have been prepared to make considerable sacrifices to ensure success, Aberdeen had to let the negotiations lapse.

NOTES

1. *Hansard*, 3rd ser., LII, 764 (28 Feb. 1840).
2. *Hansard*, 3rd ser., LVI, 96, 34 (26 Jan. 1841).
3. AAE Angleterre 658, Bourquenay to Guizot, no. 85, 7 Sept. 1841.
4. Guizot Papers, 42 AP 8, Guizot to Ste Aulaire, 18 June 1842.
5. Add. MSS 43131, Bulwer to Aberdeen, 1, 11 July 1842.
6. *Hansard*, 3rd ser., LXV 1280–2 (10 Aug. 1842).

7. FO 27/652, Cowley to Aberdeen, No. 300, 26 Aug. 1842.
8. FO 78/439, Aberdeen to Canning, No. 2, 3 Oct. 1841.
9. *Ibid.*
10. Add. MSS 43135, Lyons to Aberdeen, 30 Sept., 9, 21 Oct. 1841, Aberdeen to Lyons, 30 Oct., 13, 30 Nov. 1841; AAE Angleterre 658, Guizot to Bourquenay, No. 39, 23 Sept. 1841; FO 32/102, Aberdeen to Lyons, No. 1, 30 Sept. 1841.
11. FO 72/579, Aston to Aberdeen, No. 241, 7 Oct., No. 248, 15 Oct. 1841; FO 27/629, Bulwer to Aberdeen, No. 320, 18 Oct., No. 325, 22 Oct., No. 336, 22 Oct. 1841.
12. Add. MSS 40453, Peel to Aberdeen, 17 Oct. 1841; Add. MSS 43145, Aberdeen to Aston, 18 Nov. 1841, 'I do not care a sixpence for their liberalism. They may be as radical as they please . . . but their acts of butchery are terrible.'
13. FO 72/571, Aberdeen to Aston, No. 16, 28 Oct. 1841. Guizot's denials of complicity are borne out by his correspondence with Alphonse Pageot, the French chargé in Madrid, AAE Espagne 805, Pageot to Guizot, No. 91, 24 Oct 1841, Guizot to Pageot, No. 30, 30 Oct. 1841.
14. FO 72/571, Aberdeen to Aston, No. 23, 18 Nov. 1841.
15. FO 27/629, Bulwer to Aberdeen, No. 328, 25 Oct. 1841, 'Private and Confidential', 5 Nov. 1841.
16. Add. MSS 40455, Aberdeen to Peel, 21 Sept. 1846.
17. FO 27/629, Bulwer to Aberdeen, Conf. 25 Oct. 1841, 8 Nov. 1841; FO 27/631, Cowley to Aberdeen, Secret and Confidential, 3, 24 Dec 1841; Guizot Papers 42 AP 8, Guizot to Ste Aulaire, 26 Oct. 1841.
18. Add. MSS 40453, Peel to Aberdeen, 9 Nov. 1841; Add. MSS 43145, Aberdeen to Aston, 28 Oct., 23 Dec 1841; Aston to Aberdeen, 20 Nov. 1841.
19. AAE Angleterre 658–9, Ste Aulaire to Guizot, No. 94, 4 Oct. 1841, No. 17, 8 Mar. 1842; FO 27/647, Cowley to Aberdeen, No. 27, 21 Jan. 1842; FO 27/645, Aberdeen to Cowley, No. 13, 28 Jan. 1842; Add. MSS 43129, Aberdeen to Cowley, 11 Mar. 1842, Cowley to Aberdeen 31 Jan., 14 Mar. 1842.
20. Add. MSS 43131, Bulwer to Aberdeen, 13 Dec. 1841.
21. Add. MSS 43061, Peel to Aberdeen, 13 Oct. 1841.
22. FO 27/621, Aberdeen to Cowley, No. 22, 31 Dec. 1841; Add. MSS 43129, Aberdeen to Cowley, 31 Dec. 1841; FO 78/439, Aberdeen to Canning, No. 36. 31 Dec. 1841.
23. This is dealt with in detail in Guizot, *Mémoires*, vol. 8, Ch. XLI.
24. All the relevant documents are published in De Ridder, *Les projets d'union douanière franco-belge.*
25. Guizot, vol. 6, pp. 276–8.
26. FO 10/91, Aberdeen to Seymour, No. 9, 9 Aug. 1842.
27. The *projet de traité* of 15 Oct. 1842 and other relevant documents are in Guizot Papers 42 AP 11.
28. Add. MSS 40453, Aberdeen to Peel, 13 Oct. 1842; FO 27/653, Cowley to Aberdeen, No. 384, 21 Nov. 1842; Add. MSS 43129, Cowley to Aberdeen, 13 Oct., 21 Oct. 1842 and encls.
29. Add. MSS 43211, Robert to Aberdeen, 16 Oct., 12 Nov. 1842.
30. FO 7/304, Aberdeen to Gordon, No. 70, 28 Oct. 1842.
31. Add. MSS 43042, Albert to Aberdeen, 19, 30 Oct. 1842; Add. MSS 43051, Aberdeen to Leopold, 21 Oct. 1842.
32. Add. MSS 43051, Leopold to Aberdeen, 12 Nov. 1842.
33. Add. MSS 43062, Peel to Aberdeen, 16 Nov. 1842; Add. MSS 43131, Aberdeen to Bulwer, 9 Dec. 1842, Bulwer to Aberdeen, 12 Dec. 1842.

34. Add. MSS 43129, Aberdeen to Cowley, 29 Nov. 1842; FO 27/653, Cowley to Aberdeen, No. 418, 9 Dec. 1842; De Ridder, pp. 205–16.

35. Add. MSS 43131, Bulwer to Aberdeen, 12 Dec. 1842; Add. MSS 43128, Neumann to Aberdeen, 26 Dec. 1842 encl. Apponyi to Metternich, 17, 19 Dec. 1842 Peel was extremely exasperated, Add. MSS 43062, Peel to Aberdeen, 27, 28 Dec. 1842.

36. Add. MSS 40453, Aberdeen to Peel, 22 Nov. 1842; Add. MSS 43062, Peel to Aberdeen, 8 Dec. 1842.

37. Add. MSS 40453, Aberdeen to Peel, 26 Dec. 1842; Add. MSS 43062, Peel to Aberdeen, 27 Dec. 1842, 17 Jan. 1843.

38. Add. MSS 43129, Cowley to Aberdeen, 25 Jan. 1842.

39. Add. MSS 43131, Bulwer to Aberdeen, 8 Apr. 1842. Cowley got much information from 'secret correspondents' but some were unofficial intermediaries from Guizot, Add. MSS 43129, Cowlet to Aberdeen, 28, 31 Jan. 1842, Guizot, vol. 6, pp. 158–9.

40. Add. MSS 43129, Cowley to Aberdeen, 12 Aug. 1842.

41. AAE Angleterre 660, Guizot to Ste Aulaire, No. 55, 14 Oct. 1842; Add. MSS 40453, Aberdeen to Peel, 12, 18, 25, 29 Oct. 1842; Add. MSS 43062, Peel to Aberdeen, 15, 19, 28, 30 Oct. 1842; Add. MSS 43060, Wellington to Aberdeen, 28 Oct. 1842; Guizot, vol. 6, pp. 175–6.

42. Add. MSS 40452, Aberdeen to Peel, 15 Nov. 1842.

43. Add. MSS 43131, Bulwer to Aberdeen, 9 Dec. 1842.

44. Add. MSS 43062, Peel to Aberdeen, 14 Dec. 1842.

45. Add. MSS 43131, Bulwer to Aberdeen, 14, 17 Apr., 8 May 1843, Aberdeen to Bulwer, 25 Apr. 1843.

46. *Hansard*, 3rd ser., LII, pp. 762–5.

47. Add. MSS 43062, Peel to Aberdeen, 10 July 1842.

48. The British Commissioner, Sir Henry Pottinger, exceeded his instructions in retaining Hong Kong but the British government decided not to amend the Treaty for fear of seeming weak.

49. Guizot, vol. 8, p. 45; FO 27/621, 646, Aberdeen to Cowley, No. 6, 23 Nov. 1841, No. 143, 4 Oct. 1842.

50. Guizot, vol. 7, pp. 45–7; Guizot Papers 42 AP 6.

51. Confidential Print, Correspondence relative to the Society Islands, pp. 1, 3–5, 10, 24–5.

52. G. Pritchard, *Queen Pomare and her country*, pp. 18–21.

53. Society Islands Correspondence, pp. 61–77, 86–7.

54. Society Islands Correspondence, pp. 88–92, 98–9, 107–8, 112, 124.

55. Guizot, vol. 6, pp. 132–3; *Hansard*, 3rd ser., LVIII, 706–7.

56. FO 27/645–6, Aberdeen to Cowley, No. 17, 8 Feb., No. 34, 4 Mar., No. 129, 23 Aug. 1842; FO 6/82, Aberdeen to Mandeville, No. 14, 3 Aug. 1842.

57. FO 27/625, Cowley to Aberdeen, No. 317, 9 Sept. 1842; Add. MSS 40453, Aberdeen to Peel, 4 Oct. 1842.

58. FO 6/82, Aberdeen to Mandeville, Nos 18 and 19, 5 Oct. 1842; FO 6/84, Mandeville to Aberdeen, No. 69, 3 Aug., No. 83, 26 Aug., No. 91, 15 Oct., No. 97, 26 Nov. 1842, No. 2, 2 Jan 1843; FO 27/663, Aberdeen to Cowley, No. 33, 17 Mar. 1843; FO 27/668, Cowley to Aberdeen, No. 109, 20 Mar. 1843.

59. Add. MSS 43131, Bulwer to Aberdeen, 14, 20 Mar. 1842.

60. Add. MSS 43129, Cowley to Aberdeen, 6 June 1842; Add. MSS 43131, Bulwer to Aberdeen, 25 Nov. 1842.

CHAPTER TWENTY-TWO

The 'good understanding' with France

By 1843, although Britain and France no longer stood on the brink of war, very little seemed to have been achieved in establishing more cordial relations between them. Nevertheless, Anglophobia was declining in France. Guizot's government was stronger and, for the first time, Guizot dared to speak openly of his desire to cultivate 'most friendly' relations with Britain.[1]

The new relationship was fostered and publicised by a royal visit, to which neither government at first attributed much importance. In the summer of 1843 Queen Victoria resolved to pay a private visit to the French royal family at their country retreat of the Chateau d'Eu near Tréport in Normandy, and in August the princes of Joinville and Aumâle paid a flying visit to England to arrange it. Public opinion was cautious and Peel commented that the French 'seem very apprehensive that Her Majesty will return with a Commercial Treaty in her pocket'. Aberdeen, however, thought that it was likely to produce 'a good effect'.[2] The visit was regarded with suspicion in Vienna and St Petersburg and began to assume a diplomatic importance far beyond its initial modest beginnings.[3] Victoria was captivated by the French royal family and thereafter very unwilling to hear any ill of them. She complained in 1845 that Cowley's reports, critical of the Orleanists, were 'totally contrary to the Queen's feelings'.[4]

Aberdeen accompanied the Queen to the Chateau d'Eu[5] and was able to have long private conversations with Guizot, who had also been summoned. They discussed the whole range of international issues, Spain, the Near East, the slave trade and various commercial issues and were pleasantly surprised to find how close their views appeared to be. Guizot waxed almost lyrical with delight and wrote to a friend,

Je ne ressemble pas à Jeanne d'Arc; elle a chassé les Anglais de France; j'ai assuré la paix entre la France et les Anglais. Mais vraiment ce jour-ci est, pour moi, ce fut, que pour Jeanne d'Arc, le sacre du roi à Reims.[6]

From that point onwards both governments began to speak publicly of the good understanding between them.

The magic phrase *entente cordiale*, which was used to describe good relations between England and France at least until the time of the First World War, came into being more or less accidentally. The French *chargé d'affaires*, the comte de Jarnac, himself an Anglophile with estates in Ireland, was staying at Haddo in the autumn of 1843 when Aberdeen showed him a letter to his brother, Robert, in which he had used the phrase 'a cordial, good understanding'. Jarnac and Guizot translated the English phrase into *entente cordiale*. Louis Philippe, when the French Chambers met in December, spoke gracefully of 'la sincère amitié qui l'unissait à la reine de la Grande Bretagne' and of 'la cordiale entente' established between the two governments. Ironically Victoria's reference in her Speech from the throne a few weeks later to a 'good understanding' was regarded as 'courte et froide' in France. But Peel went out of his way to speak firmly in favour of the *entente* in the Commons.[7]

The British were able to do a small service to Louis Philipe by persuading the Duke of Bordeaux, still the Legitimist claimant to the French throne, who had become the centre of royalist demonstrations, to leave Britain, although not before there had been a meeting at a house in Belgrave Square, attended by leading Legitimists including Berryer and Chateaubriand, at which he had been hailed as 'Henri V'.[8] More serious matters were more difficult to resolve.

The situation in Greece was deteriorating. Aberdeen knew that the other Powers would have liked to have seen Sir Edmund Lyons replaced as British Minister in Athens. Lyons said indignantly that it was because he knew the country too well. Aberdeen, perhaps thinking this was true, left him there, although cautioning him that Britain had no 'exclusive interests' in Greece.[9] The Powers co-operated to resolve frontier incidents between the Greeks and the Turks in 1842, but the growing financial chaos in Greece was more intractable. In 1832 the three protecting Powers had guaranteed a loan of 60 million francs to Greece at five per cent interest, the principal to be repaid at one per cent a year. The Greeks soon defaulted. The French were more accommodating than the other Powers and the British suspected that the French were prepared to lay out money to secure political predominance in Greece.[10] Negotiations were particularly acrimonious in the summer of 1843, and British suspicions were further aroused by the news that the French were appointing a new envoy in Athens, a M. Piscatory, who had already boasted that he had been personally responsible for the overthrow of Mavrocordato in favour of Christides in 1841.

The long expected crash occurred with a revolution led by the Greek army on 15 September 1843. The army officers demanded a new ministry and the summoning of a National Assembly within a month. Lyons was impressed by the moderation and orderly nature of the revolution and Aberdeen agreed with him. He wrote to his brother in Vienna:

I am no lover of Revolutions . . . but in truth, it is only the fulfilment of promises made by the three Powers, and by the King, many years ago. All this ought to have been done quietly, voluntarily, and constitutionally. We are punished for the neglect of our engagements . . .[11]

He expressed similar sentiments so forcibly to Lyons that Peel asked him to modify his despatch, fearing that 'too extravagant praise' of a revolution in which the military had played a part, could only be embarrassing in the future. Aberdeen toned down his despatch but continued to insist that they must support the constitutional party and that, the sooner they made that plain, the more influence they would have.[12]

The National Assembly finally met on 20 November. The Russian Minister had been withdrawn in an ostentatious gesture of disapproval but Lyons and Piscatory were instructed to work together to help the Greeks formulate their new constitution. For the moment no one wanted to press the claims of the 'English' and the 'French' party. Aberdeen, although he told Guizot that he had 'no vocation' for constitution making and was diffident about imposing a constitution on the Greeks when he knew so little of local conditions, could not resist trying his hand. He and Guizot exchanged a number of private letters, full of detailed proposals and criticisms. Aberdeen wanted Otho to adhere strictly to his engagements but hoped his subjects would avoid 'wild Theories . . . respecting the extension of the Democratic Principle'.[13]

The new constitution was ready in the spring of 1844. An attempt was made to form a coalition government under Mavrocordato, still regarded as the leader of the English party, and Coletti, a former Greek Minister in Paris and a personal friend of Guizot, who was now considered the leader of the French party. In the end Mavrocordato took office alone. The calm was short-lived. General Theodore Grivas, the leader of the Anarchist party, raised a rebellion in Western Greece and the Philorthodox party revived a militant society, the Brotherhood of the Cross, which wished to annex the neighbouring Turkish provinces and replace Otho by an Orthodox prince. Coletti allied himself with the Philorthodox party and Mavrocordato was overthrown in July 1844. Lyons was convinced that Piscatory was behind what he saw as Coletti's treachery and his suspicions seemed to be confirmed when Coletti drove to the royal palace in the French Minister's official carriage to accept office as Prime Minister.[14] The Greek crisis coincided with the Tahiti crisis and Aberdeen's first reaction was one of extreme annoyance. He protested to Jarnac that it made him doubt the possibility of 'a really intimate and permanently cordial understanding with France'. 'It is clear', he complained 'that M. Guizot cannot command his own Agents: and I fear it is impossible to trust to the steadiness and consistency of the French Govt in any course of policy which shall be founded upon the existence of a good understanding with England.'[15]

Guizot replied that Mavrocordato's fall was due to the natural workings of a constitutional government and that Lyons' pique was due to 'the very publick and active patronage' that he had given Mavrocordato. As evidence Guizot showed Aberdeen every despatch from Piscatory since September 1843.[16] Aberdeen was half convinced. He instructed Lyons to adopt 'an attitude of dignified reserve' and to refrain from intervention unless British interests were directly involved. He felt that Britain could not now rely on either Russia or France in Greece.[17] Anglo-French co-operation in Greece had therefore already broken down by September 1844.

In the event, the two great crisis of 1844, which brought England and France to the verge of war, were those relating to Morocco and Tahiti. In June

1844 Guizot, under considerable pressure from General Bugeaud and Bugeaud's supporters at home, sent an ultimatum to the Emperor of Morocco, demanding that he withdraw Moroccan forces from the Algerian border and expel Abd–el–Kader from his territory. Guizot assured the British that he did not intend to seize an inch of Moroccan territory[18] but Aberdeen now doubted Guizot's ability to control his own agents. He knew Bugeaud was an independent and ambitious man and he was further perturbed when one of Louis Philippe's younger sons, the prince de Joinville, was sent to command the French fleet, despatched to the Moroccan coast. Guizot privately explained that it was to keep the young man out of worse mischief at home, where he was becoming too friendly with Thiers and the leaders of the opposition. Unfortunately, Joinville had just written a provocative pamphlet, suggesting a lightning invasion of Britain. His appointment created the worst possible impression and Peel told Aberdeen it was 'a very bad return on the part of the King and M. Guizot for all the efforts both you and I have made to smooth their difficulties in carrying on the Government'.[19]

Aberdeen did his utmost to prevent the outbreak of hostilities between France and Morocco. Guizot 'gladly accepted' Aberdeen's offer to send Drummond Hay, the British Consul at Tangiers, to persuade the Emperor to oblige the French. At the same time Aberdeen pointed out to Guizot that the Emperor was probably genuinely unable to expel Abd–el–Kader.[20] The French were suspicious, however, that the British might be secretly stiffening Moroccan resistance. They took particular exception to the deployment of a British fleet in the western Mediterranean, and the frequent journeys of the Governor of Gibraltar – none other than Aberdeen's old friend, Sir Robert Wilson – to Tangiers.[21]

Aberdeen was prepared to go very far indeed to conciliate the French. He secured the recall of H.M.S. *Formidable* from Gibraltar so that Britain should not have a larger fleet in the area than the French.[22] Peel, however, felt that conciliation had gone far enough and it was now time for precaution. He advised the maintenance of 'a considerable Naval Force in Gibraltar Bar ready to act in case of necessity and the employment of some intelligent Military Man on the frontier of Morocco to give us reports of the real state of affairs'. Remembering how France had broken her promises about Algiers in 1830 he wanted 'formal and official assurances as to their intentions towards Morocco'.[23] Aberdeen could not ignore so definite a directive from the Prime Minister and in any case he was uneasy himself by this time. Cowley presented a note to the French government on 11 July in an attempt to extract a formal reply. Guizot, however, replied in general terms and avoided specific commitments.[24] Britain was particularly concerned about the safety of Tangiers, the supply base for Gibraltar, and Cowley's 'secret correspondents' were warning him that it was to be bombarded; but Cowley, who had repeatedly been reprimanded for listening to rumours, thought it unlikely. Early in August matters seemed to be well in train for a settlement. Telegraphic despatches were received in Paris on 9 August, announcing that Drummond Hay had persuaded the Emperor to accept the French terms and Aberdeen understood that Joinville had been instructed to suspend any operations until the results of Hay's mission could be known.[25]

It therefore came as all the greater shock when London learnt that Tangiers had been bombarded on 6 August. Louis Philippe and his ministers heard of it on the evening of 14 August. Aberdeen learnt of it on the 16th, immediately after receiving letters from Cowley, assuring him that Guizot had promised Tangiers would be respected, and from Sir Robert Wilson and the commander of the British fleet, Admiral Owen, written on 5 August 'full of joy and congratulation at the pacifick termination of the affair'. The Tahiti crisis had also just reached its most dangerous point and Aberdeen hastened to Windsor to warn the Prince of the gravity of the situation.[26]

Aberdeen now had the greatest difficulty in restraining the anger of his colleagues. Peel had already written on 12 August that France had 'a menacing fleet' off Morocco and another off Tunis. France's conduct over Algeria had been 'marked by a gross violation of her Engagements towards Europe'. Unless Britain were prepared to speak and act decisively, France would soon control both Morocco and Tunis. 'I do not attach', he said 'the slightest weight to the disclaimers of M. Guizot & the King.' Against the 'professed moderation' of the French leaders he set the fact that 'the most strenuous Exertions' were being made in every French port from which England could be threatened.[27]

Reports of hostile preparations in French ports flooded in. War steamers were supposed to be ready at Rochefort, L'Orient, Brest and Cherbourg.[28] Wellington and Graham whole-heartedly supported Peel. At the Cabinet meeting on 13 August, Aberdeen alone opposed an immediate increase in the navy. Two regiments intended for service in India were detained in Ireland in case the situation in the Mediterranean worsened. On 15 August Peel 'put the Ordnance & Admiralty into actual personal Concert as to preparations for Armament' and told Haddington at the Admiralty 'not to stint the Reliefs from the fear of exceeding the number of men voted by Parliament'. Graham recommended the immediate commissioning of three or four battle ships. 'While we are hesitating,' he wrote, 'France, if the Newspapers are to be credited, is bringing forward Three more Line of Battle Ships for active service'.[29] On 21 August Peel solemnly warned Aberdeen,

Matters are in that state that the interval of 24 hours – some act of violence for which the French Ministry is not strong enough to make reparations or disavowal may not only dissipate the shadow of the *entente cordiale* but may change our relations from Peace to War. Let us be prepared for War . . . They [the French] are much more likely to presume upon our weakness than to take offence at our strength.

Everything might depend upon the result of the first naval engagement. It would decide 'whether we contend at Sea with France single-handed, or whether the United States will declare in favour of France against us. It may also materially influence the decision of the Northern Powers of Europe in respect to active co-operation and support.'[30]

Privately Aberdeen was as angry as Peel. He told Jarnac that if it was true that the French were commissioning ships, 'I would be the first person to recommend that we should commission six sail of the line without delay.'[31] He was particularly indignant because he felt he had been misled into acting as the guarantor of French intentions to the Moroccans. But he was also acutely conscious that his colleagues' anger and the growing public excitement might spark off a major war which would be disastrous for all parties. He therefore firmly opposed military preparations. He told Peel:

There is no rational ground of quarrel between the two countries and it is the business of the Government of each, by patience, good temper, and forbearance to remove if possible any accidental misunderstanding.

He was horrified to see placards posted outside the Admiralty advertising for men for the *Queen* and the *St Vincent* for foreign service and secured their removal. He attributed much of the blame to the press and protested to Peel 'If war, the greatest of all calamities is to be endured, it will be brought upon us chiefly by the press of the two countries. I still trust that we shall not play into the hands of these firebrands.' Meanwhile he suspended judgement and waited for news from Paris or Tangiers which he hoped would put the French action in a better light.[32]

Guizot was not ready with the French explanations until 17 August. He then told Cowley that Joinville had only attacked Tangiers when he was sure Hay's mission had failed and the Moroccans were playing for time until the advanced season made naval operations impossible. As for the French assurances that Tangiers would be respected, they referred only to the town. It had never been intended that Joinville should be precluded from attacking the fortifications of Tangiers, which was all he had done. Asked why Britain had not been informed of the distinction, Guizot replied that although he had a 'large idea' of the *entente cordiale*, France could not have been expected to disclose her military plans. Although the French documents on the whole bear out Guizot's explanations, it is not surprising that both Cowley and Peel disbelieved him.[33]

Aberdeen wanted to believe Guizot but he found it very difficult. He waited impatiently for Hay's despatches, which did not arrive until 20 August and, when they came, Aberdeen, by now in a fever of nervous exasperation, complained that they were illegible and so confused he could not understand them. He did, however, gather that Joinville had had no contact with Hay before the bombardment. On the contrary, Hay sailed into Tangiers Bay just as the attack ended and found that the town, including consular houses, had been damaged. Aberdeen, under pressure from his colleagues, wrote a strong despatch to Cowley on 23 August but he also sent a private letter to Cowley on the same day telling him to use his discretion as to whether he communicated it.[34] Meanwhile King Leopold played his favourite role of mediator between Louis Philippe and the British government, sending a letter to the Prince which bore out Guizot's explanations. Albert believed him and Aberdeen let himself be persuaded too. The despatch of 23 August, the only official British protest, was much modified before it was communicated.[35]

The bombardment was a *fait accompli* but the British still feared a French occupation of Moroccan territory. Guizot sent long, reassuring private letters but Peel bluntly refused to put any more faith in private assurances.[36] In fact the French refrained from further measures and peace was concluded between France and Morocco on 10 September. Years later, Guizot was frank as to why the French did not press the matter further. They feared that the Moroccan Emperor, Abdul Rhaman, might be overthrown and that their own enemy, Abd–el–Kader, would emerge as the only man with any remaining authority. They were also seriously alarmed by the possibility of European complications.[37]

This suggests that it was the firmness of Peel, rather than the conciliatory policy of Aberdeen, which restored peace in Morocco. Although British interests did not suffer any serious material damage in the Moroccan crisis of 1844, it did leave a permanent legacy of suspicion. Peel never trusted Guizot again.

The Tangiers crisis unhappily coincided with the Tahiti crisis which seemed likely to complete the Anglo-French estrangement. Aberdeen's formulation of a Pacific policy in October 1842, when he advocated the maintenance of the independence of native rulers and more 'showing the flag' by British ships, came just too late. The previous month, Admiral Dupetit Thouars had compelled the Tahitians to accept a French protectorate. Queen Pomare's sovereignty in internal matters was guaranteed. George Pritchard was still absent in London and, although his fellow missionaries and certain naval officers who were on the spot were indignant, not much could be done. Aberdeen first learnt of the protectorate in March 1843, although full reports did not arrive until the summer. The news caused a public outcry in Britain. Various missionary societies protested to the Foreign Office and to the French Ambassador and petitions were signed by Lord Ashley and a number of bishops.[38]

Aberdeen was displeased by the French action but not disposed to make a serious quarrel. He had never been convinced of the strategic importance of Tahiti and particularly disliked pressure from Exeter Hall. He hoped at first that the French government might disavow the protectorate but they never seriously thought of doing so. They were, however, prepared to give Britain assurances about other areas, notably the Hawaiian Islands, which Britain considered strategically more important. Further, they were ready to give a formal guarantee of religious toleration and protection for British missionaries, which Aberdeen thought vital to quieten the Protestant agitation at home. In these circumstances, Aberdeen was prepared to let the matter drop and in July 1843 he virtually accepted the *fait accompli*. He did, however, again urge that British warships should visit the islands more frequently and report on the treatment of Protestant missions.[39] French actions were not reassuring. In April, the Chambers had voted an extraordinary credit of nearly six million francs for France's Pacific establishments and in October it was revealed that France had three times as many warships in the Pacific as had Britain.[40]

On 1 November, Dupetit Thouars returned to Tahiti, to be followed within a few days by the new French Governor of the island, Captain Bruat, and a detachment of French troops. Dupetit Thouars took exception to the fact that Queen Pomare was flying a Tahitian flag with a crown superimposed which probably was meant as an act of defiance to the French authorities. He said that, unless it was struck immediately, he would confiscate the Queen's dominions. Pomare refused. Dupetit Thouars landed troops and carried out his threats. Pritchard formally protested and struck his consular flag 'not having been accredited . . . to a French colony.'[41]

News of these events reached Europe in February 1844 and there was an immediate outcry in Britain. Angry and embarrassed, Aberdeen told Ste Aulaire:

This is a most vexatious affair and much more important than you may imagine . . . Tahiti is really almost an English Island; and we cannot forget what our Missionaries have done there; nor the promises which have been made by Mr Canning and succeeding Ministers in this country.

He warned Ste Aulaire that it could be 'a fatal blow to the preservation of the entente cordiale'.[42] On 25 February the French Cabinet, at a meeting presided over by Louis Philippe himself, decided to revert to a simple protectorate.[43] The matter might have rested there but for the unfortunate complications which centred on George Pritchard.

Pritchard was the hero or the villain of the drama, according to the point of view. The French protested strongly at the part Pritchard had played in November and asked for his removal. Aberdeen was inclined to believe that Pritchard might have acted unwisely. He told Peel, 'It is very likely that Mr Pritchard may have been the cause of much that has happened to this unhappy Queen.'[44] He was not adverse to removing him, if J. A. Moerenhout, the French Consul, went too. Guizot forced Aberdeen's hand by announcing in the Chambers that Pritchard was being recalled. The London Missionary Society, to which Pritchard belonged, was furious but Aberdeen tartly advised them to 'confine themselves to their proper functions' and arranged to transfer Pritchard, in his role as a British Consul, to the Navigators' Islands.[45]

Events in the Pacific had, however, once again outrun decisions in London. Tahiti was in a state of chronic insurrection. On the night of 2–3 March 1844, a French sentry was attacked and his bayonet stolen. Bruat's deputy, Captain D'Aubigny, arrested Pritchard and accused him of having stirred up the rebellion. Pritchard was imprisoned and subsequently expelled from the island. He arrived in London in July, almost as soon as the news of his arrest and expulsion. The story lost nothing in the telling. Pritchard had been imprisoned in a filthy blockhouse, dark and ankle-deep in mud. When he fell ill with dysentery neither his family nor his doctor was allowed to visit him. The only British naval officer on the spot had been rudely rebuffed when he protested. Guizot wrote later, 'All the feelings which had been excited at the commencement of the Tahiti affair, and which hitherto had been kept somewhat in check, burst forth in clubs, drawing rooms, newspapers and Parliament.' Every element, nationalist or religious, which could arouse popular passion was to be found in the incident. Here was a British subject arrested and imprisoned without trial, ill-treated and ignominiously expelled from his home; a Protestant missionary persecuted by a Roman Catholic power; a British Consul insulted by a foreign government.[46]

Peel and Aberdeen at first shared the general anger and both spoke in Parliament of the 'gross outrage' committed on a British subject. Both, however, were careful to leave the way open for amicable adjustment. Peel, in a speech which he concerted with Aberdeen beforehand, emphasised that the act had been committed by a 'person in temporary authority at Papeiti' and expressed the hope that 'the French government will at once make the reparations which the country has the right to require'. Aberdeen spoke in similar terms the following day and his own anger cannot be doubted.[47] Jarnac wrote privately to him, 'You are so very fierce at present that I am afraid of going near you again this week.'[48] At the same time, Aberdeen was soon aware that public feeling in both countries had run so high that one or both governments might be manoeuvred into some position from which retreat would be impossible and, however indignant he might be, he never doubted that the incident was not worth all the calamities of a European war.

Heated discussions took place in Paris as Cowley and Guizot produced charges and counter-charges,[49] but Aberdeen was increasingly dissatisfied with Cowley as an envoy and he preferred to conduct these critical negotiations in London with Jarnac, who was not only an able diplomat but a good friend. Much of the credit for the final resolution of the crisis goes to Jarnac but weeks of difficult negotiations lay ahead, while public excitement mounted on both sides of the Channel. Guizot, complaining of the violence of the English press, protested that they could not adjust delicate affairs when 'elles feront les explosions, explosions tous les matins, explosions à Londres, explosions à Paris, mettant le feu à tout ce qui touche'. He blamed Peel's original speech. Peel was unimpressed. He told Aberdeen, 'M. Guizot has himself alone to blame for what has occurred . . . if M. Guizot can only exist by declining to do what we would under similar circumstances there is anything but advantage to us in his remaining in power'. To Peel's considerable surprise, Aberdeen showed this letter to Jarnac.[50]

The British government were seriously contemplating strong measures, in particular sending Pritchard back to Tahiti in a warship. A stern despatch to this effect was drawn up. In part it read, 'H.M. Govt have therefore determined to send out Mr Pritchard to Tahiti in H.M. Ship Collingwood, bearing the flag of Sir Geo. Seymour [the new Commander-in-Chief in the Pacific] who will be instructed to restore Mr Pritchard to his family, and to reinstate him in the full exercise of his consular functions in Tahiti.' After that they might discuss the simultaneous removal of Pritchard and Moerenhout.[51]

The despatch was never sent but its existence was made known to Jarnac. Jarnac thought that Aberdeen had prepared it unwillingly under pressure from his colleagues, but a letter from Aberdeen to Peel of 11 August rather belies this interpretation. Aberdeen, while warning Peel of the risks of sending Pritchard back, promised that he would 'continue to hold out the possibility of the speedy return of Mr Pritchard in case no reasonable alternative shall be proposed'.[52] Aberdeen in fact was playing a difficult and delicate role. Not only was he restraining his colleagues while putting pressure on the French, he was also deliberately giving the French the impression that they had better come to terms with him, before he was overborne by more extremist colleagues. This explains why he showed Peel's confidential letter of 12 August to Jarnac.

Aberdeen's tactics succeeded. Although both Guizot and Jarnac warned him that the forcible return of Pritchard could scarcely fail to lead to hostilities, confidential negotiations to find a way out had already begun. Aberdeen dropped a hint to Jarnac that Pritchard might accept financial compensation. By 11 August he was ready to suggest £1,000 'as a solatium' to Pritchard for his sufferings, the disavowal and censure of the French officers and the removal of Moerenhout, although he told Peel that he was not sure that he would be able to obtain this.[53] Leopold offered his services again, approaching the Prince to find out what exactly Britain would accept but Aberdeen preferred to deal with Jarnac.[54]

By late August the situation seemed to have deadlocked. The British government wanted something settled before Parliament reassembled at the beginning of September. The French government was prepared to censure D'Aubigny for acting improperly but had not yet offered compensation. Cowley and Princess Lieven warned Aberdeen that this was the best Guizot could do. 'Guizot', wrote Cowley, 'makes no secret of his determination to resign if his overtures are rejected by Her Majesty's Government. He is full of anxiety, which preys upon his health and he looks ill.'[55] Aberdeen and Jarnac sombrely discussed the possibility of war and Aberdeen told him that, if Guizot resigned, he would do so too, and 'nous nous retirerons ensemble, et notre politique succomberait avec nous'.[56] *The Times* recorded of Sunday, 1 September: 'In Paris, as in London on that day, the impression was general that a crisis had arrived . . .' Charles Greville wrote in his diary that it was 'a toss up whether we went to war or not'.[57]

In fact, despite the public impression, the situation may not have been as dangerous as it had been a fortnight earlier when Britain was considering sending Pritchard back to Tahiti. Jarnac, on the strength of Guizot's private letters, assured Aberdeen that he was 'morally convinced' that an indemnity would be forthcoming. The letter Aberdeen wrote to Peel on 1 September was by no means pessimistic: 'The amount of redress,' he said, 'if measured by what we have the right to expect, is little enough; but if it is estimated by what they have the power to grant, I suppose it is all that can be done.' The Cabinet met on 2 September and Aberdeen later dropped a hint to Delane which led to the, slightly premature, publication of a leading article in *The Times*, congratulating the country on the peaceful termination of the affair.[58]

On 2 September, Guizot telegraphed to Jarnac, agreeing to pay an indemnity to Pritchard. By mutual consent the amount was to be referred to the British and French admirals in the Pacific. The affair was officially at an end and Aberdeen, at Jarnac's urgent request, secured a last minute addition to the Queen's Speech proroguing Parliament to the effect that all danger of an interruption of the good understanding with France had been 'happily averted'.[59] A spirit of mutual congratulation prevailed.

Tahiti passed under complete French control, for there was little distinction in practice between a protectorate and annexation. Commercially it was no great loss to Britain and strategically it was less important than some contemporaries believed. What was felt to be at stake was national 'honour'. In the end Aberdeen secured an apology and a promise of compensation. What more, asked Graham, could any government demand? Even Palmerston later expressed his approval of the settlement Aberdeen had obtained.[60] Both knew it was not worth a European war. Aberdeen firmly resisted public clamour and patiently negotiated a settlement. On this occasion he had proved to be a safe pilot on a very stormy sea.

Unfortunately the Tahitian and Moroccan crises – and the government, if not the public, regarded the latter as much the more important – meant that after the summer of 1844 no member of the British Cabinet, except Aberdeen himself, any longer had much faith in the French *entente*. Despite this, cordiality was apparently restored. Louis Philippe, accompanied by Guizot, came to Windsor in October 1844. The visit had been promised since the Chateau d'Eu meeting the previous year, but, at the height of the crisis, it had seemed likely that it would have to be cancelled. Aberdeen and Guizot again had wide ranging discussions.[61]

The personal co-operation of the two men in the winter of 1844–5 was remarkable. Both governments were under heavy pressure to produce the papers on the Tahiti crisis. Aberdeen and Guizot agreed to suppress some documents and edit others. In December, Peel asked Aberdeen, a little sarcastically, for the *'Parliamentary* Tahiti case. The producible controversy . . .' Aberdeen was taking no chances. The originals of all the relevant despatches were removed from the Foreign Office files and the edited versions substituted. It is only his private papers which reveal what actually happened. Guizot too asked Jarnac to return the originals so that they might be destroyed.[62]

Even so Guizot saw his majority in the Chambers reduced to eight on 27 January 1845. He begged the British government to make it clear that he had not yielded to British threats. Jarnac appealed to Aberdeen to think *'à ses deux auditoires* publiques'. Princess Lieven added her voice. She told Aberdeen, 'Votre langage et celui de Sir Robert Peel, auront une influence presque décisive sur le sort du Cabinet.'[63] Peel and Aberdeen did their best to comply but they reaped a poor reward. Guizot never dared to ask the Chambers for Pritchard's indemnity and he eventually received £2,000 'on account' from the British Foreign Office.[64] The French proceeded to establish claims to other islands in the Society group, although Aberdeen protested strongly at his next meeting with Guizot at the Chateau d'Eu in September 1845.

More seriously, the British government began to fear that the French intended to occupy the island of Chusan which the British had occupied during the Opium War, but which was due to be evacuated as soon as the last instalment of the indemnity was paid in December 1845. This was particularly irritating because the government was well aware that they would have done better to have retained Chusan, rather than Hong Kong. Graham, Wellington and Haddington agreed with Peel, 'In no circumstances ought we to consent to the occupation of Chusan by France.' Even Aberdeen admitted, 'Anything would be better than ridicule so overwhelming'.[65] He warned Ste Aulaire that

Sir John Davis, the new British Superintendent of Trade in China, had been authorised to prevent any Power occupying Chusan, without awaiting further instructions, by force if necessary, and empowered to summon reinforcements from India. Guizot replied in genuine indignation that this was to put the issues of war or peace into the hands of a subordinate agent, thousands of miles from home. He categorically denied that France had ever thought of occupying Chusan.[66] Britain secured an official assurance from the Chinese that they would never alienate Chusan and the island was evacuated without incident in July 1846.

The *entente* did not seem to be bearing much fruit in other areas either. Greece was in disorder and relations between Lyons and Piscatory steadily deteriorated. Aberdeen was exasperated and told Lyons that his complaints were 'pitiable stuff'. He boldly claimed 'Let M. Piscatory and M. Coletti govern Greece if they can. Let them make Greece as French as they please, I will take good care that justice shall be done to British subjects.'[67] Unfortunately, Aberdeen had left himself with no means of ensuring that justice. He was powerless when the Greeks brusquely dismissed General Richard Church, who had been Inspector General of the Greek army since the War of Liberation, and replaced him by the notorious General Grivas, whom Aberdeen described as 'little better than a highway robber'. Even Aberdeen called the proceedings 'a deliberate insult to England'.[68] He was equally powerless in the face of Greek intransigence in refusing to fulfil their financial obligations arising from the 1832 loan. He tried to make light of the problems when challenged in Parliament, telling the Lords that Greece 'had always been inhabited, more or less, by robbers,'[69] but it is difficult to resist the conclusion that the decline of British influence in Greece in the 1840s contributed to the notorious Don Pacifico incident in 1850. Whatever Don Pacifico's claims, there was by then no way, except a direct appeal force, by which the British government could convince the Greeks that their views must be heeded.

Even the slave-trade treaties continued to give trouble. In November 1844, Guizot suggested a commission of enquiry into the operation of the 1831 and 1833 treaties.[70] The British government reluctantly agreed. Two commissioners, the duc de Broglie, and Dr Lushington, a well–known English judge, met in March 1845. A compromise was reached on 29 May. The treaties were to be suspended for ten years but both Powers committed themselves to keep at least 26 cruisers on the West Coast of Africa to act in concert to suppress the trade. What 'acting in concert' meant was deliberately left vague, especially so far as it meant verifying the nationality of a suspected vessel. They also discussed obtaining treaties with African chiefs to permit them to destroy the 'barracoons', that is places where slaves were collected prior to shipment.[71] This had been done in the past and approved by Palmerston, but Aberdeen had reluctantly come to the conclusion, after consulting the Law Officers, that this was illegal unless Britain had treaty rights. This decision embroiled him with the anti-slavery lobby.[72]

Aberdeen, however, took one bold decision in favour of suppression. In 1844 Britain's right of search treaty with Brazil expired and the Brazilians declined to renew it. Aberdeen seized on the fact that the Brazilians had condemned the slave trade as 'piracy' and insisted that the established international convention that any warship might take action against a pirate, whatever colours he was flying, therefore applied. He secured the passage of a British Act of Parliament, popularly known as Lord Aberdeen's Act, which in effect, unilaterally extended the right of search of Brazilian ships.[73] The Act was the more sensational in that the United States had also condemned slave trading as piracy, although no one seriously supposed that Britain was going to apply the same principle to American ships.

The high-handed action towards Brazil suggests that Britain regarded the South American countries as still standing in a quasi-colonial relationship to Europe. Another illustration of this is that Britain and France became involved in a new intervention in the River Plate in 1845. The initiative for a tripartite intervention in fact came from Brazil. Peel was exasperated by the continued interruption of trade, and Aberdeen disgusted by the brutality of the war between Buenos Aires and Monte Video and alarmed for the safety of British nationals.[74] In December 1844, Britain and France agreed to undertake an armed mediation. Unfortunately the exact extent of the force to be employed was not agreed, although both Aberdeen and Guizot made it clear that they were thinking only of a naval demonstration. The mediation was entrusted to William Gore Ouseley, the son of the man who had been Robert's chief in Teheran in 1811–12. Ouseley was in Paris in January 1845. He discussed the Plate situation with French diplomats and naval officers, including the Minister of Marine, and Aberdeen does not seem to have entirely appreciated the impression that these conversations made on Ouseley.[75]

Aberdeen gave Ouseley his instructions on 20 February. Although immensely long, they were not free from ambiguity. Aberdeen impressed on Ouseley that it would be very desirable to open the tributaries of the River Plate to trade. 'To open the great arteries of the South American Continent to the free circulation of commerce would be not only a vast benefit to the trade of Europe, but a practical, and perhaps the best security for the preservation of peace in America itself.' It was not made clear how far the decision to use force, if necessary, to end the war also applied to these other desirable objectives.[76] Ouseley arrived in South America in April. His first task was to tell the Brazilians that Britain and France had decided to dispense with their participation because of the bad relations between Britain and Brazil over the slave trade and other issues. This deprived Britain and France of any chance of obtaining local ground forces. The Monte Videans accepted the Anglo-French mediation, but General Rosas sharply refused. Ouseley's despatches took a long time to reach London and British commercial interests were becoming impatient at the delay in settling the question. On 8 October, Aberdeen wrote a long private letter to Ouseley advising him:

If measures of coercion have become necessary, as is but too probable, I trust that they will have been executed with vigour, & that we shall not incur the inconvenience & loss of a long blockade . . . After the relief of Mte Video shall be effected, & the retreat of Oribe secured, I presume that the first operation will be the occupation of Martin

Garcia. This cannot be attended with much difficulty, & ought to lead to the opening of the Parana.[77]

Unknown to Aberdeen, matters had already proceeded to extremities. Ouseley and his French opposite number, Baron Deffaudis, had presented Rosas with an ultimatum, with which he had not complied, demanding that he raise his blockade of Monte Video by 31 July. Chance placed some British troops at Ouseley's disposal when the 24th and 73rd Regiments of Foot called at Rio de Janeiro on their way to the East and were diverted to the Plate. In the course of the summer, the blockade of Monte Video was raised and a blockade of Buenos Aires established. In September the two diplomats decided to extend their operations to the rivers Uruguay and Parana. The Anglo–French squadron fought a major engagement at Obligado on the Parana in November 1845.[78]

News of these events did not reach Europe until the early months of 1845. By then Aberdeen had undergone a complete change of heart. The French seemed to be cooling off. He was under heavy attack from British commercial interests in Liverpool and elsewhere, whose principal ties were with Buenos Aires. The Baring Brothers, who held the Argentinian national debt, used all their influence to stop what seemed to be becoming an intervention on the Monte Videan side. On 3 December Aberdeen wrote to Ouseley, strongly disapproving the idea of any expedition up the Parana.[79] Unfortunately, his letter arrived too late to influence events. Instead, Ouseley received Aberdeen's earlier letter of 8 October, urging vigorous action. Aberdeen and Ouseley remained at cross-purposes for the rest of the Conservative administration. Aberdeen wrote insisting on the withdrawal of the Parana expedition and the despatch of the 45th and 73rd Regiments to their proper destination, but, finding that the French had again changed their minds and were now supporting the Parana expedition, he wrote again, telling Ouseley not to get out of step with his French colleague.[80]

Ouseley was extremely indignant at his chief's disavowal and wrote repeatedly to prove that he had always acted according to his instructions.[81] Peel wished to recall him, but Aberdeen was unhappily aware that Ouseley had been placed in an impossible situation. He tried to redeem the position by sending out a special mission under Hood, a former Consul-general at Monte Video.[82] Hood reached Buenos Aires just before the Conservative ministry fell. His mission was unsuccessful and peace was not finally restored until 1850. Some years later, when he was Prime Minister, Aberdeen wrote to his then Foreign Secretary, Lord Clarendon (to whom Ousely had applied for an appointment) to tell him quite frankly that although Ouseley had fallen foul of both Aberdeen and, on another occasion, Palmerston, it had not been Ouseley's fault.[83]

It would be easy to conclude that, in most parts of the world, relations between Britain and France remained much the same as they would have done without the much publicised *entente*. This is not quite true. The *entente* at least enabled the two governments to discuss their differences in a comparatively calm atmosphere in London and Paris and so prevented their rivalry from leading to open collision. Peel at any rate had never expected the *entente* to accomplish more, but he was concerned at the fact that Britain seemed to be paying a higher price than France for this co-operation. He moved steadily towards Wellington's view that Britain's security depended on her own strength and not on the good will of other Powers.

Problems of defence had not been entirely out of the government's mind since the Eastern crisis of 1840. The navy estimates for 1841–42 were increased by nearly one million pounds.[84] British diplomats and consuls sent home disturbing reports about French naval and troop movements. Guizot announced his intention of reducing the French estimates but was, more than once, overborne by the Chamber of Deputies. The British government was the more worried because of the revolution in naval warfare resulting from the development of steam navigation. Successive governments had allowed the army to atrophy – just how far was to be revealed by the Crimean War – behind what was regarded as the safe shield of the navy. The British public was appalled by the prince de Joinville's pamphlet,[85] suggesting that the British navy could be decoyed away for a few days or hours, while a fleet of French steamships, no longer dependent on wind or tide, slipped across the Channel and disembarked an invading army. Aberdeen dismissed it as a *jeu d'esprit* by a young naval officer, but Wellington calculated that no point between the North Foreland and Selsea Bill, except the beach immediately under Dover Castle, was adequately defended against such an attack. In a matter of days a comparatively small French force could sack London and the great naval dockyards.[86]

These dangers were pressed on Peel from the beginning of his administration but at first his own desire for economy and retrenchment and Aberdeen's insistence on peace and conciliation prevailed. The navy estimates were reduced year by year. The Tahitian and Moroccan crises led Peel to enquire seriously into the state of Britain's preparedness. He was appalled by what he found. In December 1844, he wrote to the Chancellor of the Exchequer, Goulburn:

There are *awful* reports from a Commission on the state of defence of all the great naval arsenals and dockyards . . . One would suppose that each was at the mercy of a handful of men, and that it will require an enormous expenditure to give to each not complete but the most ordinary works of defence.[87]

Peel, Wellington and Graham came to the conclusion that a greatly increased naval budget would be required for 1845. Wellington wanted to go even further than his colleagues.[88]

The correspondence between Peel and Wellington, together with other papers on defence, was communicated to Aberdeen by Peel late in December. Aberdeen seems to have been kept rather in the dark about defence matters by his colleagues since, in August 1844, he differed from them on the need for an immediate increase in the navy. This partially explains the violence of his reaction. He categorically condemned the whole plan for reorganising Britain's defences, contending that it would 'virtually stultify our whole policy for the last three years'. There was no real danger and they were acting 'under the influence of mere panick'. The most he would agree to would be a modest increase to cover the new demands of the African and Chinese stations.[89]

Peel showed Wellington Aberdeen's letter. The Duke was furious. 'I had no intention', he wrote, 'of stultifying our foreign policy. It may be a foolish opinion, but I think it better to rely upon our own means for our defence than upon the faith and forbearance of France . . . I will never say or write another line on the subject, and it is far from my wish to interrupt any line of policy recommended by Lord Aberdeen.' Both Aberdeen and Peel had to write soothing letters to the Duke.[90]

The cracks in the Cabinet were papered over. The navy estimates were increased to £4,962,076, the highest sum since 1841, but Peel insisted in the Commons that this was only because of Britain's increased overseas commitments. Guizot assured Aberdeen that similar increases in the French naval budget were only to remedy past deficiencies and did not mean an expansion.[91]

The anxiety of a large section of the Cabinet remained unallayed. The whole question leapt into prominence again in the late summer of 1845 with the deterioration of relations with the United States.[92] The government could no longer ignore the cumulative evidence of muddle, neglect and incompetence in the country's defences, revealed by the enquiries instituted the previous year. Moreover, the opposition had taken up the question. In July 1845, Palmerston told the Commons that there was 'no country in Europe in such a state of defencelessness as England at the present moment'. Peel made an unconvincing reply.[93] Wellington was deeply perturbed by the exchange. Palmerston had said no more than he was thinking himself. He returned to the attack, causing Peel to defend his reply in the House. 'I presume', he wrote, 'even the strictest regard for truth does not compel a Minister of the Crown publicly to proclaim that this country is in a most defenceless state.' But, in spite of himself, Peel was convinced. 'I do not question the policy,' he admitted, 'or rather I should say the necessity for additional preparations for the contingency of war, a contingency which may occur with little previous notice.' He had already authorised the Admiralty and the Ordnance to incur expenses beyond the official Estimates.[94] Sir George Murray, the Master of the Ordnance, added his voice. Britain with her industrial concentrations and sprawling and undefended capital was peculiarly vulnerable to sudden attack. Ireland too was a danger point. An attempt on Ireland or 'such an impression upon Britain itself as should create a Revolutionary impulse in any large mass of its population might lead to every fatal result'.[95] In the days of the Irish famine and the Chartists, the government was compelled to take such a warning seriously.

Peel, Wellington, Graham and Stanley began to exchange almost daily letters on the subject of re-armament. Aberdeen was once again excluded, although this time partly by chance. In August 1845, Aberdeen accompanied the Queen and the Prince on a tour of Germany, which culminated in a visit to the Prince's home at Coburg. Aberdeen derived both pleasure and first–hand information from the expedition in the course of which he had long conversations on various questions of the day with the King of Prussia and Metternich, whom he found 'looking very old'. He told Peel 'He was always *long* in his manner of treating every subject, but as he now speaks more slowly he requires a patient listener.'[96] The visit was profitable but his absence meant that he was out of touch with the development of his colleagues' views on France and defence until he received a letter from Peel, written on 31 August, telling him, among other things, that Cowley had been home on leave and had confirmed all the Duke's apprehensions.

A small matter exacerbated misunderstandings. The Queen wished to pay another visit to the Chateau d'Eu. Unfavourable public comments were beginning to be made about the Queen's continual 'jaunts' abroad[97] and most of the Cabinet thought that her prolonged German tour would rule out such a visit in 1845. Aberdeen at first agreed with them but was persuaded by King Leopold that the Queen could easily fit in an informal visit on her way back from Germany. Peel advised against it but his letter arrived too late to prevent the programme from being carried out.[98]

Aberdeen had had another chance to discuss matters with Guizot, and he returned to London with his faith in the French government largely restored. A few conversations with Peel and Graham convinced him that an unbridgeable gap had opened between his views and those of his principal colleagues, and on 18 September he offered Peel his resignation. His letter was long and carefully thought out. He wrote:

I cannot but foresee the probability of a great difference of opinion in matters connected with an important part of our Foreign Policy, which may be attended with the most serious consequences. Graham has assured me that his own views, with respect to our relations with France, have recently undergone an entire change; and such, I perceive, is also the case with yourself. A policy of friendship and confidence has been converted into a policy of hostility and distrust. This change will of course justify and call for a corresponding change in the character of the measures adopted by us. [He could not agree] It is my deliberate and firm conviction that there is less reason to distrust the French Government, and to doubt the continuance of peace, at the present moment, than there was four years ago, when your administration was first formed.

He conceded that war might come suddenly and must come some day. Reasonable precautions were justified. But the government was acting in a panic. He had heard that ships were to be recalled from the Africa squadron, that Britain was preparing her 'advanced ships' and that some had '*actually got their water aboard*'. This was absurd and could only spread alarm aboard.

He spoke with some pain of his difficulties with the Duke of Wellington, who, he supposed, must regard him as 'the only obstacle to the adoption of measures which he sincerely believes to be indispensible for the welfare and safety of the country'. This was tolerable so long as others regarded the Duke's fears as 'chimerical' but this was no longer so. He thought it better that he should retire before there was any public difference. No open controversy need ensue.

It is well known to my friends and connexions that office is not only irksome to me, but that considerations of health have more than once pretty urgently called for this proceeding. No other motive will be assigned, and it will be the more easy to sanction this, as I have no wish ever to enter the House of Lords again.

Nevertheless, he left the final decision to Peel. He had no wish to embarrass him and he added, with a touch of pride, that at present 'there may be no person altogether so acceptable to the Great Powers of Europe as myself'.[99]

Aberdeen's letter came as a great shock to Peel, who replied at once that he would consider Aberdeen's loss as 'irreparable'. He could never consent to Aberdeen retiring without assigning the real reason. It would be unfair to Aberdeen himself and quite impracticable. The Queen and the Cabinet would have to be told the truth and 'my experience of public life convinces me that a week could not pass without entailing the necessity of an explicit disclosure of the real grounds of your retirement'.[100]

Peel showed Aberdeen's letter to Graham and Wellington, under injunctions of strict secrecy. They reacted much as their leader had done. Graham replied that he was always willing to reconsider when his views differed from Aberdeen's. 'I think highly of his abilities,' he said, 'I admire his sterling honesty and pure principles . . . It is the pride and strength of your Government to have such a Man in the place which he now fills. His loss would be irreparable.' Wellington in his reply, although dwelling on possible dangers, emphasised that he agreed with the need for understanding with France. He concurred in everything Peel had said about Aberdeen's resignation.[101]

The matter was finally thrashed out between Peel and Aberdeen during a few days which they spent together at Drayton, towards the end of September. Aberdeen agreed to stay in the government but essentially they agreed to differ.[102] The basic policy difference was not resolved. Peel and the majority of his colleagues continued to look to England's defences. Aberdeen tried to establish yet closer relations with Guizot. Guizot expressed his agreement with Aberdeen: 'Des ministres devoués comme nous à la paix', he wrote on 2 October, 'seraient insensés de préparer ou de laisser préparer la guerre . . . si vis pacem, para bellum, est devenue absurde et dangereuse.' Peel, when shown the letter, was sceptical. Guizot, he replied, 'may be perfectly sincere as an individual in controverting the maxim . . . But, as the Minister of France . . . can he point to her *practice* as confirming his theory?' Aberdeen prepared an elaborate reply but did not send it.[103]

Peel and Aberdeen avoided the subject between themselves although Aberdeen could not refrain from protesting at the appointment of Ellenborough, newly returned from India, to succeed Haddington at the Admiralty in Peel's reconstituted government of December 1845. 'Knowing his military propensities,' he wrote, 'I expect to hear the "note of preparation" loudly sounded by himself as well as by the Duke. It may be difficult to resist these two "dua fulmina belli".'[104]

In fact, despite Aberdeen's apprehensions, the domestic crisis drove the military precautions from the centre of the stage. The whole matter was dropped as suddenly as it had been taken up. This *volte face* lends a certain air of unreality to what Aberdeen always described as the 'panic' of 1845. Either the country was defenceless in the face of imminent danger or it was not. If it was, it was irresponsible of the government to drop the question. If it was not, Aberdeen was right to plead for calm.

NOTES

1. FO 27/666, Cowley to Aberdeen, No. 113, 24 Mar. 1843.
2. Add. MSS 43062, Peel to Aberdeen, 3 Sept. 1843; Add. MSS 40453, Aberdeen to Peel, 3 Sept. 1843.
3. Add. MSS 43211, Robert to Aberdeen, 13 Sept., 13 Dec. 1843.
4. Add. MSS 43045, Victoria to Aberdeen, n.d. June 1845.
5. The social side of the visit is described in great detail in Charlotte Canning's Diary, (V. Surtees, pp. 86–118). Charlotte was the daughter of Stuart de Rothesay and married the second Viscount Canning who became Aberdeen's Political Under-Secretary in 1841.
6. Guizot, vol. 6, pp. 195–6.
7. Jarnac, 'Lord Aberdeen, Souvenirs et papiers diplomatiques', *Revue des deux mondes*, xxxiv (1861), pp. 451–2; FO 27/671, Cowley to Aberdeen, Secret 29 Dec. 1843; Add. MSS 43132, Ste Aulaire to Aberdeen, 31 Jan. 1844; *Hansard*, 3rd ser., LXXII, 95–7.
8. *Letters of Queen Victoria*, vol. 1, pp. 507–8; Add. MSS 40454, Aberdeen to Peel, 26 Oct., 7, 8 Dec. 1843. Aberdeen was originally sorry for the 'poor young man', asking 'What mischief can he possibly do here?'.
9. Add. MSS 43135, Lyons to Aberdeen, 22 Dec. 1841, Aberdeen to Lyons, 30 Oct. 1841, 30 Oct. 1843; 43136, Aberdeen to Lyons, 5 Jan. 1844.
10. FO 32/115, Lyons to Aberdeen, No. 91, 6 Dec. 1842.
11. Add. MSS 43211, Aberdeen to Robert, 3 Nov. 1843.
12. Add. MSS 43063, Peel to Aberdeen, 15 Oct. 1843; Add. MSS 40453, Aberdeen to Peel, 18, 26 Oct. 1843; FO 32/119, Aberdeen to Lyons, No. 38, 25 Oct. 1843.
13. Add. MSS 43134, Aberdeen to Guizot, 23 Nov. 1843, Guizot to Aberdeen, 29 Nov. 1843; Guizot Papers 42 AP 7, Guizot to Piscatory, 8 Oct. 1843; FO 32/119, Aberdeen to Lyons, No. 44, 25 Nov. 1843; Add. MSS 43136, Aberdeen to Lyons, 15, 24 Nov., 6 Dec. 1843.
14. FO 32/130, Lyons to Aberdeen, No. 84, 20 Aug. 1844; Add. MSS 43136, Lyons to Aberdeen, 20, 22, 31 July, 21, 27 Aug., 10 Sept. 1844.
15. Add. MSS 43132, Aberdeen to Jarnac, 20 Sept. 1844.
16. Add. MSS 43133, Jarnac to Aberdeen, 24, 26 Sept. 1844; Add. MSS 43136, Aberdeen to Lyons, 16 Oct. 1844.
17. Add. MSS 43136, Aberdeen to Lyons, 16 Oct. 1844; FO 32/126, Aberdeen to Lyons, No. 60, 25 Sept. 1844.
18. Add. MSS 43132, Guizot to Ste Aulaire, 15 June 1844.
19. Add. MSS 43130, Aberdeen to Cowley, 14 June 1844; Add. MSS 43132, Guizot to Ste Aulaire, 17 June 1844, Guizot to Jarnac, 3 July 1844; Add. MSS 43063, Peel to Aberdeen, 12 Aug. 1844. For further effects of Joinville's pamphlet see p. 371.
20. Add. MSS 43130, Aberdeen to Cowley, 14 June 1844; Add. MSS 43132, Guizot to Ste Aulaire, 17 June 1844; FO 27/690, Aberdeen to Cowley, No. 179, 21 June 1844.
21. Add. MSS 43132, Guizot to Ste Aulaire, 17 June 1844, Guizot to Jarnac, 3 July 1844 encl. Louis Philippe to Guizot, 29 June, Jarnac to Aberdeen, 20 July 1844 encl. Guizot to Jarnac, 18 July 1844; AAE Angleterre 663, Guizot to Ste Aulaire, No. 47, 2 June 1844.

22. Add. MSS 43130, Aberdeen to Cowley, 5, 16 July 1844.

23. Add. MSS 43063, Peel to Aberdeen, 2 July 1844.

24. FO 27/698, Cowley to Aberdeen, No. 336, 5 July, No. 350, 12 July, No. 352, 14 July 1844.

25. Add. MSS 43130, Cowley to Aberdeen, 12 July, 12 Aug. 1844; FO 27/698–9, Cowley to Aberdeen, Secret, 1 July, No. 358, 15 July, No. 403, 9 Aug. 1844.

26. The Queen was convalescing after the birth of Prince Alfred; Add. MSS 43044, Aberdeen to Albert, 16 Aug., Albert to Aberdeen, 16 Aug. 1844; Add. MSS 40454, Aberdeen to Peel, 16, 20 Aug. 1844.

27. Add. MSS 43063, Peel to Aberdeen, 12 Aug. 1844.

28. Add. MSS 40460, Peel to Wellington, 20 Aug. 1844; Add. MSS 43063, Peel to Aberdeen 21 Aug. 1844.

29. Add. MSS 40450, Peel to Graham, 9, 15 Aug. 1844, Graham to Peel, 17,18, 22, 26 Aug. 1844.

30. Add. MSS 43063, Peel to Aberdeen, 21 Aug. 1844.

31. Add. MSS 40454, Aberdeen to Peel, 20 Aug. 1844; AAE Angleterre 664, Jarnac to Guizot, 'Officielle', 22 Aug. 1844.

32. Add. MSS 40454, Aberdeen to Peel, 19, 20, 21 Aug. 1844.

33. FO 27/699, Cowley to Aberdeen, Secret, 19 Aug., No. 425, 19 Aug. 1844; Add. MSS 43130, Cowley to Aberdeen, 18, 26 Aug. 1844; Add. MSS 43133, Guizot to Jarnac, 27 Aug. 1844; Add. MSS 43063, Peel to Aberdeen, 21 Aug. 1844. Joinville's private letters are in Guizot Papers 42AP 6, and the official reports in AAE Maroc, 12 bis.

34. Add. MSS 40454, Aberdeen to Peel, 20 Aug. 1844; FO 27/691, Aberdeen to Cowley, No. 241, 23 Aug. 1844; Add. MSS 43130, Aberdeen to Cowley, 23 Aug. 1844.

35. Add. MSS 43044, Albert to Aberdeen, 20, 24 Aug. 1844 and encls; Add. MSS 43130, Aberdeen to Cowley, 24, 27 Aug. 1844.

36. Add. MSS 43133, Guizot to Jarnac, 24, 27 Aug. 1844; Add. MSS 43063, Peel to Aberdeen, 28 Aug. 1844.

37. Guizot, vol. 7, pp. 168–70.

38. Society Islands Correspondence, pp. 100–5, 173–4; The Times, 13, 21 Mar., 1 Apr. 1843.

39. AAE Angleterre 661, Ste Aulaire to Guizot, No. 29, 14 Mar., No. 30, 21 Mar. 1843; Addington to Barrow, 11 July 1843, Society Islands Correspondence, pp. 134–5.

40. FO 27/666, Cowley to Aberdeen, No. 145, 17 Apr. 1843; Society Islands Correspondence, pp. 134–6, 179–80, 213–14.

41. Society Islands Correspondence, pp. 210–17, 222, 226–9.

42. Add. MSS 43132, Aberdeen to Ste Aulaire, 20 Feb. 1844; RA B8/49, Aberdeen to Victoria, 23 Feb. 1844.

43. FO 27/693, Cowley to Aberdeen, No. 110, 25 Feb. 1844.

44. Add. MSS 40454, Aberdeen to Peel, 28 Feb. 1844.

45. Add. MSS 40454, Aberdeen to Peel, 13 Mar. 1844, London Missionary Society to Aberdeen, 20 Mar., 6, 26 Apr. 1844, Addington to L.M.S., 16 Apr. 1844, Society Islands Correspondence, pp. 236, 239, 243–7.

46. Guizot, Sir Robert Peel, p. 176, Morning Chronicle, 31 July, 1, 15 Aug. 1844; The Times, 8, 15 Aug. 1844; AAE Angleterre 664, Jarnac to Guizot, 4, 28 Aug. 1844. Punch published a cartoon of 'The London Mission – Loading the Gun at Exeter Hall', vol. 7, p. 105.

47. *Hansard*, 3rd ser., LXVI, 1575–6, 1642–6.
48. Add. MSS 43133, Jarnac to Aberdeen, 3 Aug. 1844.
49. FO 27/699, Cowley to Aberdeen, No. 392, 2 Aug. 1844, Secret, 2 Aug. 1844.
50. Add. MSS 43131, Guizot to Jarnac, 8 Aug. 1844; Add. MSS 40454, Peel to Aberdeen, 12 Aug. 1844; Add. MSS 40450, Peel to Graham, Secret, 15 Aug. 1844.
51. Add. MSS 43130, Draft despatch, n.d. Aug. 1844.
52. Add. MSS 40454, Aberdeen to Peel, 11 Aug. 1844.
53. Add. MSS 40454, Aberdeen to Peel, 11 Aug. 1844.
54. Add. MSS 43044, Albert to Aberdeen, 24 Aug. 1844 encl. Leopold to Albert, 21 Aug. 1844.
55. Lieven to Aberdeen, 1 Sept. 1844, Jones Parry, vol. 1, pp. 229–30; Add. MSS 43130, Cowley to Aberdeen, 30 Aug. 1844.
56. Jarnac, *Revue des deux mondes*, XXXIV (1861) 456.
57. *The Times*, 3 Sept. 1844; Greville, vol. 2, pp. 252–4.
58. Add. MSS 43133, Jarnac to Aberdeen, 2 Sept. 1844; Add. MSS 40454, Aberdeen to Peel, 1 Sept. 1844; Delane to Reeves, 3 Sept. 1844, quoted Laughton, vol. 1, pp. 168–70; *The Times*, 3 Sept. 1844.
59. AAE Angleterre 664, Guizot to Jarnac, Tel, 2 Sept. 1844 (the letter of the same date in FO 27/708 is edited, see p. 367); *Hansard*, 3rd ser., LXXVI, 1998.
60. *Hansard*, 3rd ser., LXXVII, 116–8.
61. Guizot, vol. 6, pp. 213–21.
62. Add. MSS 43133, Guizot to Jarnac, 9 Sept., 26 Nov. 1844, Jarnac to Aberdeen, 12 Sept., 20 Dec. 1844; Aberdeen to Jarnac, 20 Sept. 1844; Guizot Papers 42 AP 7, Guizot to Jarnac, 1, 16 Dec. 1844; Add. MSS 43064, Peel to Aberdeen, 17 Dec. 1844.
63. Add. MSS 43133, Jarnac to Aberdeen, 21 Jan. 1845; Lieven to Aberdeen, 30 Jan. 1845, Jones–Parry, vol. 1, p. 237.
64. Society Islands Correspondence, pp. 558, 572, 599; W. Pritchard, p. 48.
65. Add. MSS 43190, Graham, Memorandum, 22 Apr. 1845; Add. MSS 43244, Wellington, Memorandum, 23 Apr. 1845; Add. MSS 40455, Aberdeen to Peel, 21 Oct. 1845.
66. Add. MSS 43198, Aberdeen to Davis, 7 May 1845; Add. MSS 43133, Guizot to Jarnac, 30 Oct., 5 Nov. 1845.
67. Add. MSS 43136, Aberdeen to Lyons, 11 Nov. 1844.
68. FO 32/126, Aberdeen to Lyons, No. 71, 2 Dec. 1844; Add. MSS 43134, Aberdeen to Guizot, 20 Dec. 1844.
69. *Hansard*, 3rd ser., LXXXII, 1281.
70. Add. MSS 43134, Guizot to Aberdeen, 27 Nov. 1844; Guizot Papers, 42AP 8, Guizot to Ste Aulaire, 27 Nov. 1844.
71. *B.F.S.P.* vol. 33, pp. 4–18.
72. Mathieson, pp. 60–3.
73. *B.F.S.P.* vol. 4, p. 85, vol. 14, p. 609, vol. 34, pp. 688 ff.; Add. MSS 40454, Aberdeen to Peel, 18 Oct. 1844; Add. MSS 43125, ff. 135–258; FO 84/523–5, Correspondence with Lisboa, *passim*. Cf. Bethell, pp. 242–66.
74. FO 13/219 *passim*. Correspondence with Abrantes; Add. MSS 40454, Aberdeen to Peel, 17 Oct. 1844.
75. FO 27/701, Cowley to Aberdeen, No. 572, 6 Dec. 1844; FO 27/691, Aberdeen to Cowley, No. 287, 17 Dec. 1844; Add. MSS 43127, Ouseley to Aberdeen, 10, 20 Jan. 1845.

76. FO 6/102, Aberdeen to Ouseley, No. 4, 20 Feb. 1845.
77. Add. MSS 43127, Aberdeen to Ouseley, 8 Oct. 1845.
78. The first naval battle in which steamships played a decisive part; Add. MSS 43127, Ouseley to Aberdeen, 17 Aug., 8, 9 (2) Sept., 30 Nov. 1845; Ouseley's official reports are in FO 6/104–7.
79. Add. MSS 43127, Aberdeen to Ouseley, 3 Dec. 1845.
80. Add. MSS 43127, Aberdeen to Ouseley, 15 Jan., 4 Feb., 4 Mar. 1846; FO 6/114, Aberdeen to Ouseley, No. 26, 17 Mar. 1846.
81. Add. MSS 43127, Ouseley to Aberdeen, 31 Jan., 18, 19 Apr., 6 May, 6 June, 7, 8, 20 June, 4 July 1846.
82. Add. MSS 40455, Peel to Aberdeen, 21 Apr. 1846; Add. MSS 43126, Aberdeen to Hood, 9 Apr. 1846.
83. MSS Clar. dep. c4, Aberdeen to Clarendon, 23 Feb. 1853.
84. PP, XIV (1841) 253; PP, XXVII (1842) 345.
85. *Notes sur les forces navales de la France.*
86. Wellington to Sir John Burgoyne, 9 Jan. 1847, quoted Briggs, pp. 278–83.
87. Add. MSS 40444, Peel to Goulburn, 7 Dec. 1844.
88. Add. MSS 40460, Wellington to Peel, 24 Aug. 1844, Murray to Wellington, 29 Nov. 1844; Add. MSS 40450, Herbert, memorandum, 4 Sept. 1844, Graham to Peel, 18 Sept. 1844.
89. Add. MSS 43064, Peel to Aberdeen, 29 Dec. 1844; Add. MSS 40454, Aberdeen to Peel, 31 Dec. 1844.
90. Add. MSS 40461, Wellington to Peel, 7 Jan. 1845, Peel to Wellington, 12 Jan. 1845; Add. MSS 43060, Aberdeen to Wellington, 14 Jan. 1845.
91. PP, XXIX (1845) 173; *Hansard*, 3rd ser., LXXVII, 211–4, 464–7, 1240–1308; Add. MSS 43133, Guizot to Ste Aulaire, 20 Jan. 1845.
92. In Add. MSS 40461 there is a large section headed in Peel's own hand, 'These are important Confidential Papers relating to the defences of the Country from Invasion . . . during the autumn of 1845.'
93. *Hansard*, 3rd ser., LXXXII, 1223–33.
94. Add. MSS 40461, Wellington to Peel, 7 Aug. 1845, Peel to Wellington, 9, 13 Aug. 1845.
95. Add. MSS 40451, Murray, Memorandum, 9 Aug. 1845.
96. Add. MSS 40455, Aberdeen to Peel, 15 Aug. 1845. Aberdeen described the conversations he had in great detail to Peel; Charlotte Canning described the social side of the visit in her diary (Surtees, pp. 151–65).
97. For instance, *Punch*, 'Victoria's Voyages for the next Ten Years', 5, p. 128, culminating in one to the North Pole.
98. Add. MSS 40455, Aberdeen to Peel, 25, 29 Aug. 1845; Add. MSS 43064, Peel to Aberdeen, 31 Aug. 1845.
99. Add. MSS 40455, Aberdeen to Peel, 18 Sept. 1845.
100. Add. MSS 43064, Peel to Aberdeen, 20 Sept. 1845.
101. Add. MSS 40451, Graham to Peel, 21 Sept. 1845; Add. MSS 40451, Wellington to Peel, 22 Sept. 1845.
102. Add. MSS 43064, Peel to Aberdeen, 30 Sept. 1845.
103. Add. MSS 43134, Guizot to Aberdeen, 2 Oct. 1845; Add. MSS 43065, Peel to Aberdeen, 17 Oct. 1845; Add. MSS 43065, Aberdeen to Peel, 20 Oct. 1845 (not sent).
104. Add. MSS 40455, Aberdeen to Peel, 29 Dec. 1845.

CHAPTER TWENTY-THREE

The collapse of the *entente*

The Tsar Nicholas came to London in the midst of the Tahitian and Moroccan crises in June 1844. As early as December 1843, rumours began to circulate that the Tsar would like to come to England as a counter-stroke to the Chateau d'Eu meeting, which had annoyed the more conservative courts of Europe,[1] but the project became the prey of the Tsar's eccentricity. He failed to inform the British government when, or even whether, he was coming and by the end of May 1844, Aberdeen had made up his mind that he would not come at all. The visit was inconvenient because Victoria was about to be confined (Prince Alfred was born on 6 August) and arrangements had already been made for a visit by the King of Saxony. In the end the two monarchs arrived together and a hasty programme of festivities was mapped out for them.[2]

During a military review the Tsar seized his opportunity to make a rather theatrical remark to Victoria that all his forces were at her disposal. This was construed by some observers, including even the comte de Jarnac,[3] into the offer of an alliance against France but there is no evidence at all that the British government took the remark seriously. Much more significant, in the long run, were the conversations which took place between the Tsar and Aberdeen on the possible collapse of the Turkish empire.

It is, unfortunately, impossible to reconstruct exactly what was said in the course of these conversations. They were casual and intermittent, much interrupted by formal engagements. No written record was kept on the British side, officially or unofficially, and since all the leading members of the Cabinet were together in London, there was no need for letters. It is, however, clear that at the time Aberdeen did not attribute to these conversations anything like the importance that they were later to assume. He already regarded the Tsar as an unreliable eccentric and he knew that the Tsar's views were not always those of his ministers. In addition he had many more urgent matters, connected with the crisis with France, on his mind. It seems probable that he expressed polite agreement with the Tsar's views, without attaching too much weight to them.

The Tsar, on the other hand, thought that he had won a major victory. It was not that he was pressing for the break up of the Turkish Empire. On the contrary Russian policy was still guided by the Protocol, drawn up in 1829 by the Committee on Turkish affairs, which had declared that, from the Russian point of view, the dangers involved in the dissolution of the Turkish Empire would outweigh the advantages. The Tsar, however, foresaw that the Turkish Empire might break up of its own accord. In that event he wanted to revive the alignments of 1840 and ensure that Britain would support Russia and would not ally with France against her. This was the point which the Tsar believed he had gained in his talks with Aberdeen and, immediately on his return to St Petersburg, he sent Nesselrode to London to get the agreement put into writing. Aberdeen, still not suspecting the gravity of what he was doing, was delighted to see his old friend Nesselrode, and the latter, with Aberdeen's approval, was soon able to draw up a memorandum, based on the conversations between Aberdeen and the Tsar.[4]

This memorandum has been the subject of so much later misrepresentation that its contents must be examined in some detail. So far from being an agreement about the partition of the Turkish Empire, its emphasis was all on the preservation of that Empire. It began:

La Russie et l'Angleterre sont mutuellement penetrée de la conviction qu'il est de leur intérêt commun que la Porte Ottomane se maintienne dans l'état d'independance et de possession territoriale dont se compose actuellement cet Empire, cette combinaison politique étant celle qui se concilie le miex avec l'intérêt général de la conservation de la paix.

The British and Russian governments would therefore do their utmost to uphold the Sultan's authority, even though his tendency to break engagements with the European Powers and to persecute his Christian subjects, might occasionally necessitate joint representations. If, despite all their efforts, the Turkish Empire did break up:

la Russie et l'Angleterre s'entendent sur la marche qu'elles auront à adopter en commun . . . Sur terre, la Russie exerce envers la Turquie une action préponderante. Sur mer, l'Angleterre occupe la même position. Isolée, l'action de ces deux Puissances pourrait faire beaucoup de mal. Combinée elle pourra produire un bien réel; de là l'utilité de s'entendre préalablement avant d'agir.

The two Powers summarised their objectives thus:

Le but dans lequel la Russie et l'Angleterre auront à s'entendre peut se formuler de la manière suivante:
1 Chercher à maintenir l'existence de l'Empire Ottoman dans son état actuel, aussi longtemps que cette combinaison politique sera possible;
2 Si nous prévoyons qu'il doit crouler, se concerter préalablement sur tout ce qui concerne l'établissement d' un nouvel ordre de choses destiné à remplacer celui qui existe aujourd'hui, et veiller en commun à ce que le changement survenu dans la situation interieure de cet Empire, ne puisse porter atteinte ni à la sureté de leurs propres états et aux droits que les Traités leur assurent respectivement, ni au maintien de l'équilibre Européen.

Russia and Austria were already in agreement (since the Treaty of Münchengratz of 1833). 'Si l'Angleterre comme principale Puissance maritime agit d'accord avec Elles, il est à penser que la France se trouvera dans la necessité de se conformer a la marche concertée entre St Petersbourg, Londres et Vienne.' General agreement would be secured and peace preserved.[5]

There is nothing in Aberdeen's or Sir Robert Peel's papers to suggest that they regarded this document as in any way revolutionary. They had not departed from their policy that the Turkish Empire must be preserved. On the contrary, in so far as the Tsar's word could be relied upon, they had gained a substantial victory by securing Russia's formal adherence to that policy. It was only a decade later, in totally changed circumstances, that the memorandum assumed an importance which had never been envisaged in 1844.

Always a dangerous source of international conflict, the Near East was comparatively quiet in this period. There was nothing that the experienced Stratford Canning at Constantinople could not handle. Some warning signs had, however, appeared. The Europeans had become more prone to proselytise. One sign of this had been the setting up of an Anglo-Prussian Protestant bishopric of Jerusalem.[6] Aberdeen had here carried on the policy which he had inherited from his immediate predecessors and had had some correspondence with his old friend, William Howley, the Archbishop of Canterbury, on the subject. It had been decided that the new bishop should go out in state on a warship but it had been disconcerting to find that the only suitable warship was named *Devestation*. The French had been busy converting Syrians to Roman Catholicism. The Sultan had responded by re-enforcing old laws which prescribed the death penalty for apostasy from Islam. Stratford Canning had not approved of this missionary zeal, complaining that they had enough trouble with all the local sects of Maronites, Druses, Syrian Jacobites and the rest, without adding the complications of the Reformation. Unfortunately, many of these religious groups looked to European patrons for their protection.[7] The full implications of this too, however, were not to appear for another decade.

If the vexed problems of the Near East looked well on the way to settlement in the early 1840s, so too did the equally vexed problems of Spain. The outstanding issue was still the marriage of Queen Isabella and her younger sister. This was one of the main topics discussed between Aberdeen and Guizot at the Chateau d'Eu meeting in September 1843. The matter had become urgent because, in July 1843, Espartero had been overthrown and, in November, the thirteen year old Isabella was proclaimed of age to dispense with the need for a Regent. Palmerston later declared that the fall of Espartero was a disaster for British interests in Spain, and Arthur Aston, the British Minister in Madrid, warned his government that it was a victory for the French party; but Aberdeen, true to his principle of not supporting any particular party in Spain, took it calmly.[8]

Victoria, and still more the Prince, would have liked Isabella to have married Albert's own cousin, Prince Leopold of Saxe-Coburg.[9] Espartero was supposed to have favoured this, but Aberdeen was adamant that there must be no 'English candidate'. Isabella's marriage was a matter for the Spanish people, although he now maintained respect for the balance of power would make it impossible for Britain to look 'with indifference' on a marriage between Isabella and a French prince. Such an alliance would not be a *casus belli* but it would justify Britain in withdrawing all countenance from the Spanish government. Britain would not object to a marriage between Isabella and any other Bourbon prince but she could not concede, as the French wished, that Isabella's choice should be limited to a Bourbon.[10] The French government had made several previous attempts to secure agreement, notably in Alphonse Pageot's mission to London and Vienna in 1842 and Sebastiani's mission to London in August 1843. It had emerged that Metternich would have liked Isabella to marry Don Carlos's son – an idea to which Aberdeen was thoroughly opposed, since it would have revived all the old controversies.[11] Britain and France had made little progress towards concerting their policies before Aberdeen and Guizot met at Eu.

At Eu Guizot convinced Aberdeen that France objected to Leopold as much as Britain objected to a French prince and made it plain that Leopold's candidature would lead to a renewal of the duc d'Aumâle's claims. Aberdeen, although in theory maintaining Spain's freedom of choice, then entered into an entirely informal agreement that, in return for France excluding Louis Philippe's sons from consideration, Britain would support the choice of some other Bourbon. Only in December, at the French request, was the agreement put into writing. Peel disliked a 'formal communication', feeling that it was a derogation of Spanish sovereignty. He was also uncertain what use Guizot might make of it.[12] Part of the trouble was that the available Bourbons were singularly uninspiring. In practice there were three: the comte de Trapani (the son of the King of Naples), and two Spanish cousins of the Queen, the Duke of Cadiz and his younger brother, the Duke of Seville. It was not true, as is so often stated, that contemporary diplomats believed the Duke of Cadiz to be impotent. On the contrary, they believed that, although a homosexual, he had fathered a number of bastard children. The real problem was that Isabella herself was such a poor physical specimen, the result of generations of interbreeding, that many doubted whether she would ever be capable of bearing children. For this reason, the marriage of the Infanta was regarded as almost as important as the marriage of the Queen.

In the summer of 1844, rumours began to spread that the French favoured a marriage between the Infanta and another of the younger sons of Louis Philippe, the duc de Montpensier, and it was rightly reported that Charles Bresson, the French Minister in Madrid, was an enthusiast for it. Peel described any such suggestion as 'underhand and dishonest'.[13]

When Aberdeen and Guizot met again at the Chateau d'Eu in September 1845, Aberdeen found the Spanish marriage question to be the chief topic of interest there. Louis Philippe and Guizot had given their support to the comte de Trapani and they both explained to Aberdeen that they could not very well desert him, unless his candidature proved quite impossible, but they would then have no objection to supporting the Duke of Seville whom, at this time, Aberdeen preferred. The discussion then turned to the Infanta and Aberdeen's account, written to Peel at the time, of what he understood the French had agreed to, is very important in view of the differences of opinion to which it later gave rise.

Aberdeen told Peel: 'With respect to the Infanta they both declared in the most positive manner, that until the queen was married *and had children*, they should consider the Infanta precisely as her sister, and that any marriage with a French Prince would be entirely out of the question.' Aberdeen understood, however, that if Isabella had children, not one child, the French would consider a marriage between the Infanta and a French prince, unexceptional. Aberdeen thought these assurances satisfactory and proposed to postpone further discussion.[14]

Peel was less satisfied. He wanted to put the Montpensier marriage out of court altogether. Suppose Isabella had one or two weak or sickly infants, idiots perhaps (not at all improbable given the history of the Spanish royal family), or suppose there was a long interval after the birth of her first child, could the Infanta and a French prince be expected to wait indefinitely? He considered Britain should enter into no engagements at all.[15] Thus urged, Aberdeen spoke to Jarnac, insisting that his conversations with Guizot were unofficial and in no way binding. Guizot readily agreed. 'Il n'y a point de communication', he wrote, 'ni d'entente régulière à établir et encore moins à proclamer entre nous sur la question du mariage de l'Infanta.' He had only performed a friendly act by declaring in advance what his policy would be in certain circumstances.[16] Less than two years later, Guizot was to take advantage of these reservations in a way in which Peel and Aberdeen had not anticipated.

The winter of 1845–46 saw the practical failure of the Neapolitan marriage project and the renewal of the Coburg candidature. The latter received no countenance from Aberdeen but the British Court could not entirely conceal their conviction that Leopold would be a much more suitable husband for Isabella than a degenerate Bourbon. When Leopold and his father spent the winter in Lisbon and talked of visiting Madrid, the French scented intrigue.[17] It was in these circumstances that Guizot communicated to Ste Aulaire the famous memorandum of 27 February 1845, part of which read:

Si le mariage soit de la reine, soit de l'infante, avec le prince Leopold de Coburg, ou avec tout autre prince étranger aux descendants de Philippe V, devenait probable et imminent . . . dans ce cas nous serions affranchis de tout engagement, et libres d'agir immédiatement pour parer le coup, en demandant la main, soit de la reine soit de l'infante, pour M. le duc Montpensier.

The only way of averting such a contretemps was for Britain to join France in expediting a Bourbon marriage.[18]

When this memorandum was shown to Aberdeen he was not greatly perturbed. He had no intention of supporting a Coburg candidate and he interpreted it as a French attempt to spur the British on to be more active in support of a Bourbon. Indeed in his reply he tended to revert to an earlier position. He did not, he said, like the *limitation* of the Queen's choice to the Bourbons (who, as individuals, had little to commend them), although a Bourbon might prove to be the best choice.[19]

At this point, matters were complicated by a serious intrigue in Madrid. Henry Bulwer had succeeded Arthur Aston as British Minister there. Aberdeen had repeated his instructions that there must be no 'English candidate' but he had not concealed that he was half-hearted in his support of a Bourbon. Bulwer allowed himself to become the intermediary, if not the author, of a letter from Queen Christina to the Duke of Saxe-Coburg, suggesting a marriage between her daughter and Prince Leopold. Bulwer outlined to Aberdeen a plan for carrying through this scheme. The Spanish ministry would be reconstituted, formally reject the comte de Trapani and accept Leopold, summon the Cortes and announce the decision. Europe would thus be faced with a *fait accompli*. The Spaniards would insist on their freedom of choice but placate France by offering the Infanta's hand to Montpensier.[20]

Aberdeen was alarmed at the devious paths into which Bulwer seemed to be leading them. He rebuked him and instructed him to revert to strict neutrality. To be on the safe side, he himself told the French the substance of what had happened but he firmly rejected their request that Bulwer be recalled.[21] The Spanish Minister in London, the Duke of Sotomayer, asked what would be the British attitude if Spain chose a candidate other than a Bourbon and the French consequently tried to coerce Spain. Aberdeen replied in terms not entirely in the spirit of his earlier discussions with Guizot. Britain, he said, had always denied France's right to insist on a Bourbon. He did not think the French would act in such circumstances but, if they did, Spain would have the 'warmest sympathy' of all Europe.[22] Aberdeen may have been moved by concern for the young Queen and reluctance to see her forced into a disagreeable marriage. He was also influenced by his own court's sympathy for a Coburg candidate and a desire not to seem, either to Palmerston or to his own colleagues, to be truckling to France. He did not attempt to spell out the form the 'sympathy' of Europe might be expected to take, but it is clear that even before the Conservative administration fell, Anglo-French understanding on Spain had worn very thin.

The Conservative government was in fact now living on borrowed time. On 2 December 1845, Peel had finally told his Cabinet colleagues that, in his opinion, the solution of the Irish crisis required the immediate and permanent repeal of the Corn Laws. On 4 December Lord Stanley and the Duke of Buccleuch warned Peel that they would sooner resign. Two days later, Peel offered his government's resignation to the Queen and advised her to send for Russell. Russell, however, was unable to form an administration. An important factor in his failure was the refusal of Lord Grey to serve if Palmerston returned to the Foreign Office. Palmerston, who does not seem to have realised previously how much distrust he had roused in some quarters, set out to prove to potential colleagues that he was not unacceptable in Europe. In the spring of 1846, he visited Paris and was accorded a warm welcome by Guizot as well as by Thiers. Aberdeen, although well aware that the smooth functioning of constitutional government required such accommodations, would have been less than human if he had not felt some pique at this rapid reconciliation with his own most formidable rival and critic.[23]

After Russell's failure, Peel reconstituted his government and returned to office for a further six months. Aberdeen had been one of the first men in the Cabinet to support Peel in his growing conviction that the Irish famine could only be countered by a suspension of the Corn Laws. Even in November, when it was assumed that all that was involved was a temporary suspension and that there was plenty of time to work out any long term changes, Peel had encountered strong opposition. At the important Cabinet meeting of 6 November, only Aberdeen, followed by Graham and Herbert, had supported Peel. Aberdeen never subsequently wavered in his support.[24] His attitude depended on two factors. First, his knowledge of and concern for Ireland, which had interested him for thirty years, (although it is true that his first-hand knowledge was less since his stepson had grown up and taken over the management of the Abercorn estates). Secondly, and most importantly, his complete faith in Peel's judgement of economic issues. On foreign questions Aberdeen would argue strenuously and on equal terms with Peel, but on economic issues – on which as a young man Aberdeen had sometimes been regarded as having some expertise himself – he was content to follow Peel. After Peel's death, when he himself was the leader of the party, he still interpreted his role as being that of preserving Peel's legacy.

Despite their disagreements in November, most of Peel's senior colleagues remained with him. Only Lord Stanley finally resigned from the Cabinet. Even Buccleuch returned. Nevertheless, they had no illusions that their position was precarious. Most of the rank and file of the Tory party were hostile. The best they could hope for was to survive long enough to carry the repeal of the Corn Laws with Whig assistance. Aberdeen had his final triumph in foreign affairs with the signature of the Oregon Treaty, but it came as no surprise when Peel resigned on 29 June 1846.

Palmerston returned to the Foreign Office. Aberdeen briefed his successor on the outstanding issues, including the Spanish marriage question. He communicated a number of documents to Palmerston on the question but they did not include Guizot's memorandum of 27 February of which there was no official copy.

On 1 September, the *Journal des Débats* carried the news that there was to be a double wedding of Queen Isabella to the Duke of Cadiz and the Infanta Luisa Fernanda to the duc de Montpensier. Henry Bulwer had despatched the same unwelcome information from Madrid two days earlier. British public reaction was almost unanimously hostile, although *The Times* mistakenly supposing that some arrangement must have been reached, was initially friendly to France. The Prince wrote to Aberdeen on 1 October, 'The Spanish marriage affair is running its course, and every stage through which it goes produces new disgust in our minds. The King and, more even, Guizot, stop at no lie, at no trick to consummate the affair.' Peel was equally angry and had no doubt 'there is an end of the *entente cordiale*'. He added a few days later that Louis Philippe had been very foolish since the friendship of Victoria was worth far more to him than the hand of the Infanta.[25]

Guizot's explanation to the new British Ambassador, Lord Normanby, that he had felt himself released from all engagements by Palmerston's despatch to Bulwer of 19 July, naming three possible candidates, Leopold, Cadiz and Seville in that order, was of course absurd.[26] It in no way fulfilled the conditions of Guizot's memorandum of 27 February that a Coburg marriage was 'probable and imminent'. Guizot had rational reasons for his actions, but they would have been difficult to avow. He knew that Queen Christina still hankered for a Coburg match for her daughter. He knew also that Palmerston was anxious to re-establish British influence in Spain and, for that reason, favoured the candidature of Seville, who was associated with Espartero and the Progressistas, who had always tended to be the 'English' party in Spanish politics. Once Isabella was safely married to Seville, Palmerston could hope to defer the Infanta's marriage to Montpensier, not just until Isabella had children, but indefinitely. Even before Aberdeen fell from power, Guizot would have liked a way out of any engagements on the marriage question so France could resume an independent policy, but his own reputation for straight dealing would hardly have stood such a breach of faith. Palmerston's accession provided him with the perfect opportunity.

Aberdeen too was angry, although more prepared to wait for explanations. Jarnac wrote on 6 September to assure him that he had known nothing of plans for a simultaneous marriage.[27] Guizot himself wrote on 7 September, the first of a long series of letters full of arguments and explanations. He asserted, disingenuously, that the decision had been taken in Madrid by the Spaniards and repeated that, according to the memorandum of 27 February, Palmerston's despatch freed him from all obligations. Aberdeen replied a week later that he had explained the situation fully to Palmerston when he left office. Palmerston had approved the previous policy and he had no reason to think that Palmerston had subsequently changed his mind. Since the Queen's marriage to Cadiz was satisfactory, why rush into the Montpensier marriage?[28] Aberdeen sent a copy of his letter to the Prince who replied that, although his letter was rather mild, it did ask Guizot *why* he had departed from his engagements. Aberdeen told both the Prince and Jarnac that he did not think the marriage important in itself and he dissociated himself from most of the press comments ('Such coarse ribaldry and violence . . . are little to my taste'), but he did feel deeply the breach of faith.[29]

Peel was never convinced by the French explanations but Aberdeen began to listen to them.[30] He was angered by the extent to which Palmerston made capital out of the affair to discredit him and perhaps began to sympathise with the French view of Palmerston. He lost his temper with Delane, accusing *The Times* of deserting him for Palmerston, although Delane replied soothingly that he was no ally of Palmerston and that everyone spoke better of Aberdeen than of Palmerston. On 16 November, Aberdeen told Guizot that he did not doubt his personal good faith and 'with respect to Lord Palmerston, no one could have acted with more hostility, or more unfairly, than he did towards me during the whole time I was in office'. Aberdeen would act differently: 'The great object of his life was to occupy my place. I have not the least wish to fill his.'[31]

Thereafter Aberdeen defended Guizot to both Peel and Russell.[32] The question began to bog down in sterile discussions of detail. Aberdeen went to great lengths to persuade Guizot to accept that the understanding at the Chateau d'Eu had been that the French marriage should not take place until Isabella had not 'un enfant' but 'issue, progeny or even children' – rather a moot point by this time. Aberdeen was on stronger ground on the arguments about the real meaning of the Treaty of Utrecht of 1713. At Lockhart's request he wrote an able article for the *Quarterly Review* of March 1847, demonstrating that there were precedents for the marriage, which could in no way be regarded as a breach of the Treaty, as this only forbade the union of the crowns of France and Spain – which was not here at issue.[33]

When Parliament reassembled, in January 1847, the Spanish marriages were the focus of an attack on the whole policy of the *entente* and the peculiarly personal system of diplomacy which Aberdeen was accused of operating. Some of the fire found its mark, some did not. It can be questioned how much reality there ever was in the *entente* of the 1840s. It was at best very short-lived. It cannot really be said to exist before the Chateau d'Eu meeting in September 1843 and it seemed to have little force left in it by the summer of 1845, when Peel and Wellington were concentrating on strengthening British defences. Even the *entente* of the 1830s had more substance in it, in so far as it was an alignment of the two western constitutional powers against the more conservative powers of the east. Neither Aberdeen nor Guizot thought in those terms. It was more a *modus vivendi* than an *entente* and as such it had considerable success. With so many conflicting interests all over the world, the only alternative to conflict was an understanding. Peel, not easily deceived, explained this very clearly to the Commons. 'A bad understanding', he said, 'may prevail between distant countries and may not lead to war; but between England and France you have hardly an alternative between a cordial and friendly understanding and hostility.'[34]

This was Aberdeen's view too and accorded entirely with the underlying suspicion of France which he felt all his life. His personal friendship with Guizot was well known to the public but he was not naive in his estimate of his character. He was caustic to Peel and Bulwer, among others, about Guizot's defects and subterfuges; nevertheless he was convinced that Guizot was the only bulwark against the triumph of revolutionary parties in France and a forward foreign policy. He was not alone in this opinion, which was shared by the Austrians. As a result, Guizot had a very strong bargaining position which he did not hesitate to use. Peel quickly became exasperated. He was tired, he complained 'of the constant repetition of the same story "the existing Government in France is the only security for Peace – the Powers of Europe must support it – they can only support it by concessions to the democratic and war party in the Chambers" '.[35] There was the further danger that the price might be paid in vain. Because the *entente* was regarded as Guizot's personal policy, it shared his unpopularity and was likely to fall with him.

The break-down of understanding between Britain and France over the Spanish marriages had one immediately obvious effect. The two Powers were unable to co-ordinate a protest against the Austrian annexation of Cracow, the only surviving remnant of a free Poland in the autumn of 1846. It is unlikely, in view of the unity of the Eastern Powers on the question, that any protest would have been effective, but the end of Anglo-French co-operation was proclaimed to the world.

NOTES

1. Add. MSS 43144, Bloomfield to Aberdeen, 26 Dec. 1843.
2. Add. MSS 43044, Aberdeen to Victoria, 16 Apr., 27 May 1844; Victoria to Leopold, 4, 11 June 1844, *Letters of Queen Victoria*, vol. 2, pp. 12–16.
3. Jarnac, *Revue des deux mondes*, XXXIV (1861) 450.
4. Add. MSS 43144, Aberdeen to Brunnow, 3 Aug. 1844, Brunnow to Aberdeen, 18 Sept., 26 Nov. 1844, Nesselrode to Aberdeen, 28 Dec. 1844, Aberdeen to Nesselrode, 21 Jan. 1845.
5. There is a copy in Add. MSS 43144 marked 'Memo . . . by Count Nesselrode founded on communications received from the Emperor during H.I.M.'s visit to England in June 1844.' It is with Brunnow's letter of 26 Nov. 1844 in which he says that he returns the original of Nesselrode's Memorandum, with a corrected copy intended to replace the original: this seems to be the corrected copy. A copy was only placed in the FO archives on 29 March 1854 (FO 65/307). For its subsequent history see pp. 497–9.
6. For a full account of this see Greaves, 'The Jerusalem Bishopric', *E.H.R.*, LVIV (1949) 328–52.
7. See Temperley, *England and the Near East*, Ch. VI–IX. Some of Canning's most important despatches are printed in *BFSP*, vol. 35, pp. 864–1007.
8. *Hansard*, 3rd ser., LXXVI, 1871; FO 72/626, Aston to Aberdeen, No. 127, 27 June 1843 et seq.; FO 72/622, Aberdeen to Aston, No. 43, 12 Aug. 1843. For the whole history of the question see Jones Parry, *The Spanish Marriages*.
9. Add. MSS 43041, Victoria to Aberdeen, 14 Dec. 1841 encl. Memo by Albert.
10. FO 7/304, Aberdeen to Gordon, No. 18, 16 Mar. 1842; FO 72/622, Aberdeen to Aston, No. 34 Conf., 7 June 1843; Add. MSS 40453, Aberdeen to Peel, 6 Sept. 1843.
11. Guizot Papers, 42 AP 2, Pageot to Guizot, No. 1, 3 June 1842 (full report of mission); FO 7/304, Aberdeen to Gordon, No. 35, 26 Apr. 1842.
12. Add. MSS 40453–4, Aberdeen to Peel, 6 Sept., 19 Oct., 5, 8 Dec. 1843; Add. MSS 43063, Peel to Aberdeen, 7 Dec. 1843; FO 27/664, Aberdeen to Cowley, No. 180, 15 Dec. 1843.
13. Add. MSS 43147, Aberdeen to Bulwer, 27 Nov. 1844; Add. MSS 43064, Peel to Aberdeen, 20 Dec. 1844.
14. Add. MSS 40455, Aberdeen to Peel, 8 Sept., 9 Oct. 1845.
15. Add. MSS 43065, Peel to Aberdeen, 7 Oct. 1845.
16. Add. MSS 40455, Aberdeen to Peel, 17 Oct. 1845; Add. MSS 43133, Jarnac to Aberdeen, 16 Oct. 1845.
17. Guizot Papers, 42 AP 7, Guizot to Jarnac, 1 Aug., 6 Oct., 7 Nov. 1845.
18. Guizot Papers, 42 AP 8, Guizot to Ste Aulaire, 27 Feb. 1845.
19. Add. MSS 43147, Aberdeen to Bulwer, 14 Mar. 1846; Guizot, vol. 8, p. 251; Guizot Papers, 42 AP 8, Ste Aulaire to Guizot, 5 Mar. 1846.
20. Add. MSS 43147, Bulwer to Aberdeen, 28 Mar., 24 Apr., 6, 19 May 1846.

21. Add. MSS 43147, Aberdeen to Bulwer, 7, 8, 19 May 1846; Add. MSS 43133, Aberdeen to Ste Aulaire, 9 Apr. 1846.
22. Add. MSS 43179, Aberdeen to Sotomayer, 22 June 1846.
23. Greville, vol. 2, p. 267; Add. MSS 43130, Cowley to Aberdeen, 27 Apr. 1846; Add. MSS 43065, Peel to Aberdeen, 30 Apr. 1846; Add. MSS 43134, Aberdeen to Guizot, 5 May 1846.
24. Gash, *Sir Robert Peel*, pp. 542, 583–4, 608–9.
25. *The Times*, 3, 16 Sept. 1846; Add. MSS 43046, Albert to Aberdeen, 1 Oct. 1846; Add. MSS 43065, Peel to Aberdeen, 15 Sept., 1 Oct. 1846.
26. The Princess Lieven secured a copy of the despatch from the British Embassy in Paris and showed it to Guizot but it was an unnecessary piece of espionage. Palmerston had officially communicated it to Jarnac. Lieven to Guizot, 24 July 1846, *Lettres* (ed. Naville), vol. 3, pp. 230–1.
27. Add. MSS 43133, Jarnac to Aberdeen, 6 Sept. 1846.
28. Add. MSS 43134, Guizot to Aberdeen, 7 Sept. 1846 and encls, Aberdeen to Guizot, 14 Sept. 1846.
29. Add. MSS 43046, Albert to Aberdeen, n.d. Sept., 8 Oct. 1846; Add. MSS 43133, Aberdeen to Jarnac, 28 Oct. 1846.
30. Add. MSS 43065, Peel to Aberdeen, 21 Nov., 7 Dec. 1846.
31. Add. MSS 43246, Delane to Aberdeen, 13 Nov. 1846; Add. MSS 43134, Aberdeen to Guizot, 16 Nov. 1846.
32. Add. MSS 43066, Aberdeen to Russell, 17 Nov. 1843; Add. MSS 43065, Aberdeen to Peel, 1 Dec. 1846.
33. Add. MSS 43134, Aberdeen to Guizot, 5 Jan. 1847 (originally drafted to be sent to the Princess Lieven), Guizot to Aberdeen, 15 Jan. 1847; NLS MS 930, Aberdeen to Lockhart, 27 Feb., 4, 12 Mar. 1847.
34. *Hansard*, 3rd ser., LXXVII, 89 (4 Feb. 1845).
35. Add. MSS 43062, Peel to Aberdeen, 19 Oct. 1842.

CHAPTER TWENTY-FOUR

Revolution and reaction
1848–50

The Austrian annexation of Cracow disturbed Aberdeen. If the allied Powers themselves broke the Treaty of Vienna, they could scarcely complain if the French insisted that it was time that it was revised. In the late 1840s, as in the early 1830s, Aberdeen became intensely conservative, and for the same reason. He felt that the Vienna Settlement, which he equated with the peace and stability of Europe, was threatened. His relations with his continental conservative friends, Guizot, Metternich and Princess Lieven became very close.

Aberdeen may have been speaking the truth when he told Guizot that, personally, he had no desire to take Palmerston's place but it was a qualified truth. By 1848, he certainly wished to 'turn out' Palmerston because he had become convinced that Palmerston was a dangerous man who, intentionally or unintentionally, was giving aid and comfort to the radical and revolutionary forces which might smash the whole European system. Ironically, Palmerston was himself as conservative as Aberdeen on most issues. When they sat together in the Cabinet of 1852–5, he was well to the right of Aberdeen on almost all domestic questions. During the revolutionary upheavals of 1848–49, it was the concerted voice of conservative Europe which first cast Palmerston in the role of the radical in international affairs and, in the end, forced him to play it.

There had been some revolutionary stirrings even in the early 1840s, one of which had had a curious effect on British domestic politics. In 1844, two sons of a prominent Venetian family, the Bandiera brothers, were executed in Naples for allegedly plotting an insurrection. It was rumoured that details of the conspiracy had been revealed in letters to Mazzini, then in exile in Britain, and that these letters had been intercepted by the British government and the information passed on to the Austrians. A radical M.P., Thomas Duncombe, took up the matter in Parliament and there was a great outcry in the press. In July 1844, Peel had to consent to the setting up a Secret Committee of Enquiry.[1]

The British government were in fact innocent of any connection with the Bandiera trial but, between March and June 1844, they had opened Mazzini's letters at the request of Austria. The warrant had been issued by Sir James

Graham as Home Secretary, at Aberdeen's request.[2] The government was greatly embarrassed by the parliamentary enquiry. Aberdeen wrote to his brother, Robert:

Your Italian Refugees have given us much trouble. In consequence of Mazzini's letters having been intercepted, we have now a Committee of both Houses sitting to enquire into all the mysteries of the Post Office. Their Report will exhibit to the Publick some curious discoveries, for which they are by no means prepared.[3]

The British government in fact managed to protect some of their 'mysteries'.

What concerned the radicals was the interception of the letters of named individuals, suspected of subversion, under a special warrant issued by the Home Secretary – which applied in the Mazzini case. On this Graham was able to advance a successful defence that, although the practice was distasteful, it was both legal and necessary for the safety of the state. Potentially more embarrassing was the existence of the 'Secret Office' of the Post Office, with its private entrance in Abchurch Lane and its highly skilled staff, usually discreetly paid from the Secret Service funds, which in collaboration with the Deciphering Branch, secured and opened as much of the correspondence of foreign envoys as possible.[4] This practice was authorised by 'general warrant', and dated from the seventeenth century. It could not be entirely concealed from the Committee of Enquiry but, in order to anticipate criticism, it was suspended in June 1844, before the Committee met, and every attempt made to convey the impression that the procedure was obsolete.[5]

In fact, until 1844, references to letters seen 'in the interceptions' abound among Aberdeen's papers. In February 1845, Aberdeen felt compelled to apologise to Victoria for their continued absence. He wrote,

Lord Aberdeen is anxious to explain the cause of no *interceptions* being received at present, as the persons belonging to that Department are not now employed. Whether it may be practicable to reinstate them in their functions, will very much depend on the nature of the discussions which take place in Parliament.[6]

Aberdeen hoped that the practice could be restored and both he and his senior colleagues were angry with Lord John Russell, who when in office himself had had no qualms about the matter, for making political capital out of the 'Post Office affair' to the detriment of national security. The historian[7] who has investigated the matter the most closely suggests that the loss of the 'interceptions' after 1844 had a disastrous effect on the efficiency of British foreign policy, but against this must be set the fact that the practice was so universal in Europe at this time that precautions were commonly taken. Aberdeen himself, for example, when visiting Germany in 1845 would not send Peel an account of his conversations with the King of Prussia until he had a special messenger available.[8]

During the next few years Britain was to have a greater need than ever of an efficient intelligence network. The great revolutionary year of 1848 opened with riots in Lombardy and a rising at Palermo in Sicily. On 23 February an insurrection in Paris overthrew both Guizot and Louis Philippe. There then began eighteen months of upheaval which engulfed most of western Europe. Even Britain did not entirely escape.

Aberdeen watched the preliminaries to the great struggle with mounting anxiety, intensified by his conviction that Palmerston was handling the situation in the wrong way. In July 1847, the Austrians, nervous at what they saw as dangerous concessions by the new Pope, Pius IX, used their treaty rights to send troops to Ferrara. They were compelled by Anglo-French pressure to withdraw. Aberdeen's sympathies lay with the Austrians and he told Peel that he considered their actions to be defensive. 'We cannot', he said 'expect that Austria will quietly allow herself to be dispossessed of her Italian Provinces in order to promote the project of the Union of Italy, which is an impracticable dream, and which, if practicable, I believe would be of very doubtful advantage.'9 He was equally critical of Palmerston's support for the Swiss Liberals in the struggle which was developing between them and the Catholic cantons. Here, French sympathies, like those of Metternich, lay with the seven Catholic cantons, the Sounderbund, and Aberdeen complained to Peel 'It seems to me that England and France may almost be said to have exchanged their former systems of policy.' In the past, Britain had always supported governments against revolutionary attempts encouraged by France, but now France was trying to check revolution and England was opposing her. The only explanation seemed to be that Palmerston's policy was dominated by 'blind hatred' of Guizot's France.10

By the summer of 1847, Aberdeen feared the outbreak of a European war, which might equally well arise from, or give rise to, a revolutionary situation. The principal cause of danger, he wrote to Peel, was 'the rapid progress of the Democratic spirit throughout Europe, supported as it is by England'. The British radicals were playing with fire. 'They may', he said, 'sincerely love peace; but they love radicalism much more, and would incur any risk to promote it in any part of the world.'11 Graham was reaching similar conclusions, although his concerns were more domestic. Russell, he feared, had dangerous allies, Repealers, Chartists and Radicals. The prolongation of the divisions of the Conservative Party would give a most 'dangerous impulse' to democracy and, with Palmerston at the Foreign Office, Britain would not have a friend in Europe. Aberdeen gloomily agreed. Graham, he said, always reminded him of his old friend, Gentz, 'who began all his letters to Metternich with "Mon Prince, J'ai Peur . . ."', but this time he thought Graham was right. 'The radical and democratic tendencies so prevalent in Europe, meet with English support, but have been the means of uniting all the Great Powers of the continent against us. Spain, Italy, Switzerland, and Greece furnish abundant grounds of difference. Our difficulties in Portugal are not yet begun . . .'12

The developments in Portugal were peculiarly embarrassing for British Liberals, who had always supported Queen Maria, and seemed to justify Aberdeen's sceptical approach. When the radical Septembrist party won the general election of 1845, Maria dissolved the Cortes, annulled the constitution and conferred dictatorial powers on Marshal Saldanha. In October, the Septembrists seized Oporto and Maria asked for help under the Quadruple Treaty of 1834.

Palmerston temporised as long as possible, but in May 1847, he allowed the British navy to assist the Portuguese government in blockading Oporto. Maria was persuaded to restore constitutional government but Saldanha and his right-wing supporters remained in power.

Embarrassments in Switzerland or Portugal, however, faded into insignificance in March 1848, when, following the abdication of Louis Phillippe and the proclamation of a republic in Paris, the governments tottered in Vienna and Berlin and revolutionary fervour spread across Germany, the Austrian empire and Italy. Only Russia seemed safe from revolution. Even in England the Chartists planned a monster meeting on 10 April, on Kennington Common, from where they planned to march to the Houses of Parliament. Men not easily given to panic believed that they intended to set up a provisional government on the French model. The Duke of Wellington was put in charge of the defence of London, and thousands of special constables were enrolled. Arrangements were made to defend the Bank of England and other key locations; government offices were garrisoned and provisioned; and cannons trained on all the bridges over the Thames. 'The fools,' said Wellington, 'they have mustered on the wrong side of the river.' The Chartists were indeed amateurs and less numerous than they supposed. By the evening of 10 April they had melted away, their movement covered in ridicule. In Ireland there were sporadic risings among those who had awaited the signal from London but they were easily put down by the authorities. Nevertheless it was some time before the propertied classes were convinced that they were safe and the continent was still convulsed.

Guizot and Princess Lieven arrived in England in March, Metternich in April. Aberdeen spent a good deal of time in their company, although his reunion with Metternich was marred by a misunderstanding. Metternich did not call on him and Aberdeen heard a rumour that he was offended because he, Aberdeen, had expressed misgivings about his arrival. Aberdeen wrote a rather stiff letter, explaining that he had only meant that he feared Metternich would be ill-received because the public saw recent events in Vienna 'with very different eyes from mine'. He reminded Metternich that for the last thirty-five years he had been regarded as 'your most devoted adherent in this Country' and his political adversaries had never failed to reproach him as 'your friend and pupil'. He concluded with a broad hint that, if Metternich did not accept his explanation, it would be the end of their friendship. Metternich promptly and tactfully replied that he had not realised that Aberdeen was in London and he was unaware that he was supposed to be offended. The public would soon realise how mistaken their view of continental events was. For himself, he had quitted the political world for ever. [13]

Metternich continued his pose as a man who had entirely withdrawn from politics but this did not prevent him from taking a keen interest in British, as well as continental, politics and discussing them at length with Aberdeen. He was immediately impressed by Disraeli, whom he regarded as almost the only British politician capable of discussing political principles on a philosophical level, and sang his praises to Aberdeen who, since he still saw Disraeli primarily as a traitor to Peel, was not the most sympathetic listener.[14] This, however, led to a remarkable episode.

Disraeli too now regarded himself as a pupil of Metternich and, after the death of Lord George Bentinck in September 1848, consulted him as to whether he should agree to serve under the leadership of the elderly Herries in the Commons. Metternich promptly passed the correspondence on to Aberdeen for his advice. Aberdeen agreed that Disraeli's letter was 'most extraordinary' but Metternich would see from the correspondence which Disraeli had obligingly enclosed that Herries was 'a commander whom his troops would not respect, or obey with much alacrity'. If Metternich wished to take the responsibility of offering advice, he should try to promote 'the reconciliation and reunion of the great body of men, by whose united efforts evil may be prevented, and good government succeed', that is, the reunion of the Conservative party, without distinction of 'Protectionist' or 'Peelite'. Aberdeen was unwilling to commit too much to paper and suggested that they should discuss the matter further when they met in Brighton.[15] Metternich's reply to Disraeli, which was published by Monypenny and Buckle,[16] followed Aberdeen's suggestions very closely. Neither Disraeli, nor his biographers, ever suspected its origin.

But the cordiality of Aberdeen's relations with the conservative refugees did not escape notice. In the summer of 1848, he became the target of renewed personal attacks, for which he blamed Palmerston. An article appeared in the *Globe*, laying the responsibility for the Spanish marriages once again at Aberdeen's door. Delane replied briefly in *The Times*, although he advised Aberdeen against an extended explanation. The *Globe*, with a circulation of only eight or nine hundred, was, he said, beneath notice. The *Globe* even used the smear, which was to be repeated so often at the time of the Crimean war, that Aberdeen's continental friendships cast doubt upon his patriotism. 'Imagine', he wrote angrily to Princess Lieven, 'my loyalty being doubted, because I have seen the King and M. Guizot.'[17]

Aberdeen's complete commitment to what he regarded as Britain's best interests cannot be seriously doubted, but he unquestionably involved himself in continental politics to an extent which has passed unnoticed, partly because it was deliberately concealed by his son. Arthur was then an undergraduate at Cambridge and spent much time in his father's company. He was often present at Aberdeen's meetings with Guizot and accompanied him to Paris in 1849. Most of the time he kept a journal. Aberdeen probably did not confide all aspects of high politics to his son, but Arthur must have had a fairly good idea of what was going on. In his published memoir of his father he dismissed the 1848 revolutions in one paragraph and devoted most of the relevant chapter to domestic and family questions.[18] Writing in the 1890s, Arthur may have felt that some of the issues were still politically sensitive but even more he must have realised that Aberdeen's role in 1848–50 would win him little public sympathy, nor did it accord well with the image that Arthur wished to retain of his father, as a liberal–minded man who was almost accidentally attached to the Conservative party.

In 1848–50 Aberdeen was sternly and uncompromisingly conservative. Some of his expressions in his letters to Metternich and the Princess Lieven may have been meant to convey sympathy with their plight, rather than considered political judgements, but he did identify himself closely with their position. Like Metternich, he saw the 1848 revolutions as a threat to the whole social fabric of Europe and his experiences in 1802 and 1813 did not lead him to the conclusion that revolutions righted injustices or established a better society. In his opinion they were much more likely to lead to bloodshed, widespread devastation and general war.

Everyone agreed that the key to the situation lay in France. The revolution had taken a more extreme social form there than elsewhere and no one doubted that a European war was more likely to be triggered from Paris than from any other European capital. In the spring of 1848 it seemed possible that socialism, and not merely republicanism, would triumph in Paris. Lamartine, who had taken control of foreign affairs in the provisional government, had succeeded in preventing the tricolour being replaced by the red flag, and issued his famous circular assuring the Great Powers that France was not about to launch a crusade for freedom; but the question was how long could Lamartine keep control of the situation? When the Constituent Assembly finally met, on 4 May, it became clear that the majority were moderate Republicans but, by that time, the National Workshops had drawn thousands of unemployed men into Paris and the Socialists staged an abortive coup on 15 May. It was put down by the National Guard and, encouraged by this, the new executive government closed down the National Workshops, which were regarded as the centre of the socialist movement, on 22 June. The result was a pitched battle in the streets of Paris between the unemployed workmen and a joint force of regular soldiers and National Guardsmen, under the command of General Cavaignac, which lasted for four days before Cavaignac triumphed.

Conservative Europe breathed again but a new danger soon appeared. The Assembly approved a new constitution, which resembled the American constitution, in that a President was to be elected for a four–year term by direct suffrage, independently of the Chambers. In December 1848 Louis Bonaparte was elected by a huge majority against Cavaignac and the Socialist, Ledru-Rollin. Aberdeen had previously regarded Louis Bonaparte as a clown, notable only for the fiascos of his two earlier attempts to raise the imperial flag at Strasbourg in 1836 and Boulogne in 1840. It was clear that he had been elected solely by the prestige of the Bonaparte name, and the fact that he was the nephew of the great Napoleon. As Metternich wrote, 'Ce n'est pas *l'homme* qui a eu les voix, mais son *nom*; son *chapeau*, et non sa *tête*.'[19] He and Aberdeen were agreed that the only way a Bonaparte could hope to retain control of France was by military success. Even before the election Aberdeen had written to Princess Lieven 'The election of Louis Bonaparte to the office of President, which seems probable, will be a fact of evil augury; for in the minds of many, it must mean war. By those who elect him, it is as a captain, and not as an administrator, that the name of Napoleon is honoured.' As early as August 1849, he was convinced that Bonaparte would try to restore the Empire. He told Princess

Lieven, 'I am still inclined to think that the Empire will be the most probable means of escape from the intolerable position in which France is at present placed.'[20]

To the conservatives there was another, greatly preferable, escape route, the restoration of the monarchy. Metternich calculated that among the votes cast in the December elections, 7 million were votes for order, against 30,000 'Papageurs, ou soidisant Montagnards etc.' and 30,000 socialists. Among the first group, he thought that at least five and a half million were the enemies of the events of 24 February, that is the proclamation of the Second Republic.[21] Metternich's calculations were not unbiased but the largest party in the new Legislative Assembly was conservative and monarchist in sentiment. The problem was that there were two possible royal claimants, one Bourbon, one Orleanist; the Duke of Bordeaux, now more usually known as the Count of Chambord, the grandson of Charles X, and the Count of Paris, the grandson of Louis Philippe. If the royalists were to have a chance, they must unite behind one candidate or the other. Aberdeen was very willing to be drawn into active moves to bring about the *fusion*.

In November 1849 Princess Lieven begged Aberdeen to come to Paris, where she and Guizot had now returned. Aberdeen at first demurred on what seems to have been the genuine grounds that Lady Haddo was about to be confined and her health was giving cause for anxiety, but in December, after she had safely given birth to a daughter, he agreed to go, telling the Princess that she must advise him about hotels, since he had not been to Paris for twenty-five years. He insisted that he was coming simply to renew old acquaintances but the Princess made it clear that she was mapping out a programme of meetings with all the key political leaders and that the critical issue of the moment was the *fusion* of the Bourbon and Orleanist interests.[22]

This was certainly not news to Aberdeen. Just before Christmas, Louis Phillippe and the duc d'Aumâle had paid an unexpected and rather curious flying visit to Peel at Drayton. Aberdeen had been asked to accompany them from Euston. No sooner were they all seated in the train than Louis Philippe began to talk about the *fusion*, making it clear that he favoured it, although he thought that the moment had not yet come for formal proposals.[23]

Aberdeen arrived in Paris at the end of December 1849, and stayed until the middle of January, during which time he saw most of the leading French politicians. On his return to London, Princess Lieven sent him almost daily bulletins of the progress of affairs. They were extremely concerned about the security of their correspondence – even though Lord Brougham had assured Aberdeen in January 1849 that 'Republican virtue' had put an end to the practice of opening letters.[24] The Princess began to number her letters so that they should know if any had been abstracted. She instructed Aberdeen not to sign his letters or call her by any name. He should put his letters in an envelope, simply marked 'D' (presumably for Dorothea) with some kind of device in the corner, and enclose them in another envelope addressed to 'Monsieur Paul de Tolstoy, 7 place de la Madeleine'. He must take care not to address them in his own hand. Aberdeen was doubtful about the security of this mode of communication, telling the Princess that 'your relations with M. de Tolstoy must be sufficiently well known to afford no protection'. He still preferred to use trusted messengers but he told the Princess, 'if you have occasion to write to me otherwise than by the ordinary Post, you may put your letter under cover to John Newman Esqr 45 George Street, Euston Square. If you also put the letter D. upon the inclosure, it will be delivered to me.'[25]

Aberdeen (who had taken the precaution of telling Peel at least something of what was going on) saw Louis Philippe, who was still in exile at Claremont in Surrey, several times during February and March 1850. He consulted Guizot by letter, having 'a secure mode of conveyance' as to exactly what proposition he should put to Louis Philippe.[26] Guizot replied that he understood Aberdeen to believe that the younger, that is the Orleanist, branch should yield to the elder but that, in return, the elder branch should recognise the July Monarchy as a legitimate, not a usurping, monarchy and that they should jointly adopt the tricolour flag with the fleur de lys added. He asked Aberdeen to argue along these lines to Louis Philippe since it was essential that one branch or the other should formulate precise terms.[27] Aberdeen duly put these points to Louis Philippe in an interview which lasted some two hours. Louis Philippe told him that both he and his four sons were persuaded that Bordeaux must be king and that he would be satisfied if the legality of his own reign were recognised. He did not object to his opinions being made known to those to whom they might be useful, but he did not yet wish to make an official communication to Bordeaux. He was apprehensive as to how the Duchess of Orleans, the mother of the Count of Paris, would react, and he was also unsure of the general Orleanist reaction in France. About this time, Aberdeen passed a few days at Windsor and found the British Court in favour of the *fusion* and fearful of the establishment of a Bonaparte dynasty. He suspected that they had been in independent contact with Louis Philippe but he feared that the British government might entertain other views.[28]

Aberdeen had told Louis Philippe that, so far as he knew, Thiers was the only eminent man in Paris who did not approve of the reunion project. Louis Philippe replied that, if Thiers would come to England, he would try to persuade him.[29] Thiers duly came. So did Molé and de Broglie but little progress was made. Louis Philippe sent for Aberdeen again, while on a visit to Richmond early in March, but during a very long interview, apart from expressing distrust of those by whom Bordeaux was surrounded, the King chose to talk of other things, and Aberdeen was left puzzled as to why he had wished to see him.[30] Early in May, Aberdeen wrote again to Guizot, to suggest some action. He had not seen the King for some time but he thought the situation in France was favourable. Jarnac had just returned from a visit to Ireland and perhaps he could approach the King, although Aberdeen was reluctant to bring anyone else into these delicate negotiations.[31]

In fact, the project was hanging fire. Louis Philippe was right to be nervous of those who surrounded Bordeaux. The Legitimists were going ahead on their own. Bordeaux, Henri V to his supporters, was virtually holding a court at Wiesbaden, making arrangements for what he would do when he returned to

France, and totally disinclined to compromise on the important symbol of the flag.

Even more importantly, the conservative forces had hesitated to gamble on a counter-coup in March 1850. On 21 March, Guizot had written a very frank letter to Aberdeen, telling him that he thought they were near the big step. Public opinion had been alarmed by the results of thirty by-elections, held that month to fill the places of members of the Legislative Assembly, expelled for their part in another abortive socialist rising the previous June. Most of the seats had again been won by socialists. The party of order now felt that the moment of decision had come. They must conquer or be conquered. There was talk of Molé, Thiers and the Legitimist, Berryer, sitting together in one Cabinet and making common cause with the military chiefs. But in the end they recoiled. Dare they raise the Bourbon flag against the Republic? Instead they settled for a package of measures which would, among other things, ban political clubs and restrict the franchise by imposing a residence qualification. Guizot argued that if the Left accepted these measures the forces of anarchy would have been tamed. If they resisted, the President, the ministers and the heads of the other parties would be united against them. General Changarnier, the commander of the National Guard and of the troops in Paris, was ready for action. Guizot insisted that everything would happen as they desired if only the monarchical elements held together.[32]

Changarnier was the man they saw as their General Monk. When Guizot had been in exile in England he and Aberdeen had had many learned conversations about English seventeenth century history, which eventually resulted in Guizot's history of the Restoration,[33] but in 1848 it had been anything but an academic study. Aberdeen had been impressed by Changarnier during his visit to Paris. He told Guizot that he saw him 'as the great source of hope for the future salvation of France', and Princess Lieven, 'I think the salvation of France depends more entirely upon him, than upon any other individual'.[34] But Changarnier never had the chance to play the role of Monk. It was Louis Bonaparte who over–reached his opponents. The restriction of the franchise worked to his advantage rather than that of his enemies. Louis Philippe died in August 1850, and no compact was worked out between the Bourbons and the Orleanists. Bonaparte's tour of the conservative French provinces in the summer of 1850 was a triumph. Alarmed by the Socialists on the one hand and by the Legitimists on the other, many Frenchmen clung to the name of Bonaparte. In January 1851, Bonaparte felt strong enough to dismiss Changarnier, whose loyalty he had every reason to doubt, and a few months later had him arrested.

On 2 December 1851, the anniversary of both the battle of Austerlitz and Napoleon I's coronation, Bonaparte carried out a successful coup d'état. The Assembly was dissolved. A few weeks later, a national plebiscite gave Bonaparte an overwhelming majority to carry through a revision of the constitution. In January his term as President was extended to ten years. Few doubted that it was the prelude to the re–establishment of the Empire.

Aberdeen had continued to take the closest possible interest in events in

France. In March 1850, he had declined Princess Lieven's invitation to go to Paris again, because he feared that his activities were attracting attention and that it would cause political speculation. However, in December he arranged to go with Edward Ellice, oddly enough one of his more radical friends. He was prevented at the last moment by the dangerous illness of his eldest grandson, Lord Haddo's son, George, who was struck down by a fever at York when the family was returning from a visit to Haddo.[35]

Bonaparte's coup d'état came as no surprise to him but, he told Ellice, 'the fellow has done the business more thoroughly than I was prepared to see. In duplicity and hypocrisy he beats his uncle out of sight; and in unscrupulous violation of all law Napoleon himself could not exceed him.' If he was to keep his army faithful, he would have to give them something to do abroad and he would not care in what direction.[36]

By this time, Princess Lieven was prepared to settle for anything which gave France a secure government. Her change of front caused some caustic amusement to her friends, although Aberdeen was prepared to admit that there was something to be said for her point of view. 'For', he said 'any Government is better than the anarchy which is the only alternative . . . After all, the great mass of mankind care much more for their personal safety than for Constitutional privileges.' Military government was the strongest kind of government there was. But, more soberly, he pointed out what he saw as the real dangers in the situation:

What is to happen, and how is this immense army to be employed, after the country shall be fully tranquillized? The President has made his Uncle the model of his imitation . . . The President must find employment for his army, or he must disband it . . . Perhaps Brussels and Chambery may satisfy him; but he does not forget that his Uncle has been at Vienna, Berlin, and Moscow. Possibly he may have a fancy to revisit London in a new character; and Waterloo is still unavenged. A few years ago, we were panick stricken without a shadow of reason. The approaching danger seems to me to be much more real . . .[37]

Aberdeen had done his best to prevent the re-establishment of a Bonaparte dynasty. Perhaps he had been influenced by a scarcely acknowledged romanticism which desired to see the king have his own again, but his main motive had been to keep out Louis Bonaparte. He never ceased to regard him as an utterly unscrupulous man and a danger to England. It was a strange irony that made him, within three years, much against his will, Bonaparte's ally in a war against the Tsar of Russia, who, contrary to the popular view in England, he believed had behaved properly and responsibly in 1848–49.

Only in France did Aberdeen try to play any kind of active role during the stirring days of revolution, although he did not cease to criticise Palmerston's handling of the situation. In fact the two men were not so opposed in their views as the public believed or as perhaps they believed themselves at the time. Both were agreed that a stable Austria was essential to the European balance of power. Where they differed was that Aberdeen wanted to keep the Vienna Settlement intact, while Palmerston believed that Austria would be stronger if she shed her Italian responsibilities and concentrated on her role north of the Alps. The problem, as Palmerston saw it, was to find some other arrangement in Italy which would still keep out French influence. Aberdeen did not believe that any such alternative arrangement was practical.

Aberdeen did not believe that there was any widespread desire in Italy for the creation of a national state. On the contrary, Italian loyalties had always been local. He agreed with Metternich who assured him in August 1848, 'L'histoire preuve qu'il n'y a qu'une *Italie nominale* mais pas une Italie matériellement existante'.[38] Aberdeen did not accept, as British Liberals did, that Austrian influence in Italy had been consistently bad. On the contrary, he declared in the Lords in March 1849, that the Austrian provinces had been the 'best governed' in Italy, with property secure, justice impartially administered and prosperity steadily increasing. Far from seeing Piedmont-Sardinia as the champion of Italian nationalism and her king, Charles Albert, as a tragic hero, he regarded Charles Albert as an unscrupulous opportunist who deserved all his ill-success. He told the Lords that the House of Savoy had always regarded Lombardy as an artichoke, to be eaten leaf by leaf, but Charles Albert had such a good appetite that he thought he could swallow the whole plant at once.[39]

Both Lombardy and Venetia rose against the Austrians in March 1848. Manin proclaimed the Venetian Republic on 22 March and, the same day, the Austrian general, Radetzky, had to withdraw his forces from Milan and retreat to the strong defensive position between the Adige and the Mincio, dominated by the fortresses of the Quadrilateral. On 25 March, Charles Albert sent an army to help the Lombards. When Palmerston laid papers before Parliament, warning the Austrians that Britain would not view an attack on Sardinia 'with indifference', Aberdeen challenged him to say why the warning had been issued to Austria, when it had been Sardinia who had taken advantage of the 'portentous convulsions' round her to challenge the public law of Europe by invading the territory of a neighbour.[40]

In the summer of 1848, Palmerston was prepared to join the French in a mediation with the objective of transferring Lombardy to Sardinia and giving Venetia some kind of home rule but, while diplomatic negotiations deadlocked, the octogenarian General Radetzky acted vigorously and routed the Sardinians at Custozza on 25 July. Aberdeen wrote to the Princess Lieven:

The most remarkable of late events is the complete success of the Austrians in Italy. Our old friends have not only acted well, but promptly, which is not their usual method...I am delighted at the result. Never was there a more wanton and unprovoked aggression, and never was such aggression more signally defeated.[41]

Metternich too was overjoyed. 'Le canon', he commented, 'dissipe les nuages.' He gave Aberdeen his views on the European situation at inordinate length and seems to have been pumping him about likely British conservative reaction. He could, he said, now see no point in British mediation since the war was finished.[42]

Metternich was too optimistic. The war in northern Italy was resumed in the spring of 1849. Aberdeen, who had maintained a discreet public silence as long as there seemed to be any chance of a settlement by negotiation, launched an open attack soon after the parliamentary session began. He had told Princess Lieven the previous November, just before he returned from Haddo to London:

I shall be very curious to know what part we have really acted in all the recent affairs of Italy and Germany. From all I can learn, I fear it has been shuffling, inconsistent, and shabby. With a constant leaning to Radicalism; but with the pretence of supporting monarchical government. I hear great complaints of the duplicity of our conduct. This would be quite a new characteristic of British policy; but in these times, it is far from impossible.[43]

Aberdeen had numerous private sources of information. Metternich supplied him with an uncomplimentary dossier on Charles Albert and Aberdeen was convinced that the King was now virtually the prisoner of Mazzini and the extreme Republicans.[44] Aberdeen also received information from inside the British Foreign Office. In his private papers are some proof copies of the Italian papers laid before Parliament in 1848, with additional information written in. One is docketed in Aberdeen's writing as having been laid 'without explanation' when 'political ferment' prevailed in Italy.[45] His multiplicity of sources led to some embarrassment when he brought the matter before the House on 22 March 1849. He did not pull any punches. Apart from denouncing Charles Albert, he accused the British government of being wanting in 'justice and good faith', as well as in sound policy. Lansdowne promptly complained that Aberdeen seemed to be referring to papers which were not before the House, as well as those which were. Aberdeen had to appeal to the discretion of the Lords 'as gentlemen' but he stuck to his main point. The British government had omitted those papers which told in Austria's favour and this amounted to a *suppressio veri*.[46]

Aberdeen still pinned his hopes on Radetzky. He told Metternich that he hoped Vienna would take a firm line. 'Everything', he considered, 'promises well for the success of Raditzky [sic], which I most sincerely hope may be prompt and decisive'.[47] His confidence was not misplaced. On 23 March, Radetzky decisively defeated the Sardinians at Novara and Charles Albert abdicated in favour of his son, Victor Emmanuel, who was forced to surrender the whole of Lombardy to Austria. Aberdeen did not hesitate to praise Radetzky publicly. In the Lords, on 30 March, he referred to his 'brilliant successes' and 'magnanimous conduct'.[48] Contrary to what has usually been accepted since, Aberdeen believed that his views were those of the majority of the British public. 'There is', he said, 'scarcely a single exception to the satisfaction of men of every party at Raditzky's success.' The justice of Austria's cause must indeed be manifest, he told Metternich, if it made men forget their natural instinct to sympathise with the weak against the strong. He was satisfied that the main crisis was passed. The French would act 'reasonably' and Victor Emmanuel control 'the madness of his republican subjects'. As for the British government, they had 'received a lesson, which I hope may discourage future meddling in the cause of revolution'.[49]

The nationalist cause was collapsing elsewhere in Italy. The Austrians restored a number of lesser rulers, including the Dukes of Tuscany, Parma and Modena. By May 1849, Ferdinand II had regained control of both Naples and Sicily. Even Aberdeen found it difficult to say anything good of Ferdinand. He told the Lords that he would not enter into the merits of the insurrection but only enquire whether Britain had maintained a proper neutrality.[50] He was most caustic about the results of British policy in the Papal States. In November 1848 the Pope had fled from Rome and in February 1849 a Roman Republic had been proclaimed. The Pope appealed for the help of the Catholic Powers. Here too Aberdeen believed that Austria should have been supported. Instead, Louis Napoleon decided to make a bid for clerical support in France by answering the Pope's appeal. The French intervention was successful. The Roman Republic was crushed and Garibaldi and Mazzini forced to flee. But, said Aberdeen, what an extraordinary outcome for a policy supposed to protect British interests, to have allowed 20,000 French troops to move into the centre of Italy, with no firm assurances as to their intentions or guarantees as to when they would leave.[51]

Events in Italy seemed to bear out Metternich's prediction that ultimately everything would be settled by regular armies and Italy would have been subdued more quickly but for the situation elsewhere in the Austrian empire. Twice in 1848, the Emperor Ferdinand, who had succeeded Francis in 1835, had to flee from his capital. For Aberdeen, the blackest moment was in October when he wrote to Princess Lieven,

This morning has brought the intelligence of the late horrible excesses at Vienna, and of the anarchy now established in Austria. It is truly frightful, and the consequences must be deplorable . . . the Empire seems to be crumbling to pieces, and each portion will attempt to declare its independence.

In this extremity he was prepared to look for Russian intervention. He told the Princess:

But after all it is to your Emperor that Europe must look for safety. His prudence and moderation have hitherto been admirable; and when the proper time arrives, I have no doubt that his energy and vigour will be so too. He will maintain the cause of justice, consistency, and good faith; and this will give him strength.

He still held the same opinion the following April when he told Princess Lieven that he hoped that Metternich was wrong in anticipating a war between Russia and Turkey because 'It would be playing the game of disorganising and revolutionary principle throughout Europe; and I trust that the Emperor feels he has a greater *mission* at present. The East may be left to itself for a time. He is our anchor of safety in the west.'[52]

In the end it was in Hungary, not in Austria itself, that the Austrians invited the Russians to intervene. Aberdeen admitted to Metternich that he was puzzled by the situation in Hungary. He had always supposed the Hungarians to be particularly attached to the imperial family. But he showed a fairly detailed knowledge of the complex racial situation there, telling Metternich that he supposed that concessions to the Magyars would be oppressive to the Slavs, and speculating, 'Should there be a war of the Races I suppose the Sclavonians will be too strong for the Magyars'.[53] When the Russian intervention came, in June 1849, Aberdeen in fact regretted it on two grounds. First, it was a 'publick avowal of Austrian weakness' and second, it would 'furnish materials for the activity of Radicals in all countries'. In particular, he feared that the radicals would exploit anti-Russian feeling to subvert good order in Germany.[54]

Both Aberdeen and Metternich regarded the contest in Germany as one which was likely to be decisive for the future peace of Europe. They saw two related dangers, the advance of revolution and the advance of Prussian at the expense of Austrian power. Metternich believed that the German liberals wanted to return to Stein's schemes of 1813 and drive Austria out of Germany.[55] Both Aberdeen and Metternich were contemptuous of the amateur politicians of the Frankfort Parliament. They saw its failure to solve its immense problems with grim satisfaction, and in February 1849 Aberdeen wrote to Metternich:

The German Drama, or Farce, seems to be drawing to a close . . . and the practical question which remains is how best to get rid of the Frankfort parliament, and to establish a Diet, which shall give effect to the real and substantial union of the States of Germany.

This letter suggests that Aberdeen was not wholly unsympathetic to the concept of the national unity of Germany, which he regarded as more real than that of Italy, as long as it was clothed in a suitably conservative form.[56]

They had one fright when, at the end of March 1849, it seemed possible that Frederick William IV would accept the imperial crown from the Frankfort Parliament. The Princess Lieven wrote, 'Metternich est très *gloomy*. Il croit à l'empire républicain allemand, et à la suite de cela infailliblement à la guerre entre la Russie et la Porte, et entre la France et l'Angleterre.' Aberdeen refused to panic, insisting that a little 'firmness' would settle the matter.[57] The Frankfort Parliament was finally dissolved in June.

During all these events, Aberdeen had moved very far from the general concensus of opinion in Britain. Where he regarded the Tsar as 'an anchor of safety', most people saw him, after the Hungarian intervention, as a despot who had quenched the spark of liberty in Europe. There is much substance in the view that the Crimean War was fought at least as much about the balance of power in Europe and because of popular hostility to the Tsar because of his actions in 1848–49, as it was about Constantinople and the safety of British India – and Aberdeen saw the whole situation very differently from popular opinion. He was not opposed to orderly reform, nor did he regard the Vienna Settlement as perfect or immutable but he did see it as the framework within which European peace could be preserved and which must therefore be defended against both violence and subversion. History is usually written by the victors and, in the long run, the liberals and the nationalists of 1848 were the victors. Their cause is therefore almost universally represented as the right one. Aberdeen was on the other side. As he saw it he was defending not despotism but stability; nor did he see the liberals as heroes. On the contrary he saw most of them as, at best, misguided idealists, and at worst, as crude terrorists.

He was extremely angry with Palmerston for, as he believed, playing with fire for the sake of a little party advantage. He wrote to Princess Lieven in August 1849, 'I do not believe that he is in reality at all more radical than I am myself, but being entirely without principle, he does not hesitate to follow whatever may seem most conducive to the popularity of the moment.' A little earlier in the same letter he wrote, 'He has long been supposed to look to the Radicals in the House of Commons as his best supporters and friends . . . The sympathy of the Radicals in the country is still more extravagant.'[58]

He was also worried because the press seemed to be giving the British public such a distorted view of European events. Press coverage was a frequent topic of discussion between Aberdeen, Metternich, Guizot and Princess Lieven. Aberdeen maintained his personal friendship with Delane and *The Times* sometimes came to his aid when he was attacked. But Delane by no means shared all Aberdeen's views; for example, he believed that Austria would be stronger if Lombardy became an independent Duchy, an opinion closer to that of Palmerston than of Aberdeen.[59] In August 1848, the *Morning Chronicle*, traditionally a Whig paper, was purchased by a group of Peelites and, for a few months, its articles gave some satisfaction to Aberdeen and his friends. But by the autumn of 1849 Aberdeen was in despair. He wrote to Princess Lieven, 'The foreign articles [in the *Chronicle*] which were so admirably written last summer are now inspired from another quarter, and in a different sense. Even the "Times" although not actually connected with the Foreign Office, I believe no longer entertains the same hostility which it felt and expressed so strongly.'[60] Aberdeen's inability to find any secure base for support in the press was to be his Achilles heel during the next few years.

The aftermath of the 1848 revolutions provided one extremely embarrassing experience for Aberdeen. He had admitted that he had little personal sympathy for Ferdinand II of Naples but he had supported Stanley in attacking Palmerston's policy towards Naples and had, among other things, accused him of being gullible in believing all the radical charges against Ferdinand.[61] By chance, William Gladstone spent the winter of 1850–51 in Naples and became acquainted with some of the Neapolitan liberals. He was appalled by what he learnt of the conditions in which political prisoners were detained and became particularly interested in one case, that of the lawyer, Carlo Poerio. He hesitated as to whether more might be achieved by public denunciation or by private representations. The first might only harden the attitude of the Neapolitan government, but they were hardly likely to listen to the second from Britain's current Foreign Secretary, Lord Palmerston. On his return to London he consulted Aberdeen. Whether Aberdeen persuaded him to delay public disclosure or whether Gladstone himself volunteered to do so, if Aberdeen would undertake to make representations, is not of great importance, although it became a matter of acrimonious dispute between Gladstone and Aberdeen's son.[62] The general picture is clear. Both men agreed that, if private representations failed, Gladstone would be free to denounce the Neapolitan government publicly. Aberdeen, however, believed not unreasonably in the circumstances, that he should be the one to decide when representations had failed. Gladstone believed that the discretion remained with him.

Gladstone presented the detailed case to Aberdeen in April 1851. The first delay was imposed by the fact that Gladstone went to Paris and Aberdeen was unwilling to proceed until he had checked some of the facts with him[63] but, on 2 May, Aberdeen sent a most carefully worded letter to the Austrian Chancellor, Prince Schwarzenberg. The matter could hardly have been more delicate. Schwarzenberg was not Metternich. Aberdeen could not claim the privilege of a private word in the ear of an old friend. In fact, Schwarzenberg was one of the few Austrian statesmen whom Aberdeen disliked and distrusted.[64] Aberdeen had no official position, indeed no *locus standi* in the affair at all. He began by reminding Schwarzenberg that he had been Austria's warm friend for forty years and congratulated him on the restoration of order in the empire. He laid the facts which Gladstone had given him before Schwarzenberg, assuring him that Gladstone was no trouble-maker but 'one of our most distinguished public men and a staunch conservative and monarchist'. He understood, he said, the difficulties of the situation in Naples 'but personal vengeance, and prolonged rigour will deprive the Government of that sympathy to which it is entitled, and perhaps may not ultimately tend to its security'.[65] Aberdeen also approached the Neapolitan envoy in London, Prince Castelcicala, who stone-walled in reply; but both Aberdeen and Gladstone attached more importance to Schwarzenberg's response.[66]

Schwarzenberg replied at the end of June. The delay was partly due to his decision not to entrust his letter to normal channels but to use a special messenger. In part, his letter was a fighting defence. He was sure that some of the complaints were exaggerated 'au caractère national des Napolitains' but the public would believe anything. He complained that the radicals had denounced the death sentences passed in Hungary, but ignored the fact that most of them were not carried out and had turned a blind eye to the assassinations perpetrated by the insurgents. He also reminded Aberdeen that Britain did not have clean hands. What of the severities she had used to put down the recent insurrection in the Ionian Islands, or the treatment of the Irish deportees in Van Diemen's Land or the case of Ernest Jones? The last was a palpable hit because the Jones case seemed almost an exact parallel of Poerio's. (Jones, a lawyer of good family,[67] had been arrested for Chartist activities. He refused to conform to prison discipline on the grounds that he was not a common felon and it was generally agreed that his imprisonment ruined his health.) Having established, at least to his own satisfaction, that all governments treated their dissidents harshly when they feared for their own safety, Schwarzenberg promised that, although he would have refused to have intervened if he had been approached officially, he would because of his high regard for Aberdeen and from consideration of Gladstone's honourable character, bring the matter to the attention of the Naples government. He added that he hardly needed to say that the matter must remain entirely confidential because any act of clemency must seem to come spontaneously from the King.[68]

Despite the indignant tone – and Schwarzenberg had some reason to resent the holier than thou attitude of many British politicians – it was essentially a satisfactory reply. It would have been difficult for the Neapolitans to have refused a request from their protectors, the Austrians, and Schwarzenberg had virtually promised 'acts of clemency', presumably either the release of political prisoners or at least an amelioration of their conditions. But Gladstone had jumped the gun. He was convinced that Aberdeen's intervention had failed and, a few days before Schwarzenberg's reply was received in England, he published the first of his two 'Letters to Lord Aberdeen', denouncing the Neapolitan government.

Aberdeen was understandably angry. He had begged Gladstone to delay the publication a little longer and he had not given Gladstone permission to use his name in connection with the affair. He felt that he had been put into a totally false position but, what was worse, the publication had destroyed any chance of effectual intervention in Naples.[69] He salvaged what he could. He wrote a long but dignified letter of apology to Schwarzenberg, telling him that, in his opinion, Gladstone had been 'bound' to wait for the result of Aberdeen's representations before acting. He realised that the publication had entirely deprived Schwarzenberg of 'those confidential means of interference' which he had promised to employ. In the circumstances he did not feel that he could appeal to Schwarzenberg further although, he pointed out 'the rashness of Mr Gladstone's publication' had not altered the facts in Naples and he could only leave any action to Schwarzenberg's discretion. Schwarzenberg replied that Gladstone's 'deplorable publication' robbed him of all opportunity to intervene. Even Gladstone's friend and biographer, John Morley, admitted that the immediate effect of Gladstone's action was to worsen the condition of the Neapolitan prisoners. Poerio, and the others in whom Gladstone had been particularly interested, were not released until 1859.[70]

It says a good deal for Aberdeen's natural generosity of temperament and perhaps also for the almost paternal feeling which he had for Gladstone, which made him extend to him the same kind of indulgence which he showed to his own sons, that the incident did not cause a permanent breach between the two men. Gladstone himself was conscience–stricken. He admitted that the degree to which his own feelings were involved might have made him 'a bad judge' and he hoped Aberdeen would overlook 'any error which it is possible I may have committed' and do anything he still could for the sake of humanity. Aberdeen, although telling him bluntly that he had put him in an impossible position, accepted that Gladstone had 'acted in the whole matter under the conscientious belief that you were discharging a solemn duty imposed upon you'.[71]

Aberdeen's irritation at Gladstone was, however, mild compared with his anger at Palmerston. For European conservatives, Palmerston's actions were becoming increasingly difficult to bear. Metternich and Guizot, through Princess Lieven, continually urged Aberdeen to launch an attack on Palmerston although Aberdeen's response was not always entirely satisfactory to them.

A potentially dangerous incident developed in the autumn of 1849 when the Hungarian leader, Kossuth, and a Polish patriot, General Bem, fled to Turkey. Austria and Russia demanded the return of the fugitives. Stratford Canning advised the Sultan to refuse. When the Sultan replied that he dared not risk war with both Austria and Russia without support, Canning summoned Admiral Parker and the British Mediterranean fleet to the entrance to the Dardanelles and persuaded the French Ambassador to call the French fleet. Palmerston endorsed his action, although counselling caution since, if Parker entered the Dardanelles while Turkey was at peace, this would constitute a breach of the 1841 Convention. In fact, Parker did at one point venture into the mouth of the Dardanelles, ostensibly because of bad weather.

Princess Lieven wrote indignantly to Aberdeen, who was not entirely responsive. If he had been in office, he told her, he too would have tried to have saved 'these miserable Refugees'. So long as they were removed from the Austrian border, the Emperors had no real cause for complaint. On the other hand, he did concede that the whole affair had been 'grossly mismanaged' as a result of the 'old rancour of Stratford Canning' and 'the clamour of our whole Press'.[72]

In the eyes of European conservatives, Parker's fleet had been a kind of 'typhoid Mary' carrying sedition and revolution all round Europe but it was its next exploit which brought matters to a head. Britain had a number of long–standing disputes with the unsatisfactory government of King Otho in Greece. The Greeks had persistently defaulted on the repayment of the loan guaranteed by the Powers in 1832. Several British citizens had been unable to obtain compensation from the Greek government, notably a well-known Scots historian, George Finlay, whose garden in Athens had been confiscated to make way for a new royal palace. Then came the notorious Don Pacifico case. David Pacifico was a Spanish Jew, who claimed British citizenship because he had been born in Gibraltar, although he also held Portuguese citizenship. He already had a dubious record as a confidence trickster, but he had undoubtedly suffered loss when his house was burnt down during an anti-Semitic riot in 1847 and the Athens police had apparently stood by and watched.

Palmerston would have been less likely to have intervened in such trivial cases, but for the more serious quarrel centring on the Ionian Islands, still a British protectorate. In 1848 the then British High Commissioner, Lord Seaton, had introduced a form of constitutional government there, but the experiment had been followed by a rebellion in which the inhabitants had demanded to join Greece. Seaton's successor, Sir Henry Ward, put down the rising with a stern hand. This was the time when the British press was running a campaign against the Austrians for flogging rebels in Italy and Hungary, and it was for his part in this that the Austrian General Haynau was pitched into a horse trough at Barclay and Perkins Brewery during a visit to Britain in 1850. It was therefore embarrassing to have the spotlight turned on the fact that the British had been flogging rebels in the Ionian Islands. Princess Lieven tried to induce Aberdeen to take up a number of atrocity stories, including an allegation that a nine–year–old boy had been flogged to death. The story was untrue and Aberdeen wisely refused to touch anything which could not be proved up to the hilt.[73]

The Greek government had sympathised with the Ionian rebels and the dispute came to centre on the ownership of two small islands, Cervi and Sapienza, by way of which some of the rebels had escaped. Aberdeen himself was unsure whether Palmerston engineered a showdown with Greece in the spring of 1850, with the deliberate intention of bringing down the government which had defied him over the Ionian Islands, or whether the whole thing should be attributed to the incorrigible 'recklessness' of the Foreign Secretary.

It was certainly an extraordinary proceeding. Admiral Parker was directed to sail to Piraeus and deliver an ultimatum. Unless the British demands were met within twenty-four hours, a blockade would be established. The Russians protested and the French offered to mediate. Under pressure from his cabinet colleagues, Palmerston accepted the French mediation and the blockade was temporarily lifted. In April, a compromise agreement was reached in London between Palmerston and the Greek and French Ambassadors, but, before the news could reach Athens, the British Minister, Sir Thomas Wyse, acting on out–of–date instructions, re–imposed the blockade and the Greeks yielded to the original British demands. An angry French government recalled their Ambassador from London.

The reaction, of both Metternich and the Princess Lieven was to say, in effect, 'We've got him now'. Ever since February they had been urging Aberdeen to move in for the kill but he was extremely cautious. He himself was convinced that Palmerston must be removed from the Foreign Office if Britain were to retain her good name for honourable dealings in international affairs and if the stability of Europe was to be safeguarded. But he knew that his closest associates had other priorities. Peel was convinced that Palmerston could not be removed without bringing down Lord John Russell's government and he was determined not to be a party to letting in Stanley and the Protectionists which, he believed, would spell economic disaster for Britain. Graham agreed with Peel and as late as April 1850 wrote to him:

I make great allowances for Lord Aberdeen's soreness and impatience. He attaches primary importance to our foreign relations, and in his estimation our domestic policy is secondary. At home he is liberal, but not an enthusiast; abroad he is a zealot, in the sense most opposed to Palmerston; and having much reason on his side in condemnation of the proceedings of our Foreign Office he is impetuous and indignant, and overlooks all the consequences of the course to which he is honestly impelled.[74]

In these circumstances, Aberdeen began to move closer to Stanley and, in the spring of 1850, concerted his tactics on foreign questions very closely with him.[75]

Aberdeen obtained a great deal of confidential information from Paris to aid him in his attacks on Palmerston, but Guizot was no longer in office and occasionally the information was misleading. When Stanley and Aberdeen opened the campaign in February, Aberdeen, knowing how central the Ionian

Islands were to the controversy, was under the impression that the cession of
Cervi and Sapienza was among the British demands. Princess Lieven continued
to insist that it was but the British government was able to disprove it.[76]

The government managed to stave off the attack for some time. Aberdeen
told Princess Lieven on 23 February that he feared public interest might fade;
a week later he added, I had rather hoped we might have returned to the subject
of Greece today, and pressed Stanley to do so; but he had not sufficiently read
the Papers, which are rather voluminous.'[77] Stanley gave notice of a motion for
14 March, but Lansdowne appealed to the House not to proceed for fear of
jeopardising the negotiations then in progress and, as a disappointed Aberdeen
told Princess Lieven, 'Such appeals as these are never made in vain'.[78] The long
anticipated debate in the Lords did not take place until 17 June.

No one doubted that it was to be a full dress attack on the whole of Palmerston's policy, to be repeated in the Commons a few days later. Almost up
to the end Aberdeen was not sure that he would have the support of Peel in
the Commons.[79] He had been stung to anger by an article in *The Globe* on 29
March, inspired (and perhaps even written) by Palmerston, which boasted that
Peel's silence on foreign affairs must be construed to mean support for Palmerston's policies. Aberdeen wrote Peel a rather bitter letter, saying that he
was not surprised that such a conclusion should have been drawn but he
thought it 'very injurious in its consequences'. Peel, annoyed in his turn, wrote
to Graham that he thought Aberdeen too 'sensitive', and added, 'The letters
he receives from Paris, from Guizot and Madame de Lieven and others – all
reckless as to any other consequences, provided only they can get rid of Palmerston – make Aberdeen still more impatient.' He made it clear to Aberdeen
that he had no intention of leading a crusade against Palmerston, however much
his silence might be misconstrued, and even though both Peel and Graham
began to fear that Aberdeen's 'old high Tory habits and predilections' might
reassert themselves and he might rejoin Stanley.[80]

Stanley opened the debate on 17 June with a witty speech which put the
House in a good humour for Aberdeen's more sober and documented contribution. Aberdeen conceded that both Don Pacifico and Finlay probably had
grievances but it was quite wrong to resort to force before all legal means were
exhausted. It was incredible that Britain had not concerted her policy with her
co-guarantors, Russia and France. Greece was only the starting point for his
general attack. He traced the course of Parker's fleet since it left Britain. It had
called in the Tagus and stirred up trouble in Portugal. It called at Naples,
threatened the King, encouraged the Sicilian rebels and then abandoned them.
It went to the Ionian Islands. To do what? To deliver the cat–of–nine–tails
to flog the rebels. It proceeded to the Dardanelles, and broke the 1841 treaty
by entering the Straits – the explanation that this was because of the weather
was a 'deception'. And all to no purpose – Austria and Russia had withdrawn
their demands that the rebels be handed over before the fleet even arrived.
Aberdeen then switched to an attack on Palmerston's policy in Italy. Britain,
he said, could have stopped the Sardinian war if she had exerted herself and
the unpopular Russian intervention in Hungary would then have been unnec-

essary because Austria would have had adequate forces herself. Lansdowne and others replied on Palmerston's behalf as best they could, but Stanley's motion was carried by 169 votes to 132. Princess Lieven was ill with delight when she heard the news. She told Aberdeen that her physician had to remain at her bedside all night.[81]

The Princess's delight was premature. Russell saw that his own survival depended upon saving Palmerston. He publicly proclaimed his support for him by again casting doubt on Aberdeen's patriotism. Palmerston, he declared, 'will act not as the Minister of Austria, or as the Minister of Russia, or of France, or of any other country, but as the Minister of England'.[82] By arrangement, on 24 June, Roebuck moved a resolution in the Commons praising Palmerston. The debate, which lasted four days, ranged over the whole spectrum of foreign affairs but the great triumph was Palmerston's own. In a four–hour speech he defended his policy, including his recent actions in Greece. He made his famous declaration that, just as 'the Roman, in days of old, held himself free from indignity when he could say *Civis Romanus sum*', so a British subject should be able to feel confident in the strong protection of England. Gladstone remorselessly exposed the fallacies in Palmerston's argument – but in vain. The government had a majority of 46 in the Commons, but Palmerston's real victory was in the country. His popularity was never greater.

Aberdeen had, however, one great cause for satisfaction about the Commons debate. Peel, knowing that Russell was bound to be able to command a majority on what had become a formal issue of confidence, felt free to express all his real disapproval of Palmerston's policy. He cast it in the form of a defence of the alternative policy of Aberdeen.[83] The next day, 29 June, Peel was thrown by his horse on Constitution Hill, and died on 2 July 1850. His death was an appalling shock to Aberdeen. While Peel still fought vainly for his life, Aberdeen's children and grandchildren noticed his strange rigidity and his attempt to conceal all emotion. At night he was attacked by violent spasms which racked his whole body.[84] After Peel's death he wrote in unusually emotional terms to Lady Haddo of his pleasure that Peel's last speech in Parliament 'was made in my defence and that it was accompanied with unusual terms of affection and regard'.[85] At first sight this seems an unexpectedly egotistical reaction to the tragedy from a man who was not normally egotistical, but Aberdeen knew how close he and Peel had been to a political breach and estrangement a few weeks earlier. He was expressing his thankfulness that they were reconciled before Peel's sudden death.

NOTES

1. *Hansard*, 3rd ser., LXXV, 892–906, 973–85, 1264–1308, 1326–43, LXXVI, 212–59 (14, 17, 24 June, 2 July 1844).*The Times*, July – August 1844; *Morning Chronicle*, esp. 26 June 1844; PP, XIV (1844) 501, 505, 'Reports of the Secret Committees relative to the Post Office'.

2. Add. MSS 40455, Aberdeen to Peel, 25 Mar. 1844; *Hansard*, 3rd ser., LXXXVIII, 1341–53.
3. Add. MSS 43211, Aberdeen to Robert Gordon, 19 July 1844.
4. This is most fully described in K. Ellis, *The Post Office in the Eighteenth Century*, which also deals with the end of the 'Secret Office' pp. 65–77, 138–42.
5. PP XIV (1844), 503, 520–1.
6. Add. MSS 43045, Aberdeen to Victoria, 7 Feb. 1845.
7. Ellis, p. 141.
8. Add. MSS 40455, Aberdeen to Peel, 12, 15 Aug. 1845.
9. Add. MSS 40455, Aberdeen to Peel, 18 Sept. 1847.
10. Ibid.
11. Ibid.
12. Add. MSS 43190, Graham to Aberdeen, 6 Aug. 1847, Aberdeen to Graham, 29 Aug. 1847.
13. Add. MSS 43128, f. 294 (out of order), Aberdeen to Metternich, 26 Apr. 1848; Add. MSS 49275, Metternich to Aberdeen, 26 Apr. 1848 (copy).
14. Add. MSS 49275, Metternich to Aberdeen, 6 June 1848 (copy).
15. Add. MSS 49275, Metternich to Aberdeen, 22 Jan. 1849, 'Confidentielle et Secrète' (copy); Add. MSS 43128, Aberdeen to Metternich, 23 Jan. 1849.
16. Monypenny & Buckle, *Disraeli*, vol. 3, pp. 576–7.
17. Add. MSS 43247, Delane to Aberdeen, 23 Aug., 6 Sept. 1848, Aberdeen to Lieven, 16 Aug. 1848, Jones-Parry,.vol. 2, p. 297.
18. Stanmore, p. 196; cf. Add. MSS 49253–4, Stanmore's Diaries for various dates 1848–9.
19. Add. MSS 49275, Metternich to Aberdeen, 29 Dec. 1848 (copy).
20. Aberdeen to Lieven, 1 Nov. 1848, 18 Aug. 1849, Jones-Parry vol. 2, pp. 302, 316.
21. Add. MSS 49275, Metternich to Aberdeen, 29 Dec. 1848 (copy).
22. Lieven to Aberdeen, 27 Nov., 10, 17 Dec. 1849, Aberdeen to Lieven, 16, 26 Dec. 1849, Jones-Parry, vol. 2, pp. 349–52, 356–7.
23. Aberdeen to Lieven, 19 Dec. 1849, Jones-Parry, vol. 2, pp. 353–4.
24. Add. MSS 43194, Brougham to Aberdeen, 12 Jan. 1849.
25. Lieven to Aberdeen, 2, 21 Feb., 9 Mar. 1850, Aberdeen to Lieven, 12, 16, 19 Feb. 1850, Jones-Parry, vol. 2, pp. 373, 379, 384, 389, 393, 415.
26. Add. MSS 43134, Aberdeen to Guizot, 31 Jan. 1850.
27. Add. MSS 43134, Guizot to Aberdeen, 3 Feb. 1850.
28. Aberdeen to Guizot, n.d. Feb. 1850, BP 12/8.
29. Ibid.
30. Aberdeen to Guizot, 4 Mar. 1850, BP 12/8.
31. Aberdeen to Guizot, 3 May 1850, BP 12/8.
32. Add. MSS 43134, Guizot to Aberdeen, 21 Mar. 1850.
33. *Histoire du protectorat de Cromwell et du rétablissement des Stuarts*, (1856); cf. Add. MSS 49253, Stanmore's Diary, eg. 27 Jan. 1849.
34. Add. MSS 43134, Aberdeen to Guizot, 31 Jan. 1850; Aberdeen to Lieven, 22 Jan. 1850, Jones-Parry, vol. 2, p. 364.
35. NLS 15017, Aberdeen to Ellice, 15, 29, 30 Dec. 1850, 7 Jan. 1851.
36. NLS 15017, Aberdeen to Ellice, 13 Dec. 1851.
37. Aberdeen to Lieven, 19 Dec. 1851, Jones-Parry, vol. 2, pp. 606–7.
38. Add. MSS 49275, Metternich to Aberdeen, 24 Aug. 1848 (copy).
39. *Hansard*, 3rd ser., CIII. 1102 (22 Mar. 1849); XCVII, 1194–6 (3 Apr. 1848).

40. *Hansard*, 3rd ser., XCVII, 1194–6 (3 Apr. 1848).
41. Aberdeen to Lieven, 16 Aug. 1848, Jones-Parry, vol. 2, pp. 296–7.
42. Add. MSS 49275, Metternich to Aberdeen, 24 Aug. 1848 (copy).
43. Aberdeen to Lieven, 1 Nov. 1848, Jones-Parry, vol. 2, p. 302.
44. Add. MSS 49275, Metternich to Aberdeen, 5 May 1849 (copy); Add. MSS 43128, Aberdeen to Metternich, 23 Feb. 1849.
45. Add. MSS 43128, ff. 232 onwards.
46. *Hansard*, 3rd ser., CIII, 1086–1105 (22 Mar. 1849).
47. Add. MSS 43128, Aberdeen to Metternich, 22 Mar. 1849.
48. *Hansard*, 3rd ser., CIV, 58 (30 Mar. 1849).
49. Add. MSS 43128, Aberdeen to Metternich, 3 Apr. 1849.
50. *Hansard*, 3rd ser., CIII, 240–1 (6 Mar. 1849).
51. *Hansard*, 3rd ser., CV, 377–80 (14 May 1849).
52. Aberdeen to Lieven, 15 Oct. 1848, 18 Apr. 1849, Jones-Parry, vol. 2, pp. 299–300, 309.
53. Add. MSS 43128, Aberdeen to Metternich, 9 Oct. 1848.
54. Aberdeen to Lieven, 18 Aug. 1849, Jones-Parry, vol. 2, p. 317.
55. Add. MSS 49275, Metternich to Aberdeen, 29 Dec. 1848, 4 Jan. 1849 (copy).
56. Add. MSS 43128, Aberdeen to Metternich, 23 Feb. 1849.
57. Lieven to Aberdeen, 17 Apr. 1849, Aberdeen to Lieven, 18 Apr. 1849, Jones-Parry, vol. 2, p. 308.
58. Aberdeen to Lieven, 18 Aug. 1849, Jones-Parry, vol. 2, p. 317.
59. Add. MSS 43247, Delane to Aberdeen, 23 Aug, 6 Sept. 1848; cf. Dasent, *John Delane*, vol. 1, pp. 90–1.
60. Add. MSS 49275, Metternich to Aberdeen, 29 Jan., 17 Feb., 11 Apr. 1849 (copies); Add. MSS 43128, Aberdeen to Metternich, 16 Dec. 1848; Aberdeen to Lieven, 1 Nov. 1849, Jones-Parry, vol. 2, p. 345
61. *Hansard*, 3rd ser., CIII, 240.
62. Add. MSS 49209, Gladstone to Arthur Gordon, 17, 21 Feb. 1893. Gordon to Gladstone, 19 Feb. 1895; cf. Stanmore, pp. 203–5.
63. Add. MSS 43070, Gladstone to Aberdeen, 14 Apr. 1851, n.d. Apr. 1851 (f. 204); Add. MSS 44088, Aberdeen to Gladstone, 7 Apr. 1851.
64. *Hansard*, 3rd ser. CXXXII, 175 (31 Mar. 1854).
65. Add. MSS 43128, Aberdeen to Schwarzenberg, 2 May 1851.
66. Add. MSS 43070, Gladstone to Aberdeen, 12 June 1851.
67. His father had been an equerry to the King of Hanover, which helps to explain why the case became so well known on the continent.
68. Add. MSS 43128, Schwarzenberg to Aberdeen, 30 June 1851.
69. Add. MSS 43070, Gladstone to Aberdeen, 7, 10 July 1851; Add. MSS 44088, Aberdeen to Gladstone, 15 July 1851.
70. Add. MSS 43128, Aberdeen to Schwarzenberg, 5 Aug. 1851. Schwarzenberg to Aberdeen, 18 Sept. 1851; Morley, *Gladstone*, vol. 1, p. 401.
71. Add. MSS 44088, Gladstone to Aberdeen, 18 July 1851, Aberdeen to Gladstone, 26 Aug. 1851.
72. Aberdeen to Lieven, 26 Oct. 1849, Jones-Parry, vol. 2, p. 340.
73. Lieven to Aberdeen, 19, 26, 30 Mar. 1850, Aberdeen to Lieven, 21 Mar., 8 Apr. 1850, Jones-Parry, vol. 2, pp. 422, 424, 427–8, 437–8, 441.
74. Add. MSS 40452, Graham to Peel, 7 Apr. 1850.
75. For example, Derby Papers, Aberdeen to Stanley, 11 Feb., 4, 19 Mar. 1850. For the more general implications of this see Ch. 25.

76. *Hansard*, 3rd ser., CVIII, 262–8 (4 Feb. 1850); Aberdeen to Lieven, 6, 12 Feb. 1850, Lieven to Aberdeen, 7, 8, 9 Feb. 1850, Jones-Parry, vol. 2, pp. 373–80, Derby Papers, Aberdeen to Stanley, 11 Feb. 1850.

77. Aberdeen to Lieven, 23 Feb., 1 Mar. 1850, Jones-Parry, vol. 2, pp. 394, 403.

78. Aberdeen to Lieven, 15 Mar. 1850, Jones-Parry, vol. 2, p. 418.

79. Aberdeen to Lieven, 11 June 1850, Jones-Parry, vol. 2, p. 489.

80. Add. MSS 40455, Aberdeen to Peel, 30 Mar., 4 Apr. 1850; 43065, Peel to Aberdeen, 2 Apr. 1850; Add. MSS 40452, Peel to Graham, 3, 7 Apr. 1850.

81. *Hansard*, 3rd ser., CXI, 1293–1332, 1350–62; Lieven to Aberdeen, 20 June 1850, Jones-Parry, vol. 2, pp. 492–3.

82. *Hansard*, 3rd ser., CXII, 106 (20 June 1850).

83. *Hansard*, 3rd ser., CXII, 674–81 (28 June 1850).

84. Stanmore, p. 197.

85. HH 1/29, Aberdeen to Lady Haddo, 4 July 1850.

CHAPTER TWENTY-FIVE

The survival of the Peelites

One hundred and seventeen Conservatives voted for the repeal of the Corn Laws in the House of Commons in May 1846. As Professor Conacher has pointed out 'Free Trade Conservative' is not quite synonymous with 'Peelite'[1] but there clearly remained the nucleus of a Free Trade Conservative party, if Peel had chosen to rebuild it. He did not so choose. He was tired, unwell, angered by what he regarded as totally unjustified personal attacks on him and sensitive to the criticism that for the second time – the first had been over Catholic Emancipation – he had betrayed the fundamental principles of his party. His own inclination would have been to have withdrawn from politics altogether. He was persuaded to retain his seat in the Commons and concentrated on keeping Russell's government in office, even putting his own financial expertise at the disposal of their inexperienced Chancellor, Sir Charles Wood, until he became, as Professor Gash remarks, in some danger of being the prisoner of the government.[2]

Peel's attitude was deeply disappointing to his younger supporters and puzzling even to some of his closer friends, many of whom at first imagined that he would soon reconsider his position. Aberdeen was probably one of the first to realise that Peel's decision was irrevocable. Before Parliament reassembled in January 1847, Peel refused to give his blessing to the attempt by Goulburn and others to keep the party together by sending out the customary circular letter to all known supporters. Some party organisation survived to fight the general election of the summer of 1847. When Gladstone feared that he would lose his Oxford University seat – although because of religious rather than economic differences with his constituents – he asked Aberdeen whether there was likely to be an opening in the city of Aberdeen. Aberdeen replied regretting that, if Gladstone had applied to him earlier he might have been able to arrange something, but that there was now no vacancy.[3] In the event Gladstone retained his Oxford seat.

Overall it was difficult to calculate Peelite gains and losses, not least because Peel refused to interest himself in who might support him. He wrote to Aberdeen in August, 'Lord Brougham has made a calculation which I have not taken the trouble to make, namely the number of *Peelites* as they are called in

414

the new House of Commons. I know not whether there are 60 or 6 and rather hope they may be the latter in preference to the former or a larger number.'[4] Calculations in fact varied enormously. Lord George Bentinck, the Protectionist leader in the Commons, thought the Peelites might muster as many as 130 supporters. Brougham put it at between 80 and 90. But this was only potential strength. 'What right have we', asked Brougham, 'to call them Peelites – except some dozen or so? The others are only so reckoned because they are not known to be Protectionists & are known not to be Whigs.'[5] Everything still depended on Peel.

In September 1847, Aberdeen was invited to join the royal shooting party at Laggan. He found the Queen and the Prince Consort in good spirits but suffering 'considerable uneasiness and apprehension' at the prospect of the new House of Commons. The Queen asked him about Peelite strength. Aberdeen replied that, although two-thirds of the House probably respected Peel more than anyone else, strictly speaking Peel had no party because the only 'permanent bond of party . . . was the possession of Office, or the pursuit of it' and Peel had renounced both. The Queen expressed some surprise but, on the whole, acquiesced in Aberdeen's analysis. When Aberdeen reported this to Peel, the former Prime Minister expressed irritation that people found it so difficult to believe that politicians ever wanted to retire.[6]

But if Peel was determined not to come back into office, his followers had only two realistic alternatives to consider, to accept overtures from the Whigs, or to look to the reunion of the two wings to the Conservative party. Peelite support was well worth bidding for. Numerically they were not strong but they included virtually all the weight and ministerial experience of the old Conservative party. Russell made several offers to individual Peelites. Some such as Sir James Graham, who had first entered politics as Whigs, would not have found it too traumatic to have rejoined their old party, but for others it would have meant breaking the habits and connections of a lifetime. In the event, all those approached, Graham, Herbert, Lincoln and Dalhousie declined to join Russell's government although Dalhousie eventually accepted the Governor–Generalship of India – an appointment which Aberdeen warmly approved.[7]

At the same time attempts were made, some more serious than others, to re-unite the Conservative Party. Aberdeen himself always favoured such a reunion, as he had told Metternich and (obliquely) Disraeli, but from the beginning he made it clear that it could only take place if the Protectionists accepted the *fait accompli* of the repeal of the Corn Laws. On all other points he believed the Conservative party to be still united. From an early date Aberdeen was spoken of as a possible compromise leader who would be acceptable to both wings of the party, although he was not the only possibility. Goulburn, for example, was also considered a serious candidate. The moving spirits in the early attempts at reunion were Lord Brougham, who kept up a constant barrage of correspondence with Aberdeen,[8] Lord Londonderry (the former Sir Charles Stewart), and the one–time Chancellor, Lord Lyndhurst.

Although Aberdeen, as Edward Stanley, later the fifteenth Earl of Derby, shrewdly discerned,[9] was not so indifferent to the resumption of office as he liked to pretend, he was initially very cautious. In 1846 he was genuinely glad of the opportunity to rest. He was still suffering from the crippling headaches which had tormented him since 1842. Even after six months leisure at Haddo they were very little better and he told Gurney that he was now sceptical of his doctors' insistence that they were due to overwork. He still preferred to believe that they arose from some undiagnosed physical cause.[10]

Loss of office also enabled Aberdeen to turn his attention to his estates which had suffered some neglect while their master was almost permanently in London. He resumed his experiments with livestock, favouring Shorthorn cattle and South Down sheep and he began once more to plant trees enthusiastically. He also took advantage of one of the last Acts of Peel's government, the Public Money Drainage Act, to borrow substantial sums of money to begin new drainage schemes on the estate.[11]

He carried through some further improvements as Haddo House – some of which caused his family great inconvenience while the work was in progress[12] – but he now had a new delight, a small house which he had built on the sea cliffs near Buchan Ness. Although he feared his neighbours would call it 'Aberdeen's folly', he rejoiced in the solitude it afforded him. Although it was a wild and desolate spot, swept by the east wind from the North Sea, he found a sheltered spot in one of the ravines leading down to the shore, where he could establish a terraced garden full of unusual plants. He took refuge there, particularly in the hot summer of 1847, and loved to watch the large herring fleets of those days setting sail. The fishing village itself, however, was smelly and neglected and Aberdeen decided that it must be taken in hand. In July 1847, he told his step-daughter, Harriet's, husband, Captain Baillie-Hamilton, 'The village is much improved; and it is possible to walk through it without any sense being at all offended.' He also had a large barometer set up so that the local fishermen might have early warning of changing weather conditions.[13]

Aberdeen told his friends that over the door of his house at Buchan Ness he had inscribed the tag 'Procul negotiis beatus' (blessed is he who is far removed from business) but his life in Aberdeenshire was not quite so retired as he liked to suggest. When he was at Haddo the house was almost always full. Many of the guests were members of his now extensive family, or old friends and neighbours, but they also included a liberal sprinkling of politicians and some foreign visitors. Most of the great issues of the day were discussed at Haddo and it played an important role in the attempts to find new political alignments after the split in the Conservative party.

Both Lord Stanmore and Lady Haddo have left descriptions of the extreme formality and almost feudal state of some of those house parties. Lady Haddo even spoke of 'a little court with a somewhat rigid etiquette'.[14] Delane, a little later, called Haddo 'Very splendid, but rather cold and stiff after Glenquoich [the Ellice home].'[15] Perhaps Aberdeen rather consciously played the part of a Scottish laird. He still sometimes felt the need to apologise for his house in comparison with the great English country houses and some of his guests, like Lord Clarendon,[16] were a little patronising about it.

No one, however, ever complained of Aberdeen's hospitality. The comte de

Jarnac, visiting him in 1843, was impressed by his excellent table and his choice selection of wines. Knowing Jarnac's passion for shooting, Aberdeen sent him out every day, usually in the company of one of his sons, and Jarnac later said that he enjoyed the best sport of his life.[17] Aberdeen himself had developed an enthusiasm for otter hunting and his second son, Alexander, was as keen as his father. Aberdeen's otter hounds became famous. Landseer painted them and exhibited the picture ('The otter speared') at the Royal Academy in 1844. The same year Aberdeen took them to Blair Atholl to entertain Queen Victoria but his sense of fair play was revolted by the fact that a 'bagged' otter was produced to provide sport for Prince Albert. Aberdeen's hounds did not, perhaps, create too much havoc among the Aberdeenshire otters since he apparently considered two 'kills' a satisfactory score during a visit when they had had 'some good runs'. His activities caused some mirth among his friends and Lord Stanley, declining an invitation to Haddo, admitted that he would have been tempted to change his mind if he could be promised a sight of Aberdeen in a kilt, up to his waist in a stream, hunting otters.[18]

Victoria had parted with Aberdeen in 1846 with great regret – Lord Cowley had a story that she had burst into tears.[19] She did her best to continue to show her regard for him. Already in 1845 she had appointed him to the sinecure post of Ranger of Greenwich Park which gave him the use of the Ranger's House at Blackheath.[20] This was particularly valuable to him because, although he still had Argyll House, Bentley Priory which for many years he had used as his main London base was now in the hands of his step-son, the second Lord Abercorn and was soon to pass from the family altogether. Abercorn was extravagant and, once he had the management of his own affairs, quickly ran into serious debts. In 1848 he leased Bentley Priory to William IV's widow, Queen Adelaide. By 1850 he was confronted with the choice of selling Bentley Priory or the Irish estate at Baron's Court, and in 1852 he sold the Priory to Sir John Kelk, who had made his money in the new railways. The loss of Bentley Priory was a great wrench to Aberdeen. He told Baillie-Hamilton, 'I never go there without going to seek the dead as well as the living.'[21]

He was shocked by Abercorn's mismanagement of his affairs. The truth was apparently revealed to him by Abercorn's bankers rather than by Abercorn himself and he wrote to his step-son that the news was a 'thunderbolt'. He had known that he was embarrassed but not the 'frightful reality' that he was in debt to the tune of something like £400,000. Even in this extremity he concentrated on trying to provide practical help and support. Fortunately, his bankers, Coutts, would do their best to help him and a trust must be created. He would not remark on the events which had led up to this crisis since he was sure Abercorn already felt the matter deeply. Despite his own feelings about Bentley Priory, Aberdeen counselled his step-son to sell that rather than Baron's Court, without which he could hardly keep up his place in society, although he could not repress one rather bitter comment. 'For although in your situation', he said, 'I would rather have lived on bread and water for the rest of my days than have sold it, I could not honestly say that it was a place for a man on the brink of ruin to keep.'[22]

In 1846 Aberdeen had at last become Lord Lieutenant of Aberdeenshire, but, as he wrote to his daughter-in-law, Mary, whereas twenty years ago it would have given him great pleasure, now it would only give him trouble.[23] Perhaps there was an element of a pose in this but Aberdeen was still hesitating as to how far he wished to continue in public life. His relations with the Court remained close with visits both to Windsor and to the Queen when she was in Scotland. The fact that his second son, Alexander, was now an equerry to the Prince also provided natural opportunities for contact.

The outcome of the 1847 elections worried the Court as they worried Aberdeen and Graham.[24] Russell's government failed to deal with the Irish crisis – indeed their measures were much less effective than those of Peel had been – and, in the autumn of 1847 they were overtaken by a serious financial crisis. Nevertheless, it was the European revolutions of 1848 which really brought Aberdeen back into active politics. Despite the disclaimers with which he hedged them, his comments to Mary in the summer of 1848 show that he considered the possibility of being asked to resume office a very real one. He wrote on 30 June, 'I am assured that the Ministry cannot stand, and that I am to be sent for to form the new Government. This would be a dreadful affair, and I trust will never be realised.' A week later he thought that the immediate crisis had passed and assured Mary, 'You need not be afraid of my being again in office; for I do not think it at all likely that the present Government should be displaced; and if they were, it is my determination to preserve my own freedom'.[25]

Nevertheless the possibility of a ministry being formed under Aberdeen was still being canvassed in the winter of 1848–49. In January 1849 Brougham arrived back from Cannes, as Arthur put it, 'sick of the cowardly French, but more sick of Palm.' He wrote Aberdeen what Arthur interpreted as an 'evident feeler' to see whether Aberdeen sought office, and to make a bid for a place under him. Arthur added, 'We went to Grafton St. but he was out.' Arthur then sketched a possible Cabinet with Aberdeen as Prime Minister, Lyndhurst as Lord Chancellor, Clarendon as Foreign Secretary, Gladstone at the Colonial office, Graham at the Home Office, Brougham as Lord Privy Seal, Lincoln at the Admiralty, Herbert at the War Office, Harrowby as Lord President of the Council, and Disraeli at either the Board of Trade or the Board of Control. This may have been a mere *jeu d'esprit* but Aberdeen's hastening to Grafton Street suggests that he took Brougham's overtures seriously. Brougham, however, quickly cooled off. He called the next day but Arthur wrote in disgust, 'Who can trust that shifty fellow. He now seems inclined to hark back again.'[26]

At this time there seemed to be more chance of Aberdeen sinking his differences with Stanley. Their personal relations had always remained cordial, although Aberdeen doubted whether Stanley had 'the ballast' to be Prime Minister.[27] Stanley, well aware of how woefully short the Protectionists were of men with ministerial experience and of Aberdeen's desire to see Palmerston removed from the control of foreign policy, made a number of attempts, chronicled by his son, Edward, to lure Aberdeen back to the main body of the Conservative party with promises of the Foreign Office in any future government.

In March 1849, at a dinner party, Stanley sketched out a Cabinet in which Aberdeen would become Foreign Secretary again, although Edward admitted, 'Lord Aberdeen's acceptance of the office proposed for him is doubtful.' A month later Edward even believed that the Peelites might join the Whigs. 'We believe', he wrote 'that Lord Aberdeen would join such an administration as readily as he would join us. He takes little interest in questions of domestic policy.' He added, a few days later, 'Lord Aberdeen . . . though professing friendship [for the Stanleyites] is much distrusted.'[28]

Nevertheless, early in May 1849, the Stanleyites made another determined effort to secure Aberdeen. He was invited to dinner and they were gratified that he agreed with them in criticising the government's attitude to Canada, where Lord Elgin had just made his famous decision to accept the controversial Rebellion Losses Bill and so set Canada firmly on the path to complete internal self-government. Russell accepted Elgin's decision but the Conservatives tended to sympathise with the Canadian Loyalists who thought the Bill a bad and unjust one, which should have been rejected.

Stanley, however, failed to persuade Aberdeen to act with them on the more immediately critical question of the repeal of the Navigation Acts. The Navigation laws, which were designed to protect the British mercantile marine from foreign competition, were the one important remaining piece of protectionist legislation and even Peel had originally had some doubts about the wisdom of repealing them. Russell had little difficulty in getting the measure through the Commons but there was a real danger that it would be defeated in the Lords. Stanley begged Aberdeen to vote with the Protectionists, telling him 'if he went against us, it would be impossible to include him in the arrangements [for the formation of a Protectionist ministry], and without him as Foreign Secretary we could not succeed'. Stanley 'bade him consider well the responsibility which he was incurring'. Peel, on the other hand, asked him to vote for the measure on the principle of preserving Russell's government and Aberdeen did so. The Bill passed the Lords by ten votes. Aberdeen also voted against an amendment, proposed by Stanley himself, to limit the operation of the Act.[29]

Despite this, Aberdeen and Stanley continued to keep terms until their supporters, and their enemies, began to wonder who was using whom. Disraeli, who by this time had struck up a strange kind of alliance with Palmerston, did his best to implant doubts in Stanley's mind. He had some success with Edward but little with his father. Edward wrote in his Diary for 9 June 1850:

Lord Aberdeen was greatly suspected, D. said (and I heard the same from others) of making us catspaws in this business [the Don Pacifico debate]: intending to overthrow Lord Palmerston and then supplant him with the Whigs. I told this to my Father, who scouted the ideas, saying that he did not particularly admire Lord Aberdeen but thought him wholly incapable of such treachery as this.[30]

Stanley and Aberdeen had, in fact moved very close to one another on foreign questions in the spring of 1850 and their co-operation here was close and harmonious.[31] Their attempts to concert their policy on domestic questions were less happy. The crucial issue was the Irish franchise and Aberdeen's letters to Stanley leave no doubt that he regarded it as a vital test case as to whether the two wings of the Conservative party could re-unite. Stanley replied on 21 May, 'I share as warmly as you or any one can in the desire that the Conservative party should again be found acting together.'[32] Unfortunately they were not really agreed on the best course of action.

Russell's government introduced a measure to extend the Irish franchise to £8 ratepayers. The Protectionists were thoroughly alarmed, believing that it would place all Irish seats at the mercy of the radicals and the priests. Stanley wished to kill the Bill entirely by voting against the Second Reading in the Lords and hoped that Aberdeen would induce the Peelites to vote with him. Aberdeen, however, argued that the Conservative party had already conceded when in office that the Irish franchise must be changed to bring it more nearly into line with that of mainland Britain and he still feared the repercussions of a head–on clash between the Lords and the Commons. It would be better to let the Bill pass its Second Reading and introduce such amendments at the committee stage as would render it 'safe'. He believed that, if the amendments were moderate, the Commons would accept them.[33] Stanley reluctantly agreed and the argument now turned on what amendments would render the measure safe. Stanley believed that £15, based on rent not rates, was the minimum acceptable. If, he implied, he was prepared to follow Aberdeen's lead on foreign policy, Aberdeen should listen to him on domestic affairs. Aberdeen believed, rightly as it proved, that anything above £12 would be unacceptable to the Commons. Stanley got his £15 amendment in the Lords but, in July, the Commons reduced the figure to £12 and most leading Peelites voted with the government. Stanley was angry and complained to Aberdeen that some Peelites were only voting for the measure out of hostility to him, Stanley[34]

The problems over the Irish franchise boded ill for any reunion between the Peelites and the Protectionists in the Commons, but the Protectionists had not abandoned hope that they might recapture Aberdeen and that he might bring a substantial number of Peelite peers with him. The possibility of this was the reason for the near breach between Aberdeen and Peel in the spring of 1850. Peel's unlooked for death in fact made Aberdeen's position more difficult. He could no longer make decisions simply as an individual. Whether he wished it or not he was now looked to as the natural leader of the remaining Peelites, a small but influential and close-knit group. Loyalty, and Aberdeen was a very loyal man, compelled him to consider the wishes of the whole group.

Aberdeen had repeatedly said that what he really wanted was the reunion of the Conservative party, which he saw as an essential safeguard of stability, both at home and abroad. The Peelites were bound together essentially by their loyalty to the legacy of Peel, as the Pittites had once been bound together by their loyalty to William Pitt. They interpreted this in a surprisingly narrow way. Graham wrote to Aberdeen in the summer of 1852, 'The paramount duty; perhaps the sole remaining duty, of Peel's Friends as a Party is the Defence of his Financial and Commercial Policy.'[35] They understood it, in other words, primarily or entirely as the defence of the economic policy which had rescued

Britain from the depression of the 1840s and so averted the danger of public disorder and social upheaval. On these fairly narrow grounds, if Edward Stanley is to be believed, Aberdeen had some reservations. In February 1851, Lord Stanley challenged Aberdeen as to whether he had expected the results which had followed the repeal of the Corn Laws. Aberdeen replied simply, 'No'. Stanley then asked why he should be ashamed to admit that his anticipations had proved incorrect and to agree to modify the measure to produce the results he had originally desired. According to Edward Stanley, Aberdeen replied that he would be willing to do so in company with Graham and the other Peelites but that he would be 'ashamed', picking up Stanley's word, to do so alone.[36]

Apart from the death of Peel, the political sensation of the summer of 1850 was the papal brief conferring territorial titles on Roman Catholic bishops in England and Wales. They had already assumed territorial titles in Ireland and the possibility of extending the system to England had been amicably discussed in Rome by Lord Minto in 1848. Russell's initial reaction had been to regard the brief as 'not a matter to be alarmed at'.[37] But on 4 November he wrote his famous letter to the Bishop of Durham, virtually promising counter-measures. The excitement of Protestant England was provoked partly by the 'Romanising' tendencies in the Church of England itself, which were just starting to attract attention, and partly by the indiscreet utterances of certain Roman Catholics, led by their new Cardinal Archbishop of Westminster, Wiseman, that this was the beginning of the return of the whole of England to the Catholic fold. It was not soothed by the knowledge that the Pope himself was currently dependent on the support of the French army.

Russell's criticism of the Pope's action was accompanied by sharp words about the activities of the 'Romanisers' within the Anglican Church, which provoked a strong reaction from the High churchmen among the Peelites, notably Gladstone and Lincoln, who promptly entered the lists against Russell. Aberdeen's objections sprang from different motives. He was not a High churchman but he thought Russell's proposal to invalidate such titles foolish and unnecessary. He also suspected that it was a cheap political manoeuvre to cash in on public excitement to shore up an unstable government. In his opinion it was a government's duty to calm irrational clamour not to exacerbate it.

It was clear that Russell's government had become unstable and that, when Parliament met in February they could not always rely even on the votes of their supposed supporters. Edward Stanley cynically wrote in his Diary on 1 February, 'Lord Aberdeen, whose visits in St. James's Square become more frequent as our prospect of power brightens, has called three or four times during the last week, foretelling a crisis as a Mother Carey's chicken foretells a storm.' On one occasion, Aberdeen and Lord Stanley discussed various possible combinations. Lord Stanley subsequently recounted the conversation to his son, who recorded:

Then they began to talk of possible coalitions – my Father with the moderate Whigs, in the event of the Radicals seceding. He knew one at least who would not be scrupulous about free trade. 'Who is that?' asked Lord Aberdeen. 'The Secretary for Foreign Affairs' my Father answered, laughing. Lord Aberdeen's surprise was extreme – he rose from his chair. 'It is impossible – quite out of the question.' The hint was broad: 'if you will not join me, others will', and in this sense it seems to have produced some effect.[38]

The effect may well have been very different from that intended by Stanley. Aberdeen was not a good man to threaten and Stanley's attitude must have seemed to him one of complete cynicism and opportunism. One of the main attractions to Aberdeen of rejoining the Conservatives, even at the cost of losing his closest friends among the Peelites, was that it would finally remove Palmerston from his dangerous position at the Foreign Office – and he had believed that Stanley shared that priority. Nevertheless, further discussions took place on 9 and 10 February. But Aberdeen now made it clear that he would not join Stanley without Graham and Graham made it clear that he would not compromise on agricultural protection. Edward concluded that, for the moment, Aberdeen was lost – unless the Court could persuade him otherwise. 'For the present,' he wrote, 'Lord Aberdeen keeps aloof, he might be gained over by Court influence: but for such an attempt royal favour is necessary and we are not supposed to be in the way of obtaining it.'[39] Court influence was to be used but not in that way.

The crisis came on 20 February. Locke King introduced his almost ritual motion for the equalisation of the borough and county franchises. It passed in a thin House by 100 votes to 52. Russell was under no constitutional obligation to resign and some of his ministerial colleagues thought him unwise to do so, but Russell had lost his temper. If he could not rely on the votes of his supposed supporters, they could look for another Prime Minister. The Queen, very properly, sent for Lord Stanley as the leader of the next largest party.

Stanley saw the Queen and Prince Albert on the afternoon of 22 February. He was remarkably frank about his difficulties. His party contained hardly any men of talent and experience. Disraeli, the ablest, had no ministerial experience. Unless he could persuade some of Peel's old front bench to rejoin him, he could not form an administration. Only Aberdeen and Palmerston were serious possibilities for the Foreign Office and he hinted that Aberdeen was not adamant on the Free Trade issue. He told the Queen that he would have to re-impose a duty on corn to protect the landed interests and the figure of six shillings was mentioned. This alarmed the Prince, who thought six shillings much too high, and warned Stanley that it might arouse 'a violent spirit' among the working classes which could render a dissolution dangerous.[40] Edward Stanley may well be right in supposing that his father wanted the discussions to break down because he did not wish to be pressurised into a premature attempt to form a government, but apparently serious negotiations went on for some days, in which the Stanleyites had not yet abandoned the hope of capturing Aberdeen.[41]

Stanley himself suggested the alternative possibility of a Whig–Peelite coalition to the royal couple, and the Prince wrote to Aberdeen, Graham and Russell, asking them to come to Buckingham Palace. The separate messages led to misunderstandings and the talks began in some confusion. The 22nd of February was a Saturday and Aberdeen and Graham were both out of Town.[42]

Russell arrived almost immediately, Graham at six o'clock, Aberdeen not until after nine. The discussions were interrupted by a long-arranged royal dinner party at which the Duke of Wellington was present. The Prince saw the three political leaders separately as they arrived. Graham agreed that there would be 'universal commotion' if any attempt were made to re-impose the Corn Duties and he did not believe that Aberdeen would ever join a government that abandoned Peel's principles. Wellington too expressed the opinion that there would be 'civil commotion' if a dissolution was granted to a protectionist government. Graham also made it clear that he would not take office if Palmerston remained at the Foreign Office – a view fervently endorsed by the Queen herself. Graham also expressed uneasiness at the implications of Russell's recent declaration in favour of further parliamentary reform. When Aberdeen arrived, as the Prince put it, 'We went over the same ground with him.' Aberdeen made his position very clear, although some of it may have been surprising to some of his audience. He would not, he said, join a Protectionist ministry. 'He did not pretend to understand the question of Free Trade, but it was a point of honour with him not to abandon it, and now, since Sir R. Peel's death, a matter of piety.' He agreed that a dissolution on the question 'of imposing a tax upon bread' would be very dangerous. 'He had no difficulty upon the Franchise, for though he was called a *despot*, he felt a good deal of the Radical in him sometimes.' He disapproved of Russell's 'Papal Bill' and also of a current proposal to abolish the Irish Lieutenancy.

Little agreement could be reached at such a preliminary meeting. According to the Prince's memorandum, 'Lord John put it to Lord Aberdeen, whether *he* would not undertake to form a Government, to which Lord Aberdeen gave no distinct reply.' The meeting went on until nearly midnight and broke up 'with the Queen's injunction that *one* of the three gentlemen *must* form a government, to which Lord Aberdeen laughingly replied: "I see your Majesty has come into [sic] the Président de la République." '[43]

Russell drew up a memorandum setting out the conditions on which he would be prepared to form an administration, including both Whigs and Peelites. He proposed a Cabinet of not more than eleven members, to be chosen solely on grounds of fitness. They should agree on five conditions; the present commercial policy should be maintained, the present year's financial measures might be revised, the preamble and first clause of the projected Ecclesiastical Titles Bill should be maintained but the rest of the measure abandoned, a franchise reform measure should be introduced after Easter and an enquiry held into corrupt electoral practices in the cities and boroughs of the United Kingdom.[44] The Queen saw Aberdeen and Graham again on Sunday, 23 February, but they had not had time to consider Russell's proposals.[45] The following day Aberdeen wrote their joint reply at Argyll House. They saw no difficulties about the first two conditions. The Ecclesiastical Titles Bill was, however, another matter. The measure would still have condemned the papal brief and imposed some financial penalties for the assumption of the titles. Aberdeen and Graham held this to be an entirely unsatisfactory compromise. It would not satisfy the excited Commons or public and it would still offend the Roman

Catholics. They themselves condemned the 'tone' of the papal brief and of Cardinal Wiseman in his pastoral letter, but they saw no need for 'legislative interference' and would not be parties to it. They could not agree to give notice of a measure to extend the franchise without knowing what it was intended to contain. The proposed Commission of Enquiry into electoral corruption, unobjectionable in itself, might lead to unforeseen proposals, perhaps even the secret ballot. It seemed unnecessary to comment on the restriction of the Cabinet to eleven, since the other base for agreement did not exist, but they hinted that they had reservations about the implication that Russell should be the judge of 'fitness'.[46]

Russell was moved to explain his memorandum further, assuring them that the idea of restricting the Cabinet in this way was only intended to ensure that it should not be constructed on the basis of four from one party and four from another. Aberdeen, however, replied that his explanations did not 'materially affect the principal point of difference', namely the Ecclesiastical Titles Bill, 'and as the negociation is now closed, it cannot be necessary to carry this discussion further'. Aberdeen and Graham promised to keep Russell's written communications absolutely confidential, 'unless compelled by unforeseen circumstances, which they cannot anticipate, to recur to it in their own defence'. Russell replied on 25 February that he hoped that they would at least be able to act cordially together in Parliament.[47]

At this point it seemed likely that they would be acting together in opposition, if at all. Russell gave up his attempt to form a government on 24 February. There had been problems besides the Ecclesiastical Titles Bill. Aberdeen and Graham had made it clear to the Prince that the Peelites would expect to be 'on an equality' with the late ministers, an interesting insistence in the light of December 1852.[48] But a great deal turned on the possession of the Foreign Office and the relative positions of Aberdeen and Palmerston. The Queen urged Russell to take the Foreign Office himself but he insisted that he could not combine it with leading the House of Commons. He told her that he would be happy to accept Lord Clarendon, Lord Granville or even Graham but he 'would not like' Aberdeen at the Foreign Office. Aberdeen and Graham, on the other hand, were at first agreed that it was impossible to have Palmerston in the Cabinet. Graham told the Prince bluntly that, after seeing him intrigue with the radicals to coerce his colleagues, he would rather have him as the Protectionist leader on the benches opposite. When the Prince told them that Russell had considered giving Palmerston the lead in the Lords, Aberdeen 'looked very black' and said that the House would never submit to that. He would have preferred Palmerston to be offered the Lord Lieutenancy of Ireland with a peerage. Aberdeen, however, then said that he would not object to sit in the Cabinet with him but, when they had been in office together before under Wellington, they had had constant disputes on foreign policy which had been anything but pleasant. Prince Albert was under no illusions that Aberdeen expected the Foreign Office and he knew that Russell would not consent to it.[49]

Late on the evening of 24 February, Victoria asked Aberdeen himself whether he would attempt to form a government. Aberdeen replied that he feared that he would have no chance of success. Far from being reluctant to take office, Aberdeen and Graham made it clear that they had considered every possible combination and had only very regretfully come to the conclusion that there was no way. Their resistance to the Ecclesiastical Titles Bill had made them 'the two most unpopular men in England'. Ironically, the only people they had pleased were the radicals and they were not prepared to trust to their support. Graham had now had the chance to consult some of the other Peelites, including Lincoln who had just succeeded his father as Duke of Newcastle, and Herbert, and they were agreed that Stanley must be given the chance to form an administration and bring in his proposed legislation.[50]

The Queen and the Prince were again alarmed at the prospect of serious civil disorder and of obstructive tactics in parliament which would bring all orderly government to an end. Graham assured them that he and Russell would manage the opposition in a responsible manner and that such an alliance would thereby be forged between the Whigs and the Peelites that they would be able to return to office together with none of the present jealousies and suspicions. The Prince noted 'Lord Aberdeen would save his influence in the House of Lords, which he would probably have lost if he had joined the Whigs in office.'[51]

The Queen sent again for Lord Stanley. Aberdeen made it clear that it was out of the question for him to take the Foreign Office but he commended the appointment of Lord Canning, the eldest surviving son of George Canning, who had been his Under-Secretary at the Foreign Office from 1841 to 1846. He told Canning that it was a 'fine thing', presumably meaning fine experience, to be Foreign Secretary even for a short time.[52] His motives for this rather odd action are not altogether clear. Perhaps he believed that he would be able to exercise some influence, by proxy as it were, on the Office and it must be remembered that Aberdeen still regarded European events as more important than purely domestic British ones. Canning declined the appointment.

Stanley failed in his attempt to form a government and Russell resumed office with a purely Whig administration on 3 March. Aberdeen wrote to Hudson Gurney that, but for the Pope and the cardinals, he might have been forming a ministry. He commented that, having seen Peel's 'torments' in 1841, he was not sorry to be spared but stated quite categorically, 'I should certainly have undertaken the task, if I could have hoped to bring people to their senses in the matter of this "Papal Aggression".' He added jokingly that he expected to be included in 'the list of Popish Martyrs'. He recognised that these negotiations had probably ended any likelihood of him rejoining Stanley. 'Graham and I', he told Gurney, 'are probably now united for the future, unless the approach of age should induce me to prefer a sleeping partnership in the concern. He is a very able man, and of good resource. I am not quite so sure about his courage.'[53] Graham did indeed lack courage, or at least confidence in his own ability to assume the highest office, and it was this that left the way open for Aberdeen's final unchallenged assumption of the leadership of the Peelites.

The Prince too believed that the negotiations had finally shipwrecked on the Ecclesiastical Titles Bill and in 1855, in a moment of irritation, he addressed a letter of uncharacteristic sharpness to Aberdeen. The Peelites, he said, had taken the Pope's side against the Queen's Government and, when Russell's government broke down in 1851, Victoria had had to go through a 'fruitless Ministerial Crisis', which had caused many of the anomalies from which they were now suffering 'on account of the peculiar position in which your party had placed itself.'[54] Prince Albert was the more disappointed because he had worked very hard to secure an arrangement. On 27 February, Baron Stockmar had visited Aberdeen, ostensibly in connection with the Prince's subscription to Peel's monument. Aberdeen told him that he thought it unlikely that Stanley would succeed in forming a government. Stockmar replied that the next attempt would have to be made by Aberdeen or Russell. Aberdeen said that Graham thought it must come to him, Aberdeen, since he could work with Stanley with less difficulty than anybody else. Aberdeen then said what were, on the face of it, some curious things. He told Stockmar, 'I hope the Queen is not afraid of the Radicals, for we must now hold strong language and rather talk in the way of Roebuck.' Stockmar answered that the Queen had better keep a free hand and noted, 'Lord Aberdeen replied, I think so too, but don't mention that I have said so.'[55] Victoria herself wrote to King Leopold, 'Alas! the hope of forming a strong coalition Government has failed for the present.'[56]

Russell's government survived until February 1852. In December 1851, Russell had insisted that Palmerston should resign from the Foreign Office on the grounds of his premature recognition of Louis Napoleon's coup d'état. Aberdeen, although glad to see Palmerston go at last, commented to Edward Ellice that a dozen better opportunities had been lost. It was singular, he thought, that no one knew with which party Palmerston would now connect himself, whether he would turn to the Radicals or to the Protectionists. He was under no illusion that the dismissal of Palmerston would seriously weaken Russell's administration. Either Russell would have to strengthen it, perhaps by recruiting Sir James Graham – and Aberdeen saw nothing to prevent the juncture – or there would have to be, what Aberdeen thought would be the best thing for the country, 'the formation of an entirely new Administration on a broad and liberal basis'. He wished to make it clear that he saw no difference on foreign policy between himself and Russell's government freed from Palmerston. He told Ellice,

It is all very well to declare that the Foreign Policy of the Government is not changed. But I must observe that the Programme which appeared in the 'Globe' the other day, and which I take to be dictated by Lord John, is precisely that which I have frequently written myself, and to which of course I shall now readily subscribe. It is not of the principles of Foreign Policy of the Government, as announced by them, that I have ever complained; but of a deviation from those principles, by which this policy was made a policy of passion, personality and hatred.[57]

Palmerston quickly had his revenge by securing Russell's defeat on the Militia Bill, and Stanley, now Lord Derby, finally formed an administration with Lord Malmesbury at the Foreign Office. The long-delayed informal opposition 'coalition' of Whigs and Peelites could now take effect. Derby's

Cabinet was almost entirely composed of inexperienced nonentities and no one thought it would last long. Derby, as expected, asked for a dissolution and fresh elections were held in July 1852. The results were not very comforting for the Derbyites since they failed to gain an overall majority but for the surviving Peelites they were disastrous. The Derbyites increased their numbers in the Commons from about 280 to about 310. The basic weakness of the Peelites is shown by the fact that no one knew any longer who to include among their adherents. *The Times* described 111 candidates as 'liberal conservatives' but that could cover many things. Calculations of Peelites or 'liberal conservatives' elected varied from 30 to 58. Some leading Peelites, including Cardwell, lost their seats. Their position was further damaged by the fact that, in the previous House of Commons, they had clearly been able to hold the balance between Whigs and Protectionists. The balance was now held, much more dangerously in the eyes of many, by Radicals and Irish Repealers, the notorious 'Irish brass band'.[58] The nature of the House of Commons which emerged from the 1852 elections was to be one of the crucial underlying weaknesses of Aberdeen's government of 1852–5.

The elections of 1852 gave a further impetus to discussions between the Whig and Peelite leaders. Aberdeen, like other thoughtful men, was disquieted by the elections. He considered that the Protectionists had employed thoroughly dishonest tactics, refusing to state candidly where they now stood on the whole question of agricultural protection. He was alarmed by their efforts to rouse religious bigotry for electoral purposes. He and Graham were annoyed by what they saw as attempts to use religious questions to capture the Peelite High churchmen such as Gladstone and Newcastle, although they believed that the whole Derbyite position on this had become so self-contradictory that it must fail. But it was the conduct of the election itself which convinced Aberdeen that fundamental reform could not be long delayed and that, dangerous though the attempt might be, the system was now so corrupt that change could hardly make it worse. He would have had little difficulty in agreeing with the radical *Economist* that there was 'more truckling, more corruption, more fanaticism and more debauchery, than on any previous occasion'. His only fear was that politically motivated attempts, possibly against a background of public excitement and foreign difficulties, would make 'real amendment' difficult.[59]

It was Russell who made the first overtures towards the Peelites, in the summer of 1852. Aberdeen spent the summer at Haddo, but he played a central role in co–ordinating the discussions. Russell had written in friendly terms to Graham in June before the election, but this could hardly be regarded as an approach to the Peelites as a body since at this time Graham had apparently separated himself from the Peelites and was on the point of returning to his old political allegiance as a Whig. In March his Carlisle constituents had asked him, as a Free Trader, to run in harness with a Liberal for the two-member constituency. Graham had agreed and had made a speech in Carlisle reminding his audience of his record as a reformer in the 1830s, and despite his doubts in February 1851, pledging his support for parliamentary reform, only stopping short of acceptance of the secret ballot. Aberdeen was almost alone among the Peelite leaders in refusing to accept that, by his Carlisle speech, Graham had severed himself from them. Gladstone was particularly intransigent in his condemnation.[60]

Russell's first approach to Aberdeen was an oblique one. He wrote to him on 2 July to offer a virtual apology for a speech which Palmerston had made in the Commons on 29 June. He hoped that Aberdeen would not be misled, as the press had been, into supposing that his (Russell's) administration had 'sought to wrest Northern Italy from Austria'. He then entered into a long explanation of his Italian policy. Aberdeen replied a little tartly (and the many alterations he made to his draft suggest that he did not find it an easy letter to write) that he had never supposed that Palmerston's opinions were shared by Russell's government as a whole but they should have made their position clear at the time.[61]

When most of the election results were known, Russell wrote to Aberdeen with a much more explicit offer. The government had done rather better than he expected and would stand on 'two legs', first abusing Peel's Corn Law and pressing the right of the agricultural interest to compensation, and secondly, 'hounding on the Protestants to run down the Catholics'. Sir Robert Peel's friends could not support such policies and must choose between three courses: first, remain aloof as they had done since Peel's death, but this would only prolong the uncertain life of a bad and weak government; secondly, act in friendly concert with the Whigs but preserve their independence of action; or thirdly, join the Whigs in a 'fusion', with or without Cobden, that is, with or without the more radical wing. More immediately, they should concert their course when Parliament met. Russell did not favour a vote of no confidence on the Address but rather an amendment affirming the wisdom of the commercial policy pursued since 1842 and especially in 1846. There should be a vigorous attack on the corruption of the late election. Any proposal for parliamentary reform should be deferred until February, when they had ample time to discuss it. He was not prepared to accept the secret ballot or go below a £5 rating in the boroughs but he favoured a £12 rating in the counties. He asked Aberdeen to discover how far these views were agreeable to Gladstone, Herbert and Newcastle. Finally he suggested that he, Russell, knowing his own unpopularity with the Radicals and Irish members – because of the Ecclesiastical Titles Bill – would be quite happy to support a liberal ministry out of office.[62]

Aberdeen willingly undertook to consult his fellow Peelites, although it was not easy in late July. Herbert was in Germany and the rest scattered about the United Kingdom. He hoped that, if Russell were coming north, he would come to Haddo so that they could discuss the question. He also tried, without success, to arrange a meeting with Newcastle, Gladstone and Herbert but, in the event, the negotiations were carried on almost entirely by letter, which had the advantage of leaving an exceptionally full record. Russell was still independently in touch with Graham, but Graham chose to write to Aberdeen and, in effect, to associate himself with the Peelite negotiations.

Aberdeen told Newcastle that he was not surprised by Russell's overture, although it had arrived a little earlier than he expected. Although the recent election had thinned their ranks, the country still looked to them as the representatives of Peel's policy and as 'the party of conservative progress'. He thought the government strong enough to meet Parliament but a proposal might be made to Peel's friends. He then told Newcastle quite bluntly that his own feelings towards the Derbyites were 'much changed'. When the government was formed he thought that the only question between them was Protection but in fact no 'intelligible issue' had been put to the electorate. The only test proposed at the election had been that of religious bigotry 'pregnant with mischief for the future, and more objectionable to me than Protection itself'. The whole proceeding of the government was dishonest and every principle would be sacrificed to gain parliamentary support. He could derive no satisfaction from the government's continuance in office but, so long as the opposition was divided, they could survive. 'If', he said 'I could realize my own individual wishes, it would be to see Lord John at the head of a Government, supported and in some measure directed by a portion of Peel's friends, although not in office myself.' He was told that some Whigs, as well as the Irish and the Radicals, would not serve under Lord John. If that were so, another combination must be found but Russell must be included in the government.

He saw no great difficulty in the Peelites acting with the Whigs. They agreed on Free Trade and financial policy. Their differences on education and the Church were more theoretical than practical. He thought the Whigs had learnt their lesson and would do nothing further to interfere with religious freedom. The only practical difficulty might be parliamentary reform. He thought himself that what Russell said was reasonable and the details were open to discussion. 'For myself,' he added, 'I must confess that I think our whole system of Representation is attended with so much real corruption, whether in the shape of personal influence, intimidation, or direct venality, that I am by no means reluctant to attempt some change. I should view even the Ballot itself without much dread, if I did not think it calculated to increase, rather than to diminish the evil.' He approved of the course Russell advocated on the meeting of parliament, that is refraining from an immediate vote of no confidence. 'Disraeli should be forced to produce his measures, and exhibit the *hocus pocus* tricks by which he hopes to gull his supporters.' Most members would see and resent the dishonesty of the course pursued.

Aberdeen was also able to add some information, recently acquired from Graham. In some ways, Russell had spoken more freely to Graham than to Aberdeen. In particular, he had gone into the difficulties about his own position. He realised that he was no longer an acceptable leader to many of his party but he 'rejects as personal degradation, the notion of his being in any subordinate situation'. In his view, he could only support such a ministry from the outside as an elder statesman.[63] Russell's extreme touchiness about his own position and his conviction that a former Prime Minister could not accept subordinate office was to be the great stumbling block to the desired 'fusion'.

Newcastle replied in two long letters, the first of which was largely devoted to analysing the situation in the new House. His conclusion was that union with Derby was impossible, isolation was pleasant but unpatriotic and therefore 'Co-operation with other Liberals is *requisite.*' On the delicate question of who should head such a combination, Newcastle reluctantly concluded that Russell could not; Lansdowne was a possibility but at seventy-two he was almost certainly too old; there remained Aberdeen. Newcastle thought that, if Russell agreed, '*you* could best unite and consolidate the various elements which ought to be collected together in a Liberal Government'. He knew that Aberdeen pleaded ignorance of finance and was less associated with domestic adminis-tration than was usual in a Prime Minister but that must be weighed against the fact that the times were peculiar and the state of the parties unprece-dented.[64]

The following day Newcastle wrote a second very important letter, making what his fellow negotiators rightly saw as a very radical suggestion. He told Aberdeen:

It strikes me forcibly that with a view to a real fusion of all Liberals in one party the name of Whig as well as Peelite should as far as possible be abandoned. In the eyes of the public names are things and I am convinced that the late Government and its Friends would act wisely if they followed the example of 1832 when we abandoned the unpopular and unmeaning name of *Tory* and adopted that which at the moment was significant and distinctive – *Conservative.*

The previous change of 'nickname' had drawn to Peel many who would never have joined a Tory opposition. It would be a sacrifice for Russell but there were many who would never 'join the Whigs' who would join an administration which included Russell, Clarendon and Sir George Grey. If a new 'Liberal Party' was to be constructed and that was what the country wanted, it must be on a new basis and not a simple matter of one party joining another.[65]

In his reply, Aberdeen expressed entire agreement with Newcastle except on his suggestion that he, Aberdeen, should head such a government. The only thing which would induce him to do so, he said, was if that was the only way in which Russell felt that he could honourably take subordinate office. If, on the other hand, Russell intended in any case to remain out of office, Newcastle was better qualified to assume the lead.[66] Aberdeen presumably had in mind that it would be less difficult for Russell to serve under a man nearly ten years his senior, who had been Foreign Secretary before Russell even attained Cabinet office.

As requested, Newcastle had sent the correspondence on to Gladstone and had also spoken to Cardwell who, being temporarily out of Parliament, had not originally been consulted. Gladstone's answer was much less favourable than Newcastle's. Although he disapproved of many aspects of Derby's conduct – for which he blamed Disraeli – he launched into a long denuncia-tion, going back to the 1830s, of the sins of the Whigs, against both sound economic policy and religious toleration.[67]

Aberdeen was disappointed. Perhaps rashly, he sent both Gladstone's and Newcastle's replies to Russell, believing at the time that they had been intended for communication. He thought Gladstone 'hampered by his Oxford constituency' but was convinced that he would not join Derby. He saw no difficulty about co-operation when Parliament met, but he did not know what would happen in the future. 'It is evident', he wrote rather sadly, 'that I am at present considerably in advance of my friends; although I do not despair of seeing them ultimately brought to an entire agreement with me.' If he thought that he himself, or any of his friends, could form a government he would have seen it with 'satisfaction' as the 'natural triumph' of Peel's policy and an end to the contests of the last six years. But that was out of the question, so cordial co–operation with Russell was the most becoming course for Peel's friends to adopt.[68] Russell replied thanking him for his frankness and giving it as his opinion that Gladstone would have joined Derby but for Disraeli. He asked Aberdeen's permission to show the correspondence to Sir George Grey, Lord Minto and Lord Panmure. Aberdeen, perhaps regretting his complete frankness, felt unable to agree to this. Russell ignored Aberdeen's scruples. Grey agreed with Russell's interpretation of the letters. Russell told Graham, 'He came to my conclusions; that Ld Aberdeen already agrees with the liberal party; that the D. of N. does so in all essential points; & that Mr G. is only anxious to re–unite with the Tories.'[69]

Russell wrote again several times during the next few days, apparently as he digested the Peelite answers. He expressed great indignation at Gladstone's strictures, complaining that Peel had supported him cordially but after his death his supporters had contributed to bring down his government.[70] He questioned some of Newcastle's calculations, particularly his belief that true Whigs were now nearly as rare as Peelites. 'I count here as Whigs', he told Aberdeen, 'what he might call Conservative Liberals, or Liberal Conservatives, such as Graham & Cardwell, but no Radicals & no Peelites, keeping separate as such'. He felt strongly about the name 'Whig'. 'As to the name of Whig,' he wrote, 'a name of which Mr Pitt (as Lord Harrowby assured me) was as tenacious as Mr Fox, it does not belong to me to give it up.' At the same time he did not object to using the term 'liberal'.[71] The name began to assume an inordinate importance. It had also been discussed between Aberdeen and Graham and, despite Russell's cunning reference to Pitt, Aberdeen was as reluctant to assume the title as Russell was to abandon it. He told Graham 'You may fall back upon the Whiggism, in which you were bred; but I was bred at the feet of Gamaliel, and must always regard Mr Pitt as the first of Statesmen.'[72]

Aberdeen made another attempt in September to persuade Russell to consider the possibility of another name. He and Newcastle, he said, could not become Whigs. They could not abandon a 'Conservative policy'. On the other hand, Russell could not act with them unless he was convinced their views were liberal. He suggested,

Although the term may appear a little contradictory, I believe that 'Conservative Progress' best describes the principles which ought to influence the conduct of any Government at the present day. This was Peel's policy, and I think will continue that of all his friends. For one, looking at the actual state of affairs, I have no objection that the progress should be somewhat more rapid than perhaps he ever intended.

Russell made short work of this. If he agreed to abandon the name, Whig, he said, others would not. 'It has the convenience of expressing in one syllable what Conservative Liberal expresses in seven, & Whiggism in two syllables means what Conservative Progress means in another seven. [sic]'[73]

This discussion of name was not so sterile as it might seem. Most men knew what they meant by the term 'Conservative', as it had been defined by Peel. 'Whig' had too long a history to have been consistent in its use but again most men knew accurately enough what they understood by it in the mid–nineteenth century. 'Liberal' was the undefined term. It had come a long way since it had been applied to a group of Spanish radicals. To Aberdeen it seems to have meant the reforming policies of Pitt and Peel, applied at a more rapid pace to suit the exigencies of the times but without abandoning their underlying principles. In this sense he could say without intentional paradox that no government could be too liberal for him so long as it was conservative. He told Goulburn 'I think it clear that all Government in these times must be a Government of progress; conservative progress, if you please; but we can no more be stationary, than reactionary.'[74] But to Graham he defined the limits of his liberalism. He would be glad, he said, to see Russell at the head of a government surrounded by some of Peel's friends but he could not support him as the head of Whig/Radical government. 'I hope', he wrote 'that I am not deficient in liberal views either at home or abroad; but I cannot altogether renounce my Conservative character . . . I am thoroughly convinced of the necessity of a Government of progress, and am prepared to advance more rapidly than probably was ever contemplated by Peel himself; but this progress must be Conservative in principle.'[75]

The question of leadership was still unresolved. Russell felt compelled to explain what might seem an ungracious phrase that he would not lead in the Commons for any 'peer Prime Minister' in the Lords, which he knew had got back to Aberdeen through Graham. He meant, he said, that if Irish and radical hostility made him unacceptable as Prime Minister, they would make him equally unacceptable as Leader of the House. He added, 'If you would take the lead in a Ministry I should be ready out of office to give you my cordial support.' Aberdeen did not like the idea. He told Russell, 'You have made a suggestion respecting myself, which there is no necessity to discuss; but which under the most favourable circumstances would be entertained by me with the utmost reluctance, and of which I cannot even contemplate the possibility.'[76]

Quite different possibilities were being canvassed for a compromise leader. Aberdeen learned of these mainly through Graham. This was the so-called 'Lansdowne project' to bring the elderly Lord Lansdowne out of retirement to head a ministry. After it had failed, a number of people found it politic to deny that it had ever had any real existence but the Peelites were well informed on these Whig manoeuvres.[77] Graham first learned of it from Lord Dunfermline who enclosed a letter from Ellice, who derived his information from the Duke of Bedford and the third Lord Melbourne. As here revealed, it was a discreditable scheme for a juncture between Palmerston and Lansdowne, which it was hoped the Peelites would join and which would ultimately entrain a large proportion of the Whig aristocracy and many of Lord Derby's supporters. The basis of this arrangement would be resistance to any disfranchising Reform Bill 'and the adoption of one, which shall have the semblance of change with the minimum of the Reality'. Ellice thought it dangerous and impracticable, and Dunfermline thought that it would discredit 'both Classes of the Aristocracy' – which may explain why they allowed the project to be made known. Graham was puzzled. Russell apparently knew nothing of it, which was strange if Bedford was a party to it. He could not believe that Newcastle or Gladstone would be parties to a sham Reform Bill and, all in all, he thought the plan crude and destined to come to nothing.[78] Two days later, on 7 August, Graham managed to have a long conversation with Bedford. The Duke told him that it was perfectly true that Palmerston had opened negotiations to place Lansdowne at the head of a government which would include many Whigs, those Peelites who would join, and possibly some Derbyites. Melbourne had opened the project to Bedford with the intimation that Palmerston would serve with Russell but not under him and that Lansdowne was ready to take the premiership if Russell concurred in asking him to do so. Graham told Bedford that such a scheme would not attract the Peelites and Bedford seemed to acquiesce in thinking it foredoomed to failure. Bedford expressed pleasure at the good relations developing between Russell and Aberdeen, but dropped a hint that Gladstone and Palmerston seemed to be becoming very intimate. Despite Graham's scepticism, Aberdeen considered the 'Lansdowne combination' a very real possibility.[79]

Graham, who remained in London during most of August, was a very useful source of information for Aberdeen about the gossip and intrigue which abounded. The two men did not always see eye to eye and, in September, came near to a quarrel, but ultimately their discussions cemented the alliance which had been forged in February 1851. On 11 August, Graham told Aberdeen that, although Clarendon would prefer to serve under Lord John, fear of parliamentary reform might drive him to Lansdowne. Graham was sure that Palmerston and Lord John would not be reconciled and that Palmerston would not agree to go to the Lords – which, no doubt, relieved Aberdeen's mind. Graham still did not believe that the Lansdowne project could succeed, but he did think it possible that, if Derby were overthrown, Palmerston and Disraeli might raise the flag of resistance to parliamentary reform, and so many would flock to it from all sides that they might be able to form an administration.[80]

Aberdeen scouted the idea of a Palmerston-Disraeli government but he still thought a Lansdowne ministry with Clarendon at the Foreign Office perfectly feasible. He told Graham that Russell had promised that if he, Aberdeen 'would take the concern [i.e. the premiership] he should be ready out of office to give me his cordial support', but he was emphatic to Graham, as he had been to others, that he would only head a government if Russell would join it. He had, he said, advised Russell to wait and see. He added cryptically that Graham knew all that had passed 'by means of Stockmar' and so knew what might be expected in that quarter. He would himself wait and see. The existing government might hold on.[81]

433

Other rumours too abounded. Aberdeen heard from both Graham and Brougham that Palmerston might take the Home Office under Derby. This time it was Aberdeen who was sceptical but both Graham and Goulburn thought it likely. Graham pointed out that it would make a convenient smoke screen to cover the abandonment of protection; it would place the management of the Militia in the competent hands of its greatest champion; and by superseding Disraeli without offence from the lead in the Commons, it would facilitate the juncture of Gladstone and other useful recruits. Aberdeen was more concerned about the fate of the Foreign Office, having heard a rumour that Malmesbury was to leave it. He was relieved to hear that Palmerston had told Derby that he would never go back there. 'But how could it be filled?' he asked Graham. One possibility was Stratford Canning, now Lord Stratford de Redcliffe, who had been considered before Malmesbury, although it was known that his appointment would be very much disliked by the Russians. 'What' Aberdeen enquired of Graham, 'are Lord Stratford's relations with the Government?'[82]

Both Aberdeen and Graham feared Gladstone's defection to the Derbyites. Aberdeen thought the balance of probabilities against it — Gladstone would find it very hard to stick Disraeli — but he feared that there would be further exploitation of the religious issues. He speculated that the government would make sure in the ensuing session that religion would take up more time than Free Trade or parliamentary reform, and commented 'what a prospect'. Brougham told him a little later that 'Convocation' was the bait with which Derby meant to catch Gladstone. Aberdeen did not believe either that Convocation could be restored or that Gladstone desired it. One of the attractions of the restoration of Convocation in the eyes of the High church party was that it might provide them an alternative appeal tribunal so that they would never again have the humiliation of seeing the verdict of an ecclesiastical court set aside by the Judicial Committee of the Privy Council as had happened in the notorious Gorham judgment in 1850. Aberdeen himself thought that the establishment of a specific tribunal to judge heresy cases and including both lay and clerical members, as proposed by the Bishop of London, would be preferable to the restoration of Convocation which would be likely to precipitate the great schism between the two parties in the Church of England, which he feared was approaching. On some points Aberdeen proved a bad prophet. Convocation was restored in 1853 and Gladstone did support it, although not very warmly. But his underlying fear, that Derby thought only of electoral advantage, was probably correct. The same motives that made Derby 'submit' to Free Trade would make him adopt the cry of 'No Popery'. Aberdeen told Graham bluntly that he 'dreaded' a religious war in Ireland.[83]

Gladstone did not defect but, in September, Graham moved so close to Russell that Aberdeen felt that he had left them. On 27 September he returned the correspondence between Russell and Graham, which the latter had sent him, with the comment that he saw that their alliance, offensive and defensive, was now signed and ratified and regretting that he could not follow him so far. He was sorry to see him leave the Peelites but he still hoped that events might bring about a fusion which discussions had apparently failed to produce.[84] Graham replied at once in real distress of mind. He had been influenced, he said, by his conviction that the first priority was to get the Derby-Disraeli ministry out of office, which would not be easy, especially if Palmerston and Gladstone joined them. He had always been completely open with Aberdeen and did not wish to be separated from him by a 'hair's breadth'. He did not think he had said in his Carlisle speech, as Aberdeen supposed, that he had ceased to be a Peelite when Peel died but what he had said then on parliamentary reform had been repudiated by the Peelites and he had been 'drummed out of the Regiment, you alone, with Cardwell, refusing to forego all political connexion with me'. He declined Aberdeen's invitation to Haddo because of what seems to have been a genuine attack of gout.[85]

Aberdeen was not the man to make no response to such a plea. He had meant only, he said, that Graham had placed himself in a relationship with Russell in which he himself could not fully participate. He could co-operate with Russell as a 'liberal conservative' but not join him as a Whig. He believe that, by this time, the negotiations had, if not broken down, gone as far as they could. It depended on events whether the two groups would move closer. In the meantime he, Aberdeen, would 'preserve my character of spectator' as he had 'really no object of my own'. Aberdeen's proclamation of disinterest is not altogether borne out by the fact that he was still entertaining Peelite colleagues, including Cardwell and the Duke of Argyll, at Haddo, conducting a wide correspondence with Goulburn and Brougham among others and hinting that Graham should see Stockmar, that 'able and disinterested adviser'. Aberdeen himself had just returned from a visit to Balmoral. Earlier, he had been unsure whether he would receive his usual invitation, or whether it would give rise to too much political speculation. In the course of the visit, he had what he described as 'three or four very full conversations', which he could not very well commit to paper. He assured Graham that they had been 'perfectly satisfactory' and he was anxious to tell him about them.[86]

The negotiations had been conducted between a small group of party leaders and had turned very largely on personalities and, in Russell's case, personal susceptibilities. Nevertheless, they had not been totally unaware of feelings in the country, the importance of the reactions of other groups, especially the Irish and the Radicals and the need to clarify their views on certain specific issues.

Who would secure the votes of the Irish members was of critical importance. 'There is a notion', Aberdeen wrote to Graham at the end of August, 'that the Government have come to an understanding with a portion of the Irish band. This seems scarcely credible, but our representative system is becoming every day more wonderful, and not more respectable.' The suspicion was not entirely without foundation. Disraeli was planning to court the Irish by introducing legislation to help agricultural tenants. The Peelites also had tenuous links with the Irish through their mutual opposition to the Ecclesiastical Titles Act, and Newcastle and Graham derived some modest capital from this.[87]

Even more central was the question of parliamentary reform. Russell had drafted a Reform Bill in 1851 and introduced it at the beginning of the 1852 session. His Cabinet was deeply divided and the fall of his administration put an end to the project. Even among those who doubted the general principles of reform, the blatant corruption of the 1852 election had persuaded many of the desirability of disfranchising some particularly notorious constituencies. Aberdeen, as he pondered the matter in the summer of 1852, was torn between the conviction that the system must be reformed, and doubts as to whether this was the right moment to undertake it. The revolutionary tumult in Europe had only just subsided, although Aberdeen seems to have been convinced that authority had triumphed and democracy – which to men of his generation bore a meaning not far removed from 'revolution' – was in retreat. When Russell raised the question at the outset of the negotiations in July, Aberdeen warmly commended reform to Newcastle. A few days later he wrote more cautiously to Ellice, although there may have been an element of political tactics in this. Lord John's abortive Reform Bill had, he complained, made matters more difficult. 'I am not', he said, 'myself afraid of the effects of the Reform; and the evils of our Representative system are perhaps great enough to justify those who wish for change; but I think that real amendment will be very doubtful; and unquestionably there is much apathy on the part of the Publick.' In principle it might be desirable to 'pause' but that would now be difficult.[88]

Graham was once again the channel of communication by which Aberdeen learnt of the views of the Radicals, at least as explained by that experienced campaigner, Joseph Parkes. Aberdeen was relieved to learn that Parkes did not want to press ahead too fast. He repeated that he thought the public apathetic. He feared that a moderate measure might be lost or a sweeping measure carried with public support but only after excitement, violence and confusion – presumably orchestrated by an interested minority in the face of general indifference. Graham was cynical about the real attitude of the Whig magnates, suspecting that Russell's declaration that he could not agree to the disfranchisement of the smallest boroughs without the consent of the Whig party, really meant that he could not disfranchise Calne, Arundel and Morpeth without the consent of Lansdowne, Norfolk and Carlisle.[89]

The attitude of the Whig magnates was important but so too was that of the Radicals. 'What', Aberdeen asked Graham, 'are the Radicals doing? They may probably become more organized and more formidable. I do not much fear Reform in the abstract; but the special measure will be attended with enormous difficulty. To make it the great *cheval de bataille* of a Party would be for me a painful extremity.' He also saw the danger that the Derbyites would find a new bogy to frighten the electorate and the Commons. 'It is clear', he said, 'that the rallying cry of the Government will not be Protection to Agriculture, but Protection against Democracy. Free Trade is our really strong ground, and it is upon this that the Government should be compelled to fight, when the proper time shall arrive.'[90]

Nevertheless, Aberdeen was committed to reform. At first sight it was a surprising conversion for a man who had adopted so uncompromisingly conservative a stance towards events in Europe. It may perhaps bear out Graham's judgement: 'At home he is a liberal, but not an enthusiast; abroad he is a zealot, in the sense most opposed to Palmerston.'[91] But Aberdeen himself would have argued that he had applied reasoned commonsense to both situations. In Europe he wanted not blind reaction, but stability and respect for the sanctity of treaties. In Britain he wanted not radical change but orderly reform, especially of the franchise, where first–hand observation had led him to much the same conclusion as that reached by many modern scholars, namely that the 1832 Act had increased, not diminished, corruption and violence.

He had been compelled to think out his position carefully on many issues between 1847 and 1852. Always a serious man, he devoted time and energy to studying any subject before him. In 1846 he had perhaps genuinely believed that, already in his sixties, with an honourable career behind him, it was time to retire and devote himself to his family and estates. His anger at what he saw as Palmerston's irresponsibility brought him back into politics. He believed that Palmerston must be replaced at the Foreign Office, not necessarily by himself, but no mock modesty concealed from him that he was the obvious alternative. By 1852, he seems to have become convinced that Derby was a totally irresponsible Prime Minister, prepared to do anything for short-term electoral advantage. He did not see himself as the only alternative Prime Minister but, from 1851, he was not reluctant to undertake the job. He did not intrigue for it, but he was a volunteer, not a conscript. Perhaps he felt that he could not do worse than his old colleagues.

NOTES

1. Conacher, *The Peelites and the Party System*, pp. 15–16.
2. Gash, *Sir Robert Peel*, pp. 628–32.
3. Add. MSS 43070, Gladstone to Aberdeen, 30 July, 1 Aug. 1847; Add. MSS 44088, Aberdeen to Gladstone, 31 July 1847.
4. Add. MSS 43065, Peel to Aberdeen, 19 Aug. 1847.
5. Conacher, *The Peelites*, p. 77.
6. Add. MSS 40455, Aberdeen to Peel, 18 Sept. 1847; Add. MSS 43065, Peel to Aberdeen, 22 Sept. 1847.
7. Add. MSS 43190, Graham to Aberdeen, 6 Aug. 1847.
8. These letters are in 43193–4. They are almost illegible but the most important are printed in BP 12/7. Brougham's projects would also have included Whigs.
9. *Disraeli, Derby and the Conservative Party: The Political Journals of Lord Stanley, 1849–69* (ed. J. R. Vincent). See pp. 418–9, 421–2.
10. Gurney Papers, RQC 334/111, Aberdeen to Gurney, 24 Jan. 1847, /112, 20 Aug. 1847.
11. HH 1/28, Aberdeen to Chalmers, 22 Dec. 1846. 8 Dec. 1853.
12. See Arthur's bitter comments, Add. MSS 49254, Journal, 31 July, 2 Aug. 1849.
13. Stanmore, pp. 192–3; Aberdeen to Baillie-Hamilton, 28 June, 15 July 1847, BP 12/7; RA 83/3, Peel to Albert, 4 Sept. 1846.
14. Stanmore, pp. 193–4; cf. Add. MSS 49254, Journal, 31 July, 8, 18 Aug. 1849, which suggests a young man's boredom with family parties.

15. Dasent, vol. 1, p. 257.
16. Clarendon told Victoria that the 'house is rather ugly but very comfortable. The gardens are extremely pretty & they have all been laid out by Ld. Aberdeen', Clarendon to Victoria, 14 Sept. 1857, RA B16/79.
17. *Revue des deux mondes*, xxxiv (1861), pp. 446–7.
18. V. Surtees, *Charlotte Canning*, pp. 138, 146. Although Aberdeen commissioned Landseer's picture, its stark savagery is very different from the picture Aberdeen requested, cf. R. Ormond, *Sir Edwin Landseer*, 1962, pp. 184–6.
19. Lord Howden to Aberdeen, 9 Oct. 1846, BP 12/7.
20. RA M53/3, Albert to Aberdeen, 19 Jan. 1845; /4, Aberdeen to Albert, 20 Jan. 1845.
21. HH 1/32, Aberdeen to Baillie-Hamilton, 29 Nov. 1848.
22. HH 1/28, Aberdeen to Abercorn, 20 Apr. 2 Oct. 1850.
23. HH 1/29, Aberdeen to Lady Haddo, 1 May 1846.
24. Add. MSS 40455, Aberdeen to Peel, 18 Sept. 1847.
25. HH 1/29, Aberdeen to Lady Haddo, 30 June, 8 July 1848.
26. Add. MSS 49253, Journal, 29, 30 Jan. 1849.
27. Gurney Papers, RQC 334/111, Aberdeen to Gurney, 24 Jan. 1847. He added, 'It is imposible not to like him; but he has some queer companions.'
28. *Disraeli, Derby and the Conservative Party* (ed. J. R. Vincent), pp. 2, 5–6 (23 Mar., 20 Apr. 1849). Although obviously partisan, Stanley's Journals are an invaluable source for these negotiations which both Aberdeen and Stanley were shy of committing to paper.
29. Vincent pp. 6–7 (2, 5 May 1849); *Hansard*, 3rd ser., CV (8 May 1849), 756 (21 May 1849).
30. Vincent, pp. 19–20.
31. See Ch. 24.
32. Derby Papers, Aberdeen to Stanley, 12, 15, 20 May 1850; Add. MSS 43072, Stanley to Aberdeen, 21 May 1850.
33. Derby Papers, Aberdeen to Stanley, 12, 15 May 1850.
34. Derby Papers, Aberdeen to Stanley, 20, 26 May, 22 July 1850; Add. MSS 43072, Stanley to Aberdeen, 21, 17 May, 5 June 1850; Add. MSS 44088, Aberdeen to Gladstone, 30 May 1850.
35. Add. MSS 43190, Graham to Aberdeen, 15 Sept. 1852.
36. Vincent, pp. 37–8 (6 Feb. 1851).
37. Russell to Victoria, 25 Oct. 1850 *Letters of Queen Victoria*, vol. 2, pp. 272–3.
38. Vincent, pp. 35, 37–8 (1, 6 Feb. 1851).
39. Vincent, p. 39 (9, 10 Feb. 1851).
40. The interview was very fully recorded by Prince Albert, RA C46/12, 14, Albert, Memoranda, 22, 23 Feb. 1851.
41. Vincent, pp. 42–7 (22–5 Feb. 1851).
42. RA C46/16, 18, Albert to Aberdeen, 22 Feb. 1851, Aberdeen to Albert, 22 Feb. 1851.
43. RA C46/21, Albert, Memorandum, 23 Feb. 1851.
44. Add. MSS 43066, Russell, Memorandum, 'Saturday night', 22 Feb. 1851.
45. Victoria to Russell, 23 Feb. 1851, *Letters of Queen Victoria*, vol. 2, pp. 296–7.
46. Russell Papers, PRO 30/22/9B, Aberdeen, Memorandum, 24 Feb. 1851.
47. Add. MSS 43066, Russell to Aberdeen, 24, 25 Feb. 1851; Russell Papers, PRO 30/22/9B, Aberdeen to Russell, 25 Feb. 1851 encl. Memorandum by Aberdeen.

48. RA C46/31, Albert, Memorandum, 24 Feb. 1851.
49. RA C46/29, Albert, Memorandum, 23 Feb. 1851, /31, the same, 24 Feb. 1851, /35, the same, 24 Feb. 1851 (Monday evening).
50. RA C46/36, Aberdeen to Victoria, 24 Feb. 1851, /39, Albert, Memorandum, 25 Feb. 1851; Victoria to Russell, 24 Feb. 1851, Victoria to Leopold, 25 Feb. 1851, *Letters of Queen Victoria*, vol. 2, pp. 299–300.
51. RA C46/39, Albert, Memorandum, 25 Feb. 1851.
52. RA C46/72, Stockmar, Memorandum, 27 Feb. 1851; Vincent, pp. 46–8 (25–7 Feb. 1851).
53. Gurney Papers, RQC 334/116, Aberdeen to Gurney, 3 Mar. 1851.
54. RA G32/21, Albert to Aberdeen, 3 June 1855.
55. RA C46/72, Stockmar, Memorandum, 27 Feb. 1851.
56. Victoria to Leopold, 25 Feb. 1851, *Letters of Queen Victoria*, vol. 2, p. 299.
57. NLS, MS 15017, Aberdeen to Ellice, 4 Jan. 1852.
58. Stewart, *The Politics of Protection*, p. 199.
59. NLS, MS 15017, Aberdeen to Ellice, 3 Aug. 1852; Graham Papers, 124, Aberdeen to Graham, 2, 28 Aug., 10 Sept., 20, 24 Oct. 1852; Add. MSS 43190, Graham to Aberdeen, 29 Sept., 22 Oct. 1852; *Economist*, quoted Stewart, p. 202.
60. Graham Papers, 124, Aberdeen to Graham, 27 Sept. 1852; Add. MSS 43190, Graham to Aberdeen, 29 Sept. 1852.
61. Add. MSS 43066, Russell to Aberdeen, 2 July 1852; Russell Papers, PRO 30/22/10C, Aberdeen to Russell, 5 July 1852 (drafts in Add. MSS 43066).
62. Add. MSS 43066, Russell to Aberdeen, 21 July 1852.
63. Add. MSS 43197, Aberdeen to Newcastle, 25 July 1852.
64. Add. MSS 43197, Newcastle to Aberdeen, 2 Aug. 1852.
65. Add. MSS 43197, Newcastle to Aberdeen, 3 Aug. 1852.
66. Add. MSS 43197, Aberdeen to Newcastle, 12 Aug. 1852.
67. Add. MSS 43070, Gladstone to Aberdeen, 5 Aug. 1852.
68. Russell Papers, PRO 30/22/10D, Aberdeen to Russell, 8 Aug. 1852.
69. Add. MSS 43066, Russell to Aberdeen, 11 Aug. 1852; Russell Papers, PRO 30/22/10C, Aberdeen to Russell, 13 Aug. 1852; Graham Papers, 124, Russell to Graham, 18 Aug. 1852.
70. Add. MSS 43066, Russell to Aberdeen, 13 Aug. 1852. The reference seems to be to the meeting of the Peelites which Newcastle called at Clumber in January 1852. Aberdeen went to this, but Graham regarded it as an anti–government cabal and refused to attend.
71. Add. MSS 43066, Russell to Aberdeen, 21 Aug. 1852.
72. Graham Papers, 124, Aberdeen to Graham, 27 Sept. 1852.
73. Russell Papers, PRO 30/22/10D, Aberdeen to Russell, 16 Sept. 1852; Add. MSS 43066, Russell to Aberdeen, 18 Sept. 1852.
74. Add. MSS 43196, Aberdeen to Goulburn, 2 Sept. 1852.
75. Graham Papers, 124, Aberdeen to Graham, 27 Sept. 1852.
76. Add. MSS 43066, Russell to Aberdeen, 13 Aug. 1852; Russell Papers, PRO 30/22/10D Aberdeen to Russell, 28 Aug. 1852.
77. Graham Papers, 124, Aberdeen to Graham, 31 Aug. 1852.
78. Graham Papers, 124, Graham to Aberdeen, 5 Aug. 1852 and encls.
79. Add. MSS 43190, Graham to Aberdeen, 7 Aug. 1852; Graham Papers, 124, Aberdeen to Graham, 9 Aug. 1852.
80. Add. MSS 43190, Graham to Aberdeen, 11 Aug. 1852.

81. Graham Papers, 124, Aberdeen to Graham, 15 Aug. 1852.
82. Add. MSS 43190, Graham to Aberdeen, 27 Aug. 1852; Graham Papers, 124, Aberdeen to Graham, 31 Aug. 1852.
83. Graham Papers, 124, Aberdeen to Graham, 31 Aug. 6, 10 Sept., 7, 20 Oct. 1852; Add. MSS 43190.
84. Graham Papers, 124, Aberdeen to Graham, 27 Sept. 1852.
85. Add. MSS 43190, Graham to Aberdeen, 29 Sept. 1852.
86. Graham Papers, 124, Aberdeen to Graham, 7 Oct. 1852.
87. Graham Papers, 124, Aberdeen to Graham, 31 Aug. 1852; Whyte, p. 95; Stewart, p. 207.
88. Add. MSS 43197, Aberdeen to Newcastle, 25 July 1852; NLS MS 15017, Aberdeen to Ellice, 3 Aug. 1852.
89. Add MSS 43190, Graham to Aberdeen, 25 Aug. 1852; Graham Papers, 124, Aberdeen to Graham, 28 Aug. 1852.
90. Graham Papers, 124, Aberdeen to Graham, 31 Aug., 10 Sept. 1852.
91. See above p. 408.

CHAPTER TWENTY-SIX

The formation of the Aberdeen coalition

Walter Bagehot, no mean judge of nineteenth–century politics, called the Aberdeen Cabinet 'the ablest we have had' since the Reform Act, 'eminently adapted for every sort of difficulty save the one it had to meet'. It was potentially a great reforming Cabinet in the tradition of Pitt and Peel and its record, before it was overtaken by the Eastern crisis, was impressive in both achievement and promise.[1] Even the difficult circumstances of its birth did not at first seem to impair its efficiency in domestic politics.

Disraeli had told the Commons in December 1852, 'England does not love coalitions.' Many on the other side of the House tended to agree with him and Whig and Peelite leaders continued to discuss whether they were forming a 'combination' or a 'fusion'. Aberdeen wanted a 'fusion'. He did not envisage the rump of the diminishing Peelite party attaching itself to an unregenerated Whig party, with a tactical alliance with the radicals. He wanted to see a new party emerge which, like Newcastle, he would have been content to call 'Liberal', although he would have preferred to have named it 'Liberal Conservative', in which Peelite doctrine would have as much weight as Whig or radical thinking. He had agreed that 'fusion' could not be forced and must wait on events but he saw the defeat of the Derbyites in December 1852 as an opportunity for trying to put it into practice. This belief in the genuine newness of the party being formed and the essential equality of the traditions being fused, explains his intransigence (Russell would have said his unreasonableness) in the face of the vast numerical superiority of the Whig-Radicals over the Peelites in the Commons. Once such a fusion was safely achieved, he had no objection to leaving the lead to someone else, but he regarded himself as well qualified to bring it about and, as a Conservative elder statesman, who had all his life had cordial personal links with the leading Whig families, he had good claims to be the ideal man. He saw this restoration of stability to British politics, which he had at first sought in vain in the reunion of the Conservative party, as his last service to his country. He was, after all, approaching his seventieth year and, although his own health seems to have been a great deal better in 1852 than it had been in 1846, he had new family problems in the illness of his son and heir, Lord Haddo.

Lord Derby met Parliament in November 1852. Despite some attempts to compel the government to admit that Free Trade was the right policy, when they were only prepared to concede that the re-imposition of the Corn Laws was politically impracticable, the opposition was agreed that the administration must be given the opportunity to present its measures and in particular Disraeli must present his Budget. In the opinion of many, including Aberdeen, this was simply a matter of giving them enough rope to hang themselves but to some, notably Gladstone, it was a matter of waiting to see what the Conservatives really meant to propose, and judging whether their proposals might be acceptable. Disraeli had a difficult task. He was called on to present a Budget in the middle of the financial year when calculations were particularly difficult. The country was sufficiently nervous about the intentions of Louis Napoleon, who was on the point of converting his life Presidency into the restoration of the Empire, to demand increased spending on defence. Some gesture had to be made towards the agricultural interest – it was found in the reduction of the malt tax and in income tax concessions to farmers – but the towns and those who derived their income from trade and the professions had to be persuaded that they were not being sacrificed to the countryside. The extension of the income tax to Ireland was likely to alienate the Irish Brigade, whose support was important to the government. Disraeli knew that he did not have the requisite financial expertise and he was not comforted by Derby's airy assurance that there was no need to worry because 'they give you the figures'. He cobbled together a Budget of expedients and presented it with some panache but it could not deceive an expert such as Gladstone. The great confrontation between Gladstone and Disraeli took place in the Commons on the evening of 16 December. When the vote was taken, in the early hours of the next morning, the Derbyites were reduced to their hard core vote of 286. Their opponents mustered 305.[2]

Derby at once went to see the Queen, who was holidaying at Osborne on the Isle of Wight and recommended her to seek the advice of Lord Lansdowne. He declined to advise her to send for Aberdeen although he had heard 'from good authority' that the Whigs and Peelites were ready to form an administration under him, on the grounds that, if he, Derby, were known to have tendered such advice, many of his own supporters would take it as a hint that, if he withdrew from public life, they should join Aberdeen. When the Prince pointed out that, constitutionally, it did not rest with him to advise on his successor, he treated the intervention as a quibble, and when Victoria indicated that she had thought of sending for Lansdowne and Aberdeen together, he said this would 'do very well'. He added with grim satisfaction that so many Whigs and Peelites would feel entitled to office that they would not be able to get away with a Cabinet of less than 32 – an impossible figure – and entered into some inaccurate speculation about who had been offered what.[3]

Derby's information may have been defective but he was entirely right in supposing that plans for an amalgamation were far advanced. He may have been ignorant as to how active a part the Court had played in the rapprochement. The intermediary had been Lord John's brother, the Duke of Bedford.

Apparently prompted by Stockmar, he had invited Aberdeen and Newcastle to Woburn, together with his brother, Lansdowne and Clarendon. The party, except for Lansdowne who was ill, assembled on 15 December. Prince Albert's private secretary, Colonel Phipps, joined them, and both Bedford and Phipps wrote full accounts of the discussions.[4] Bedford told Stockmar, 'I think our little meeting of politicians here . . . has been of infinite use, by putting the parties in good humour with each other & by smoothing jealousies and asperities, for a common object . . .' The news of Derby's defeat on 17 December broke up the gathering. Bedford, about to set out with the Woburn Hunt, scribbled a long and rather incoherent letter to Stockmar, relating the latest developments. 'This morning', he wrote, 'Ld Aberdeen was called unexpectedly to London, but came to my room before he left, & we had a full & clear understanding on all points of importance. He is very friendly, both personally & politically to my Brother, & will take no steps without communicating with him.' The Duke of Newcastle, who was still at Woburn, was also very friendly and would do his best to facilitate the formation of a government by a 'fusion of Whigs & Peelites'. Russell would do whatever Lansdowne and Aberdeen thought best. Bedford was aware that both Peelites and Irish would find it difficult to follow Russell. Palmerston was still a potential joker in the pack. He would serve with Lansdowne as Prime Minister and Russell as Leader of the House, but not with Russell as Prime Minister. 'Aberdeen,' Bedford told Stockmar, 'I believe, wd. not object to act with him, except as head of a Govt or Sect. of State for F. affairs – both entirely out of the question.' When Bedford's letter arrived, Stockmar transmitted it to the Queen with the comment that she would be surprised that no coalition had yet been formed but he was grateful to the Duke for revealing 'the secrets of his political circle'.[5]

Phipps' information did not differ substantially from Bedford's. He had talked at length with Clarendon and Newcastle. Clarendon was gloomy. He feared that most Peelites and some Whigs would not serve under Russell but the Liberals would object to Aberdeen alone. He saw one great difficulty. Phipps asked if he meant Cobden and the Manchester School. Clarendon replied that he did not – he meant Palmerston. When Phipps protested that Palmerston had no following, Clarendon replied that , if he were left out, he would ally with Disraeli and be a formidable opponent. Newcastle confirmed that the Peelites would not serve under Russell as Prime Minister, although they would accept him as Leader of the House. He added that he and Gladstone had influence with many of Derby's followers.

The suggestion that the Queen should send for Aberdeen and Lansdowne to tender their joint advice came from both Newcastle and Clarendon although Bedford, who had originally agreed, wrote on 18 December urging categorically that Aberdeen should become Prime Minister and Russell, Leader of the House.[6]

The Queen duly sent for Aberdeen and Lansdowne. Lansdowne who was still incapacitated by a severe attack of gout, could not travel. Aberdeen, knowing the delicate state of negotiations, going right back to the 'Lansdowne project' in the summer, refused to go to Osborne alone, until he was sure that this would be acceptable to the Queen.[7] He did not, however, waste time while he awaited her answer.[8] First he called on Lansdowne.[9] Lansdowne indicated that he was unwilling to take the premiership himself, although Palmerston and others had urged him to do so. He was opposed to parliamentary reform and did not think that some Peelites would serve under him. He thought that Aberdeen was better qualified than he was to become Prime Minister and promised his co–operation. At the same time he dropped a hint that he expected a joint commission to be extended to Aberdeen and Russell. Aberdeen then called on Graham at his house in Grosvenor Place. Graham was strongly opposed to the idea of divided authority. If Aberdeen became Prime Minister it must be with all the normal powers of a Prime Minister to choose his own colleagues. Aberdeen acquiesced in this. Walking back from Graham's house to Argyll House across Hyde Park, he happened to meet Russell. Unfortunately their later recollections of what was said during that informal meeting differed. Aberdeen told Sidney Herbert that Russell, acting on the Duke of Bedford's advice, had clearly agreed to take the Foreign Office and to lead the House of Commons. Aberdeen had naturally 'jumped at his offer'. Russell subsequently maintained that he had never done more than indicate that he would consider such a course. Of the two, Aberdeen, who had at times an almost obsessive regard for accuracy, is probably a better witness than Russell, whose impulsive nature not infrequently led him to contradict himself. But, whatever was actually said in the park that afternoon, Aberdeen certainly set off for Osborne the next day, Sunday, 19 December, believing that he had Russell's agreement and shaped his course accordingly.[10]

Aberdeen spent only an hour at Osborne, arriving at three o'clock and leaving at four. In fact he and the royal couple were already largely in agreement. He told the Queen that he had already had a chance to consult Lansdowne, Russell and his own 'friends'. Victoria replied that Lansdowne was too old and infirm for 'such arduous duties' and asked Aberdeen to take the commission himself. Aberdeen then made his position very clear. He alone must be responsible and 'the new Government should not be a revival of the old Whig Cabinet with the addition of some Peelites, but should be a liberal Conservative Government in the sense of that of Sir Robert Peel'. He thought that this would 'meet with the confidence of the country, even if it excluded the Radicals'. He indicated that he would propose Russell as Foreign Secretary and Leader of the House and had reason to believe that he would accept it. He would consult Russell about appointments and make sure that he was 'satisfied' but he alone would be responsible. He repeated to the Queen what he had previously said to many of his political friends, that he believed that Russell's unpopularity with the Whigs (as distinct from the Irish and the radicals) was undeserved, and indeed inexplicable, and that it would pass. He hoped for the support of many of the outgoing Conservatives and, for this reason, it was important that the two Secretaries of State should be Peelites. They then discussed Palmerston, whom it would be 'imprudent' to leave to combine with Disraeli. Aberdeen hopefully suggested that he might be persuaded to go to Ireland but the Queen and the Prince rightly thought that unlikely. Aberdeen hinted that he might like to translate Graham or Herbert to the Lords, well aware that alone he was no match for Derby. As for measures, he was cool about parliamentary reform, which could be postponed, and thought that the Budget and, more particularly, the income tax presented the most immediate problems. He left, having kissed hands as Prime Minister.[11]

The key figure of the planned administration was obviously Russell, and Aberdeen saw him again immediately on his return to London on the Sunday evening. Russell still seemed co-operative and Aberdeen went to bed reasonably confident that he would be able to form an administration. But Russell had second thoughts and at eight o'clock the next morning scribbled a note to Aberdeen to say that a night's reflection had convinced him that he was not equal to the work of the Foreign Office and the leadership of the Commons. He would come to Argyll House immediately after breakfast and, in the meantime, asked Aberdeen to do nothing. Contemporaries, especially Sir James Graham, had little doubt that Russell had been persuaded by his family and friends, and particularly by his wife, that he would be demeaning himself by taking any office under Aberdeen. His plea that he could not undertake both offices may not have been entirely spurious. His health was not robust and the attempt to combine the Foreign Office with the management of the Commons had killed both Castlereagh and Canning. He suggested that he should support Aberdeen's government from outside, while advising his friends to accept office. Aberdeen asked him to take a day to think it over. He told Russell bluntly that, if he had known this before he saw the Queen, he would have acted differently and he wrote to Victoria expressing grave doubts as to whether he could form an administration without Lord John's participation. The Queen had already written to Lord John urging him to make a 'patiotic sacrifice of personal interests' to assist Aberdeen. During the next few days the Duke of Bedford, Lord Lansdowne and T. B. Macaulay eventually triumphed over the discontent of Lady John.[12]

Lord John at first suggested that he should join the Cabinet and lead the Commons 'without an office'. He could not face either the Foreign or the Home Office and the only Cabinet office with virtually no departmental duties which could traditionally be held in the Commons, the Duchy of Lancaster, was universally regarded as too junior for him. He added the rather ambiguous phrase that he would take 'general charge' of government business in the Commons. He appealed to the precedent of the Duke of Wellington, who had led the Lords and sat in Peel's Cabinet in 1841 without office.[13]

Aberdeen himself would probably have reluctantly agreed to this arrangement. No one knew better than he did that the Foreign Office was probably 'the most labourious' of all the great offices of state. Later, on 20 December, he wrote to Clarendon, apparently acquiescing in Russell's decision, and offering Clarendon the Foreign Office.[14] But Aberdeen's Peelite friends, and particularly Sir James Graham, were adamant that Russell's offer must not be accepted. It was unprecedented for the Leader of the Commons not to hold departmental office. Their arguments were rather confused as to whether it would weaken him because he could not speak with ministerial authority, or strengthen him because he could, in some measure, dissociate himself from unpopular ministerial decisions. Underlying their misgivings, however, was, fairly obviously, a fear that a discontented Lord John would be able to exploit the situation to his own advantage. Graham also suspected that Russell had made the unusual suggestion because he feared to vacate his seat and fight a by-election, as he would have to do on taking office under the Crown. Russell sat for the City of London and it was commonly rumoured that the Rothschilds had withdrawn their support because of the failure of the Bill to allow Jews to become M.P.s. When he heard of this Aberdeen, who had previously mildly opposed the Bill, shrugged his shoulders and expressed his willingness to support it. This rather unusual cynicism probably reflects real doubts in his mind. The logic of the peculiar relationship between Parliament and the Church of England demanded that only members of the established Church be M.P.s but, in a House that already contained Roman Catholics and Dissenters (as well no doubt as covert atheists), the logic of the position was increasingly difficult to maintain. Russell, however, scotched this particular rumour by offering to take the Chiltern Hundreds, on accepting the Leadership, and fight a by-election.[15]

On 21 December Russell changed his mind and agreed to take the Foreign Office with the Leadership on the understanding that if the double burden proved too much he could resign the Foreign Office to Clarendon but retain the Leadership. Lady John believed that her husband had secured a definite promise from Aberdeen that he would resign the premiership itself to her husband, as soon as circumstances permitted. Aberdeen's own recollection – and again he is probably the more exact and conscientious witness – was that there had been no specific promise and certainly Russell's entry into his ministry had not been contingent upon it.[16] But he made no secret of the fact that he saw his role as bringing the coalition into being and that once its future was secure he intended to retire. He had always believed that the hostility of many Whigs to Russell was irrational and would pass and, in that case, Russell would be his obvious successor. But this prognosis was always hedged around with qualifications. He would not voluntarily break up the ministry to give the succession to Russell. He would yield place to him only if the Cabinet were agreed. This would almost certainly mean only if Russell were prepared to continue the equal fusion of Whigs and Peelites. This misunderstanding of the basis of their alliance was fundamental to the tensions which arose between the two men during the next two years.

Russell was the key figure but Palmerston was also important. The Derbyites were still the largest party in the Commons. They lacked only leaders. A combination of Palmerston and Disraeli would have been devastatingly effective. Aberdeen called on Palmerston on 21 December and offered to include him in the arrangements. Palmerston's first instinct was to decline. He told Aberdeen that they had 'stood so long in hostile array one against the other, that it was too late now to join' and the combination would not be acceptable to either party. He added, ominously for the future, that even if there were no other objection, the fact that the new ministry would be committed to parliamentary reform would be an insuperable one. The next day Palmerston reconsidered and delicately conveyed, through Lord Lansdowne, the information that he was available. An equally delicate offer of the Home Office went back through Lord Lansdowne. Graham was beginning to have misgivings and confided to his diary, 'There is no room for Disraeli and Lord Derby. Otherwise we had better all kiss and be friends at once.' He called on Palmerston and found him courteous but 'embarrassed'.[17] The Queen and the Prince were also a little startled by this development. Aberdeen assured them that when he saw Palmerston, even though he had then declined office, he had been very cordial and 'even reminded him that in fact they were great friends (!!!) of sixty years' standing, having been at school together'. Albert added, 'We could not help laughing heartily at the *Harrow* Boys and their friendship.'[18] No one, however, was under any illusion that the real reason why Palmerston had been included was that he would have been too dangerous in opposition.

Aberdeen was able to present a tentative list of Cabinet appointments to the Queen on her return to Windsor, on the evening of Wednesday, 22 December. Russell's acceptance of the Foreign Office the next day enabled Aberdeen to draw up what he hoped was his final list. Graham had no doubts about the difficulties ahead, writing in his journal:

I have great faith in the strong Cohesion of Office: otherwise it might be difficult to bind together the Materials, of which the Cabinet will be composed. It will embrace, however, great administrative Talent and Debating Power, and will present a more formidable Front to the Protectionists than they believed possible. The difficulties of agreement respecting Parliamentary Reform are the seeds of future dissension.

The Cabinet, as then envisaged, included seven Peelites, five Whigs and one radical (Sir William Molesworth as the First Commissioner of Works). Graham hoped that Russell and Palmerston would balance each other. He mused, 'It is a powerful team, but it will require good driving. There are some odd tempers and queer ways among them, but on the whole they are gentlemen, and they have a perfect gentleman at their head, who is honest and direct, and who will not brook insincerity in others.'[19]

Russell's reaction was what might have been expected. He complained at once that the government was too Peelite. 'I am seriously afraid', he wrote on 23 December, 'that the whole thing will break down from the weakness of the old Liberal party (I must not say Whig) in the Cabinet.' In addition, Peelites were being proposed as President of the Board of Trade, Postmaster General and Chief Secretary for Ireland. Russell warned Aberdeen that the proposed distribution of Irish places was so unsatisfactory that the fifty–seven Irish MPs who might be expected to support the government, meant to 'go as a body'. Aberdeen replied that he could not see him immediately to discuss this, as he had to go to Windsor, but that he did not think the distribution of offices unfair on the basis of individual merit. Aberdeen was, of course, turning against Russell the argument that Russell himself had used in February 1851, namely that office should be determined by personal suitability, and not by party numbers.[20]

Russell no longer recognised this argument. He replied vigorously the next day:

While I admit that you have had every wish to act fairly, I must submit to you the following results of your proposals:
Of 330 members of the H. of Commons
270 are Whigs & Radicals
30 Irish Brigade
30 Peelites.
To this party of 30 you propose to give 7 seats in the Cabinet.
To the Whigs & Radicals 5
To Lord Palmerston 1–13
Of the four important offices not in the Cabinet you propose to give 3 to the 30 Peelites, 1 to the 270.
I am afraid the Liberal party will never stand this & that the shame will overwhelm me.

He suggested three additional Whigs in the Cabinet, Lord Granville as Lord President, Francis Baring as President of the Board of Trade and Clarendon as Chancellor of the Duchy of Lancaster. He pointed out that ten former Whig Cabinet ministers were omitted, as against two Peelites, and that Aberdeen wanted to bring in an additional Peelite, the Duke of Argyll, who had never held office, as Lord Privy Seal. Argyll was by way of being a personal protegé of Aberdeen – Delane subsequently referred to him as 'old Aberdeen's little Scotch terrier' – and he wanted his support in the Lords. Russell also argued that the minor appointments should be re–cast with 'less disproportion'.[21]

Aberdeen went some distance, but not very far, to meet Russell's demands. He agreed to strengthen the Whigs by bringing in Granville as Lord President and Lansdowne as minister without portfolio. He had already agreed to accept Lord Cranworth as Lord Chancellor, although he would himself have liked to have retained Derby's Chancellor, Lord St Leonards, and he thought that he might have been acceptable to Russell because he had continued the law reforms initiated by Russell's former Chancellor, Lord Cottenham. He insisted on keeping the Board of Trade for Cardwell, and the Postmaster-Generalship for Viscount Canning, but these were not to be in the Cabinet. The Cabinet, as finally agreed, consisted of six Peelites and six Whigs, plus Molesworth. Graham was slightly surprised that Victoria agreed to Molesworth since he was known to be an advocate of the secret ballot.[22]

The final list read:

Prime Minister: Earl of Aberdeen (Peelite)
Lord Chancellor: Lord Cranworth (Whig)
Lord President of the Council: Earl Granville (Whig)
Lord Privy Seal: Duke of Argyll (Peelite)
Chancellor of the Exchequer: W. E. Gladstone (Peelite)
Home Secretary: Lord Palmerston (Whig)
Foreign Secretary: Lord John Russell (Whig)
Secretary for War and the Colonies: Duke of Newcastle (Peelite)
First Lord of the Admiralty: Sir James Graham (Peelite)
President of the Board of Control (India): Sir Charles Wood (Whig)

First Commissioner of Works: Sir William Molesworth (Radical)
Secretary at War: Sidney Herbert (Peelite)
Minister without portfolio: Marquis of Lansdowne (Whig).

The Times revealed most of the truth to its readers on Christmas Day. No one doubted that it had got its inside information directly from Aberdeen who had talked openly to his old friend, Delane. The paper praised the selection. 'If', said the leading article, 'experience, talent, industry, and virtue are the attributes required for the government of this empire, we are likely to have a good Government now as ever within the period of Parliamentary history and responsible Governments.' Naturally partisans complained about the distribution of offices, but since both sides complained, it was probably fair. Opponents were bound to harp on its 'composite character' but all governments were to some extent coalitions, based on compromises. *The Times* did not believe that its members disagreed on any really important point. Unfortunately, Delane decided to poke a little fun at the allocation of some offices. Wood knew nothing about India and it was odd that Molesworth, who was an expert on the colonies, should have to look after 'parks and gardens'. But it was the reference to Russell which did the damage. 'Lord John Russell', he remarked, 'has so little of the accomplishments required for his new office, that we can only suppose he is keeping it for a successor, most probably Lord Clarendon, who otherwise will not have a seat in the Cabinet.' The mixture of inside knowledge and innuendo – although Aberdeen was not responsible for the latter – infuriated Russell and, during the next few days of hard bargaining about the minor appointments, including Irish and Scottish appointments, he was less inclined to be co-operative than he otherwise might have been.[23]

Aberdeen met Graham, Newcastle, Herbert, Russell and the Whig whip, W. G. Hayter, at Argyll House on the evening of 26 December (the day before he had to announce his new government in Parliament) to discuss non-Cabinet offices and Household appointments.[24] In the end, to Aberdeen's private irritation, most of the Scottish offices had to go to Whigs because the Scottish Conservatives were Derbyites almost to a man. Most of the major offices in the Royal Household were amicably enough conceded to the Whigs as were the majority of minor ministerial appointments.[25] The one which caused most difficulty was the Duchy of Lancaster. Russell proposed Edward Strutt but Gladstone objected that Strutt was a Unitarian and it would be improper to give him the large church patronage enjoyed by the Duchy. After tedious enquiries Aberdeen established that Strutt took communion in the Church of England.[26] As always, Ireland presented almost insuperable problems. The Whigs had to agree to accept Lord St. Germans, a Peelite, as Lord Lieutenant. They fought hard for Sir Thomas Redington as Chief Secretary, but he was unacceptable to the Irish because of his support for the Ecclesiastical Titles Act, and another Peelite, Sir John Young, was appointed. Aberdeen did what he could to conciliate the Whigs over minor Irish appointments and also proposed to restore the Protestant, Lord Roden, to the Irish magistracy. Roden had been put out of the Commission of the Peace for allegedly encouraging an Orange demonstration which had led to armed conflicts with the Catholics. Aberdeen

449

remarked that his Protestant friends could hardly restore him but that he, Aberdeen, was such an impeccable 'Papist' that he could take the risk.[27]

The number of minor offices secured by the Whigs was more in proportion to their overall numbers but this did not affect their comparative weakness in the Cabinet. Hobhouse may have exaggerated a little when he wrote, 'Russell goes into the Cabinet with scarcely a personal or even a party friend in it', but Lady John was right in saying that the Liberal members of the Cabinet were not those she would have chosen. They were not a cohesive group. Molesworth was a radical, Palmerston still at odds with many old colleagues, Lansdowne virtually retired, and Cranworth interested in little except technical legal matters. Lady John wrote to her mother that she would like to have seen Lords Minto, Carlisle and Granville, with Sir George Grey and Sir Francis Baring in office but 'of these but one is in office, and instead of the others, alas, alas, Lds Clarendon, Lansdowne, Palmerston, and Sir C. Wood.'[28]

The Peelites on the other hand felt that Aberdeen had performed miracles in forming a government at all. Gladstone and Argyll were convinced that he was the only man who could have achieved it. Graham wrote in his journal: 'Lord Aberdeen's patience and justice are exemplary; he is firm and yet conciliatory, and has ended by making an arrangement which is on the whole impartial, and quite as satisfactory as circumstances admit.'[29] The Court too was immensely relieved. They had feared that, once again, the coalition would not be formed. Stockmar made an agonised appeal to Aberdeen on 21 December, 'For God's sake don't suffer at this moment Hesitation, Indecision anywhere. Manliness, Energy and Patriotism is what we want at this Hour . . . God bless and prosper you my dear Lord. Every yours sincerely and very affectionly. Stockmar.'[30] When success seemed assured the Queen wrote to her uncle Leopold of the Belgians in enthusiastic terms: 'The success of our excellent Aberdeen's arduous task and the formation of so brilliant and strong a Cabinet would, I was sure, please you. It is the realisation of the country's and our *most* ardent wishes, and it deserves success, and will, I think, command great support.'[31] Victoria's reaction might seem over–sanguine but Gladstone too thought the Cabinet potentially very strong. He wrote later: 'I must say of this cabinet of Lord Aberdeen's that in its deliberations it never exhibited the marks of its dual origin . . . [The Eastern] question and the war were fatal to it. In itself I hardly ever saw a cabinet with greater promise of endurance.'[32]

Aberdeen had to meet Parliament on Monday, 27 December, before his government was finally complete. Derby, in announcing his resignation to the Lords in a singularly bad–tempered speech, had only reluctantly asked for several days adjournment at Aberdeen's request, complaining that as the Whigs, radicals, Irish and Peelites had been combining for several months to bring down his government, he thought they would have needed less than twenty-four hours to settle their arrangements. He also expressed astonishment that Aberdeen could continue to call himself a Conservative in view of his present associates.[33]

Aberdeen felt compelled to answer Derby before expounding the policy of the new government.[34] There had, he said, been no conspiracy to overthrow

Derby, and personally, he had no wish to displace him. He assured the House that he was not expressing merely conventional reluctance to assume the premiership; the House knew that he rarely spoke except on foreign affairs; he was approaching seventy years of age and when Derby's government was defeated he had been making arrangements to spend the winter in Nice.

Without making any direct reference to the fact that he was now sitting with Palmerston he felt compelled to make clear both where he stood on foreign questions and why he felt that there was no inconsistency in his present position. Equally unspoken, but understood by the House, was the assumption that any foreseeable danger was likely to come from France:

The truth is, my Lords (he said), that for the last thirty years the principles of the foreign policy of this country have never varied. There may have been differences in the execution, according to the different hands intrusted with the direction of that policy: but the foundation of the foreign policy of this country has been, I repeat, for the last thirty years the same. It has been marked by a respect due to all independent states, a desire to abstain as much as possible from the internal affairs of other countries, an assertion of our honour and interests, and, above all, an earnest desire to secure the general peace of Europe by all such means as were practicable and at our disposal.[35]

Britain may have looked with sympathy on constitutional states but her first principle had always been to respect their independence and not interfere in internal questions. He hoped that they would retain the goodwill of all states and, if they had to interfere, 'my earnest desire, my great hope is, that we shall never be called upon to act except to exercise the blessed office of the peacemaker'. At the same time they should not relax their precautions but, since these were purely defensive, they could not properly give offence to any Power.

Aberdeen's assertion of the essential continuity of British foreign policy caused understandable surprise, but he had worded the statement very carefully and there was, perhaps, an element of casuistry in it. The public did not know of the letters which had passed between himself and Russell in which both men appeared to regard Palmerston's conduct, or at least recent conduct, of foreign affairs as freakish.

When he turned to domestic affairs, Aberdeen proclaimed that the government's 'mission' would be to maintain Peel's commercial and financial system and to protect free trade. The matter of the Budget was urgent, but Aberdeen would not be drawn on details. His treatment of other prospective reforms, including education, the law and the parliamentary franchise, although cautious, was firm and definite. He left his hearers in no doubt that the government intended to introduce such reforms. Aberdeen himself had always believed as passionately as any Benthamite in the crucial importance of education ever since he had contrasted the situation of his Scottish and his Irish tenants. Education must be general and universal. The Church must have due influence but it should be consistent with the 'perfect right and freedom' which all men were entitled to expect in Britain. The new government would vigorously pursue the law reforms, initiated under Russell's last government. Education and law reform together should materially improve the 'social condition' of the people. He was more cautious on parliamentary reform but he made it clear that he envisaged amendments 'not rashly or hastily undertaken, but . . . safe, well-considered measures'.

He took up Derby's taunt that he could not be a Conservative in his present company. 'My Lords,' he said, 'I declare to the noble Earl that in my opinion no Government in this country is now possible except a Conservative Government: and to that I add another declaration, which I take to be as indubitably true, that no Government in this country is now possible except a Liberal Government.' The distinction was now meaningless and Russell would not have associated himself with Aberdeen unless he thought him in a real sense a Liberal or he with Russell, unless he had believed him to be a Conservative.

Finally, he challenged Derby's attempt to rally support by making men's flesh creep with fears of democracy. There would always be violent men, ready for any outrage, but they were not a present danger to stability. The country had never been more prosperous or tranquil. 'I have great confidence', he said, 'in the people of this country.' The attempt to stir up alarm was almost 'a libel on the people'.

Derby rose to reply and instantly proved himself a much cleverer parliamentarian than Aberdeen. He came close to saying that Brutus was an honourable man. Of course, he accepted Aberdeen's word that there had been no conspiracy against himself, but he hoped Aberdeen would never have to meet such 'factious opposition' or 'unprincipled coalition'. There must have been great concessions of opinion to have allowed such a coalition to have been formed. He laughed at the idea that there were no disagreements about foreign policy and found Aberdeen's pronouncements on parliamentary reform oracular. He concluded that he felt no personal hostility to Aberdeen but he had no confidence in his government.[36]

In saying that he felt no personal hostility, Derby was probably less than truthful. Even the Queen was sufficiently curious to try to find out what had caused such a 'chill' between the two men. Derby's explanation was that he had been quite taken by surprise by Aberdeen's actions since, up to the end of the last session, he had believed him to be friendly and Aberdeen had even sent him messages that he would never join the Whigs. Aberdeen entirely denied this and made it clear that it was Derby's unprincipled conduct during the 1852 election which had estranged him. It seems, however, that Derby did think Aberdeen guilty of the 'treachery' of which he had once told his son he believed him to be incapable.[37] The announcement of the Conservative government's retirement had led to bitter recriminations in the Commons as well as in the Lords, but the debate there on 27 December was conducted with better humour than in the Lords and Disraeli virtually apologised to Graham for some of the things he had previously said. Graham had been the original target for the Conservatives' strongest attacks but, as Aberdeen emerged as the Coalition leader, the fire naturally transferred to him.

Throughout his period of office, the Conservatives continued to make bitter personal attacks on Aberdeen, which he was ill-equipped to meet. The content of his first speech as Prime Minister was generally acknowledged to be good but it was badly delivered and he missed an important political trick by failing to refer with sufficient cordiality to Russell and Lansdowne. If Greville is to be believed, Aberdeen himself was very dissatisfied and wished he could have made his speech again.[38] His inability to speak effectively in the Lords, which had so haunted him as a young man, but which he seemed partially to have overcome in the 1830s and 1840s, returned in full force when he was Prime Minister.

It was not an easy premiership. Aberdeen was the leader of a minority government which could only secure a majority in the Commons with the unpredictable support of the Irish Brigade. His personal following was tiny. He claimed fifty Peelites in the Commons but most estimates accorded him only thirty. Russell, the leader of the majority party in the government and of the second strongest party in the Commons, was still deeply dissatisfied and waiting impatiently for the reversion of the leadership. Even if Russell had been a less sensitive and difficult man, he would still have been under pressure, as the Whig leader, from his disappointed followers who were angry that the Peelites had a share of offices so obviously out of proportion to their numbers. Aberdeen did, however, have the cordial support of the Court. The Queen, and still more the Prince, had gone close to the limits of constitutional propriety in their attempts to find a stable government in the chaos of parties which had followed the schism in the Conservative party in 1846. The public, without knowing the full facts, sensed that the connections between Aberdeen's administration and the Court were unusually close. When his government became unpopular, a highly distorted notion of its relationship with the Court was to be dangerously compromising to both parties. The wonder was that the coalition worked as well as it did for a year, and that, despite the *débâcle* of the Crimean War, it laid the foundations for a completely new alignment of British politics.

NOTES

1. Bagehot, *The English Constitution*, p. 26. Its domestic achievements were first properly discussed in Conacher, *The Aberdeen Coalition* (1968).
2. Blake, pp. 328–47; Conacher, *The Peelites*, pp. 162–8.
3. RA C28 'Papers concerning the Change of Government Dec. 1852', /1, Albert, Memorandum, 18 Dec. 1852.
4. RA C28/7 Bedford to Stockmar, 17 Dec. 1852, /12, Phipps to Albert, 18 Dec. 1852.
5. RA C28/6, Stockmar to Victoria, 18 Dec. 1852.
6. RA C28/19, Bedford to Stockmar, 18 Dec. 1852; Add. MSS 43248, Bedford to Aberdeen, 19 Dec. 1852.
7. RA C28/5, Aberdeen to Victoria, 18 Dec. 1852.
8. The fullest account of these negotiations is in the Diary kept by Graham, Graham Papers, 124, headed 'Change of Government' and covering 17–29 Dec. 1852, but it is confirmed at numerous points by other letters.

9. RA C28/11, Lansdowne to Victoria, 'Sunday morning'.

10. Stanmore, p. 231; Spencer Walpole, vol. 2, pp. 160–1; Graham, Diary, 20 Dec. 1852 (under date 18 Dec.).

11. RA C28/13, Albert, Memorandum, 19 Dec. 1852.

12. Add. MSS 43066, Russell to Aberdeen, '8 a.m.' 20 Dec., 22 Dec. 1852; Graham, Diary, 20, 21 Dec. 1852; RA C28/14, Victoria to Russell, 19 Dec. 1852, /21, Aberdeen to Victoria, 19 (corrected to 20) Dec. 1852; Spencer Walpole, vol. 2, pp. 162–3; Add. MSS 43248, Lansdowne to Aberdeen, 'Monday' (20 Dec. 1852).

13. Add. MSS 43066, Russell to Aberdeen, 22 Dec. 1852.

14. MSS Clar. Dep. C525, Aberdeen to Clarendon, 20 Dec. 1852; cf. Greville, vol. VII, p. 21 (22 Dec. 1852).

15. Graham, Diary, 21, 22 Dec. 1852; Add. MSS 43066, Russell to Aberdeen, 22 Dec. 1852.

16. Spencer Walpole, vol. 2, pp. 163–4.

17. Graham, Diary, 21, 23 Dec. 1852.

18. RA C28/38, Albert, Memorandum, 22 Dec. 1852; RA C28/43, Aberdeen to Victoria, 23 Dec. 1852.

19. Graham, Diary, 23 Dec. 1852; RA C28/44, Aberdeen to Victoria, 23 Dec. 1852.

20. Add. MSS 43066, Russell to Aberdeen, 23 Dec. 1852, Confidential, Aberdeen to Russell, 23 Dec. 1852.

21. Add. MSS 43066, Russell to Aberdeen, 24 Dec. 1852. For the development of Aberdeen's friendship with Argyll see Argyll, *Autobiography and Memoirs*, vol. 1, pp. 301–2, 369–72; Dasent, vol. 2, p. 332.

22. Graham, Diary, 21, 24 Dec. 1852; RA C28/38, Albert, Memorandum, 22 Dec. 1852.

23. *The Times*, 25 Dec. 1852; Prest, pp. 356–7.

24. Graham, Diary, 26 Dec. 1852.

25. Albert cautioned him against letting the Whigs 'deal out' places in the Household, before he had taken the Queen's pleasure: RA C28/57, Albert to Aberdeen, 26 Dec. 1852.

26. Add. MSS 43070, Gladstone to Aberdeen, 25 Dec. 1852; RA C28/63, Aberdeen to Victoria, 27 Dec. 1852.

27. Add. MSS 43188, Aberdeen to Clarendon, 14 Jan. 1853.

28. Quoted Prest, p. 356.

29. Graham, Diary, 28 Dec. 1852.

30. Add. MSS 43248, Stockmar to Aberdeen, 21 Dec. 1852.

31. Victoria to Leopold, 28 Dec. 1852, *Letters of Queen Victoria*, vol. 2, p. 428.

32. Quoted Morley, vol. 1, p. 450.

33. *Hansard*, 3rd ser., CXXIII, 1698–1705 (20 Dec. 1852).

34. *Hansard*, 3rd ser., CXXIII, 1721–7 (27 Dec. 1852).

35. *Hansard*, 3rd ser., CXXIII, 1724.

36. *Hansard*, 3rd ser., CXXIII, 1727–41.

37. RA C28/60, Albert, Memorandum, 27 Dec. 1852 (The version in *Letters of Queen Victoria*, vol. 2, pp. 425–6 is a good deal shortened.) Vincent, p. 20.

38. Greville, vol. VII, pp. 25, 27–8 (28 Dec. 1852).

CHAPTER TWENTY-SEVEN

Liberal–Conservatism in action: the legacy of Pitt and Peel

The new Cabinet met for the first time at dinner at Argyll House on the evening of 29 December 1852. Despite Graham's fears that they would 'look somewhat strangely at each other',[1] the dinner was a convivial one at which good talk flowed.

The youngest member of the Cabinet, Argyll, retained vivid memories of that first meeting, his sense of the historic significance of the occasion heightened by the fact that it took place in what had for many generations been his own family's London home. It was a remarkable group of men who assembled round Aberdeen's table that evening. 'Taken together', wrote Argyll, 'it was a body of men who, in personal experience, spanned the whole political history of the country from the days of Pitt and Fox . . . Within the limits of our own constitutional contests, it embraced every school of politics which had been of any distinction for more than half a century.' Aberdeen and Lansdowne were living links with Pitt and Fox. Lansdowne had been Chancellor of the Exchequer as early as 1806. Palmerston, Graham and Russell made up the rest of the older statesmen. The rising generation was represented by Molesworth, Newcastle, Herbert, Granville (the son of the former Harriet Cavendish), Gladstone and Argyll himself. The Benthamite, Molesworth, was at first sight the incongruous element in the Cabinet, but his social origins were little different from the rest – he was a Cornish landowner – and Gladstone soon found his views to be closer to those of the Peelites than of the Whigs. Of the new generation, Newcastle and Herbert, like Molesworth, were to die in middle life but Granville and Argyll went on to hold high office in Liberal Cabinets for the next thirty years, while Gladstone was to emerge as the true heir of the great coalition of 1852. Like Gladstone who maintained that the Cabinet never exhibited its 'dual origin', Argyll too, immediately felt 'a sense of comradeship'.[2] Such judgements might seem sanguine in view of the storms ahead, but the clashes were always those of strong personalities and rarely followed the old party lines. In domestic politics at least something like the desired 'fusion' was achieved.

The next few weeks were taken up by those ministers, who were also members of the House of Commons, fighting the necessary by-elections. They

caused few problems and reassured the coalition of its acceptability to the country.[3] A series of Cabinet meetings was held in late January and early February
which gave rise to some, generally unfounded, speculation in *The Times* about
differences on policy. With no secure majority in the Commons, the government had decided to move cautiously. By general agreement, the Budget was
the only urgent issue.

Since Parliament had only been adjourned, not prorogued, there was no
Queen's Speech when it met again on 10 February. Instead, Russell, as the
Leader of the House of Commons, announced the government's programme.
Apart from the Budget, legal reforms and education would take priority but
the question of Jewish disabilities and some colonial questions, including transportation to Australia and the vexed question of the Clergy Reserves in Canada,
would be tackled. Consideration of parliamentary reform would be postponed
for a year to allow for further study and until more urgent legislation was out
of the way. All these issues would first be raised in the Commons and it had
been agreed that the announcement should be left to Russell.[4] Aberdeen did
not intend to add anything to the general statement he had made the previous
December. Perhaps the criticisms which his speech had attracted, even from
his friends, made him uneasy. That excellent parliamentarian, Lord Derby, at
once sensed that he had him at a disadvantage. He maintained that it was
improper for the Lords to learn of the government's policy from press reports
of the Commons. The Prime Minister must make a statement. Aberdeen was
not going to walk into a trap, and he declined. When Derby pressed him
further he merely bowed and sat down.[5]

Charles Greville was scathing. He wrote: 'The scene was rather ridiculous, and
not creditable, I think, to Aberdeen. He is unfortunately a very bad speaker
at all times, and what is worse in a Prime Minister, has no readiness whatever.
Lord Lansdowne would have made a very pretty dexterous flourish, and
answered the question.' But the importance of that bad beginning can be
exaggerated. Greville did not persist long in his belief that Lansdowne would
have made a better Prime Minister. Less than three weeks later he wrote:
'Aberdeen has done very well in the House of Lords, his answers to "questions"
having been discreet, temperate, and judicious.' He noted with some surprise
that Aberdeen had no intention of being a figure-head: 'Aberdeen seems to have
no notion of being anything but a *real* Prime Minister.' By late March he was
almost enthusiastic: 'Aberdeen likes his post and enjoys the consciousness of
having done very well in it. He is extremely liberal, but of a wise and well-
reasoned liberality. As it has turned out, he is far fitter for the post he occupies
than Lansdowne would have been, both morally and physically.'[6]

Greville was entirely right in his estimate of Aberdeen's 'liberality'. During
the next two years he consistently threw his weight on the side of reforming
ministers, despite strong opposition, sometimes from within the Cabinet. A
number of important measures would not have got through without his intervention. Others were lost because of the great tragedy of the outbreak of the
Crimean War, but, even here, foundations were often laid which later governments could build upon.

The first great test was Gladstone's Budget. Gladstone immediately plunged into a morass of figures and calculations from which he emerged with what contemporaries were eventually to agree was a masterly Budget, worthy of Peel himself, which shed lustre on the new coalition. But it was a hard struggle to get it adopted.[7]

The most sensitive, as well as the most immediate question, was the income tax. Income tax was a very unpopular form of taxation, partly because of its 'inquisitorial' nature, partly because of the unfairness with which it was supposed to weigh on 'precarious' (i.e. earned) as opposed to 'permanent' (i.e. unearned) sources of income. The income tax was still regarded, as Gladstone himself described it, as 'an engine of gigantic power for great national purposes' but not as a normal and routine form of taxation. William Pitt had introduced it as a temporary expedient during the Napoleonic wars. Peel had re-introduced it in 1842 – at the modest rate of 7d in the £1 – for a period of three years, to tide over the loss of customs duties resulting from his first free trade Budget. He anticipated that the recovery of trade would quickly make good the deficiency and enable the tax to be abandoned but it was renewed for three year periods until 1851, after which the Commons declined to renew it for more than one year at a time. The current vote was due to expire at the end of June 1853.

Gladstone's objective was to carry out Peel's programme by gradually reducing the income tax and abolishing it altogether by 1860. To do this he had to try to calculate the probable revenue not for one year but for eight years ahead. Paradoxically, he wanted, in the short run, to increase the return from the income tax. He needed this additional money for two reasons. First, a nervous public was demanding an increase in the Army and Navy Estimates in the face of events in France. Secondly, and a good deal closer to Gladstone's heart, he wanted some leeway to continue the Peelite policy of the liberalisation of trade. He proposed to reduce substantially the import duty on tea and to abolish the excise duty on soap. Both these measures involved major losses of revenue but it was calculated that they would greatly benefit the poorer customer and the latter measure had important implications for public health. In addition, import duties on most semi–manufactured goods were to be abolished and the remaining customs duties on food imports reduced. The Budget also provided for the reduction of a whole range of miscellaneous duties, including the stamp duty on newspapers.

To obtain this additional revenue, Gladstone proposed to lower the threshold at which the income tax became payable from £150 to £100 and to extend the tax to Ireland. He argued that, since only the well-to-do paid in any case, it was not logical to exempt Ireland on the plea of poverty. He refused to differentiate, as many wished, between earned and unearned incomes, on the grounds that the latter included the modest investments of widows in the government funds and the former the large profits of merchants and manufacturers. He did concede, however, that those who derived their income from their own exertions in trade and the professions were more precariously situated than those who derived it from property. To redress the balance he proposed tax exemptions on the purchase of life assurance from earned income and, much more controversially, the extension of the legacy duty, first introduced by Pitt, to real property. This, the 'succession duty', was extremely unpopular with the Tory landowners.

Gladstone outlined his proposals to the Cabinet on 9 April. Only Aberdeen knew them in detail in advance. He spoke for three hours and his colleagues were silenced by the boldness of his ideas and his mastery of his material. Argyll wrote, 'It was like the flow of some crystal stream . . . The order was perfect in its lucidity, and the sentences as faultless as they were absolutely unhesitating.'[8]

His colleagues' stunned acquiescence did not, however, last long. When the Cabinet met again on 11 April they had had time to consider how unpopular some of the proposals would be. Aberdeen had had no illusions about how difficult it would be to persuade either the Cabinet or the Commons to accept the whole package. He wrote to the Prince (the Queen being confined for the birth of her fourth son) after the first Cabinet meeting, 'If Gladstone can make it as intelligible to the House of Commons as he did to us, I shall feel sanguine with respect to the result; but the subject is complicated and difficult, and it would be, indeed, the triumph of reason against prejudice'.[9] Aberdeen himself had some reservations about the rejection of the arguments in favour of differential taxation and of the extension of the income tax downwards.

At the meeting on 11 April doubts were raised, especially about the succession duties and the practicability of extending the income tax to Ireland. These doubts hardened at another meeting the following day. By this time, Lansdowne, Graham, Wood, Palmerston and Granville all wanted important modifications, and Palmerston felt so strongly about the succession duties that he declined to join his colleagues in warning the Commons that, if the Budget were rejected, the government would ask for a dissolution. At one time on 12 April only Newcastle and Molesworth seemed inclined to stand by Gladstone's original proposals, but Aberdeen had come to the conclusion that the proposals were indivisible. Gladstone himself noted, 'Lord Aberdeen came in to help and said it was better to take the whole: the more you cut off from it, the less the remainder hung together.' Wood was particularly embarrassed because, in criticising Disraeli's Budget, he had virtually pledged himself against the extension of the income tax to Ireland.[10]

By the next Cabinet meeting on 15 April, Gladstone had almost come to the conclusion that he could not force his proposals through, and he put forward an alternative strategy, suggested by Cardwell; but, once convinced, Aberdeen was determined to stiffen Gladstone's resolve to stand out for the whole measure. A compromise was found so far as Ireland was concerned. The income tax was to be extended, but in return certain Irish debts, the 'consolidated annuities', were to be remitted. Wood felt that this relieved him of his obligation to resign and gradually the whole Cabinet swung round. They agreed to Gladstone's Budget on 16 April.[11]

Gladstone presented the Budget to the Commons on 18 April in a great speech lasting almost five hours. Russell gave his opinion that 'Mr Pitt in the days of his glory might have been more imposing, but he could not have been more persuasive.'[12] Aberdeen told Leopold of the Belgians that Gladstone had 'placed himself fully on the level of Sir Robert Peel'.[13] Many of the congratulations went to Aberdeen and he passed them on to Gladstone, rather with the air of a proud father congratulating a son. The same personal note was struck by Gladstone in his reply to Aberdeen. 'I had the deepest anxiety with regard to you, as our Chief,' he said, 'lest by faults of my own, I should aggravate the cares and difficulties into which I had at least helped to bring you.' Aberdeen had no doubt that, on the contrary, Gladstone's Budget had strengthened his administration. 'If the existence of my government shall be prolonged,' he told him, 'it will be your work.' He told Princess Lieven a month later that his government was 'infinitely better and stronger than I ever expected to see it' and that it was largely due to Gladstone who had given it a 'strength and lustre' it could have derived from nowhere else.[14]

Great as Gladstone's oratorical triumph had been on 18 April it took some weeks to consolidate the position. The Irish were not so hostile to the income tax proposals as had been feared and a number of Derbyites voted with the government. The income tax measure passed the Commons on 6 June. Aberdeen himself introduced its Second Reading in the Lords and it received the royal assent on 28 June. The Succession Duties Bill was hotly contested in both Commons and Lords. Aberdeen had to come in to support it in the Upper House and it was finally accepted on 28 July.

Gladstone's calculations in his Budget were not fulfilled in every particular, but the Budget produced a healthy surplus of £2,500,000. After seven years of inept financial management, both Parliament and the public were impressed. Only the outbreak of the Crimean War devastated Gladstone's careful strategy for a complete reform of the taxation system.

Aberdeen also gave powerful support to Sir Charles Wood's India Bill.[15] Wood had not been an effective Liberal Chancellor and he was a poorish speaker in the Commons. Russell blew hot and cold on the measure and, but for Aberdeen, the Bill would have been abandoned. Some measure was imperative because the East India Company's Charter had last been renewed in 1833 for a period of twenty years but there was a considerable lobby in favour of simply extending the existing measure for a short period.

Since Pitt's Act of 1784, British India had been governed by a complex dual system of the Crown and the Company which, it was generally conceded, had given rise to many anomalies. While Derby was in power in 1852, both Houses of Parliament appointed committees to enquire into the renewal of the Charter. Lord Dalhousie, the Peelite, whose appointment as Governor General Aberdeen had so warmly applauded, submitted a long report, upon which Wood founded many of his recommendations. In the circumstances, Aberdeen was not impressed by the argument that the government had insufficient information upon which to act.

The matter was discussed at an important Cabinet meeting on 20 March. Aberdeen admitted to the Queen there was a growing feeling in favour of passing an Act for one year only and he felt that the only way in which that could be avoided was to propose wide reforms. He therefore suggested that all patronage should be abolished and young men appointed to go out to India on merit after 'due examination'. This was a revolutionary proposal, favoured by Sir Charles Trevelyan, Macaulay's brother-in-law and himself an experienced Indian administrator, who was to make similar proposals for the British Civil Service. The reform of the Court of Directors was also discussed by the Cabinet and a committee, consisting of Aberdeen, Russell, Argyll, Graham, Granville, Wood, Herbert and Molesworth, appointed to consider the whole question over Easter. If they could not agree, Aberdeen told the Queen, they would have to accept the one year proposal.[16]

Discussions were interrupted by the first stirrings of the Eastern crisis, and further delayed by the priority initially given to education questions and by the more urgent problem of the Budget but the committee's recommendations eventually went to the Cabinet on 21 May. The Cabinet expressed general approval of the proposals but Russell got cold feet and doubted whether he could pilot the measure through the Commons. Graham and Wood saw Russell and 'remonstrated strongly' but without success. Aberdeen took advantage of a Cabinet dinner at Herbert's on 25 May to argue at length with Russell but no firm conclusion was reached. Aberdeen admitted to the Queen that it would be very embarrassing to withdraw the measure now because Russell had already told the Commons that he would bring it forward on 3 June.[17] The Cabinet met on 28 May and decided to postpone the Bill but they met again on 31 May and reversed their decision. Gladstone privately recorded the extraordinary ebb and flow of the discussion. At the outset only Aberdeen, Wood and, amazingly (since he had made all the difficulties) Russell were for going ahead that session. Palmerston, who admitted that he had changed his mind ten times in as many minutes, eventually sided with them. Clarendon (who had joined the Cabinet in February), Newcastle and Argyll also came over and the decision to go ahead was accepted by one vote.[18]

Wood introduced the measure into the Commons on 3 June. The dual system of government was to be preserved but the composition of the Court of Directors much modified. Patronage was to be abolished and entry to Haileybury, the training college for the Indian Civil Service, was to be by examination. Provision was also made for some long overdue administrative re—organisation in India. The Governor-General was no longer to be also the Governor of Bengal. The important codification of the Indian laws, initiated by Macaulay in the 1830s, was to be taken up again. Although not a thoroughgoing Benthamite measure, there were considerable traces of Benthamite thought in Wood's Bill. Macaulay warmly supported it, although Hume and some other Radicals attacked it. The idea of recruitment by competitive examination was particularly roughly handled by the critics, who saw no correlation between academic brilliance and practical ability. They were effectively answered by Macaulay and the knowledge that the alternative to competition was patronage was fatal to their case. Russell's fears of not being able to get the measure through the Commons proved unfounded and, although voting crossed party lines, the government secured a majority on the Second Reading of 322 to 140.

Ellenborough, who was no friend of Aberdeen's government, and had his own reasons for disliking the Court of Directors (they had secured his recall in 1844) made difficulties in the Lords, but the Bill passed without serious hindrance. The government introduced one important amendment in the Lords at the instance of Benjamin Jowett, the famous master of Balliol. He persuaded several members of the Cabinet, including Aberdeen, that the age limit for the competitive examination should be raised from 19 to 21 in order to admit university graduates.[19] As a result the universities replaced Haileybury as the main source of supply for the Indian Civil Service.

Although the settlement of 1853 was overtaken by the Mutiny in 1857 and the final surrender of the Company's powers, the Act was an important landmark in Anglo-Indian relations. Apart from its introduction of the competitive principle, it allowed in its administrative reorganisation in India for the setting up of a Legislative Council to advise the Governor General, and, although this was at first confined to Europeans, Dalhousie allowed it to function as a miniature parliament and its status was already established when Indians were first admitted to it in 1861. The codification of the laws was completed by the issue of the three great Codes, the Penal Code and the Codes of Civil and Criminal Procedure between 1859 and 1861. Wood also strengthened the 1835 decision to foster a system of higher education in English for an élite who could provide leadership for their own people. This did not please those who would have preferred vernacular education for the masses but this was generally condemned by contemporary liberals as designed to keep the Indians as ignorant helots. Like Gladstone's Budget, Wood's India Act charted a new course.

Education for British children should have been one of the central themes of the coalition's first year in office. At the Cabinet meeting on 2 April it was agreed that Russell would propose an increase in the education grant of at least £250,000 per annum for England and Wales, under the direction of a Privy Council committee. A Scottish measure would follow later.[20] Russell duly gave notice in the Commons on 4 April of the government's intention to bring in a far-reaching measure which in many ways foreshadowed Forster's Act of 1870 by putting the onus on the local authorities. The idea quickly fell victim to the fears and vested interests of the various religious groups. Aberdeen, while not denying the Church a place in education, was irritated, but the Bill was crowded out of the legislative programme. On 29 July, in reply to a question from Brougham, Aberdeen had to say 'with great regret' that it would be 'utterly impossible' to proceed that session.[21] But for the Crimean War the government would undoubtedly have returned to the problem but, as it was, only the increased money grants survived.

The coalition was rather more successful in its dealings with the two ancient universities. In 1850 Russell had appointed a Royal Commission to enquire into the state of Oxford and Cambridge. Aberdeen was no stranger to Royal Commissions on university reform. Despite both the Crimean War and strenuous internal opposition, the Oxford University Reform Act, largely drafted by Gladstone, went through in 1854. Cambridge escaped until 1856.

The attempt to bring about a radical reform of the Civil Service foundered for lack of time but much important preliminary work was done. Between January and August 1853, Sir Charles Trevelyan and Sir Stafford Northcote, a Tory but a friend of Gladstone's, were asked to enquire into the running of a number of civil service departments. In April they were asked to draw up a general report on the state of the Civil Service and especially on its methods of recruitment. The famous Northcote-Trevelyan Report appeared in November. After a scathing indictment of the short-comings of the patronage system, it recommended a partial change to recruitment by competitive examination.[22] Significantly, it was the Peelites, despite some misgivings on Graham's part, who supported the Northcote–Trevelyan proposals and the old Whigs who feared them.[23] The outbreak of the Crimean War and the fall of the coalition prevented the implementation of the proposals but a qualifying examination for civil servants was introduced in 1855 and entry became fully competitive in 1870.

Important, although highly technical, legal reforms proceeded quietly. The Charitable Trusts Act, which established the modern Charity Commissioners, although it did not do all its enthusiastic sponsors claimed, began to cut a path through the jungle of ancient and chaotic charities. Three Chancery Reform Acts, the Evidence Amendment Act and three important Acts dealing with the care and protection of lunatics were also passed. Palmerston, his energy diverted to home affairs, strengthened the Factory Acts, tried unsuccessfully to improve the sewerage system of London and, rather more successfully, pioneered the first Smoke Abatement Act. An important issue, which straddled the jurisdiction of the Lord Chancellor and the Home Secretary, was that of transportation, which had become acute because the colonies, except Western Australia, no longer wished to receive convict labour. Aberdeen, who had always disliked transportation as an 'inequitable' punishment,[24] was glad to see it replaced by the Penal Servitude Act, which made imprisonment in the United Kingdom the normal punishment for serious crimes.

Canada came back to haunt the one time Colonial Secretary, now Prime Minister. Pitt's Act of 1791 had set aside certain lands, the Clergy Reserves, for the upkeep of a Protestant clergy, which was at first interpreted to mean Anglican clergy. In 1840 the Act was amended to make it possible to use the revenue for other Protestant and even Catholic clergy. Under strong pressure from the Canadians, Aberdeen's government resolved to finally transfer control of these lands to the Canadian legislature; but they then made the embarrassing discovery that the support of the then Archbishop of Canterbury, William Howley, had only been secured for the 1840 measure by the promise that the imperial government would continue to guarantee an annual payment to the Protestant clergy. Howley had been dead for five years but Aberdeen determined to honour the promise to his old friend. An amendment to continue the guarantee was bound to provoke opposition but, he told the Queen, 'a well founded accusation of breach of good faith would have been much more formidable'.[25] Combining the two sensitive issues of colonial autonomy and religious prejudice, it was a contentious measure but it passed both Houses with safe majorities.

The Bill to admit Jews to Parliament was an even more delicate matter. It passed the Commons, as previous Jewish Disability Bills had done in 1848, 1849 and 1851, but the real stumbling block was the House of Lords. Even in the Commons, one Peelite junior minister, Lord Alfred Hervey, felt compelled to vote against it. Aberdeen refused to ask for his resignation. He told Russell, 'I was so late a convert myself, that I felt it would be unreasonable to do so.'[26] He was surprised to find his government not more divided.

With considerable courage he decided to introduce the Second Reading in the Lords himself. He reminded the House that, although he had not taken part in the discussion, he had voted against the Bill two years earlier. He had, he said, changed his mind early in 1852 and spoken of the matter to Gladstone and Newcastle. He strongly denied that he had changed his position because of the 'recent political combination'. Graham's Diary certainly gives a rather different impression of his conversion [27] and, although he was usually uncomfortably clear-sighted about his own motives, he may for once have been deceiving himself. If so, he made up for it by the quality of his speech.

He chose to put the matter in the whole context of anti-semitism. Men had felt justified in persecuting the Jews on the grounds that they had committed a crime of 'inconceivable magnitude' and had deliberately taken it upon their own heads. But, even if that were the case, Christians should remember that it was not for them to take vengeance. A Jew was the only person still precluded from full civil and political rights in Britain. Since they assumed all the other obligations of Englishmen, they could not continue to be treated as aliens. Logically Parliament should be confined to members of the established Church but it already included dissenters and, Aberdeen hinted, atheists. Technically Jews were excluded not by law but by the need to swear an oath on 'the true faith of a Christian'. Such oaths, he stated quite boldly, were not in concert with modern views. Finally, he warned his hearers of the still continuing danger of a constitutional clash between Lords and Commons. Aberdeen had obviously devoted much thought to his speech and the principles behind it, but he spoke in vain. The opposition was led by Lord Shaftesbury, who dwelt on the principle that only a Christian had the right to make laws which bound a Christian Church. The second Reading was defeated by 49 votes,[28] and Jews were not admitted to Parliament until 1866.

Irish religious issues continued to bedevil the government's path. They successfully warded off several attempts to reduce or abolish the grant to Maynooth College. A serious clash occurred at the end of May when a number of Irish Catholic MPs moved for a Select Committee to enquire into the ecclesiastical revenues of Ireland. Russell, who had burnt his fingers on the question in the 1830s, replied with unnecessary sharpness in a speech which threw doubt on the loyalty and patriotism of all Catholics.[29] The Catholic members of the government, William Keogh, the Irish Solicitor General, William Monsell, who was Clerk of the Ordnance, and John Sadleir, a Lord of the Treasury, felt compelled to offer Aberdeen their resignations. A defiant Russell offered his resignation instead. This was out of the question. As Graham wrote to Aberdeen: 'Lord John's secession from your Government at this juncture, as a Martyr to his strong Protestant convictions, would convulse the country, and would overthrow your Administration.'[30] On the other hand, the loss of Irish support would have been disastrous in view of the government's precarious majority in the Commons. The Duke of Newcastle was persuaded to exert his influence with the Irish. Aberdeen himself wrote a letter to Monsell, rejecting the idea of a Select Committee, but assuring him that Russell's views were not shared by the rest of the Cabinet. Irish support was retained but at the cost of offending Russell.[31]

A sorely-tried Aberdeen attempted to hold the balance in all Irish matters, even the Six Mile Bridge affair. During the 1852 election, a mob had attacked some soldiers escorting voters to the poll in County Clare. The soldiers had opened fire killing two men, and a local coroner's jury had wanted to indict them for murder. Protestant opinion was outraged but Aberdeen would have seen no objection to such a course so long as the leaders of the mob were also brought to trial.[32]

Even Irish issues paled beside the great crisis of parliamentary reform. Aberdeen had hesitated many times about parliamentary reform but, as with Jewish disabilities, once his mind was made up he became deeply committed. Throughout his battle for parliamentary reform inside the Cabinet in the last months of 1853, Russell was supported by the Peelites and opposed by a number of the old Whigs – and of the Peelites Aberdeen and Newcastle were by far the most radical. In the spring of 1854, when Russell concluded that, in the face of the worsening international situation, parliamentary reform would have to be abandoned, it was – contrary to public belief – Aberdeen who tried hardest to persuade him to go on.[33]

Russell had announced to the Commons in February 1853 that the reform question would be taken up in the 1854 session and it was during a holiday in Scotland, in the summer of 1853, that he began to draft his plans. The notorious corruption of the 1852 election, which had led to a seemingly endless succession of election petitions, was an additional spur. Russell broached the matter in Cabinet in November and a committee, consisting of Graham, Newcastle, Granville, Palmerston and Wood, in addition to Russell himself, was chosen to consider the question. Serious difficulties might have been anticipated from the beginning because Palmerston had made it clear when the coalition was formed that he, like Lansdowne, was opposed to reform but at first Aberdeen was optimistic. He told the Queen on 19 November that there had been more agreement in the committee than he expected and three days later he assured her that the Cabinet had agreed to Russell's proposals, although some ministers had reservations about some portions of them. 'So far as Lord Aberdeen is himself concerned', he added, 'he could have wished that the franchise had been more extended, and the measure somewhat more liberal.'[34]

The reforms, as they evolved during the next few months, covered a very wide field. Two Bills were drafted to deal with bribery at elections. Aberdeen himself had been interested in proposals which Lord Shaftesbury had put forward earlier to abolish voting booths and allow voting papers to be collected by officials. The voting papers would have been signed but could be handed to the official Collector sealed. This novel suggestion, which would have made both bribery and intimidation difficult, was not followed up.[35]

The most important measure, however, dealt with re-distribution and the extension of the franchise. Russell proposed to take 29 seats from 19 boroughs which had fewer than 300 voters or a population of less than 5,000. 33 boroughs, which had fewer than 500 electors or 10,000 population, would be allowed to retain one member. In addition, St Albans and Sudbury were to be disfranchised for corruption. This would give 66 seats for re-distribution. It was suggested that county constituencies with more than 100,000 inhabitants should have three members each. Some towns with more than 100,000 inhabitants would also qualify for a third member. Salford, with a population of 80,000 should have two (instead of one) members. Three 'new towns', Birkenhead, Burnley and Stalybridge, with populations of more than 10,000 should be given one member each. London should have four additional members and the graduates of London University should have their own member, as Oxford and Cambridge already had. In a more modest measure for Scotland, Edinburgh and Glasgow were to gain two members each and the Scottish Universities one.[36] Argyll was enthusiastic for the last proposal; Aberdeen was not.[37] At first sight, the proposals increased the influence of the county, that is landed, interest at the expense of the disfranchised boroughs but it was soon appreciated that this was misleading. The most populous counties to which the seats would be given were collections of towns rather than rural constituencies.

The franchise presented a bigger problem. Everyone agreed that the 'freemen', who had retained the vote in 1832, should be eliminated. They were notoriously bribable. Aberdeen called them 'odious in the publick eye'. But the freemen were for the most part working men and it was also felt that they must be replaced by more respectable representatives of the working class. Aberdeen himself wrote to Newcastle: 'I think the great distinctive nature of our Bill is the admission of the working Classes to the possession of the electoral franchise; and we ought to take care that this admission is really and liberally granted, avoiding anything like mere pretence.' The argument turned on whether the borough franchise should be lowered from £10 to £6 or to £5 or even to the 'household franchise' used in municipal elections. Aberdeen himself doubted whether £6 was low enough although if, as some argued, it would lead to a considerable increase in the electorate, 'all is well'. Aberdeen also felt that other proofs of 'prudence' and 'responsibility', such as £50 in a savings bank, might entitle a man to the vote.[38]

At the end of November, Aberdeen still believed that the tendency of his Cabinet colleagues was 'to make the Bill more liberal in some respects than as proposed by Lord John Russell'.[39] He was quickly disillusioned. Early in December Palmerston made it clear that he regarded it as a resigning matter. On 10 December he sent Aberdeen copies of correspondence he had had with Lansdowne. He had warned Lansdowne that there were three things he could not accept: the extent of the disfranchisement, the extent of the enfranchisement (that is, redistribution), and the changes in the borough franchise. Russell's plan would transfer representations from one class to another. He was not prepared to defend a measure of which he disapproved either in the House or at an election. He would be sorry to resign but he was not prepared to be 'dragged through the dirt by John Russell'. Lansdowne's reply had been less supportive than Palmerston had no doubt hoped. The measure, he argued, was mainly intended to remedy the defects of the 1832 Act, and it was universally agreed that bribery had increased since 1832. Aberdeen sent a soothing but pessimistic reply on 11 December and a firmer one on 14 December when, after consulting Graham and Russell, he told him that he could see no way of meeting his objections.[40]

There were those who would have been delighted to have seen Palmerston go. The Eastern Question had now reached a critical stage. Aberdeen warned the Queen of the possibilities on 6 December, after his first conversation with Palmerston.

Lord Aberdeen [he wrote] thinks it by no means improbable that Lord Palmerston may also desire to separate himself from the Government, in consequence of their pacific policy and in order to take the lead of the War Party and the Anti-Reformers in the House of Commons, who are essentially the same. Such a combination would undoubtedly be formidable; but Lord Aberdeen trusts that it would not be dangerous. At all events, it would tend greatly to the improvement of Lord John's Foreign Policy.[41]

The Queen replied that she was not at all surprised by Palmerston's attitude and added,

The Queen wd. very much advise Lord Aberdeen to let him go at once. He will be a source of mischief to the Country as long as he lives but the Queen has now had ample & varied experience that the mischief he is able to do in Office *exceeds any* he can do in opposition. If he is to go, – as he most probably will anyhow – let it be on the *reform question* wh. is unpopular ground, & not on a popular question of his choosing for wh. he has plenty of ingenuity.

Prince Albert too was extremely suspicious and, after consulting Russell, advised Aberdeen to get Palmerston's objections in writing 'to make all future misrepresentation impossible'. Russell complained that, if he did amend the measure, he would be attacked for want of liberality and Palmerston would stay in the background and retain his reputation as 'the real friend of liberty'. The Prince was however, alarmed by Russell's declaration that on foreign affairs he found himself closer to Palmerston than to Aberdeen and begged Aberdeen to end any misunderstandings with Russell.[42]

When Palmerston's resignation seemed to be a *fait accompli*, Aberdeen invited another leading Whig, Sir George Grey, to take the Home Office. Grey declined, possibly because he thought the ministry could not survive.[43] Others were doubtful too and, when Palmerston dropped hints through third parties that his decision was not final, Wood, Gladstone and, more particularly, Newcastle undertook to use their good offices. Aberdeen said that he would not stand in the way.[44]

466

The Queen was furious. She believed Palmerston 'has long meditated to drive out Lord Aberdeen, & this failing to break up the Government'. Palmerston had hoped to overthrow Russell at the same time but, because Lansdowne had refused to support him, he had failed and he had also realised that he had 'chosen unpopular ground' which would expose him to the condemnation of 'his former Radical Admirers'. She thought fears of Palmerston in opposition were 'unduly exaggerated' and would expect his character to suffer 'did she not know his unscrupulous dexterity' which would enable him to represent himself as 'an innocent injured man'.[45]

Aberdeen was unmoved by this plea. Whatever his private thoughts, when Palmerston wrote to him on 23 December to say that he had misunderstood Aberdeen's letter of 14 December to mean that no further amendments to the Bill could be considered, he accepted his explanation – although he did permit himself the tart comment that he did not see how Palmerston could have misunderstood when he was himself a member of the committee still revising the Bill.[46]

The incident led to unfortunate exchanges in the press. On 16 December *The Times* assured their readers that Palmerston had resigned on parliamentary reform, not on the Eastern Question. So far they were no doubt following government hints, but *The Times* also carried a leader, witty but offensive, suggesting that Palmerston was liable to these brain storms at certain seasons, and coming near to calling him a lunatic. Curiously enough, the style was rather like that of the young Aberdeen of Bentley Priory days. It is most improbable that the Prime Minister had anything to do with it, but suspicions lingered[47] and helped to fuel the personal nature of the attacks made on Aberdeen by the pro-Palmerston press.[48]

Aberdeen himself believed that Palmerston really did resign on the domestic and not the foreign question and he was probably right. Palmerston's instincts seem to have been to have gone on fighting on the Eastern Question from within the government, where the majority was now moving on to his side.[49] He felt deeply and bitterly about parliamentary reform, which he saw as the destruction of the social order. He wrote to Aberdeen on 12 February 1854 that the new voters would be 'Ignorant, poor and dependent . . . The System of organization which universally prevails among them by means of the Trade Unions, gives to their agitating Leaders an absolute Despotism over the Masses . . . Can it be expected that men who murder their children to get £9 to be spent on Drink will not sell their vote for whatever they can get for it?'[50] This hysteria from the darling of the radicals contrasts very strangely with the bold acceptance of real change and confidence in the working classes shown by the supposed reactionary and friend of despots, Aberdeen.

In the end, however, the outbreak of the Crimean War killed the Reform Bill. Despite the Eastern crisis, the new Bill was announced in the Queen's Speech on 31 January 1854 and Russell introduced it into the Commons on 13 February. It soon became clear that it would meet widespread opposition in the House, and on 25 February Russell suggested to Aberdeen that the measure should at least be postponed until after Easter. Aberdeen reacted sharply. Postponement, he said, would be tantamount to defeat and 'a regard for our honour and consistency demands that we should persevere'. He thought the Bill had found favour with the public 'as a liberal, wise and honest measure'.[51]

Graham stood by Aberdeen but Gladstone, Herbert and Wood all began to have doubts in view of the international situation, as Wood succinctly put it to Russell: '[The country] is now bent on war, & will not trouble itself about Reform.'[52] In vain Aberdeen contended that a war and the inevitable widening of taxation and other burdens was an argument for extending the franchise, not for postponing the measure. Palmerston had never ceased to fight to kill the Bill altogether. At the Cabinet meeting of 3 March the majority would have liked to have postponed the Bill for a year but, in the face of opposition from Aberdeen and Graham, they agreed only to postpone it until the end of April.[53]

On 23 March Russell told Aberdeen that he thought the best course would be for him (Russell) to resign and the government to abandon the Bill for the foreseeable future. Aberdeen still fought a rearguard action. He regretted that they had not proceeded with the Bill on 13 March. He might, he said, have been more sympathetic if he had thought that there was any prospect of a quick decisive war which would soon leave the way open for a return to domestic reforms. He now proposed that the Bill be postponed, but with a definite pledge to re–introduce it, come what might, the next year. He was unable to carry his Cabinet with him and Russell now seemed to be almost the firmest in his opposition to any such promise. Aberdeen made a final effort at the Cabinet meeting of 8 April to secure a definite pledge that the Bill would be re–introduced, although without any promise as to date. Palmerston, now supported by Lansdowne, held out against even this. Russell persisted in his determination to resign and the break up of the Cabinet seemed imminent.[54] In the end Russell was persuaded to remain and to announce to the Commons the reasons for the abandonment of the Bill. He did so in an unusually emotional speech in which he impressed the House by the sincerity of his attachment to Reform.[55] Very few suspected that it was Russell who had lost his nerve and Aberdeen who would have gone on.

Even in the short space of little more than one parliamentary session the coalition's record in domestic legislation was substantial. If it had been able to carry through its whole programme it would have been, as Bagehot saw, a great ministry. It was the Crimean War which was fatal to its plans, as it was to the reputation of its leader.

NOTES

1. Graham Papers, Diary, 23 Dec. 1852.
2. Argyll, *Memoirs* vol. 1, pp. 374–83.
3. Add. MSS 43191, Graham to Aberdeen, 4 Jan. 1853.
4. *Hansard*, 3rd ser., CXXIV, 17–23; RA A23/7 Aberdeen to Victoria, 6 Feb. 1853.

5. *Hansard*, 3rd ser., CXXIV, 10–17 (10 Feb. 1853).
6. Greville, vol. VII, pp. 39, 45–6, 56 (11 Feb., 1, 24 Mar. 1853).
7. Morley deals with the Budget at length, *Gladstone*, vol. 1, pp. 458–75. It is also discussed in detail by F. W. Hirst, *Gladstone as Financier and Economist*.
8. Argyll, *Memoirs* vol. 1, pp. 422–3.
9. RA C47/1, Aberdeen to Albert, 9 Apr. 1853.
10. Morley, vol. 1, pp. 465–6. Morley's account is based on memoranda which Gladstone himself kept, now in Add. MSS 44778; RA C47/2, Aberdeen to Albert, 12 Apr. 1853.
11. Add. MSS 44778, Memorandum, 13 Apr. 1853; RA C47/3, 4, Aberdeen to Albert, 15, 16 Apr. 1853.
12. RA C47/7, Russell to Victoria, 19 Apr. 1853.
13. Add. MSS 43051, Aberdeen to Leopold, 4 May 1853.
14. Add. MSS 43070, Gladstone to Aberdeen, 19 Apr. 1853; Add. MSS 44088, Aberdeen to Gladstone, 19 Apr. 1853; Aberdeen to Lieven, 23 May 1853, Jones–Parry, vol. 2, p. 644.
15. The Bill is most fully discussed in R. J. Moore, *Sir Charles Wood's Indian Policy, 1853–66*.
16. Add. MSS 43047, Aberdeen to Victoria, 20 Mar. 1853.
17. RA C47/32, 34, Aberdeen to Victoria, 21, 26 May 1853, /36, Victoria to Russell, 27 May 1853.
18. RA G3/8, Aberdeen to Victoria, 28 May 1853; RA C47/38, Albert, Memorandum of a conversation of Stockmar with Graham on 28 May 1853, /40, Aberdeen to Victoria, 31 May 1853; Add. MSS 44778, Gladstone, Memorandum, 10 June 1853.
19. R. J. Moore, 'The abolition of patronage in the Indian civil service', *Historical Journal* vii (1964), pp. 246–67.
20. RA E45/19, Aberdeen to Victoria, 3 Apr. 1853. A Scottish Bill was brought in in 1854 but it too fell a victim to the Crimean War and vested interest.
21. *Hansard*, 3rd ser., CXXIX, 972–3.
22. PP, XXVII (1854) 1–31, 'Report on the organisation of the permanent civil service'.
23. RA A23/71, Aberdeen to Victoria, 26 Jan. 1854; Add. MSS 44163, Graham to Gladstone, 4 Jan. 1854.
24. RQC 334/87, Aberdeen to Gurney, 19 Feb. 1836; RA A23/26, Aberdeen to Victoria, 11 May 1853.
25. RA A23/17, Aberdeen to Victoria, 13 Mar. 1853.
26. PRO 30/22/10H, Aberdeen to Russell, 25 Feb. 1853.
27. Graham Papers, Diary, 21 Dec. 1853.
28. *Hansard*, 3rd ser., CXXVI, 753–9, 759–67, 795 (29 Apr. 1853).
29. *Hansard*, 3rd ser., CXXVII, 942–955 (31 May 1853).
30. Add. MSS 43250, Monsell to Aberdeen, 2 June 1853; Add. MSS 43067, Russell to Aberdeen, 2 June 1853; Add. MSS 43191, Graham to Aberdeen, 2 June 1853.
31. Add. MSS 43188, Clarendon to Aberdeen, 2 June 1853 – Clarendon suggested the letter; Add. MSS 43067, Aberdeen to Russell, 2 June 1853, Russell to Aberdeen, 2 June 1853 (2nd letter); Add. MSS 43250, Aberdeen to Monsell, 3 June 1853; Whyte, pp. 99–100.
32. *Hansard*, 3rd ser., CXXIV, 31, 32, 338 (11, 21 Feb. 1853); Add. MSS 43049, Aberdeen to Palmerston, 24 Feb. 1853; RA A23/14, Aberdeen to Victoria, 27 Feb. 1853.

33. Greville, vol. VII, p. 153 (15 Apr. 1854).

34. Add. MSS 43048, Aberdeen to Victoria, 10, 19, 22 Nov. 1853; Graham Papers, Diary, 21 Dec. 1852; cf. Greville, vol. VII, p. 104 (12 Nov. 1853).

35. RA F10/28, Aberdeen to Albert, 15 July 1853 encl. /29, Shaftesbury's Bill. Aberdeen thought it 'deserved consideration' but Russell opposed it because it was very like the secret ballot; Add. MSS 43067, Aberdeen to Russell, 14 July 1853, Russell to Aberdeen, 15 July 1853.

36. RA F11/45, 46, Drafts of reform measures.

37. PRO 30/22/11B, Aberdeen to Russell, 31 Dec. 1853. See above p. 290.

38. Newcastle MSS, Ne 10017, Aberdeen to Newcastle, 30 Dec. 1853; cf. PRO 30/22/11B, Aberdeen to Russell, 31 Dec. 1853 Greville was mistaken in thinking that Aberdeen would not go as low as £5, Greville, vol. VII, p. 104 (12 Nov. 1853).

39. RA F10/44, Aberdeen to Victoria, 23 Nov. 1853.

40. Add. MSS 43049, Palmerston to Aberdeen, 10 Dec. 1853 encl. Palmerston to Lansdowne, 8 Dec. 1853 and Lansdowne to Palmerston, 9 Dec. 1853, Aberdeen to Palmerston, 11, 14 Dec. 1853.

41. RA F11/1, Aberdeen to Victoria, 6 Dec. 1853.

42. Add. MSS 43048, Victoria to Aberdeen, 7 Dec. 1853, Albert to Aberdeen, 9 Dec. 1853 (2nd letter).

43. Add. MSS 43197 Aberdeen to Grey, 17 Dec. 1853, Grey to Aberdeen, 19 Dec. 1853; PRO 30/22/11B, Aberdeen to Russell, 20 Dec. 1853.

44. Add. MSS 44088, Gladstone to Aberdeen, 18 Dec. 1853; PRO 30/22/11B, Aberdeen to Russell, 20 Dec. 1853; Newcastle Papers, Ne 10015, Aberdeen to Newcastle, 22 Dec. 1853; Stanmore, p. 273.

45. Add. MSS 43048, Victoria to Aberdeen, 21 Dec. 1853. Victoria's indignation against Palmerston was building up to a dangerous pitch. In September she was annoyed when Aberdeen insisted on her receiving Palmerston as minister in attendance despite the scandal in 1840 when Palmerston had entered a lady's bedroom at Windsor Castle. Aberdeen who was not so shocked as the royal couple, insisted that, as Home Secretary and, in the interests of the government, Palmerston must be received. Add. MSS 43047, Victoria to Aberdeen, 8 Sept. 1853, RA A81/42, Aberdeen to Victoria, 11 Sept. 1853, cf. Connell, p. 121. Victoria never ceased to complain of him, e.g. Add. MSS 43048, Victoria to Aberdeen, 21 Nov. 1853, when she protested that he should not have received a deputation on foreign affairs.

46. Add. MSS 43049, Palmerston to Aberdeen, 23 Dec. 1853, Aberdeen to Palmerston, 24 Dec. 1853.

47. *The Morning Herald* of 17 December bluntly accused Aberdeen of having written it.

48. *The Times* 16 Dec. 1853, *Morning Chronicle* 17 Dec. 1853, *Morning Post, Daily News*, 17, 27, Dec. 1853. All the relevant press cuttings are preserved in RA A81.

49. He said as much in his letter to Lansdowne, Add. MSS 43049. Palmerston to Lansdowne, 8 Dec. 1853.

50. Add. MSS 43049, Palmerston to Aberdeen, 12 Feb. 1854.

51. Add. MSS 43067, Russell to Aberdeen, 25 Feb. 1854, Aberdeen to Russell, 26 Feb. 1854.

52. Add. MSS 43191, Graham to Aberdeen, 26 Feb. 1854; PRO 30/22/11C, Wood to Russell, 28 Feb. 1854.

53. Add. MSS 44778, Gladstone, Memorandum, 3 Mar. 1854.
54. Add. MSS 43067, Russell to Aberdeen, 23 Mar. 1854; PRO 30/22/11C, Aberdeen to Russell, 24 Mar. 1854; RA F11/97, 98, 99, 100, Albert, Memoranda, April 1854.
55. *Hansard* 3rd ser., CXXXII, 836–44 (11 Feb. 1854); Greville, vol. VII, p. 154 (15 Apr. 1854); Spencer Walpole, vol. II, p. 209.

CHAPTER TWENTY-EIGHT

The Eastern Crisis, 1853–1854

Aberdeen and Palmerston were entirely agreed on one thing as they entered upon the coalition. They must prepare for war. But they prepared for the wrong war. The war they expected was with France, where Louis Napoleon had been proclaimed Emperor on 4 December. A mood of tension and excitement began to grip the British public which was eventually to find an outlet in war with Russia and which found immediate expression in the unusual willingness of Parliament to vote increased Army and Navy Estimates.

Palmerston told Aberdeen that he did not expect war immediately. 'We are safe', he wrote, 'for 1853 and I should hope for 1854.' But he had no doubt that Napoleon III was 'working hard to place himself in such a Position of relative Strength as to enable him to strike a stunning Blow whenever a dispute may arise, or whenever it may suit his Purpose to do so.' Since parliamentary opinion was fickle, it would be unwise to spend the additional money on extra men, who might have to be discharged the next year. They should rather spend it on permanent works, dockyards, harbours of refuge, fortification in the Channel Islands and the completion of the steam engine factory at Plymouth. He wanted to have regular meetings with Lord Hardinge, the Commander-in-Chief, about defence policy. Aberdeen entirely endorsed Palmerston's views. He no longer rejected the motto, *Bellum para pacem habebis*. Napoleon III was not Louis Philippe. 'The danger of war', he replied, 'is by no means imminent, although quite sufficient to justify our reasonable precautions.'[1]

The belief that the real danger came from Napoleon III determined British policy at the beginning of 1853, although Aberdeen's suspicions were not quite so strong of those of Graham, who told Palmerston in May that they could never rely on the French in the East since 'Nicholas may be suspected; but Napoleon is known to set at nought all moral obligations.' Once Britain was thoroughly committed, Graham feared, France might well do a deal with Russia to expel Britain from the Mediterranean, in which France would get Egypt, Malta and Minorca, and Russia would get Constantinople, Greece and the Ionian Islands. Plausibility was lent to such suspicions by Napoleon's grandiose ambitions and the hints he dropped in March 1853 that he no longer regarded the treaties of 1815 as binding and that he would certainly regard them as cancelled in the event of a new European war.[2]

It is therefore ironic that the Crimean War should have been ascribed to the supposed pacificism of the British Prime Minister. Aberdeen was never a pacifist, conscious though he was that war was the last terrible arbitrament, justifiable only when all other means had failed. He gave one unfortunate hostage to fortune when, in July, he used the phrase 'peace at any price' to the Piedmontese envoy, D'Azeglio, although his explanation to Graham of how that came about is almost certainly accurate. D'Azeglio told Aberdeen during an after-dinner conversation at Stafford House, that he was returning to Turin immediately and, when Aberdeen expressed some surprise, 'he said he thought it probable that out of the complications in the East something might arise which would be advantageous for Italy & that he wished to be on the spot'. Aberdeen was determined to nip any such suggestion in the bud. He replied, 'I see what you want, you expect to get another leaf of the artichoke; but we must have no war; *il nous faut la paix à tout prix.*' He assured Graham, 'This was said half jestingly & in some surprise at the declaration of Azeglio to me.' Nevertheless the story was very quickly round London.[3]

Lord Strangford's anecdote that Princess Lieven told him that Aberdeen wrote to her when the Russian forces crossed the Pruth (in July), assuring her that he would never be associated with a government engaged in war, seems to be a *canard*. He had written on 23 May, 'I hope you do not at Paris expect a European war quite so much as we do in London' and spoken vaguely of his own possible retirement, but this was clearly in a domestic context. It might be a reference to his letter of 8 September, in which he said that he would spare no effort to preserve the peace and that, although public opinion was very excited, he did not think that a government which declared war would last three months. But Princess Lieven was never a reliable witness.[4]

It is no doubt true that the Tsar thought Aberdeen's government was likely to be more friendly to Russia than its immediate predecessor had been. He attached more importance to the 1844 conversations than did the British government. Throughout the troubles of 1848-49 Aberdeen had proclaimed his attachment to the *status quo* in Europe and had never represented the Tsar as a despot hostile to the liberties of Europe. When the coalition government was formed in December 1852, Brunnow, the Russian Ambassador in England, hailed the advent of his old friend with the greatest delight and, as early as 24 December, sent him a note asking for a private interview to talk about affairs in the East.[5] During the early months of 1853 Aberdeen and Brunnow saw each other and corresponded quite frequently. Palmerston came to have grave suspicions of Aberdeen's private dealings with Brunnow, fearing that the Prime Minister was giving the Russians the impression that they had nothing in reality to fear from British policy. At the outset Aberdeen saw no harm in continuing his old friendship with Brunnow. He had always believed that much might be accomplished by informal diplomacy and had not hesitated to have long and confidential correspondence with Guizot and Metternich. The wisdom of the Prime Minister conducting a private correspondence with a foreign ambassador with the imperfect knowledge of the Foreign Secretary may be questionable but, in any case, the correspondence almost ceased after September 1853, that is to say when the crisis became acute.[6]

The Tsar's decision to embark on what became known as the Seymour conversations and to look for a new understanding with Britain, was taken before he knew that Aberdeen was to be the British Prime Minister.[7] The situation in the East had suddenly deteriorated as a result of Austrian and French, not Russian actions. The Austrians had some excuse for their intervention. A complicated local quarrel had led Omer Pasha, the Turkish Governor of Bosnia, to invade the quasi-independent state of Montenegro. The Austrians, with Russian approval, sent Count Leiningen to Constantinople with peremptory demands that peace be made with Montenegro and Omer Pasha removed from Bosnia. The Turks gave in, although they refused to accept some additional terms which would have given the Austrians the right to protect Christians in Bosnia. The Russians did not fail to note the speed with which Turks yielded to a threat of force.

The French intervention was harder to justify. Louis Napoleon, bent on gaining the support of the clerical party, chose to re–assert the long–neglected French rights over the Holy Places, including the Church of the Holy Sepulchre in Jerusalem. Nicholas, as the champion of the Orthodox Church, could hardly fail to respond. The Sultan, under heavy pressure from both sides, made contradictory promises. In 1852, however, the French seemed to be having the better of the contest. In February the Sultan granted most of the Latin Church's demands and, in May, the powerful French warship, the *Charlemagne*, sailed through the Dardanelles bringing the French Ambassador, Charles Lavalette, back from leave. The passage of the *Charlemagne*, although not a breach of the letter of the 1841 Convention, which allowed for the ceremonial use of warships on such occasions, was universally recognised as a breach of its spirit. In the East, as elsewhere, the French seemed to be embarking on an aggressive course.

It was not unnatural in the circumstances that the Tsar should seek to open discussions with the British Ambassador, Sir Hamilton Seymour, to find out where Britain stood. It was only in retrospect when these conversations were published, together with the 1844 Memorandum, when public excitement was already uncontrollable, that they came to assume any sinister significance. Seymour may have encouraged the Tsar more than he realised when (by his own account in order to induce the Tsar to speak freely) he expressed sympathy. In any case, the Tsar's views were what the British government wished to hear. He still preferred to keep the Ottoman empire intact. If it collapsed, Britain and Russia must concert their policy. The contingency planning which would have given Russia control of Moldavia and Wallachia and Serbia, Britain control of Egypt and perhaps Crete, and have ensured that Constantinople remained independent would at least have been preferable to Graham's nightmare scenario of a Franco-Russian deal, reminiscent of Tilsit. The sentence which was least acceptable to the British government was the Tsar's hint that he might, in some circumstances, be compelled temporarily to occupy Constantinople.[8] Aberdeen, like most of his Cabinet colleagues, was unwilling to be drawn into speculation about future arrangements. Lord John Russell, as Foreign Secretary, sent back an essentially non-committal reply, pointing out that the Ottoman empire might yet survive for a long time.[9]

Russell was also responsible for the decision to send Stratford Canning, now Lord Stratford de Redcliffe, back to Constantinople. Stratford was currently on leave in Britain and had indicated his wish to give up his post. Russell, however, told Aberdeen that he thought it would be 'expedient' if Stratford went back, at least for a short time, mainly because he was the only British diplomat with much influence over the Turks. Stratford in fact served his government loyally during the next few years. Far from being a war-monger, the only occasions that he bent his instructions a little were when he tried to prevent precipitate action.[10] At the same time he was known to be *persona non grata* with the Russians, who had declined to receive him as Ambassador in 1833. More seriously, he was deeply distrusted by many members of his own government. Their private comments on him were often virulent. Graham spoke of his 'adverse influence'. Clarendon complained of his 'ungovernable temper' and said that he seemed to think his own government 'not worth communicating with'.[11] Aberdeen shared in the general distrust but his attitude to Stratford was always tinged with unease, perhaps dating back to a suspicion that in 1829 he had been right and Aberdeen had been wrong. In any case, once Stratford had been sent back, it became impossible to recall him without creating even more serious misunderstandings about British policy.

It was Russell who began to formulate Stratford's general instructions but Clarendon who completed them. As the parliamentary session approached, Russell again insisted that he could not combine the Leadership of the House with the Foreign Office. Aberdeen had already been annoyed by an item which had appeared in the *Globe* on 15 January, which probably originated with Russell himself, saying that he would resign the Foreign Office at the beginning of the session on public, not personal, grounds. The Queen had immediately queried this and Aberdeen assured her that, if a change were made, it would be entirely for Russell's convenience.[12] Russell insisted, relying on some notes kept by his wife the previous December, that Aberdeen and Clarendon had given 'their words of honour as gentlemen' that he should resign the Foreign Office when Parliament met, adding petulantly, 'It is not my fault that all this was not stated to the Queen at the time.' He ruled out the idea that he would take the Duchy of Lancaster but suggested he might take the Home Office. An exasperated Aberdeen replied that Russell could have taken what office he liked the previous December but the Home Office was now filled. He still felt grave doubt about the constitutional propriety of Russell retaining the Lead without a substantive office and felt that there would be an obvious absurdity in Russell resigning without meeting Parliament. Later in the session, he suggested, it would be easier.[13] There was a certain lack of logic in Aberdeen's position. Either there was a constitutional barrier to Russell's proposal or there was not. If there was not, and Aberdeen conceded that Russell could judge the Commons' likely view of the convention better than he could, there was nothing to be gained by delay. Since he had not taken a minute of the earlier conversation himself at the time, he could not challenge Lady John's minute, but he had understood that, if Russell gave up the Foreign Office, he would take the Duchy. Russell got his way. Aberdeen concluded the correspondence by saying that they must now leave it to parliament and the public to judge. If they were to continue to work cordially together, this kind of 'conversation', that is recrimination about what had and had not been said, must cease.[14] The matter was smoothed over but the fragile foundations of the coalition had been revealed.

Clarendon became Foreign Secretary on 21 February. While still in London, Stratford had submitted a memorandum of the instructions he would like to receive. Much was unexceptional but, as Russell warned Aberdeen, 'Lord Stratford evidently wishes to have the Mediterranean fleet at his command. This you will hardly like.'[15] Aberdeen did not like it. His reply to Russell shows very clearly the preconceptions with which he first confronted the Eastern Question. They included a deep distrust of the Turks and a mixture of respect and unease towards Stratford. He counselled Russell to be very cautious:

'The awareness of prompt and effective aid on the approach of danger' given by us to the Porte, would in all probability produce war. These Barbarians hate us all, and would be delighted to take their chance of some advantage, by embroiling us with the other Powers of Christendom. It may be necessary to give them our moral support, and to endeavour to prolong their existence; but we ought to regard as the greatest misfortune, any engagement which compelled us to take up arms for the Turks.

He complained that Stratford was not very consistent in his description of the Turkish Government:

He refers to their present course of rashness, vacillations and disorder; and speaks of their mal-administration as hopeless. At the same time, he looks to their power of carrying into effect a system of internal improvement, particularly in the essential branches of justice, revenue, roads, police and military defence.

'I do not believe', he continued, 'that any Power at this time, entertains the intention of overthrowing the Turkish Empire; but it is certainly true that any quarrel might lead to this event; or, as Lord Stratford says, it might take place without any such a deliberate intention on the part of any one of these Powers.' Britain should be careful to retain her independence and freedom to act as circumstances might require. 'Above all', he concluded, 'we ought not to trust the disposal of the Mediterranean fleet, which is Peace or War, to the discretion of any man.'[16]

In the short run, however, the Eastern Question seemed less pressing than terrorism in Europe and some irritating new quarrels with the United States. There was an attempt to assassinate the Austrian Emperor by a Hungarian on 18 February and fresh disturbances in Milan. The Austrians believed that both events were instigated by Kossuth and Mazzini and co–ordinated from London, by a mysterious body called 'the London Committee'. They also suspected the British of supplying arms. Russell admitted after the Milan rising, 'The "poignards of London make" and the "London Committee" are rather awkward.'[17] All Aberdeen's continental friends combined to put pressure on him. Guizot told him that events in Milan and Vienna had caused a sensation and everyone asked why London harboured such men. The Princess Lieven demanded, 'Kossuth et Mazzini peuvent-ils conserver des droits à l'hospitalité britannique lorsqu'ils se vantent patemment d'envoyer les révolutions et les poignards sur le Continent et que nous voyons les fruits de leur atroces prédications?' It was Metternich who supplied chapter and verse. The orders for the assassination, he said, were dated from London. He begged Aberdeen to stop giving asylum to men 'qui font des appels à tous les genres de desordre, y compris le meutre et la spoliation'. He could not believe that England had no law to cover the situation. Leopold of the Belgians also protested.[18]

The British government was acutely embarrassed. Although Aberdeen told Leopold that they could only act within the existing law, they certainly had no wish to be known as the terrorist capital of Europe.[19] Clarendon thought they must do as other Courts had done and send a special envoy to congratulate the Emperor on his escape. He persuaded *The Times* to express indignation at the misuse some refugees had made of their asylum in Britain. Clarendon told Aberdeen that he would like to know what grounds there were for saying that the orders for the murders came from the Central Committee in London and added wistfully, 'I must say our Police give us very little assistance. I knew everything that happened in Dublin in 1848.'[20] In fact the government was kept fairly well informed of the activities of the leading refugees[21] but they were adamant that they could not introduce new legislation to deal with the situation, although they would prosecute if the refugees offended against British law. Although he treated the matter with his usual calm, Aberdeen was not unaffected by the idea that there might be an international revolutionary conspiracy afoot and it strengthened his reluctance to see Britain plunge into an international conflict which could only destroy the stability of Europe and give the revolutionaries their chance.

The quarrels with America, although apparently trivial in themselves, also made Aberdeen anxious, as he had been in 1841, to keep the peace in Europe. The first dispute, which concerned fishing rights in territorial waters off the North American coast, was settled in June 1854 by a reciprocal agreement between the United States and British North America.[22] The Mosquito Coast dispute was more troublesome and basically more serious because what was at stake was the control of the crucial area of Central America through which any canal from the Pacific to the Atlantic must pass. The Californian gold rush had once again brought the project to the attention of the public. Britain was unwilling to see the region completely dominated by the United States and determined to keep her own stake in the area, consisting of Belize and the Mosquito Coast Protectorate. In 1850 the two Powers signed the Clayton–Bulwer Treaty to demarcate their claims, but its meaning was in dispute from the beginning. In 1852 Britain offended the Americans by confirming her jurisdiction over the Bay Islands, south of Belize. A local dispute led to an American warship bombarding Greytown on the Mosquito Coast. Clarendon and Graham, as well as Palmerston, spoke seriously of the possibility of war with the United States. In the end it was the Crimean War which persuaded the British government to extinguish their quarrel with the Americans.[23]

The Eastern Question began to move towards a crisis in February 1853, when the Tsar despatched Prince Menshikov to Constantinople to get guarantees of the position of the Orthodox Church which would offset the concessions which the Sultan had granted to the Catholics. Noting Leinigen's success, the Russian government instructed Menshikov to be peremptory in his demands, although Menshikov was hardly the man to need such instructions. The French Ambassador, Lavalette, promptly responded by summoning the French fleet to the Eastern Mediterranean. The British chargé d'affaires, Colonel Rose, sent a similar request to the British fleet at Malta but their commander, Admiral Dundas, refused to move without the direct authorisation of the Admiralty.

The first important decision was thus left clearly to the Cabinet in London. As the crisis developed, the Cabinet divided into hawks and doves, corresponding roughly, although only roughly, to the old division of Whigs and Peelites. Palmerston and Aberdeen emerged as the protagonists of the two policies. Ironically, they started from the same premise, that the Tsar did not want war. Palmerston, however, believed that the best way of avoiding war was to issue clear warnings to the Tsar, to respond to any forward moves with counter-moves, especially fleet movements, which would show the Tsar that he was standing into danger and, Palmerston believed, almost certainly persuade him to alter course. Aberdeen, on the other hand, believed that the whole crisis could be settled by quiet behind–the–scenes diplomacy, employing if necessary the good offices of the Great Powers of Europe. In this strategy threats and fleet movements would be counter-productive because they would make it difficult, if not impossible, for the Tsar to alter his course. Either policy, carried through consistently, might have brought success. What was to prove fatal was the mixing of the two. No one was more conscious than Aberdeen, in bittter retrospect, that on two vital occasions, in September and December, 1853, he had surrendered to the hawks. Each time he had done so because his belief in the Tsar's essentially pacific intentions had been understandably, although temporarily, shaken.

In assessing Aberdeen's responsibility for what ensued one must also take into account the fact that Aberdeen's position within his own Cabinet was exceptionally weak. It was not simply the fact that he was the Prime Minister of a coalition government. His own parliamentary support was almost derisorily small. He did not have the Prime Minister's usual ultimate weapon of threatening resignation and appealing to the country. His most powerful colleague, Russell, had made it all too apparent that he was waiting impatiently for the succession which he felt was rightfully his. At best Aberdeen could only negotiate with his own Cabinet. He could not command it.

He could, of course, have resigned as an individual. He later told Hudson Gurney that he wished he had done so.[24] He would certainly have been spared a burden of personal guilt and his posthumous reputation would have been better. He did not do so for a number of reasons. The wishes of the Court played some part.[25] More importantly, he believed that his opponents were wild men. His distrust of Palmerston's foreign policy in 1848–49 had been deep and sincere. Now a piece of ill-timed bluster could easily take Europe over the edge of the precipice. By 1854 Palmerston was widening the issue from the defence of Constantinople, where Aberdeen agreed with him, to grandiose plans for Poland and Italy.[26] It was understandable if Aberdeen felt that he alone represented sanity. More than that, he felt that if he was allowed to carry out his own policy, he was the right man to find a peaceful solution. Clarendon, himself overstrained by unremitting anxiety, complained that Aberdeen haunted him constantly seeking him out to discuss what should be done.[27] Aberdeen was conscious of his own long experience and his good record of settling dangerous disputes. He over-estimated his powers, but he does not emerge from these critical months, as he is so often portrayed, as a weak man. He stuck to his post because he felt it was his duty to do so. He made an obstinate, but ultimately unsuccessful, stand for his policy.

Aberdeen was able to carry his colleagues with him when the Eastern Question first came before the Cabinet in late March. They endorsed Graham's opinion that Dundas had acted wisely in refusing to move, although Graham himself suggested to Clarendon that they should reinforce the Mediterranean fleet.[28] Aberdeen's own first impression had been that the Russian demands were reasonable and that the fault lay entirely with the French. He had written to Russell at the end of January,

The case is this. About a year ago, the Sultan issued a Firman, accompanied by an Autograph letter to the Emperor of Russia, which confirmed certain privileges possessed by the Greeks in the Holy Land. This Firman, in consequence of the exertions of M. Lavalette, and the threat of a French fleet on the Coast of Syria, has not been executed; and this is what the Emperor now demands.

He believed that Lavalette was about to be recalled and told Russell with satisfaction that this was 'of good augury as disavowing the mischievous activity which has been the origin of this dispute'.[29]

The French fleet movement led Brunnow to disclose a little more about Menshikov's instructions to the British government. Aberdeen still thought them satisfactory. He told the Queen that they related only to the Greek Church at Jerusalem. The demands might humiliate Turkey and wound French vanity but there was no question of territorial aggression. At the same time he had misgivings. If the Turks were 'obstinate', the situation could become serious but he believed that the Tsar would consult Britain before taking any action. Much would depend on the personal character of Menshikov. He hoped that they would all await the arrival of Stratford when he was sure that the matter could be settled without proceeding to 'extremities'. The Queen replied rather tartly that Russian actions at Constantinople were not those one would expect towards 'a sick friend for whose life there exists much solicitude'.[30]

Stratford arrived in Constantinople on 5 April and, with his help, the original dispute about the guardianship of the Holy Places was settled early in May.

But it now became apparent that Menshikov's demands were much wider than Aberdeen had supposed them to be. On 5 May Menshikov presented the Turks with what was virtually an ultimatum demanding that they agree to a new Convention. The first Article of this asked for a guarantee of the rights, privileges and immunities which the Orthodox Churches had enjoyed *ab antiquo* in the Ottoman Empire; the second that any rights granted to other Churches should be automatically extended to the Orthodox Church. The problem about the first was that it could mean almost anything from a pious, but empty, assertion of traditional rights, to a claim for a virtual Russian protectorate over the twelve million Orthodox Christians within the Ottoman Empire. Menshikov's bullying tactics led both the Turkish government and western statesmen to believe that it meant something closer to the second rather than the first interpretation. It probably did not require any argument by Stratford to persuade the Turkish government that the ultimatum must be rejected. Menshikov left Constantinople on 22 May.

The British government, although absorbed in difficult domestic questions, had now to decide what course to take. The two parties in the Cabinet came into open conflict for the first time. Palmerston wrote to Graham on 29 May, marshalling the arguments in favour of sending the fleet to the Bosphorus, even though this would be a clear breach of the 1841 Convention. Graham told Aberdeen: 'Palmerston's Tone is eager and uncompromising. I am afraid that he meditates mischief or early separation.' Palmerston emphasised that British policy had always been to defend Turkey against Russia. He countered the argument that this would be to support 'a barbarous Mahommedan against a Civilised Christian Power' with a rather over-strained plea that Turkey was now more civilised than Russia. Much of his letter was taken up with combating the navy's opinion, represented by Sir Baldwin Walker, that a British fleet in the Bosphorus would be in a very dangerous position because a Russian force could slip across the Black Sea to Bourgas, take Constantinople from the land side, and then march down the Dardanelles, and trap the fleet.[31]

Aberdeen remembered precisely the same argument in 1829. He counter attacked with energy. To send the fleet to Turkish waters would look like a 'vigorous and decisive step' to the public but in fact would be nothing of the sort. The only effect would be to release the Tsar from the obligations he had 'voluntarily contracted'. It certainly would not protect the Turks. Aberdeen entirely agreed with Admiral Walker. 'I know the spot well', he added rather crushingly. The Russians could land 15 or 20 miles from Constantinople and advance from the land side, even if there were a British fleet in the Dardanelles. Aberdeen drew on his own experience again to point out that, at this time of the year, when the northerly winds blew, ships could be delayed a long time sailing up the Bosphorus. The logic of this was that if they really wanted to protect Constantinople they would have to send the fleet into the Black Sea, with all that this would imply in terms of a direct challenge to Russia. Aberdeen argued that until they knew more about the circumstances in which the diplomatic rupture represented by Menshikov's departure had taken place, they should not assume that it meant war. If the Tsar violated his engagements to

Britain, 'if we act at all, we ought to resent it worthily, and not by a poor demonstration, which only insults him, and does nothing effectual either for us, or for the Power we desire to protect.' For good measure, he ridiculed Palmerston's new-found admiration of the Turk. He would, he told Graham, 'as soon think of preferring the Koran to the Bible, as of comparing the Christianity and civilization of Russia to the fanaticism & immorality of the Turks.'[32] Aberdeen's low opinion of the Turks, formed so many years before, was still a factor in his estimate of the situation in 1853.

Brunnow, who had been in occasional confidential communication with Aberdeen since the beginning of the Menshikov mission, asked him for an interview on 18 May and sent him a draft of the proposed Convention on 21 May with assurances that there was nothing in it that encroached on the independence, integrity or dignity of the Ottoman Empire. Russia only wanted confirmation of existing privileges. The next day he sent a memorandum of all his conversations with Russell and Clarendon since the beginning of the ministry, asking Aberdeen to tell him if he objected to anything. He, Brunnow, only wanted to avoid misconstructions. Aberdeen returned the memorandum with the simple comment that it seemed to be accurate. Brunnow wrote again on 29 May, asking to see Aberdeen before he sent to St Petersburg on 31 May, commenting, 'You remember, I am sure, the Duke of Wellington saying: now, we have got into a mess, let us see how we shall get out of it. In fact, this *is* the question. All the rest, as you often say, is stuff.'[33]

Aberdeen was not unduly impressed by Brunnow's special pleading. He told Clarendon on 30 May that the real question was whether the first Article of the projected Convention was compatible with Russia's previous promises. He himself thought that Russia's demands were unreasonable and should be resisted. The key to his position was the next sentence. 'I cannot yet believe', he wrote, 'that it will be necessary to do so by war, if the Emperor should hitherto have been acting in good faith; if his whole conduct should have been a cheat, the case is altered.'[34]

Aberdeen's attempt to keep the temperature of the dispute low, was not acceptable to all his Cabinet colleagues. Russell had not been happy about the lack of a British response in March. He wrote then to Clarendon, 'The Emperor of Russia is clearly bent on accomplishing the destruction of Turkey, & *he must be resisted*' but, with his usual lack of consistency, he thought that the Turks should have accepted Menshikov's terms, even though it would mean 'a miserable existence for Turkey'.[35] At the end of May he was again in favour of action. Like Graham, he now feared that Britain might be betrayed by both France and Russia. The Tsar, he suspected 'having failed with us may offer to France Egypt & Candia as her part of the spoils of Turkey'. He thought the fleet should 'approach the neighbourhood of Turkey without entering Turkish waters'. Two days later, on 31 May, he was in favour of the fleet going at once to the Dardanelles.[36] Clarendon, under pressure from the French Ambassador, Walewski, as well as from Russell, also began to favour action. Walewski asked that Stratford be authorised to summon the fleet. Clarendon wrote to Aberdeen: 'I think we ought to do this. I wish we had done it a fortnight ago, though I doubt it being of any use now; for if a *coup de main* is intended, it will be a fait accompli within 10 days from this time.' He did not believe that the Tsar had deliberately deceived them but he feared the violence of his reaction when he learnt of Menshikov's failure.[37]

Aberdeen was very reluctant to give such permission. He told Clarendon:

The authority given to Lord Stratford to call up the fleet to Constantinople, is a fearful power to place in the hands of any Minister, involving as it does the question of peace or war. The passage of the Dardanelles being a direct violation of the treaty, would make us the aggressors, and give to Russia a just cause of war. It is most important therefore, that Lord Stratford should not have recourse to such a step except under the pressure of actual hostilities, or under circumstances fully equivalent to such a state.[38]

He must have felt that his caution was more than justified when, a few days later, Graham communicated to him letters from Admiral Dundas, including information from Captain Slade, a British officer in the Turkish service. 'You will observe', Graham commented 'that Capt. Slade states, "Ld. Stratford told me he had advised the rejection of Prince Menshikoff's Ultimatum" ' and that Stratford's note to Dundas indicated that he intended to use the fleet if it were placed at his disposal.[39]

But, by this time, the die was cast. The Cabinet meeting of 28 May had agreed to postpone a decision until they had more information.[40] The Cabinet met again on 4 June in a very different mood. In advance of the meeting Aberdeen had been compelled to agree that if the majority of the Cabinet wished it the fleet should be sent to Besika Bay outside the Dardanelles, which would not violate any agreement. Russell told Clarendon on 1 June that he, Clarendon, Lansdowne and Palmerston were agreed on this. No one, except possibly Graham, supported Aberdeen in opposing it.[41] Aberdeen told Victoria on 5 June: 'With orders given to Your Majesty's fleet to leave Malta, & a power extrusted to Ld. Stratford to call the force up to Constantinople, it is impossible to say how soon the state of affairs may become so complicated as to render a peaceful solution much more difficult.'[42] He used much less guarded language to Clarendon. 'As we are drifting fast towards War,' he wrote on 7 June, 'I should think the Cabinet ought to see where they are going.' He had told him some days previously, 'It is right that we should know on what grounds the Parliament and the People of this country, short of the occupation of Constantinople by a foreign force, would be prepared to enter into a war on behalf of such a State as Turkey.'[43] But as the month of June passed Aberdeen detected some re-assertion of, as he saw it, common sense among his colleagues, if not among the public. He wrote to the Queen on 25 June that he was glad to say 'in proportion as the war mania has increased in the country, a decided improvement has taken place in the sentiments of the Cabinet, & that the desire of peace is more decided, as well as more practical. This has been a great relief to Lord Aberdeen, who had recently been under considerable apprehensions on the subject.'[44]

The only alternative to war seemed to be international negotiations and this was always Aberdeen's preferred policy. The chances of a successful international mediation appeared at first to be diminished by the fact that the Tsar's reaction to the Turkish rebuff to Menshikoff was as sharp as Clarendon had feared it would be. On 31 May the Russians despatched an ultimatum to the Turks, threatening to occupy Moldavia and Wallachia until they received full satisfaction. The occupation was carried out at the beginning of July. It has sometimes been argued that the Russians had rights of intervention in the Principalities which meant that the occupation was not strictly an act of war. This was never the view of the British Cabinet. None of Russia's treaty rights was remotely applicable to the present situation. The British government, including Aberdeen, held uncompromisingly that the invasion of the Principalities was a *casus belli* to which the Turks would have been perfectly entitled under international law to respond by a declaration of war. Whether the Turks would be wise to do so was a different matter and British advice was that they should seek a settlement by other means.[45] The Russian passage of the Pruth, although the first resort to arms in the war, in fact galvanised the chancelleries of Europe into seeking compromise solutions.

Everyone had a project. Aberdeen gave short shrift to the King of Prussia's draft Convention. 'This', he wrote to Clarendon, 'is the most impracticable proposition ever made and is quite worthy of its origin.'[46] The British government were drawing up their own project. They were rather embarrassed by the fact that, at the outset of the dispute, they had expressed some sympathy with the Russian desire to reassert their claims against French encroachments. Matters had moved so far that most members of the Cabinet seemed to have entirely forgotten their original position.[47]

The most hopeful development, however, was the ambassadorial conference which the Austrian Foreign Secretary, Count Buol, agreed, after some prompting from Britain and France, to call in Vienna in July. Aberdeen no longer felt quite the same high regard for Austria as he had done in the past. He disliked her bullying tactics towards Turkey at the time of the Leiningen mission and he was much more critical than he had been before of her policies in Italy.[48] Nevertheless, Vienna was the most obvious neutral capital in which an agreement could be worked out. The Russian Ambassador pleaded that he had no instructions, but the Ambassadors of the other four Great Powers arrived at a formula for a peaceful settlement: the Vienna Note, which was despatched to St Petersburg on 1 August. The Russians quickly accepted it.

In late July everything seemed to be in train for a successful settlement. At home the parliamentary session was drawing to a close with a good record of work accomplished and a clear programme for the next session. Aberdeen felt that he could honourably retire. He was well into his seventieth year and he had achieved his objective of bringing a Liberal Conservative coalition into being. Although he did not believe, as Lord John apparently did, that he had made any specific promise to resign in his favour, he had always regarded this as the natural and expected course. He had, however, made it clear that he would only do so if this were acceptable to the other Peelites. Gladstone, who of all the Peelite leaders still felt closest to the traditional Conservative party,

was the most difficult to persuade. Aberdeen had hoped to discuss the proposition with him at Haddo after the parliamentary session ended in August,
but Gladstone was taken ill on a visit to Dunrobin and, for several vital weeks,
was out of touch with his colleagues, while Aberdeen himself was prevented
from going to Scotland at all by a deterioration in the Eastern situation.[49]

When the Russian acceptance of the Vienna Note became known in London,
there was a general disposition to think that the affair was settled. Greville
recorded in his Diary: 'The Government are in high spirits at the prospect of
winding up this prosperous Session with the settlement of the Eastern Question: nothing else is wanting to their success.' [The credit went to Aberdeen.
Even the Whig, Granville] 'says it will be principally owing to Aberdeen, who
has been very staunch and bold in defying public clamour, abuse, and taunts,
and in resisting the wishes and advice of Palmerston, who would have adopted
a more stringent and uncompromising course.'[50] Aberdeen permitted himself
briefly to join in the general relief. He later wrote to his daughter-in-law, Lady
Haddo: 'Do you remember one day in the summer at Blackheath, when I told
you that everything was settled? That was a happy moment! It was believed
to be certain; and had it been fully confirmed, there would have been great
credit, reputation, and triumph.'[51]

But privately both Aberdeen and Clarendon were aware that there was still
plenty of opportunity for slips. The British government themselves had suggested some last minute alterations in the Vienna Note and were uneasy at the
Tsar's insistence that he would only accept the Note word for word as it stood
and was not prepared to negotiate. More importantly, the Turks had not yet
agreed. That same Sunday at Blackheath, Aberdeen wrote to Clarendon: 'As
I have never despaired, and have long felt that we were *landed*, the despatch
[announcing Russia's acceptance] does not surprise me. I have some misgivings
about the answer from Constantinople.'[52]

Aberdeen's misgivings were entirely justified. The Turks, who resented the
fact that they had not been consulted in Vienna and had already drawn up a
counter-proposal of their own, which became popularly known as 'the Turkish
ultimatum', rejected the Vienna Note on 20 August. When the Turkish refusal
was known, Greville noted, 'Granville told me that what had occurred showed
how much more sagacious Aberdeen had been as to this affair than Palmerston,
the former having always maintained that there would be no difficulty with
the Emperor, but if any arose it would be from the Turks; whereas Palmerston
was always sure the Turks would make none, but that the Emperor would
refuse all arrangements.'[53] Even before the Turkish reply was received the government's misgivings were such that they decided to alter the wording of the
Queen's Speech at the prorogation of parliament – very much against Victoria's
own wishes – from 'confident expectation' of a settlement to 'good reason to
hope' for one.[54]

Unfortunately the government was also steadily losing confidence in their
Ambassador in Constantinople. Stratford had been unwilling to press the
Vienna Note on the Turks and Aberdeen regretted that they had not sent him
more specific instructions at the outset as he himself had wished. He told Clar-

endon on 18 August: 'This demur on his part is alarming enough as indication of his intentions.' The next day he wrote again, this time from Osborne: 'I fear Stratford intends to give us some trouble, otherwise he might have acted on the telegraphic despatch, as the other Ministers were ready to do . . . We must at last be plain with him, as well as his friend Reschid.'[55]

When the Turkish rejection became known, Aberdeen, still at Osborne, suggested to the Queen that Stratford be replaced. He found her agreeable to the idea. 'Stratford', he told Clarendon, 'will have a bad case.' His delay in obeying Clarendon's telegraphic orders would in itself justify his recall. The problem was to find a replacement. 'What', Aberdeen asked 'has become of Bulwer?' He would, he thought, be the best choice both from the point of view of ability and local knowledge.[56] Considering Bulwer's independent actions at the time of the Spanish marriage negotiations, when he had come near to committing his government to Leopold's candidature, it is curious that Aberdeen should have believed him more cautious and amenable to instructions than Stratford.

The British reaction to the Turkish demand for modifications was initially to lose all sympathy with the Turkish case. Aberdeen wrote to Clarendon:

The Turkish modifications, although not absolutely altering the sense of the Note, are not insignificant. I cannot say what the Emperor may be disposed to do for the sake of peace; but I am sure we have no right to ask him to agree to further alterations, after what has already been done. He accepted our first proposal, in its full context, without the least hesitation. He agreed as promptly to an alteration proposed by the English Govt in the interests of the Porte. I should not think it probable that he would submit to have the work of the Four Powers altered by the Porte. Indeed, he made an express stipulation to this effect . . . The conduct of the Porte is suicidal, and some fatal influence must be at work. It can only be explained by a desire that the affair should end in war.

He repeated the next day his view that the Turks evidently wanted war. 'I think', he commented, 'the Turks, and the friends of the Turks, have overshot the mark.'[57]

Aberdeen's attitude was totally changed by the revelation in a German newspaper early in September, of Nesselrode's own interpretation conveyed to the Russian Ambassador in Vienna, of the meaning of the Vienna Note. Aberdeen had always believed that the Russians only wished to safeguard their ancient rights in connection with the Orthodox Church within the Ottoman Empire. Until July, the danger seemed to be that a quarrel about these might tempt the Russians to attack Constantinople or that a war might, very much against the will of the participants, precipitate the collapse of the Empire. Nesselrode's 'interpretation', however, spoke of Turkey's obligation to 'take account of Russia's active solicitude for her co-religionists in Turkey', in other words, a claim to exercise a general protectorate over the Orthodox Church and its adherents, or the most extreme possible interpretation of the meaning of the Menshikov demands. Experienced observers were astonished that an 'old fox' such as Nesselrode should have committed such a 'niaiserie'.[58] Brunnow delivered an explanation which conceded the essential truth of the German report.

The effect on Aberdeen was shattering. Neither he nor Clarendon could bring themselves to admit that Stratford had been right in his reservations but Aberdeen's whole strategy had been based on the assumption that Russian policy was honest and, in the last resort pacific, while the Turks were totally unreliable. Now it seemed to be proven that the Russians were guilty of double-dealing and, even more alarming, that they might be planning to take the Ottoman Empire by sap rather than by storm.

Still shocked by this realisation, Aberdeen agreed with Clarendon on 23 September that Stratford should be, not merely authorised, but instructed to summon the fleet to Constantinople. Until then Aberdeen had been vehement in his arguments that there must be no breach of the 1841 Convention and had insisted that sending the fleet to Constantinople must be a decision for the whole Cabinet. The excuse for the move was that the war fever in Constantinople had now become so violent that European lives and property, and even the Sultan himself, were in danger. Aberdeen emphasised to Clarendon, 'Our main object in going to Constantinople is for the protection of British life and property, and if necessary, of the person of the Sultan.' That protection extended only to the person of the Sultan, not to his political authority. Aberdeen also insisted that they must explain to the Tsar, through Seymour, that it was not intended to menace Russia.[60] Aberdeen may have persuaded himself that this was so but Clarendon's recollection was that it was essentially a reply to the revelation of Russia's real position. Certainly he wrote to Stratford the next day, 'The only real likelihood now is war.'[61]

Aberdeen, although badly shaken, was still not committed. On 28 September he wrote to Lady Haddo:

I am sorry to say that the political prospect is very gloomy, and that it is becoming worse and worse. There is a general desire of war, or, as it is called, supporting the honour of the country, which it will be difficult to resist. I shall personally continue my pacifick policy as long as I am able; but, when I am overborne, as I see that I shall be, I will readily leave the execution of a different policy to others. It is a matter of inescapable comfort that my conscience is clear, and that I have no misgivings of the wisdom and justice of my course.[62]

He sent for Delane on 4 October and repeated similar sentiments to him. He would, he said, resign rather than be a party to a war with Russia 'on such grounds as the present'.[63]

Yet, when the Cabinet met on 7 October, (for the first time for six weeks), Aberdeen was 'overborne' but still decided against resignation. There had been two important developments in the previous fortnight. The Tsar had met the Emperor of Austria at Olmütz and assured him that he sought only the maintenance of the status quo and that he would withdraw his troops from the Principalities as soon as the Vienna Note was signed. By implication he repudiated Nesselrode's interpretation of the Note. But the news from Constantinople was less encouraging. The war party had finally triumphed and on 3 October Turkey had declared war on Russia. The Cabinet knew this by 7 October, although official confirmation had not yet arrived.

In England during the previous few weeks consultations had been going on between various members of the Cabinet, particularly those who were now dissatisfied with Aberdeen's handling of affairs. Russell wrote uncompromisingly to Clarendon on 27 September that the British fleet must not retire from Constantinople until the Russians left the Principalities. The Turks should declare war. 'I know something', he went on bombastically, 'of the English people, & I feel sure that they would fight to their stumps for the honour of England. To have held out such encouragement to the Turks as we have done, & afterwards to desert them would be felt as deep disgrace and humiliation by the whole country.' He told Clarendon a few days later, 'I do not believe in the note from Olmütz any more than you.' He thought it 'intended only to deceive'. On 4 October he drew up an elaborate memorandum, rehearsing the history of the question and concluding that, if Russia would not make peace on 'fair' terms, the British must appear in the field 'as auxiliaries of Turkey'. He hoped they would act with France and perhaps with Austria. He applauded the Turkish declaration of war, which showed that Turkey 'has some spirit left', although he admitted, 'These telegraphic dispatches are the very devil. Formerly Cabinets used to deliberate on a fact & a proposition from foreign Govts. Now we have only a fact. To be sure it is a great fact.'[64]

Palmerston was equally uncompromising. He was contemptuous of the excuse for the British fleet movement, which would not deceive the Russians, but he told Aberdeen that he ought to maintain a 'mysterious indefiniteness & uncertainty' in his communications with Brunnow about what assistance Britain would render to Turkey in the event of war. Aberdeen replied that Brunnow was already 'frightened out of his wits at the prospect and, most assuredly, he hears nothing from me to diminish his alarm'. He thought that fear of an open rupture with England and France was already exercising a salutary influence on the Tsar.[65]

On the morning of 7 October, Palmerston sent Aberdeen his proposals now that war had actually broken out. He had already told Clarendon that, since all treaties between Russia and Turkey were now at an end, the Olmütz proposals were mere 'après dîner moutarde'. Britain should conclude a Convention with the Sultan, promising him such naval assistance as he might require and allowing British subjects to enter his service. In return the Sultan should agree to consult them about any peace treaty. More immediately, a British squadron should enter the Black Sea 'and should send word to the Russian admiral at Sebastopol that in the existing state of things any Russian ship of war found cruizing in the Black Sea would be detained and given over to the Turkish government.'[66]

The Cabinet meeting was very long and the deep divisions could not be concealed. Graham was absent at Balmoral. Molesworth was also absent by a misunderstanding. Graham's absence may well have been decisive. He was a clear-sighted man and it is difficult to believe that he would have deceived himself, as Aberdeen did, about the significance of what was decided. Aberdeen assured both Graham and the Queen that the outcome was satisfactory. He told Graham:

The aspect of the Cabinet was, on the whole, very good, Gladstone, active and energetic for Peace; Argyll, Herbert, C. Wood, and Granville, all in the same sense. Newcastle, not quite so much so, but good; Lansdowne, not so warlike as formerly; Lord John warlike enough, but subdued in tone; Palmerson urged his views perseveringly, but not disagreeably.

Palmerston's proposition to send a fleet into the Black Sea to detain any Russian ships it found there, received no real support but the Cabinet eventually agreed to Clarendon's 'compromise' proposal that the fleet should remain in the Bosphorus for the time being, but enter the Black Sea if the Russians attacked the Turkish coast or crossed the Danube, which would be interpreted as the first step towards a land attack on Constantinople. Aberdeen insisted that the measures were purely 'defensive' and assured both the Queen and Graham that there was little real danger that they would be put into force. 'As there is very little chance', he wrote to the Queen, 'of Russia undertaking any active hostilities of the nature apprehended, it may reasonably be hoped that no actual collision will take place.'[67] The Cabinet met again the next day to finalise their instructions to Stratford and Dundas. They also discussed the Olmütz proposals but only Aberdeen and Sidney Herbert took them at all seriously.[68]

The decisions of 7 October seem to have been arrived at by a tired and divided Cabinet who had talked themselves to a standstill but felt compelled to agree to something. Argyll immediately had misgivings and wrote to Russell that night, emphasising how careful they must be about their instructions. They must make it clear, particularly to the Turks, that they were purely defensive. Otherwise the situation would be 'very dangerous'.[69] Aberdeen too, by the next day, doubted whether it would be possible in practice to maintain the distinction between defensive and offensive operations. Victoria strongly disapproved. The Prince wrote: 'It was evident that Lord Aberdeen was, against his better judgement, consenting to a course of policy which he inwardly condemned, that his desire to maintain unanimity at the Cabinet led to concessions which by degrees altered the whole character of the policy, while he held out no hope of being able permanently to secure agreement.'[70] Graham too expressed strong dissent. The decision up to the anchorage in the Bosphorus was correct but the contingent agreement on operations in the Black Sea was 'at least premature'. It put the decision in the hands of the men on the spot. How if the Turks were the assailants, were repulsed and the Russians followed up their advantage? 'Are we bound in that case to be dragged into hostilities by a Barbarian whom we are unable to control?' Nothing had happened since early September when a solution seemed in sight, except Nesselrode's incautious letter to the Russian Ambassador in Vienna. Surely, they could get a retraction of that.[71]

The Prince returned to the attack on 21 October with a long memorandum in which he spelt out the dangers of Britain being dragged into war as the 'auxiliaries' of Turkey. They might, in the last resort, have to go to war to preserve the Turkish Empire but they must be sure to fight for European, not

Turkish, objectives. In particular, they must ensure that the end result would be an entirely new arrangement in the Balkans and not the re-imposition of the 'ignorant, barbarous & despotic yoke of the Mussulman'.[72]

It was too late to recall the instructions of 8 October and Aberdeen did not try to get the Cabinet decision reversed but the conflict seems to have strengthened his resolve not to resign. Russell was now actively intriguing for the succession. Graham wrote to Aberdeen on 13 October, 'A new Game is about to be opened.'[73] Russell seems to have concluded that a peaceful succession was not now possible and that he must first break up the ministry. The only thing that seemed to be in doubt was whether he would play the Turkish or the parliamentary reform card. Aberdeen challenged Russell openly on more than one occasion in Cabinet as to his intentions. When Russell suggested that Parliament ought to be recalled to consider the Eastern Question, despite the alarm that this was likely to generate, 'Lord Aberdeen told Lord John quite plainly he knew what the proposal meant – he meant to break up the Government.' When Russell admitted that he had his parliamentary reform plans ready, but saw no point in bringing them forward, Aberdeen replied, 'You mean unless you sit in the chair which I now occupy?' According to Aberdeen's account to the Prince, 'Lord John laughed'.[74]

Only a few weeks earlier Aberdeen had been preparing to resign in Russell's favour, and to take active steps to persuade his more reluctant colleagues. He announced his change of mind to Graham on 22 September. He admitted,

This Eastern question affects my own position a good deal. Of course I never took it into my calculations, and concluded that it would be settled in some way or other, long before it was necessary for me to act. This may still be the case; and if so, I should have no difficulty; but I should not like to have the appearance of running away from an unfinished question of real importance, and of a most complicated description.[75]

Far from being resolved, the Eastern Question steadily became more complicated and more dangerous.

For some weeks it seemed that Graham's hope, that the decisions of 7 October would prove 'harmless', would be fulfilled. Stratford received Clarendon's orders of 23 September to summon the fleet on 4 October but did not act on them until 23 October after he had received the further orders of 8 October. The Russians received the Turkish ultimatum requiring the evacuation of the Principalities within a fortnight, on 10 October, and Omer Pasha's army crossed the Danube on 27 October. However, no serious fighting had as yet taken place and international negotiations continued. At the end of November, the Russians accepted the proferred good offices of Britain, France, Austria and Prussia and early in December the Turks too agreed to accept the mediation of the Great Powers. Clarendon tried to resurrect the British draft Convention which he believed the Turks had always preferred to the French project on which the Vienna Note had been founded.

All hopes for peace disintegrated with the news of the so-called 'massacre of Sinope' on 30 November which was known in London on 12 December.

Most modern authorities have argued that Sinope was a perfectly legitimate act of war. The Turks had declared war on the Russians. If a Russian squadron found a Turkish squadron in the Black Sea, they had every right to sink it. Technically, this was no doubt correct but it was not how it appeared in London, even to Aberdeen. The Tsar had given the other Great Powers to understand that, so long as negotiations continued, he would do nothing to worsen, in the modern phrase to 'escalate', the situation. If they were attacked the Russians would defend themselves but they would not take the initiative.[76] But Sinope was in no way a defensive operation. The small Turkish squadron involved was no threat and it was caught immediately off the Turkish coast. The whole operation looked dangerously like the Russian descent on the Turkish coast, which the Cabinet had envisaged on 7 October would require an immediate British response. For a time Aberdeen hoped that the action had been a breach of the Tsar's orders but it was not repudiated. On the contrary the Tsar openly rejoiced.[77] Coming after Nesselrode's 'violent interpretation' of the Vienna Note, it looked like further evidence of Russian double-dealing. Aberdeen felt helpless before the hawks in the Cabinet.

Aberdeen asked Brunnow personally for details of what had happened at Sinope. Brunnow, obviously holding that attack was the best form of defence, made counter-charges against the Turks, alleging that they had crucified customs house men at Tiflis.[78] Palmerston believed that Aberdeen had allowed himself to be threatened by Brunnow, who said he would be recalled if a British fleet entered the Black Sea. Palmerston was not entirely immune to the fears that the Turks might have deliberately trailed their coat in order to compel the British to come to their aid but he had no doubt that Sinope was 'an occurrence disgraceful to the Two Powers' [Britain and France] and that 'Something ought to be done to wipe away the Stain'. Palmerston believed, or professed to believe, that this was all part of a general forward policy on the part of Russia, directed at Persia as well as Turkey. He advocated occupying the island of Karrack in the Persian Gulf and giving the Turks command of the Black Sea by insisting that the Russian fleet return to Sebastopol and stay there.[79]

Palmerston was absent from all the crucial Cabinet meetings of late December because of the quarrel about parliamentary reform but his ghost dominated them. It is possible that the Cabinet came to more extreme conclusions than they would have done if he had been present, for fear of the political capital he would be able to make if they showed weakness. Public excitement was now almost out of hand. The press was practically unanimous in its demands for war to protect Turkey and British interests in the Eastern Mediterranean against the Russian despot. Even *The Times* which, under Aberdeen's direct influence had been a moderating force, commented on Sinope that Russia had now thrown down the gauntlet to the maritime powers and that they must be ready to protect Turkey if necessary.[80] Aberdeen's own reaction, as at the time of Tahiti crisis, was that they must ignore public clamour. Popularity was a bad guide, he warned. He remembered that Alcibiades asked when the crowd applauded, whether he had said anything unusually foolish.[81] This lofty view was not shared by his colleagues. Beyond a certain point they were not prepared to risk popular displeasure.

Matters now really turned on what the British government would regard as a *casus belli*. Even before Sinope, Russell had wanted strong arm tactics. He had suggested that Admiral Dundas should intercept troops and stores going from one Russian port to another and order them to Sebastopol, and argued, unconvincingly, that this could be done without war.[82] Apart from the command of the Black Sea, the other vital question was the danger of an advance on Constantinople by land. Most of the Cabinet were inclined to make a Russian passage of the Danube the critical test. Aberdeen would have preferred to name the Balkan. Graham explained to Clarendon on Aberdeen's behalf, 'The passage of the Danube does not necessarily portend a march on Constantinople; the passage of the Balkan does; and there in is the difference.'[83] Both Aberdeen and Graham were troubled by the fact that Turkey had begun the fighting, against the clear advice of the allies she now expected to assist her, and also by the idea of defending such a 'barbarous' Power at all. They could not, like Palmerston, maintain the convenient fiction that Turkey was now a reformed Power. Aberdeen, with his long experience of diplomacy, was scandalised by the idea of resorting to force without a formal declaration of war, which his colleagues, especially Russell, airily dismissed as of little consequence. More importantly, he pleaded that they should at least await the outcome of the pending international negotiations before they did anything irreparable. But step by step he was driven back.[84]

The Cabinet met on 17 December. The previous night the four leading Peelites, Aberdeen, Graham, Newcastle and Gladstone, met at the Admiralty. The meeting lasted from just after 10 p.m. until 1.30 a.m. but they failed to find any new policy. The full Cabinet agreed to order the British fleet into the Black Sea, although they believed that they would only be confirming what Stratford would already have done under his instructions of 8 October. In this they were mistaken. The supposedly warlike Stratford had not sent the fleet into the Black Sea. But the French had decided, not only to send their fleet into the Black Sea but also to require the Russian fleet to return to Sebastopol.[85]

The Cabinet met again on 20 December to approve instructions arising from the meeting of 17 December; but it was the meeting of the afternoon of 22 December, which considered the French proposals, that was decisive. It was as long and as confused as the meeting of 7 October and, as on the previous occasion, members seem to have failed to appreciate the full significance of what they had decided. Gladstone argued strongly against Britain and France 'occupying' the Black Sea unless they got a number of guarantees from Turkey. Both Newcastle and Wood objected that this would tie their hands and that they would be better without any obligations. Perhaps many members voted in the end as Wood himself did because 'it seemed to me to be such a tissue of confusions, that I advocated the simple course [of accepting the French proposals].'[86]

The experienced Aberdeen cannot have been under any illusions that to demand that the fleet of a Great Power return to port was tantamount to a declaration of war. His report to the Queen explains why he acquiesced. He believed that war was now virtually certain and it was vital to keep in step with the French. He wrote:

It is possible, and even probable, that this decision may so far provoke the resentment of the Russian Government, as either to lead to a declaration of war, or to acts of retaliation; but Lord Aberdeen believes that the accidental collisions which under the present state of things would inevitably have taken place, render the proposed instructions not more dangerous.

He admitted that he would have hesitated if the continuation of the French alliance had not depended on it. The tone of the French communication was 'exacting and peremptory' but, if Britain did not agree, the French would either act alone or withdraw their fleet to Toulon. He thought the peremptoriness of the French communication was mainly due to the excitement in France as a result of Sinope, 'and unfortunately public opinion in this country would not permit the risk of dissolving the alliance at this juncture by the assertion of a little more independence.'[87]

The actual war took an extraordinarily long time to break out and, right to the end, Aberdeen still clung to the hope that peace might yet be preserved. Negotiations were still going on in Vienna and new proposals being forwarded to both Constantinople and St Petersburg but, as Aberdeen had feared from the beginning, the Tsar had now been forced into a position where he could not afford to lose face by agreeing to them. The British and French fleets entered the Black Sea on 3 January and three days later the Russian fleet was warned to return to Sebastopol. It was not until 11 January that Sir Hamilton Seymour officially informed Nesselrode of the instructions sent to the British and French Black Sea fleets. On 15 January Brunnow, who had learnt of the instructions from Russell, came to Aberdeen to ask if it were true. When Aberdeen told him that it was, Brunnow replied that Clarendon had not told him and he feared that consequently he had misled his government.[88] The Russians naturally enquired whether similar undertakings to remain in port had been required of the Turks. When they received an unsatisfactory reply they recalled their ambassadors from London and Paris. Brunnow asked for his passports on 4 February.

Aberdeen still refused to despair. He told Clarendon on 12 February, 'I still say that war is *not inevitable*; unless, indeed, we are determined to have it, which, perhaps, for aught I know, may be the case', and Russell the same day, 'Only let us have peace, which I persist in saying is *not hopeless*, and we may defy all opposition or intrigue.' Gladstone had become uneasy about the grounds on which they were breaking with Russia. It would be no great comfort if the Tsar was in the wrong sometime ago if they were in the wrong now. Their proceedings in the Black Sea might be very difficult to defend.[89]

It was, perhaps, for this reason that the British became anxious to switch the grounds for the quarrel back to Russia's original illegal act, the occupation of the Principalities, and away from their own attempts to 'police' the Black Sea. On 27 February Clarendon addressed a direct demand to Nesselrode that the Principalities be evacuated by the end of April. The French sent a similar demand. Both Aberdeen and the Queen would have preferred to have waited until Austria joined Britain and France in making it.[90] The demand was an ultimatum. If the Russians did not answer, the two Western Powers would consider themselves at war. The terms of the ultimatum appeared in *The Times* the next day, 28 February. Aberdeen was extremely angry. He knew that publicity must destroy what little chance there was of the Russians accepting.[91] Russell was now prepared to argue that their course was justified because war could only have been avoided by complete surrender to the Russians.[92] Aberdeen would have none of this. He replied that, 'On the contrary, I believe that there were two or three occasions when, if I had been supported, peace might have been honourably and advantageously secured.' In particular, he thought that the Olmütz proposals should have been taken more seriously. Aberdeen himself, with his usual clear-sightedness, correctly identified those occasions in September, October and December when different decisions could have been taken which might have averted disaster. He told Russell, 'My conscience upbraids me the more, because seeing as I did from the first, all that was to be apprehended, it is possible that by a little more energy and vigour, not on the Danube, but in Downing Street, it [the war] might have been prevented.'[93] That, rather than abstract considerations of the justice of the war, was the basis of his later self-reproach. War was declared on 28 March 1854.

NOTES

1. Add. MSS 43049, Palmerston to Aberdeen, 10 Jan. 1853, Aberdeen to Palmerston, 10 Jan. 1853.

2. MSS Clar. Dep. C3, Graham to Palmerston, 30 May 1853. On the possible connection between Louis Napoleon's ambitions in the East and on the Rhine see Puryear, *England, Russia and the Straits Question*, pp. 242–53 and Conacher, pp. 143–4.

3. Graham Papers, 124 Aberdeen to Graham, 11 July 1853.

4. Croker, vol. 3, pp. 298–9; Aberdeen to Lieven, 23 May, 8 Sept. 1953, Jones-Parry, vol. 2, pp. 644, 646–7. For the likelihood that the Princess Lieven's views got back to the Tsar see Jones–Parry, vol. 1, p. xxi.

5. Add. MSS 43044, Brunnow to Aberdeen, 24 Dec. 1852.

6. The letters between Aberdeen and Brunnow in Add. MSS 43044 become infrequent and formal after September 1853, although they did discuss Sinope. This impression is confirmed by R. E. Howard, who had access to Brunnow's side of the correspondence, in his 'Brunnow's reports on Aberdeen', *Cambridge Historical Journal*, iv (1934), pp. 312–21. For Palmerston's suspicions see Ashley, vol. 2, pp. 40–1 and MSS Clar. Dep. C15, Palmerston to Clarendon, 22 Aug. 1854.

7. H. W. V. Temperley, *England and the Near East: The Crimea*, pp. 270–1. This is still the best single account of all these intricate negotiations.

8. FO 65/424, Seymour to Russell, No. 13, 11 Jan. 1853, No. 24, 22 Jan. 1853, No. 87, 21 Feb. 1853, No. 88, 22 Feb. 1853 (all 'Secret and Confidential'). Aberdeen told the Queen that the Tsar 'appeared to expect an early dissolution

of the Turkish Empire, and was prepared in such a case to act in perfect concert with [the] British Government', Add. MSS 43046, Aberdeen to Victoria, 8 Feb. 1853; cf. Temperley, p. 461.

9. FO 65/420, Russell to Seymour, No. 38, 9 Feb. 1853, Secret and Confidential.

10. Add. MSS 43066, Russell to Aberdeen, 5 Feb. 1853. Stratford's conduct has been minutely scrutinised by many historians, notably H. W. V. Temperley 'Stratford de Redcliffe and the origins of the Crimean War', *E.H.R.*, xlviii (1933), pp. 601–21 and xlix (1934), pp. 265–98.

11. Add. MSS 43191, Graham to Aberdeen, 19 Sept. 1853; Graham Papers, 124, Clarendon to Graham, 1853; Add. MSS 43188, Clarendon to Aberdeen, 27 Sept. 1853.

12. Add. MSS 43046, Victoria to Aberdeen, 18 Jan. 1853; RA C28/88, *Globe* article marked 'evidently sent in by Ld John Russell', /89, Aberdeen to Victoria, 18 Jan. 1853, /91, Albert, Memorandum, 23 Jan. 1853.

13. Add. MSS 43066, Russell to Aberdeen, 19, 21 Jan. 1853; PRO 30/22/10G, Aberdeen to Russell, 19 Jan. 1853.

14. PRO 30/22/10G, Aberdeen to Russell, 21 Jan. 1853.

15. Add. MSS 43066, Russell to Aberdeen, 14 Feb. 1853.

16. MSS Clar. Dep. C4, Aberdeen to Russell, 15 Feb. 1853.

17. Add. MSS 43066, Russell to Aberdeen, 14 Feb. 1853.

18. Add. MSS 43134, Guizot to Aberdeen, 27 Feb. 1853; Lieven to Aberdeen, 25 Feb. 1853, Jones-Parry, vol. 2, p. 640; Metternich to Aberdeen, 22 Feb. 1853, BP 12/10; Add. MSS 43051, Leopold to Aberdeen, 2 Mar. 1853.

19. Add, MSS 43051, Aberdeen to Leopold, 7 Mar. 1853; cf. MSS Clar. Dep. C4, Aberdeen to Clarendon, 8 Mar., 1 Apr. 1853, RA A23/14, Aberdeen to Victoria, 27 Feb. 1853.

20. Add. MSS 43188, Clarendon to Aberdeen, 'Friday night', 7 Mar. 1853.

21. Aberdeen himself, for example, learnt from his secretary who was married to the daughter of the banker, Roberti, that Kossuth had just drawn £300 worth of foreign gold coins. He hoped that it meant he intended to leave England, MSS Clar. Dep. C4, Aberdeen to Clarendon, 21 Apr. 1853.

22. C. C. Tansill, *The Canadian Reciprocity Treaty of 1854*. The Peelites had been inclined to rejoice at the difficulties this problem had caused Derby's government, Graham Papers, 124, Aberdeen to Graham, 9 Aug. 1852; Graham to Russell, 16 Aug. 1852; MSS Clar. Dep. C4, Aberdeen to Clarendon, 21 Apr. 1853.

23. MSS Clar. Dep. C4, Graham to Clarendon, 4 Apr., 18 May, 17 Nov. 1853; C14, Aberdeen to Clarendon, 17 Apr. 1854.

24. 'My only cause for regret is, that when I found this [the preservation of peace] to be impossible, I did not at once retire.' Gurney Papers, RQC 334, Aberdeen to Gurney, 5 Aug. 1857.

25. For discussion of this see below pp. 499, 504–5.

26. MSS Clar. Dep. C15, Palmerston to Clarendon, 4 Mar. 1854.

27. Maxwell, vol. 2, p. 30.

28. RA A23/18, Aberdeen to Victoria, 17 Mar. 1853; Add. MSS 43047, Aberdeen to Victoria, 20 Mar. 1853; MSS Clar. Dep. C4, Graham to Clarendon, 19 Mar. 1853; Add. MSS 43044, Brunnow to Aberdeen, 19 Mar. 1853, Aberdeen to Brunnow, 23 Mar. 1853.

29. PRO 30/22/10G, Aberdeen to Russell, 31 Jan. 1853.

30. Add. MSS 43047, Aberdeen to Victoria, 22, 24 Mar. 1853, Victoria to Aberdeen, 23 Mar. 1853.

31. Add. MSS 43191, Graham to Aberdeen, 29 May encl. Palmerston to Graham, 29 May 1853.
32. Add. MSS 43191, Aberdeen to Graham, 31 May 1853.
33. Add. MSS 43044, Brunnow to Aberdeen, 18, 21, 22, 29 May 1853, Aberdeen to Brunnow, 25 May 1853.
34. MSS Clar. Dep. C4, Aberdeen to Clarendon, 30 May 1853.
35. MSS Clar. Dep. C3, Russell to Clarendon, 20 Mar. 1853.
36. MSS Clar. Dep. C3, Russell to Clarendon, 29, 31 May 1853.
37. Add. MSS 43188, Clarendon to Aberdeen, 29 May 1853.
38. MSS Clar. Dep. C4, Aberdeen to Clarendon, 1 June 1853.
39. Add. MSS 43191, Graham to Aberdeen, 9 June 1853.
40. RA G3/8, Aberdeen to Victoria, 28 May 1853.
41. MSS Clar. Dep. C3, Russell to Clarendon, 1 June 1853.
42. RA G3/42, Aberdeen to Victoria, 5 June 1853.
43. MSS Clar. Dep. C4, Aberdeen to Clarendon, 1, 7 June 1853.
44. RA G3/96, Aberdeen to Victoria, 25 June 1853.
45. FO 352/36, Clarendon to Stratford Canning, 8 June 1853, Private; Add MSS 43049, Palmerston to Aberdeen, 12, 15 July 1853, Aberdeen, Memorandum, 13 July 1853, Aberdeen to Palmerston, 15 July 1853.
46. MSS Clar. Dep. C4, Aberdeen to Clarendon, 27 June 1853.
47. MSS Clar. Dep. C4, Aberdeen to Clarendon, 20 June, 10, 20 July 1853.
48. MSS Clar. Dep. C4, Aberdeen to Clarendon, 8 Mar. 1853, *Hansard*, 3rd ser., CXXX1, 175 (27 Mar. 1854).
49. Graham Papers, 124, Aberdeen to Graham, 22 Sept., 3 Oct. 1853; Stanmore, pp. 267-8.
50. Greville, vol. VII, p. 80 (8, 9 Aug. 1853).
51. HH 1/29, Aberdeen to Lady Haddo, 28 Sept. 1853.
52. MSS Clar. Dep. C4, Aberdeen to Clarendon, 'Sunday' Aug. 1853.
53. Greville, vol. VII, pp. 81-2 (27 Aug. 1853).
54. MSS Clar. Dep. C4, Aberdeen to Clarendon, 19 Aug. 1853.
55. MSS Clar. Dep. C4, Aberdeen to Clarendon, 18, 19 Aug. 1853.
56. MSS Clar. Dep. C4, Aberdeen to Clarendon, 26 Aug. 1853.
57. MSS Clar. Dep. C4, Aberdeen to Clarendon, 26, 27 Aug. 1853.
58. Maxwell, vol. 2, p. 26.
59. Add. MSS 44089, Aberdeen to Gladstone, 2 Sept. 1854; Add. MSS 43251, Aberdeen, Memorandum, 9 Sept. 1853; Graham Papers, 124, Aberdeen to Graham, 22, 24 Sept. 1853.
60. MSS Clar. Dep. C4, Aberdeen to Clarendon, 23 Sept. 1853.
61. *Edinburgh Review*, cxvii (1836), p. 326.
62. HH 1/29, Aberdeen to Lady Haddo, 28 Sept. 1853.
63. Greville, vol. VII, p. 95 (6 Oct. 1853).
64. MSS Clar. Dep. C3, Russell to Clarendon, 27 Sept., 4 Oct. 1853 encl. Memorandum.
65. Add. MSS 43049, Palmerston to Aberdeen, 2 Oct. 1853, Aberdeen to Palmerston, 5 Oct. 1853.
66. Add. MSS 43049, Palmerston to Aberdeen, 7 Oct. 1853; MSS Clar. Dep. C3, Palmerston to Clarendon, 3 Oct. 1853.
67. Graham Papers, 124, Aberdeen to Graham, 7 Oct. 1853; RA G6/11, Aberdeen to Victoria, 7 Oct. 1853.
68. RA G6/15, Aberdeen to Victoria, 8 Oct. 1853: MSS Clar. Dep. C4 to Clarendon,

5 Oct. 1853: Stanmore, *Sidney Herbert*, vol. 1, pp. 185–7.

69. PRO 30/22/11B, Argyll to Russell, 7 Oct. 1853 (marked, apparently by Russell, 'Important').

70. Add. MSS 43047, Victoria to Aberdeen, 10 Oct. 1853; Albert, Memorandum, 10 Oct. 1853, *Letters of Queen Victoria*, vol. 2, p. 454.

71. Add. MSS 43191, Graham to Aberdeen, 9 Oct. 1853.

72. Add. MSS 43047, Albert to Aberdeen, 21 Oct. 1853 encl. Memorandum.

73. Add. MSS 43191, Graham to Aberdeen, 13 Oct. 1853.

74. RA G6/44, Albert, Memorandum, 16 Oct. 1853.

75. Graham Papers, 124, Aberdeen to Graham, 22 Sept. 1853.

76. By the circular despatch of 31 Oct. 1853, Anderson, p. 130; cf. PP LXXI (1854), 642–3.

77. Temperley, p. 373. But the Russian Admiral did give the Austrian Consul at Sinope a reasonable explanation, later privately communicated to Aberdeen. The Turks had attacked in the Caucasus and he had been sent to find the Turkish ships supplying the Circassians with powder: Add. MSS 43251, Douglas McDonald, *Britannia* to unknown recipient, 11 Dec. 1853. This letter also revealed that two English ships were present, one was destroyed, one escaped.

78. Add. MSS 43044, Brunnow to Aberdeen, 15 Dec. 1853.

79. MSS Clar. Dep. C3, Palmerston to Clarendon, 13 Dec. 1853.

80. *The Times*, 13 Dec. 1853. For a detailed analysis of press influence see Kingsley Martin, *The Triumph of Lord Palmerston*.

81. Add. MSS 43049, Aberdeen to Palmerston, 4 July 1853.

82. MSS Clar. Dep. C3, Russell to Clarendon, 4, 5 Dec. 1853.

83. MSS Clar. Dep. C4, Graham to Clarendon, 13 Dec. 1853.

84. Add. MSS 43191, Graham to Aberdeen, 8 Oct. 1853; Graham Papers, 124, Aberdeen to Graham, 19 Dec. 1853.

85. Morley, vol. 1, p. 490; RA F11/24, Aberdeen to Victoria, 17 Dec. 1853.

86. Add. MSS 43048, Aberdeen to Victoria, 20 Dec. 1853; RA G8/6, Aberdeen to Victoria, 22 Dec. 1853; Morley, vol. 1, p. 491.

87. RA G8/6, Aberdeen to Victoria, 22 Dec. 1853.

88. MSS Clar. Dep. C14, Aberdeen to Clarendon, 16 Jan. 1854.

89. Add. MSS 43071, Gladstone to Aberdeen, 26 Jan. 1854.

90. Add. MSS 43048, Aberdeen to Victoria, 26 Feb. 1853, Victoria to Aberdeen, 26 Feb. 1853; MSS Clar. Dep. C14, Aberdeen to Clarendon, 21 Feb. 1854.

91. MSS Clar. Dep. C14, Aberdeen to Clarendon, 28 Feb. 1854.

92. Add. MSS 43067, Russell to Aberdeen, 3 Mar. 1854.

93. Add. MSS 43067, Aberdeen to Russell, 28 Feb., 3 Mar. 1854.

CHAPTER TWENTY-NINE

The War

Aberdeen delivered the Queen's Message, announcing the outbreak of war with Russia, to the Lords on Monday, 27 March 1854..Derby spoke briefly, warning the government that the opposition would expect a full explanation. The following Friday, 3 March, was set as the day the House would debate the Address in reply.

Aberdeen's handling of the crucial debate was disastrous. The partial mastery of the House, which he had acquired over the years, seemed to desert him and he repeated all the faults of his youth. Age, and perhaps the onset of deafness,[1] accounted for something but, more fundamentally, he was sick at heart at having to defend a policy in which he did not really believe. All his life he had few powers of dissimulation. During the 1853 session he had spoken fairly frequently, and not badly, on domestic affairs but only twice, and very briefly, on the Eastern Question. He left Clarendon to open the debate on 31 March. Clarendon made a clever, but by no means great speech, contending that the Tsar had deliberately deceived the rest of Europe about his intentions since the despatch of the Menshikov mission. He refused to be specific about Britain's war aims beyond saying that the Russians must be kept out of Constantinople, but he also appealed to the vigorous stream of anti-Russian sentiment in Britain by referring to Russia's generally aggressive and anti-liberal policies which had already made some German states virtually dependent upon her.[2] It would in any case have been a difficult speech for Aberdeen, whose views in 1848–49 were well-known, to follow. Derby made it impossible for him. Derby began by saying that the country must be united but he heaped all the blame, not so much on the government generally – he deliberately acquitted Russell of mistakes – as on the Prime Minister personally. The war was now necessary for the liberties of Europe but, at the outset, it could have been avoided. The foundations for Derby's attack had been laid in Disraeli's new journal, the *Press*.

Derby had plenty of ammunition. Earlier in the month *The Times* had revealed that conversations had taken place between the Tsar and the British government about the possible dissolution of the Turkish Empire. Aberdeen at first supposed that the leak had come from inside the British Foreign Office but, in fact, the revelations had come from the *St Petersburg Gazette*, which insisted that the British government had misled the Russians.[3] Determined to put the record straight, on 17 March, the British government laid before Parliament not only Seymour's reports of his conversations with the Tsar and Russell's reply but also Nesselrode's Memorandum of the 1844 conversations. Aberdeen had some doubts about communicating the latter but he told Clarendon, 'As we profess to give everything, I see no good reason for suppressing it; although it has no necessary connection with the recent negotiations'.[4]

Derby made these revelations the centre piece of his attack. It was not, he said, as Clarendon had tried to maintain, the British who had been deceived by the Russians but the Russians who had been misled by the British, or rather by Aberdeen. 'I believe', he thundered, 'this war would never have taken place, these pretensions never would have been put forward, if, at the particular time of these particular difficulties arising, the noble Earl opposite had not been the Minister at the head of the Government.' He dwelt on the 1844 Memorandum, this 'secret memorandum', 'this document . . . of a very remarkable character', which was not official, not placed in the Foreign Office but passed privately down by Secretaries of State. When Brunnow asked Derby and Malmesbury about it in 1852, Derby had to tell him that he knew nothing of it. But, when Aberdeen came to power, the Tsar immediately returned to the document. The Russians, Derby maintained, had been quite open about their claims to a protectorate over the Christians in the Ottoman Empire at the beginning of 1853 and the British government had acquiesced, perhaps not realising what they were doing. He accused Aberdeen of 'political blindness' since, he said, he did not want to accuse him of 'political connivance', when he told the House on 25 April that they had received satisfactory assurances from Russia. Aberdeen foolishly challenged him, 'What did we connive at?', only to provoke the devastating reply, 'The noble Earl knows that better than I do. It certainly is not for me to pry into the secret recesses of the imperturbable mind of the noble Earl opposite, who certainly contrives to keep his own counsel, both here and elsewhere, by dint of a solemn and persevering silence such as I have seen in no other Minister.'[5] When they acted as a team, Derby's wit and Aberdeen's gravity could be devastating, as they proved in the Don Pacifico debate. When they were on opposite sides, Aberdeen was completely outclassed.

Aberdeen was totally thrown by Derby's personal attack. He began his reply with an ill-judged sneer. Derby had spoken of unity. The House would see the nature of his support but he supposed they 'must be grateful for what we have received'. He could hardly avoid replying to Derby's personalities but he let himself be distracted by them. Derby had said he was too easily flattered by royal attention, what of the way Derby himself had positively grovelled in response to Austrian flatteries in 1852? He then launched into a detailed explanation of the 1844 conversations which, although true, impressed nobody. He did not make the obvious defence that he had told Palmerston of them in 1846 and so could hardly be held responsible for the ignorance of any subsequent Foreign Secretary. Palmerston, after all, was still a member of his government. Nor could he very well say in public that withholding very confidential papers from the Foreign Office, which was inclined to leak information, was a common practice with which he had been familiar since 1813.

Only then did he turn to the war itself. He admitted that even though he had 'deprecated and resisted' the war he believed it to be just and necessary and would not be found wanting in carrying it on but, at the same time, 'I make peace my first object and my first vow.' He reminded his hearers that the most virtuous character of the English Civil War (Fairfax), even while arming himself for battle, continued to murmur 'Peace! Peace!' It was not a speech any Prime Minister should have made when taking his country into war.[6]

He made matters worse a few weeks later. On 19 June Lord Lyndhurst made a bellicose speech, saying that no faith could be put in Russian promises, and deploring Austrian and Prussian attempts to restore peace. Since the time of Catherine the Great, Russia had considered Turkey her 'predestined prey'. Russia was a 'semi-barbarous' Power, who always meditated aggression, and, if she could establish herself 'in the heart of Europe', it would be 'the heaviest and most fatal calamity that could fall on the civilised world'.[7] Clarendon made the main reply for the government but Aberdeen was then unfortunately moved to add his comments. He began with a personal attack, telling the House that twenty-five years ago he had introduced Lyndhurst to the French Ambassador who afterwards commented, 'Chancellor, did you call him? Surely he is a colonel of dragoons.' Lyndhurst's bellicosity was, he said, quite unnecessary. The country was too much roused already. Perhaps recalling events even longer ago, he warned the House that it was easy to make demands but peace terms depended on military events. If the Russians got to Constantinople, the terms would be very different from what they would be if the Allies were at St Petersburg. He did not himself believe in Russian aggressiveness. At the time of Adrianople they had been within fifty miles of Constantinople but they had not demanded any territory. Reminded of Russia's Asian gains at this time, he amended that to 'an inch of territory in Europe'. Since then they had not fought Turkey or sought territory. On the contrary, they had defended Turkey from Mehemet Ali. 'There has been no war, there has been no aggression, but only a singular service rendered to Turkey by Russia.' What Aberdeen said was true but it may be imagined that, after this, his promise to prosecute the war with vigour did not appease the House.[8]

The Queen and the Prince were horrified. Even in March, Victoria had written to Leopold, reproaching him for writing to Aberdeen, assuring him of the Tsar's peaceful intentions. 'I think', she said, 'you are *not* aware of Lord Aberdeen's *feelings* on the *subject of this War*. He has *so strong an aversion* for *War* of *any kind* that he has several times *hinted* that he wd. *resign*. I need not tell you *how* alarming and serious this wd. be, for it wd. throw us at once into the arms of the *War Party*.' She and the Prince were now bending their energies to keeping Aberdeen 'up to the mark' and persuading him that now war was declared it must be carried on 'vigorously & enthusiastically'.[9] After his reply to Lyndhurst on 19 June, she advised him to dispel the misapprehensions to which it had given rise as soon as possible. She assured him that she knew what he meant 'but the public . . . is impatient and annoyed to hear at this moment the first Minister of the Crown enter into an *impartial* examination of the

Emperor of Russia's character and conduct'. She feared that his 'candour and his courage in expressing opinions . . . opposed to the general feelings of the moment' was 'dangerous' to him.[10]

Aberdeen's colleagues also complained. Clarendon told him that his speech had 'jarred against public opinion, which is now running breast–high against Nicholas' and warned him that it would not be wise to dampen down the excitement under which great sacrifices are made.[11] Russell sent him an angry letter from his constituents in the City of London, thanking Russell and Clarendon for their 'manly and truly British declarations' and deploring Aberdeen's 'imprudent and unstatesmanlike speech' which might lead the Tsar to think that he could restore the *status quo ante bellum*.[12] Under this pressure, Aberdeen made clumsy amendment by moving for a copy of his own despatch on the Treaty of Adrianople. This despatch, really drafted by Wellington and disapproved of by Aberdeen at the time, virtually contradicted everything he had said on 19 June. Clanricarde rose to say that he was glad that Aberdeen had 'retracted' and, although Aberdeen called out 'No', it was for all practical purposes a retraction.[13] In terms of public relations, Aberdeen was proving to be the world's worst war leader.

The firmness of the Queen and the Prince was ironic in view of the popular suspicions which culminated in the absurd rumour that Albert had been consigned to the Tower as a traitor.[14] The royal couple and Aberdeen were alike the victims of the war hysteria which swept the country, expressing itself first in enthusiasm for the war and then, when victory did not immediately arrive, in a search for scapegoats.

The Crimean War was certainly no more horrible, no more costly in lives and suffering, and probably no worse managed than the Napoleonic Wars, but its details were infinitely better known to the public. It was the first war for which there was real press coverage, aided by the new telegraphs. Since the news was for all practical purposes uncensored, the reporting was franker than it was to be during either of the two World Wars. This first glimpse of the real sufferings of war had much the same effect on the British public of the 1850s as the television coverage of the Vietnam War had on the American public of the 1960s. Inevitably, they looked for someone to blame.

Some of the hysteria grew out of the lunatic propaganda of David Urquhart, who believed not only that the Tsar of Russia was the personification of all evil but that the British government, even Palmerston, were his agents.[15] Urquhart's simple black and white view in which Russia was the great threat to European liberties, had its appeal to the radicals until it was overtaken by the saner opposition of Richard Cobden and John Bright.

The first press campaign really grew out of the controversy over Palmerston's resignation in December 1853. The attacks on the 'unconstitutional' position of Prince Albert, including the fact that he was present when the Queen saw her ministers, and his suspect correspondence with foreigners, came mainly from the radical press but they found echoes in some conservative organs. The close connection of the ministry with the Court, more felt than understood in most quarters, made political sense of what would otherwise seem to be pure irrationality. The royal couple found the attacks very distressing and appealed to Aberdeen for protection. The Queen wrote to him on 5 January that 'a *systematic & most infamous Attack* appears daily in the Mor. Herald & Standard' and that she could no longer doubt that there was 'some design' in this.[16] Aberdeen replied in sympathetic and reassuring terms. He did not believe that any serious consequences could follow 'these contemptible exhibitions of malevolence and faction'. At the same time he felt compelled to admit that the position of the Prince in the constitution was 'somewhat anomalous' and to emphasise that the ministers alone were responsible for policy. He could not ignore the fact — although he did not think it tactful to mention it to the Queen at this juncture — that Albert's desire to reorganise the army, however much the next few months might demonstrate that it was amply justified, had aroused resentment in quarters which were certainly not radical. He had, he said, some information on the origins of the attacks but it was as yet 'vague and uncertain'. To the horror of the government, it seemed possible that Sir Robert Peel's son might raise the matter in the Commons. Aberdeen still tried to be reassuring. He told the Queen: 'As he is half mad, it is difficult to say what he may not do; but although he would utterly disgrace himself, nothing could more expose the monstrous absurdity of the whole affair.'[17]

Victoria was not altogether appeased. She disliked what she regarded as a 'very injudicious' article in *The Times*, which emphasised her dependence on the Prince. Aberdeen had to reply that *The Times* was under 'no control'. Delane had in fact asked Aberdeen whether he should join in the controversy. Aberdeen, after some hesitation, replied that it would be better to answer the libels in Parliament. But, he told the Queen, 'They have not only violated Ld Aberdeen's injunctions but have done it in bad taste.' The Queen was better pleased by an article which Gladstone contributed to the *Morning Chronicle*.[18]

Victoria was even reluctant to open Parliament in person, fearing that she would be subjected to insult. Aberdeen thought her absence would be 'most unfortunate' and she was persuaded to be present but Edward Stanley recorded in his diary that her reception was less good than the press made out and that some of the crowd hissed.[19] In the debate on the Address in reply to the Speech, Derby attacked Aberdeen for leaks to *The Times* for which he held him personally responsible. Aberdeen took advantage of the opening thus accorded him to deplore the wild attacks on Prince Albert and to suggest that it ill became Derby to complain of the irresponsibility of the press when papers with which he was known to be connected carried such material. Derby replied but on that occasion Aberdeen had the better of the exchange.[20]

The questioning of Albert's position had cut Victoria to the quick. On 22 January Albert himself wrote a long memorandum on the army, protesting that Wellington had wanted Albert to succeed him as Commander–in–Chief and he had only declined because he thought he should sink his individual existence in that of the Queen. A week later Victoria revived a proposal, first made in 1850, that Albert should assume the title of Prince Consort. It must, she said, be settled before the children grew up. Otherwise they would have the embarrassing anomaly of the royal princes taking precedence over their father.[21]

Aberdeen was well aware that the moment was most unpropitious for making Albert Prince Consort and the suggestion was allowed quietly to lapse.

While he was doing his best to defend Prince Albert, Aberdeen himself was being subjected to a political smear campaign of unusual ferocity and considerable professional expertise, from which his reputation has never really recovered to this day. He was handicapped by having no reliable organ through which he could reply. Even the Peelite *Morning Chronicle* was increasingly sympathetic to Palmerston. When Palmerston returned to the Cabinet at the end of 1853, it expressed its relief and called Palmerston 'a symbol of pluck and public spirit'.[22] *The Times* could no longer be depended upon. Aberdeen told Clarendon in February 1854: 'Unfortunately it is believed that the Times is especially my organ: although in fact there is seldom an Article in it from which I do not entirely dissent.'[23] Aberdeen kept up his personal friendship with Delane, but Delane printed what he liked and increasingly became the most strenuous critic of the deficiencies of the war administration.

Aberdeen met with some criticisms from the political left. The radical *Daily News* complained on 19 December, 'The indignation against Lord Aberdeen, as the wet blanket which is turning the national fire into smoke, is very strong and nearly universal.' But the strongest criticisms came from the Conservative journals, the *Morning Herald* and, above all, Disraeli's weekly, the *Press*. The *Herald*, like the *Chronicle*, expressed its preference for Palmerston. In December 1853 it proclaimed: 'The one [Aberdeen] was Russian, the other [Palmerston] English to the backbone' and complained that Aberdeen and the Peelites had thwarted all attempts to act with 'manly vigour'.[24]

Aberdeen's inept performances in the Lords on 27 March and 19 June 1854 gave every opening for hostile criticism but the attacks had begun long before that, at the time when Aberdeen's government was enjoying domestic success and when a peaceful outcome of the Eastern Question still seemed very possible. The *Press* opened the campaign on 4 June 1853 with an article written by Disraeli himself. It proclaimed:

His mind, his education, his prejudices are all of the Kremlin school. Now that he is placed in a prominent position, and forced to lead English gentlemen, instead of glozing and intriguing with foreign diplomatists, not a night passes that his language or his demeanour does not shock and jar upon the frank and genial spirit of our British Parliament. His manner, arrogant and yet timid – his words, insolent and yet obscure – offend even his political supporters. His hesitating speech, his contracted sympathies, his sneer, icy as Siberia, his sarcasms, drear and barren as the Steppes, are all characteristic of the bureau and the chancery, and not of popular and aristocratic assemblies animated by the spirit of honour and the pride of gentlemen. If war breaks out – and the present prospect is that war will break out – this dread calamity must be placed to the account of this man, and of this man alone.

Disraeli's accusing Aberdeen of being no gentleman had its comic side, and the comment on his contacts with foreign diplomatists was cool from a man who had gone out of his way to take Metternich's advice on English politics, but as a piece of character assassination it was brilliant. Like a cruel caricature it had just enough truth to carry conviction, or at least raise doubts.

There was worse to follow. A week later Disraeli wrote: 'The curse of "antiquated imbecility" has fallen in all its fulness, on Lord Aberdeen. His temper, naturally morose, has become licentiously peevish. Crossed in his Cabinet, he insults the House of Lords, and plagues the most eminent of his colleagues with the crabbed malice of a maundering witch.' After this, repeated reference to the 'incompetence' of British foreign policy in subsequent issues was almost an anti-climax. The attacks in December were equally vicious. Aberdeen, the *Press* said, 'will betray the honour and interests of our country – it is the law of his nature and the destiny of his life.' It is scarcely surprising that Aberdeen complained in the Lords of the *Press's* 'malignity'.[25]

At first sight the venom of the attacks might seem incomprehensible but they were carefully calculated. Gladstone saw this when he said a little later that the personal attacks on Aberdeen came from two quarters, first, those who were fanatical about the Eastern Question 'and secondly, those who, knowing his weight and the importance of his position, desire to eject him as the keystone out of the arch, and use this Eastern Question as a lever for the purpose.'[26] Aberdeen was holding the coalition together. Disraeli, although not perhaps Derby, believed that if Aberdeen were driven from office by whatever means, the Conservatives would be able to form the next government. For several leading British politicians the priority was not to unite to win the war but to exploit the war to bring about the desired re–alignment in British politics. Disraeli, and to some extent the radicals, exploited it in opposition. Russell exploited it within the Cabinet. Aberdeen personally was every man's target, not just because some believed that a man so openly committed to peace could never be a successful war leader – a perfectly honourable and reasonable position – but also, and much less defensibly, because he was the man who stood in the way of other ambitious men determined to seize power.

Aberdeen had perhaps enough Scottish obstinacy in his character to be determined not to yield to attacks such as these. The reasoned criticisms of men like John Bright distressed him much more than the venom of Disraeli. Bright made one desperate personal appeal on the very eve of the war. Some, said Bright, seemed to want war on any terms but he believed that Aberdeen wanted peace as much as he did. He assured him that the majority of the British people would be with him. A portion of the London press wanted war but the 'quiet and intelligent classes have many doubts; the House of Commons is not warlike'. Disraeli's approbation of war had given displeasure to many of his supporters. On Bright's side of the House, except for a few 'enthusiasts who want to fight both Russia and Austria', the feeling was strongly for peace. Bright admitted that he had written in the belief that the proposals still being discussed in Vienna were known to Russia and had a chance of being accepted and 'if it is not the case, then my argument falls to the ground'. But, Bright argued, Aberdeen had more interest than anyone in preserving the peace. 'Your administration will not be known in our Annals as the *Russell*, or the *Palmerston*, but as the *Aberdeen* administration.' It was to him that 'posterity and impartial history' would award the praise or the blame.[27] Aberdeen was all too painfully aware of that, and on 22 March, Bright came to Argyll House at Aberdeen's

request. Aberdeen had to tell him that his (Bright's) hopes about the negotiations still in progress, were mistaken. War now seemed inevitable but he
'would avail himself of any proposal for mediation and for peace', even if he
stood alone. He spoke more freely to Bright than to almost anyone else, telling
him that, 'His grief was such that at times he felt as if every drop of blood
that would be shed would rest upon his head'.[28]

He seriously discussed the possibility of resignation with Gladstone in February, arguing that he could not lead the country in what was likely to become
an offensive war against Russia. Gladstone used his very considerable persuasive
powers to convince him that they were still talking of a defensive and entirely
justified war. In the end Aberdeen decided against resignation. Victoria showed
her distress at the idea of being left to the 'War Party' and Aberdeen was deeply
imbued with Wellington's philosophy that 'the King's government must be
carried on'. If the coalition broke up, what was the alternative? At home it
would probably have meant the recrudescence of the faction fighting of 1851
and 1852. His youngest son, who was very close to him at this time, had no
doubt that he remained to restrain the wild men, who would have liked to
have broadened the basis of the war, and because he believed that he had the
best chance of persuading Austria to side with Britain and France, and, perhaps, even at this late stage of negotiating an acceptable peace.[29]

The question of war aims was vital. For Aberdeen, the objective was simple
and, in itself, entirely defensible – his doubts turned entirely upon whether
it could have been achieved without recourse to war. Russia must be prevented
from getting undue influence over the Ottoman Empire and, more particularly,
from obtaining permanent control of Constantinople and the Straits. He had
no quarrel with the Tsar as the champion of European conservatism. He had
not particularly liked the Polish settlement in 1815 but he had never been
attracted by the idea of a radical crusade to free Poland from Russia.

These were not the views of some of his colleagues. As early as 4 March
1854, Palmerston wrote a long letter to Clarendon, sketching some of the
possible results of a war with Russia. The Aaland Islands and Finland could
be restored to Sweden; Poland re–established in its ancient limits as an independent state; the mouth of the Danube restored to Turkey, unless a new
arrangement could be made for carrying Austria to the Black Sea; the Crimea
taken, the Russian Black Sea fleet destroyed, and Sebastopol, with its docks
and arsenals, razed to the ground; the Crimea could then be returned to Turkey,
Circassia made independent and Georgia given either to Circassia or to Turkey.[30] Aberdeen though this ridiculous fantasy and said so. Such terms could
only be dictated at the gates of Moscow. In April he told Russell that they
ought to be clear about their objectives. He wrote:

I had imagined them [the objectives] to be the protection of Turkey against Russian
aggression, the evacuation of Turkish territory by the Russian forces, and generally,
the independence of the Sultan in his domestic administration, as well as the integrity
of his Empire. I have recently heard much of securing the independence of Europe, the
progress of civilization, and the overthrow of barbarism. These are objects too vague
to be easily understood, or practically to regulate our proceedings . . .[31]

Clarendon, however, was tending towards Palmerston's side. He wrote to Aberdeen:

The war was, undoubtedly, defensive in its character at the commencement. The Porte defended itself against unjust aggression; but now England and France have taken part in it on European grounds and for the defence of Ottoman territory, the character of the war is changed, and we are fighting for a state of things which will render peace durable.

At the least, they must look afresh at all former treaties.[32] In August Palmerston could ask indignantly, 'Is it *possible* that Aberdeen can have discouraged the Idea of the re—establishment of a Kingdom of Poland?'[33] By then, Palmerston seems to have believed the rest of the Cabinet to be in favour of it.

By July Aberdeen was completely isolated. When the Vote of Credit for the war came before the Commons on 24 July, he was once again the subject of bitter attacks, led by Disraeli and Henry Layard, the diplomat and archaeologist, whose knowledge of the Near East could cap Aberdeen's own.[34] None of Aberdeen's friends tried to reply. This time Aberdeen had had enough. He poured out his feelings to Graham. He was, he said, about to go to Osborne and he would have a great deal to say to the Queen; 'it will require a little time for me to recover my equanimity, after having been made the subject of repeated attacks during a long debate, without a single syllable being said in defence . . . I should have no pleasure in meeting the Cabinet to-day at dinner.'[35]

Graham replied that their interview the previous day 'grieved me very deeply' and Aberdeen's note had not diminished 'the painful impression'. If Aberdeen felt that he had failed him as a friend or as a colleague, 'I am sure the error is mine; for you are just and forbearing, and I regret the error from my heart.' He assured him that, since the death of Peel, he had regarded Aberdeen as 'my most faithful and familiar friend'. He explained that he had been ready to speak but that the brunt had fallen on Russell and he had hesitated, not knowing what had happened in the Lords and fearing to do more harm than good.[36]

Aberdeen had recovered command of himself the next day. He replied to Graham, 'You may be assured that I blame no one except myself. I ought to have acquired sufficient philosophy to meet an occurrence like that of Monday without repining. Fortunately, I have expressed my feelings to no one but to yourself, and, in a much less degree, to Gladstone; neither shall I say anything more of the matter.' He assured him that he felt complete confidence in his friendship. 'There is no change; let us, therefore, be satisfied, and turn to other matters.' While he was at Osborne, Victoria had put Cowes Castle at his disposal and he now offered it to Graham. Graham, however, declined, suggesting that it had better go to a distinguished military officer.[37]

It was Aberdeen's son, Arthur, who wrote to explain his father's distress to Gladstone. Gladstone replied, offering several explanations as to why he had not spoken. He did not feel 'fully master' of the Eastern Question. He was commonly supposed to be 'tarred with the same stick' as Aberdeen – that is, too pacific – and it was difficult to keep a 'defence from a presumed accomplice from being positively mischievous to the defended'. 'You speak', he said, 'of setting Lord Aberdeen right with the public.' Perhaps Aberdeen felt that he needed it. but Gladstone did not. Aberdeen was in the bad grace of only two sections of the public, the 'fanatics' of the Eastern Question, and those who for political reasons wanted to eject him as the 'keystone of the arch'. 'No one', he insisted 'can fail to see that, whoever has lost, Lord Aberdeen has not lost by the formation of the present Government. The act itself was an achievement which no other man could have accomplished. Before he became Minister it might be said that his reputation was more Continental than British, but he has become a great historical figure in domestic politics.'[38]

Aberdeen soldiered on. He still believed that he understood the continental situation better than most of his colleagues. The Austrians were suspected in 1854, as they had been in 1813, of endless vacillation and indecision but Aberdeen had no difficulty in comprehending the difficulties of their position. He told Clarendon in July that he was not surprised that the Austrians continued to hold pacific language. If Austria joined the Allies, the Tsar would probably foget Turkey and turn on her. 'I am only surprised', he added 'that he did not say he would give his answer [to the latest Austrian approach on the Principalities] in Vienna.'[39] The old description of the Crimean War as a series of negotiations punctuated by battles is not inapt. Even after the fighting had begun the negotiations went on. Ultimately, this was Aberdeen's justification for his belief that he must be in office to take advantage of any opportunity for an honourable peace which presented itself.

Despite their reluctance to join in a war which would put their very existence at stake, the Austrians had more reason than anyone else to complain of the presence of Russian troops in Moldavia and Wallachia and, in the summer of 1854, they persuaded the Russians to evacuate their forces, in return for a promise that the Austrians themselves would garrison the Principalities and prevent them from being seized by the Turks or their allies.

Attempts to involve the Austrians also led to the formulation by the Austrians and the French of the 'Four Points' on which peace might be made. They were: first, the renunciation by Russia of any special rights of intervention in the Principalities or Serbia; second, the free navigation of the Danube; third, the revision of the Straits Convention of 1841 'in the interests of the balance of power', which was later extended to mean the neutralisation of the Black Sea; and fourth, the renunciation by Russia of any protectorate over the Christian subjects of the Sultan – instead the Sultan should promise them rights under the general guarantee of Europe. When the British Cabinet first discussed these proposals on 19 July, they were not keen to tie themselves down to specific proposals but at the end of the month in order to keep in step with the French and Austrians, they accepted them as the bases for negotiation.[40]

The Russian evacuation of the Principalities had a profound effect on Anglo-French war strategy. It could be said that by September 1854 the allies had achieved all the objectives for which they had originally gone to war, but practically nobody except Aberdeen (and Richard Cobden and his supporters) drew the obvious conclusion that it would now be sensible to make peace. Constantinople was safe and the Russians out of the Principalities.

There had been a revealing exchange of letters between Aberdeen and Russell at the end of April. Both were agreed that, with an Anglo–French force in the Black Sea, Constantinople was safe from attack by sea but its land defence was less certain. Russell recalled that when the forces were first despatched there were plans for the establishment of a perimeter defence some twenty miles from Constantinople on the model of the lines of Torres Vedras, but he doubted the validity of the analogy. The Portugese had been on Wellington's side. If the Turks fell back on Constantinople, the Christian population would rise and welcome the Russians and the Tsar would have the whole of European Turkey in his grasp. They must therefore hold Schumla and the line of the Balkan River for as long as possible. Aberdeen entirely agreed that the defence must be made on the Balkan or even the Danube. At the same time, he saw the grim irony of the fact that Russell at last appreciated the real attitude of the Christian population in Turkey. Every Christian in the Ottoman Empire, as Aberdeen put it, would be praying for the Tsar's success. 'This', he told Russell 'is the great original vice of our position, which from the first I have endeavoured to point out, and which will become more embarrassing every day.'[41]

Other embarrassments were appearing too, particularly in Greece and the Baltic. The Greeks were keen to take advantage of Turkey's difficulties to improve their own frontiers. The French eventually sent a garrison to Athens to restrain the Greeks but Aberdeen was adamant that it would be impossible to employ British troops against them.[42] Difficulties in the Baltic turned on the position of Sweden. Some people were anxious to recruit Sweden as an ally. Aberdeen, perhaps remembering all the difficulties of 1813, was not enthusiastic. There was another good reason too. The only inducement for Sweden to enter the war would be the possibility of her acquiring Finland from Russia. This would have greatly widened the scope of the war aims and introduced issues quite separate from the defence of Turkey. Aberdeen was determined to avoid this if possible.[43] The naval operations in the Baltic, which Aberdeen whole–heartedly supported, achieved some success. In August Admiral Napier in conjunction with the French, captured the Aaland Islands, including the Russian naval base of Bomarsund.

The main theatre however, was still the Black Sea. From the beginning there had been those who advocated the destruction of Sebastopol. It was argued that Constantinople would never be really secure so long as the Russian Black Sea fleet and its base remained intact. Late in June the Cabinet decided in favour of an attack on Sebastopol.[44] The most economic form of attack would have been a naval bombardment and this seems to have been what Aberdeen himself would have favoured. But the British Admiral in the Black Sea, Admiral Dundas, advised that the destruction of Sebastopol by naval means was impossible. He attacked the port once but his ships stood too far out to sea, and he achieved little.[45] Dundas attracted much criticism throughout the Crimean campaign, notably for allowing the Russian garrison of Anapa to return to Sebastopol by sea without interception. Much pressure was brought to bear on Aberdeen to recall him, but the Prime Minister refused on the grounds that there was no firm evidence that Dundas was guilty of dereliction of duty.[46] Throughout the campaign he showed the same loyalty to other commanders.

The Guards sailed in April, among them Aberdeen's own son, Alexander. Alexander wrote very frequently to his father and Aberdeen hardly needed the famous denunciations of W. H. Russell in *The Times* to tell him of all that was going wrong with the military organisation in the Crimea. Alexander wrote with vigorous anger and he also found it hard to stomach their Turkish allies. Although he fought bravely in all the great battles of the Crimean War, he made no secret of the fact that his own sympathies were with the Russians. Aberdeen, who shared many of his son's views, must have groaned in spirit, not least at the possibility of Alexander's opinions becoming known. Alexander also had a genuine grievance in that he was persistently denied the promotion that came to brother officers who fought in the same battles. The excuse was always the same. They could not promote Alexander because his father was Prime Minister.[47]

Alexander's first surviving letter is dated from Scutari on 5 May 1854. He told his father that he did not know when they would be able to move because they had such difficulty in getting baggage animals. So far, not a single cavalry soldier except Lord Lucan had arrived. He supposed that when they did, they too would be landed on the Scutari side of the Bosphorus, in order to put that river as well as the Danube between them and the Russians. They should have made camp at Pera. He found Constantinople a great disappointment. 'It is quite time that some civilised nation should get possession of it and build a proper town instead of the present collection of wigwams.'[48]

A few weeks later he complained that he was not getting letters from home. Everyone was furious at the inadequate postal arrangements. It was said letters were kept at Malta until someone paid the postage and there was no one there to do so. The Light Division had sailed for Varna but they could not follow because the Commissariat was not ready. Aberdeen should send out orders that Lord Raglan was in command, not General Filder. Filder, like many other Crimean War generals was a Peninsula veteran and Alexander recounted with relish how during that campaign General Picton had wished to hang this 'Fidler'. Alexander had seen St Sophia, then a mosque, and remarked wistfully that they could make it a Christian Church again in a few hours. He thought it symbolic that a wall painting of Christ or the Virgin had begun to show through the covering paint just above where the high altar used to stand.[49]

Early in August he wrote from near Varna that preparations were apparently being made for them to embark for Sebastopol but he found it hard to believe that they were about to begin the siege of Sebastopol at the end of the summer with cholera, typhoid and dysentery already in the camp. 7000 French soldiers had died of cholera. 'You seem to think', he told his father, 'we are on the Danube – I wish we were – and we should have been if your Treasury Regulations would permit us. We promised Austria & Omer Pasha that we would go there, and we might have taken up our winter quarters at Bucharest with the greatest ease; there would have been some point gained and we should have been in a forward position to commence again next year.' A month later, although Raglan kept his plans 'very close', Alexander understood that they were to land fifteen miles from Sebastopol. He was glad that his wife, Caroline, was in good hands because 'Sebastopol cannot be taken without some loss'.[50]

Aberdeen believed that the decisions must be left to the military commanders on the spot but he knew enough of the area to have grave doubts about the advisability of an army wintering in the Crimea. He saw no particular virtue in occupying Sebastopol for the winter and certainly did not want to give it, as Palmerston had suggested, to the Turks. He agreed with Russell that the important thing was that it should be destroyed as a naval base.[51]

The Queen begged him to leave London for Balmoral and take the opportunity of a few days rest at Haddo. The siege of Sebastopol was likely to take some time and it would be after it had fallen that he must be in London to take decisions. She had heard from his doctors, Clarke and Holland, that he was not well and she was becoming seriously concerned about his health. His health, she told him, was not 'his *own* alone but that she and the country have *as much* interest in it as he and his own family'. He should come to Scotland to take in a 'stock of health' for the winter.[52] Aberdeen was now racked not only by public anxieties but also by concern for Alexander in the Crimea and for the failing health of his eldest son, George. At the end of September he gave in and went to Scotland.

While he was there, there came the news not only of the battle of Alma, which was represented as a great and complete victory, but also of the reported fall of Sebastopol. Aberdeen was cautious but in the end he too became convinced that the news must be true. The war seemed to be won. Graham wrote in exultation on 30 September, 'Do not lose sight of your great opportunity; take the tide at its rise, and let us have a new Parliament'.[53] The disappointment when it became apparent that Sebastopol had not fallen was all the crueller. Stanmore is probably right in saying that it was the sharpness of the reaction which intensified the criticisms of the next few months.[54]

Alexander, writing from 'Before Sebastopol', kept his father all too well informed of what was going wrong. The Russians had been able to bring up massive reinforcements of both men and guns. By late December Sebastopol was 'five times stronger' than when first attacked on 17 October. The heavy rains in November broke up the roads and made the bringing up of either food or ammunition difficult. The horses were dying of starvation and cold. Winter clothing should have been sent much earlier. The November hurricane which destroyed the supply ships was almost the final straw. When Sir de Lacy Evans, another Peninsula veteran but an intelligent soldier, was invalided home because of his age, Alexander told his father, 'His parting advice to Raglan was "My Lord, Save your Army, and raise the siege". I believe the same advice would be given by every General and Officer of experience in this Army, *if his opinion were asked.*'[55]

By December, Alexander was making no secret of the fact that he hoped for peace. He was now Assistant Quarter Master General and well placed to see both the magnitude of the disaster and the brave, but usually unsuccessful, efforts which were being made to combat it. Food was short. Men, like the horses, were dying of cold and hunger. Three hundred men had died in the last four days of cholera and cold. The boots sent out from England were too small and the men preferred to go bare-foot in the trenches in the snow. As a result many were crippled by frost-bite. So many men were sick that they had had to reduce the guards on the batteries and spike the guns. Huts had at last arrived from England but they were too heavy to move easily. They were building a railway to replace the damaged road but they had no 'stationary engines' and the trucks were too large to be pulled easily by horses. He asked his father whether he remembered him saying before he left England, ' "Do you (the Government) know what you have undertaken?" ' Alexander, who was certainly no coward, saw no real alternative to negotiating a peace but he added grimly, 'I should think the "Times" had enlightened the Emperor of Russia too much as to the present state of our army here to make *him* wish for peace.'[56]

The British army, which suffered a great deal more than the French, was paying for the many years of peace–time neglect of the army and its support services. The government was understandably angered by the fact that some of their severest critics in Parliament were those who had themselves neglected to remedy the situation when they were in power. The Duke of Newcastle was doing his conscientious, if laboured, best to improve matters. When the war broke out it had been appreciated that no man could continue to combine the offices of Secretary of State for the Colonies and for War. The question was how they should be re–distributed. A number of proposals were put forward. In May, Russell suggested three possible arrangements. Newcastle should keep the War Office and Sir George Grey come in to take the Colonies; or Newcastle should move to the Home Office, Palmerston to the War Office and Grey again come in for the Colonies; or Newcastle should keep the Colonies, Palmerston take the War Office and Sir George Grey the Home Office.[57] Russell favoured the last, which would almost certainly have been the best. Palmerston, who had a long experience of the War Office dating from the Napoleonic Wars, was perhaps the only man who could have infused real vigour into that Department. At the same time, it is easy to see why Aberdeen hesitated. Palmerston's views on the war objectives were very far removed from his own.

What complicated the situation still further was that Russell could not make up his mind what he wanted to do. He almost agreed to take the Colonial Office: then decided that he might prefer the Presidency of the Council. Aberdeen would have been agreeable to that, although there were some con- stitutional difficulties because the Presidency was normally held by a member of the House of Lords. What Russell really wanted was the Premiership. Every- one knew that much of his vacillation was due to the influence of his wife. Gladstone lost his temper and told Arthur that he doubted 'if there was any man in England, except Lord Aberdeen, who could have borne what he has had to bear during the last seventeen months from *Lady John*'. Aberdeen did his best to find an accommodation, although he knew it would be embarrassing to bring Sir George Grey in while Canning and Cardwell were still outside the Cabinet. In the end, even he became irritated and told Russell that, since the offices had originally been adjusted to suit him, he would have to help Aberdeen to explain why a reshuffle was necessary. The re–arrangement fell through. Aberdeen declined to move Newcastle from the War Office.[58] It would have been bound to have looked like a vote of no confidence and, apart from the fact that Newcastle was one of his most reliable Peelite allies, Aberdeen believed that he was doing his best and achieving considerable results in the face of almost impossible difficulties. It was, however, a case of loyalty and a sense of fair play triumphing over political expediency. Neither Newcastle, nor Sidney Herbert, the Secretary at War, was best suited to his office.

Russell remained profoundly dissatisfied. He tried to break up the ministry by manufacturing a quarrel with Gladstone over the dismissal of a connection of his own, Thomas Kennedy, from the Department of Woods and Forests.[59] In the end, perhaps common sense persuaded him that this was hardly an issue on which he could take a public stand, and towards the end of the year he reverted to the much more serious question that the unsatisfactory progress of the war demanded a change at the War Office and that Palmerston must replace Newcastle. Aberdeen still refused. Russell threatened to resign but subsequently withdrew his threat. By now he had lost the sympathy of all his colleagues. It was not only Aberdeen's own friends, Graham, Gladstone and Herbert, who were indignant. The Prince rightly thought that it would really turn on whether Palmerston supported Russell. Palmerston did not. After a particularly unpleasant Cabinet dinner on 4 December Clarendon described Russell as a 'spoilt child' and Wood told him that it would be 'treason' to break up the government at present.[60]

Parliament met for a short session in December. Aberdeen was now more hopeful than he had been for many months of an end to the war. Complete stalemate had been reached in the Crimea but Aberdeen had always put more faith in negotiations than in battles. On 2 December Austria finally signed a treaty with Britain and France in which she undertook to press the Four Points upon Russia. At the beginning of January 1855, the Russians agreed to accept them as the basis for negotiations. Although Victoria, Clarendon and even Aberdeen feared that the Tsar was merely playing for time, Aberdeen at least hoped that a peace conference might be speedily assembled in Vienna. He also hoped that Lord John might be persuaded to attend it as the British representative and that he might be able to make a compromise peace acceptable to the British public. Aberdeen told Lady Haddo, 'Of this . . . I am quite determined; if reasonable terms should be within my reach, I will make peace, or some one else shall carry on the war.'[61] A few weeks later his whole strategy had collapsed, largely sabotaged by Lord John.

Parliament was due to meet again on 23 January. Russell attended the Cabinet meetings of 16 and 20 January and joined in the discussions on domestic measures, giving no hint that he intended to leave the government. He also pressed on a number of occasions for more vigorous measures in the Crimea but so did other members of the Cabinet. By now public opinion was becoming thoroughly excited by the first–hand reports of conditions in the Crimea which were appearing in *The Times* and elsewhere. Newcastle had told Aberdeen privately that he wished to resign but had asked for a delay in the announcement.[62]

When Parliament met, Roebuck immediately gave notice that he would move for a Committee of Enquiry into the conduct of the war. That evening Aberdeen returned to Argyll House to dinner. After dinner his son, as his private secretary, opened the despatch boxes. The first document that came to hand was a letter of resignation from Lord John. Aberdeen's first reaction was one of scepticism. Lord John had resigned too often. But this time even Aberdeen had had enough and his mood soon changed to a determination to accept the resignation. Arthur was despatched to fetch Graham from the Admiralty.[63] Russell's decision seems to have been taken impulsively but the reason he gave and to which he stuck was that Roebuck's motion could not be resisted. Russell believed that the Commons had the right to insist on such an enquiry if they wished. Aberdeen did not.[64] But, behind this disagreement on constitutional proprieties, lay the fact that Russell was unwilling to defend the government's war record.

Before the Cabinet met on 24 January, Aberdeen saw Newcastle and Palmerston. Newcastle again offered to resign in favour of Palmerston but the Cabinet did not feel that, at this juncture, they could use him as a scapegoat. Palmerston expressed strong disapproval of Russell's conduct. The Whig members of the Cabinet did, however, accept Russell's view that the Commons had the right to ask for a committee. There seemed no alternative to resignation and Aberdeen left for Windsor. The Queen, in great distress, begged Aberdeen to stay on.[65] Russell, realising that he had miscalculated and had few supporters, made a number of indirect overtures to Aberdeen but this time Aberdeen turned a deaf ear. There seemed no alternative to going down fighting.[66] Russell, explaining his resignation to the Commons on 26 January, told them that he could not oppose Roebuck's motion. Late on the evening of 29 January Roebuck's motion was carried by 305 to 148.

On 30 January Aberdeen went to Windsor in a snow storm to tender his government's final resignation.[67] The Queen was intensely distressed. Unlike the public, she had been able to follow the drama from the inside and she made no secret of the fact that her sympathies were with Aberdeen. A few days later she took the opportunity, while writing about a minor ecclesiastical appointment 'to say what she hardly dares to do verbally without fearing to give way to her feelings; she wished to say what a pang it is for her to separate from so kind & dear and valued a friend as Lord Aberdeen has ever been to her since she has known him'. The day he became her Prime Minister was 'a very happy one'. He had always been her 'Kindest and wisest adviser' and she hoped that she and the Prince could continue to rely on his advice.[68]

His advice and assistance were soon to be needed. On the resignation of the ministry, the Queen very properly sent for Lord Derby. Derby approached Palmerston for support but, when he refused, Derby, to Disraeli's chagrin, declined to try to form a government.[69] The Queen then sent for Russell, still the titular leader of the Whigs, but all his former Cabinet colleagues refused to join him. Some of them made their opinions of his recent 'treachery' very clear.[70] Palmerston now became, in his own words, 'l'inévitable'.

Even Palmerston could not form a ministry without the support of the former Peelites and Aberdeen, in what he himself recognised to be a supreme piece of irony, exerted himself to bring a Palmerston government into being by persuading his reluctant colleagues, particularly Graham and Gladstone who were very unwilling to serve, to join it. It was even suggested that Aberdeen himself should join it but this, he told Sidney Herbert, was quite out of the question. The humiliation would be unbearable and he would rather die. Palmerston was well aware of the sacrifice he had already made and thanked him warmly for his 'handsome conduct' and 'energetic exertions', without which the formation of his government would have been quite impossible. Aberdeen, in his reply, while not entirely concealing his indignation at what had occurred, acquitted Palmerston of having had any share in it. Relations between Aberdeen and Palmerston in fact became remarkably cordial and they frequently dined together.[71]

The leading Peelites did not long remain in the ministry. Graham, Gladstone and Herbert resigned at the end of February. Canning left in July to become Governor General of India. Only Argyll stayed on. Nevertheless, Aberdeen continued to play the role of elder statesman outside the Cabinet. The Prince remained in close touch with him. So did Clarendon.

Popular acclaim had brought Palmerston to power but there was no sudden turn for the better in the Crimea, although Sebastopol was finally captured on 9 September 1855. Peace came about more as a result of international diplomacy than of military success. The terms of the Treaty of Paris of March 1856 were based on the Four Points, of which Aberdeen had approved and which he had believed they were quite close to securing in December 1854, if his ministry had been given a little more time. The wilder ideas of freeing Poland and returning the Crimea to Turkey had all been forgotten. Aberdeen realistically consoled himself that Palmerston could present peace terms to the British people which they would not have accepted from him.[72] As a final irony, in the Treaty of Paris Palmerston surrendered all Britain's old definition of maritime rights and the right of search, which had caused Aberdeen such agonising problems in 1813 and 1842. No one even noticed.

NOTES

1. Charlotte Canning had suspected as early as 1843 that Aberdeen could not hear as well as he thought he could, Surtees, p. 102 (6 Sept. 1843).
2. *Hansard*, 3rd ser., CXXXII, 14053.
3. Add. MSS 43252, Delane to Aberdeen, 13 Mar. 1854; *History of The Times, 1841–1884*, pp. 159–60; Malmesbury, pp. 327–8 (14, 17 Mar. 1854); Greville, vol. VII, pp. 147–8 (20 Mar. 1854). Delane's letter dispels any suggestion that Aberdeen was his informant. Curiously, he says *inter alia* that the fact that the Tsar made proposals in London in 1844 had been published and discussed many times.
4. PP LXXI (1854), 833, 863; MSS Clar. Dep. C14, Aberdeen to Clarendon, 16 Mar. 1854.

5. *Hansard*, 3rd ser., CXXXII, 153–74.
6. *Hansard*, 3rd ser., CXXXII, 174–80.
7. *Hansard*, 3rd ser., CXXXIV, 306–19.
8. *Hansard*, 3rd ser., CXXXIV, 331–4.
9. RA Y99/12, Victoria to Leopold, 31 Mar. 1854.
10. Add. MSS 43049, Victoria to Aberdeen, 26 June 1854.
11. Add. MSS 43189, Clarendon to Aberdeen, 26 June 1854.
12. Add. MSS 43068, Russell to Aberdeen, 23 June 1854.
13. *Hansard*, 3rd ser., CXXXIV, 640–50 (26 June 1854).
14. Malmesbury, p. 323 (15 Jan. 1854); Greville, vol. VII, pp. 127–32 (15, 16, 25, 29 Jan 1854); Kingsley Martin, pp. 178–86.
15. Urquhart's peculiar position is best discussed in A. J. P. Taylor, *The Troublemakers*, pp. 46–50, 58–60.
16. Add. MSS 43048, Aberdeen to Victoria, 5 Jan. 1854.
17. RA A81/121, Aberdeen to Victoria, 6 Jan. 1854, G9/15, Aberdeen to Victoria, 17 Jan. 1854.
18. Add. MSS 43251, Delane to Aberdeen, 20 Jan. 1854; Add. MSS 43048, Victoria to Aberdeen, 16, 18 Jan. 1854; RA G9/32, 33, Aberdeen to Victoria, 19, 20 Jan. 1854.
19. Add. MSS 43048, Victoria to Albert, 21 Jan. 1854, Aberdeen to Victoria, 21 Jan. 1854; Vincent, p. 118 (31 Jan. 1854).
20. Hansard, 3rd ser., CXXX, 74–6, 100–4 (31 Jan. 1854).
21. Add. MSS 43048, Albert, Memorandum, 22 Jan. 1854, Victoria to Aberdeen, 29 Jan. 1854.
22. *Morning Chronicle*, 26 Dec. 1853.
23. Mss Clar. Dep. C14, Aberdeen to Clarendon, 28 Feb. 1854.
24. *Morning Herald*, 17 Dec. 1854.
25. The *Press*, 4, 11, 18 June, 16 July, 3 Sept., 16 Dec. 1853; *Hansard*, 3rd ser., XXXII, 177–8, (31 Mar. 1854). Monypenny and Buckle, who published the more striking passages, felt compelled to defend Disraeli, vol. 3, p. 521.
26. Add. MSS 44319, Gladstone to A. Gordon, 28 July 1853.
27. Add. MSS 43252, Bright to Aberdeen, 16 Mar. 1854.
28. *The Diaries of John Bright* (ed. R. A. J. Walling), pp. 164–6 (22 Mar. 1854).
29. Add. MSS 44778, Gladstone, Memorandum, 22 Feb. 1854, printed Morley, vol. 1, pp. 491–3. Stanmore, pp. 257–8.
30. MSS Clar. Dep. C15, Palmerston to Clarendon, 4 Mar. 1854. Albert was convinced in October that Palmerston was manipulating the war to pursue his favourite projects, 'depriving Austria of her Italian possessions & restoring Poland', RA G17/89, Albert, Memorandum, 7 Oct. 1854.
31. Add. MSS 43068, Aberdeen to Russell, 27 Apr. 1854.
32. Add. MSS 43189, Clarendon to Aberdeen, 26 June 1854.
33. MSS Clar. Dep. C15, Palmerston to Clarendon, 22 Aug. 1854.
34. *Hansard*, 3rd ser., CXXXV, 653–62, 668–80.
35. Add. MSS 43191, Aberdeen to Graham, 26 July 1854 (original). The Graham Papers contain copies, not the originals of this correspondence, apparently as the result of Stanmore's request that it should not be published, Graham Papers, 125.
36. Add. MSS 43191, Graham to Aberdeen, 26 July 1854.
37. Add. MSS 43191, Aberdeen to Graham, 27 July 1854; Add. MSS 43191, Graham to Aberdeen, 28 July 1854.

38. Add. MSS 44319, Gordon to Gladstone, 27 July 1854. Gladstone to Gordon, 28 July 1854.
39. MSS Clar. Dep. C14, Aberdeen to Clarendon, 5 July 1854.
40. Add. MSS 43049, Aberdeen to Victoria, 19, 29 July 1854; Henderson, *Crimean War Diplomacy*, pp. 153–68.
41. Add. MSS 43068, Russell to Aberdeen, 27 Apr. 1854, Aberdeen to Russell, 27 Apr. 1854.
42. MSS Clar. Dep. C14, Aberdeen to Clarendon, 25 Apr., 12 May 1854.
43. MSS Clar. Dep. C14, Aberdeen to Clarendon, 23 Apr., 16 Aug. 1854; Add. MSS 43253, f. 42, Aberdeen, Memorandum, 20 May 1854.
44. For a detailed analysis see Conacher, pp. 251–6, 451–3; Aberdeen, Memorandum, n.d. June 1854, in which he cites the memoranda by other members of the Cabinet 'All agree in thinking that the destruction of Sebastopol and the Russian fleet ought to be the great object in view . . . I agree in this opinion.'
45. Among other sources Alexander complained to his father of this, Add. MSS 43225, Alexander to Aberdeen, 18 Oct. 1854.
46. Graham agreed with Aberdeen but Newcastle was sharply critical, Add. MSS 43191, Graham to Aberdeen, 7, 8 Oct. 1854, Aberdeen to Graham, 8 Oct. 1854; Newcastle Papers, NeC 10024, Aberdeen to Newcastle, 15 Oct. 1854. Albert suspected an intrigue against Aberdeen himself: 'There is a good deal of intrigue in fact, chiefly against Lord Aberdeen', RA G17/89, Albert, Memorandum, 7 Oct. 1854.
47. Add. MSS 43225, Alexander to Aberdeen, 2 Feb. 1855 (encl. his letter to Major General Yorke, 1 Feb. 1855), 6, 20, 23 Mar., 28 May 1855. His father apparently told him to be careful what he said, Alexander to Aberdeen, 11 Jan. 1855.
48. Add. MSS 43225, Alexander to Aberdeen, 5 May 1854.
49. Add. MSS 43225, Alexander to Aberdeen, 30 May 1854. Alexander was particularly concerned about the lack of letters because his wife was expecting their first child.
50. Add. MSS 43225, Alexander to Aberdeen, 8 Aug, 4 Sept. 1854.
51. Add. MSS 43189, Clarendon to Aberdeen, 10, 14 Sept. 1854; Add. MSS 43068, Russell to Aberdeen, 11 Sept. 1854; MSS Clar. Dep. C14, Aberdeen to Clarendon, 15 Sept. 1854.
52. Add. MSS 43049, Albert to Aberdeen, 17 Sept. 1854, Victoria to Aberdeen, 22, 25 Sept. 1854.
53. Add. MSS 43191, Graham to Aberdeen, 30 Sept. 1854; MSS Clar. Dep. C14, Aberdeen to Clarendon, 1 Oct. 1854; RA G17/83, Aberdeen to Victoria, 6 Oct. 1854.
54. Stanmore, p. 261.
55. Add. MSS 43225, Alexander to Aberdeen, 8, 13, 17 Nov., 26 Dec. 1854.
56. Add. MSS 43225, Alexander to Aberdeen, 3, 13, 26 Dec. 1854, 11, 25 Jan. 1855.
57. Add. MSS 43253, Russell Memorandum, 24 Apr., 20, 31 May 1854, Aberdeen, Memorandum, 20 May 1854; Add. MSS 43068, Russell to Aberdeen, 5, 29, 31 May 1854.
58. Add. MSS 43068, Aberdeen to Russell, 30 May, 5, 7 June (2 letters) 1854, Russell to Aberdeen, 5, 8, 9 June 1854; Add. MSS 44319, Gordon to Gladstone, 6 June 1854; Add. MSS 43071, Gladstone to Aberdeen, 8 June 1854.
59. The correspondence on this is massive. Stanmore printed some of the most impor-

tant in an Appendix to BP 12/11, pp. 345–71. The case is summarised in RA G20/118, Albert Memorandum, 13 Dec. 1854.

60. Add. MSS 43068, Russell to Aberdeen, 17, 18, 23, 28 Nov., 3 Dec. 1854, Aberdeen to Russell, 18, 21, 30 Nov. 1854; Add. MSS 43050, Victoria to Aberdeen, 25 Nov., 1, 7 Dec. 1854; RA G20/78, Albert, Memorandum, 4 Dec. 1854, /101, 9 Dec. 1854; file in RA A84, 'Papers concerning the part which Lord John Russell took in breaking up Lord Aberdeen's Government, Nov. 1854 – Feby. 1855'; cf. Conacher, pp. 493–503, which describes the crisis in detail.

61. RA G21/73, Aberdeen to Victoria, 2 Jan. 1855, G22/21, Aberdeen to Victoria, 11 Jan. 1855; MSS Clar. Dep. C14, Note by Aberdeen, 10 Dec. 1854, Aberdeen to Clarendon, 26 Dec. 1854; HH 1/29, Aberdeen to Lady Haddo, 7 Jan. 1855. Arthur noted that Aberdeen 'rejoiced' at the Russian reply, Add. MSS 49269, Diary, 8 Jan. 1855.

62. Stanmore, Diary, 22 Jan. 1855, BP 12/11, pp. 378–9; Stanmore, p. 283.

63. Stanmore, Diary, 23 Jan. 1855, BP 12/11, pp. 380–1.

64. Walpole, vol. 2, pp. 238–9.

65. RA G23/1, Albert, Memorandum, 25 Jan. 1855.

66. Stanmore, p. 283; RA G23/5, Victoria, Memorandum, 25 Jan. 1855; Add. MSS 43049, Palmerston to Russell, 24 Jan. 1855.

67. Stanmore, Diary, 30 Jan. 1855, BP 12/12.

68. Add. MSS 43050, Victoria to Aberdeen, 7 Feb. 1855.

69. Vincent, pp. 129–32.

70. Prest, p. 371; Argyll, *Memoirs*, vol. 1, p. 526.

71. Argyll, *Memoirs*, vol. 1, pp. 526–31; Stanmore, *Herbert*, vol. 1, pp. 251–62; HH 1/29, Aberdeen to Lady Haddo, 24 Feb. 1855; RA Y183/113, Albert to Aberdeen, 6 Feb. 1855; Add. MSS 43197, Aberdeen to Herbert, 6 Feb. 1855; Add. MSS 43049, Palmerston to Aberdeen, 12 Feb. 1855, Aberdeen to Palmerston, 13 Feb. 1855.

72. Palmerston can venture to make a peace, for which the country will thank him: but for which if I had made, they would have talked of cutting my head off', Gurney Papers, RQC 334/122, Aberdeen to Gurney, 12 Feb. 1855.

CHAPTER THIRTY

Last years

It would be quite wrong to think that Aberdeen emerged from the Crimean War a broken man. Although he was now over seventy and despite his own insistence that he was now a mere 'spectator', he still had several years of active political life before him. In January 1855, he had an attack of faintness and giddiness which alarmed both himself and Sir James Graham, but his doctors pronounced it to be merely a passing stomach upset and, generally, he was fitter and showed less signs of overt strain as Prime Minister than he had done as Foreign Secretary.[1] Nor, despite what he had said to Bright in 1854, was he entirely consumed by a sense of guilt or remorse about the war. He admitted to close friends that his conscience upbraided him, mainly for not having been firm enough with his colleagues, and he sometimes went over the events which had led up to the war, trying to diagnose where a different decision might have preserved the peace. But it is doubtful whether Aberdeen could have imposed his will on his Cabinet, made up as it was of strong personalities, many of whom had much more political backing than he had himself.

Like Gladstone he believed that the war itself was 'just', in the sense that Britain was defending her legitimate interests as a nation, which would have been damaged by Russian domination of the Ottoman Empire. He was not a pacifist. He believed that a nation had the right, indeed the duty, to defend its vital interests. What he did doubt was whether the war had been 'necessary'. He spelt this out very clearly in the winter of 1855, when he wrote:

I have never entertained the least doubt of the justice of the war in which we are at present engaged. It is unquestionably just, and it is also strongly marked by a character of disinterestedness. But although just and disinterested, the policy and the necessity of this war may perhaps be less certain . . . It is true that every necessary war must also be a just war; but it does not absolutely follow that every just war must also be a necessary war.

In this case he believed that, if public opinion had been less excited and his colleagues more reasonable, Britain's objectives could have been achieved without recourse to war.[2]

He gave a very sane analysis of the situation to Edward Ellice in October 1855. Speaking of the peace negotiations still in progress he said,

I admit that it requires much courage to resist the popular voice, and to incur the certainty of great odium; but we have seen this at all times; and it is an evil to which we must submit. Of course, if the objects of the war are not yet attained, we must persevere; but in this respect I think we seem to be rather abroad, and not to know very well what we desire. Certainly, for one, I entered into the war for the protection of Turkey, and for the repression of Russian aggression; but I never contemplated the necessity of making war of civilization against barbarism, or of freedom against despotism . . . Still less did I ever think of making war to liberate Europe from the dire thraldom of Russian influence.

He added that he thought that the question of war or peace really lay in Louis Napoleon's hands rather than Palmerston's and 'Whatever we may have gained by the war, it is certain that the power of France has been immeasurably increased.'[3]

He told Hudson Gurney in 1857 that Gurney was 'quite right in supposing that I look back with satisfaction to the efforts made by me to preserve peace'. He only regretted that when this became impossible he did not resign 'instead of allowing myself to be dragged into a war, which although strictly justified in itself, was most unwise and unnecessary. All this will be acknowledged some day but the worst of it is, that it will require fifty years before men's eyes are opened to the truth.'[4]

He was even philosophical about the attacks on himself and Newcastle. He wrote to Gurney as early as February 1855,

I cannot be surprised that the Publick should be enraged at the state of our Army in the Crimea. It is clear that great blame must be due somewhere; but I am at a loss to say in what quarter it ought to be assigned. I can only assert that I never knew a more laborious, indefatigable, and zealous man than the Duke of Newcastle; and I have no belief that Lord Panmure [his successor] can exceed, or even equal him in activity and ability. But the People must have a victim; and it is natural that he and I should be selected, 'sequitur fortunam, ut semper'.[5]

For all the trials and tribulations he had had to withstand he even admitted to Mary that he regretted being out of office. He told her, about the same time, 'I do not know how I shall bear being out of office. I have many resources and many objects of interest; but after being occupied with great affairs, it is not easy to subside to the level of common occupations.'[6] The fact that, for many months, he allowed Clarendon to show him the despatches and tell him of Cabinet discussions, (a proceeding of doubtful propriety) and offered detailed comments and advice on them, suggests that he had not lost confidence in his own judgement.[7]

The final irony was that Lord John Russell himself came to seek his advice. Palmerston had asked Russell, as Aberdeen had intended to do, to represent Britain at the conference convened in Vienna to discuss peace terms based on the Four Points. Russell himself would have been prepared to have agreed to an interpretation of the third point, acceptable to both Russia and Austria, to the effect that Russia and the western Powers should have parity of forces in the Black Sea. Even though Sebastopol had not yet fallen, Palmerston and the Cabinet in London were determined to stand out for the total destruction of the Russian naval power in the Black Sea. After he arrived back in London at the end of April 1855, Russell sought out Aberdeen to enlist his sympathy and to pour out his grievances against his colleagues.

Aberdeen would have needed to be a saintly character not to have resented Russell's campaign against him in 1854 and his final treachery over Roebuck's motion and he had expressed his anger and indignation to a few relatives and non-political friends at the time. He wrote to Lady Haddo on 7 January 1855 of 'the intrigue which has existed during the whole of my administration' and told her 'I should care little for the loss of office; but it is hard to be the victim of treachery and deceit.' On 25 January he wrote, 'It is a sad business; for there has been much intrigue, and underhand dealing.'[8] Publicly he conducted himself with great dignity. Gladstone marvelled at his self-control. He told him in February 1855, 'Your whole demeanour has been a living lesson to me; and I have never gone, with my vulnerable temper and impetuous moods, into your presence, without feeling the strong influence of your calm and settled spirit.'[9]

Graham could not contain his indignation at Russell's appeal to Aberdeen's sympathy. He wrote, 'Lord John is indeed unfathomable . . . He was bound in honour to defend your Government, of which he remained a member till the eve of an attack, when he ran away leaving the door open for a triumphant entry of the enemy into the fortress. To talk of peace *now*, and to profess friendship and concert, is absurd.' But Aberdeen's strong sense of humour came to his rescue. Only Russell could have failed to have seen the absurdity of the situation. Aberdeen gravely told him that he now looked to him as 'the man of peace'.[10]

Perhaps Aberdeen agreed with Graham that, after all his intrigues, Russell's 'present position is punishment as severe as an implacable adversary could desire'. Family relationships made it difficult to sever relations entirely. Aberdeen's step-son, Lord Abercorn, was still married to Russell's half-sister. The two men still met frequently socially. Aberdeen's feelings about Russell remained ambivalent, as well they might. In 1858 he told Hudson Gurney, who had criticised Russell, 'In truth I am not bound to take up the cudgels for him. For he treated me very scurvily. I have, however, forgiven him, seeing that age and infirmity remove me from the possibility of any personal competition or interference with him, or anyone else.'[11]

Aberdeen was called upon to make one public defence of his government's record. The 'Sebastopol Committee' set up in consequence of Roebuck's motion summoned him to appear as a witness on 15 May. Although Roebuck was in the chair, it was Henry Layard who launched the main attack on Aberdeen. On the whole he seems to have acquitted himself well. Challenged as to why the attack on Sebastopol had been mounted too late in the year, in September, he replied that that was properly a matter for the judgement of the military authorities on the spot. Asked why he had not undertaken a major re-organisation of the War Departments, he replied that the middle of a war was not the best time for such an activity. When the Committee pressed him as to whether the absence of Cabinets between August and October 1854 had not delayed vital decisions, even though the service ministers and himself were in London, he told them that they misunderstood the role of the Cabinet.[12] Devastatingly, he presented the Committee with all the correspondence between himself and Russell about the division of the War and the Colonial Offices.[13] The Report was ready in June. It analysed correctly many of the things which had gone wrong in mounting the Crimean operation, but it was easy to be wise after the event.[14] When Roebuck moved a resolution in the Commons laying the blame on every single member of Aberdeen's administration, there were too many members of the government who had also been members of the previous administration. He was defeated by a procedural device. Perversely, some of the Peelites maintained that they wanted the question debated to the bitter end to establish the real responsibility. Aberdeen too would probably have preferred 'a direct negative'.[15]

The Queen continued to sympathise and to show what public support she properly could. In May 1854 the Bishop of Oxford, Samuel Wilberforce, who was on terms of close friendship with Arthur, suggested very confidentially to Prince Albert that it might be some comfort to Aberdeen in face of the repeated public attacks upon him, if he were given the vacant Garter.[16] Aberdeen hesitated to accept it and suggested other possible recipients, including Lord Cardigan, but in January 1855 he agreed.[17] It was not, he explained to Gurney, bestowed because he was leaving office. It had all been settled before Parliament met. By special dispensation he was allowed to keep the Order of the Thistle, which he had held since 1808, as well, which was unusual although not unprecedented.[18] Arthur was pleased because his father was pleased, although he was a little nervous that there might be political repercussions at it being bestowed when his father was so unpopular. Aberdeen himself wrote to Mary that these were empty honours but he valued them as 'proofs of real regard'. When he went to Windsor to receive the Garter the Queen did not try to hide her feelings. He told Mary that when, in the course of the ceremony, he kissed the Queen's hand she, to his great surprise, 'squeezed my hand with a strong and significant pressure'.[19] A few days after his resignation, Victoria presented him with a bust of herself by Marochetti. Aberdeen, who had not forgotten his old skills as a courtier, replied that his descendants would value it as a memorial to Her Majesty's 'gracious favour to their fortunate Predecessor' but 'For himself, he will only say that Your Majesty's image already exists in his heart.'[20]

Aberdeen now had time to turn to his family and his neglected private affairs. He was not happy about the condition of his estates. He told Mary that he was rather 'hampered' by lack of money. He was once again missing his official salary and 'I believe there has been much bad management of my affairs; and I have now placed all matters under the control of Mr Lindsay of Edinburgh which I hope will lead to an improvement.'[21] The estate records show a healthy increase in rents during this period of prosperity for British agriculture, from £15,351 in 1842, to £17,215 in 1852 and £21,657 in 1862, but the problem seems to have been with the manangement of Aberdeen's own account and he told Gurney that he had made the 'disagreeable discovery' that the previous two years had produced more confusion that he would have thought possible.[22]

Financial problems were, however, small compared with family anxieties. Aberdeen's only sister, Alicia, had died, after a good deal of suffering in 1847, and the same year his brother Robert had dropped dead very suddenly of apoplexy at his home at Balmoral.[23] William died at Exmouth in 1858.[24] Alexander and Charles had been dead for many years and, apart from Aberdeen himself, only his youngest brother, John, now survived.

Two of his sons, Douglas and Alexander, had married. Douglas made a suitable, if not particularly exciting, marriage to a cousin, Lady Susan Douglas, the daughter of the Earl of Morton, and proceeded sedately on his career in the Church, raising a family of six children. In 1852 Alexander married Caroline Herschel, the eldest daughter of Sir John Herschel. The Herschels were an intellectually brilliant family, originally of German Jewish descent although by this time Protestant. Sir John, like his father William who had arrived penniless from Hanover, was one of the foremost astronomers of his age. But the family was neither wealthy nor well-connected and Aberdeen grumbled to Haddo that Caroline 'did not have a farthing'.[25] Their first child, a daughter, was born while Alexander was in the Crimea and the Queen offered to stand godmother. She made it clear that her offer was not simply because Alexander had been the Prince's equerry but was intended to show her regard for the child's grandfather.[26] The christening took place at Windsor in November 1854. Arthur, rather ungraciously, recorded that the Queen had particularly asked the ladies to wear white and many of them, including the Queen, looked 'hideous'.[27]

It was, however, his eldest son, Lord Haddo, who gave Aberdeen the most anxiety at this time. In 1853 he began to suffer from a mysterious wasting illness and in the summer of 1854 he became a resident patient of Dr William Gully at Malvern. Gully was a fashionable doctor with an exaggerated faith in the then-popular treatment of diseases by hydrotherapy. Haddo's illness was never properly diagnosed, although tuberculosis seems the most likely of several possibilities. By the autumn his weight had dropped to under eight stones and Gully told him frankly that he would be unlikely to see another spring. It was decided to send him out to Egypt for a few months, less in any real hope of a cure, than to spare him the discomfort of an English winter.[28]

The Egyptian Pasha's yacht was at Southampton, where it had been undergoing a refit, and he was graciously pleased to put it at the disposal of the English Prime Minister's son. In August 1854 Aberdeen begged Victoria to excuse him from attending her at Osborne so that he could see off his son whom, 'humanly speaking', he could never expect to see again.[29] The Haddos were treated almost like Royalty in Egypt and Aberdeen feared that when he lost office there would be a sharp change in their treatment, although he hoped that the Egyptians understood that 'ex Grand Vizier's' did not usually have their heads cut off in England.[30] To everyone's astonishment, Haddo rapidly improved in Egypt and one of the few consolations his father had in 1855 was when he returned apparently cured.

Some time before the onset of his illness Haddo had undergone one of the extreme Evangelical conversions beloved of the Victorians and Mary, after a few days of bewilderment, apparently decided that the only thing she could do was to join him in his new found convictions. Haddo seems indeed to have become somewhat mentally unbalanced. He became convinced that many of society's ills could be traced to the fact that nude models were used in art classes and waged a crusade against it. He spent his second visit to Egypt in 1860, trying to convert the Copts to his own form of Evangelical Protestantism.[31]

Despite these eccentricities, Haddo's political ambitions had revived. He had refused to take an interest when his father tried to obtain a parliamentary seat for him in 1838, but, in 1847 he decided that he would like to enter Parliament. As Aberdeen pointed out, he had chosen a very inconvenient moment. His father was now out of office and had 'no interest to procure a seat and no money to fight a contest'. He believed that a few years earlier, when Peel was in office, he could have procured a peerage for his son without difficulty.[32] It was not then practical to turn William out of the Aberdeenshire seat and only in 1854 did it become vacant when William became Admiral of the Nore. Haddo was duly elected in 1854, while too ill to visit his constituency, a curious proceeding for a Prime Minister pledged to bring about parliamentary reform.[33]

Provision had also to be made for Arthur. Arthur had become a rather pious young man when an undergraduate at Cambridge although his taste, unlike his brother's, turned to the Anglo-Catholic party. His diary is full of his attendance at chapel (when he could get up in time) and ecclesiastical chit chat of various kinds. His father dissuaded him from taking orders, telling him that one parson in the family was enough.[34] In the early 1850s he acted as his father's private secretary and general factotum and repaid some of the devotion which his father had showered on him as a sickly child. His father was, perhaps, more aware than Arthur realised that this was sometimes irksome to his son and he told Newcastle that Arthur must have a career.[35] In 1854 he obtained a parliamentary seat at Beverley and his father even hoped that Palmerston would give him an office in 1855. Perhaps wisely, for it would have looked rather strange, Palmerston did not. In 1857 Arthur even lost the Beverley seat when its patrons found another candidate.[36] In 1858 he accompanied Gladstone when the latter went out on a special mission as High Commissioner to the Ionian Islands. Unfortunately, he managed to irritate Gladstone who always remained convinced that Arthur was an unworthy son of his admired mentor, and did less to help his future career than Aberdeen had hoped.[37]

If Aberdeen hoped that Arthur, the most intelligent of his sons, might one day take his place in British politics, he had not entirely relinquished his own role. He rarely spoke in the Lords and then usually on rather technical matters, often with a Scottish connection. But eminent politicians continued to visit Haddo. Inviting Newcastle in 1857, he told him that Clarendon had just left and he was expecting Lady Jersey 'from whom of course I shall hear abundance of news, true and false'. Granville too was coming. The journey was much easier now that there was a convenient railway connection to Inverurie. It was very different from the days when it had taken a fortnight to get from London to Aberdeen. It might be expected that his fellow Peelites, Graham, Herbert and

Gladstone, would come, but so too did John Bright. Delane was another visitor. Aberdeen was delighted to welcome foreign statesmen and Guizot and Jarnac both came.[38]

Graham said that he was 'the common friend to whom we all resort when we want comfort and advice'.[39] His most important single act in domestic politics was to dissuade Gladstone from rejoining the Conservative party. Derby tried hard to recapture Gladstone for the Conservatives. He first approached him as early as 1855 and made further overtures in the spring of 1856. Gladstone was unwilling to act without consulting Aberdeen, Graham and Herbert and they advised him against listening to Derby. For Gladstone, the fact that it would be difficult to displace Disraeli as the Leader of the Commons was a formidable barrier but he was also finding it increasingly difficult to continue to support Palmerston's government.[40]

In this Aberdeen sympathised. Once the Crimean War was over, Palmerston seemed to have reverted to all his old recklessness and irresponsibility in foreign affairs. Britain became involved in two wars in 1857, one with Persia, the other with China. Aberdeen condemned both wars as unnecessary and believed that they sprang largely from the sense of public frustration because the Crimean War had not ended in a decisive military victory.[41] Cobden, supported by Gladstone, condemned Palmerston's policy in China in the Commons in March 1857 and the government was defeated. Palmerston immediately appealed to the country and won a decisive victory at the ensuing general election.

Among the casualties were many of the small remaining band of Peelites. It was generally acknowledged that the Peelites had finally ceased to exist as a party. It was now very difficult for Gladstone to resist Derby's overtures but Aberdeen once again threw his weight on the side of persuading Gladstone to at least maintain his independence. His letters to Gladstone show how far his own opinions had moved and how irrevocable he believed the 'fusion' of December 1852 to have been. He told Gladstone that he was convinced that 'there is [now] no such thing as a distinctive Peelite party in existence'. He believed that 'when my Government was formed, an amalgamation of Peel's friends with the Liberal party took place'. He was prepared to go even further. He told Gladstone, 'I believe, too, that in this age of progress the Liberal party must ultimately govern the country; and I only hope that their supremacy may be established without mischief or confusion.'[42] His distrust of Palmerston's irresponsible foreign policy was such that he held Lord John Russell, despite all he had personally suffered at his hands, to be the less dangerous man and hoped that he would resume the leadership of the Liberal party. He even told Lord John in March 1857 that if the Queen asked his advice after Palmerston's defeat, he would advise her to send for Lord John and that he hoped that Gladstone and Herbert would join his ministry.[43] Russell, however, was a man well into his sixties and it was obvious that he could not be the party leader for very long. Aberdeen had few doubts that the man who must ultimately come to the fore as the leader of what he hoped would be a party of moderate reform at home and responsible policy abroad, was Gladstone himself. He was grieved that Gladstone did not seem to have established the kind of command of the Commons that he would have expected from a man of his great talents and he bent his own energies to trying to ensure that Gladstone would do nothing which would compromise his own future.[44]

Gladstone came near to taking office with Derby in 1858. After his triumph of 1857 Palmerston had fallen foul of the very spirit of jingoism which he had done so much to arouse. In January 1858 an Italian nationalist, Felice Orsini, tried to assassinate Napoleon III. There was some evidence for the suspicion that the plot had been hatched in London. Palmerston agreed to introduce a Conspiracy to Murder Bill to strengthen the law. Interestingly, Aberdeen maintained the view he had held in 1853 that the existing law was strong enough. Palmerston's government was defeated in the Commons by a rather unholy alliance of his opponents and Derby formed a minority government. Politics were again in a state of confusion and it even seemed, briefly, that Aberdeen might once again be called upon to head a coalition. According to his son, he would not have been unwilling. He wrote in his diary, 'H. L. [i.e. His Lordship] . . . suddenly seized the idea of its being possible for him to regain the Premiership & certainly now entertains the wish.'[45]

The moment passed but Aberdeen continued to be the elder statesman, constantly consulted. The Queen herself consulted him on the difficult question of the royal prerogative of dissolution. Derby, faced by all the problems of controlling the Commons with a minority government, wanted the Queen's authority to tell the Commons that, if he were defeated, he had the Queen's consent to a dissolution. Aberdeen returned through the Prince's secretary, Sir Charles Phipps, what seems to have been very sound constitutional advice. Derby had no right to ask for such a prospective promise. The Queen had the right to refuse a minister a dissolution but, if she did so, any minister who succeeded would have to take responsibility for the act and defend it in Parliament.[46]

Aberdeen's close interest in the Indian Mutiny of 1857–58 rose in part from the fact that his own protegé, Viscount Canning, was still Governor General, but his comments were shrewd and far-sighted. In August 1857 he wrote to Gurney: 'The important question which is not yet clearly answered, is whether the revolt is a military mutiny, or a national movement. Should it be the latter, our tenure cannot be very secure.' He approved of Canning's conciliatory policy, which earned him the derisive nickname of 'Clemency Canning', for as he told Gurney, 'The exhortations of our Papers, in recommending indiscriminate slaughter, are abominable; but they are also suicidal; for we could never long exist in India, after having taken such means to create the most inveterate spirit of revenge.'[47]

But, if his views on India were liberal, his views on Italy were not. He never altered his opinion that there was no real demand for an Italian national state among the Italian people, that they were being exploited by outsiders and that northern Italy was more prosperous under Austrian rule that it would be if dominated by Piedmont or France. Like the Prince he had feared that Palmerston was using the Crimean War to get Austria out of Italy and he had only reluctantly agreed to accept a Piedmontese contingent on the Allied side, desperate though the British need for additional forces had become. He saw the implications quite clearly and told Clarendon in November 1854 that he thought his letter to Hudson, the British Minister in Turin, 'a little equivocal, and [likely] to provoke the Sardinian appetite'. 'It seems rather strange', he said 'that while you are on the point of signing a Treaty of offensive and defensive alliance with Austria, you should engage to protect Piedmont from Austrian attacks. I suppose, however, that you intend, during the war, to protect Lombardy from the much more probable contingency of the renewal of the Sardinian invasion.'[48]

The Prince sought his views when the French went to war to aid the Sardinians against Austria in 1859. Aberdeen replied in a long and carefully—worded letter which showed that, greatly as his views had changed on domestic questions, on European questions his opinions remained consistent throughout a long political life. Austria, he said:

Was fighting the battle of Europe, and defending not only her own right but a settlement which Europe contributed to make, and no Power more eagerly than this country. The war therefore was most iniquitous, and without the shadow of a pretext; but was really founded on the hypocritical declarations and ambitious projects of the King of Sardinia . . . The situation of England is inconsistent and indeed whimsical. The prevalent feeling of the whole kingdom is dread of the Emperor Napoleon. But it has been thought more prudent to join a cry against the bad government of Austria in Italy; and while making a barren declaration of adherence to treaties, practically to unite in the destruction of a settlement which more than any other power, England had contributed to make; and this destruction for the advantage of the very power which at this moment we dread more than any in the world.

He thought that Britain had a much stronger moral obligation to defend the Austrians against the French in Italy, than she had ever had to defend Turkey against the Russians in the Principalities. However, he did not recommend that Britain should physically intervene. He was well aware that politics was the art of the possible.[49]

Aberdeen did not carry Gladstone with him in his views on Italy and, rather ironically, this was the point on which Gladstone decided that he did have more in common with Palmerston than with Derby and joined Palmerston's second Cabinet as Chancellor of the Exchequer in June 1859.[50]

The question of the Prince's place in the constitution continued to haunt Aberdeen. The Queen appealed to him again in 1856 and enlisted his support for Albert assuming the title of Prince Consort. Aberdeen exerted himself quite considerably. He consulted his fellow Peelites and discussed the matter with the Lord Chancellor. It is not quite clear who first proposed that the title should be bestowed, not by Act of Parliament, which might have entailed many difficulties, but by Letters Patent, but the proposal was certainly supported by Aberdeen. It was carried into effect in 1857.[51]

Aberdeen's relations with the Court remained close. He was regularly invited to Balmoral when the Queen was in residence and, in 1857, she suggested that she should visit Haddo. The visit disconcerted Aberdeen, who still had slight feelings of inferiority about his home,[52] but it passed off very successfully. The

Queen recorded it in her own journal. They arrived at Haddo at a quarter past four in the afternoon after a long drive from Balmoral. All Aberdeen's tenants, about 600 of them, met her on horseback and escorted her to the house 'which is plain, about 100 years old'. It was a family occasion. Apart from Aberdeen, Lord and Lady Haddo and their six children were there, Alexander and his wife and their 'pretty little girl Victoria' and Lord Abercorn. Victoria noted, 'We walked out onto a very pretty Terrace, on the other side of the House & down some steps. Lord Aberdeen has laid everything out & planted *all* the trees, excepting the very oldest.' They had walked with Aberdeen and other members of the party down a fine walk, something like the Long Walk at Windsor, at the end of which was the gate opening into the Deer Park, where there was a fine road of old Scotch firs and 'a fine piece of artificial water, made by Ld Aberdeen. All he has done is beautifully planned out.' All the same she missed the mountains which surrounded Balmoral. At dinner she sat between Aberdeen and Abercorn and noticed that the room was narrow like the one at Frogmore and 'contained some fine pictures'. She did not note, although the *Aberdeen Journal* did, that she planted two trees to commemorate the occasion.[53] Her visit, although partly a courtesy to a neighbour who had been instrumental in procuring Balmoral for the Prince Consort, was probably like the bestowal of the Order of the Garter, a public demonstration of her continuing affection and confidence in her former Prime Minister, who had been so badly treated both by colleagues and the public.

Very shortly after Victoria's visit, Aberdeen was struck down by a serious illness and his condition was critical for several days. He was insistent that it was not due to over-exertion during the royal visit[54] and in fact he had had symptoms before it. Arthur recorded in his diary in July that his father had fallen in his room during the night and had lain for some time in the cold before anyone found him. When Victoria saw him at Balmoral, shortly before her visit to Haddo, she noticed that he was 'a good deal aged'.[55] Nevertheless, Aberdeen made a rapid recovery and in November removed, on his doctors' advice but against his own inclinations, to London.

It was the following spring before he was well enough to go out much in society[56] but he was again politically active by the summer, speaking several times in the Lords on the old vexed question of how to check the identity of a slave ship which was flying false colours and on a Scottish Universities measure.[57] He was tempted to speak against his old adversary, Ellenborough, who had got himself into an embarrassing predicament at the India Office but Ellenborough had resigned and, as Aberdeen told Newcastle, 'unless it is proposed to bring Ellenborough to the block, I do not see what more can be expected than his resignation'.[58] His speech on 26 July on the suppression of the Slave Trade (soon to be an obsolete issue with the outbreak of the American Civil War) was to be his last in the House of Lords.[59] The wheel had come full circle. His first vote in the House had been fifty-one years before against the Slave Trade.

His health finally began to break in 1859. The exact cause was never diagnosed and Aberdeen had some contempt for the doctors' attempts.[60] It may have been some form of progressive heart failure. His relatives spoke only of steadily increasing weakness. A final blow was struck by the fact that his eldest son had suffered a relapse and in May 1860 left for Egypt again.

Aberdeen was determined to spend the summer of 1860 at Haddo.[61] His condition was now so serious that Mary returned from Egypt to see him. She seems to have found him in a state of senile depression. She told her husband, still in Egypt, 'Of course he cried for a moment at first but not more than he often did on coming to Blackheath.' A few days later she added, 'That hysterical crying is worse some days than others, but he is alive to all that is going on, and likes one to sit & talk to him in the evening as he used always to do.' Sometimes he rallied. Mary was pleased that one evening 'he sat by me talking about our boat and discussing the Suez Canal & Egyptian affairs as he might have done years ago'. He did not give in without a struggle. Mary wrote, 'He has once or twice walked . . . with two sticks, otherwise he is generally wheeled in his chair, & carried down the steps to the carriage or terrace in a chair of a very nice construction which was invented for the Duke of Devonshire. He sits at the head of the table, helps the soup but does not carve.' He even insisted on going to Buchan Ness and took douche baths of cold sea water which Mary thought 'hardly safe with his feeble circulation'.[62]

Haddo was trying to convert the Copts and, unfortunately, Mary felt it her duty to try to convert her father-in-law to her own fervent Evangelicalism. Aberdeen's own beliefs to the end seem to have been the moderate, rational, even agnostic, ones which he had adopted as a young man. In 1856 Gladstone had tried to enlist Aberdeen's support for Archdeacon Denison who had been condemned for believing in the Real Presence. Aberdeen, although he regarded transubstantiation as a superstition,[63] replied mildly that 'to inflict penalties upon a man for believing more than his neighbour, in a matter neither of them can comprehend' certainly seemed unfair.[64]

Mary did her best to have 'little talks' with Aberdeen which he foiled by staying in the Drawing Room 'very late, till 11 o'clock sometimes'.[65] She read the Bible to him but he tended to fall asleep. He did, however, express some regret that he had not read it more seriously as a younger man. He had once, years before, told Hudson Gurney that, if one believed the Bible seriously, one would wish to read no other book.[66] Finding him too weak for sustained reading, she, and Haddo in his letters from Egypt, plied him with short Biblical texts. Aberdeen expressed his appreciation, although perhaps he enjoyed better the sketches which his son, who was a very talented artist, sent him.

It was from these sad days at the end of his life that there dates the story, related by his son, of how Aberdeen refused to rebuild the parish church at Methlic for reasons which no one could understand at the time and how after his death they found that he had written repeatedly on scraps of paper a text from Chronicles:

And David said to Solomon, My son, as for me, it was in my mind to build an house unto the name of the Lord, my God: but the word of the Lord came to me, saying, Thou has shed blood abundantly, and hast made great wars: thou shalt not build an house unto my name, because thou hast shed much blood upon the earth in my sight.

The story was repeated by Professor Temperley in his standard work on the Eastern Question and it has come to be regarded as Aberdeen's considered judgement on his role in the Crimean War.[67] It probably was not. That can be found in his correspondence with his colleagues and friends immediately after the war. What it did mark was the final breaking point of a man whose life had been constantly shadowed by tragedy.

Aberdeen returned once again to London in the autumn of 1860. He was occasionally well enough to see friends[68] but no one doubted that the end was near. When it came it was peaceful. He began to sink on 6 December. His three younger sons and Abercorn took it in turns to watch over him. He died in the early hours of 14 December, one hand held by Arthur and the other by his eldest grandson, Haddo's son, George, who had only been brought in a few minutes earlier 'to spare his young mind too long a witness'. Arthur told Mary, 'He passed away calmly and tranquilly without pain or struggle holding my hand and Dod's . . . Life had become to him a weary burden & the end was a painless release.'[69]

He was buried on 21 December in the old church at Stanmore and laid to rest between Catherine and Harriet in the Abercorn family vault. The Bishop of Oxford, Samuel Wilberforce, officiated at his own request. Graham, Newcastle, Clarendon, Gladstone, Cardwell and Dalkeith acted as pall bearers. The Queen sent her carriage as a token of her own mourning.[70]

NOTES

1. Add. MSS 49269 and BP 12/11, pp. 380–1, Stanmore, Diary, 6, 7, 23 Jan. 1855; HH 1/19, Aberdeen to Lady Haddo, 4 Oct. 1853.
2. Stanmore, pp. 303–4.
3. NLS MS 15017, Aberdeen to Ellice, 27 Oct. 1855.
4. Gurney Papers, RQC 334/126, Aberdeen to Gurney, 5 Aug. 1857.
5. Gurney Papers, RQC 334/122, Aberdeen to Gurney, 12 Feb. 1855.
6. HH 1/29, Aberdeen to Lady Haddo, 7 Feb. 1855.
7. MSS Clar. Dep. C30, *passim*.
8. HH 1/29, Aberdeen to Lady Haddo, 7, 25 Jan. 1855.
9. Add. MSS 43071, Gladstone to Aberdeen, 10 Feb. 1855. Clarendon too contrasted Aberdeen's demeanour with Russell's 'spoilt child' act, Maxwell, vol. 2, p. 54.
10. Add. MSS 43191, Graham to Aberdeen, 28 June 1855, Aberdeen to Graham, 29 Jan. 1855; MSS Clar. Dep. C30, Aberdeen to Clarendon, 3 May 1855.
11. Gurney Papers, RQC 334/129, Aberdeen to Gurney, 3 Mar. 1858.
12. PP IX (1854–45) Pt. III, 289–98. Aberdeen was not satisfied with his own performance because, speaking without notes, he confused some dates, Newcastle Papers, MSS NeC 12442, Aberdeen to Newcastle, 16 May 1855.
13. PP IX (1854–55) Pt. III, 355–60; Add. MSS 43068, Aberdeen to Russell, 16 May 1855. Russell had previously referred to the letters in the Commons.
14. PP IX (1854–55) Pt. III, 367–87.

15. *Hansard*, 3rd ser., CXXXIX, 954–66, 1185 (17 July 1855); Newcastle Papers, MSS NeC 12443, Aberdeen to Newcastle, 25 June 1855.
16. RA M54/4, Wilberforce to Albert, 16 May 1854, Most Private. For his relations with Arthur see Add. MSS 49269 *passim*.
17. Add. MSS 43050, Victoria to Aberdeen, 10, 11 Jan. 1855, Aberdeen to Victoria, 10, 11, 13 Jan. 1855.
18. Gurney Papers, RQC 334/122, Aberdeen to Gurney, 12 Feb. 1855.
19. Add. MSS 49269, Stanmore, Diary, 22 Jan. 1855, also BP 12/12, p. 379; HH 1/29, Aberdeen to Lady Haddo, 7 Feb. 1855.
20. RA F38/25, Aberdeen to Victoria, 20 Feb. 1855.
21. HH 1/29, Aberdeen to Lady Haddo, 23 Aug. 1855.
22. PP XVI (1896), 516, 'Royal Commission on Agriculture; Haddo House Estates'; Gurney Papers, RQC 334/124, Aberdeen to Gurney, 22 Feb. 1855.
23. HH 1/29, Aberdeen to Lady Haddo, 24 Apr. 1847; *Aberdeen Journal*, 28 Apr., 13 Oct. 1847.
24. Gurney Papers, RQC 334/128, Aberdeen to Gurney, 12 Feb. 1858.
25. HH 1/19, Aberdeen to Lady Haddo, 23 Oct. 1852.
26. Add. MSS 43050, Victoria to Aberdeen, 27 July 1854.
27. Add. MSS 49269, Stanmore, Diary, 7 Nov. 1854.
28. Haddo attracted a deeply pious biography from his former tutor, the Rev. E. B. Elliott, *Memoir of Lord Haddo*, in which he printed a number of letters between Haddo and his father, For Haddo's illness see pp. 58–80; cf. HH. 1/19, Lady Haddo to Aberdeen, n.d. Aug. 1854, Aberdeen to Lady Haddo, 21 Aug. 1854.
29. RA A23/143, Aberdeen to Victoria, 28 Aug. 1854.
30. Elliott, pp. 117–8; HH 1/19, Aberdeen to Lady Haddo, 25 Dec. 1854.
31. Elliott, pp. 15–20, 170–3, 197–217. When his eldest son came of age, instead of the usual celebrations, he presented all his tenants with a copy of *The Pilgrim's Progress*. History does not record their reactions.
32. HH 1/29, Aberdeen to Lady Haddo, 28 May 1847.
33. Elliott, pp. 158–9. Aberdeen does not seem to have been the moving spirit in this. He told Mary it was a 'mockery' to think of George entering Parliament in his present state of health, HH 1/19, Aberdeen to Lady Haddo, 24 July 1854.
34. Add. MSS 49253–4, Stanmore, diary, 31 Jan, 23, 29 May 1849.
35. Newcastle Papers, MSS NeC 12455, Aberdeen to Newcastle, 30 Nov. 1859.
36. Stanmore, Diary, 7 Feb., 7 Dec. 1855, quoted Iremonger, pp. 317–8.
37. Gurney Papers, RQC 334/130, Aberdeen to Gurney, 28 Nov. 1858; Conacher, 'A visit to the Gladstones in 1894', *Victorian Studies*, ii (1958), pp. 155–60. Arthur himself wrote a rather obscure apology, Add. MSS 44319, A. Gordon to Gladstone, 12 Nov. 1860.
38. Newcastle Papers, MSS NeC 12447, 12450, 12471, Aberdeen to Newcastle, 28 Aug., 15, 25 Sept. 1857; *Revue des deux mondes*, xxxiv (1861), p. 470; Walling, p. 249; Dasent, vol. 1, pp. 257, 269; Gurney Papers, RQC 334/130, Aberdeen to Gurney, 28 Nov. 1858.
39. Parker, vol. 2, p. 346.
40. Add. MSS 43071, Aberdeen to Gladstone, 5, 11 Dec. 1856; Add. MSS 43192, Aberdeen to Graham, 17 Jan. 1857; Morley, vol. 1, pp. 551–2, 556, 560–6; Stanmore, *Herbert*, vol. 2, pp. 64–5, 70–2, 77; Parker, vol. 2, pp. 292–6, 338–40, 344–51.
41. Gurney Papers, RQC 334/126, Aberdeen to Gurney, 5 Aug. 1857.

42. Add. MSS 44089, Aberdeen to Gladstone, 3, 8 Apr. 1857; Add. MSS 43071, Gladstone to Aberdeen, 31 Mar., 4 Apr. 1857.
43. Walpole, vol. 2, p. 287.
44. Newcastle Papers, MSS NeC 12447, Aberdeen to Newcastle, 28 Aug. 1856; Add. MSS 44089, Aberdeen to Gladstone, 5 Dec. 1856.
45. Add. MSS 49269, Stanmore, Diary, 21 Mar. 1858.
46. Memorandum by Sir Charles Phipps, (?) 15 May 1858, *Letters of Queen Victoria*, vol. 3, pp. 286–9.
47. Gurney Papers, RQC 334/126, 127, Aberdeen to Gurney, 5 Aug., 9 Nov. 1857.
48. MSS Clar. Dep. C14, Aberdeen to Clarendon, 29 Nov. 1854.
49. RA 121/104, Aberdeen to Albert, 18 July 1859.
50. Stanmore, *Herbert*, vol. 2, pp. 179–80; Add. MSS 44319, Gordon to Gladstone, 12 Nov. 1860. To his son, Aberdeen called Gladstone 'that renegade Italian attorney'. See also Gladstone to Gordon, 21 Apr. 1861.
51. Add. MSS 43050, Victoria to Aberdeen, 19, 20, 26 Mar., 18 Apr., 19 May 1856, 23 Mar., 22 June 1857, Aberdeen to Victoria, 22, 26 Mar., 23 May, 27 June 1856, 24 Mar., 23 June 1857; Newcastle Papers, MSS NeC 12445, Aberdeen to Newcastle, 22 June 1856, 12446a, Newcastle to Aberdeen, 22 June 1856.
52. NLS MS 15017, Aberdeen to Ellice, 16 Oct. 1857; Newcastle Papers, MSS NeC 12451, Aberdeen to Newcastle, 25 Sept. 1857.
53. RA, Victoria's Journal, 14 Oct. 1857; *Aberdeen Journal*, 14, 21 Oct. 1857.
54. Add. MSS 44319, A. Gordon to Gladstone, 31 Oct., 14 Nov. 1857; RA B16/93, Clarendon to Victoria, 26 Oct. 1857; Gurney Papers, RQC 334/127, Aberdeen to Gurney, 9 Nov. 1857.
55. Add. MSS 49256, Stanmore, Diary, 29, 30 July 1857; RA, Victoria's Journal, 21 Sept. 1857.
56. HH 1/29, Aberdeen to Lady Haddo, 20 Apr. 1858.
57. *Hansard*, 3rd ser., CL, 2214–5 (17 June 1858); CL, 2085–8, 1359–61, 1369 (13, 26 July 1858).
58. Newcastle Papers, MSS NeC 12452, Aberdeen to Newcastle, 22 May 1858.
59. *Hansard*, 3rd ser., CLI, 2085–8 (26 July 1858).
60. Gurney Papers, RQC 334/127, Aberdeen to Gurney, 9 Nov. 1857. Arthur frequently wrote his letters for him after September 1859 (e.g. HH 1/28, estate correspondence with Chalmers) but Aberdeen wrote some of his own letters until Feb. 1860, e.g. MSS Clar. Dep. 525, Aberdeen to Clarendon, 12 Feb. 1860. HH 1/28, Aberdeen to Lady Haddo, 29 Feb. 1860, docketed 'The last letter he ever wrote to me'.
61. HH 1/28, Alexander Gordon to Lady Haddo, 9 July 1860.
62. HH 1/21, Lady Haddo to Lord Haddo, 25, 28–31 Aug., 4 Sept. 1860.
63. Add. MSS 43225, Aberdeen to Baillie Hamilton, 28 Oct. 1850.
64. Add. MSS 43071, Gladstone to Aberdeen, 13 Aug. 1856; Add. MSS 44089, Aberdeen to Gladstone, 17 Aug. 1856.
65. HH 1/21, Lady Haddo to Lord Haddo, 28–31 Aug., 4, 6–8 Sept. 1860.
66. RQC 334/107, Aberdeen to Gurney, 30 Nov. 1842.
67. Stanmore, pp. 302–3; Temperley, p. 385.
68. Add. MSS 44319, Arthur Gordon to Gladstone, 14 Nov. 1860; Newcastle Papers, MSS NeC 12456, Arthur Gordon to Newcastle, 8 Dec. 1860.
69. HH 1/28, Arthur Gordon to Lady Haddo, 16 Dec. 1860, Douglas Gordon to Lady Haddo, 17 Dec. 1860, Alexander Gordon to Lord Haddo, 17 Dec. 1860.
70. HH 1/28, Arthur Gordon to Lady Haddo, 26 Dec. 1860, Alexander Gordon to Lord Haddo, 25 Dec. 1860.

Conclusion
The English Aristides

Aberdeen was buried at Stanmore among those he had most loved but some ten years after his death his friends placed his bust in Westminster Abbey with the simple inscription △IKAIOTATOE – 'Most Just'.[1] John Bright too called him the 'English Aristides' – the Athenian statesman to whom the soubriquet was first applied. What did these men, steeped in the classics, mean to convey by that?

The Victorians saw Aristides as an aristocrat who had come to terms with democracy. In foreign affairs he had made one great mistake (when he opposed Pericles' plans for the navy) but his record was otherwise an honourable one. Such an analysis might be, very roughly, applied to Aberdeen's career but the implication was probably more subtle. Aristides stood as the type of the good man, who was not also a good politician. This was probably the view even of William Gladstone. Soon after Aberdeen's death he wrote, at Arthur Gordon's request, an appreciation of his character which was published in part in the *Edinburgh Review* in 1883 and subsequently in Gordon's biography.[2] In it he dwelt not only on Aberdeen's exceptional love of justice but also on his extraordinary absence of suspicion which made him like 'a little child'. Gladstone feared that what he had written would be misunderstood and it has been. Intentionally or not, he had drawn the portrait of a supremely honest but naive man. Aberdeen was not a naive man. His private papers show him to have been a very shrewd, as well as a very independent, observer of the political scene.

Perhaps the word 'observer', or as Aberdeen himself would frequently have said 'spectator', gives the clue. Kingsley Martin, in his *Triumph of Lord Palmerston*, came as near to understanding him as anyone ever has when he said that he was fifty years in politics but he never became a politician, and this is profoundly true.[3] Aberdeen entirely lacked the instinctive flair for politics which Disraeli or Palmerston, or even Gladstone, possessed. His fundamental shyness and inability to project himself to the public was an important factor but it was not the whole of it. Perhaps he was too intellectual. His very ability to think for himself, to stand out against public clamour and excitement, however admirable, made him a poor politician. He seems to have had no 'gut' reactions. What other Prime Minister would have stood up in the House of Lords and defended the Tsar of Russia a few weeks after the outbreak of the Crimean War?

531

Should one then conclude that Aberdeen was a man of great talents and great private virtues but that the real tragedy of his life was the accident that introduced him into Pitt's household and persuaded him to become a politician? Even this may be too simple. Aberdeen himself maintained that his only real interest in public life was in foreign affairs and to this he devoted practically the whole of his career. Yet he was often at his weakest in the confrontational atmosphere of foreign policy. As Palmerston discerned, he could not bluff. His temperament remained that of a scholar, able to see many sides of a question, and anxious to reach a conclusion by reasonable argument. Sometimes this paid handsome dividends. It is very doubtful whether any British interest would have been advanced by a showdown with either France or the United States in the 1840s. Even at the time of the Crimean War, if Aberdeen's policy had been consistently followed, peace could probably have been preserved with no real loss of British interests. Yet his conduct of affairs always aroused uneasiness. Foreign affairs, like the English legal system, are essentially adversatorial. A Foreign Secretary, even in some circumstances a Prime Minister, is expected to behave like an advocate. When he begins to behave like a judge instead, weighing the issues instead of presenting the case, he is in danger of sending the wrong signals. This Aberdeen did on more than one occasion. Significantly Aberdeen's pupil, William Gladstone, aroused Bismarck's ire for exactly the same reasons. They were not playing the game according to the accepted rules.

Aberdeen usually professed little interest in domestic politics but, ironically, his judicious approach might have been much better adapted to practical reforms at home where some degree of concensus is vital. Gladstone said that no man but Aberdeen could have brought the 1852 coalition into being. This is probably true. He alone had the necessary contacts right across the political spectrum, the requisite patience to deal with so many difficult characters and the essential trust of the leading protagonists, at least at the beginning. Aberdeen was no mere figure-head. He insisted on a real 'fusion' of the Peelite and the Whig-Radical traditions. Even later, when the coalition government itself had so ignominiously collapsed, he insisted that the 'fusion' must endure and he stopped Gladstone from drifting back to the Conservative party. In that sense he, much more than Palmerston, even more than Gladstone, was the true father of the late nineteenth—century Liberal party. If this is true, the final irony may be that Aberdeen always mistook his métier and that the real tragedy was not that he became Pitt's ward but that he accompanied William Drummond to Constantinople in 1803 and became convinced that his destiny lay in foreign affairs.

NOTES

1. Gladstone seems to have proposed the bust after Arthur had complained that his father had no memorial but his Correspondence, the publication of which Gladstone was obstructing. The bust was executed by Matthew Noble. Add. MSS

44320, A. Gordon to Gladstone, 20 Jan. 1871, Gladstone to A. Gordon, 9 May 1871.

2. Add. MSS 44319, A. Gordon to Gladstone, 19 Dec. 1860, Gladstone to A. Gordon, 21 Apr. 1861; *Edinburgh Review*, clviii (1883), pp.573–7; Stanmore, pp. 307–8.

3. Kingsley Martin, *The Triumph of Lord Palmerston*, p. 77.

Bibliography

MANUSCRIPT SOURCES

Aberdeen's Diaries, Greek and Roman Department, British Museum.

Aberdeen Papers, British Library.

Aberdeen Papers, Haddo House, Aberdeenshire.

Aberdeen University Library, Sederunt Book of Lord Aberdeen's Trust in favour of his natural children and miscellaneous other manuscripts.

Bathurst Papers, British Library.

Canning Papers, Harewood MSS, Leeds City Libraries, Archives Department.

Castlereagh Papers, Public Record Office of Northern Ireland, Belfast.

Clarendon Papers, Bodleian Library, Oxford.

Colonial Office records, 1834–35, Public Record Office.

Derby Papers, currently in Oxford.

Ellice Papers, National Library of Scotland.

Foreign Office records, 1813–14, 1828–30, 1841–46, 1853–54, Public Record Office.

Gladstone Papers, British Library.

Graham Papers, microfilm, Bodleian Library, Oxford.

Guizot Papers, Archives Nationales, Paris.

Gurney Papers, Norfolk Record Office, Norwich.

Gurney's Journal, in private hands.

Harrowby MSS, Sandon Hall, Staffordshire.

Haus–, Hof–u. Staatsarchiv, Vienna.

Heytesbury Papers, British Library.

Howley Papers, Lambeth Palace Library.

Liverpool Papers, British Library.

Longley Papers, Lambeth Palace Library.

Melbourne Papers, Windsor Castle.

Ministère des Affaires Étrangères, Paris.

National Library of Scotland, miscellaneous manuscripts in addition to the collections separately listed.

Newcastle Papers, Nottingham University Library.
Peel Papers, British Library.
Royal Archives, Windsor Castle.
Royal Society, Journal Books.
Russell Papers, Public Record Office.
Scottish Record Office, Edinburgh, Haddo House Papers and miscellaneous other manuscripts.
Society of Antiquaries, miscellaneous papers.
Society of Dilettanti, Minute Books.
Stanmore Papers, British Library.
Stratford Canning Papers, Public Record Office.
Stuart de Rothesay Papers, National Library of Scotland.
Wellington Papers, Historical Manuscript Commission and British Library.
Wilson Papers, British Library.
Wordsworth Papers, Lambeth Palace Library.

PRINTED BUT UNPUBLISHED SOURCES

Selections from the Correspondence of the Fourth Earl of Aberdeen, Privately printed, 13 volumes. These are fuller on the 1850s than on earlier periods. They contain some letters not in the Additional Manuscripts in the British Library. Most of the missing letters are at Haddo House but a few seem to have disappeared altogether. These volumes are cited by their British Library numbers, i.e. BP 12 (1–12a).
Correspondence relative to the Society Islands, 1822–46, Privately printed for the use of the Cabinet. Copy in Rhodes House Library, Oxford. (Other 'Confidential Prints' of this kind are in the Aberdeen Papers and are so cited.)

PUBLISHED OFFICIAL AND SEMI–OFFICIAL SOURCES

Acts of the General Assembly of the Church of Scotland 1638–1842.
British and Foreign State Papers.
British Parliamentary Papers.
Hansard's Parliamentary Debates, 2nd and 3rd series.
House of Lords Journal.
Miller, D. Hunter, *Treaties and other international acts of the United States of America*, Department of State, Washington, 1934–37.
Parliamentary History, vol. VI.
Richardson, J. D. *Messages and Papers of the Presidents.*
USA Executive Documents.
USA Senate Documents.

NEWSPAPERS

Aberdeen Journal, Courier, Globe, London Gazette, Morning Chronicle, Morning Herald, Morning Post, Standard, Sun, The Times

PERIODICALS

Annual Register, Archaeologia, Edinburgh Review, Examiner, Moniteur, Punch. Quarterly Review, Revue des deux mondes

SECONDARY WORKS

(Place of publication is London unless otherwise stated.)

ABERDEEN, Earl of, *An Inquiry into the Principles of Beauty in Grecian Architecture; with an Historical View of the Rise and Progress of the Art in Greece*, 1822.

ABERDEEN, Earl of, *Correspondence of Lord Aberdeen and Princess Lieven*, 2 vols, Camden Society, 3rd ser., nos 60, 62, (ed. E. Jones–Parry), 1938–39. (Cited as Jones-Parry.)

ADAMS, E. D. *British Diplomatic Correspondence, Texas, 1836–46*, Austin, Texas, 1918.

ADAMS, E. D. 'English interests in the annexation of California', *American Historical Review*, xiv (1909), pp. 744–63.

ANDERSON, M. S. *The Eastern Question*, 1966.

ARBUTHNOT, H. *The Journals of Mrs Arbuthnot, 1820–1832*, (ed. F. Bamford and the Duke of Wellington), 2 vols, 1950.

ARGYLL, 8th Duke of *Autobiography and Memoirs*, 2 vols, 1906.

ASHLEY, E. *The Life of Henry John Temple, Viscount Palmerston, 1846–1865*, 2 vols, 1876.

ASPINALL, A. 'The Coalition Ministries of 1827', *English Historical Review*, xlii (1927), pp. 201–26.

ASPINALL, A. *The Formation of Canning's Ministry, February–August 1827*, Camden Society, 3rd ser., vol. 59, 1937.

BAGEHOT, W. *The English Constitution* (World's Classics Edition), 1961.

BAGOT, J. F. *George Canning and his Friends*, 2 vols, 1909.

BALFOUR, F. *Life of George Hamilton Gordon, Fourth Earl of Aberdeen*, 2 vols, 1922.

BARTLETT, C. J. *Castlereagh*, 1966.

BARTLETT, C. J. *Great Britain and Sea Power, 1815–1853*, 1963.

BESSBOROUGH, *Lady Bessborough and her family circle; Journals and Correspondence*, (ed. Earl of Bessborough), 1940.

BETHELL, L. *The Abolition of the Brazilian Slave Trade, 1807–1859*, Cambridge, 1970.

BINDOFF, S. T. *British Diplomatic Representatives, 1789–1852*, Camden Society, 3rd ser., vol. 50.

BLAKE, R. *Disraeli*, 1966.

BOLSOVER, G. H. 'Nicholas I and the partition of Turkey', *Slavonic and East European Review*, xxvii (1948–49), pp. 115–45.

BOURNE, K. *Britain and the Balance of Power in North America, 1815–1908*, 1967.

BOYD, T. D. 'The arch and the vault in Greek architecture', *American Journal of Archaeology*, lxxxii (1978), pp. 83–100.

BRIGGS, J. H. *Naval Administrations, 1827–92*, 1897.

BROCK, M. *The Great Reform Act*, 1973.

BULLEN, R. *Palmerston, Guizot and the Collapse of the Entente Cordiale*, 1974.

BULLOCH, J. M. *House of Gordon*, vol. 1, Aberdeen University Studies, No. 8, 1903.

BULLOCH, J. M. *Gordons under Arms*, House of Gordon, vol. 3, Aberdeen University Studies, No. 59, 1912.

BULLOCH, J. M. *Gordons of Cluny*, Privately printed, 1911.

BULWER, H. L. (Baron Dalling), *The Life of Henry John Temple, Viscount Palmerston (to 1846)*, 3 vols, 1871–4.

BURNET, GILBERT, *Bishop Burnet's History of his own times*, 2 vols, 1724.

CASS, L. *An Examination of the questions now in discussion concerning the Right of Search*, Baltimore, 1842.

Cambridge History of British Foreign Policy, 1783–1919, 3 vols, 1922–23.

CHALMERS, DR, *The Correspondence between Dr Chalmers and the Earl of Aberdeen in the years 1839 and 1840*, Edinburgh, 1893.

CHAMBERS, R. (ed.) *The Songs of Scotland prior to Burns*, Edinburgh, 1862.

CHAPMAN, J. K. *Arthur Hamilton Gordon, First Lord Stanmore, 1829–1912*, Toronto, 1964.

Complete Peerage (ed. V. Gibbs), vols I and VI, 1910, 1926.

CONACHER, J. B. *The Aberdeen Coalition, 1852–1855*, 1968.

CONACHER, J. B. *The Peelites and the Party System, 1846–52*, Newton Abbott, 1972.

CONACHER, J. B. 'A visit to the Gladstones in 1894', *Victorian Studies*, ii (1958–59), pp. 155–60.

CONNELL, B. *Regina v. Palmerston*, 1962.

COOK, J. M. *The Troad; an Archaeological and Topographical Study*, Oxford, 1973.

COREY, A. B. *Canadian Historical Association Annual Report*, Toronto, 1936.

CRAWFURD, GEORGE, *The Lives and Character of the Officers of the Crown and of the State in Scotland . . .* vol. 1, 1726.

CRAWLEY, C. W. *The Question of Greek Independence: a study in British foreign policy, 1821–1833*, 1930.

CURTIS, G. T. *Life of Daniel Webster*, 2 vols, New York, 1970.

CUST, L. and COLVIN, S. *History of the Society of Dilettanti*, 1898.

DAKIN, D. *British and American Philhellenes during the War of Greek Independence, 1821–1833*, Thessaloniki, 1955.

DASENT, A. I. *John Delane, 1817–1879*, 2 vols, 1908.

DERRY, J. W. *Castlereagh*, 1976.

DOUGLAS, R. *The Peerage of Scotland*, 2 vols, Edinburgh, 1813.

DOUGLAS, R. *The Scots Peerage*, vol. 1, Edinburgh, 1907 edition.

DU BOIS, W. E. B. *The Suppression of the African Slave Trade to the USA*, Cambridge, Mass., 1896.

DUTENS, M. L. *Recherches sur le Tems, le plus reculé de l'Usage des Voutes chez les Anciens*, nouvelle edition, 1807.

ELLENBOROUGH, Lord, *Political Diary 1828–1830*, 2 vols, 1881.

ELLIOTT, E. B. *Memoirs of Lord Haddo, later the fifth Earl of Aberdeen*, 1866.

ELLIS, K. *The Post Office in the Eighteenth Century*, 1958.

EVANS, JOAN, *The History of the Society of Antiquaries*, 1956.

FERGUSON, J. *The Sixteen Peers of Scotland. An Account of the Elections of the Representative Peers of Scotland, 1707–1959*, Oxford, 1960.

FOOTE, A. H. *Africa and the American Flag*, New York, 1853.

FOSTER, H. L. VERE- *The Two Duchesses: Georgiana, Duchess of Devonshire, Elizabeth, Duchess of Devonshire, Family Correspondence, 1779–1859*, 1898.

FOORNIER, A. *Der Congress von Chatillon: Die Politik im Kreige 1814*, Vienna and Prague, 1900.

GANONG, W. F. 'Monograph of the evolution of the boundaries of the Province of New Brunswick', *Transactions of the Royal Society of Canada 1901–02*, pp. 140–447.

GARRISON, G. P. *Diplomatic Correspondence of the Republic of Texas*, 3 parts, 1907–08.

GASH, N. *Politics in the Age of Peel*, 1953.

GASH, N. *Mr Secretary Peel*, 1961.

GASH, N. *Sir Robert Peel*, 1972.

GELL, W. *The Topography of Troy and its Vicinity*, 1804.

GLOVER, M. *A Very Slippery Fellow; the life of Sir Robert Wilson, 1777–1849*, 1978.

GORDON, COSMO, *A Souvenir of Haddo House*, 1958.

GORDON, THOMAS, *History of the Greek Revolution*, 2 vols, 1832.

GREAVES, R. W. 'The Jerusalem Bishopric', *English Historical Review*, lxiv (1949), pp. 328–52.

GREVILLE, C. *Memoirs*, (ed. H. Reeve), 8 vols, 1888 (all references are to this edition unless otherwise stated).

GREVILLE, C. *The Greville Diary*, (ed. P. W. Wilson), 1927.

GUIZOT, F. *Mémoires pour servir à l'histoire de mon temps*, 8 vols, Paris 1858–67.

GUIZOT, F. *Sir Robert Peel*, 1857.

HAMILTON, H. (ed.) *An Aberdeenshire Estate*, 1946.
Harrow School Register 1571–1800, 1934.

HENDERSON, G. B. *Crimean War Diplomacy and other Essays*, Glasgow, 1947.

HIDY, R. W. *The House of Baring in American Trade and Finance*, Cambridge, Mass., 1949.

HINDE, WENDY, *George Canning*, 1973.

HIRST, F. W. *Gladstone as Financier and Economist*, 1931.

HOBSBAWM, E. J. and RUDÉ, G. *Captain Swing*, 1970.

HODDER, E. *Life and Work of the Seventh Earl of Shaftesbury*, 3 vols, 1887.

HOWARD, H. E. 'Brunnow's reports on Aberdeen, 1853', *Cambridge Historical Journal*, IV (1934), pp. 312–21.

HUMPHREYS, W. H. (ed. Sture Linner), *First Journal of the Greek War of Independence*, Stockholm, 1967.

INGLE, H. H. *Nesselrode and the Russian rapprochement with Britain, 1836–1844*, Berkeley, 1976.

IREMONGER, L. *Lord Aberdeen*, 1978.

JACOBS, M. C. *Winning Oregon*, Caldwell, Idaho, 1938.

JARNAC, COMTE DE, 'Lord Aberdeen, Souvenirs et papiers diplomatiques', *Revue des deux mondes*, xxxiv (1861), pp. 429–72.

JONES, W. D. *Lord Derby and Victorian Conservatism*, 1956.

JONES, W. D. *Lord Aberdeen and the Americas*, Athens, Georgia, 1958.

JONES, W. D. *Prosperity Robinson: The Life of Viscount Goderich, 1782–1859*, 1967.

JONES-PARRY, E. 'Review of the relations between Guizot and Lord Aberdeen, 1840–52', *History*, xxiii (1938), pp. 25–36.

JONES-PARRY, E. *The Spanish Marriages 1841–1846*, 1936.

JONES-PARRY, E. 'Under Secretaries of State for Foreign Affairs 1782–1855', *English Historical Review*, 1934, pp. 304–20.

JOINVILLE, Prince de, *Notes sur les forces navales de la France*, 1844.

KENNEDY, W. *The Rise, Progress and Prospects of the Republic of Texas*, 2 vols, 1841.

KERNER, R. J. 'Russia's new policy in the Near East after the Peace of Adrianople', *Cambridge Historical Journal*, v (1937), pp. 280–90.

LANE-POOLE, S. *Life of Stratford Canning*, 2 vols, 1888.

LASCARIDES, A. C. *The Search for Troy, 1553–1874*, Newcastle 1974.

LAUGHTON, J. K. *Memoir of the Life and Correspondence of Henry Reeve*, 2 vols, 1898.

LAWRENCE, W. B. *Visitation and Search*, Boston, 1858.

LEVESON-GOWER, G. and PALMER, I. (eds), *Hary—O: The Letters of Lady Harriet Cavendish, 1796–1801*, 1940.

LIEVEN, PRINCESS, Correspondence with Lord Aberdeen, see under Aberdeen.

LIEVEN, PRINCESS, *Correspondence of Princess Lieven and Earl Grey*, (ed. and trans. Guy le Strange), 3 vols, 1890.

LIEVEN, PRINCESS, *Lettres de Francois Guizot et de la Princesse de Lieven*, (ed. J. Naville), 3 vols, Paris, 1963–64.

LIEVEN, PRINCESS, *The Lieven–Palmerston Correspondence, 1828–1856* (ed. and trans. Lord Sudley), 1843.

LIEVEN, PRINCESS, *The Unpublished Diary and Political Sketches of Princess Lieven*, (ed. H. Temperley), 1925.

LODGE, *Peerage, Baronetage and Knightage*, 1908 edition.

MALMESBURY, Earl of, *Memoirs of an ex-Minister*, 1885.

MARTIN, B. K. *The Triumph of Lord Palmerston: a Study of Public Opinion in England before the Crimean War*, new ed. 1963.

MATHIESON, W. L. *Great Britain and the Slave Trade, 1839–1865*, 1929.

MAXWELL, H. *The Life and Letters of George William Frederick, fourth Earl of Clarendon*, 2 vols, 1913.

MERK, F. 'British government propaganda and the Oregon Treaty', *American Historical Review*, xl (1934), pp. 38–62.

METTERNICH, PRINCE, *Autobiographie et Mémoires*... (ed. M. A. de Klinkowstroem), vols 1 and 2, 4th ed. Paris, 1886.

MONYPENNY, W. F. and BUCKLE, G. E. *The Life of Benjamin Disraeli, Earl of Beaconsfield*, 6 vols, 1910–20.

MOORE, R. J. *Sir Charles Wood's Indian Policy 1853–1866*, Manchester, 1967.

MOORE, R. J. 'The abolition of patronage in the Indian Civil Service', *Cambridge Historical Journal*, vii (1964), pp. 246–67.

MOORE, THOMAS, *The Works of Lord Byron*, vol, 1, 1832.

MORLEY, J. *Life of Gladstone*, 3 vols, 1903.

ORMOND, R. *Sir Edwin Landseer*, 1982.

PARKER, C. S. *Life and Letters of Sir James Graham, 1792–1861*, 2 vols, 1907.

PARKER, C. S. *Sir Robert Peel*, 3 vols, 1891–99.

POLK, J. K. *The Diary of a President* (ed. A. Nevins), New York, 1929.

PREST, J. *Lord John Russell*, 1972.

PRICE, C. (ed.) *The Letters of Richard Brinsley Sheridan*, 3 vols, Oxford, 1966.

PRITCHARD, G. *Queen Pomare and her country*, 1879.

PURYEAR, V. J. *England, Russia and the Straits Question, 1844–1856*, Berkeley, 1931.

PURYEAR, V. J. *International Economics and Diplomacy in the Near East, 1834–1853*, Stanford, 1935.

DE RIDDER, A. (ed.) *Les projets d'union douanière franco-belge*, Commission Royale d'Histoire, vol. 43, 1933.

RIDLEY, J. *Lord Palmerston*, 1970.

RUSSELL, LORD JOHN, *The Later Correspondence of Lord John Russell, 1840–1878*, (ed. G. P. Gooch), 1925.

ST CLAIR, W. *Lord Elgin and the Marbles*, 1967.

ST CLAIR, W. *That Greece might still be free*, 1972.

SINCLAIR, J. *General Report of the Agricultural State and Political Circumstances of Scotland. Drawn up for the Board of Agriculture*, 6 vols, Edinburgh, 1814.

SMITH, A. HAMILTON, 'Lord Elgin and his collection', *Journal of Hellenic Studies*, xxxvi (1916) pp. 163–370.

Society of Antiquaries, Occasional Papers II, *Presidents of the Society*.

SOULSBY H. G. *The Right of Search and the Slave Trade in Anglo-American Relations, 1814–1862*, Baltimore, 1933.

STANMORE, LORD (Sir Arthur Gordon), *The Earl of Aberdeen*, 1893.

STANMORE, LORD, *Sidney Herbert*, 2 vols, 1906.

STEWART, R. *The Politics of Protection: Lord Derby and the Protectionist Party, 1841–1852*, 1971.

STUART, C. H. 'The Formation of the Coalition Cabinet of 1852', *Transactions of the Royal Historical Society*, 5th ser., vol. 4 (1954), pp. 45–68.

SURTEES, V. *Charlotte Canning*, 1975.

TANSILL, C. C. *The Canadian Reciprocity Treaty of 1854*, Baltimore, 1922.

TAYLOR, A. J. P. *The Trouble Makers: Dissent over Foreign Policy, 1792–1939*, 1957.

TEMPERLEY, H. W. V. *England and the Near East: the Crimea*, 1936.

TEMPERLEY, H. W. V. 'Stratford de Redcliffe and the origins of the Crimean War', *English Historical Review*, xlviii (1933), pp. 601–21 and xlix (1934), pp. 265–98.

The Times, History of The Times, 4 vols, 1935–52.

TWISS, SIR TRAVERS, *The Oregon Question examined*, 1846.

VINCENT, J. R. (ed.) *Disraeli, Derby and the Conservative Party; the Political Journals of Lord Stanley, 1849–1869*, 1978.

WALKER, J. W. *Wakefield, its History and People*, 2nd ed. Wakefield, 1939.

WALLING, R. A. J. (ed.) *The Diaries of John Bright*, 1930.

WALPOLE, ROBERT, *Memoirs relating to European and Asiatic Turkey*, 1817.

WALPOLE, ROBERT, *Travels in various Countries of the East . . .*, 1820.

WALPOLE, SPENCER, *The Life of Lord John Russell*, 2 vols, 1889.

WEBSTER, C. K. *British Diplomacy 1813–1815*, 1921.

WEBSTER, C. K. *The Foreign Policy of Castlereagh, 1812–1815*, 1931.

WEBSTER, C. K. *The Foreign Policy of Castlereagh, 1815–1822*, 1925.

WEBSTER, C. K. *The Foreign Policy of Palmerston, 1830–1841*, 2 vols, 1951.

WEBSTER, C. K. 'Palmerston, Metternich and the European system', *Proceedings of the British Academy*, xx (1934).

WEBSTER, DANIEL, *The Diplomatic and Official Papers of Daniel Webster*, New York, 1848.

WEINBERG, A. K. *Manifest Destiny*, Baltimore, 1935.

WELLINGTON, Duke of, *Despatches, Correspondence and Memorandum . . . in continuation of the former series* (ed. A. R. Wellesley, Duke of Wellington), 1867–80. (Cited as Wellington, *Correspondence*.)

WHITTINGTON, G. D. *An Historical Survey of the Ecclesiastical Antiquities of France* (with a Preface and Notes by G. Gordon, Earl of Aberdeen), 1809.

WHYTE, J. H. *The Independent Irish Party, 1850–1859*, 1958.

WIGHT, A. *The Present State of Husbandry in Scotland*, 4 vols, Edinburgh, 1778–84.

WILKINS, W. *The Civil Architecture of Vitruvius* (with introduction by the Earl of Aberdeen), 1812.

WILSON, ROBERT (ed. H. Randolph), *Private Diary*, 2 vols, 1861.

WINSOR, J. *Cartographical History of the North East Boundary Controversy* (privately printed from the Proceedings of the Massachusetts Historical Society), Cambridge, Mass., 1887.

WOODWARD, E. L *The Age of Reform, 1815–1870*, Oxford, 1938.

ZIEGLER, P. *Melbourne*, 1978 edition.

Maps

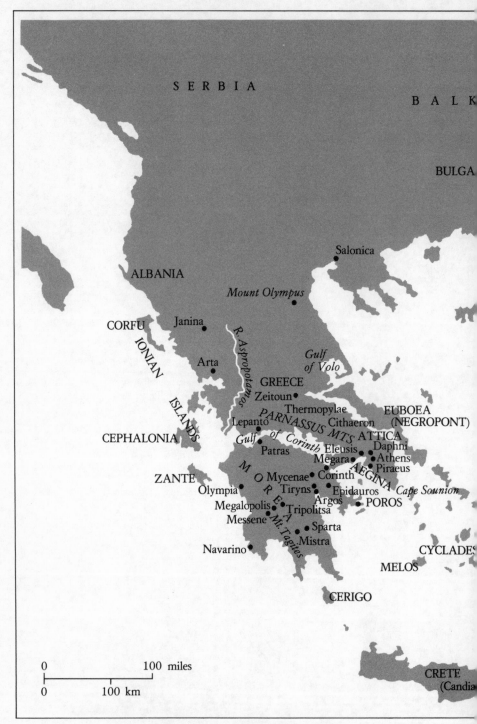

Map 1. The Aegean in the early 19th century

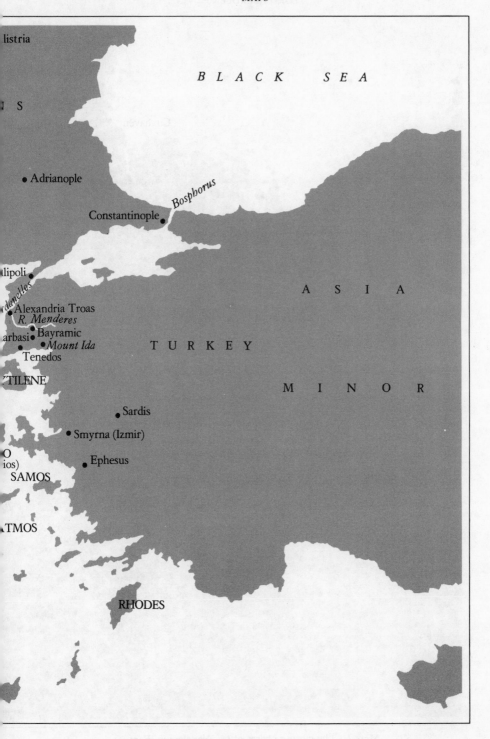

BLACK SEA

listria

IS

Adrianople

Bosphorus

Constantinople

lipoli

rdanelles

Alexandria Troas
R. Menderes
arbasi
Bayramic
Mount Ida
Tenedos

'TILENE

Sardis

Smyrna (Izmir)

O
(ios)
SAMOS

Ephesus

TMOS

RHODES

A S I A

T U R K E Y

M I N O R

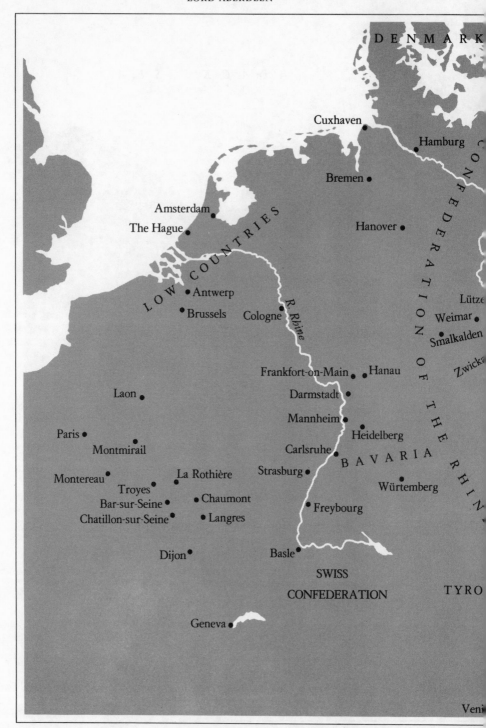

Map 2. The closing phases of the Napoleonic Wars

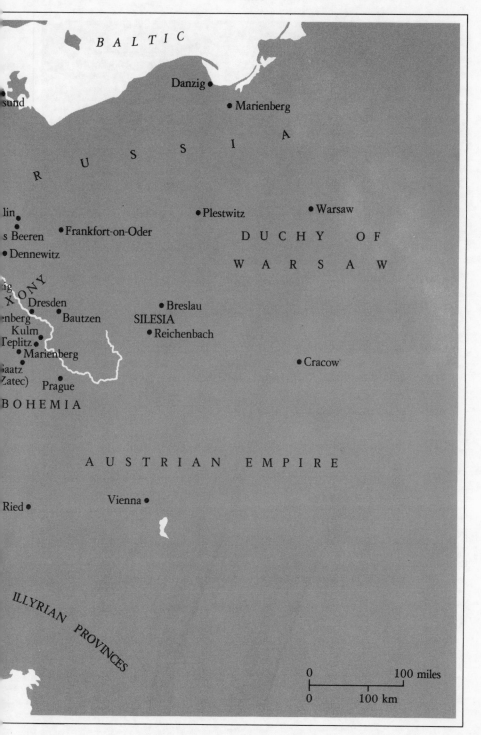

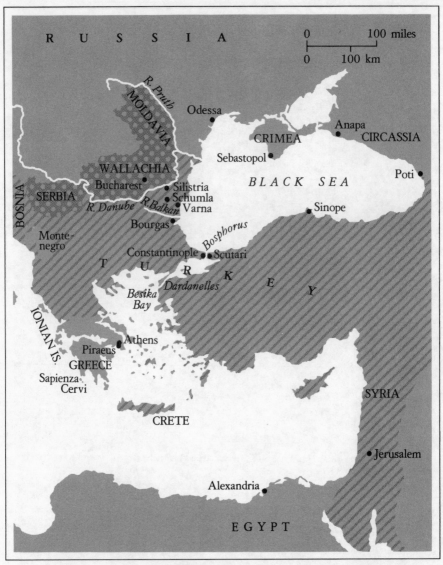

Map 3.   The Ottoman Empire at the time of the Crimean War

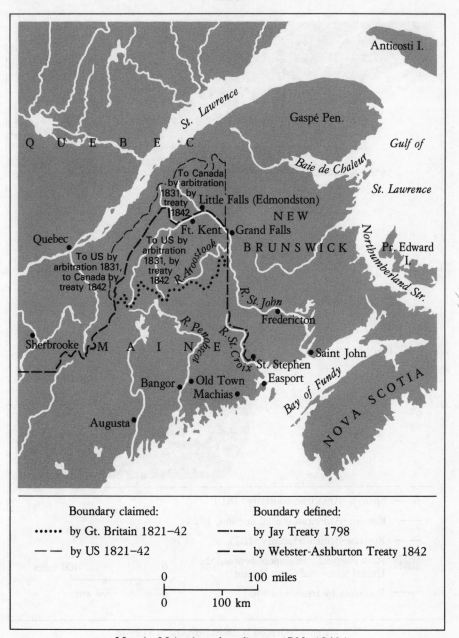

Map 4. Maine boundary dispute, 1783–1842

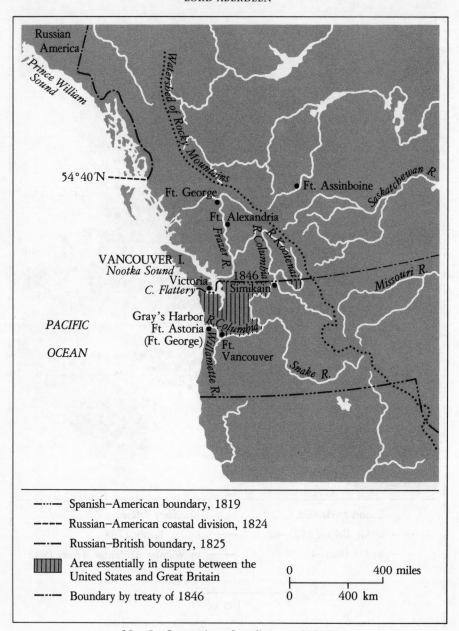

Map 5. Oregon boundary dispute, 1819–46

-----· Spanish–American boundary, 1819

---- Russian–American coastal division, 1824

--·- Russian–British boundary, 1825

Area essentially in dispute between the
United States and Great Britain

--·- Boundary by treaty of 1846

0   400 miles

0   400 km

Index

Aaland Islands, 504, 507

Abbeville, 31, 33

Abd-el-Kader (Algerian nationalist leader), 347, 360, 363

Abdul Mejid (Sultan of Turkey), 284, 344, 381, 407, 474, 478, 486, 506

Abdul Rhaman (Emperor of Morocco), 360, 363

Abercorn estates, 81, 82, 176–77, 194, 385

Abercorn family, 48–51, 61, 92, 178, 528

Abercorn, Anne, Marchioness of (3rd wife of 1st Marquess), 109, 110, 174

Abercorn, James Hamilton, 2nd Marquess of, 175, 176, 180–1, 260, 263, 264, 385, 417, 519, 526, 528

Abercorn, John James Hamilton, 1st Marquess of, 49–52, 54–6, 67, 82, 86, 94, 95–9, 101, 101–2, 111, 112–13, 116, 117–18, 124, 143, 157–8, 158–9, 160, 161, 162, 163–5, 166–7, 169, 172, 173, 174–5, 176

'Aberdeen Act' (Brazilian Slave Trade, 1844), 369

'Aberdeen Act' (Church of Scotland, 1843), 292–3

Aberdeen, city of, 14, 15, 20, 55, 82, 253, 258, 263, 292, 414

Aberdeen, Anne, Countess of (wife of 1st Earl), 15

Aberdeen, Anne, Countess of (3rd wife of 2nd Earl), 16

Aberdeen, Catharine Elizabeth, Countess of (wife of 3rd Earl), 17–18, 25–6, 58, 83

Aberdeen, Catherine Elizabeth, Countess of (1st wife of 4th Earl), 4, 7, 17–18, 49–56, 75, 93, 96, 102, 106–9, 111, 112, 157, 158, 174, 175, 176, 178, 181, 184, 258, 528

Aberdeen, Harriet, Countess of (2nd wife of 4th Earl), 4, 5, 74, 175–83, 187, 188, 197, 260–1, 263, 274, 528

Aberdeen, Mary, Countess of (2nd wife of 2nd Earl), 16

Aberdeen, Susan, Countess of (1st wife of 2nd Earl), 16

Aberdeen, George Gordon, 1st Earl of, 15

Aberdeen, George Gordon, 3rd Earl of, 17–21, 24, 31, 82, 111
  illegitimate descendants of, 18, 24–6, 263
  Will of, 18, 21, 24–6, 80

Aberdeen, George Gordon, 4th Earl of, appearance, 6–7
  biographies of, 2–6
  botanical interests, 30, 33, 38, 74, 76, 86–7, 182, 416
  character and reputation, 5–6, 8, 50, 195–6, 265, 282, 295, 306–7, 374, 394, 410, 447, 456, 478–9, 506, 512, 531–2
  classical scholar, 1, 5, 23, 34–44, 62–72
  collector, as a, 30, 32, 37, 40, 56–8
  correspondence and papers of, 1–5, 9
  estates, attitude to, 5, 30, 46, 79, 81–8, 177–8, 416
  financial difficulties, 79–81, 175, 177–8, 257–8, 264, 520
  health, 50, 125, 175, 176, 293, 306,

416, 441, 497, 509, 517, 526−8

humour, sense of, 7, 74, 519

languages, interest in, 22, 32, 34, 37, 65, 119, 182

liberalism, 3, 10, 184−5, 408, 456

claim to be real founder of Liberal party, 428−32, 441, 444, 452, 453, 455, 523, 532

Lords, fear of speaking in, 5, 6, 99−101, 106, 110, 452−3, 497−8

nationalism, attitude to, 9, 189, 199, 201, 224, 230, 392, 400, 403

Ottoman empire, special interest in, 102

reform, attitude to, 10, 185, 189, 197, 252−5, 259, 260, 423, 426, 429, 436−7, 451−2, 456, 458, 464, 467

religious views, 4−5, 61−2, 108−9, 172, 188, 260−1, 527

revolution, attitude to, 8, 31, 33, 187, 258−9, 395, 436

Scotland, attitude to, 5, 33, 46, 61−2, 92, 100, 187−9, 256, 259, 289−93, 465, 522, 526

science, growing interest in, 74, 75−6, 86

theatre, interest in, 22, 32, 52−4

toryism, 3, 8, 9−10, 184, 230, 235, 272, 390, 392, 395, 403, 408, 409

United Kingdom peerage, desire for, 91, 93, 94, 99, 112, 158−9

not a Victorian, 3

war, attitude to, 8, 125, 126, 134−5, 143, 186, 211, 244, 271, 272, 312, 472−3, 493, 499, 517−18, 527−8

Aberdeen, George Gordon, 4th Earl of, biographical chronology

ancestry, 13−20

birth (1784), 20

death of parents, 4, 20

education at Harrow, 20−1, 22

education at Cambridge, 21, 23−4

inherits titles and estates (1801), 24−6

travels in France and Italy, 30−4

travels in Ottoman empire, 34−44

undertakes management of estates, 46−7, 81−7

1st marriage (1805), 50

birth of daughters, 55−6

early writings, 62−6

member of Dilettante Society, 66−7

President of Society of Antiquaries, 73−5

Trustee of British Museum, 75

Fellow of Royal Society, 75

elected Scottish representative peer, 98

death of 1st wife (1812), 4, 56, 108

British ambassador to Vienna (1813−14), 1, 2, 4, 102, 112, 115−19, 122−69

United Kingdom peerage (1814), 169

Elgin Marbles controversy, 67−71

2nd marriage (1815), 175

birth of sons and daughter, 106, 175, 176

death of daughters, 4, 179, 182, 183

occasional interest in politics (1815−28), 183−90

assumes name Hamilton-Gordon (1818), 176

Royal Commission on Scottish universities (1826−7), 289−90

Chancellor of Duchy of Lancaster (1828), 194

Foreign Secretary (1828−30), 6, 75, 195−247

Great Reform Act (1832) and consequences, 255−9

death of 2nd wife (1833), 260

death of youngest daughter (1834), 4, 261

attitude to foreign affairs (1830−41), 268−72, 282−6

Colonial Secretary (1834−5), 10, 272−82

Scottish Church affairs (1835−43), 290−3

Foreign Secretary (1841−6) 297−385

attitude to 1848 revolutions, 390−410

desires re-union of Conservative party but emerges as the leader of the Peelites (1846−52), 414−37

formation of the coalition government, (1852), 10, 441−53

domestic reforms of coalition ministry (1852−5), 10, 455−68

Crimean war, 472−520

active in politics after 1855, 517−18, 523−6

mortal illness of heir, 4, 441, 521, 527
death (1860), 528
Aberdeen, William Gordon, 2nd Earl of, 15–17, 25, 95
'Aberdeen head', 43
Aberdeen Journal, 47, 526
Aberdeen, John Campbell Hamilton-Gordon, 1st Marquess of, 4
Aberdeen, university of, 15, 26, 289–90
King's College, 188, 289–90
Marischal College, 289–90
Aberdeenshire, 6, 13, 14, 99, 177, 178, 256–8, 522
Lord Lieutenancy of, 17, 417–18
3rd Aberdeenshire Militia, 31, 263
Aberdour, 14
Abergavenny, Henry Nevill, 2nd Earl of, 261
Aboyne, George Gordon, 5th Earl of, 96, 97, 98
Academical Questions, 62
A'Court, Sir William *see* Heytesbery, Lord
Adams, Sir Frederick, 216
Adams, James, 16
Adams, Robert, 16
Adams, William, 16
Addington, H. U., 245, 299
Adelaide, Queen, 417
Adrianople, 222
Adrianople, Treaty of (1829), 219–20, 499, 500
Advocates, Faculty of, 290
Afghanistan, 302, 304
Africa, 229, 237
North, 236–7, 301, 346
West, 301
West Coast of, 312–14, 343, 350–1, 371
Aix-en-Provence, 33
Aix-la-Chapelle, Congress of (1818), 241
Akkerman, Convention of (1826), 206–7, 220
Alabama (ship), 332
Albany, Countess of, 34
Albert, Prince (later the Prince Consort), 88, 262, 298, 300, 348, 361, 362, 372, 381, 385, 386, 415, 466, 501–2, 513, 520, 521, 524, 525, 526
and political crises of 1851–2, 422–6
and coalition, 442–4, 447, 453, 458,

488, 489, 499–502, 511, 512
Alcibiades, 490
Alexander the Great, 66
Alexander I, Tsar of Russia, 113, 172, 200, 201, 221, 295
and Napoleonic wars, 125, 128, 131, 132, 133, 139, 140, 141, 142, 147–8, 151, 152, 155, 158, 163, 166, 173, 199
Alexandria, 212
Alexandria, Convention of (1828), 8, 212
Alexandria Troas, 40, 65
Alfieri, Vittorio, Count, 34
Alfred, Prince, 379
Algeria, 197, 236–7, 268, 271, 272, 346–7, 360, 361
Ali Pasha (of Janina), 198
'All the Talents', ministry of, 93–4, 99–101
Alma, battle of, 509
Alps, 123, 141, 144–5, 149
Altenberg, 134–5
ambassadors, quality of, 8–9, 299
Amherst, William Pitt, 1st Earl, 278
instruction to (1835), 280–1
Amiens, 31, 32, 36, 72, 113
Amiens, Peace of (1802), 30, 42
Amyclae, 43, 62–3
Anapa, 217, 220, 507
Ancona, 271
Angelo Castro, 43
Anglesey, Henry Paget, 1st Marquess of, 194
Anglicanism *see* Church of England
Anglo-Saxon Chronicle, 73–4
Annard, David, 14
Annandale, Marquess of, 16
Anne, Queen
Annual Register, 234
Antibes, 33
Antiquaries, Society of, 5, 72, 73–5, 110, 184
Antiquities of Athens, 67
Antiquities of Attica, 67
Antiquities of Eleusis, 67
Antwerp, 7, 149, 153, 168, 243, 244
Apsley House, 57, 196
Arbuthnot, Charles, 195, 272
Arbuthnot, Mrs Charles, 6
Arbuthnot, Colonel, 58

Arbuthnot, John, 8th Viscount, 97
arch, history of, 65–6
Archaeologia, 73
Ardlach, 14
Ardlethan, 15
Argentina, 246–7, 354, 370
    see also Buenos Aires
Argos, 43
Argyll House, 56, 80, 107, 110, 172, 178, 179, 224, 272, 417, 423, 445, 449, 455, 503, 512
Argyll, George Douglas Campbell, 8th Duke of, 3, 7, 81, 293, 435, 448, 450, 455, 458, 460, 465, 488, 513
Argyll, John Douglas Campbell, 7th Duke of, 96, 97
Argyll, Archibald Campbell, 1st Marquess of, 15
Aristides, 531
Aristotle, 65, 72
Aroostook Valley, 326
Arroya Grande, battle of, 354
art treasures, looted, 168
Arta, Gulf of, 213
Arundel, 436
Ashburnham, Lord, 87, 179, 180, 182
Ashburton, Alexander Baring, 1st Baron, 316, 331
Ashburton–Webster negotiations, 8, 316–27, 334–5
Ashburton–Webster Treaty (1842), 326–7
Ashley, Lord see Shaftesbury, 7th Earl of
Aspropotamos River, 206, 209, 224
Aston, Arthur, 346, 381, 383
Aswanley, Laird of, 13
Athenian Society, 67, 70
Athens, 36–7, 41–2, 43, 65, 67, 212, 213, 214, 407, 408, 507
Atkinson, Miss, 109
Atreus, treasury of (tomb of Agammenon), 43, 65
Attica, 209, 212, 214, 217
Auchmalladie, 15
Auchmedden, 15, 25
Auchneve, 15
Auchterarder, 291, 292
Augustus, Emperor, 66
Aumale, Duke of, 346, 357, 382, 396
Australia, 352, 456, 462
Austria, 186, 189–90, 198, 200, 208, 210,

217, 221, 242, 244, 245, 271, 272, 283, 302, 304, 313, 348–50, 357, 380, 387, 390, 428, 476–7, 498, 503, 504, 524–5
    and Napoleonic wars, 113–69 *passim*
    and 1848 revolutions, 392, 393, 399–407, 409–10
    and Crimean war, 474, 483, 486, 489, 499, 506, 508, 511, 518
Austrian Netherlands, 123, 242
    see also Belgium
Avignon, 33
Axone, 42
Ayas, 39
Aylmer, Matthew, 5th Baron, 278
Azeglio, Marquis D', 473
Azores, 233–4, 269

Backhouse, John, 188, 299
Bagehot, Walter, 441, 468
Bagot, Sir Charles, 242–5
Bahamas, 314, 320
Baillie, Dr, 107
Baillie, George (of Jerviswood), 264
Baillie, Grizel, 264
Baillie, Miss Joanna, 52, 109
Baillie, Mary see Haddo, Mary, Lady
Baillie-Hamilton, Captain (later Admiral), William Alexander, 416, 417
Baird, Charlotte (Charles) see Haddo, Charlotte, Lady
Baird, General Sir David, 19, 20, 79
Baird, William, 19
balance of power, 186, 305, 403, 506
Balcarras, Alexander, 6th Earl of, 96
Balfour, Lady Frances, 3, 4, 49
Balkan Mountains, 216, 219
Balkan River, 491, 507
Ballogie, 16
ballot, secret, 424, 427, 428, 429, 448
Balmoral, 88, 90 n42, 307 n7, 435, 509, 520, 525, 526
Baltic, 142, 156, 507
Baltimore, Democratic Convention at (1844), 334, 338
Bandiera brothers, 390
Banffshire Journal, 85
Bankhead, Charles, 334
Banks, Sir Joseph, 67, 73
Barbecena, Marquis de, 233

Barbour, John, 23–4
Barcelona, 345
Barclay de Tolly, Field Marshal Prince Mikhail, 128, 133, 134, 151
Baring Brothers, 244, 310, 316, 370
Baring, Francis, 448, 450
Baron's Court, Co. Tyrone, 55, 87, 109, 178, 417
Barry, Dr, 23
Bar-sur-Seine, 166
Basle, 162, 163
Basque country, 283
Bassano, Duke of, 146, 152
Batavian Republic, 33
Bates, Joshua, 339
Bath, Order of the, 159, 215
Bathurst, Benjamin, 124
Bathurst, Henry, 3rd Earl, 116, 158, 160, 167, 174, 179, 187, 196, 199–200, 205, 206, 232
Bathurst, Lady Louisa Georgiana, 174
Batoni, Pompeo, 19
Bautzen, battle of, 117
Bavaria, 128, 130, 131, 143, 160
Bay Islands, 477
Bayramic, 39
Beauvale, Lord see Lamb, Frederick
bedchamber crisis (1839), 294
Bedford, Francis, 7th Duke of, 327, 432, 433, 442–3, 444, 445
Bedford, John, 6th Duke of, 93, 178, 183, 186, 260
Belgium, 268, 269, 270–1, 283, 301, 305
  1830 Revolution in, 197, 242–5
  projected Franco-Belgian Customs Union, 301, 305, 347–50
Belhaven, William, 7th Baron, 97
Belize, 477
Bellegarde, Marshal, 161
Bem, General, 407
Bennigsen, General, 133, 134
Benthamites, 10, 200, 259, 451, 455, 460
Bentinck, Lord George, 394, 415
Bentinck, Lord William, 185
Bentley Priory, 3, 49, 51–4, 56, 72, 79, 87, 107, 124, 174, 175, 176, 179, 182, 194, 263, 417, 467
Bérard, Auguste Simon Louis, 239
Berlin, 44, 124–5, 393
Bernadotte, Marshal, (Prince Royal of Sweden), 114, 124, 130, 133, 134, 140, 142, 143, 147, 161–2
Berri, Duchess of, 273
Berry Pomeroy, 142
Berryer, Antoine Pierre, 358, 398
Berwickshire, 13
Besika Bay, 482
Betty, William Henry, 52
Beverley, 522
Binning, Lord see Haddington, 9th Earl of
Birkenhead, 465
Birmingham, 252
Bismarck, Otto von, 532
Black Sea, 208, 217, 220, 221, 480, 487, 488, 490, 491, 492, 504, 506, 507, 518–19
Black Stone of Essar-Haddon, 75
Blackheath, 417, 484
Blackstone, William, 247
Blair Atholl, 46, 293, 417
Blair, Robert (Scottish Solicitor-General), 26
Blantyr, Lord, 96
Bloomfield, Lord, 303
Blücher, Marshal, 133, 134, 161, 166
Boddam, 16, 25
Boers, 273, 276–7
Bohemia, 133
Boileau, 56
Bomarsund, 507
Bonaparte, Carolina, 124
Bonaparte, Joseph, 32, 57
Bonaparte, Louis, 143
Bonaparte, Louis-Napoleon see Napoleon III, Emperor
Bonaparte, Napoleon see Napoleon I, Emperor
Bonham, F. R., 258
Bordeaux, 166, 352
Bordeaux, Duke of ('Henri V'), 238–40, 273, 358, 396–8
Bosnia, 474
Bosphorus, 206, 208, 218, 219, 220, 221, 480, 488, 508
Boulogne, 31, 395
Bourbons, restoration of, 162, 164, 167–8, 173
Bourgas, 480
Bournabashi, (Pinarbaşi), 39, 63–4
Bourquenay, M, 343
Braganza, House of, 233, 234

Brazil, 229–35, 269–70, 313, 319, 368–9

Breadalbane, Elizabeth, Lady (wife of 2nd Marquess), 264

Breadalbane, John Campbell, 4th Earl of, 97

Brebner, James, 80–1, 256–7, 263, 264

Brechin, 14

Bremen, 155

Breslau, 125

Bresson, Charles, 382

Bridgewater, Duke of, 57

Bright, John, 500, 503–4, 517, 523, 531

Brighton, 158, 178, 179–80

Bristol, 253

British and Foreign Anti-Slavery Society, 332

British Critic, 39

British Library, 4

see also British Museum

British Museum, 4, 34, 35, 42, 43, 67, 68–9, 75

Aberdeen, a Trustee of, 5, 75, 110, 112, 184

Broglie, Duke of, 284, 368, 397

Brooks, Lord (later 3rd Earl of Warwick), 35, 50

Brotherhood of the Cross, 359

Brougham, Henry, 1st Baron, 251, 300, 333, 396, 414–15, 418, 434, 435, 461

Bruat, Captain, 363, 364

Brunnow, Baron, 304, 473–4, 479, 481, 485, 487, 490, 492, 493 n6, 498

Brussels, 80, 243, 244

Bryant, Jacob, 39

Brysea, 62

Buccleuch, Walter Scott, 5th Duke of, 289, 384, 385

Buchan Ness, 416, 527

Buchanan, James, 336, 337, 338, 339

Bucharest, 508

Buckingham and Chandos, 1st Duke of, 186

Buckland, William, 78 n54

Buenos Aires, 246–7, 353–4, 369–70

Bugeaud, Marshal, 347, 360

Bülow, von General, 133

Bülow, Henri von (Foreign Minister of Prussia), 348, 349–50

Bulwer, Henry, 302, 326, 344, 347, 349, 351, 354, 383–4, 385, 387, 485

Bunsen, Baron, 349

Buol, Count, 483

Burdett, Sir Francis, 185, 193, 197

Burghersh, Lord (later 11th Earl of Westmorland), 127, 136, 158, 159, 299

Burke, Edmund, 71–2

Burlington House, 68

Burnet, Bishop, 15

Burnett, John, 26

Burnett, Sir Thomas, 257

Burnley, 465

Bute, John, 1st Marquess of, 96

Byron, George Gordon, 6th Baron (the poet), 6, 19, 64, 69–70, 198, 200

Byron, Admiral the Hon. John, 19

Byron, Captain John ('Mad Jack'), 19

Byzantine Empire, 198

Cadiz, Duke of, 382, 385, 386

Cairnbulg, 25, 82

Caithness, James Sinclair, 12th Earl of, 97

Calais, 31

Calhoun, John, 333, 335

California, 334, 477

Calne, 436

Campbell, Colen, 16

Cambridge, 2, 61, 91

Cambridge University, 23–4, 30, 47, 52, 61, 66, 93, 98, 263, 290, 394, 461–2, 522

Canada, 242, 262, 282

internal problems, 10, 273, 277–81, 311, 312, 324, 339, 419, 456, 462–3

involved in disputes with U.S.A., 246, 311–12, 321–6, 339

Candia see Crete

Canmore, House of, 13

Cannes, 33, 418

Canning, Charles, 2nd Viscount, 5, 299, 425, 448, 510, 513, 524

Canning, Charlotte (wife of 2nd Viscount), 293

Canning, George, 1st Viscount, 5, 94–5, 102, 106, 118, 119, 160, 203 n3, 258, 299, 445

as Foreign Secretary, 101–2, 118, 187, 202, 205–7, 209, 230, 231, 235, 246

as Prime Minister, 193–4, 203

Canning, Stratford (later Lord Stratford de Redcliffe), 6, 119, 203 n3, 246, 305, 407, 434
  as Ambassador to Constantinople (1826–9), 9, 195–6, 203, 208–25, *passim*
  his quarrel with Aberdeen (1829), 213–15, 216, 226 n39, 336
  as Ambassador to Constantinople (1841–6), 299, 304, 345, 347, 381
  as Ambassador to Constantinople (1853–5), 475, 476, 479–93 *passim*
Canningites, 194–5, 205–7, 231
Canova, Antonio, 66, 69
Canterbury, 52
Canterbury, Archbishops of, 75
  see also Howley, William
Canterbury, Charles, 1st Viscount, 278
Cape Horn, 247, 315
Cape of Good Hope, 79, 247, 270
Cape Province, 273, 275–7
Capodistrias, Count Ioannis, 201, 212, 213
Caracciolo, 36
Cardigan, James Thomas Brudenell, 7th Earl of, 520
Cardwell, Edward, 427, 430, 435, 448, 458, 510, 528
Caribbean, 246, 315
Carinthia, 44
Carlisle, 73, 427–8, 435
Carlisle, George Howard, 6th Earl of, 436, 450
Carlisle, Nicholas, 74
Carlos, Prince of Spain, 234–5, 283, 345, 382
Carlotta, Queen of Portugal, 231
Carlsruhe, 162–3
Caroline, Queen (wife of George IV), 110, 136, 184, 185
Caroline incident, 311–12, 317, 326, 331
Carret, Father, 353
Cass, General, 314, 318, 326
Cassilis, Archibald, 12th Earl of, 94
Castelcicala, Prince, 405
Castlereagh, Lady (wife of Viscount), 51, 110, 168
Castlereagh, Robert Stewart, Viscount (later 2nd Marquess of Londonderry), 3, 9, 94, 102, 106, 110, 173, 186, 188, 195, 230, 235, 258, 305, 445

  and Napoleonic Wars, 105, 114–19, 122–69 *passim*
  goes to the continent himself, 160, 163
  State Paper of 1820, 189–90
  and Greek war, 200–1, 202
Cathcart, William Schaw, 1st Earl
  and 1806 peerage election, 96, 97
  as Ambassador to Russia (1812–14), 114, 115, 117, 117–18, 122, 123, 126–32, 139–41, 147–8, 151–2, 155, 158–9, 160–1, 163, 164–6
Catherine the Great, Empress of Russia, 499
Catholic measures *see* Roman Catholic Church
Caulaincourt, Armand (later Duke of Vicenza), 141, 152, 164, 165–6, 169
Cavaignac, General, 395
Cavendish, Anne, 4, 111–12, 157, 173–4
Cavendish, Lady George, 111–12, 157, 174
Cavendish, Lord George, 68, 111–12, 157, 174
Cavendish, Lady Georgiana (later Lady Morpeth, wife of 6th Earl of Carlisle), 50, 110, 111, 173–4
Cavendish, Lady Harriet (later Lady Leveson-Gower, wife of 1st Earl Granville), 48, 49, 50–1, 53–4, 110, 111, 179, 183, 455
Cephalonia, 216
Cerigo, 216
Cervi, 408–9
Ceylon, 2
Chalmers, Dr Thomas, 291–2
Chalmers, James, 530 n60
Chalus, 13
Chamberlain, Neville, 10
Champlain, Lake, 323
Chambord, Count of *see* Bordeaux, Duke of
Chancery Reform Acts (1853), 462
Chandler, Richard, 67
Changarnier, General, 398
Channel Islands, 239, 241, 472
Chantilly, 31
Charitable Trusts Act (1853), 462
Charlemagne (ship), 474
Charlemont, Lady, 182
Charles I, King, 15
Charles II, King, 15

Charles X, King of France, 235, 236, 237, 271, 396
  and 1830 Revolution, 237–41
Charles Albert, King of Piedmont-Sardinia, 400–1
Charles, Captain, 135
Charles, Prince of Bavaria, 223
Charles, Prince of Mecklenburg, 223–4
Charles, Prince of Prussia, 218
Charlewood, Captain, 332
Charlotte, Princess, 176–223
Chartists, 372, 392, 393, 405
Chateaubriand, François René, 358
Chatillon, Conference of, 164–6, 169, 172, 173
Chaumont, Treaty of (1814), 166
Chaucer, Geoffrey, 24
Cherbourg, 239, 240
Chesterhall, 19
Chevalier, Jean Baptiste Le, 38–9
China, 297, 302, 304, 351, 367–8, 371, 523
Chios (Scio), 41, 199
Chiswick House, 51, 110
Choiseul-Gouffier, Count of, 38
Christides, 345, 358
Christina, Queen of Spain, 234, 283, 345, 346, 384, 386
Church of England, 62, 110, 196, 260, 421, 434, 445, 449, 451, 461, 463
Church, General Richard, 212, 215, 368
Chusan, 367–8
Cincinnati, Democratic Convention at (1843), 334
Circassia, 504
Civil Code (French), 33
Civil Service, reforms, 462
Clanricarde, Lord, 234, 299, 500
Clapham Sect, 274
Clare, County, 197
Clarendon, George William Villiers, 4th Earl of, 8, 12 n26, 87, 300, 327, 335, 370, 416, 418, 424, 430, 433, 443, 445, 446, 448, 449, 450, 460, 475, 476–513 passim, 518, 522, 525, 528
Clarke, Dr, 509
Clarke, Edward, 42, 70
Clayton–Bulwer Treaty (1850), 477
Cleveland, Row, 48

Clifton, 20
coat-of-arms, family, 176–7
Cobbett, Williams, 185
Cobden, Richard, 428, 443, 500, 506, 523
Cockburn, Henry, 257
Codrington, Admiral, 202–3, 210, 211–12, 219
coinage
  in ancient world, 62, 187
  in 19th century, 187
Cole, General, 106
Coletti, Jean, 359
colonial assemblies, Aberdeen's views on, 275, 277–81
Colonial Office, 246, 273–82
Columbia River, 315, 334, 335, 338, 339
commercial discussions (with France), 344, 354
Comotau, 133, 157
Complete Peerage, 17
Conacher, Professor, 414
Congress system, 166, 202
Conservative party
  foundation of, 260, 430
  Aberdeen's desire to re-unite (1846–52), 392, 394, 415, 420–1, 441
Conspiracy to Murder Bill, 524
Constantinople, 8, 34, 40, 42, 43, 101, 102, 156, 263, 283, 304, 347, 532
  Aberdeen visits (1803), 37–8
  and Greek War at Independence, 199, 206–21 passim
  and Crimean War, 403, 472, 474–5, 478–93 passim, 497, 499, 504, 507, 508
'continental peace', 7, 113, 115, 117, 144, 145
Continental System, 113–14
Contini, 238
Convocation, 434
Copenhagen, 79, 105
Coquette (ship), 269
Corfu, 44, 48, 79, 200, 201, 209, 216, 261
Corinth, 43, 209, 212
Corn duties
  after Napoleonic Wars, 177
  in 1828, 194, 196
  repeal of 1845–6, 339, 384–5, 414, 415, 421
Corniche, 33, 182

Cornwallis, Charles, 1st Marquess, 32
Corporation Act, 194, 196
Correggio, 57
Cortona, 34
Corunna, 106
Cossacks, 133
Cottenham, Charles Popys, 1st Earl of, 448
cotton supplies, 315, 333
Courier, the, 152
Coutts, Bank, 80, 239, 240, 417
Court, interest in formation of Aberdeen's coalition, 422, 425–6, 435, 442–3, 445, 450, 452, 479
Covenanters, 14, 15
Cowes Castle, 505
Cowie, Alexander, 82
Cowley, Henry Wellesby, 1st Baron, 208, 236, 299, 301, 344, 348, 349, 350, 352, 354, 357, 360–1, 362, 365, 366, 417
Cowper, Lady (formerly Emily Lamb, later Lady Palmerston), 261, 293
Cracow, 387–8, 390
Craddock, Colonel 239–40, 248 n48
Cranworth, Lord, 448, 450
Crawford, Earls of, 14
Crawfurd, George, 15
Crawley, C. W., 207
Creole incident, 314, 317, 320–1, 331
Crete (Candia), 44, 202, 211, 213, 214, 215, 224, 236, 474, 481
Crichie, 16
Crimean, 8, 504, 409, 513
Crimean War, 1, 22, 186, 195, 219, 262, 284, 304, 306, 371, 394, 399, 403, 453, 459, 461, 462, 467–8, 477, 528, 532
   causes of, 478–93
   course of, 497, 500, 506–13, 518
   end of, 513
   British war aims in, 504–5, 507
Croft, Dr, 55
Croker, John Wilson, 75, 255, 300–1, 337
Crombie, Alexander, 26, 50, 82, 83, 84, 86, 99, 177–8, 253, 254, 256
Crown, role of in foreign policy, 223–4, 297–9, 397, 479
Cruden, 84
Cruickshanks, Elizabeth, 13
Cuba, 245–6, 319

Cumberland, Duchess of, 223–4
Cumberland, Duke of, 223
currency problems, 187
Custozza, battle of, 400
Cuxhaven, 155
Cyclades, 209
Cyprus, 38, 199

Daily News, 502
Dalhousie, George Ramsay, 9th Earl of, 96, 98
Dalhousie, James Ramsay, 10th Earl of, 415, 459, 461
Dalkeith, Lord (later 6th Duke of Buccleuch), 528
Dalmatia, 150
Dalzel, Andrew, 38
Danube, River, 198, 218, 220, 488, 489, 491, 493, 504, 506, 507, 508
Daphnis, 36
Dardanelles, 37, 206, 210, 218, 219, 220, 284, 407, 409, 474, 480, 482, 504
Darmstadt, 162
Darwin, Charles, 76
Dashwood, Sir Francis, 66
D'Aubigny, Captain, 364, 366
David, Jacques Louis, 33
Davis, Sir John, 368
defence
   crisis of 1844–5, 301–2, 370–4
   estimates, 338, 371, 372, 442, 457, 472
Deffaudis, Baron, 370
Delane, John Thaddeus 6, 300, 339, 366, 386, 394, 404, 416, 448, 449, 486, 501, 502
Denison, Archdeacon, 527
Denmark, 105, 114, 129, 130, 143, 149, 159
Dennewitz, battle of, 133
Derby, 253
Derby, Edward Stanley, 14th Earl of (Lord Stanley until 1852), 260, 274, 275, 279, 280, 297, 312, 372, 384, 385, 404, 408, 409, 410, 417, 441, 442, 443, 444, 447, 449, 459, 512, 523–4, 525
   and political manoeuvres 1849–52, 418–37 *passim*
   opposition to coalition, 450–2, 456, 497–8, 501, 503

Dering, Mrs, 18, 25, 86

Devonshire, William, 5th Duke of 48, 67, 79, 111–12

Devonshire House, 49, 92, 94, 111–12, 173

Dickens, Charles, 310

Diebitsch, General, 218, 220, 222

Dijon, 167

Dilettanti, Society of, 5, 57, 66–7, 68, 184

Dionysius, cave of, 36

Directory, French, 32, 237

Disbrowe, Sir Edward, 298

Disraeli, Benjamin, 7, 393, 418, 419, 422, 429, 430, 431, 433, 434, 435, 443, 444, 446, 447, 512, 523, 531

    consults Metternich, 394, 415

    budget (1852), 442, 458

    opposition to coalition, 452, 497, 502–3, 505

dissolution of parliament, royal prerogative of, 524

Dodwell, Edward, 70

Donnelson, Major, 333

Douce, Francis, 73

Douglas, Harriet see Aberdeen, Harriet, Countess of

Douglas, Sir Howard, 243, 322

Douglas' Peerage of Scotland, 13, 14

Douglas, Lady Susan, 521

Dover, 31, 371

Doyle, Percy, 333

Drayton, 261, 294, 374, 396

Dresden, 117, 130, 133, 146

Drummond, William, of Logie Almond, 34, 35, 36, 38, 42, 44, 47, 48, 50, 52, 57, 62, 63–5, 67, 91, 101, 532

Drury, Joseph, 22

Dublin, 477

Dubois de Saligny, 333

Dudley, John William Ward, Earl of, 70, 100, 188, 193, 194–5, 196, 205, 206, 207, 231, 232

Dumira, 21, 26, 46

Duncombe, Thomas, 390

Dundas, Henry (later 1st Viscount Melville), 4, 17, 20–2, 26, 34, 49, 50, 53, 80, 83, 91, 93, 94, 95, 99, 101, 105, 107, 184

    becomes Aberdeen's guardian, 21

    impeached, 22, 91–2, 93, 94

Dundas, Admiral James, 478, 479, 482, 488, 491, 507–8

Dundas, Jane (Lady Melville), 20, 34, 55, 56, 93, 182

Dundonald, Archibald, 9th Earl of, 97

Dunfermline, Lord, 432–3

Dunkirk, 354

Dunmore, John, 4th Earl of, 97

Dupetit-Thouars, Admiral, 352–3, 363–4

D'Urban, Benjamin, 275–7

Durfee, Amos, 311

Durham, John George Lambton, 1st Earl of Durham, 79, 278, 281

    Report on Canada (1839), 280

Dutens, Louis, 65–6

Dysart, Wilbraham, 6th Earl of, 97

Earl of Aberdeen (ship), 178

East Retford, 194, 196

Eastern Question see Ottoman empire

Ecclesiastical Antiquities of France, 30, 72

Ecclesiastical Titles Act, 423–4, 425–6, 428, 435, 449

Economist, The, 427

Edinburgh, 15, 20, 33, 38, 46, 75, 81, 96, 97, 98, 107, 289

    George IV's visit to (1822), 188

    Royal Society of, 38

Edinburgh Review, 5, 63–5, 300, 531

education, Aberdeen's enthusiasm for, 10, 186, 274, 281, 429, 451

    measures of coalition government, 451, 456, 460, 461

Egina (Aegina), 42

Eglinton, Hugh Montgomerie, 12th Earl of, 97

Egypt, 39, 65, 211–12, 213, 284, 472, 474, 481, 521–2, 527

Eight Articles (on Belgium, 1814), 243

Elba, 186

Elbe, River, 113, 133, 147

elections, general

    1806, 95–99

    1807, 99

    1812, 99, 112

    1830, 251

    1831, 252

    1833, 256–7, 294

    1835, 257, 259, 294

    1837, 257, 294

1841, 294
1847, 414, 418
1852, 427, 428, 429, 436, 452
1857, 523
Eleusis, 36–7, 42, 65
Elgin, James, 8th Earl of, 419
Elgin, Thomas, 7th Earl of, 34, 41–2, 56, 68–70, 96, 97, 156
Elgin Marbles, 5, 41–2, 56, 66, 67–71, 73, 184
Elibank, Alexander, 7th Baron, 97
Ellenborough, Edward Law, 1st Earl of, 184, 189, 190, 297, 334, 374, 461, 526
  in Wellington's government, 194–5, 195–7, 205, 206, 207, 211, 217, 224, 232
  jealousy of Aberdeen, 6, 195–6
Ellice, Edward 'Bear', 284, 399, 416, 426, 432–3, 436, 517–18
Elliot, Charles, 333–4
Ellon, 18, 24, 25, 82, 86
  Presbytery of, 290, 291–2
Elphinstone, John, 13th Baron, 278
Elster River, 133, 134
Englefield, Sir Henry, 73
entails
  on the Haddo estate, 16, 25, 46, 55, 83, 103, 116
  legislation on, 188–9
  entente cordiale
  nature of, 370–1, 387
  origins of phrase, 357–8
Ephesus, 41, 65
Epidaurus, 42
Erroll, William Hay, 17th Earl of, 96
Espartero, Baldomero (Duke de la Victoria), 345, 346, 381, 386
estates, family, 5, 6, 14, 15, 16, 26, 46–7, 54–5, 79, 81–8, 174–5, 176–8, 416, 520
  Articles and Regulations settled by George, Earl of Aberdeen (1804), 83–5
  stock-breeding experiments, 86, 416
Ethwald, 52
Etna, Mount, 36
Eu, Chateau d'
  1843 meeting, 303, 357, 367, 379, 381, 382, 387

1845 meeting, 367, 373, 382–3, 386–7
Euboea (Negropont), 209, 213, 224
Evans, Sir de Lacy, 509
Everett, Edward, 300, 317, 318, 324, 331, 333, 335, 338, 339
Evidence Amendment Act (1853), 462
Examiner, the, 300–01
Exeter Hall, 363
  see also 'Saints'
extradition
  treaty with U.S.A. (1842), 321
  treaty with France (1843), 344

factory legislation, 462
Faden, 326
Fairfax, Thomas, 3rd Baron, 499
Fairfax, Thomas, 9th Baron, 97
Falkland Islands, 246–7
Falmouth, 233
Falmouth, Edward, 1st Earl of, 255
Fedderat, 16
Fenwick, Mr, 35,
Ferdinand, Emperor of Austria, 402
Ferdinand II, King of Naples, 404–5, 409
Ferdinand VII, King of Spain, 144, 190, 230, 234, 283
Ferrara, 392
Filder, General, 508
Findlay, Mr, 35
Finland, 114, 504, 507
Finlay, George, 407, 408
fiorin grass, 86
Fishery Convention (with France, 1843) 344
fishery quarrels (with U.S.A.), 477
Fitzgerald, Brian Vesey, 197
Flaxman, John, 66, 69
Florence, 30, 34, 182
Fontainebleau, Treaty of (1814), 186
Forbes, James, 17th Baron, 96
Foreign Enlistment Acts, 194, 269–70
Foreign Office, 9, 497, 498–9
  organisation of, 299–300
  relations with Aberdeen when out of office, 401
Formartine see Gight
Forrest, Mrs Janet, 18, 25
Forsyth, John, 312
Forster's Education Act, 461
Foster, Augustus, 42, 46, 47, 48, 51, 59nll,

64, 67, 91, 92, 110, 175, 310

Foster, Lady Elizabeth (later Duchess of Devonshire), 42, 48, 51, 59 n11, 92

Foulerton (Foullarton) family, 14

Fourmont Abbé, 62–3

'Four Points' (to settle Crimean War), 506, 511, 513, 518

Fox, Charles James, 57, 93, 431, 455

Fox, Henry, 312, 316, 335

France, 42, 47, 70, 173, 190, 285–6, 408, 410, 421, 457, 472–3, 532

    Aberdeen's distrust of, 8, 186, 235, 268–72, 343

    Aberdeen's tour in 1802–3, 7, 30–3

    and Napoleonic Wars, 7, 36, 105–6, 110, 113–69 passim

    'natural frontiers' of, 141–2, 144–5, 149, 152, 164, 166, 168, 222

    colonies, 135, 144, 147, 155, 159, 168

    and Greek War of Independence, 202–3, 206–25, 236

    and Iberian Peninsula (in 1820s and 1830s), 229–34, 283

    and Algeria, 197, 236–7

    and July Revolution (1830), 197, 237–41, 251

    and Belgian Revolution, 242–5

    and Italy, 400, 402, 524–5

    and Mehemet Ali crisis, 283–5

    royal visits to, 303, 357, 367, 381, 382–3, 386–7

    quarrels with (1840–2), 284–5, 297–307 passim, 312–14, 315, 343–54

    attempt to create 'understanding' (1842–6), 8, 332–3, 336–8, 344, 353–4, 357–70, 381–4

    collapse of entente, 385–8, 392

    1848 revolutions and rise of Louis Napoleon, 391, 392, 395–9

    Aberdeen's attempts to secure restoration of the monarchy, 8, 396–8

    and Crimean War, 472, 474, 489, 491–3, 504, 506, 507, 508, 510, 518

Francis I, Emperor of Austria, 113, 125, 126, 127, 128, 133, 140, 142, 143, 144, 162, 167, 172, 173, 174, 182, 190, 272, 295, 402

Francis Joseph, Emperor of Austria, 476–7, 486

Frankfort-on-Main, 119, 142, 143, 161, 163

    negotiations at (1813), 117, 141–53, 155, 164, 166, 167

    Declaration of (1813), 146, 149, 164

Frankfort Parliament (1848), 403

Frankfort-on-Oder, 125

Franklin, Benjamin, 325, 326

Frederick William III, King of Prussia, 113, 125, 128, 172, 223

Frederick William IV, King of Prussia, 351, 372, 391, 403, 483

Frederiction, 322

Freemasonry, 20, 289

Free Trade, defence of 1846–52, 415, 420–1, 422–3, 427, 428, 429, 434, 436, 442, 451, 457

Fréjus, 33

Freybourg, 162

'Friends of the People', 93

Gale, Mrs, 109, 181–2, 183

Gallipoli, 37

Galloway, John Stewart, 7th Earl of, 97

Garibaldi, Guiseppe, 402

Garter, Order of the, 159, 173, 174, 520, 526

Gash, Professor, 414

Gaul, James, 82

Gell, Sir William, 47, 55, 63–5, 66, 67, 209

Genoa, 33–4, 142, 182

Gentleman's Magazine, 20

Gentz, Friedrich von, 119, 121 n56, 392

George III, King, 100–1

George IV, King

    as Prince Regent, 57, 75, 94, 106, 110, 123, 135, 176, 184

    as King, 184, 188, 210, 216, 223–4, 233, 325, 251, 297, 298

Georgia, 38, 220, 504

Germany, 113, 199, 301, 242, 245, 309 n46, 497

    in Napoleonic Wars, 7, 115, 119, 123, 130–2, 135, 144, 145, 152, 162–3

    royal visit (1845), 303, 372–3

    revolutions (1848–9), 393, 401, 403

Gibraltar, 65, 136, 233, 360, 407

Gight (Formartine), 19–20, 25, 178

Giordano, 34

Girard, 33

Gladstone, 3, 5, 61–2, 88, 180, 198, 224, 260, 410, 414, 418, 421, 513, 517, 519, 522, 523–4, 525, 527, 528, 531, 532

and Aberdeen correspondence, 1–2

Under Secretary at Colonial Office, 281–2

'Neapolitan letters' (1850), 404–6

political manoeuvres of 1852, 427, 428, 430–6, 442

and coalition, 443, 448, 449, 450, 455, 460, 463, 466, 483–4, 488, 491, 492, 501, 503, 504–6, 510, 511

budget (1853), 457–9

and parliamentary reform, 2, 467

Glasgow, 465

Glasgow, George Boyle, 4th Earl of, 96

Glasgow, university of, 289

Globe, the, 263, 394, 409, 475

Goethe, Johann Wolfgang von, 56

Gooch, Dr, 75

Gordons, Dukes of, 6, 13, 14

Gordon, Jane, née Maxwell, Duchess of (wife of 4th Duke), 46, 48, 93

Gordon, Alexander, 4th Duke of, 21, 92, 188, 254, 289

Gordon, George, 1st Duke of, 13

Gordon, Adam, 13

Gordon, Sir Adam, 13

Gordon, Alexander, 1st Earl of Huntly, 13

Gordon, Alexander, (illegitimate son of 3rd Earl of Aberdeen), 18, 25–6

Gordon, Alexander, (brother of 4th Earl of Aberdeen), 20, 56, 57–8, 79–80, 86, 105, 107, 168, 175, 520

in Peninsular War, 79, 105–6, 114

death of, at battle of Waterloo, 79, 176

Gordon, Alexander (son of 4th Earl of Aberdeen), 176, 262, 417, 418, 520, 526

in Crimea, 508–9, 509–10

Gordon, Alice (daughter of 4th Earl of Aberdeen), 55–6, 88, 109, 116, 118, 156–7, 175, 178–83

Gordon, Alicia (sister of 4th Earl of Aberdeen), 20, 80–1, 176, 520

Gordon, Anne (daughter of 3rd Earl of Aberdeen), 18, 25, 26

Gordon, Arthur (later 1st Baron Stanmore, son of 4th Earl of Aberdeen), 1–3, 5, 62, 75, 252, 260, 262, 263, 265, 282, 339, 394, 404, 418, 504, 505–6, 512, 520, 521, 522, 524, 526, 528, 531

biography of his father, 2–3, 5, 8, 9, 14, 17, 21, 22, 34–5, 86, 101, 108–9, 111, 116, 135, 168, 174, 175, 182, 183, 184, 193, 241, 252, 273, 192, 394, 416, 504

Gordon, Caroline (daughter of 4th Earl of Aberdeen), 55–6, 109, 116, 156–7, 175, 178–9

Gordon, Catherine (daughter of 3rd Earl of Aberdeen), 18

Gordon, Catherine, 13th Laird of Gight (mother of Lord Byron), 19

Gordon, Charles (illegitimate son of 3rd Earl of Aberdeen), 18, 25–6

Gordon, Charles (brother of 4th Earl of Aberdeen), 10, 20–1, 57–8, 79–81, 86, 176, 180, 182, 257, 261, 520

Gordon, Charles (of Abergeldie), 35, 39, 41

Gordon, Charles (of Cluny), 45, 180

Gordon, Cosmo, Colonel (half-brother of 3rd Earl of Aberdeen), 21

Gordon, Cosmo (of Ellon), 17

Gordon, Douglas (son of 4th Earl of Aberdeen), 260, 262–3, 520

Gordon, Elizabeth, 13

Gordon, Frances (daughter of 4th Earl of Aberdeen), 4, 176, 261

Gordon, George ('Dod', grandson of 4th Earl of Aberdeen and later 6th Earl of Aberdeen), 399, 528

Gordon, Isabella (illegitimate daughter of 3rd Earl of Aberdeen), 18, 25–6

Gordon, James (son of 'Jock'), 14

Gordon, James (fl. 1469), 14

Gordon, James (fl. 1582), 14

Gordon, James (d. 1623), 14

Gordon, Jane (daughter of 4th Earl of Aberdeen), 55–6, 109, 110, 116, 156–7, 175, 178–82

Gordon, Sir John (of Strathbogie) and his sons, 13–14, 24

Gordon, John ('Jock'), 13–14

Gordon, John (royalist, executed 1644), 14–15

Gordon, John (d. 1665), 15

Gordon, John (illegitimate son of 3rd Earl of Aberdeen), 18, 25–6

Gordon, John (brother of 4th Earl of Aberdeen), 20, 80, 176, 180, 182, 183, 520

Gordon, Mary (daughter of 3rd Earl of Aberdeen), 18, 25

Gordon, Patrick (d. 1452), 14

Gordon, Patrick (fl. 1479), 14

Gordon, Penelope (illegitimate daughter of 3rd Earl of Aberdeen), 18, 25–6

Gordon, Richard (fl. 1170), 13

Gordon, Sir Robert (brother of 4th Earl of Aberdeen), 4, 20, 53, 79–80, 88, 111–12, 113, 117, 119, 156, 172, 173–4, 176, 183, 242, 245, 251, 306, 348, 358, 520
   in Teheran, 57–8, 86
   in Constantinople, 195–6, 215–23, 236
   in Vienna, 299, 302–3, 391

Gordon, Susan (daughter of 3rd Earl of Aberdeen), 18, 26

Gordon, Susan (illegitimate daughter of 3rd Earl of Aberdeen), 18, 26

Gordon, Thomas ('Tam'), 13

Gordon, Thomas (of Cairncross), 200

Gordon, Victoria (granddaughter of 4th Earl of Aberdeen), 521, 526

Gordon, William (of Fyvie, half-brother of 3rd Earl of Aberdeen), 21

Gordon, William (2nd son of 3rd Earl of Aberdeen), 18, 21, 25–6, 34, 83

Gordon, William (brother of 4th Earl of Aberdeen), 20–1, 25, 79–81, 116, 176, 180, 256–8, 520, 522

Gore, Captain, 35, 36

Gorham judgment, 434

Gosford, Archibald Acheson, 2nd Earl of, 281

Gosford's Close, 75

Gothenberg, 124

Gothic architecture, 30, 34, 61, 72–3

Gourdon, Bertrand de, 13

Goulburn, Henry, 232, 260, 371, 414, 415, 435

Grafton, George Fitzroy, 4th Duke of, 174

Graham, Sir James, 10, 260, 300, 312, 361, 367, 371–4, 385, 390–1, 392, 408,
409, 415, 418, 421, 422, 513, 517, 519, 522–3, 528
   and Aberdeen's correspondence, 2
   and political manoeuvres of 1851–2, 422–36
   and formation of coalition, 444–50
   in coalition, 455–68 passim, 472, 474, 475, 479, 482, 487–93, 505, 509, 511, 512

Grant, Charles, 196, 281

Grant, Rev. Ludovic, 291

Grants of Monymusk, 82

Granville, G. Leveson-Gower, 1st Earl of, 51, 179, 183, 235, 299

Granville, G. Leveson-Gower, 2nd Earl of, 424, 448, 450, 455, 458, 460, 464, 484, 488, 522

Gravesend, 270

Great Lakes, 336, 338

Greece, 36, 40, 47, 64, 65, 67, 70, 109, 230, 326, 242, 269, 271, 283, 301, 305, 345, 368, 392
   Aberdeen's travels in (1803), 34, 41–4
   War of Independence, 195, 197–225
   boundaries of, 206, 209, 212–14, 216, 222, 224, 269
   selection of a monarch for, 213, 215, 216, 223–4, 269
   loan, 224, 358, 368, 407
   revolution of 1843, 358–9
   and Don Pacifico affair, 368, 407–10
   and Crimean War, 472, 507

Greek architecture, 65, 67, 71–2

Greenwich Park, Ranger of, 417

Gregorios, Patriarch, 199

Gregory XVI, Pope, 271

Grenville, William, Baron, 93–4, 98, 100

Greville, Charles, 285, 300, 316, 326, 327, 339, 366, 453, 456, 484

Grey, Charles, 2nd Earl, 184, 194, 246, 261
   and Reform Act, 251–6
   and foreign policy, 268–72

Grey, Sir George, 430, 431, 450, 466, 510

Grey, Henry, 3rd Earl see Howick, Lord

Greytown, 477

Griquas, 276

Grivas, General, 359, 368

Grogan case, 312, 321

Gropius, Herr, 70

Guadeloupe (ship), 332

Guilleminot, M., 236

Guillemot, M., 273

Guizot, François, 8, 261, 262, 390, 391, 406, 408, 409, 473, 477, 523
- character of, 286, 387
- French prime minister, 284–6, 299, 313, 336, 338, 343–73, 392
- Memorandum of 27 February 1846, 9, 383, 385, 386
- in exile, 393, 404
- and attempts to restore French monarchy, 396–8

Gully, Dr William, 521

Gurney, Hudson, 23–4, 50, 61, 73–4, 81, 91, 176–7, 185, 265, 271, 293
- tours France and Italy with Aberdeen (1802–3), 23, 30–4
- lifelong correspondent of Aberdeen, 7, 21, 44, 48, 182–3, 187, 194, 197, 211, 253, 254, 257, 259, 261, 282, 416, 425, 478, 518, 519, 520, 524, 527

Gustavus, Prince of Sweden, 223

'H', Lady, 112

Habeas corpus, 186

Haddington, Charles Hamilton, 8th Earl of, 96, 97, 98

Haddington, Thomas Hamilton, 9th Earl of, 97, 187–8, 193, 254, 256, 259, 297, 312, 361, 367, 374

Haddington, George Baillie-Hamilton, 10th Earl of, 264

Haddo, 14, 18, 24, 46–7, 54–5, 81–8, 117, 174–5, 176, 180, 181, 253, 256, 257–8, 261, 264–5, 290, 416, 509, 527
- see also estates, family

Haddo House, 4, 19, 42, 46, 54, 111
- building and rebuilding of, 16, 87–8, 175, 178, 416, 526
- as a political centre, 88, 358, 416–17, 427–35, 484, 522–3

Haddo, Charlotte, Lady (mother of 4th Earl of Aberdeen), 17, 18, 20

Haddo, Mary, Lady (wife of 5th Earl of Aberdeen), 79, 262, 264–5, 396, 410, 416, 418, 484, 486, 511, 518, 519, 520, 521–2, 526, 527, 528

Haddo, George, Lord (father of 4th Earl of Aberdeen), 6, 18–20, 21
- death of (1791), 20

Haddo, George Lord (later 5th Earl of Aberdeen), 4, 45, 62, 176, 258, 262, 263–5, 521–2, 526
- attempt to find parliamentary seat for, 258, 522
- marriage, 264–5
- illness, 441, 509, 521, 527

Hadrian, Emperor, 68, 70

Haileybury College, 460

Halifax, Canada, 231, 322

Hamburg, 142, 154 n37, 242, 246

Hamilton, Catherine see Aberdeen, Catherine, Countess of

Hamilton, Claud (step-son of 4th Earl of Aberdeen), 180–1

Hamilton, Frances (sister-in-law of 4th Earl of Aberdeen), 49

Hamilton, General, 315, 324, 331

Hamilton, Harriet (step-daughter of 4th Earl of Aberdeen), 180–1, 261, 416

Hamilton, James, Lord (brother-in-law of 4th Earl of Aberdeen), 157–8, 172, 175

Hamilton, Maria (sister-in-law of 4th Earl of Aberdeen), 4, 49, 52, 110–11, 157–8
- Aberdeen's letters to, during the Napoleonic Wars, 124–7, 133–5, 142–3, 156–7, 162–3
- death of (1814), 172

Hamilton, Sir William (British Ambassador in Naples), 67, 68, 73

Hamilton, William Richard (Lord Elgin's private secretary and later Under Secretary at the Foreign Office), 68, 74, 143

Hamilton-Gordon, Aberdeen assumes the name, 177

Hanau, 143

Hannah (ship), 39, 40, 41

Hanover, 123, 129, 144, 149, 521

Hanseatic towns, 117

Hanson, Catharine Elizabeth see Aberdeen, Catharine, Countess of

Hanson, Oswald, 17

Hardenberg, Baron, 129, 165

Hardinge, Lord, 472

Hardwick, Lady, 112

Harrison, William, 312
Harrow school, 20–1, 22, 159, 262, 263, 447
    Aberdeen, a governor of, 22–3
Harrowby, Susan, Lady, 173
Harrowby, Dudley Ryder, 1st Earl of, 87, 110, 111–12, 112, 116, 124, 172, 173–4, 187, 254–5
    Aberdeen's correspondence with, during the Napoleonic Wars, 126, 128–9, 129, 158, 159, 160, 161, 163, 167–8, 169
Harrowby, Dudley Ryder, 2nd Earl of, 418
Harper, Canea, 14
Hartington, Lord, 48
Hatfeild Hall, 17
Hawkesbury, Lord see Liverpool, 2nd Earl of
Hawaiian Islands, 363
Hay, Drummond, 360–1
Hay, Robert, 274, 278–80
Haydon, B. R., 71
Haynau, General, 407
Hayter, W. G., 449
Heidelberg, 162–3
Heligoland, 282
Helvetic Republic, 33
Henri IV, King of France, 32
Herbert, Sidney, 2, 260, 385, 415, 418, 428, 513, 522–3, 523
    and political manoeuvres of 1851–2, 425
    in coalition, 444, 445, 449, 455, 460, 467, 488, 510
Herries, J. C., 196, 232, 394
Herschel, Caroline, 509, 521, 526
Herschel, John, 521
Herschel, William, 521
Heyden, Admiral, 210, 218
Heytesbury, William A'Court, 1st Baron, 208, 210–11, 216–17, 219, 220–2, 229, 230, 242, 244
Hervey, Lord Alfred, 463
Hervey, Lord William, 298–9
Hobhouse, Arthur, 450
Holbein, Hans, 34
Holland, 348
    and Napoleonic Wars, 123, 129, 135, 141, 142, 143, 144, 145, 149–50, 151, 162
    and Belgian revolution (1830), 242–5, 270–1

Holland, Dr, 509
Holland House, 49, 284
Holland, Lady, 112, 183
Holland, Henry Fox, 3rd Baron, 183, 190, 233, 234, 242, 272, 284
Holloway, Miss, 109, 183
Holy Alliance, 200, 229
Holy Places, 474, 479
Holy Roman Empire, 130
Holyrood House, 98, 241
Home, Alexander, 10th Earl of, 97
Homer, 39, 64, 198
Hong Kong, 351, 367
Honiton, 258
Hood, Consul, 370
Hope, John, 100, 189, 292
Hottentots, 277
Howick Act (1831), 277, 279
Howick, Lord (later 3rd Earl Grey), 277, 278, 282, 287 n40, 384
Howley, George, 109
Howley, William, 56, 61, 108–9, 172, 254, 260–1, 262–3, 381, 462
Hudson Bay Company, 315, 336, 338–9
Hudson, James, 525
Hume, Joseph, 460
Hungary, 139, 476
    and revolutions of 1848–9, 8, 402–3, 405, 407, 409
Hunt, Henry, 187
Huntly, Alexander Gordon (Seton), 1st Earl of, 13, 14
Huntly, George, 2nd Marquess of, 14
Huntly, George, Lord (later 5th Duke of Gordon), 99
Huskisson, William, 194, 196, 231
Hyndford, Lord, 96, 97
Hypselantes, Alexander, 198

Iberian peninsula, 115, 197, 283, 285
    see also Portugal and Spain
Ibrahim Pasha, 202–3, 206, 210, 211–12, 213, 215, 283–4
Ida, Mount, 39, 40, 64
Illyrian Provinces, 113, 117
impressment, 319–20
income tax, 337, 442, 444, 457
Indemnity Acts, 196
India, 20, 47, 48, 195, 247, 278, 297, 361, 368, 403, 415, 449, 513

renewal of East India Company Charter (1813), 110

India Act (1853), 459–61

introduction of competitive examinations for Indian Civil Service, 460, 461

Mutiny (1857), 461, 524

Inglis, Sir Robert, 7

Inquiry into the Principles of Beauty in Grecian Architecture, 71–2

interception of letters and despatches, 8, 115, 130, 216, 236, 390–1, 396–7

Ionian committee, 67

Ionian Islands, 109, 112, 199, 201, 214, 216, 217, 405, 407–9, 472, 522

Ireland, 82, 86, 91, 101, 116, 176, 177, 186, 197, 260, 272, 302, 337, 358, 361, 372, 384–5, 393, 397, 404, 418, 423, 424, 434, 442, 444, 447, 449–50, 457–9, 463–4

    Aberdeen offered Lord Lieutenancy of, 194

    Irish Church, 260, 463

    Irish franchise, 197, 291, 420

    Irish party (in 1850s), 427, 428, 429, 432, 435, 442, 443, 444, 450, 453

Iremonger, Lucille, 4

Isabella II, Queen of Spain, 234–5, 283, 345, 346, 381–7

Isle of Wight, 107, 442

Italy, 8, 66, 113, 115, 123, 130, 135, 136, 141, 142, 143, 144, 145, 161, 168, 182, 186, 189, 199, 242, 271, 272, 428, 473, 479, 483, 524–5, 525

    Aberdeen's tour in 1803, 33–4

    lack of sympathy with Italian nationalism, 392, 400, 524–5

    and 1848 revolutions, 391–2, 393, 400–2, 407, 409

Itabayana, Count, 233

Ivers, Mr, 239

Jackson, George, 129, 151

Jackson, John (Rector of St. James, Picadilly, later Bishop of Lincoln), 76 n4

Jacobi, Baron, 116

Jacobite traditions, 15–16, 17, 32, 240

Jamaica, 274–5

    problems with Assembly, 275

James II, King, 15

James V, King of Scotland, 73, 75

Jarnac, comte de, 358, 359, 365–7, 379, 383, 386, 397, 417, 523

Jeffrey, Francis, 63–5

Jersey, Lady, 51, 173, 522

Jerusalem, 38, 41, 474, 479

Jerusalem, Bishopric of, 381

Jewish Disabilities Bills, 456, 463

John VI, King of Portugal, 229–30

John, Prince of Saxony, 223

'joint cruising' arrangements, 318–19, 331, 368

Joinville, Prince of, 357, 360, 362, 371

Jones, Ernest, 405

Jowett, Benjamin, 461

July Revolution (1830), 237–41

Kabul (Caboul), 302, 304

Kalisch, Treaty of (1813), 113

Kandahar, 304

Karageorgevitch, Prince Alexander, 304

Karrack, 490

Kelk, Sir John, 417

Kellie, Lord, 92, 96

Kelly, lands of, 14

Kemble, John, 49, 52, 53, 109, 176, 193

Kemble, Mrs John, 109, 176

Kempt, Sir James, 278, 322

Kennedy, Thomas, 511

Kent, 251

Keogh, William, 463

Khiva, 304

Kimberley diamond fields, 276

King, P. J. Locke-, 422

King, William, 338

Kinnaird, 8th Baron, 96

Kinnoull, 11th Earl of, 291

Knight, Richard Payne, 49, 56–7, 63, 64, 67–71, 73, 87, 110

Knighton, Dr, 107

Konieh, battle of, 283

Kossuth, Lajos, 407, 476–7, 494 n21

Kulm, battle of, 133

Lafayette, marquis de, 241

La Ferronays, comte de, 210

Laggan, 415

Lamartine, Alphonse, 395

Lamb, Caroline, 51

Lamb, Frederick (later Lord Beauvale and

subsequently 3rd Viscount Melbourne), 116, 119, 122, 299, 432
  accompanies Aberdeen on his mission to Vienna (1813), 124–5, 156
  in Portugal, 231–3
Lamb, George, 53
Lamb, Mrs George, 175
Lamb, William see Melbourne, 2nd Viscount
Lancashire, 302
Lancaster, Duchy of, 194, 196, 445, 449, 475–6
Landseer, Edwin, 417
Lane-Poole, S., 6, 195
Langres, 163, 164
Lann, 125
Lansdowne, Henry Petty, 3rd Marquess of, 93, 174, 200, 242, 284, 327, 401, 409, 410
  political manoeuvres of 1851–2, 430, 436
  'Lansdowne project', 432–3
  and coalition, 442–5, 447, 448–9, 450, 453, 455, 456, 458, 464–8, 482, 488
Laon, battle of, 166
La Rothiere, battle of, 166
Lauderdale, James Maitland, 8th Earl of, 93–4, 97, 98
Laurium, mines of, 62
Laval, Duke of (French Ambassador in London), 237, 499
Laval, Father, 353
Lavalette, Charles, 474, 478, 479
Lavalette, comte de, 137
Lawrence, Sir Thomas, 6, 49, 53, 67, 69, 110
Layard, Henry, 504, 519
Ledru-Rollin, Alexandre, 395
Leeds, George, 6th Duke of, 97
legal reforms, 456
Legitimists, French, 8, 9, 241, 358, 396–8
Leiningen, Count, 474, 478, 483
Leipzig, 133, 135, 140, 142, 144
  battle of, 8, 134–5, 140, 141, 150, 162, 169, 201
Lemprière, Dr, 199
Leonidas, 43
Leopold I, King of the Belgians, 176, 223–4, 228 n77, 271, 298, 348–9, 362, 366, 373, 426, 450, 459, 477, 499

Leopold, Prince of Saxe-Coburg, 381, 382, 383, 384, 385, 485
L'Estocq, General, 125
Levant, 34, 200, 214, 297, 301, 345, 347
  see also Ottoman empire
Leven, Alexander Melville, 7th Earl of, 95, 96
Leveson-Gower, Lady see Cavendish, Harriet
Liberal party, creation of the new, 428–32, 441, 444, 452, 453, 455, 523, 532
Liberia, 313
Lieven, Count (later Prince), 116, 140, 148, 206–7, 208, 211, 216, 217, 218, 221, 236
Lieven, Dorothea, Princess, 216, 217, 261, 389 n26, 390, 393
  hostility to Aberdeen during his first period at the Foreign Office, 228 n77, 261
  supposed liaison with Aberdeen, 261–2
  intrigues to restore the French monarchy, 396–9
  correspondence with Aberdeen, 257, 259, 261–2, 272, 282, 285, 286, 293, 294, 297, 343, 366, 367, 394, 395, 400–1, 402, 403, 404, 406–10, 459, 473, 477
Lincoln, Lord, see Newcastle, 5th Duke of
Lindsay, Mr, 520
Linlithgow Palace, 75
Lisbon, 86, 107, 229, 230, 231, 233, 269
Liverpool, 332, 370
Liverpool, Robert Banks Jenkinson, 2nd Earl of, 75, 94, 99, 110, 112, 116, 158, 160, 187, 189, 193, 194
Liverpool, 3rd Earl of, 7
Livingstone, Captain, 18–19
Lizardi and Co., 332
Lockhart, Anne, 15
Lockhart, J. G., 75, 387
Lombardy, 142, 391, 400–1, 404, 525
London, City of, 238, 446, 500
London Committee (revolutionary), 476–7
London Conference (on Belgium), 244–5, 270–1, 283
London Conference (on Greece), 206–25 passim
  Protocol of 22 March 1829, 215, 216, 217, 222

Protocol of 3 February 1830, 224, 269

London Greek Committee, 200

London Missionary Society, 352, 353, 364

London, parliamentary representation of, 465

London, sewerage reform for, 462

London, Treaty of (1827), 202, 205–9, 210, 213, 218, 219

London, Treaty of (1839), 283, 347

London, university of, 465

Long, Charles, 68

Lords, House of, Aberdeen doubtful of its survival, 254, 258–60

Lothian, William Kerr, 5th Marquess of, 97

Louis XVIII, King of France, 167, 168

Louis Philippe, King of the French — see also Orleans, Duke of, 8, 241, 242, 271, 284–6, 301, 302, 303, 305, 337, 343, 346, 347, 348, 350, 358, 361, 367, 382, 391, 393, 472

and attempt to secure *fusion* with Legitimists, 396–8

Louvre, 32, 168

Low, Mr, 83

Low Countries, 7, 113, 115, 142, 143, 149, 161, 283, 285, 347

see also Belgium

Lucan, George Bingham, 3rd Earl of, 508

Luisa Fernanda, Infanta of Spain, 346, 381–7

lunatics, reforming legislation on (1853), 462

Lurde, Baron de, 354

Lushington, Dr, 368

Lusieri, Giovanni Battista, 41–2, 43

Lutzen, battle of, 117

Lyndhurst, John Copley, Baron, 194, 254, 415, 418, 499

Lyons, 33, 182

Lyons, Admiral Sir Edmund, 264, 345, 358–9, 368

Lysons, Samuel, 73

Macaulay, Thomas Babbington, 310, 460

Macdonald, Flora, 238

Macdonald, Marshal, 134

Madawaska Settlements, 321, 324

Madrid, 57, 283, 305, 345, 383, 386

Magnesia, 41, 65

Maguire, Mrs, 49

Mahmud II (Sultan of Turkey), 202, 207–21 *passim*, 236–7, 283–4

Maine, 246, 311, 323–6, 338

see also United States of America, North East Boundary dispute

Mair, Lord, 97

Maison, General, 211, 215

Majendie, Dr, 53

Malcolm, Admiral Sir Pultney, 219

Malmaison, 32

Malmesbury, James Harris, 3rd Earl of, 426, 434, 498

Malta, 36, 38, 65, 472, 478, 482, 508

Malvern, 521

Manchester, 187, 252

Manchester School, 443

Manchope, John, 26

Mandeville, J. H., 354

'Manifest Destiny', 311, 334, 335

Manin, Daniele, 400

Mannheim, 146

Mansfield, David William, 3rd Earl of, 97

maps, affair of secret, 8, 325–6

Maria II, Queen of Portugal, 230–4, 242, 283, 392–3

Maria Christina see Christina, Queen of Spain

Marie Louise, Empress of France, 113, 162

Marienberg, 133

maritime rights, 7, 114, 135, 140, 144–9, 152–3, 166, 312, 320, 513

Marochetti, Carlo, 520

Marquesa Islands, 352

marriage settlements, 25, 49–50, 103, 264

Martignac, vicomte de, 215, 235

Martin Garcia, island of, 369–70

Martin, Kingsley, 10, 531

Martin, Matthew, 83

Mary of Guise, 75

Mary II, Queen, 15

Mary, Queen, of Scots, 33, 75

Massachusetts, 323–5

Matuscewitz, Count, 217, 218

Mauritius, 2

Mavrocordato, Alexander, 345, 358–9

Maximilian, Archduke, 223

Maynooth College, 463

Mazzini, Guiseppi, 8, 390–1, 401, 402, 476–7

McDonald, Douglas, 496 n77

McGill College, Montreal, 280

McLane, Louis, 338
McLeod, Alexander, 311–12, 316, 326
Medusa, head of, 42
Medusa (ship), 35, 36
Megalopolis, 43
Mehemet Ali, Pasha of Egypt, 304, 344
    and Greece, 202, 211–12
    and Algeria, 236–7
    and Ottoman empire, 283–4, 499
Melbourne, William Lamb, 2nd Viscount,
        6–7, 53, 116, 272, 278, 283, 286,
        292, 293, 294, 295
Melbourne, 3rd Viscount, *see* Lamb,
        Frederick
Mellish, Richard, 300
Melos, 36
Melville, Lady *see* Dundas, Jane
Melville, 1st Viscount *see* Dundas, Henry
Melville, Robert Dundas, 2nd Viscount, 232
Memoirs relating to . . . Turkey, 62–3
Menderes River, 39, 64
Menshikov, Prince, 478–83, 497
Menton, 33
Merfeldt, General, 134, 141, 142, 143, 144
Messene, 43
Messina, Straits of, 35–6
Methlic, 14, 47, 290, 291–2, 527
Metternich, Prince, 74, 118, 119, 172,
        173, 190, 200, 208, 217, 218–19,
        236, 245, 302–3, 304, 306, 345,
        372, 382, 390, 405, 415, 473, 477,
        502
    Aberdeen's opinion of, 119, 127–8,
        150–1, 152
    and the Napoleonic Wars, 115, 116,
        117, 127–65 *passim*
    visits London (1814), 172
    in exile, 393–6, 400–8
Mexico, 245, 311, 314, 315, 331–4, 338,
        339
Miguel, Prince of Portugal, 9, 229–34,
        242, 269, 283
Milan, 182, 400, 476–7
Mincio River, 130, 400
Minorca, 472
Minto, Gilbert Elliot, 2nd Earl of, 421,
        431, 450
Mistra, 43
Mnesikles, 37
Modena, 402

Moerenhout, J. A., 364, 365, 366, 367
Moldavia, 198, 206, 220, 221, 474, 483,
        487, 506
Molé, comte de, 242, 243, 313, 397, 398
Molesworth, William, 447, 448–9, 450,
        455, 458, 460, 487
Monguls, 133
Moniteur, 352
Monk, General, 398
Monsell, William, 463–4
Mont Cenis, 182
Montenegro, 474
Montereau, battle of, 166
Monte Video, 353–4, 369–70
Montmirail, battle of, 166
Montpensier, duc de, 382, 383, 384, 385,
        386
Montreal, 278, 279, 323
Montezuma (ship), 332
Montreuil, 31
Monymusk, 82–3, 87
Moore, Sir John, 105–6
More, Mrs, 110
Morea, 36, 47, 236
    Aberdeen's exploration of (1803), 42–4
    in Greek War of Independence, 197–
        203, 206–24
Morier, David, 119, 124, 126
Morley, John, 406
Morning Chronicle, 263, 300, 327, 404, 501,
        502
Morning Herald, 300, 501, 502
Morning Post, 54, 300
Morocco, 301, 347, 359–63, 367, 371,
        379
Morpeth, 436
Morpeth, Lady *see* Cavendish, Georgiana
Morritt, John, 39
Morton, George Douglas, 16th Earl of, 96,
        98
Morton, George Douglas, 17th Earl of, 521
Moscow, 113
Mosquito Coast, 477–8
Mowat, Lewis, 85
Muirfield, George, 85
Mulgrave, Lord (later 1st Marquess of Nor-
        manby), 274
Münchengrätz Agreement (1833), 272, 283,
        380
Municipal Corporations Act, 259

Münster, Count, 116
Murat, Joachim, 123–4, 130, 143
Murphy, Thomas, 332, 333
Murray, Sir George, 197, 232, 246, 278, 279, 322, 372
Murray, Mr, 86
Mycenae, 43, 65
Mytilene, 40

Nanking, Treaty of (1842), 351
Nantes, 352
Napier, Admiral Charles, 507
Napier, Francis, 8th Baron, 96, 98
Naples, 34, 35, 36, 67, 115, 123–4, 130, 189, 214, 297, 390, 404, 409
  'Neapolitan letters', 2, 404–6
Napoleon I, Emperor of France, 7, 32–3, 47, 113–69 passim, 173, 185, 327, 395, 399
  Aberdeen meets (1802), 32 44 n4
Napoleon III, Emperor of France, 8, 402, 426, 442, 472–3, 524, 525
  rise to power of, 395–9
  and Crimean War, 474, 518
Napoleonic Wars, 1, 7, 81, 91, 101, 105, 110, 113–69, 177, 269, 500
  Britain's war aims during, 115, 122–3, 129, 149–50, 164, 166
  'Grand alliance' against Napoleon, 132–3, 139–41, 155–6, 159–60, 166
Nassau, 314
National Gallery, 5, 110
nationalism, 150
  German, 113, 124, 130–2, 430
  Greek, 9, 189, 199, 201, 224
  Italian, 392
native rights, 274, 276–7
Navarino, 203, 205–6, 211–12
Navigation Acts, 419
Navigators' Islnds, 364
Neale, Mr, 258
Neilson, John, 278
Negropont (Euboea), 209, 213, 224
Nelson, Admiral Lord, 31, 67
Nesselrode, Count, 141, 143, 144–5, 146, 147–8, 151, 159, 160, 163, 165, 201, 206, 207, 208, 220–1, 299, 304, 380, 485, 486, 488, 490, 492

Nesselrode Memorandum (1844), 9, 380–1, 474, 497–8
Netherlands, 168, 242–5
  see also Low Countries and Holland
Neumann, Baron, 349
New Brunswick, 246, 311, 324
  see also United States of America, North East Boundary dispute
New Orleans, 314
New South Wales, 352, 353
New York Herald, 316
New York State, 311–12
New Zealand, 352
Newcastle, Henry Pelham, 4th Duke of, 253
Newcastle, Henry Pelham, 5th Duke of, 1, 415, 418, 421, 445, 518, 522, 526, 528
  and political manoeuvres of 1851–2, 425, 427, 428–36
  and coalition, 448, 449, 455, 458, 460, 463, 464–6, 488, 491, 510–12, 518
Newcastle, Thomas Pelham-Holles, 1st Duke of, 17
Newman, John, 397
Ney, Marshal, 133, 168
Niagara River, 311
Nice, 33, 182–3, 452
Nicholas I, Tsar of Russia, 202, 208, 210, 211, 217, 221, 303–5, 381, 531
  visit to England (1844), 379–80, 473
  and 1848 revolutions, 8, 399, 403, 473
  and Crimean War, 472–3, 478–93 passim, 497–8, 500, 504, 507, 510, 511
Ninety Two Resolutions (Canadian), 273, 278
Nollekens, Joseph, 3, 66, 69, 110
Nootka Sound Convention, 315
Norfolk, Charles Howard, 11th Duke of, 73
Norfolk, Henry Howard, 13th Duke of, 436
Norfolk, Henry Howard, 14th Duke of, 264
Normanby, Constantine Phipps, 1st Marquess of, 385
North Cray, 115
Northcote, Sir Stafford, 462
Northcote–Trevelyan Report, 462
Norway, 114, 129, 143, 148–9, 159
Norwich, 52, 91

Nottingham, 253
Nova Scotia, 14, 324
Novara, battle of, 401

Oakes, General, 36
oats, duty on, 196
Obligado, battle of, 370, 378 n78
Obrenovitch, Prince Michael, 304
O'Connell, Daniel, 197, 259
Odessa, 198, 210
Oedipus Judaicus, 62
Old Sarum, 252
Oldenburg, Duke of, 125
Olmütz, Proposals, 486–7, 488, 493
Olympia, 41
Olympus, Mount, 37
Omer Pasha, 474, 489, 508
Oporto, 231, 233, 269, 392–3
Orange, Prince of, 116, 243, 244
Orange, Prince Frederick of, 218, 223
Oregon, 314–15, 331, 334–9
    Oregon Treaty (1846), 339, 385
Oribe, General, 353, 369
Orleanists, 8, 396–8
Orleans, Duchess of, 397
Orleans, Duke of, 224, 238–41
    see also Louis Philippe, King of the French
Orleans, Duke of (eldest son of King Louis
    Philippe), 305, 351
Orsini, Felice, 524
Oroonoko, 53
Osborne House, 442, 443, 444, 485, 521
Osman Bey, 39–40
otter hunting, 417
Otho I, King of Greece, 269, 345, 358–9,
    407
Ottoman empire, 9, 44, 47, 70, 195, 302,
    305, 344–5, 357, 379–81, 402,
    407, 525
    Aberdeen's travels in (1803–4), 3, 7,
        34–44
    and Greek War of Independence, 197–
        225
    and Mehemet Ali crisis, 283–5
    and Crimean War, 472–5, 476, 478–
        93, 497–513, 517–18
Oudinot, Marshal, 124
Ouseley, Sir Gore, 57
Ouseley, William Gore, 310, 369–70
Overhill, 14

Owen, Admiral, 361
Oxford, 61, 67, 109, 290, 414, 430–1,
    461–2
Oxford Movement, 72
Oykhorne, 15

Pacific, 301, 335, 336, 337, 351–3, 363
    trade in, 247, 315, 351
Pacifico, Don, 368, 407–10, 419, 498
Padua, 44
Pageot, Alphonse, 338, 382
Paine, Lieutenant, 313–14, 318
Pakenham, Richard, 332, 333, 335–9
Palermo, 391
Palladio, Andreas, 16
Palmella, Count, 233
Palmerston, Henry John Temple, 2nd Vis-
    count, 8, 9–10, 22, 93, 101, 119,
    184, 208, 298, 306–7, 310, 339,
    346, 384, 437, 498, 516 n72, 524,
    531, 532
    sits in Wellington's Cabinet with Aber-
        deen, 196, 205, 206, 207, 424
    Foreign Secretary (1830–41), 235, 245,
        246–7, 268, 283, 284–6, 295,
        297, 301, 304, 311–15, 317–
        18, 323, 343, 345, 353, 368
    criticisms of Aberdeen (1841–6), 299,
        300, 318, 327, 331, 339, 344,
        367, 372, 381, 384
    Foreign Secretary (1846–51), 385–6,
        390, 392, 393, 394, 399–407,
        419, 421–2, 426
    and Don Pacifico, 407–10, 419
    and political manoeuvres of 1851–2,
        424, 428, 433, 434
    joins coalition government, 443, 444,
        446–7, 448, 450
    in coalition, 451, 455, 458, 462, 470
        n45, 472, 473, 477, 478–93 *pas-
        sim*, 500, 502, 503, 504–5, 509,
        510, 512
    and parliamentary reform, 464–8
    Prime Minister (1855–65), 513, 518,
        522, 523–5
Panama, 315, 351
Panmure, Fox Maule, 2nd Baron, 431,
    518
'Papal Aggression', 421, 425
    see also Ecclesiastical Titles Act

Papal States, 402
  see also individual Popes
Papineau, Louis, 278, 279
Parana River, 370
Paris, 164, 166, 167, 173, 183, 186, 231,
    238, 284, 314, 326, 384, 399, 473
  Aberdeen visits in 1802, 32–3
  Aberdeen visits in 1814, 167–8
  and revolution (1848–9), 391, 393,
    395, 396
Paris, comte de, 305, 396–8
Paris, 1st Treaty of (1814), 167–9, 208,
    243
Paris, 2nd Treaty of (1815), 208, 229, 241
Paris, Treaty of (1856), 513
Parker, Admiral, 407, 408, 409
Parkes, Joseph, 436
parliamentary papers, presentation of, 268–
    9, 300, 307 n16, 367
parliamentary reform, 197
  Great Reform Bill crisis (1830–2), 10,
    251–6
  effects of 1832 Act, 10, 256–60
  in 1850s, 422, 423–4, 427, 428, 429,
    433, 434, 435–6, 437, 444,
    445, 447, 451–2, 456, 464–8,
    490
  see also Irish franchise
Parma, 402
Parthenon, 36–7, 41–2, 67, 68–71
Patmos, 41
Patras, 43, 44
Pausanias, 62
Pedro I, Emperor of Brazil, 229–30, 233,
    235, 269–70
Peel, Sir Robert, 5, 9, 10, 22, 67, 75, 79,
    136, 180, 187, 193, 196, 197, 206,
    208, 232, 254, 255, 257, 260, 261,
    272–3, 285, 289, 294, 334, 393,
    420–1, 423, 426, 430, 431, 441,
    444, 459
  Prime Minister (1834–5), 273, 278,
    281, 282, 283, 295
  Prime Minister (1841–6), 293, 297–
    306 *passim*, 312, 316, 318, 323,
    324, 325, 327, 331, 335, 337,
    339, 343–85 *passim*, 387, 390,
    391, 416, 418, 425, 457
  attitude after 1846, 385–6, 392, 396–
    7, 408–10, 414–15, 420

  death of (1850), 410, 420, 421
Peel, Sir Robert (son of the Prime Minister),
    501
Peelites, survival of as a political group, 404,
    414–53 *passim*, 523
Pekin, 302
Pemberton, Dr, 107
Pembroke, George Augustus Herbert, 11th
    Earl of, 140
penal reform, 259, 462
Penal Servitude Act (1853), 462
Peninsular War, 7, 105–6, 114, 229, 269
Pennsylvania, 310
Penrhyn, 194, 196, 258
Pericles, 37, 65, 198
Persepolis, 58
Persia, 297, 304, 490, 523
Persian Gulf, 490
Perth, 46–7
Peterloo, 186–7
Petty, Lord Henry *see* Lansdowne, 3rd Mar-
    quess of
Phidias, 69
Philike Hetaireia, 198
Philip V, King of Spain, 346, 383
Philip, Prince of Hesse-Homburg, 223
Phillip, Captain Arthur, 352
Phipps, Colonel (later Sir) Charles, 443, 524
Phygalia marbles, 69
Picardy, 33
Piedmont-Sardinia, 9, 143, 242, 400–1,
    473, 524–5
Piombo, 54
piracy, 318, 369
  in Aegean, 37, 236
  on Barbary coast, 236–7
Piraeus, 36, 408
Pisa, 34
Piscatory, M. 358–9, 368
Pitt, William (the Younger), 4, 5, 6, 10,
    17, 21, 22, 30, 32, 34, 49, 53, 57,
    66, 91, 92, 94, 98, 102, 115, 123,
    166, 184, 252, 260, 277, 420, 431,
    432, 441, 455, 457, 458–9, 462,
    532
  becomes Aberdeen's guardian, 21
  death of, 22, 92–3
Pitt Club, 263
Pius VII, Pope, 123
Pius IX, Pope, 392, 402, 421

Place, Edward, 26
Planta, Joseph, 169, 215
Plate River, 353–4, 369–70
    United Provinces of the, 246–7
    see also Buenos Aires
plate, family, 26
    attempts to replace, 58
Plato, 37
Platoff, General, 128
Plestwitz, Armistice of (1813), 117
Plutarch, 65
Plymouth, 233, 472
Pnyx, 37, 42
Poerio, Carlo, 404, 406
Poland, 113, 132, 133, 173, 221, 304,
    387, 479, 504–5, 513
    see also Duchy of Warsaw
Polignac, prince de, 215, 235, 236, 237,
    238
Polk, James K., 335–9
Pomare, Queen, 363–4
Poniatowski, Marshal, 134
Ponsonby, Lord, 299
Poor Law reform, 259
Popham, Sir Home, 80
Poros
    Conference of, 210, 211, 213, 214
    Protocol of (1828), 213, 215
Portendic case, 343, 351
Portland, William Henry Cavendish, 3rd
    Duke of, 99, 101
Portmore, Lord, 97
Portugal, 58, 313, 409, 507
    in Napoleonic Wars, 105, 123, 132,
        148–9
    crises of 1820s and 1830s, 9, 229–35,
        242, 268, 269–70, 272, 283
    crisis of 1847, 392–3
    see also Peninsular War
Postal Convention (with France, 1843), 344
Post Office
    Committee of Enquiry (1844), 390–1
    Secret Department of, 8, 391
Poti, 217, 220
Pozzo di Borgo, Count, 151–2, 155, 159,
    160, 236
Prague, 117, 125, 126, 129, 132, 143, 146
Presbyterian church see Scotland, Church of
press, 6, 300–1, 313, 365, 404, 407, 490,
    500–3

    see also individual newspapers
Press, the, 497, 502–3
Preux, 39, 40, 41
Price, Uvedale, 49, 87
Prince Regent see George IV
Principalities, the Danubian, 487, 489,
    492, 506–7, 525
    see also Moldavia and Wallachia
Pritchard, George, 353, 363–7
private letters, use of in diplomacy, 8–9,
    147–8, 221, 232, 239–40, 243,
    323, 336–7
protectionism and protectionist party after
    1846, 408, 415, 418–37 passim
Proudhon, Pierre-Paul, 33
Prussia, 173, 208, 243, 244–5, 283, 302,
    305, 313, 348–50, 388, 403
    in Napoleonic Wars, 113–69 passim
    and Crimean War, 483, 489, 499
Pruth River, 473, 483
Public Money Drainage Act, 416
public opinion in Britain, 327, 364–5
    during Napoleonic Wars, 7, 150, 164,
        167, 169
    and Crimean War, 474, 490–1, 492,
        499–501, 511–12, 517–18
Puget Sound, 315
Pyreness, 123, 141, 144–5, 149

Quadruple Alliance (1834), 283, 392
Quadruple Alliance (1840), 284
Quarterly Review, 56, 300, 387
Quebec, 273, 277, 279–80, 321–6
Quebec Act (1774), 277
Quebec Revenue Act (1774), 277, 279
Queen's Affair, 184, 185
    see also Caroline, Queen
Queensberry, William Douglas, 4th Duke
    of, 96
Quintuple Treaty (Slave Trade, 1841), 313,
    314, 317, 350

Radetzky, Field Marshal, 8, 400–1
Radicals (as a party after 1846), 392, 404,
    421, 425, 426, 427, 428, 429, 432,
    435, 436, 444, 450, 460, 500
Radzlock, 57
Raglan, Field Marshal Lord, 508–9
Raphael, 32
Rawkstone (Raxton), 15

Razumovsky, Count, 165
Reay, Eric Mackay, 7th Baron, 96
Rebellion Losses Bill (Canada), 419
Redington, Sir Thomas, 449
Reeves, Henry, 285, 338
Regency Bill, 17
Reichenbach, Treaty of (1813), 116–17, 144
Reid, Stuart, 2
religious questions, exploited for political purposes, 421, 427, 428, 429, 434
Reschid Pasha, Grand Vizier of Turkey, 485
Revette, Nicholas, 67
revolutionary outbreaks and unrest, 200, 242, 251, 390–1
  in Austrian empire, 393, 402–3
  in Belgium, 242–5
  in Britain, 113, 121 n44, 177, 186–7, 302, 372, 393, 422–3, 425
  in Germany, 199, 242, 393, 403
  in Ireland, 177, 302, 393
  in Italy, 199, 242, 391, 393, 400–2
  in Russia, 217
  in Spain, 199, 229
Reynolds, Governor, 334
Reynolds, Sir Joshua, 53, 110
Rheims, 31
Rhine, Confederation of the, 113, 129
Rhine River, 115, 123, 129, 131, 140, 141, 144–5, 149, 153, 161, 162, 168, 301, 347
Rhodes, 38, 199
Ricardo, David, 187
Richard I, King, 13
Richardson, William, 86
Richmond, Charles Lennox, 5th Duke of, 260
Ridley, Jasper, 22
Ried, Treaty of (1813), 131
right of search (Slave Trade), 302, 313–14, 315, 317, 319, 350–1, 368–9
  see also maritime rights
right of visit (Slave Trade), 313, 317–18, 319, 331
de Rigny, Admiral, 210
Rio de Janeiro, 229, 370
Ripon, 1st Earl of see Robinson, Frederick
Rivals, The, 53–4
Robert II, King of Scotland, 14
Robespierre, Maximilien, 32

Robert the Bruce, King of Scotland, 13
Robinson, Frederick (later 1st Earl of Ripon), 21, 22, 91, 168, 194, 260, 274, 277, 279, 280, 297
Rochette, R., 63
Rockville, Alexander Gordon, Lord (half-brother of 3rd Earl of Aberdeen), 21
Rocky Mountains, 314, 335, 337
Roden, Robert Jocelyn, 3rd Earl of, 449
Roderick Dhu (ship), 331
Roebuck, John Arthur, 410, 426, 512, 519, 520
Rollo, John, 8th Lord, 97
Roman Catholic Church
  relief measures, 99, 100–1, 106
  Catholic emancipation, 186, 193–4, 196–7, 273, 414
  'Papal Aggression', 421, 425
Rome, 34, 65, 71, 242, 283, 421
Rosas, General, 353–4, 369–70
Rose, Colonel, 478
Rosebery, Archibald John, 4th Earl of, 188
Rothschild, House of, 216, 220, 238–9, 244, 446
Rouse's Point, 322–3, 324
Royal Academy, 49, 69, 72, 110, 417
Royal Commission on Scottish agriculture, 85
Royal Commission on Scottish universities, 289–90
Royal Society, 5, 65, 73, 75, 184
Royal Society of Literature, 74
Royston, Lord, 23, 61, 124
Rubens, 57
Russell family, 260
Russell, Lady John, 445, 446, 450, 475–6, 510
Russell, Lord John, 49, 75, 196, 251, 260, 292, 299, 327, 384, 386, 391, 392, 408, 410, 414, 415, 418, 419, 421, 518–19, 520, 523
  and political manoeuvres of 1851–2, 422–37
  and formation of coalition, 441–53
  in coalition, 455–68 passim, 475–6, 478–93 passim, 497, 500, 503, 507, 509
  breaks up the coalition, 510–12
Russell, Lady Louisa, 260, 519
Russell, Lord William, 299

Russell, W. H., 508

Russia, 47, 100, 105, 236, 242, 244–5, 272, 283, 284, 313, 314–15, 345, 408, 434, 525

and Napoleonic Wars, 91, 110, 113–69 *passim*

and Greek War of Independence, 197–203, 205–25

British relations with (1841–6), 302, 303–5, 306, 348, 357, 358–9, 379–81, 388

and 1848 revolutions, 393, 402–3, 407, 409

and Crimean War, 473–5, 478–93, 497–513, 517–19

Ruthvens, 16

Ryder, Lady Susan, 111–12, 173–4

Saatz (Zatec), 133

Sadleir, John, 463

St. Aignan, Baron, 141

negotiations with (1813), 141–53, 167, 171 n55

memorandum of, 144–7, 166

St. Albans, 465

St. Andrews, university of, 289, 290

Ste. Aulaire, comte de, 313, 336, 343, 346–7, 350–1, 367, 383

St. Clair, William, 198

St. Denis, 31–2

St. George, island of, 269

St. Germans, Edward Granville Eliot, 3rd Earl of, 449

St. James, Picadilly, 62

St. John's College, Cambridge, 23

St. John River, 321–6

St. Lawrence River, 277, 279, 324–5

St. Leonards, Edward Sugden, 1st Baron, 448

St. Petersburg, 47, 48, 202, 208, 499

Protocol of (1826), 202, 207, 216

St. Petersburg Gazette, 9, 497

St. Stephen, Order of, 159

'Saints', 310–11

see also Clapham Sect

Saldanha, General, 231, 233, 392–3

Salford, 465

Salisbury, 72

Salisbury, Robert Cecil, 3rd Marquess of, 225

Samos, 41, 213, 215, 224

San Francisco, 315, 334

Sandon Park, 87

Sapienza, 408–9

Sardinia, 115, 123, 173, 400–1, 409, 525

see also Piedmont

Sardis, 40–1

Savock (Saphak), 14

Savona, 33

Savoy, 168, 173

Saxe-Coburg, Duke of, 383, 384

Saxony, 117, 128, 131–2, 133–4, 140, 173, 242, 379

Scamander River, 39–40, 63–4

Schumla, 507

Schwarzenberg, Field Marshal Prince, 117, 127, 128–9, 133, 134, 135, 140, 161

Schwarzenberg, Prince (Austrian Chancellor), 405–6

Scio (Chios), 41

Scotch College, Paris, 32

Scotland (Scottish), 5, 15, 21, 31, 33, 46, 79, 92, 94, 112, 259, 263, 289–93, 449, 522

agriculture, 81–7

banking system, 5, 187

Church of, 61–2, 259, 289, 290

disruption of, 290–3

Conservative party, 289

courts, 5, 100, 189, 291, 293

electoral system, 255–6, 257, 290, 465

legislation affecting, 5, 100, 188–9

National Library, projected, 290

Record Office, 17

representative peers, 91, 94, 95–9, 112

universities, 256, 289–90, 465, 526

Scott, Sir Walter, 49, 75, 110, 176, 188

Scutari, 1, 508

see power, British, 301–2

see also defence *and* maritime rights

Seaforth, Lord, 19

Seaton, Lord, 322, 407

Sebastiani, Marshal, 382

Sebastopol, 487, 490, 491, 492, 504, 507, 508–9, 513

Committee, 519–20

Seditious Meetings Bill, 186

Select Specimens of Antient Sculpture, 67

Selim III, Sultan of Turkey, 38

Selkirk, Lord 98
Senior, Nassau, 300
Sense and Sensibility, 108
Seraglio, palace of, 37–8, 206, 220
Serbia, 221, 304–5, 474, 506
Seton, Alexander (assumed name of Gordon),
    13
Seville, Duke of, 382, 385, 386
Seymour, Admiral Sir George, 365
Seymour, Sir Hamilton
    in Brussels, 348
    in St. Petersburg, 474, 492, 498
Shaftesbury, Anthony Ashley-Copper, 7th
    Earl of, 284, 363, 463, 465
Shand, Alexander, 26, 82, 84
Sheridan, Richard Brinsley, 49, 53–4, 99,
    101
Sicily, 57, 123–4, 129, 132, 148–9, 185,
    391, 409
    Aberdeen offered embassy to, 101–2,
        193
Siddons, Miss, 109
Siddons, Mrs, 32, 52, 109
Silesia, 133
Silistria, 216
Simois River, 39–40, 64
Simpson, Archibald, 88
Simpson, Sir George, 336
Sinclair, Sir George, 336
Sinope, massacre of, 489–91, 492, 496 n77
Six Acts, 186
Six Mile Bridge affair, 464
Slade, Captain, 482
Slavery
    abolished in British empire, 10, 273,
        274–5, 276–7, 310
    campaign for abolition in U.S.A., 310–
        11, 315, 332–3
    in Turkey, 38
Slave Trade, 99, 274, 311, 312–14, 317–
        19, 331, 350–1, 357, 368–9,
        526
Sligo, Howe Peter Browne, 2nd Marquess of,
        274–5
Smalkalden, 140
Smith, Ashbel, 332
Smith, John, 88
Smoke Abatement Act (1853), 462
Smyrna, 40, 41, 199
socialism, 395, 398

Society Islands, 352, 367
    see also Tahiti
Solly, Mr, 154 n37
Somerville, Lord, 96
Sophia Matilda, Princess, 80
Sotomayer, Duke of, 384
Soult, Marshal, 272
Sounion, 41
South Africa, 10, 282
    see also Cape Province
Spa Fields riot, 186
Spain, 7, 57, 58, 86, 105–6, 199, 245,
        246, 259, 301, 305, 313, 315, 331,
        345–6, 357, 392
    and Napoleonic Wars, 123, 129, 132,
        135, 144, 161, 165
    and crises of 1820s and 1830s, 190, 229,
        230, 231, 234–5, 242, 283
    Spanish marriage question, 9, 346, 381–
        8, 394, 485
    see also Peninsular War
Sparkes, Jared, 325, 326
Sparta, 43
Spon, Jacob, 41
Spencer, George, 2nd Earl of, 95
Spencer, John, 3rd Earl of, 327
Spring-Rice, Thomas, 274
Stadion, Count von, 165
Stael, Madame de, 163, 168
Stalybridge, 465
Standard, the, 300, 501
Stanley, Lord *see* Derby, 14th Earl of
Stanley, Edward (later 15th Earl of Derby),
        415–16, 418–19, 421–2, 452,
        501
stamp duty, 85
Stanmore, Middlesex, 49, 50, 175, 261,
        263, 528, 531
Stanmore, Lord *see* Gordon, Arthur
Stein, Baron, 113, 131–2, 403
Stephen, James, 274, 278–80, 281
Stevenson, Andrew, 312, 314, 317–18
Stewart, Sir Charles (later 3rd Marquess of
        Londonderry), 106, 110, 114–15,
        117, 122, 126–9, 135–6, 139–41,
        147–9, 151–2, 155, 159, 160–1,
        163, 164–6, 415
Stockholm, Treaty of (1813), 114
Stockmar, Baron, 426, 433, 435, 443, 450
Strafford Arms, 17–18

Straits Convention (1841), 284, 407, 409,
474, 480, 486, 506
Stralsund, 124, 125
Strangford, Lord, 233, 473
Strasbourg, 395
Strathbogie, 13, 292
Strathmore, Lord, 96
Stromboli, 35
Strutt, Edward, 449
Stuart, House of, 32, 75
Stuart, Charles Edward Prince (the Young
Pretender), 17, 34, 238
Stuart, Sir Charles *see* Stuart de Rothesay,
Lord
Stuart, James, 36, 67
Stuart Papers, 32, 75
Stuart de Rothesay, Charles Stuart, Lord, 9,
210, 229
in Paris, 235–42, 243, 244, 245, 271
in St. Petersburg, 299, 303
Sudbury, 465
succession duties, 458–9
Sussex, 251
Suez Canal, 527
Sweden, 114, 123, 124, 129, 132, 140,
148, 152, 504, 507
Swing, Captain, 251
Switzerland, 115, 123, 150, 161–2, 201,
242, 392, 393
Syracuse, 36
Syria, 283–4, 344, 381, 479

Tagites, Mount, 43
Tagus River, 231, 270, 409
Tahiti, 9, 301, 351, 352–3, 359, 361,
363–6, 371, 379, 490
Talleyrand, Prince, 145, 168, 245
Tangiers, 360–3
Tarland, 16
Tartars, 133
Tarves, 14, 86
Tauroggen, Convention of (1812), 113
Taylor, William, 85
Taymouth, 264
Teheran, 58, 86, 113, 119, 221
Temperley, Professor, 528
Temple, Henry John *see* Palmerston, 2nd
Viscount
Temple, William, 208, 217
Tenedos, 219

Teplitz (Teplice), 119, 125–33, 143, 144,
162
Treaty of (1813), 132
Subsidy Treaty (1813), 129, 130, 156
Terceira, 233–4, 235, 269
terrorism, 476–7
Test Act, 194, 196
Texas, 311, 315–16, 331–4
theatre, 22
in Paris, 32
at Bentley Priory, 52–4
Thiers, Louis Adolphe, 284–5, 360, 384,
397, 398
Thistle, Order of the, 17, 520
Thomas the Rhymer, 19, 20
Thuringian Forest, 127, 140
Tiflis, 490
Tillicairn, 15
Times, The, 6, 9, 98, 152, 394, 404, 426,
449
in the period 1841–6, 300, 311, 314,
327, 339, 349, 366, 385, 386
in the Crimean War period, 456, 467,
490, 492, 497, 501, 502, 507,
510, 511
Tilsit, Treaty of (1807), 474
Tiryns, 43
Tolquhon, 15
Tolstoy, Paul de, 396–7
Tom Jones, 270
Topography of Troy, The, 63
Torphichen, James Sandilands, 9th Baron,
97
Torres Vedras, lines of, 507
Toulon, 492
Townley, Charles, 67, 68
Townshend, George, 2nd Marquess of, 73
transportation, 259, 456, 462
Trapani, Count of, 382, 383, 384
Travels in various countries of the East, 62, 63
tree planting, 55, 87, 178, 180
Trevelyan, Sir Charles, 460, 462
Tripoli, 237
Tripolitsa, massacre of, 199–200
Troad, 39, 40
see also Troy
Troy, 35, 38–40, 63–4, 127
Troyes, 164
Tucker, Captain, 313–14, 318
Tuileries, palace of, 32, 350

Tunbridge Wells, 107, 216, 261
Tunis, 237, 347, 361
Turin, 182, 473, 525
Turkey *see* Ottoman empire
Tuscany, 142, 402
Tyler, John, 312, 313, 316, 317, 319, 333, 335
Tyrol, 44, 123, 130, 131, 142, 150
Tyrone, County, 54, 82, 178, 186

Union, Act of (1707), 15, 95, 189, 255
United Kingdom peerage
   Aberdeen's desire for, 91, 93, 94, 99, 112, 158–9
   achieved, 169
United Provinces *see also* Holland, 115
United States of America, 229, 236, 239, 242, 246, 281, 297, 300, 301, 302, 306, 310–40, 351–2, 361, 369, 372, 476, 477–8, 526, 532
   War of Independence, 114, 310
   War of 1812, 140, 312
   North East Boundary dispute, 246, 311, 314, 317, 321–7, 331
   North West (Oregon) Boundary dispute, 311, 314–15, 317, 331
   and Slave Trade, 302, 312–14, 317–19, 331
   and *Creole* case, 314, 317, 320–1, 331
   and *Caroline* case, 311–12, 317, 326, 331
   and Extradition Treaty, 321, 331
   and Texas, 314, 315–16, 331–4
university reform
   Scottish Royal Commission (1826), 289–90
   English Royal Commission (1850), 461
   Oxford University Reform Act (1854), 462
   Cambridge University Reform Act (1855), 462
   see also individual universities
Unkiar Skelessi, Treaty of (1833), 283
Upshur, Abel, 335
Urquhart, David, 500
Utrecht, Treaty of (1713), 387

Vancouver Island, 335–8
Vandamme, General, 133
Van Diemen's Land, 405

Van Dyke, Sir Anthony, 34
Varna, 508
Vaughan, Dr Charles, 22
Vendée, La, 168, 273
Venice (Venetia), 42, 44, 48, 123, 130, 390, 400
Vera Cruz, 333
Vergennes, comte de, 325
Vermont, 312
Vernet, Louis, 246
Verona, 44
   Congress of (1822), 190, 229
Versailles, 32
Versailles, Treaty of (1783), 246, 321
Veto Act, 291–3
Vetusta Monumenta, 73
Victor Emmanuel, King of Piedmont-Sardinia, 401
Victoria, Queen, 6, 7, 87, 236, 293, 294–5, 298–9, 358, 374, 379, 381, 385, 391, 415, 417, 418, 520, 521, 523, 524, 525, 528
   visits abroad, 295, 303, 337, 357, 372–3
   and political crises of 1851–2, 422–6
   and coalition government, 442–5, 447, 450, 452–3, 458, 459–60, 466–7, 470 n45, 475, 479, 482, 484–5, 487–93 *passim*, 499–502, 504, 509, 511, 512
   visits Haddo (1857), 525–6
   Journal of, 6–7, 526
Vienna, 44, 156, 183, 195, 208, 220, 382, 393, 477, 483, 484, 492, 503–4, 506, 511, 518
Vienna, Aberdeen as Ambassador to, 1, 4, 102, 112, 115–19, 122–69
   general instructions, 122
   detailed instructions, 122–4
   efficient organisation of his embassy, 126, 274
Vienna, Congress of (1814–15), 168, 173, 312
   Aberdeen asked to attend, 173
Vienna Note (1853), 483–4, 490
Vienna, Treaty (Settlement) of, (1815), 8, 207, 208, 229, 241, 243, 268, 390, 399–400, 403, 472–3
Vietnam War, comparison with Crimean War, 500

Virgil, 34
Virginia, 314
Visconti, Ennio Quirino, 68
Vitoria, battle of, 57, 114, 169
Vitruvius, 71
Volo, Gulf of, 206, 209, 213

Wakefield, 17
Wakefield, Edward Gibbon, 280
Wales, Princess of see Caroline, Queen
Walewski, Count, 481
Walker, Admiral Sir Baldwin, 480
Wallachia, 198, 206, 220, 221, 474, 483,
    487, 506
Walpole, Captain, 233
Walpole, Horatio, 62
Walpole, Robert, 62–3, 102
Warburton, Henry, 185
Ward, Sir Henry, 407
Ward, J. W. see Dudley, Lord
Warsaw, Duchy of, 117, 148–9
Washington, 48, 102, 246, 310, 316, 323,
    324, 335, 338
Washington-on-the-Brazos, 333
Waterboer, Andries, 276
Waterloo, battle of, 79, 176
'Waverers', 244–5, 265 n11
Webster, Professor Sir Charles, 11 n13, 160
Webster, Daniel, 312, 314, 316–27, 331,
    334–5
'Wee Frees', 290, 293
Weimar, 140, 141
Wellesley, Arthur see Wellington, Duke of
Wellesley, Henry, 299
Wellesley Richard, Marquess, 102, 160
Wellington, Arthur Wellesley, 1st Duke of,
    4, 5, 7, 8, 9, 57, 79, 114, 159, 178,
    190, 193, 202, 260, 272–3, 282,
    285, 289, 295, 343, 344, 393, 423,
    481, 500, 501
  and Napoleonic Wars, 105, 106, 153,
    161, 162, 166, 168, 507
  as Prime Minister (1828–30), 194–247
    passim, 251–2, 261, 278
  and parliamentary reform, 251–2, 253,
    254–5, 259
  opposition to Grey's foreign policy, 268–
    71
  in Peel's Cabinet (1841–6), 297, 301–

2, 312, 321–3, 361, 367, 371–
    4, 387, 445
Wessenberg, Baron Von, 115, 116, 122, 160
West, Sir Benjamin, 69, 110
West Indies, 273, 274, 276, 282, 310–11,
    315
Westminster Abbey, 3, 193, 531
Wheler, Sir George, 70
Whitbread, Samuel, 91
White's Club, 94
Whittington, George, 23–4, 47, 48, 50, 52,
    53, 55, 58, 61, 64, 66, 72, 91, 92–3,
    99, 100, 111, 182
  accompanies Aberdeen to France and Italy
    (1802–3), 23, 30–4
Whyte, Rev. James, 291–2
Wicklow, Lord, 182
Wiesbaden, 397
Wight, Andrew, 82
Wilberforce, Samuel, 75–6, 520, 528
Wilberforce, William, 274
Wilkins, William, 56, 71, 176
William III, King, 15
William IV, King, 241, 242, 251, 252,
    254–5, 272, 273, 294, 298
William I, King of the Netherlands, 242,
    244, 246, 269, 270
  arbitrates on Maine boundary dispute,
    246, 311, 321, 322, 323, 324
Willis, N. P., 7
Wilson, General Sir Robert, 126–7, 133,
    135–6, 137 n21, 138 n73, 139,
    158, 184, 185, 360, 361
Wimbledon, 22, 50, 54, 64, 93
Winchester, Charles Paulet, 13th Marquess
    of, 56
Windsor, 196, 224 233, 264, 361, 367,
    397, 418, 447, 512, 520, 521, 526
Wiseman, Cardinal, 421, 424
Wiscombe Park, Devon, 18
Wittgenstein, Field Marshal, 128
Woburn, 179, 260, 443
Wood, Sir Charles, 414, 448, 449, 450,
    458, 464, 466, 467, 488, 491, 511
  and India Act (1853), 459–61
Wood, Robert, 38, 39
Wordsworth, Christopher, 262
Wordsworth, William, 123
Wortley, Stuart, 55, 79, 92, 281

Wurtemberg, 128
Wurtembrg, Prince Eugene of, 125
Wyatt, James, 72, 73
Wyse, Sir Thomas, 408

Yarmouth, 124, 156, 318
Yorck, General, 113
York, 14, 71, 399

York, Duke of *see* James II, King
Young, Sir John, 449
Ystad, 124

Zacheriah, 43
Zante, 216
Zollverein, German, 305, 348, 350
Zwickau, 134